T5-CPW-413

History of Multicultural Education, Volume V

Students and Student Learning

History of Multicultural Education

Edited by Carl A. Grant and Thandeka K. Chapman

Volume I: Conceptual Frameworks and Curricular Issues

Volume II: Foundations and Stratifications

Volume III: Instruction and Assessment

Volume IV: Policy and Policy Initiatives

Volume V: Students and Student Learning

Volume VI: Teachers and Teacher Education

History of Multicultural Education, Volume V

Students and Student Learning

Edited by

Carl A. Grant
University of Wisconsin, Madison

Thandeka K. Chapman
University of Wisconsin, Milwaukee

Montante Family Library
D'Youville College

 Routledge
Taylor & Francis Group

NEW YORK AND LONDON

First published 2008
by Routledge
270 Madison Ave, New York, NY 10016

Simultaneously published in the UK
by Routledge
2 Park Square, Milton Park, Abingdon, Oxon OX14 4RN

Routledge is an imprint of the Taylor & Francis Group, an informa business

© 2008 Taylor & Francis

Typeset in Sabon by
RefineCatch Limited, Bungay, Suffolk

All rights reserved. No part of this book may be reprinted or reproduced or utilized in any form or by any electronic, mechanical, or other means, now known or hereafter invented, including photocopying and recording, or in any information storage or retrieval system, without permission in writing from the publishers.

Trademark Notice: Product or corporate names may be trademarks or registered trademarks, and are used only for identification and explanation without intent to infringe.

Library of Congress Cataloging in Publication Data
History of multicultural education / edited by Carl A. Grant and Thandeka K. Chapman.
 p.cm.
Includes bibliographical references and index.

ISBN 978-0-8058-5439-8 (hardback, volume i : alk. paper) – ISBN 978-0-8058-5441-1 (hardback, volume ii : alk. paper) – ISBN 978-0-8058-5443-5 (hardback, volume iii : alk. paper) – ISBN 978-0-8058-5445-9 (hardback, volume iv : alk. paper) – ISBN 978-0-8058-5447-3 (hardback, volume v : alk. paper) – ISBN 978-0-8058-5449-7 (hardback, volume vi : alk. paper)

1. Multicultural education–United States.   I. Grant, Carl A.   II. Chapman, Thandeka K.
LC1099.3.H57 2008
370.1170973–dc22   2008016735

ISBN10: 0–8058–5447–9 (hbk)
ISBN10: 0-415-98889-6 (set)

ISBN13: 978–0–8058–5447–3 (hbk)
ISBN13: 978-0-415-98889-6 (set)

LC
1099.3
,H57
2008
vol. 5

CONTENTS

PREFACE TO THE SIX-VOLUME SET

How we came to this work

We were invited by a large publishing house to create a multi-volume set on what we are calling the history of multicultural education. A change within the organizational structure of the publishing house resulted in the discontinuation of the initial project. However, over the course of the last seven years, the project was embraced by a second publishing house that later merged with our first publishing home. Our 360 degree turn has been both a professional challenge and an amazing opportunity. The project has grown and expanded with these changes, and given us the opportunity to work with many different people in the publishing industry.

We relate this series of events for multiple reasons. First we want to encourage new scholars to maintain their course of publication, even when manuscripts are not accepted on the first or second attempt to publish. Second, we would like to publicly thank Naomi Silverman and Lawrence Erlbaum Associates for throwing us a necessary lifeline for the project and for their vision concerning this project. Lastly, we would also like to thank Routledge Press for warmly welcoming us back to their publishing house and providing ample resources to support the publication of the six-volume set.

What we got out of it and what we saw

Over the course of six years, we have worked to complete these volumes. These volumes, separately or as a set, were marketed for libraries and resources rooms that maintain historical collections. For Thandeka it was an opportunity to explore the field of multicultural education in deep and multifaceted ways. For Carl, it was a bittersweet exploration of things past and an opportunity to reflect on and re-conceptualize those events and movements that have shaped multicultural education. Collectively, the time we spent viewing the articles, conceptualizing the volumes, and writing the introductions was also a meaningful chance to discuss, critique, lament, and celebrate the work of past and present scholars who have devoted time to building and expanding the literature on equity and social justice in schools.

Looking across journals and articles we noticed patterns of school reform that are related to political and social ideas that constantly influence and are influenced by the public's perceptions of the state of education and by professionals working in the field of education. We would also like to recognize authors who have made consistent contributions in journals to multicultural education. These authors have cultivated lines of inquiry concerning multicultural education with regard to teachers, students, parents, and classroom events for decades. Although we would like to list these scholars, the fear of missing even one significant name keeps us from making this list.

Moreover, we recognize that a good deal of the significant work in the field was not published in journal articles or that articles were greatly altered (titles, tone, examples, word choice) to suit the editors and perceived constituents of the journal. There are many stories that are told between the lines of these articles that may go unnoticed by readers who are less familiar with the field, such as the difficulty authors had with finding publication outlets, and questions and criticism from colleagues about conducting research and scholarship in the areas of multicultural education. Although these pressures cannot be compared across groups, scholars of color, white scholars, men and women all felt marginalized because they chose to plant their careers in the rich but treacherous soil of multicultural education.

Just as we can see career patterns, we also saw patterns of journals that were willing to publish articles that focused on multicultural education. While many journals have created an *occasional* special issue around topics of equity, social justice, and students of color, there are journals that have consistently provided outlets for the work of multicultural scholars over the past three decades.

Our hopes for the use of the volumes

We began this project with the desire to preserve and recount the work conducted in multicultural education over the past three decades. As scholars rely more heavily on electronic resources, and funding for ERIC and other national databases is decreased, we are concerned that older articles (articles from the late 60s thru the early 80s) that may never be placed in this medium would eventually be lost. The volume set is one attempt to provide students, teacher educators, and researchers with a historical memory of debates, conceptualizations, and program accounts that formed and expanded the knowledge-base of multicultural education.

GENERAL INTRODUCTION TO THE VOLUMES

Multicultural education's rich and contested history is more than thirty years old; and is presently having an impact on the field of education, in particular, and society in general. It is time to provide a record of its history in order that the multiple accounts and interpretations which have contributed to the knowledge base, are maintained and documented. Whereas this account is not comprehensive, it nevertheless serves as a historically contextualized view of the development of the field and the people who have contributed to the field of multicultural education.

The paradigm of multicultural education as social reconstruction asserts the need to reform the institutional structures and schooling practices that maintain the societal status quo. These reforms are fashioned by socially reconstructing the ways that educators and politicians approach issues of equity and equality in our public schools. Multicultural education has become the umbrella under which various theoretical frameworks, pedagogical approaches, and policy applications are created, shared, critiqued, and implemented through on-going struggles for social justice in education. These campaigns for educational reform influence and benefit all citizens in the United States.

As a movement, multicultural education has brought forth an awareness of and sensitivity to cultural differences and similarities that continues to permeate the highest institutional infrastructures of our nation. Although the movement is rooted in struggles for racial equality, multicultural education readily includes physical disabilities, sexual orientation, issues of class and power, and other forms of bias affecting students' opportunities for academic and social success. The inclusion of other forms of difference beyond skin color is one way that multicultural education acknowledges diversity in a myriad of forms and dismantles the assumptions of homogeneity within racial groups.

The purpose of this set of volumes on the history of multicultural education is to locate, document, and give voice to the body of research and scholarship in the field. Through published articles spanning the past thirty years, this set of books provides readers with a means for knowing, understanding, and envisioning the ways in which multicultural education has developed; been implemented and resisted; and been interpreted in educational settings. By no means consistent in definition, purpose, or philosophy, multicultural education has influenced policy, pedagogy, and content in schools around the United States and the world. In addition, it has stimulated rigorous debates around the nature and purpose of schooling and how students and teachers should be educated to satisfy those purposes.

This set of volumes draws attention to how scholars, administrators, teachers, students, and parents have interpreted and reacted to various political and social events that have informed school policy and practices. Each volume in the set documents and tells a story of educators' attempts to explicate and advocate for the social and academic needs of heterogeneous and homogeneous communities. Through their struggles to achieve access and equity for all children, different scholars have conceptualized the goals, roles, and participants of multicultural education in numerous ways. Through the academic arena of scholarly publications, and using diverse voices from the past thirty years, the *History of Multicultural Education* acknowledges the challenges and successes distinguished through struggles for equity in education.

Methods for collecting articles and composing the volumes

It is because of the multifaceted nature of multicultural education that we have taken multiple steps in researching and collecting articles for this volume set. Keeping in mind the many ways in which this set of volumes will enrich the study and teaching of education, we have approached the task of creating the texts using various methods. These methods reflect the spirit of inclusion intrinsic to scholarship in multicultural education and respect for diversity in the academic communities that promote and critique multicultural education. This was a multiple step process that included the following stages of data collection.

In the Spring of 2000, we began collecting articles using an electronic data bank called the *Web of Science*. This program allows the Editors to discover the number of times articles have been referenced in a significant number of refereed journals. We submitted proper names, article titles, and subject headings to create lists of articles that have been cited numerous times. The number of citations gave us an initial idea of how frequently the article had been cited in refereed journals. Using the *Web of Science* we established a list of articles, which because of their extensive referencing, have become seminal and historical works in the field of multicultural education. The authors cited in these pieces generated the names of over forty scholars who are both highly recognized or not immediately recognized for their scholarship in the area of multicultural education.

To extend the breadth and depth of these volumes, we returned to the *Web of Science* and used various subject headings to uncover other articles. The articles found in our second round of searching were also highly referenced by various scholars. The two searches were then cross-referenced for articles and authors. Through this process we attempted to reveal as many significant articles that dealt with multicultural education as possible. Some articles are foundational pieces of literature that have been copiously cited since their publication, while other articles represent a specific area of scholarship that has received less attention. For example, articles specific to early childhood and middle school education were not as easily identified as conceptual pieces that articulated various aspects of multicultural education.

The *Web of Science* program has some limitations. Articles that were published in less mainstream or more radical journals may not appear. The creation of a list of articles based solely on this program begs the questions of "What knowledge is of most worth?" and "How do we validate and acknowledge those significant contributions that have been marginalized in educational discourses?"

As multicultural educators, we were cautious not to re-instantiate those very discourses and practices that marginalize academic conversations. Therefore we used other educational and social science databases and traditional library-stack searches to present a more comprehensive set of texts that represent the field of multicultural education. For example, the reference sections in the first two searches were cross-referenced for articles that may not have appeared on-line. These articles were manually located, assessed, and used for their reference pages as well.

The main program limitation that haunted us was the lack of articles from the late 1960s and early 1970s that appeared in the electronic searches. We realized that educational research is lacking a comprehensive knowledge of its history because many scholars only cite articles written in the last ten to fifteen years when reporting their findings in academic journals. The lack of citations from the early years of multicultural education scholarship forced us to take a third approach to researching articles.

Using the ERIC files from 1966–1981 and manually sifting through bounded journals from the 1960s and 1970s, we were able to uncover other significant articles to include in the volumes. The decision to include or exclude certain articles rested primarily on the editors and other scholars who reviewed earlier drafts of the introductions to each volume and the references cited for that volume. We used the feedback from these scholars to complete our search for articles.

The volumes are a reflection of the field of research in multicultural education as well as a reflection of the community of scholars who contribute to the discourse(s) concerning issues of equity and equality in public schools. Our concern with shouldering such an awesome responsibility and our desire to include the voices from the many communities of multicultural education scholarship lead us to the final approach to finding quality articles. We solicited the opinions of over twenty multiculturalists. We asked them to choose the articles they believed belong in the volumes and suggest articles or areas that were not represented. Several scholars such as Sonia Nieto, Carlos Ovando, and Christine Sleeter answered our request and provided us with valuable feedback.

Polling various academic communities made the project a more inclusive effort, but also served as a tool to communicate the work of multicultural scholars. We appreciated the opportunity to engage with other scholars during the creation of these volumes. The multi-step research methodology for this project strengthens and enhances the finished product, making the volumes a valuable contribution to the field of education. This set of volumes, because it represents the voices of many scholars, is a spirited set of articles that reflects the tenets of multicultural education, its history, its present, its ideas for the future, and the people who believe in equity and social justice for all citizenry.

Features of the volumes

Each volume in the set includes a diverse group of authors that have written in the field of multicultural education. The array of work is based on the article's contribution to educational scholarship; they represent well-known and lesser-known points of view and areas of scholarship. The volumes do not promote one scholar's vision of multicultural education, but include conflicting ideals that inform multiple interpretations of the field.

Many of the articles from the early 1970s and 1980s are difficult for students to obtain because technology limits the number of years that volumes can be accessed through web databases. Volumes in the set provide students with access to the foundational articles that remain solely in print. Students and veteran scholars doing historical research may be especially interested in the volumes because of the rich primary sources.

The volumes are delineated by six subject groupings: *Conceptual Frameworks and Curricular Content, Foundations and Stratifications, Instruction and Assessment, Policy and Governance, Students and Student Learning*, and *Teachers and Teacher Education*. These six, broadly defined areas reflect the diversity of scholarship dealing with issues of equity and social justice in schooling. The articles illustrate the progression of research and theory and provide a means for readers to reflect upon the changes in language and thought processes concerning educational scholarship. Readers also will see how language, pedagogical issues, policy reforms, and a variety of proposed solutions for equity attainment have been constructed, assimilated, and mutated over the thirty year time period.

Volume I: Conceptual Frameworks and Curricular Issues

The articles in this volume illustrate the initial and continued debates over the concepts, definitions, meanings, and practices that constitute multicultural education. The authors articulate how best to represent the history and citizens of the United States, what types of content should be covered in public schools, and the types of learning environments that best serve the needs of all students. For example, this volume shows how multicultural education challenged the representations of people of color that are presented or ignored in textbooks. Conversely, articles that challenge conceptions of multicultural education are also included. Content wars over the infusion of authors of color, the inclusion of multiple historical perspectives, and an appreciation for various scientific and social contributions from people of color that reflect challenges to Eurocentric knowledge and perspectives are presented in this volume.

Volume II: Foundations and Stratifications

This volume presents theoretical and empirical articles that discuss the institutional factors that influence schooling. Issues such as the historical configurations of schools, ideologies of reproduction and resistance, and administrative structures that often maintain imbalances of power and equity in schools are discussed. In addition, articles explicating the various ways that students and educational opportunities are racially and socio-economically stratified are present in this volume.

Volume III: Instruction and Assessment

The articles in this volume elucidate general pedagogical approaches and specific instructional approaches with consideration given to content areas and grade level. Diverse instructional practices and the relationships between students and their teachers are discussed. Although content and pedagogy are difficult to separate, the work in this volume addresses the dispositions of the teacher and his/her awareness of learning styles, and his/her ability to incorporate aspects of students' culture and community affiliations into pedagogy. Also included in this volume are theories and models of multicultural assessment tools that reflect the needs of diverse learning communities.

Volume IV: Policy and Policy Initiatives

This volume on policy and governance explores the effects of federal and state mandates on school reforms dealing with equity in education. The articles in this volume show how educational organizations and associations have attempted to influence and guide school policy, instructional practices, and teacher-education programs. In addition, the volume presents articles that discuss how interest groups (e.g., parents and concerned teachers) influence enactments of education policy in schools.

Volume V: Students and Student Learning

This volume on "Students and Student Learning" focuses on students as individuals, scholars, and members of various social and cultural groups. The articles highlight different aspects of students' lives and how they influence their academic behaviors and includes students' affective responses to their schooling and their beliefs about the value of education. The articles also address how schools socially construct student learning through the lenses of race, class, and gender. In addition, the articles show how students act as political agents to structure, direct, and often derail their academic progress. Arguing that multicultural education is necessary for everyone, the articles highlight specific racial and cultural groups as well as offer generalizations about the academic needs of all students.

Volume VI: Teachers and Teacher Education

The teacher education volume addresses issues of multicultural education for preservice and experienced teachers. The articles cover the racial and social demographics of the past and current teaching force in the United States and the impact of these demographics on the structure of multicultural teacher education programs. Several articles speak to the role(s) of the university concerning multicultural preservice and in-service education classes, field placements, and institutional support for veteran teachers. These articles explore the nature of teaching for social justice in higher education, the desire to attract teachers of color, and the juncture between theory and practice for newly licensed teachers.

ACKNOWLEDGEMENTS

There are many who deserve a public thank you for their support of and participation in this project. We would like to thank the many colleagues and graduate
students who offered constructive criticism, suggested articles, read drafts of the
introductions, and helped to conceptualize the placement of articles in the different volumes. These people include: Barbara Bales, Anthony Brown, Keffrelyn
Brown, Nikola Hobbel, Etta Hollins, Gloria Ladson-Billings, Sonia Nieto, Carlos
Ovando, Christine Sleeter, and Michael Zambon.

We would like to offer a special thank you to the journals that, because of the
nature of the project, reduced or forgave their fees for re-printing.

Thanks to Director JoAnn Carr and the staff in the Center for Instructional
Materials and Computing (CIMC) for putting up with our large piles of bound
and unbound journals that we pulled from the shelves and made unavailable for
others for days at a time. Thank you for re-shelving all the publications (sometimes over and over again) and never reprimanding us for the amount of work we
created.

A super big thank you to Jennifer Austin for compiling, organizing, and maintaining our files of publishers' permission requests. Jennifer also contacted and
reasonably harassed folks for us until they gave her the answers we needed. Brava!

Thank you to our families for their support and only occasionally asking
"Aren't you finished yet?"

STATEMENT CONCERNING ARTICLE AVAILABILITY AND THE CONFLICT WITH REPRINT COST

During this insightful, extensive process, the goal was to share re-printings of all the articles with our readers. However, as we moved to the end of our journey, we discovered that it was financially unfeasible to secure permissions from the publishers of all the articles. We found most publishers more than willing to either donate articles or grant us significant breaks on their re-printing prices. Other publishers were more intractable with their fees. Even if the budget allowed for the purchasing of the 200-plus articles, the price of the books would have become prohibitive for most readers. Therefore, the printed articles found in the volumes do not represent all the articles that met the criteria outlined in the Preface and are discussed in each of the volumes' introductions.

At first we decided not to summarize these articles and use them solely as support for the rest of the volume(s). As we refined our introductions and re-read (and read again) the articles, we could not discount how these pieces continued to provide significant knowledge and historical reflections of the field that are unique and timely. Therefore, if the volumes are to represent the most often referenced examples and keenly situated representations of multicultural education and paint a historically conceptualized picture of the field, we had no choice but to include the works of these scholars in our introductions. Unfortunately, for the reasons explained here, some of these articles are not included in these volumes. In Appendix 2, we have provided a list of all the publishers and publishing houses so that individuals and organizations may access these articles from their local or university libraries or web services free of charge.

LIST OF JOURNALS REPRESENTED IN THE SIX-VOLUME SET

Action in Teacher Education
American Association of Colleges for Teacher Education
American Educational Research Association
American Journal of Education
American Sociological Association
Anthropology and Education
Association for Supervision and Curriculum Development
Comparative Education Review
Curriculum and Teaching
Education
Education and Urban Society
Educational Horizons
Educational Leadership
Educational Research Quarterly
Educators for Urban Minorities
English Journal
Exceptional Children
FOCUS
Harvard Educational Review
Interchange
Journal of Curriculum Studies
Journal of Curriculum and Supervision
Journal of Teacher Education
Journal of Research and Development in Education
Journal of Negro Education
Journal of Literacy Research (formerly *Journal of Reading Behavior*)
Journal of Educational Thought
Journal of Teacher Education
Language Arts
Momentum
Multicultural Education
National Catholic Educational Association
National Council for the Social Studies
National Educational Service
Negro Educational Review
Peabody Journal of Education

Phi Delta Kappan
Race, Class, and Gender in Education
Radical Teacher
Researching Today's Youth: The Community Circle of Caring Journal
Review of Educational Research
Southeastern Association of Educational Opportunity Program Personnel
    (SAEOPP)
Teacher Education and Special Education
Teachers College Record
The American Scholar
The Educational Forum
The High School Journal
The Journal of Educational Research
The New Advocate
The Social Studies
The Teacher Educator
The Urban Review
Theory into Practice
Viewpoints in Teaching and Learning
Young Children

INTRODUCTION TO VOLUME V

In many ways the student volume of the *History of Multicultural Education* series is the most important. There are no schools, teachers, administrators, or teacher educators without the students to teach. Students are the primary element of schools. Although their needs are often overlooked and their experiences undervalued (Lincoln, 1995), students are the reason that schools exist. Yet, we know very little about what learning environments work best for students and why certain students are more successful at negotiating public schools than others.

Although we would argue that multicultural education benefits all students and is not only directed toward students of color, we recognize that the bulk of the literature in educational research, theory, and practice most often constructs multicultural education as a tool to be used to engage students of color and to promote equitable policies and practices regarding marginalized groups where great imbalances exist. Ironically, by using white middle-class students as the norm and the control for experiments and value standards, research focused on students of color often provides significant information about white students as well. Thus the binding of race to multicultural education holds both positive and negative outcomes for research that focuses on the needs of students from racially and culturally diverse backgrounds. Using white middle-class students as the norm automatically positions all students who statistically differ as abnormal. In the case of certain Asian American groups that have outscored white students on standardized tests, these students gain the reputation as being overly studious, easy to teach, and easy to ignore. At the other end of the spectrum, those students who continue to score below white middle-class students on achievement tests become the objects of endless speculation that attempts to pinpoint the root of their social or cognitive deficits. Given this preoccupation with differentiated student achievement in opposition to a more heterogenous normative group, educational research primarily explores various groups of students through lenses of deficit and difference.

In the case of students of color, questions concerning what practices and contexts best promote student learning become more complex and difficult to answer than those focused on the more homogenous group of white middle-class students. The past thirty years of research on students of color (eg. their pathways to learning, their (dis)connection with schools, and their motivation to achieve and their resistance to conform to the structures of U.S. schools and classrooms) is flooded with generalizations and particularizations that have not significantly changed the way teachers teach or schools are run (Deschenes *et al.*, 2001). These generalizations and the dissolution of these restrictive conversations are enmeshed in the social contexts and political movements of the United States.

Certain debates about children of color have been sustained in social science research and in social and economic policy reforms. Researchers and policy makers continue to debate theories of cultural difference and cultural deficit when looking at ways to best serve communities that have been marginalized by race, gender, ethnicity, and economics. Innumerable scholars either wish to change the child and help him/her assimilate into the dominant Euro-centric culture or desire to change schools to reflect the styles of learning and collaboration that are found in the smaller communities of the child's home. We see these arguments reflected throughout the six volumes in the series. Each volume in some way addresses the problem of *who* or *what* should change to make all children have the opportunity to experience academic success. Do we change the child to fit the schools so that he/she will supposedly have an easier transition into the world of work, or do we change the schools so that the child experiences more immediate success that later may be jeopardized by unchanging paradigms of professionalism and performances of accept-able behavior as they matriculate through their careers? These two questions have no agreed-upon answers. Research on the child of color and his/her relationship to public schools revolves around this binary stratification. Education researchers have taken different approaches to trying to understand the lives of children.

The research of the seventies explored the various factors of student achievement and motivation. Sociologists looked at the impact of race, gender, and socioeconomic status to predict student success. These studies attempted to bracket students into successful and unsuccessful groups by delineating their achievement in a codification of race and class that is difficult to measure or standardize (Henderson, 1980). In his review of this research, Banks (1988) points out that very few studies have the same definition for social class measures, nor do the studies ask the same questions of their subjects. According to Banks, these early studies did not take into account the fluidity of socioeconomic status within groups and families. What does it mean to be middle-class? Grant and Sleeter (1988) found that most students identify themselves as middle-class even when their income level identifies them as low-income or upper middle-level-income students.

Attribution Theory and its Legacy in Research on Students

Attribution theory, the exploration of locus of control, was a primary means to explain why students of color across all income levels exhibited more external locus of control than white students (Henderson, 1980). An external locus of control means that a person more often believes that his/her levels of success are heavily impacted by factors outside their personal control. An internal locus of control means that a person is more likely to believe his/her destiny and success primarily depends on their individual effort. White middle-class stu-dents most often demonstrate high levels of internal locus of control, while students of color demonstrate high levels of external locus of control. High external locus of control is viewed as a detriment to students of color because they are less likely to take personal credit for their success and failure in schools. Seen as a roadblock to higher motivation, educators began to develop ways that students of color could increase their internal motivation and see themselves as the primary agents of their success. While these instruments measured the range of students' locus of control, they did not answer *why* students of color functioned under external locus of control.

Given the United States' history of racism and classism it is understandable that students of color would quickly learn, either explicitly through their families' stories of injustice and oppression or implicitly through their own experiences with racism, that their ambition and progress would always be tempered by race and racism beyond their control (Nieto, 1994). Moreover, when looking at the role of religion in communities of color, students would be less likely to take credit for their own achievement and success when the emphasis in church is on the value of the community and the will of God (Gibson, 1982; Schwartz,

1971). In the early literature on marginalized groups, external locus of control was seen as a deficit in children of color, not a phenomenon that could be explained by an exploration of history, contexts, and culture.

The shift to exploring the reasons for differing loci of control ushered in Ogbu's (1983) work on voluntary and involuntary minority status. Much of the work in education that focuses on students of color and achievement challenges or supports Ogbu's idea that Black students (involuntary minorities) experience great difficulty in reconciling formal schooling and their racialized community values. Conversely, Ogbu theorized that those students whose ancestors willingly came to the United States (voluntary minorities) and were not tainted by generations of oppression in the U.S. were far more likely to adopt the values of meritocracy and hard work that are encouraged by U.S. schools. Researchers who focus on groups of students have used their work to complicate and interrogate Ogbu's work (Fordham, 1996; Lee, 1996).

Combining the work of Ogbu with principles of multicultural education, other researchers have explored instructional models and strategies that value students' home communities and push for rigorous academic work (Baker, 1983; Cummins, 1986; Larke, 1991; Moll & Gonzalez, 1994). Researchers who try to bridge students' home communities with their formal schooling experiences have put forth learning style models, frameworks for understanding culture (Heath, 1983; Hollins, 1996) conceptualization of language learning (Cazden, 1988), models of good teaching (Ladson-Billings, 1994), and assessments of good schools (Lawrence-Lightfoot, 1983) to assist teachers and administrators with the task of creating meaningful and supportive learning environments for students of color. However, even within a dialogue concerning effective pedagogical strategies for students of color in public schools, researchers consistently acknowledge that there are no generalizations that will hold true for all students of a particular racial or ethnic group. What the research on students of color has given to teachers and teacher educators is a broad set of guidelines and considerations to help teachers reflect on their choices and act in ways that leave space for students to feel valued and empowered so that learning can happen.

The articles in this volume give insight into how educators have arrived at certain guidelines and considerations. Starting from 1971 and continuing until the new millennium, these articles show the progression of what we, as education researchers, know about students of color and how we know it. This selection of articles is also significant because it demonstrates the evolution of research in the field of education. In this volume several authors critique quantitative sociological research methods as the primary vehicle for understanding issues of student success and failure. Just as these researchers extend our knowledge about U.S. students, they challenge the types of questions and methods that have been privileged in educational research to explore these issues. The expansion of research and research methods often does not bring clarity to the field of education research; instead these new traditions add complexity and depth to the previous body of work.

Rather than present these articles in a chronological format, they are presented in three overarching areas of research: students and their experiences with schools, students different cultural backgrounds and family structures, and the intersections of race, class, and gender in student identity. Each area overlaps with other areas, but also provides a distinct focus that comes from the articles and the following analysis.

Single Group Studies

In the field of educational research there is a significant amount of work that deals with the perceptions, families, communities, and achievement of students from different racial groups. This research often confirms or debunks generalizations about all students or particular racial groups that have been marginalized in education research. The interplay between generalizability and specificity strongly comes across in the two articles concerning Asian American students.

Young and Pang (1995) and Kao (1995) each attempted to define the diversity with the Asian American umbrella and demonstrate the political unity of the term. They refute Ogbu's work with their empirical studies of high and low achieving Asian American students. They describe the ethnic, class, and generation differences between groups of kids in K-12 schools. They state that the model-minority myth hurts those students who do need help and continues to position Asian Americans as "other" to whites and other minority groups. Using quantitative measures to compare the reading and math scores of Asian Americans to white students, Grace Kao further attacked the myth of academic excellence among all Asian Americans. Her data analysis showed that not all groups of Asian American students outperform white students. The students' performances on standardized tests vary with regard to cultural and behavioral differences. Young and Pang moved their argument a step further to state that different ethnic groups often conflict because of their histories outside the United States. They explained that not only must teachers understand that the groups have different histories with the U.S., but that they have complicated histories with each other which may impact classroom dynamics and student learning.

Similarly, the reading on American Indians reinforces the notion that teachers must understand the historical and present contexts of American Indian students. Chiago (1981) provided a brief background on historical events and legal documents that impact the historical and present day education resources of American Indians. Chiago spoke in general terms about American Indians, while Deyhle (1995) used the Navajo Nation to dispel stereotypes about American Indians and refute Ogbu's theory of involuntary minorities. Her ethnographic research spans a ten-year period in which she documented how pervasive racism, both in and out of schools, works to oppress Navajos on and off the reservation. Both Chiago and Deyhle make reference to city-dwellers and reservation dwellers. These distinctions help readers to better understand the complexity of group affiliation and pushes readers past stereotypes and historically petrified notions of American Indians.

Robert Sizemore's (1981) early piece points to classroom dynamics and the interactions between teachers and students as relevant to the learning process. He utilized a teacher perceiver test to assess the difference between the ways white and black students view their teachers and their learning needs. This early attempt to categorize students' perceptions of teachers by race is one example of a significant body of work connecting affective elements of teaching and learning to academic outcomes.

Scott-Jones and Clark (1986) looked to the social environment of science class to answer questions about African American female students' academic performance. While socioeconomic status and race can be used as indicators of success in science, these indicators do not take into account how teachers transmit bias through their practices or how students assess their own ability to understand science. The authors contended that race is a mediating factor that is significantly bound with gender in science classrooms.

Pohan and Bailey (1997) provide ways for teachers and administrators to create a more welcoming and inviting atmosphere for gay and lesbian youth using multicultural education as a fully inclusive practice. Although gay and lesbian students do not constitute a racial or ethnic group, we are defining them as a cultural group that faces similar issues of bias and oppression in schools. Ginsberg (1999) articulated elements of group culture and behavioral characteristics that define gay and lesbian youth as a marginalized group. Both articles describe the dangers associated with gay and lesbian youth that involve being physically ostracized from family and friends and targeted for physical abuse by other groups in the school.

Intersections of Race, Class, and Gender

The articles on gay and lesbian students are significant segues to discussions of the intersections of race, class, and gender because homosexuality does not belong to one racial or ethnic categorization. In addition, mixed-race children are often overlooked when researchers explore issues of race and schooling. Cortes (1999) reminds the multicultural community that mixed-race students face the stereotypes of their racial groups and the conflicts between them. Regardless of the students' mixed background, these students are besieged with conflicting images of their identity and often forced to make choices to align themselves with one race. At a time when there are more mixed-race children than in previous years, it should be recognized that generalizations about students are subject to breakdown with regard to multiple racial affiliations and diverse family backgrounds.

Although generalizations and flexible concepts about the ways in which students from diverse communities and racial groups learn and interact in classrooms are valuable knowledge, it should always be balanced and tempered by other social issues that deeply impact the lives and experiences of children. The next section of articles explores the intersections of race, class, and gender in the lives and expectations of students.

Researchers who study diversity must continue to assert that intra-group diversity can be more profuse and complex than inter-group diversity. Historically, researchers sought to highlight the divisions between groups because the groups seemingly functioned in significantly different ways. Politically, it is a good strategy to create solidarity among racial groups in order to press forward with an agenda for school reform. However, it is difficult to sustain such cohesion when groups are inherently splintered by various experiences, forms of oppression, and histories with their home countries and the U.S.

Hawkins and Furst (1971) replicated an earlier study on student anxiety to correlate race and socioeconomic standing with elementary students' levels of stress. This study is one example of a substantial line of research that explores the relationships between various social indicators and student achievement. The authors concluded that African Americans experience more stress than white children, which affects their ability to be academically successful. Similar to this study, other quantitative representations, such as *The Bell Curve* (Herrnstein & Curray, 1983), pose African American students as deviant and separate from the norm.

To investigate the ways in which race, class, and gender have been addressed in educational research, Grant and Sleeter (1986) reviewed four leading education journals over a period of ten years. They found that these issues continued to be considered separately and argued for an integrated analysis. In their second piece, crafted from their larger book, Grant and Sleeter (1988) enacted their vision of research by providing readers with a longitudinal look at a group of junior high school students. The seven-year time span and the integrated analysis make this a rare seminal work in multicultural education.

Nieto's (1994) article almost ten years later is another seminal piece. Instead of focusing on the obstacles preventing student achievement, Nieto highlights the characteristics of these diverse students that help them to succeed. Nieto is one of the first multicultural scholars to advocate for the use of student voice in teacher education and policy arenas. In this article, she makes a case for listening to students talk about their experiences with schools.

Matching the Needs of Diverse Students to Elements of Schooling

The fourth section of the volume explores the connections that students make to their schools and their experiences as students. Capturing the essence of schooling is a difficult task. Researchers rely on qualitative research to measure student progress and resistance, they use interviews and observations with students or reflections from adults to better understand what keeps students in school, what motivates them to continue, and what pushes them away from completing their education. This information is then organized into prototypes of curriculum and pedagogical practices that are meant to enhance the learning of different groups.

An early example that depicts the breach between the culture of the students and the culture of their schools is Gibson's (1982) ethnography of students in St Croix. Although this is not based on U.S. schools, the changing demographics of teachers, the conflicts between schools and parents, the larger social issues concerning employment opportunities, and the implications for future research closely mirror urban contexts in the U.S. Gibson's work is one of the first descriptive accounts of students and their experiences in and out of schools. Her work serves as a template for qualitative research on schools and students that supports other educational theory and research.

The belief that the conflict between students and schools is greater than teacher/student interactions in the classroom (Cummins, 1986; Deschenes *et al.*, 2001; Henderson, 1980) is further explored in several of the articles. These articles represent three different time periods and shifting ideologies concerning the disconnect between schools and students. Henderson (1980) proposed that it is the students who must be changed through a series of classroom procedures. This article represents the cultural deficit theory of students of color. He contributes to an on-going line of research that uses attribution theory, or locus of control, to explain why students of color are less likely to believe they control their destinies.

Later articles show how the question of student achievement is an outcome of school structures that are designed to privilege a small minority of students. Cummins (1986) asserted that relationships between schools and communities must change before the schools will be able to serve racially diverse communities. His focus on the needs of language minority students is a necessary contribution to discussions on the changing roles of schools.

Banks (1988) further articulates a desire to see schools be more reflective of student populations. Using a meta-analysis of research on attribution theory, cultural deficit theories, and cultural difference hypotheses, he contended that the frameworks for research students of color were flawed and oversimplified because they did not take into account aspects of students' experiences that cannot be quantified. Similar to the Grant and Sleeter (1986) article that called for an integrative analysis, Banks made the push for new ways of researching students of color that would reflect their community alliances and family histories.

Banks's article supports Baker's (1983) call for administrators and teachers to learn about students' culture and multiple communities in order to motivate them. Baker asserted that teachers can overcome the disconnect between school and home by becoming more culturally literate and aware of content being used in classrooms. Similarly, Moll and Gonzalez (1994) advocated for teachers to cultivate a culturally relevant focus that involves seeing students' strengths instead of focusing on their perceived weaknesses.

In order to confront stereotypes of Latino and African American families, Moll and Gonzalez developed a "funds of knowledge" approach to teaching. By asking teachers to research their students' families and communities, the teachers were able to observe many of the positive community and familial structures in the lives of their students. They stated, "One implication, and a most important one, is debunking ideas of working-class, language minority households as lacking worthwhile knowledge and experiences" (Moll & Gonzalez, 1994, p. 444). These observations helped the teachers to make deeper connections between the students' homes and communities and their schooling experiences.

Deschenes *et al.* (2001) ended their articles with suggestions for reform. In the millennium, they echo other authors' calls for school transformations. Although it was published outside the time span of the other articles in the volume, their historical perspective on the institutions of school is a significant contribution to research on students and schools.

Conclusions

These articles serve as teaching tools and learning experiences for teachers, researchers, and education scholars. Looking at the progression from the early eighties to the beginning of the millennium, there is an evolution of particular arguments. Multicultural education has attempted to move the field of research to do more complex and in-depth analysis of students' lives and experiences. For MCE scholars, the responsibility for connecting academic learning with students has been firmly placed on the school. This argument has moved from a discussion of students of color as deficit and in need of alteration, to a critique of the role(s) of public schooling. And while no side of any debate ever disappears in education, the field of research concerning students has greatly expanded and continues to expand to include diverse perspectives on how and why students do or do not achieve in public schools.

References

Baker, G. C. (1983). Motivating the culturally different student. *Momentum, 14,* 44–45.

Banks, J. A. (1988). Ethnicity, class, cognitive, and motivational styles: Research and teaching implications. *Journal of Negro Education, 57*(4), 452–466.

Cazden, C. (1988). *Classroom Discourse: The language of teaching and learning.* Portsmouth: Heinemann.

Chiago, R. K. (1981). Making education work for the American Indian. *Theory into Practice, 20*(1), 20–25.

Cortes, C. (1999). Mixed-race children: Building bridges to new identities. *Reaching Today's Youth: The Community Circle of Caring Journal, 3*(2), 28–31.

Cummins, J. (1986). Empowering minority students: A framework for intervention. *Harvard Educational Review, 56*(1), 18–36.

Deschenes, S., Cuban, L., & Tyack, D. (2001). Mismatch: Historical perspectives on schools and students who don't fit them. *Teachers College Record, 103*(4), 525–547.

Deyhle, D. (1995). Navajo youth and angle racism. *Harvard Educational Review, 65*(3), 403–444.

Fordham, S. (1996). *Blacked Out: Dilemmas of race, identity, and success at Capital High.* Chicago: University of Chicago Press.

Gibson, M. (1982). Reputation and respectability: How competing cultural systems affect students' performance in school. *Anthropology and Education, 13*(1), 3–27.

Ginsberg, R. W. (1999). In the triangle/out of the circle: Gay and lesbian students facing the heterosexual paradigm. *The Educational Forum, 64*(Fall), 46–54.

Grant, C. A., & Sleeter, C. E. (1986). Race, class, and gender in education research: An argument for integrative analysis. *Review of Research, 56*(2), 195–211.

Grant, C. A., & Sleeter, C. E. (1988). Race, class, and gender and abandoned dreams. *Teachers College Record, 90*(1), 19–40.

Hawkins, T. H., & Furst, N. F. (1971). Race, socio-economic situation, IQ, and teacher ratings of student behavior as factors relating to anxiety in upper elementary school children. *Sociology of Education, 44*(3), 333–350.

Heath, S. B. (1983). *Ways with Words: Language, life and work in communities and classrooms.* Cambridge: Cambridge Paperback Library.

Henderson, R. (1980). Social and emotional needs of culturally diverse children. *Exceptional Children, 46*(8), 598–605.

Herrnstein, R. J., & Curray, C. (1983). *The Bell Curve: Intelligence and class structure in American life.* New York: Free Press.

Hollins, E. R. (1996). *Culture in School Learning: Revealing the deep meaning.* Mahwah, New Jersey: Lawrence Erlbaum.

Kao, G. (1995). Asian Americans as model minorities? A look at their academic performance. *American Journal of Education, 103,* 121–159.

Ladson-Billings, G. (1994). *Dreemkeepers: Successful teachers of African American students.* New York: Macmillan.

Larke, P. J. (1991). Multicultural education: A vital investment strategy for culturally diverse youth groups. *SAEOPP,* 11–22.

Lawrence-Lightfoot, S. (1983). *The Good High School.* New York: Basic Books.

Lee, S. (1996). *Unraveling the "Model Minority" Stereotype.* New York: Teachers College Press.

Lincoln, Y. S. (1995). In search of students voices. *Theory into Practice, 34*(2), 88–93.

Moll, L., & Gonzalez, N. (1994). Lessons from research with language-minority children. *Journal of Reading Behavior, 26*(4), 439–457.

Nieto, S. (1994). Lessons from students on creating a chance to dream. *Harvard Educational Review, 64*(4), 392–426.

Ogbu, J. (1983). Minority status and schooling in plural societies. *Comparative Education Review, 27*(2), 168–190.

Pohan, C. A., & Bailey, N. J. (1997). Opening the closet: Multiculturalism that is fully inclusive. *Multicultural Education, 5*(1), 12–15.

Schwartz, A. J. (1971). A comparative study of values and achievement: Mexican-American and Anglo youth. *Sociology of Education, 44*(4), 438–462.

Scott-Jones, D., & Clark, M. L. (1986). The school experiences of black girls: The interaction of gender, race, and socioeconomic status. *Phi Delta Kappan,* 520–527.

Sizemore, R. W. (1981). Do black and white students look for the same characteristics in teachers? *Journal of Negro Education, 50*(1), 48–62.

Young, R. L., & Pang, V. O. (1995). Asian Pacific American students: A rainbow of dreams. *Multicultural Education, 3*(2), 4–7.

PART 1

ATTRIBUTION THEORY AND ITS LEGACY IN RESEARCH ON STUDENTS

CHAPTER 1

SOCIAL AND EMOTIONAL NEEDS OF CULTURALLY DIVERSE CHILDREN (1980)

Ronald W. Henderson

Teachers and administrators are now well accustomed to being admonished that schools must do a better job of meeting the special needs of children from socially and culturally diverse backgrounds. The prevailing assumption behind this advice seems to be that if children differ culturally from the White, middle class dominated traditions of the schools, their needs must also differ. Thus, for example, educators are advised to match instructional strategies to the cognitive styles that are assumed to differentiate culturally diverse children from their Euro-American peers.

The consequences of following this advice are not clear. While some attempts to match instruction to different cultural styles have been reported as successful, other attempts have produced effects opposite to the hypothesized benefits of instructional matching (Kagan & Buriel, 1977). Moreover, the research base upon which the notion that ethnic groups differ along such cognitive style dimensions as field dependence/independence does not provide entirely consistent results (Knight, Kagan, Nelson, & Gumbiner, 1978). Similarly, inconclusive findings have been reported for such developmental characteristics as self esteem (Gray-Little & Applebaum, 1979) and locus of control (Knight, et al., 1978). In brief, while there is wide agreement that instruction should take culturally determined characteristics into consideration in order to reduce the undesirable effects of discontinuities between home and school learning, there is disagreement about the nature of the differences, their distribution within given groups, and how instruction should be adapted to take these factors into account.

If scientific information concerning the specific nature of cognitive needs among culturally diverse groups of children served by the schools is something less than definitive, knowledge of conditions required to promote their social and emotional well-being is even less clear. It seems unlikely that the basic needs of culturally diverse children vary on the basis of differences in their social and cultural characteristics. Rather it appears that a variety of social and cultural factors interact in ways that serve to curtail the probability that these needs will be met adequately within the context of schooling as presently constituted. While social scientists have shown a long standing interest in the ways in which sociocultural factors influence development, efforts to sort out the influences of complexly intertwined factors have been frustrated by both methodological and definitional problems.

Some of the problems that cloud the understanding of these interactions will be reviewed in this article, and a path model of reciprocal influences will be proposed with implications for the social and emotional well being of children whose cultural background deviates from the implicit expectations of the schools. Social and emotional well-being is too broad and ill defined a set of variables with which to explore the path model hypothesis. Therefore a more restricted aspect of social and emotional adjustment, functional adaptation, will serve to focus the premise explored in the latter portion of the article.

Cultural diversity and stereotypes
Basic concepts

The terms *culture* and *society* are used in varied and often undefined ways by social scientists and educators. In their examination of uses of the concept of culture, Kroeber and Kluckholm (1952) found over 160 definitions of the term in the social science literature. What most of the definitions had in common was the idea that culture is composed of habitual patterns of behavior that are characteristic of a group of people. Those shared behavioral patterns are transmitted from one generation to the next through symbolic communication (Kroeber & Kluckholm, 1952) and through modeling and demonstration (Henderson & Bergan, 1976). Culture includes the goals and values that serve to instigate behavior and determine priorities within a social group.

While British anthropologists use the term society to designate the concept that most American social scientists call culture (Evans-Pritchard, 1951; Radcliffe-Browne, 1957), Americans generally use the term society to designate an aggregation of individuals who live together in an organized population (Linton, 1936). Thus, *society* refers to a collective of people while *culture* focuses on the customary behaviors that are shared among people in the group. The terms are often used interchangeably when it is not considered important to distinguish between an aggregate of people and their customary patterns of behavior. The temptation to avoid making this conceptual distinction probably accounts for the popularity of the more general term, *sociocultural*.

People of differing statuses within a society play various roles, and the total set of roles make up the social structure of that group. These roles include those that define social stratification within a society.

The United States is a complex society in which a number of diverse groups may be identified. The members of any of these groups display a distinct way of life and social scientists often designate the group as a subculture. Valentine (1968, cited in Laosa, in press) has noted that the variety of units to which distinctive life ways have been attributed include such diverse groupings as ethnic collectives, socioeconomic strata, age groups, and regional populations. From this perspective it is certainly possible to talk about the subculture of public education as well. But subculture are distinct from the larger culture only in the limited sense that any part may be distinguished from the whole in which it is embedded (Laosa, in press), and it is in this limited sense that, for lack of a better designation, educators often refer to children who are members of identifiable groups— whose life ways deviate in certain ways from the dominant pattern—as *culturally diverse*, the term employed in this discussion.

Stereotypes

The pitfalls involved in distinguishing the influences of socialization experiences in a subculture are not easy to avoid, even by researchers who are aware of them. During the 1960's educators were introduced to studies that described the cultural characteristics of various ethnic groups. It was assumed that this information would help teachers to acquire a better understanding of the pupils in their charge. While every subcultural group is characterized by substantial heterogeneity (Laosa, in press), that diversity was largely ignored and stereotyped views were conveyed. For instance, motivational problems with Black children were attributed, in part, to a matriarchal family structure (Moynihan, 1967), a pattern that is less pervasive than the generalizations would suggest (English, 1974). Similarly, male dominance was seen as a hindrance to independence, mobility, and achievement among Mexican American youth (Heller, 1966); yet more recent work among migrant farm labor families found the most common mode of decision making to be egalitarian (Hawks & Taylor, 1975).

A number of studies have reported on the motivational characteristics of children from minority backgrounds. For example, the belief system of Hispanic Americans has been described as highly fatalistic (Heller, 1966; Madsen, 1964; Paz, 1961), a characteristic that has been blamed for hampering educational, social, and economic advancement. Yet when Farris and Glenn (1976) compared fatalism among Anglos and Mexican Americans in a Texas sample, they found no differences between the groups when they controlled for level of education.

Given findings that have helped to dispel cultural stereotypes, it should be remembered that in most ways members of subcultures within United States society are culturally more similar to each other than they are different, and in most cases within group variation exceeds between group variations. The world of subcultures is one of overlapping distributions.

Methodological problems

In an ideal world it should be possible to distinguish between the influences of various intertwined cultural and social structural variables. Many studies that compare ethnic or racial minority and nonminority children fail to control for socioeconomic status (Laosa, in press). Thus the results are ambiguous at best and usually misleading. Chan and Rueda (1979) rightly argued that researchers should be careful to distinguish between the effects of poverty and culture in their analyses, but that is more easily said than done. There is little research available on the social or emotional development of ethnic minority children that has accomplished such separation with clarity. Chan and Rueda (1979) made the point that poverty mediates both biomedical health and the socialization environment. Their point is especially well taken with reference to health, but the distinction begins to get more vague when the socialization environment is discussed. For example, they attributed lack of socialization information among the poor to their reliance on the electronic media rather than books, which may be considered an expensive luxury. It is at least as reasonable to attribute this pattern to culturally patterned preferences and values as to poverty in itself.

The difficulty of making clear distinctions between cultural and social structural influences is important because a disproportionate number of children who are from minority group subcultures are also poor. Not all minority children are poor, and not all poor children are minorities. However, poor children, whether minority or not, may display culturally acquired behavior that deviates from the expectations implicit in the culture of the school. To the extent that this is true, they also may be considered "culturally diverse" for purposes of the present discussion.

Social and emotional well-being

Problems of social and emotional well-being for culturally diverse children may be examined in a number of alternative ways. For example, as a result of discontinuities between home and school, many culturally diverse children encounter aversive experiences at school that could be explained by conditioning principles. The approach selected for present purposes is to focus on a specific aspect of social competence. The term *social competence* has an appealing ring to it, but as many observers have commented (Anderson & Messick, 1974; Zigler & Trickett, 1978), experts are far from agreement on the meaning of that construct. Recent work (Monson, Greenspan, & Simeonsson, 1979) has conceptualized social competence with reference to interpersonal functioning in social settings such as classrooms. Dimensions of this conceptualization that have been examined include interest, curiosity, or assertiveness and conformity to rules and expectations (Kohn & Rosman, 1972; Monson, Greenspan, & Simeonsson, 1979). These conceptions are compatible with Laosa's (1979) position that social competence involves functional adaptations to specific environments. Each environment may have its own specific demand characteristics for functional adaptation, and for a child success in two different environments may depend on the degree of overlap in the demand characteristics of the environments (Laosa, 1979).

Within the school environment, demand characteristics to which functional adaptations are required include such behaviors as appearing interested in school work, paying attention, and persisting at tasks. The present discussion focuses on the possible consequences for culturally diverse children who are unable to make a functional adaptation to the interpersonal setting of the school. But implicitly, the conceptualization presented here assumes that a condition required for primary prevention is for educators to know something about the child's environmental organization (Laosa, 1979), and to make adaptations in the interpersonal environment of the classroom that will enable the child to adapt to the requirements of school culture.

A path model for children at risk

A substantial body of research reviewed by Brophy and Good (1974) shows quite uniformly that teachers hold differential expectations regarding the academic performance of children who vary in personal characteristics such as sex, age, ethnicity, race, and even physical attractiveness (Brophy & Good, 1974; Henderson, in press). It could be argued that these expectancies are based on actual knowledge of children's motivation and achievement characteristics, but it is instructive to note that teachers may express stereotyped expectations based upon labels assigned to children even when the objective behavioral evidence runs contrary to those expectations.

This point is illustrated in a study (Foster & Ysseldyke, 1976) in which teachers viewed a videotape of a normal fourth grade boy engaged in various test taking and free play activities. Different groups of teachers who viewed the tapes were told that the child whose behavior was depicted on the tape suffered from a different disorder: emotional disturbance, learning disability, or mental retardation. One group of viewers was informed that the child was normal. After viewing the tape, teachers expressed negative expectancies consistent with the deviance label they had been given. Differential expectations were expressed in spite of the fact that the behavior they witnessed was inconsistent with the label.

While the subjects in this study were not minority group children, the results seem particularly relevant to circumstances involving culturally diverse children, because these children have been so heavily overrepresented among those to whom deviance labels have been assigned (Richardson, 1979), and a number of studies have demonstrated that teacher expectations tend to be lower for minority than for majority children. The obvious question to ask, then, is whether or not variations in expectations are associated with differential behavior toward students. The answer seems to be yes.

Research reviewed by Good and Brophy (1974) revealed a fairly uniform pattern showing that whenever investigators have looked for differential treatment of students who vary in sex, achievement, or socioeconomic status, they have found it. An examination of the nature of these differences suggests that teacher communications toward children from lower socioeconomic status and/ or racial and ethnic minority backgrounds is more likely to be aimed at controlling or managing behavior than is the case for their peers. Communications to majority, middle class children, in contrast, are more likely to be relevant to the content or skills of instruction than those teacher behaviors that are directed to children from culturally diverse backgrounds (Henderson, in press; Laosa, 1977).

While there is little direct information on the specific effects of differential teacher behaviors on the school achievement of culturally diverse children, an accumulation of research results does establish the general case that level of student involvement in academic tasks and the nature of teacher-student interactions are consistently related to achievement (Hoge & Luce, 1979). These findings are of particular interest when viewed in relationship to research on locus of control and learned helplessness, which provides a theoretical framework to explain how differences in teacher expectancies and interaction patterns may affect both the socioemotional development and achievement patterns of children with diverse socialization experiences outside the school.

Perceptions of personal efficacy

Locus of control

Locus of control is a personality construct that refers to the tendency of different individuals to perceive the events that influence their lives either as the consequence of their own actions (internal control), or as the result of external forces beyond their influence (external control). There is generally a positive relationship between internal perceptions of control and academic achievement (Henderson, in press; Lefcourt, 1976). Minority and poor children tend to score more toward the external end of the scale than their nonminority and more affluent peers (Henderson & Bergan, 1976).

Attribution theory

Differences in locus of control have been explained on the basis of learned expectancies of reward as a consequence of behavior (Rotter, 1966), but more recently Heider's attribution theory (Weiner, 1979) has been used to amplify conceptions of locus of control and the closely related concept of learned helplessness. Individuals who find themselves unable to control aversive stimuli to which they are exposed often come to perceive themselves as helpless. Where the aversive experience is failure at a task that such individuals believe to be important, they may come to see themselves as incapable of overcoming failure. Failure leads to anxiety and deterioration of performance. Following failure experiences these individuals are likely to perform unsuccessfully even on tasks at which they were previously proficient. Children who experience repeated failure at the tasks assigned to them at school are likely to come to perceive themselves as incapable of accomplishing other tasks of the same kind. If the cognitive skills and behavioral norms a child has learned in the subculture of the home differ from those the school culture is prepared to build on, a disproportionate number of such children are likely to experience failure that is beyond their control and subsequently they will come to attribute failure to inability.

Causality may be attributed to a number of internal factors such as ability or effort, or to external factors such as luck or task difficulty (Heider, 1958). For example, an individual may perceive success or failure at a task as the result of ability (or inability), or level of effort. Within the norm referenced world of the classroom, children may be unable to discern their progress in relation to their own past performance, because implicit and explicit comparisons with peers are so salient (Henderson & Hennig, 1979). The influence of failure experiences on the learning of helplessness has been documented in a large number of studies with animal (e.g., Abramson, Seligman, & Teasdale, 1978) and human (e.g., Wortman, Panciera, Shusterman, & Hibscher, 1976) subjects. In those studies that hold the clearest implications for children with exceptional needs, and more especially for those from culturally diverse backgrounds, the uncontrollable, aversive events that have led to perceptions of inability have involved the manipulation of feedback that lead subjects to believe they have failed problems that measure important human abilities (Roth & Kubal, 1975).

Effects of learned helplessness

In a series of studies, Dweck and her associates (Diner & Dweck, 1978; Dweck, 1975; Dweck & Busch, 1976; Dweck & Reppucci, 1973) found that children who have learned to feel helpless when confronted with difficult problem tend to attribute their failure to inability, while their nonhelpless peers often display improved performance following failure. Their improvement may be attributed to increased effort.

Helpless children are likely to see aversive situations as insurmountable and thus fail to display effort on subsequent tasks of the same sort. They are less likely to be willing to initiate a task or persist at it than are individuals who perceive their own effort as an important cause of success or failure outcomes. This is an important point, since there is evidence that differential instructional behaviors of teachers may be more associated with teacher judgments of pupil motivation to do school work than with achievement expectations (Luce & Hoge, 1978). This finding is particularly relevant in association with data showing that the behavior of teachers is markedly influenced by aspects of functional adaptation such as attending and nonattending behavior of students. Together these strands of evidence suggest that if helpless children respond to failure by declining to expend effort on subsequent tasks, teachers may react with negative expectations. Consequently, their interactions may be directed toward behavioral control rather than skill and content instruction.

Thomas (1979) has drawn attention to the striking parallels between the learned helplessness pattern and the characteristics of children classified as learning disabled. While the learning disabilities concept designates a diverse array of problems, Thomas noted that a common characteristic of children to whom this label is applied is that they are often convinced that they cannot learn. Consequently, a good deal of teaching is aimed at getting them to expend sufficient effort to achieve success (Thomas, 1979). The stronger a child's history of failure is, the more likelihood there is of self attributions of inability, and the likelihood of effortful, attentive behavior is concomitantly reduced. It seems that the nature of some schools in the United States almost predestines certain children to experience repeated failure, beginning with their earliest classroom experience. Since the socialization experience of culturally diverse children may not be highly congruent with the curricular and behavioral expectations of the middle class oriented school, a disproportionate number of them are at risk of falling into this group.

Failure, linked to perceptions of personal inability, may be coupled with negative affect (Ames, Ames, & Felker, 1977). Failure may be experienced as a painful, punishing event, and the nature of responses to aversive stimuli are well documented. One response is escape or avoidance. Another is counter aggression (Henderson & Bergan, 1976). In the school context, either may be interpreted as alienation. Aversive failure experiences often produce anxiety, and a substantial body of research has documented the inverse relationship between anxiety and student ability to profit from instruction in school. Anxiety is linked to a range of academic indicators, including academic achievement and dropout rates (Tobias, 1979).

Facilitating environments and therapeutic approaches

A number of instructional characteristics appear to facilitate perceptions of internal control and efficacy, while other procedures have been effective in increasing children's effort attributions. When children perceive a role in determining their own activities, they appear more likely to accept personal responsibility for success or failure than children in classrooms where no such opportunity to participate in the setting of objectives is provided (Arlin & Whitley, 1978; Wang & Stiles, 1976). It has also been demonstrated that the effects of success and failure are mediated by the kinds of social situations in which they occur. Classrooms constitute one of the few social settings in which children are routinely subjected to public comparisons of performance, and social comparisons are especially salient in those classrooms that employ competitive goal structures (Ames, Ames, & Felker, 1977; Henderson & Hennig, 1979). Failure is less likely to result in self deprecation in classrooms that employ a cooperative goal structure than in those characterized by norm referenced competition (Ames, Ames, & Felker, 1977).

A variety of therapeutic procedures have proved effective in changing dysfunctional attributions of cause (Henderson, in press). Since repeated failure experiences are implicated in the development of maladaptive attributions, it may seem logical that the way to change attributions from perceptions of inability to those of insufficient effort would be to provide generous portions of success. This appears not to be the case. Dweck (1975) found that a success-only intervention did not improve the ability of helpless children to sustain effort following a failure experience. In fact, after a success-only intervention, many children showed a subsequent increase in sensitivity to failure. Children who were given a program of cognitively oriented attribution retraining displayed subsequent increases in effort attributions and improved adaptation to failure.

Both environmental control programs and self regulation programs have been found effective in changing socially and academically maladaptive classroom behavior. However, the effectiveness of a given procedure seems to interact with children's perceptions of causation. Bugenthal, Whalen, and Henker (1978) have recommended beginning with therapy that is in line with the child's perceptions of causation, and moving toward procedures that provide greater self control through the application of self regulation strategies.

Conclusions and implications

Culturally diverse children are at risk of entering school with behaviors that differ from the cognitive and social norms governing the expectations of teachers who have been socialized into the school culture. These differences appear to play an important role in the reciprocal relationships among the child's capabilities, his or her actual behaviors, the teacher's expectancies, and the teacher's responses to the child. Differences in children's ability to adapt to school norms appear closely related to the level of formal education their own mothers have attained (Laosa, in press). Behaviors such as attentiveness and persistence at the kinds of tasks teachers consider important tend to influence the expectancies teachers hold, and these expectations, in turn, often influence the manner in which they interact with children.

Children whose behavior is discrepant from the norms of the school culture are likely to experience repeated failure. If, as a result, they develop feelings of helplessness in the school setting, they may well exert less and less effort, which in turn leads to more failure. An important social need of these children is to experience a feeling of personal efficacy. While it has been suggested that patterns of failure among culturally diverse children might be eliminated if the school would build systematically on abilities acquired by children in their home environments, it has proved more difficult than anticipated to put this suggestion into practice (Gallimore & Au, 1979).

One thing that can be done is to help teachers become aware of their own expectancies and variations in their instructional interactions with different children. Research on learned helplessness also suggests that it may help to structure classroom social environments in less competitive ways than has been traditional. In addition, children may be helped to gain a greater sense of efficacy if they are taught to set some of their own goals and to employ self regulation procedures. But therapeutic procedures based on experimental demonstrations are doomed to fall short if they are tagged on as remedial procedures in isolation from the on-going activities of a classroom. To do so would only provide an illusion of personal control, and set children up for additional failure.

Bilingual and multicultural programs that enable children to experience cultural and linguistic pride certainly have an important role to play in meeting the social and emotional needs of children from diverse backgrounds (Gibson, 1978; Goebes & Shore, 1978), but they cannot fully accomplish their purposes unless children are helped to experience genuine feelings of personal and social competence within the total school setting. Existing research provides only indirect evidence relative to how reciprocal influences in classrooms might be turned to a better advantage for culturally diverse children. More specific research addressed to these dynamics is urgently needed.

References

Abramson, N. L., Seligman, M. E. P., & Teasdale, J. D. Learned helplessness in humans: Critique and reformulation. *Journal of Abnormal Psychology*, 1978, *87*, 49–74.
Ames, C., Ames, R., & Felker, D. W. Effects of competitive reward structure and valence of outcome on children's achievement attributions. *Journal of Educational Psychology*, 1977, *69*, 1–8.
Anderson, S. B., & Messick, S. Social competence in young children. *Developmental Psychology*, 1974, *10*, 282–293.
Arlin, M., & Whitley, T. W. Perceptions of self-managed learning opportunities and academic locus of control: A causal interpretation. *Journal of Educational Psychology*, 1978, *70*, 988–992.
Brophy, J. E., & Good, T. *Teacher-student relationships: Causes and consequences.* New York: Holt, Rinehart & Winston, 1974.
Bugenthal, D., Whalen, C. K., & Henker. Causal attributions of hyperactive children and motivational assumptions of two behaviour change approaches: Evidence for an interactionist position. *Child Development*, 1977, *48*, 874–884.
Chan, K. S., & Rueda, R. Poverty and culture in education: Separate but equal. *Exceptional Children*, 1979, *45*, 422–428.
Diner, C. I., & Dweck, C. S. An analysis of learned helplessness: Continuous changes in performance, strategy, and achievement conditions following failure. *Journal of Personality and Social Psychology*, 1978, *36*, 451–462.
Dweck, C. S. The role of expectations and attributions in the alleviation of learned helplessness. *Journal of Personality and Social Psychology*, 1975, *31*, 674–685.
Dweck, C. S., & Bush, E. S. Sex differences in learned helplessness: I. Differential debilitation with peer and adult evaluators. *Developmental Psychology*, 1976, *12*, 147–156.
Dweck, C. S., & Reppucci, N. D. Learned helplessness and reinforcement responsibility in children. *Journal of Personality and Social Psychology*, 1973, *25*, 109–116.
English, R. Beyond pathology: Research and theoretical perspectives on black families. In L. E. Gary (Ed.), *Social research and the black community: Selected issues and priorities.* Washington DC: Institute for Urban Affairs and Research, Howard University, 1974.
Evans-Pritchard, E. E. *Social Anthropology.* Glencoe IL: The Free Press, 1951.
Farris, B. E., & Glenn, N. D. Fatalism and familism among Anglos and Mexican Americans in San Antonio. *Sociology and Social Research*, 1976, *60*, 393–402.
Foster, G., & Ysseldyke, J. Expectancy and halo effects as a result of artificially induced teacher bias. *Contemporary Educational Psychology*, 1976, *1*, 37–45.
Gallimore, R., & Au, H. The competence/incompetence paradox in the education of minority culture children. *The Quarterly Newsletter of the Laboratory of Comparative Human Cognition*, 1979, *1*, 32–37.
Gibson, G. An approach to identification and prevention of developmental difficulties among Mexican-American children. *American Journal of Orthopsychiatry*, 1978, *48*, 96–113.
Goebes, D. D., & Shore, M. F. Some effects of bicultural and monocultural school environments on personality development. *American Journal of Orthopsychiatry*, 1978, *48*, 398–407.
Good, T. L., & Brophy, J. E. Changing teacher and student behavior: An empirical investigation. *Journal of Educational Psychology*, 1974, *66*, 390–405.
Gray-Little, B., & Applebaum, M. I. Instrumentality effects in the assessment of racial differences in self-esteem. *Journal of Personality and Social Psychology*, 1979, *37*, 1221–1229.
Hawkes, G. R., & Taylor, M. Power structure in Mexican and Mexican-American farm labor families. *Journal of Marriage and the Family*, *37*, 1975, 807–811.
Heider, F. *The psychology of interpersonal relations.* New York: Wiley, 1958.

Heller, C. S. *Mexican-American youth: Forgotten youth at the crossroads.* New York: Random House, 1966.

Henderson, R. W. Personal and social causation in the school context. In J. Worell (Ed.), *Developmental psychology for education.* New York: Academic Press, in press.

Henderson, R. W., & Bergan J. R. *The cultural context of childhood.* Columbus OH: Charles E. Merrill, 1976.

Henderson, R. W., & Hennig, H. Relationships among cooperation-competition and locus of control in academic situations among children in traditional and open classrooms. *Contemporary Educational Psychology,* 1979, *4,* 121–131.

Hoge, R. D., & Luce, S. Predicting academic achievement from classroom behavior. *Review of Educational Research,* 1979, *49,* 479–496.

Kagan, S. & Buriel, R. Field dependence-independence and Mexican-American culture and education. In J. L. Martinez (Ed.), *Chicano psychology.* New York: Academic Press, 1977.

Knight, G. P., Kagan, S., Nelson, W., & Gumbiner, J. Acculturation of second and third generation Mexican-American children. Field independence, locus of control, self-esteem, and school achievement. *Journal of Cross-Cultural Psychology,* 1978, *9,* 87–98.

Kohn, M., & Rosman, B. L. A social competence scale and symptom checklist for the preschool child. Factor dimensions, their cross-instrument generality, and longitudinal perspectives. *Developmental Psychology,* 1972, *6,* 430–444.

Kroeber, A. L., & Kluckhohn, C. *Culture: A critical review of concepts and definitions.* New York: Vintage Books, 1952.

Laosa, L. M. Inequality in the classroom: Observational research on teacher-student interactions. *Aztlan International Journal of Chicano Studies Research,* 1977, *8,* 51–67.

Laosa, L. M. Maternal behavior: Sociocultural diversity in modes of family interaction. In R. W. Henderson (Ed.), *Parent-child interaction: Theory, research and prospect.* New York: Academic Press, in press.

Laosa, L. M. Social competence in childhood: Toward a developmental, socioculturally relativistic paradigm. In M. W. Kent & J. E. Rolf (Eds.), *Primary Prevention of Psychopathology* (Vol. III). Hanover NH: University Press of New England, 1979.

Lefcourt, H. M. *Locus of control: Current trends in theory and research.* Hillsdale NJ: Lawrence Erlbaum Associates, 1976.

Linton, R. *The study of man.* New York: Applenton-Century-Crofts, 1936.

Luce, S. R., & Hoge, R. D. Relations among teacher rankings, pupil-teacher interactions, and academic achievement: A test of the teacher expectancy hypothesis. *American Educational Research Journal,* 1978. *15,* 489–500.

Madsen, W. *The Mexican-American of South Texas.* New York: Holt, Rinehart & Winston, 1964.

Monson, L. B., Greenspan, S., & Simeonsson, R. J. Correlates of social competence in retarded children. *American Journal of Mental Deficiency,* 1979, *83,* 627–630.

Moynihan, D. P. *The Negro family: The case for national action.* Washington DC: US Department of Labor, March, 1967.

Paz, O. *The labyrinth of solitude: Life and thought in Mexico.* New York: Grove Press, 1961.

Radcliffe-Browne, A. R. *A natural science of society.* Glencoe IL: The Free Press, 1957.

Richardson, J. G. The case of special education and minority misclassification in California. *Educational Research Quarterly,* 1979, *4,* 25–40.

Roth, S., & Kubal, L. The effects of noncontingent reinforcement on tasks of differing importance: Facilitation and learned helplessness effects. *Journal of Personality and Social Psychology,* 1975, *32,* 680–691.

Rotter, J. B. Generalized expectancies for internal versus external control of reinforcement. *Psychological Monographs,* 1966, *80,* (1, whole No. 609).

Thomas, A. Learned helplessness and expectancy factors: Implications for research in learning disabilities. *Review of Educational Research,* 1979, *49,* 200–221.

Tobias, S. Anxiety research in educational psychology. *Journal of Educational Psychology,* 1979, *71,* 573–582.

Wang, M. C., & Stiles, B. An investigation of children's concept of self-responsibility for school learning. *American Educational Research Journal,* 1976, *13,* 159–179.

Weiner, B. A theory of motivation for some classroom experiences. *Journal of Educational Psychology*, 1979, *71*, 3–25.

Wortman, C. B., Panciera, L., Shusterman, L., & Hibscher, J. Attributions of causality and reactions to uncontrollable outcomes. *Journal of Experimental Social Psychology*, 1976, *12*, 327–345.

Zigler, E., & Trickett, P. K. IQ, social competence, and evaluation of early childhood intervention programs. *American Psychologist*, 1978, *33*, 789–798.

CHAPTER 2

A COMPARATIVE STUDY OF VALUES AND ACHIEVEMENT (1971)

Mexican-American and Anglo youth[*]

Audrey James Schwartz

The research reported here was stimulated by the impoverished conditions of many Mexican-Americans in the Southwestern United States. As a group, Mexican-Americans have relatively low educational attainment and inadequate family income, and generally have been outside the mainstream of American life. Since education traditionally has played a major role in the development of the economic and consensual bases of American society, despite diverse cultural groups, an exploration of value orientations which might inhibit the educational achievement of Mexican-Americans was undertaken.

With specific reference to California, which has the highest concentration of Mexican-Americans in the country, the U.S. Census of Population (1960) has reported the median number of school years completed by Spanish surname males over age 14 as 7.1 years; this group has less formal education than any other identifiable subpopulation in California. The continuing proportion of Mexican-American youth who drop out of school, even in urban areas, is alarming. For Los Angeles, which ranks first among American cities in the number of Mexican-Americans, Sheldon (1961:24) has concluded that one-third of the Mexican-American pupils enrolled in secondary schools do not finish. The California State Advisory Committee to the U.S. Commission on Civil Rights (1968:3) has found that the highest school-leaving rate in that city is in predominantly Mexican-American schools; in these schools only 46 to 53 per cent of entering students graduate.

Although Mexican-Americans may leave school for various reasons, the fact that as a group their in-school experience is less successful than that of their Anglo contemporaries is more than adequately documented (California State Advisory Committee to the U.S. Commission on Civil Rights, 1968; Coleman, et al., 1966; Fogel, 1965; Gordon, et al., 1968; Samora and Lamanna, 1967). Some Mexican-Americans do achieve academically; about nine per cent of California's Spanish surname adult population have completed one or more years of higher education (California State Department of Industrial Relations, 1964:3) and current college enrollments suggest that this figure is rising. Despite this optimistic note, however, the aggregated educational achievement of Mexican-Americans is both qualitatively and quantitatively lower than the educational achievement of their Anglo counterparts.

Earlier research concerning differences between Mexican-American and Anglo cultures suggests that personal value orientations may provide a partial explanation of differences between the educational achievement of Mexican-American and Anglo children. In Parsons' influential description of the two cultures (1951:180–199), he views the "Spanish-American" society as having a predominantly particularistic-ascriptive value orientation pattern in contrast to the dominant American or Anglo universalistic-achievement pattern. Parsons notes that the Mexican-American structure characteristically is one of high affectivity, of immediate gratification through expressive behavior; the Anglo structure is one of affective neutrality or of disciplined behavior leading to later gratification. Personal relations within the Mexican-American structure tend toward broad, diffuse involvement, with people treated as "ends-in-themselves," whereas relations within the Anglo structure tend toward narrow, specific involvement and are limited to some particular purpose or task. Mexican-Americans are more concerned with the quality or the ascriptive component of social roles, while Anglos are concerned with the performance or achievement aspect. Finally, the evaluative standards employed by the two social structures differ: Mexican-Americans tend to emphasize particularism and employ emotional criteria which credit the relationship between individuals; Anglos tend to emphasize universalism and employ impersonally-implemented rational criteria.

Much of Parsons' description was documented by Kluckhohn and Strodtbeck in their report of an isolated Mexican-American community in New Mexico. They concluded (1961:335) that the value orientation system of Mexican-Americans is, in most respects, the "mirror image" of the dominant American culture: the orientation toward "time" is to the present rather than the future, toward "activity" is to being rather than doing, and toward "nature" is to subjugation rather than mastery.

Subsequent research has supported many of these observations and has indicated that the cultural orientation of rural Mexican-Americans is sufficiently distinct from the Anglo orientation so that it will persist even when transplanted to the *barrios* or ethnic enclaves of a metropolitan area like Los Angeles (Dworkin, 1969; Samora and Lamanna, 1967). The Mexican-American culture continually is reinforced in cities of the Southwest by the in-migration of other Mexicans from the rural areas of the United States and Mexico and by the fact that larger cities have intense ethnic residential segregation (Moore and Mittelbach, 1966). Special caution should be exercised, however, in generalizing these observations to all Mexican-Americans. Moore (1966:44) has pointed out that much of the early literature is based upon easily studied and often isolated areas, leading us to believe that the Mexican-American population is more homogeneous than it actually is. The most recent studies of this subpopulation have tended to emphasize the variations within it (Grebler, Moore, and Guzman, 1970).

The gross differences that have been reported between the value orientations of Mexican-American adults and the larger American society imply specifically that children reared entirely within the Mexican-American social structure will differ from children reared within the Anglo structure in several ways which may contribute importantly to variations in their scholastic achievement. Value orientations are salient to achievement in that they determine the desirable; this includes both the ends a person elects and the means he views as appropriate for their attainment. Value orientations provide the criteria by which he formulates his definition of the situation. They delimit the scope and intensity of his interpersonal relations which, in turn, affect his activities.

Fewer Mexican-American children will identify long-range goals for themselves; their orientation toward activity will be more expressive and less instrumental. The positive relationship between scholastic achievement and a commitment to institutionalized school goals, with acceptance of school tasks as appropriate to these goals, has been demonstrated both for Anglos (Kahl, 1953; Straus, 1962) and Mexican-Americans (Gill and Spilka, 1962).

In addition, more Mexican-American children will tend toward particularism in their evaluation of others and toward fatalism or passive acceptance in their orientation toward their own future. The relationship between one's sense of control over external factors and achievement is well documented (Central Advisory Council for Education, 1967; Coleman, et al., 1966; Rosen, 1965; Seeman, 1963; Seeman and Evans, 1962; Strodtbeck, 1958). However, the supposition that achievement in secondary institutions like schools requires "impersonal confidence," so that pupils can interact effectively with relative strangers, requires further demonstration.

Finally, more Mexican-American children will be oriented toward the authority structure of the nuclear family. Stronger family orientation might impede the acquisition by Mexican-American children of alien values which relate to achievement. It also may be critical to achievement if success implies upward mobility and at least the possibility of separation from the family (Whyte, 1966:108).

The following hypotheses guided this exploratory study:

I.   There are substantial differences between Mexican-American pupils from blue-collar and from white-collar families on a number of selected value orientations.
II. The value orientations of Mexican-American pupils from white-collar families are more similar to those of Anglo pupils than are the value orientations of Mexican-American pupils from blue-collar families.
III. Within categories of socioeconomic status, Mexican-American pupils with value orientations most similar to those of Anglo pupils have higher levels of academic achievement than Mexican-American pupils with dissimilar values.

Research design

The data for this inquiry were obtained in the spring of 1966 from questionnaire responses and official school records of a sample of 9th and 12th grade pupils enrolled in the Los Angeles City School District.[1] At that time, administrators of the District, which serves a large, multi-ethnic and diverse socioeconomic population, exercised strong central control and claimed to allocate resources equally among the 620 school units regardless of the composition of the population served.

The sampling procedures were two-fold—first, a nonrandom, nonprobability, purposive technique which selected the universe to be sampled in accord with predetermined socioeconomic and ethnic criteria; second, a stratified quota technique which sampled from this universe until the desired number of cases from the two grade levels was obtained (Schwartz, 1967:19–47). Nonprobability selection of schools was preferred over random selection to prevent inclusion of schools in which few or no Mexican-American pupils were enrolled, thereby loading the sample with a disproportionate number of Anglos, and also to ensure access to pupils enrolled in schools with different socioeconomic and ethnic densities. Eight junior high schools and five high schools into which they feed were chosen on the basis of their pupil characteristics, estimated from census tract data and information supplied by the District.

At the request of the District, questionnaires were administered to entire classrooms rather than to individual pupils. A sufficient number of classes was selected randomly from mandatory courses so that 68 per cent of the 12th grade and 56 per cent of the 9th grade enrollment of each school would be sampled. The District also stipulated that signed consent forms had to be received from parents or guardians before data could be collected from pupils and again before they could be collected from official record files. Questionnaires were administered to about 70 per cent of the proposed junior high sample and 60 per cent of the proposed senior high sample.

To determine the reliability of these samples, the socioeconomic status and ethnicity of the pupils surveyed in each school were correlated with the school's estimated social rank and with the findings of an official school racial census taken in the fall of 1966. Both Spearman and Pearson coefficients were sufficiently high to conclude that the questionnaire samples were not biased substantially (Schwartz, 1967:38–40).

The stipulation for a second consent form presented another possible source of bias since 40 per cent of the 9th grade and 20 per cent of the 12th grade questionnaire respondents did not return signed forms granting access to their official records. To evaluate the extent of this bias, pupils with complete and with incomplete data were compared on a number of variables. Although similar proportions of Mexican-Americans and Anglos returned both forms, these pupils were of higher socioeconomic status and reported themselves to have better school marks than those who did not return the forms. The median IQ of pupils with complete data did not significantly differ from the recorded median IQ of the schools in which they were enrolled (Schwartz, 1967:41–47).

Since the pupils studied were not selected by probability techniques, the findings cannot be generalized confidently to the entire Mexican-American and Anglo pupil populations of Los Angeles. However, both the Mexican-American and Anglo samples appear to be affected similarly by any biases which the selection process might have produced; these data *can* be used confidently for comparing the different sub-samples of pupils.

Ethnicity was coded from information obtained from observing the respondent, the respondent's surname, and questionnaire precoded items stating the place of birth of pupil and parents and the language most frequently used in the home. Socioeconomic status was coded from pupil responses to open-ended items about the work of parents. A primary distinction in occupational classification was made between parents who work with their "hands" and those who work with their "heads," that is, between blue-collar and white-collar labor. Because Mexican-Americans are represented more heavily among blue-collar workers, the sample is biased toward the lower socioeconomic pupils of the district. A description of the questionnaire sample by socioeconomic status and ethnicity is presented in Table 2.1.

Reading comprehension scores obtained from the California Achievement Tests for 9th grade pupils and from the Cooperative English Test for 12th grade pupils were selected as the best general measure of academic achievement. The use of school marks was thought invalid, particularly at the 9th grade level, since a comparison between these marks and objective test scores suggested that they reflect a high component of teacher ascription (Gordon, et al., 1968:76–85; Grebler, et al. 1970:166–169).

The value orientations reported here and the questionnaire items that operationalize them, grouped according to their expected functions, are presented in

Table 2.1 Questionnaire sample by grade level, ethnicity, and socioeconomic status (percentages)

	9th Grade			12th Grade		
	M–A	Anglo	Other	M–A	Anglo	Other
Upper White-Collar[a]	2.3	14.4	10.2	2.1	16.8	9.4
	(20)	(80)	(23)	(14)	(79)	(25)
Intermediate White-Collar	3.6	13.0	9.3	4.1	13.6	12.9
	(32)	(72)	(21)	(27)	(64)	(34)
Lower White-Collar	7.7	14.0	16.0	10.1	9.6	14.3
	(69)	(78)	(34)	(67)	(45)	(38)
Upper Blue-Collar	21.7	31.4	22.3	23.4	34.3	23.8
	(195)	(175)	(50)	(156)	(162)	(63)
Lower Blue-Collar	50.3	23.9	33.0	50.1	21.8	36.2
	(452)	(133)	(74)	(334)	(103)	(96)
Unknown	14.6	3.6	9.8	10.4	4.3	3.3
	(131)	(20)	(22)	(69)	(20)	(9)
Total	100.2[b]	100.3	100.6	100.2	100.4	99.9
	(899)	(558)	(224)	(667)	(473)	(265)

[a] Occupational classifications are as follows:
  Upper-white collar—professional and managerial occupation, owners of large businesses;
  Intermediate white-collar—skilled nonmanual occupations, owners of small or medium-sized businesses;
  Lower white-collar—semi-skilled nonmanual occupations;
  Upper blue-collar—skilled manual occupations, foreman, self-employed craftsmen;
  Lower blue-collar—unskilled and semi-skilled manual occupations.
[b] Variation in percentage totals is due to rounding errors.

Table 2.2. The value orientations in Group I pertain to the individual's view of the desirable and the congruence of his view with that assumed to be institutionalized in the school. These include the Index of Idealized School Goals, the Instrumental Orientation Scale, the Expressive Orientation Scale, and the Formal School Compliance Scale. Those in Group II pertain to the individual's definition of the situation—whether or not he believes that he can attain his goals. Included are the Faith in Human Nature and the Future Orientation Scales. The value orientations in Group III treat the individual's interpersonal relations—his autonomy from both his family and his peers and the reference group most salient to his behavior. They consist of the Independence from Peers and Independence from Family Authority Scales and a single item that asks "Which of these would be hardest for you to take: your parents' disapproval, breaking with your best friend, or your teacher's disapproval?"

With the exception of the last variable, value orientations are composed of several questionnaire items, each with four choices ranging from strongly agree to strongly disagree (Schwartz, 1967: Appendix I). These multi-item variables were constructed according to the Guttman technique, which reveals both the number of items and the actual items endorsed and implies that only one underlying

Table 2.2 Value orientation variables: Total sample by grade level

I. The Desirable

Idealized School Goals (Index)

	Variable score			
	I	II	III	IV
School should train me for my future job (+ agree)	+	+	+	–
School should help me get along with the different people I will meet in my lifetime (+ agree)	+	+	–	–
School should help me understand the world I now live in (+ agree)	+	–	–	–
	Percentages			
9th Grade (N = 1664)	83.8	13.0	3.0	.2
12th Grade (N = 1403)	83.0	13.8	2.8	.4

Instrumental Orientation (Scalogram)

	I	II	III	IV
Going to school now will not help me get a better job later (+ disagree)	+	+	+	–
Doing my schoolwork will make things easier for me after I get out of school (+ agree)	+	+	–	–
Going to school will not help my future in any way (+ disagree)	+	–	–	–
	Percentages			
9th Grade (N = 1675)	74.2	23.4	1.6	.8
12th Grade (N = 1405)	75.4	22.6	1.6	.3

	Coefficient of reproducibility	Minimum marginal reproducibility
9th Grade (N = 1675)	.96	.88
12th Grade (N = 1405)	.93	.86

(Continued)

Table 2.2 (Continued)

Expressive Orientation (Scalogram)

	I	II	III	IV	V
I think of school mainly as a place for having fun (+ agree)	+	+	+	+	–
The main thing I enjoy about school is being with friends (+ agree)	+	+	+	–	–
I usually enjoy my classes here at school (+ agree)	+	+	–	–	–
In general do you like or dislike school? (+ like)	+	–	–	–	–

	Coefficient of reproducibility	Minimum marginal reproducibility	Percentages				
			I	II	III	IV	V
9th Grade (N = 1674)	.97	.86	13.1	59.4	23.8	1.7	2.0
12th Grade (N = 1404)	.97	.85	7.7	61.4	23.9	4.5	2.5

Formal School Compliance (Scalogram)

	I	II	III	IV
Even when they punish the whole class, I feel that teachers are usually right (+ agree)	+	+	+	–
Mary works in the library. Betty, who is Mary's best friend, needs a certain book to write a report. Betty knows that many other pupils also need the book so she asks Mary to hide it until she can come for it. Mary thinks it is wrong to do this. Do you . . . (+ agree)	+	+	–	–
Bill is grading tests for his class. John, who is Bill's best friend, is just below passing. If Bill gives him a break he can help him pass. John thinks Bill should help him. Do you . . . (+ disagree)	+	–	–	–

	Coefficient of reproducibility	Minimum marginal reproducibility	Percentages			
			I	II	III	IV
9th Grade (N = 1667)	.98	.65	47.5	31.4	16.1	5.0
12th Grade (N = 1405)	.91	.66	42.5	31.7	17.3	8.5

II. The Definition of the Situation

Faith in Human Nature (Scalogram)

	I	II	III	IV
In general, people can be trusted (+ agree)	+	+	+	–
Most people make friends because they are able to use them (+ disagree)	+	+	–	–
When you get right down to it, people are no good (+ disagree)	+	–	–	–

Percentages

	I	II	III	IV
9th Grade (N = 1660)	37.4	30.9	23.2	8.5
12th Grade (N = 1404)	62.6	27.7	5.7	4.0

	Coefficient of reproducibility	Minimum marginal reproducibility
9th Grade (N = 1660)	.92	.70
12th Grade (N = 1404)	.90	.73

Future Orientation (Scalogram)[a]

	I	II	III	IV
People should not expect too much out of life so they won't be disappointed (+ disagree)	+	+	+	–
Planning only makes a person unhappy since your plans hardly ever work out anyhow (+ disagree)	+	+	–	–
The wise person lives for today and lets tomorrow take care of itself (+ disagree)	+	–	–	–

Percentages

	Coefficient of reproducibility	Minimum marginal reproducibility
9th Grade (N = 1657)	.92	.67
12th Grade (N = 1404)	.99	.67

III. Interpersonal Relations

Independence from Peers (Scalogram)

	I	II	III	IV	V
I wouldn't mind being thought of as an "odd ball" (+ agree)	+	+	+	+	–
I feel upset if the group doesn't approve of me (+ disagree)	+	+	+	–	–
I never do things just to make others think well of me (+ agree)	+	+	–	–	–
If I disagree with what the group decides I would never say no (+ disagree)	+	–	–	–	–

(Continued)

Table 2.2 (Continued)

	Coefficient of reproducibility	Minimum marginal reproducibility	Percentages				
			I	II	III	IV	V
9th Grade (N = 1652)	.89	.62	9.9	25.9	31.4	21.9	10.9
12th Grade (N = 1403)	.89	.65	18.9	13.9	20.9	39.4	7.3

Independence from Family Authority (Scalogram)

	I	II	III	IV	V
Children should obey all the rules their parents make for them (+ disagree)	+	+	+	+	—
Teenagers should never date a person against their parents' wishes (+ disagree)	+	+	+	—	—
Teenagers should make their own decisions instead of their parents telling them what to do (+ agree)	+	+	—	—	—
Even if their parents disapprove, they should not stop teenagers from seeing their friends (+ agree)	+	—	—	—	—

	Coefficient of reproducibility	Minimum marginal reproducibility	Percentages				
			I	II	III	IV	V
9th Grade (N = 1660)	.90	.65	18.8	12.8	23.0	31.6	13.8
12th Grade (N = 1396)	.89	.65	20.9	26.0	19.4	22.4	11.3

Concern for Family over Peer Disapproval (Item)[b]
Which of these would be hardest for you to take/

	Percentages	
	9th Grade (N = 1410)	12th Grade (N = 1225)
Your parents' disapproval	59.9	60.9
Breaking with your best friend	34.4	34.2
Your teacher's disapproval	5.6	4.9
	99.9	100.0

[a] The second and third items of the Future Orientation measure were adapted from Fred L. Strodtbeck's V-scale (McClellend, 1958:169).
[b] Adapted from the Attitude Questionnaire developed by James S. Coleman (1961).

concept is present in each variable. The Coefficients of Reproducibility are above the conventional .89 acceptance level for each of these value orientations except Idealized School Goals. In spite of its lower validity, this variable has been retained as an "index" because of its unique concern with the respondent's prescription for the functions of formal education. The zero-order correlation coefficients among the value orientation variables are .2 or below (Schwartz, 1969:75–76), indicating their statistical independence.

For ease of presentation, scores on the value orientation variables were dichotomized into categories of "high" and "low." The cutting point is located at the variable score that most evenly divides a total sample of 3086 pupils. This sample includes ethnic subpopulations not treated in this report.

Findings

To summarize briefly, some but not all of the measured value orientations, lend support to the three hypotheses posed above. For variables that relate to school goals and to instrumental activity leading to the attainment of these goals, all subpopulations are unexpectedly similar; in general, high scores on idealized school goals are associated with high academic achievement.

For variables that relate to personal mastery over the environment and to the evaluation of other people, comparisons between and within ethnic subpopulations produce the anticipated differences. These orientations have the predicted relationships with achievement.

For variables that relate to the acceptance of family authority and to concern for family, peer, or teacher approval, the findings are as anticipated: Mexican-American pupils are more oriented, significantly, toward family than are Anglo pupils, but the distributions within the Mexican-American subpopulation are unexpectedly similar. Mexican-Americans who express greater independence from the family have significantly higher academic achievement at the 12th grade than those Mexican-Americans who do not.

Achievement

Comparisons between the mean reading comprehension scores of selected subpopulations show that the academic achievement of the sample of Mexican-American pupils is consistently and significantly below the achievement of the sample of Anglo pupils and below the means of the national samples to which the tests were standardized (Table 2.3). In addition, comparisons within ethnic samples show the achievement of pupils from white-collar families to be higher than the achievement of pupils from blue-collar families and the achievement of 12th grade pupils to be higher, in terms of national norms, than the achievement of 9th grade pupils. The differences between the reading comprehension scores of boys and girls within the same subpopulations are small and nonsignificant.

The desirable

The similarity between Mexican-American and Anglo pupils with respect to value orientations related to the functions of formal education is unexpected (Table 2.4). Most notable is the agreement among all pupils that every objective in the Index of Idealized School Goals—which deals with the ends the pupil believes the school ought to help him attain, regardless of whether it does or not—is important.

Table 2.3 Mean reading comprehension scores by ethnicity, socioeconomic status, and sex

	Mexican-American			Anglo		
	$\overline{X}$[a]	S.D.	N	$\overline{X}$	S.D.	N
9th Grade						
Blue-Collar						
Boys	3.54[b]	1.85	(229)	4.91	1.99	(89)
Girls	3.62	1.70	(204)	4.88	1.75	(78)
Total	3.58	1.78	(433)	4.90	1.88	(167)
White-Collar						
Boys	4.14	2.12	(37)	5.32	2.00	(72)
Girls	4.17	2.12	(42)	5.77	1.63	(65)
Total	4.15	2.11	(79)	5.53	1.84	(137)
12th Grade						
Blue-Collar						
Boys	4.42	1.92	(196)	5.51	2.02	(114)
Girls	4.27	1.64	(213)	5.64	1.49	(95)
Total	4.37	1.78	(409)	5.57	1.79	(209)
White-Collar						
Boys	4.64	1.90	(56)	6.51	1.75	(73)
Girls	4.78	1.93	(36)	6.37	1.45	(95)
Total	4.70	1.90	(92)	6.43	1.58	(168)

[a] All differences between means of Mexican-American and Anglo pupils and between blue and white collar pupils from the same subpopulation are statistically significant; $p \le .05$, 1-tailed t-test.
[b] Reading Comprehension scores are standardized into the stanine scale which ranges from a low of one to a high of nine; the mean is set at five and the standard deviation is two. Stanine scores are equally spaced steps on the achievement scale and should not be confused with percentiles which are equal proportions of the population.

About 80 per cent agree that (a) school should help them get along with the different people they will meet through life, (b) it should help them to understand the world they now live in, and (c) it should train them for their future jobs. There is also agreement that school succeeds in performing these functions. About 75 per cent respond positively to the items in the Instrumental Orientation Scale, a measure of the pupil's evaluation of the future utility of school-prescribed activity; fewer than one per cent maintain that going to school will not help them in any way in the future.

Most pupils also indicate expressive gratification from school attendance. About 60 per cent agree that (a) in general, they like school, (b) they enjoy their classes at school, and (c) the main thing they like about school is being with friends. The responses of 9th grade blue-collar boys show that they receive significantly less gratification than do most of their age-mates.

The Formal School Compliance Scale scores, which indicate the choices the pupil says he would make if confronted with conflicting expectations from the formal school and from his peers and the extent of his uncritical acceptance of

Table 2.4 Distribution of value orientation scores by ethnicity, socioeconomic status, grade level, and sex (percentages)

| | Blue-collar | | | | | | White-collar | | | | | |
| | Mexican-American | | | Anglo | | | Mexican-American | | | Anglo | | |
Value orientations[a]	Boys	Girls	Total	Boys	Girls	Total	Boys	Girls	Total	Boys	Girls	Total
9th Grade												
Idealized School Goals	83	86	85	82	88	85	81	77	79	83	84	83
Instrumental Orientation	75	75	75	76	74	75	69	72	71	69	79	74
Expressive Orientation	75	79	77	63	75	69	75	78	76	69	69	69
Formal School Compliance	54	49	51	42	49	46	58	39	50	37	46	41
Faith in Human Nature	27	27	27	48	58	53	47	34	41	51	50	51
Future Orientation	22	16	19	37	34	35	33	24	28	53	41	47
Independence from Peers	36	32	34	43	33	39	36	29	33	37	34	34
Independence from Family	47	47	47	64	62	63	55	51	52	64	69	66
Concern for Family over Peer	63	64	63	56	51	53	60	64	61	51	55	53
N =	(332)	(312)	(644)	(158)	(151)	(309)	(63)	(58)	(121)	(124)	(105)	(229)
12th Grade												
Idealized School Goals	82	86	84	85	88	86	73	86	79	77	78	78
Instrumental Orientation	77	74	75	75	82	78	79	78	79	81	74	77
Expressive Orientation	67	76	72	67	74	70	63	72	67	58	63	60
Formal School Compliance	42	44	43	36	44	40	49	37	43	36	38	37
Faith in Human Nature	61	66	63	68	67	67	61	59	60	59	62	61
Future Orientation	37	37	37	54	55	54	39	36	37	69	65	67
Independence from Peers	37	30	33	30	24	28	34	20	27	38	37	37
Independence from Family	66	59	62	73	74	73	52	74	61	76	71	73
Concern for Family over Peer	68	69	68	49	55	52	64	61	63	50	53	51
N =	(246)	(244)	(490)	(140)	(125)	(265)	(63)	(43)	(106)	(86)	(102)	(188)

[a] The value orientation scores are dichotomized at the point that most evenly divides the entire sample. Cell entries show the percentage of respondents with "high" scores.

teacher authority, suggest the existence of tension between individual pupils and the authority structure of the school. More than half of the pupils disagree with the statement "Even when they punish the whole class, I feel that teachers are usually right." On the other hand, responses also indicate that pupils are more accepting of the universalistic regulations of the school than of the particularistic demands of personal friendship. Sixty per cent agree that if working in the school library, they would not hide a book from other readers in order to reserve it for a friend; 80 per cent disapprove of a student aide who purposely raised the test score of a friend. The very favorable orientation toward Formal School Compliance shown by 9th grade Mexican-American boys is of special interest. Unlike the blue-collar Anglo boys who score much lower than blue-collar Anglo girls, the Compliance scores of both blue-collar and white-collar Mexican-American boys are higher than those of the other subpopulation groups.

Definition of the situation

Just as there are marked similarities between subpopulations in their conceptions of the "desirable," there are marked differences in their evaluations of the "situation" leading to its attainment (Table 2.4). Scores on the Faith in Human Nature Scale, which inquires into the individual's orientation toward other people regardless of his personal knowledge of them, indicate that significantly fewer blue-collar Mexican-American pupils have confidence in their fellow man than have either white-collar Mexican-American or blue-collar Anglo pupils. Confidence increases with grade level, however, and differences between the value orientations of 9th and 12th grade pupils are significant.

Even more striking is the ethnic variation indicated by the Future Orientation Scale which measures the belief that the individual can exercise control over his environment and thereby affect his own destiny. In every comparison between ethnic groups, more Anglo than Mexican-American pupils express greater future orientation. In comparisons within ethnic groups, more 9th grade white-collar than blue-collar Mexican-Americans express greater future orientation. The future orientation of blue-collar Mexican-American pupils, like their faith in human nature, increases with grade level; the differences in scores between 9th grade and 12th grade pupils are statistically significant.

Interpersonal relations

The variables in this category, bearing on the concept of autonomy, are divided into two separate notions (Table 2.4). The Independence from Family Authority Scale inquires into the legitimacy of parental control over pupil activity. The Independence from Peers Scale inquires into the sensitivity of the pupil to the opinions of his age-mates. To determine which of the possible reference groups has most influence over individual behavior, a single item variable asks "Which of these would be harder for you to take —your parents' disapproval, breaking with your best friend, or your teacher's disapproval?"

The responses of pupils from both ethnic groups to the measure of independence from peers are similar. However, significantly more Mexican-American than Anglo pupils indicate greater concern for parental than peer approval and, with the exception of 12th grade white-collar Mexican-American girls, also express less independence from family authority. Independence from family authority is much greater at the 12th than at the 9th grade for most blue-collar pupils regardless of ethnicity; it also is greater for white-collar Mexican-American girls.

Values and achievement

Our hypotheses suggest that differences in scholastic achievement of Mexican-American and Anglo pupils can be explained in part by differences in value orientations derivative of their cultural backgrounds. The subpopulations were divided by their value orientation variable scores into "high" and "low" categories, as described above. The mean reading comprehension scores of the pupils in the two categories of each value orientation variable were compared using Student's t. Controls for ethnicity, socioeconomic status, and grade level were employed in all comparisons. To simplify the presentation (Table 2.5), controls for sex have been omitted since the relationship between value orientations and achievement is similar for boys and girls (unpublished data).

In general, high Idealized School Goals are positively related to academic achievement; the mean reading comprehension scores of pupils with high goals are considerably higher than the mean scores of pupils of similar background who have low goals. The relationships between the other "desirable" variables and achievement are neither strong nor consistent.

The two "definition of the situation" variables, both having to do with an optimistic outlook, are positively related to academic success. Faith in Human Nature is related statistically to the achievement of all blue-collar pupils, Mexican-American and Anglo alike; Future Orientation is related to achievement for all but one subpopulation comparison.

With respect to the "interpersonal relations" variables, Independence from Family Authority is related significantly and positively to the achievement of some subpopulations and not to the achievement of others; Independence from Peers is unrelated to achievement. Among Anglo pupils, independence from family authority is associated with the achievement of blue-collar pupils in the 9th grade, yet bears no relationship in the 12th grade. The reverse is true for Mexican-American pupils; independence from family authority is unrelated to achievement in the 9th grade and has a significant positive relationship to achievement of both blue-collar and white-collar pupils at the 12th grade level.

Discussion
Commonly shared values

The data reflect certain significant and unexpected commonalities. The fact that there seem to be no differences within the Mexican-American sample with respect to some value orientations and between the Mexican-American and Anglo samples with respect to others suggests that there are some persistent Mexican value orientations that are unaffected by contact with the dominant American society. Findings with respect to other value orientations indicate that more acculturation has occurred than has been revealed by most of the earlier research into the Mexican-American culture. Regardless of ethnicity and socioeconomic background, over 80 per cent of all pupils scored high on idealized school goals, and 75 per cent of all pupils believe that their own school attendance leads to the attainment of these goals.

Table 2.5 Mean reading comprehension scores by level of value orientation scores

Value orientations[a]	SES	High			Low		
		$\overline{X}$	S.D.	N	$\overline{X}$	S.D.	N
Mexican-American 9th Grade							
Idealized School Goals	BC	3.70[b]	1.75	(372)	2.91[c]	1.79	(58)
	WC	4.24	2.18	(59)	3.90	1.89	(20)
Instrumental Orientation	BC	3.66	1.77	(317)	3.39[c]	1.78	(114)
	WC	4.38	2.16	(55)	3.62	1.93	(24)
Expressive Orientation	BC	3.61	1.80	(382)	3.54	1.70	(99)
	WC	4.14	2.19	(62)	4.18	1.84	(17)
Formal School Compliance	BC	3.63	1.70	(230)	3.55	1.87	(200)
	WC	3.97	2.01	(38)	4.32	2.21	(41)
Faith in Human Nature	BC	4.14	1.70	(117)	3.39[c]	1.77	(312)
	WC	4.56	1.77	(35)	3.91	2.33	(44)
Future Orientation	BC	3.92	1.91	(89)	3.50[c]	1.74	(342)
	WC	4.60	2.21	(20)	4.00	2.07	(59)
Independence from Peers	BC	3.65	1.84	(143)	3.59	1.74	(284)
	WC	4.25	1.98	(24)	4.11	2.17	(55)
Independence from Family	BC	3.60	1.91	(199)	3.58	1.66	(232)
	WC	4.26	2.24	(42)	4.03	1.96	(37)
Concern for Family over Peer	BC	3.57	1.72	(275)	3.77	1.90	(134)
	WC	4.26	2.14	(50)	4.09	1.92	(22)
Mexican-American 12th Grade							
Idealized School Goals	BC	4.37	1.75	(343)	4.21	1.96	(66)
	WC	4.86	1.84	(73)	4.05[c]	2.07	(19)
Instrumental Orientation	BC	4.38	1.76	(315)	4.23	1.85	(94)
	WC	4.66	1.90	(74)	4.94	1.95	(18)
Expressive Orientation	BC	4.40	1.77	(290)	4.24	1.81	(118)
	WC	4.52	1.94	(64)	5.11	1.77	(28)
Formal School Compliance	BC	4.35	1.86	(183)	4.34	1.72	(226)
	WC	4.63	1.84	(43)	4.76	1.89	(49)
Faith in Human Nature	BC	4.51	1.75	(263)	4.04[c]	1.80	(146)
	WC	4.95	1.81	(56)	4.31	2.00	(36)
Future Orientation	BC	4.66	1.91	(151)	4.16[c]	1.68	(258)
	WC	5.09	1.97	(33)	4.47[c]	1.84	(59)
Independence from Peers	BC	4.46	1.69	(142)	4.30	1.82	(266)
	WC	5.15	1.70	(27)	4.51	1.96	(65)
Independence from Family	BC	4.49	1.82	(251)	4.14[c]	1.68	(156)
	WC	4.97	1.69	(59)	4.21[c]	2.18	(33)
Concern for Family over Peer	BC	4.28	1.72	(274)	4.60	1.89	(110)
	WC	4.53	1.96	(57)	5.00	1.90	(31)

Anglo 9th Grade

Idealized School Goals	BC	5.08	1.85	(144)	3.86^c	1.58	(22)
	WC	5.59	1.84	(115)	5.33	1.82	(21)
Instrumental Orientation	BC	5.02	1.81	(127)	4.52	2.06	(40)
	WC	5.62	1.75	(92)	5.41	2.00	(44)
Expressive Orientation	BC	4.82	1.80	(113)	5.06	2.03	(54)
	WC	5.48	1.83	(93)	5.70	1.85	(43)
Formal School Compliance	BC	4.67	1.89	(84)	5.18^d	1.80	(82)
	WC	5.75	1.94	(57)	5.44	1.74	(78)
Faith in Human Nature	BC	5.27	1.71	(94)	4.47^c	1.96	(72)
	WC	5.61	1.87	(75)	5.48	1.80	(61)
Future Orientation	BC	5.56	1.82	(63)	4.54^c	1.79	(102)
	WC	6.17	1.45	(60)	5.09^c	1.96	(75)
Independence from Peers	BC	4.72	2.03	(61)	5.05	1.75	(104)
	WC	5.62	1.79	(46)	5.55	1.81	(89)
Independence from Family	BC	5.11	1.82	(105)	4.60^c	1.91	(60)
	WC	5.62	1.88	(88)	5.47	1.73	(47)
Concern for Family over Peer	BC	5.08	1.79	(88)	4.88	1.81	(66)
	WC	5.73	1.86	(78)	5.39	1.77	(49)

Anglo 12th Grade

Idealized School Goals	BC	5.65	1.79	(180)	5.07^c	1.77	(29)
	WC	6.40	1.62	(132)	6.49	1.48	(35)
Instrumental Orientation	BC	5.54	1.85	(164)	5.69	1.44	(45)
	WC	6.47	1.53	(127)	6.29	1.62	(41)
Expressive Orientation	BC	5.56	1.69	(146)	5.59	2.03	(63)
	WC	6.39	1.42	(102)	6.48	1.82	(66)
Formal School Compliance	BC	5.45	1.79	(88)	5.65	1.80	(121)
	WC	6.49	1.62	(63)	6.39	1.57	(105)
Faith in Human Nature	BC	5.70	1.77	(142)	5.28^c	1.82	(67)
	WC	6.47	1.54	(106)	6.35	1.66	(62)
Future Orientation	BC	6.04	1.64	(114)	5.00^c	1.81	(95)
	WC	6.62	1.36	(117)	5.98^c	1.95	(51)
Independence from Peers	BC	5.74	1.91	(58)	5.50	1.75	(151)
	WC	6.38	1.69	(65)	6.46	1.52	(103)
Independence from Family	BC	5.58	1.79	(158)	5.47	1.78	(49)
	WC	6.51	1.59	(123)	6.16	1.55	(44)
Concern for Family over Peer	BC	5.46	1.85	(107)	5.71	1.71	(95)
	WC	6.29	1.74	(85)	6.50	1.40	(76)

[a] Value orientation scores are dichotomized at the point that most evenly divides the entire sample.   [b] Table is read as follows: the mean reading comprehension score of 9th grade blue collar Mexican-American pupils with high Idealized School Goals scores is 3.70; the mean score of comparable Mexican-American pupils with low Idealized School Goals scores is 2.91.   [c] $p \leq .05$, one-tailed t-test of significance for differences between mean reading comprehension scores.   [d] $p \leq .05$, two-tailed t-test of significance for differences between mean reading comprehension scores.

Value differences

Certain of our findings bear upon the current problem of participation by Mexican-Americans in the larger society. The observed dissimilarities between the two ethnic groups largely are those to which earlier literature comparing the two social structures has been addressed. Larger proportions of Mexican-American than Anglo pupils accept family authority of wide scope, view their fellow man with caution, view their own destiny with resignation, and are expressively oriented—even toward the instrumental activity within the school. All but the last of these factors is obviously related to academic achievement.

Mexican-American pupils rank lower than Anglo pupils on the "definition of the situation" variables, concerned with optimism about the general social order and the extent of shared expectations and understandings within it; blue-collar Mexican-Americans rank lowest of all. One aspect of this definition, future orientation, reflects the feasibility of some control over the environment and provides motivation for goal-oriented activity; the other aspect, faith in human nature, reflects generalized confidence in mankind and supports interpersonal relations in a presumedly affectively neutral, universalistic society. There are wide gaps between the values of the 9th grade Mexican-American and Anglo pupils; some of these are narrowed at the 12th grade level.

Perhaps the school socializes pupils to the more positive value orientations or perhaps pupils who do not hold them drop out of school between the 9th and 12th grades. Which of these is the more accurate interpretation cannot be ascertained directly without specific information concerning the value orientations of the many Mexican-American pupils who leave school at sixteen, the legal school-leaving age of the Los Angeles District. Whatever the reason, the number of years the Mexican-American child spends in secondary school is related empirically to his more favorable definition of the situation, a definition in accord with participation in the larger society.

Mexican-American girls

In the light of common beliefs about rigid sex-role distinctions within the Mexican-American culture and usual assumptions concerning sex-linked differences in child-rearing practices, that there are so few observed differences in value orientations and in achievement between boys and girls is unexpected. Nevertheless, the few observed differences may be of substantive importance. More white-collar Mexican-American girls than boys have high Idealized School Goals and express Independence from Family Authority; both are value orientations that have a positive relationship to achievement. It is curious, however, that despite these orientations, the mean reading comprehension score of the girls is not significantly higher than the mean of comparable boys. (See Table 2.3.)

A striking contrast occurs between the 12th grade white-collar and the 9th grade blue-collar Mexican-American girls. About half of the younger girls drop out of school before graduation (California State Advisory Committee to the U.S. Commission on Civil Rights, 1968:3). The academic achievement of blue-collar Mexican-American girls is low compared to the national mean (Table 2.3) and their definition of the situation is unfavorable for further achievement. According to most accounts, Mexican-American girls who leave school prematurely have little additional contact with formal education and the continuing socialization it may provide.

Conclusion

Several value orientations and their relations with school achievement have been examined for a sample of 9th and 12th grade Mexican-American pupils in the Los Angeles City Schools; these data have been contrasted with similar data for a sample of Anglo pupils. The findings show that, at least for this sample, those Mexican-American pupils with value orientations most similar to those of Anglo pupils have the highest scholastic achievement. While it is recognized that pupils' values and achievement are substantially interdependent, the findings of this study suggest that affective factors in the cultural background of many Mexican-American pupils hinder their general academic achievement.

Earlier studies have concluded that children reared in the traditional Mexican-American culture have lower goal orientations; are more expressive, more particularistic, more fatalistic; and have a greater orientation toward authority than those reared in Anglo culture. This study supports these conclusions for all values except goal orientation. Here, the study finds that Mexican-American and Anglo pupils are similar. Of those values that distinguish the two cultures, particularism and fatalism—operationalized in this research as low Faith in Human Nature and low Future Orientation—are related significantly and negatively to achievement for *all* pupils, while orientation toward family authority (but not school authority) is related negatively to achievement for both Mexican-American and blue-collar Anglo pupils.

These conclusions in general suggest that the problems of the American school system with respect to Mexican-American pupils may be more intractable when approached through traditional means than has been realized. And the similarity of the goal orientations of Mexican-American and Anglo children makes those problems even more acute. For the Mexican-American children have not experienced significant academic achievement, the principal route through which their goals have been heretofore attained.

Notes

*   This article is based upon research conducted for the Los Angeles education substudy of the Mexican-American Study Project, Graduate School of Business Administration, UCLA. Financial support was provided by the Mexican-American Study Project and by the Center for the Study of Evaluation, Graduate School of Education, UCLA; both sources are gratefully acknowledged. The writer also wishes to thank C. W. Gordon for his invaluable suggestions and criticisms. For the final report of the education substudy see Gordon, et al. (1968); for the final summary of the entire Mexican-American Project see Grebler, Moore, and Guzman (1970).
1   This study also provided the data for the very recent path analysis of Warren D. TenHouten, et al. (1971). As that article points out (TenHouten, et al., 1971:105), Deluvina Hernandez (1970) has written a paper which is highly critical of the value assumptions and survey procedures used in the collection and analysis of these data.

References

California State Advisory Committee to U.S. Commission on Civil Rights.
  1968   "Education and the Mexican-American community in Los Angeles." (April).
California State Department of Industrial Relations.
  1964   Californians of Spanish Surname. San Francisco.
Central Advisory Council for Education.
  1967   Children and Their Primary Schools. London: Her Majesty's Stationery Office.

Coleman, James S.
1961   The Adolescent Society. New York: The Free Press.
Coleman, James S., E. Q. Campbell, et al.
1966   Equality of Educational Opportunity. Washington, D.C.: U.S. Government Printing Office.
Dworkin, Anthony Gary.
1968   "No siesta mañana: the Mexican-American in Los Angeles." Pp. 387–439 in Raymond W. Mack (ed.), Studies of Desegregation. New York: Random House.
Fogel, Walter.
1965   "Education and income of Mexican-Americans in the southwest." Advance Report 1, Mexican-American Study Project. Los Angeles: University of California.
Gill, Lois J., and Bernard Spilka.
1962   "Some intellectual correlates of academic achievement among Mexican-American secondary school students." Journal of Educational Psychology 53(June):144–156.
Gordon, C. Wayne, Audrey J. Schwartz, Robert Wenkert, and David Nasatir.
1968   "Educational achievement and aspirations of Mexican-American youth in a metropolitan context." Occasional Report 36, Center for the Study of Evaluation, Los Angeles: University of California.
Grebler, Leo, Joan Moore, and Ralph Guzman.
1970   The Mexican-American People. New York: The Free Press.
Hernández, Deluvina.
1970   "Mexican-American challenge to a sacred cow." Monograph 1 (March). Los Angeles: Mexican-American Cultural Center, Los Angeles: University of California.
Kluckhohn, Florence R., and Fred L. Strodtbeck.
1961   Variations in Value Orientations. Evanston: Row Peterson.
Kahl, Joseph A.
1953   "Educational and occupational aspirations of 'common man' boys." Harvard Educational Review 23(Summer):186–203.
Moore, Joan W.
1966   "Mexican-Americans: problems and prospects." Institute for Research on Poverty Special Report, Madison: University of Wisconsin.
Moore, Joan W., and Frank G. Mittelbach.
1966   "Residential segregation in the urban southwest." Mexican-American Study Project Advance Report 4. Los Angeles: University of California.
Parsons, Talcott.
1951   The Social System. Glencoe: The Free Press.
Rosen, Bernard.
1956   "The achievement syndrome: a psychocultural dimension of social stratification." American Sociological Review 21 (April):203–211.
Schwartz, Audrey James.
1967   Affectivity Orientations and Academic Achievement of Mexican-American Youth. Ed. D. Dissertation, UCLA. Ann Arbor: University Microfilms.
1969   "Comparative values and achievement of Mexican-American and Anglo pupils." Center for the Study of Evaluation Report 37, Los Angeles: University of California.
Seeman, Melvin.
1963   "Alienation and social learning in a reformatory." American Journal of Sociology 69 (November): 270–284.
Seeman, Melvin, and John W. Evans.
1962   "Alienation and learning in a hospital setting." American Sociological Review 27 (June):326–335.
Sheldon, Paul M.
1961   "Mexican-Americans in urban public schools: an exploration of the drop-out problems." California Journal of Educational Research 12 (January):21–26.
Straus, Murray A.

1962 "Deferred gratification, social class, and the achievement syndrome." American Sociological Review 27(June):326–335.

Strodtbeck, Fred L.
1958 "Family integration, values, and achievement." Pp. 135–194 in D. McClelland, et al. (eds.), Talent and Society. Princeton: Van Nostrand.

TenHouten, Warren D., et al.
1971 "School ethnic composition, social contexts, and educational plans of Mexican-American and Anglo high school students." American Journal of Sociology 77(July):89–107.

United States Bureau of the Census.
1960 United States Census of Population, 1960: State Volumes. Washington D. C.: U. S. Government Printing Office.

Whyte, William F.
1943 Street Corner Society: The Social Structure of an Italian Slum. Chicago: University of Chicago Press (1966).

CHAPTER 3

MINORITY STATUS AND SCHOOLING IN PLURAL SOCIETIES (1983)

John U. Ogbu

Most nations today are plural societies with one or more minority groups. In the more industrialized and urbanized societies, where formal education has become institutionalized as the route to full adult status, minority education has become more problematic in many ways. Most important is the disproportionate school failure of some minority groups, even with efforts to improve their school success. This situation raises doubts about the possibility of using education to reduce social and economic inequality between dominant and minority groups. It also raises questions about the educability of some minority groups. Only in the United States have the twin problems of inequality and educability received such attention, though they are also major concerns in Britain, Israel, New Zealand, and other nations.[1]

Elsewhere I have suggested the need to conceptually distinguish among different kinds of minorities.[2] Minority status per se is not always associated with persistent school failure, as some critics rightly point out.[3] We need, therefore, to specify what kinds of minorities experience disproportionate school failure and the reasons for it. Consequently, I have distinguished among autonomous, immigrant, and castelike minorities.

This paper applies such distinctions to the school experiences of one castelike minority group (black Americans) and one immigrant minority group (Chinese Americans) to show why the former but not the latter is characterized by persistent disproportionate school failure. Our interest in comparing Chinese and blacks dates back to our ethnographic research in Stockton, California, from 1968 to 1970, where, although the two groups had experienced similar discriminatory treatment and came from similar socioeconomic backgrounds, they performed differently in the same schools. The present paper is largely based, however, on our study of the history of the educational and other experiences of the two minorities in the United States as a whole. In the rest of this paper we shall first describe the distinguishing features of autonomous, immigrant, and castelike minorities. A conceptual framework for the comparison is presented next; this is followed by a comparative description of the structural position and educational experiences of blacks and Chinese.

A typology of minority groups

In this paper minority status is not synonymous with numerical status; it refers, rather, to the quality of power relations between groups. We define a population as a minority if it occupies some form of subordinate power position in relation to another population in the same society. With this definition in mind, we have classified minority groups into autonomous, immigrant, and castelike minorities. What are their distinguishing features?

Autonomous minorities are represented in the United States by groups such as the Amish, Jews, and Mormons. These are minorities primarily in a numerical sense; they are not totally subordinated by the dominant group politically or economically. In general, autonomous minorities may have a distinctive racial, ethnic, religious, linguistic, or cultural identity that is guaranteed by national constitution or by tradition. Such minorities may, as in many African and Asian nations, occupy and control distinct geographical domains while participating in supralocal politics. Their separate existence is not, however, based on a specialized economic, political, or ritual denigrated role. They may be victims of prejudice, but are not subordinated groups in a system of rigid stratification. Often such minorities have a cultural frame of reference that encourages and demonstrates success. At least in the United States, autonomous minorities are not characterized by disproportionate and persistent school failure.

Immigrant minorities are people who have moved more or less voluntarily to their host society.[4] They may initially occupy the lowest rung of the occupational ladder, lack political power, and possess low prestige. However, this objective structural position does not reflect their entire status in the social hierarchy because subjectively immigrants may not think of their position the same way as their hosts do. Immigrants may not, in fact, understand the invidious definitions the dominant group attaches to their menial positions. And if they do, they may deliberately reject them because they are strangers who are not a part of the local status system. Furthermore, immigrants may even consider their menial positions better than what they had prior to emigration.[5] As strangers they can operate psychologically outside established definitions of social status and relations. They may be subject to pillory and discrimination, but have not usually had time to internalize the effects of discrimination or have those effects become an ingrained part of their culture. Another distinguishing feature of immigrants is the location of their reference groups. Both autonomous and castelike minorities look to affluent members of the dominant group, but for immigrants the reference group is their own peers back in their "homeland" or in the immigrant neighborhoods. It is to these that they compare themselves, and here they often find much evidence of their own self-improvement and good prospects for their children because of "better opportunities."[6] Their more or less voluntary immigration is usually motivated by a desire to accumulate wealth or other means of achieving self-advancement "back home"—not by a desire to compete for equal status with elite members of their host society. This often acts as a strong incentive to exploit anticipated and unanticipated opportunities and to maintain instrumental attitudes toward economic and educational opportunities even in the face of prejudice and discrimination. It does not, of course, mean that immigrants altogether eschew protest against maltreatment.

Still another feature of immigrants is that their relationship to the dominant group may be subject to external influences. The latter include diplomatic and economic ties between the migrants' country of origin and their host society. Sometimes such factors act to rigidify the rules of subordination; sometimes they make subordination more flexible. Finally, unless they are political émigrés, immigrants have at least a symbolic option to return to their "homeland" or reemigrate elsewhere if present conditions become intolerable. This option means that immigrants can export academic and other skills to some other place where they can more fully utilize such skills and receive more adequate rewards for them. We do not mean that reemigration is possible for all nonpolitical émigrés, but the option is more available to them than to castelike minorities. Immigrant minorities are usually not characterized by persistent disproportionate school failures. In the United States these minorities include Chinese, Cubans, Filipinos, Japanese, and Koreans.

Castelike minorities are the polar opposite of autonomous minorities. Unlike immigrants, castelike minorities have usually been incorporated into their societies more or less involuntarily and permanently. Their only means of escape from such an involuntary and permanent position is through "passing" or emigration—routes not always open. Black Americans are a good example: they were brought to America as slaves and after emancipation relegated to castelike status through legal and extralegal devices.[7] Indians, Mexican Americans, and Puerto Ricans also share with blacks the experience of involuntary incorporation and relegation to subordinate status. Indians, the original owners of the land, were conquered and then forced onto reservations; Mexican Americans were conquered and displaced from power in the Southwest, and those who immigrated subsequently from Mexico were accorded the same subordinate status as the conquered group. Puerto Ricans think they are more or less a colonial people both in Puerto Rico and on the mainland.[8]

Membership in a castelike minority group is often permanent and acquired at birth. This is, however, much less true for Indians, Mexican Americans, and Puerto Ricans than for blacks partly because of the wide range of color difference within each group, which vary from pure white to pure black.[9] It is also partly because Mexican Americans and Puerto Ricans are officially classified as "white"—a classification based more on political considerations than biological reality. The variation in color permits members of these minorities to "pass" into the dominant group in order to overcome castelike barriers in social, political, and occupational positions.[10] Official classification as white makes it psychologically easier for those who "pass" to adjust to their new status. Rules of affiliation are also more flexible than for blacks because offspring of "mixed matings," that is, between Mexican Americans or Puerto Ricans on the one hand and the dominant "Anglo" whites, who possess white features (e.g., white skin color, hair, speech, etc.), may "pass" more easily. In general, the treatment of Mexican Americans and Puerto Ricans depends more on their physical appearance than on their official classification as white.

Like castelike minorities everywhere, blacks, Indians, Mexican Americans, and Puerto Ricans have traditionally been regarded by the Anglo white as inferior and ranked lower than whites in all desirable respects. Castelike minorities often have little or no political power—a reality reinforced by economic subordination. Economically they tend to be relegated to menial jobs, a situation which is then used to argue that they are naturally suited for their low status. Once the structural subordination is firmly established, appropriate cultural features, including some overarching ideology, develop to support and rationalize their position. Castelike minorities do not necessarily accept the rationalizing ideology, such as that they are biologically or culturally inferior to the dominant group. However, they do not totally escape the influence of the ideology and its behavioral concomitants.[11] For their part, castelike minorities not only reject the rationalizing ideology, they also devote disproportionate effort to fighting for political, social, and economic equality with the dominant group members. It is the castelike minorities that experience disproportionate school failure.

The typology is not static. Some internal and external forces can change the status of a given minority group. Under certain circumstances, an autonomous minority may evolve into a castelike minority. Immigrants may achieve autonomous status. Under the impact of urbanization, industrialization, and egalitarian ideology, castelike minority groups increasingly seek both emancipation from traditional menial roles and equality with the dominant group. Some minorities may eventually assimilate into the dominant group, but assimilation is not the goal of all minorities. In the next section we briefly present a framework for analyzing the educational consequences of castelike and immigrant minority statuses.

A conceptual framework: the status-mobility system and educability

We first present a conceptual framework for analyzing the educational experiences of any group or society. Then we show how the model is modified and applied to minorities.

Three assumptions underlie the approach. One is that in contemporary urban industrial societies, achieving full adult status is tantamount to holding a good job with good pay and good chances for promotion. The second is that schools are designed to recruit people into the labor market. Third is that under structured inequality, unequal opportunity in the labor market affects the design and operation of minority education. We may incorporate these assumptions under the concept of the status-mobility system.[12] A status-mobility system consists of content, folk theory, and method of self-advancement or social mobility.

Jobs are the most important content of the status-mobility system of any modern industrial society. As Inkeles points out, in the United States, for example, full adult status, especially for males, is measured in terms of the ability to compete for and obtain a desirable job, to earn a reasonably good income, to manage one's affairs, and to participate in the social and political life of one's community and establish and maintain a good and stable home and family.[13] Others have written that to achieve full adult status in American epistemology means first and foremost to have a good job that pays well.[14] Without such a job and income it is very difficult for an American male to manage his own affairs, participate effectively in politics, and/or establish and maintain a stable family life. In the words of Herman P. Miller, "It is the job that counts."[15]

Inkeles also suggests that school plays a crucial role among institutions entrusted by society to prepare children to achieve full adult status. That is, education plays a crucial role in recruiting people into the labor market.[16] School attempts to fulfill this crucial role in three ways: teaching children beliefs, values, and attitudes that support the economic system; teaching them skills and competencies required to make the system work; and credentialing them to enter the work force. During their education children develop appropriate cognitive maps or shared knowledge of how the economic and status-mobility systems work.[17]

School succeeds in recruiting people to participate in the economic and status-mobility systems when the recruits, especially as they get older, come to believe that their chances of getting ahead lie in succeeding in school and obtaining educational credentials. They usually arrive at this conclusion by observing older members of the community and by listening to and interpreting the experiences of older generations. Furthermore, for school to succeed in teaching beliefs, values, and attitudes, children must see these confirmed by the experiences of older people around them. Positive perceptions and experiences among members of a population or community eventually result in instrumental school behavior becoming culturally sanctioned. That is, they approve of and insist on working hard to get good grades to get credentials as the right thing for children to do. People who are successful in school as well as in adult life become success models influencing parents in raising their children and also influencing children's ideas of who they want to be like as they get older.

Under structured inequality involving minorities two elements emerge that modify the status-mobility pattern and responses to education. One is the unequal power relation that permits the dominant group to control minority access to both jobs and schooling. The other is introduction of a job ceiling against the minorities that limits their range of occupational choices. A job ceiling is the highly consistent pressures and obstacles that selectively assign minorities to jobs at a low level of status, power, dignity, and income, while allowing dominant-group members to compete more easily and freely for more desirable jobs above that ceiling on the basis of individual ability and qualification. It is as if the status mobility operates with one set of rules for the dominant group and another for the minorities for self-betterment. These developments affect the epistemologies of groups about the status-mobility system and minority schooling. The situation is represented schematically in figure 3.1.

Basically, unequal power relations and the job ceiling cause the dominant and minority groups to define "reality" for the minorities differently. These definitions, of course, tend to change when there are changes in the power relations or in the job ceiling or the minorities' opportunity structure. For example, the dominant group may determine at some time that minorities cannot advance in the status-mobility system beyond a certain level regardless of training and ability, or because the minorities are incapable of achieving the necessary educational qualifications. At other times they may hold a utopian view of the status-mobility system, claiming that it is an open system in which everyone with necessary educational credentials or "qualifications" can achieve self-advancement or join "the mainstream." The underrepresentation of minorities in the more desirable job categories may then be explained as due to their individual or collective faults. Consistent with their view of how things are or ought to be, dominant-group members tend to provide minorities with education (in terms of access and treatment) that recruits them to their "appropriate" place in the job market. Any relative lack of school success on the part of the minorities might be attributed to

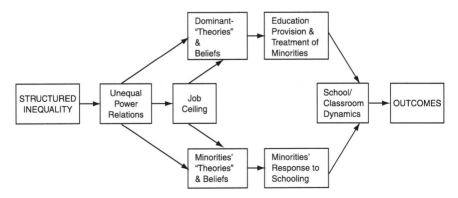

Figure 3.1 Structured inequality, epistemologies, and minority schooling

some "cultural, language, social or genetic" disadvantage of the minorities. Where they occur, dominant-group members rarely see the contradictions between their epistemology and practice.

The epistemology of the minorities—their definition of "reality"—is usually different. Minorities rarely are content with their menial position or endorse educational ideas that advocate preparing them for such positions. They do not see the status-mobility system as open or fair; however, different kinds of minorities tend to perceive and interpret the situation differently. Castelike minorities, for example, often develop an institutional discrimination perspective whereby they argue that they cannot advance into the mainstream through individual efforts in school or by adopting the cultural practices of the dominant group.[18] They may believe, in contrast to the dominant group, that collective rather than individual efforts and other strategies offer the best chances for advancement.[19] The minorities' perceptions of schooling and their educational efforts tend to be consistent with their perceptions and interpretations of the status-mobility system and other options. These perceptions, interpretations, and options determine the extent to which the minorities define school success as a satisfactory cultural goal, accept the school's criteria for success, and culturally sanction and implement instrumental behaviors that enhance that success.

The black- and Chinese-American examples: castelike status, immigrant status, and educability

An analysis of the pattern of school performance or the problem of educability of a subordinate minority group, according to the above model, involves answering three related questions: First, how does the status-mobility system operate with respect to the minority group? Second, what is the role of the education system in recruiting minorities into the status-mobility system? Third, how do the minorities perceive the status-mobility system, and how do their perceptions affect their perceptions of and responses to schooling? It is with respect to the third question that immigrant and castelike minorities differ.

The American status-mobility system and minorities

We noted earlier that the most important aspect of the American status-mobility system is jobs that are ranked and remunerated accordingly. The need to train people to perform at different levels of the job hierarchy and people's desire for an opportunity to advance are strong motivating forces behind both societal provisions of schooling and individual pursuit of educational credentials. Myrdal's description of how the American status-mobility system operates from a societal point of view helps us to understand the deviation with respect to minorities and its significance. According to him, American society "does not demand equality of economic rewards independent of an individual's luck, ability, and push [effort]. It merely demands equality of opportunity."[20] That is, the competition for desirable social and economic roles and rewards should be free and fair. The qualification for this competition is school credentials. It is widely believed that those who have more or better educational credentials have a better access to desirable jobs and wages. This belief is supported by local and national employment and earning statistics: generally, people with a high school diploma have a better chance of working at more desirable jobs and earning more money over a lifetime than their peers with only elementary schooling, and high school graduates, in turn, have less chance of working at desirable jobs and earning more money over a lifetime than their peers with college degrees.[21] This model reflects the experience of the dominant white group very well. Historically, a large proportion of whites have found jobs and earned wages commensurate with their educational credentials. This experience has influenced white epistemology or folk theory of how the system works as well as white responses to schooling. White families, particularly middle-class families for whom the system works best, as well as the school and other institutions, communicate to children in many ways the strong linkage between school success and getting a job and good income in adult life.

The American status-mobility system treats subordinate minorities differently in two respects. One is the imposition of a job ceiling; the other is the requirement of additional qualifications above school credentials for those who wish to advance. The jobs above the job ceiling roughly correspond to those comprising the four top occupational categories, namely, (*a*) professional/technical, (*b*) managerial, official and proprietary, (*c*) clerical and sales, and (*d*) skilled crafts and foremanship. In the American cultural idiom these are the more desirable jobs; they require more education and demonstrate where education pays off. The jobs below the job ceiling are (*e*) semiskilled operatives, (*f*) personal and domestic work, (*g*) common labor, and (*h*) farm labor. These are the least desirable jobs, requiring less schooling and yielding lower returns for education.

Black Americans

Experience with the status-mobility system: the job ceiling

Up to the mid-1960s, blacks were generally (1) not permitted to compete freely as individuals for any types of jobs that they desired and for which they had the educational credentials; (2) were largely excluded from jobs above the job ceiling solely because of race; and (3) because of these exclusions most blacks were confined to jobs below the job ceiling. Space does not permit as detailed a presentation of the data as we have given elsewhere, but the situation was the same in the South and in the North.[22]

The other way that blacks are treated distinctively in the status-mobility system is the requirement of an additional qualification, namely, clientship, or "Uncle Tomming." Blacks have learned since slavery that the way to get ahead even within the limited universe open to them in the status-mobility system is not through merit and talent but through white patronage or favoritism. They have also learned that the way to solicit that favoritism is by playing some version of the "Uncle Tom" role, being compliant, dependent, and manipulative.[23] A number of studies have described instances in different parts of the country and at different times in which blacks have had to rely on white patronage to get loans, buy land or a home, or obtain good jobs, decent wages, and promotions on the job.

Although black employment opportunities appear to have improved, especially for those with a college education, since the civil rights legislations of the 1960s, the job ceiling has not disappeared, nor have the improvements been progressive and consistent to equalize black and white experiences. For example, the *Wall Street Journal* reports that black "executives" and "vice-presidents" of many corporations have often been recruited to occupy specially created personnel positions in public relations departments to handle minority affairs.[24] They have not attained their present positions through a normal merit system and have neither the experience nor the hope to advance to the top of the companies or institutions.[25]

College-educated blacks, but not whites, still rely on government patronage in the form of affirmative action to obtain desirable jobs and achieve middle-class status. Furthermore, black adult unemployment in June of 1982 was about 18 percent, or twice the national average, and black teenage unemployment is more than 52 percent, exceeding the rates in the 1960s before the "improvement" in opportunity structure began.

White epistemology and black education

Research findings on black job opportunity and educational histories indicate that at various periods the nature of the opportunity structure determined their access to education.[26] A good illustration of this is seen in the shift from an emphasis on industrial education for blacks in the 1930s. Before that time blacks were said to need "industrial education"—chiefly training in low-grade manual skills. State support and money from northern philanthropists for black schools were channeled into "industrial education" programs. However, in the 1930s, when the nation's industrial economy needed more and more workers with industrial skills, and the state and federal governments began to finance industrial education courses in the public schools, the participation of blacks became progressively restricted. Black schools could emphasize an academic or classical curriculum, if they wished, but not receive enough funds to provide blacks with the training for industrial employment. On this point Myrdal notes that southern whites, in theory, believed that blacks should get industrial education so long as that did not mean preparing them to compete effectively with whites for skilled and economically rewarding jobs.[27] It seems to us, too, that the concerned efforts to redesign and improve black education in the 1960s through school integration and compensatory education can be interpreted as an attempt to prepare blacks for their new status brought about by civil rights legislations. In the 1960s the civil rights movement enhanced black political status and raised significantly the job ceiling through legislative and other measures, giving blacks access to higher-level jobs requiring more and better education than previously available. It was therefore logical for the dominant group to "improve" black education to ensure that recruits to these new positions have the appropriate training or qualification.

Black response

There is strong evidence that, on the one hand, blacks understand and "share" the folk assumptions underlying the American status-mobility system—namely, that jobs are hierarchically ranked, and that advancement in the job hierarchy depends on educational credentials. Like whites, blacks desire both job advancement and the required education: studies show that blacks usually have high job and high educational aspirations.[28] On the other hand, blacks know from a long history of experience that the status-mobility system does not operate for them according to the American folk theory; they know that the model "go to school, get a credential to get a job" works better for whites. Blacks have also generally perceived that they are given different (even segregated) and inferior education, which they interpret as designed to prevent them from competing effectively with whites for desirable jobs. Many believe, too, that those who manage to get appropriate educational credentials either cannot find appropriate jobs or earn wages commensurate with their training and ability. Our research suggests that these perceptions might have discouraged a large segment of the black population from sanctioning school success as a cultural goal, from accepting school's criteria of success, and from culturally sanctioning the instrumental behaviors that enhance school success. Instead they have led to responses that contribute to school failure, such as survival strategies, disillusionment, and conflict with the schools.

Survival strategies are directly related to job and economic opportunities and fall into two categories. The first includes collective struggle and clientship, used to increase job and other opportunities within the conventional economy. Collective struggle includes what the dominant whites legitimate as civil rights struggle. It also includes any other collective activity, such as rioting, which produces more jobs or better economic conditions.[29] Collective struggle has two opposing effects on black schooling. On the one hand, it increases job opportunities that could encourage more educational efforts. But on the other hand, it teaches children that "the system is to be blamed" for the high unemployment and other ills among blacks, and eventually they learn to blame "the system," including the school, for their own academic failure. The other strategy, clientship, contributes to the problem of school failure because successful "Uncle Toms" do not make effective models for white, middle-class school and societal success, both assumed to be based on open contest and individual ability.[30] The rules of behavior for achievement in the American status-mobility system are supposedly designed to give equal opportunity to everyone to win or lose by his or her own efforts—as in sports. Clientship, on the other hand, teaches black children the manipulative knowledge, skills, attitudes, and behaviors used by their parents to deal with whites and white institutions. Children entering school with this disposition may run into conflicts with school requirements stressing the white middle-class pattern.

Other survival strategies are used to exploit nonconventional economic resources, or the "street economy." These include hustling and pimping.[31] Three aspects of these strategies probably contribute to the school-failure problem. The first is the reverse work ethic, which, in hustling, insists that one should "make it" by not working, especially for whites, but by manipulating others to work for you. Children with this attitude, it has been reported, tend to reject doing their schoolwork because "it is the white man's thing."[32] The second aspect is the assumption that every social interaction should be an opportunity to manipulate people for some exploitation. When children play such manipulative games with teachers or their fellow students in class they generally cause disruption of learning. Finally, the repertoire of skills required by these survival strategies may on the whole be incongruent with those enhancing academic success.

Another type of response detrimental to school success is disillusionment about the job ceiling and the resulting effect on academic efforts. Perceptions of limited opportunity because of the job ceiling cause blacks to question the real value of schooling. This later probably led to a lack of development of persevering academic efforts or "effort optimism" as a culturally sanctioned behavior. Shack has suggested how this lack of academic effort and optimism may have developed as a result of the contrasting experiences of blacks and whites in the status-mobility system. He suggests that the absence of a job ceiling against whites allowed them to develop "effort optimism," summed up by the white maxim, "If at first you don't succeed, try, try again."[33] But black encounters with the job ceiling have taught them that jobs, wages, and promotions are not based on educational credentials and individual ability and efforts; consequently, they have developed a different maxim: "What's the use of trying?" Our observations in the classroom and in homes in Stockton, California, showed that the children did not take their schoolwork seriously and did not persevere at it. This lack of effort optimism is particularly serious among older children. At the same time, the children and their parents expressed high educational aspirations. The parents also tended to espouse the need to work hard in school.[34] But it seems that black children fail to do so because of three things: (*a*) it has not developed as a part of their cultural tradition to persevere at academic tasks; (*b*) the actual texture of their parents' lives of unemployment, underemployment, and discrimination convey a powerful message that counteracts parental verbal encouragement; and (*c*) children learn from observing older members of their community that schools success does not necessarily lead to jobs and other necessary and important things in adult life.

School performance is also affected by conflicts and distrust between blacks and the public schools. Hostility grew out of the treatment of blacks almost from the beginning of the public schools. It began with the exclusion of blacks, then segregation, and later the use of gross and subtle mechanisms that adversely affected the quality and amount of education blacks received. Blacks have generally perceived the exclusion and discrimination as designed to prevent them from qualifying for the more desirable jobs open to whites. Consequently, a significant part of their collective struggle has gone toward forcing schools and the whites controlling them to provide equal education for blacks. The conflicts have generated the belief among blacks that public schools cannot be trusted to educate black children. For their part, schools appear to be forced to deal with blacks defensively or to seek to control them paternalistically or through suppression in open conflict. It is our contention that in this context of hostile and suspicious relationships it is difficult for black children to internalize the values of the schools, accept school criteria for success, or follow school rules of behavior for achievement. This situation, along with other black responses, as well as provision of inferior education and negative treatment by the dominant whites, cause the disproportionate school failure among blacks.

Chinese Americans

Immigrant minorities in the United States, particularly nonwhites, often experience the same degree of subordination as castelike minorities. They are, for example, subjected to social and residential segregation, the job ceiling, and inferior education. But this condition does not necessarily cause persistent disproportionate school failure among immigrants. We use Chinese Americans as an example of immigrant minorities successful in the public schools in spite of structural and cultural subordination.

Immigration

Chinese immigration to the United States began about 1847, and by 1880 there were some 105,456.[35] These immigrants consisted of three groups: (1) laborers, who came to work in gold mines and other laboring jobs on the West Coast; (2) merchants and shopkeepers, who settled primarily in San Francisco; and (3) temporary visitors, including state officials, teachers, and students. Beginning in 1882, Congress passed a series of laws restricting Chinese immigration. These laws did not entirely stop the immigration, for, as Sung points out, up to 1943, when the laws were repealed, some Chinese continued to arrive in this country almost every year.[36] Following the repeal of the exclusion laws, the Chinese were granted an immigration quota of 105 a year in 1944, and Chinese Americans were permitted to bring their wives from China after the passage of the War Brides' Act of 1946. More Chinese were admitted under later immigration laws, including the Displaced Persons Act of 1948 and the Immigration and Nationality Act of 1952. The immigration between 1944 and 1965 was primarily selective, favoring the most highly educated, professional, and technically skilled Chinese. The law of 1944, for example, stipulated that 50 percent of the Chinese annual quota should be reserved for people with high education, technical training, specialized experience, and exceptional ability whose services, as determined by the attorney general, were needed by the United States. The number of immigrants has increased and their composition changed tremendously since 1964, when Congress passed a more liberal immigration law.[37]

Subordination and status mobility

From the beginning Chinese immigrants were highly subordinated in the areas of economic, political, and social relations, as well as in housing and education. They were denied civil rights: as aliens they were excluded from playing a major political role outside of "Chinatowns." In some states intermarriage between Chinese and whites was illegal, and where intermarriage occurred the offspring were usually defined as Chinese and accorded the same status as their Chinese parents.[38] For example, the San Francisco board of education refused school admission to a 10-year-old girl because one of her parents was Chinese.[39] The immigrants were residentially segregated and the formation of "Chinatown" in San Francisco and other places followed the same process as black ghetto formation.[40] In the area of employment the immigrants were relegated to menial jobs in the mines or worked as cooks, laundrymen, and domestic servants in the city. They were paid wages far below rates acceptable to local whites, and merchants and shopkeepers suffered from restrictive competition. Those who completed their education in America were either not hired or faced a job ceiling; as a consequence, the immigrants received little reward in the United States for their educational efforts.[41]

Chinese subordination began to change, however, during the Second World War. Following the Japanese invasion of China in 1937, and particularly after Japan attacked Pearl Harbor in 1941, America and China became allies, leading Americans to redirect their anti-Asian racism toward the Japanese. They also began to develop a new image of Chinese as "faithful allies, heroic fighters, and tragic victims."[42] The new developments resulted in repealing the Chinese Exclusion Acts in 1943. The new Chinese image, coupled with a manpower shortage in the United States after World War II, made white employers hire the Chinese for high-level jobs; that is, the job ceiling against the Chinese was raised. As a result, the proportion of Chinese professional workers rose from 2.9 percent in 1940 to 18 percent in 1960 and to 26 percent in 1970.[43] Residential segregation also began to break down; real estate agents began to sell homes in predominantly white areas to the Chinese, especially to the new professional immigrants who could afford to buy such homes.

White epistemology and Chinese education and success

Initially, white Americans regarded the Chinese as inferior people unfit to attend public schools or attend school with white children. Along with blacks and Indians, Chinese were, for example, excluded from the public schools in San Francisco. Later they were given segregated and inferior education. Schools generally ignored their culture and language.[44]

In spite of the job ceiling and other barriers, and in spite of attempts to give them inferior education, the immigrants did and have generally done well in school. For example, in our research in Stockton, California, we found that Chinese students did better than their black and white peers at the junior and senior high schools in terms of grades.[45] Their success in the public schools is also illustrated by their representation at Lowell, a college-preparatory high school that draws its pupils from the public junior high schools throughout San Francisco. Although the Chinese comprised a small proportion of the total public school population, they made up 25 percent of Lowell's students in 1965, 35.8 percent in 1972, and about 50 percent in 1976.[46] A high proportion go on to complete college degrees. Thus it is reported that in 1960, 16.7 percent of Chinese males, as compared to 8.0 percent of white males and 2.2 percent of black, had completed 4 or more years of college. The comparable figures for the females were 12.3 percent, 5.3 percent, and 2.8 percent, respectively.[47] In 1970 about 25 percent of Chinese males and 15 percent of females had completed 4 or more years of college.[48] What accounts for the Chinese school success?

Conventional explanations

Conventional explanations of Chinese school success are twofold: that the immigrants brought a cultural respect for learning and value of education as a means of self-advancement, and that their family structure and relationship encouraged children to work hard in school.

With regard to cultural tradition and values, Sung writes that "Chinese respect for learning and for scholars is a cultural heritage. Even when a college degree led to no more than a waiter's job, the Chinese continued to pursue the best education they could get, so that when the opportunities developed, the Chinese were qualified and capable of handling their job."[49] This explanation is true to some extent. The trouble with it is that it makes no distinction between the behavior and values of peasants and those of the higher classes. Consequently, it does not explain why peasants' immigrant children are academically successful in the United States while their peers in China were not. Although we have not seen studies of peasant educational values and attitudes in China, there is some relatively good information about their high degree of illiteracy. Most immigrants, the sojourners, were illiterate, and studies of peasant communities in China show their peers to be equally illiterate throughout the first half of the twentieth century. For example, Buck estimated that in 1933 84 percent of the rural population could not pass the most elementary literacy test.[50] A survey of the rural agricultural population in the late 1930s found that in all regions 69.3 percent of the men and 98.7 percent of the women were illiterate. Snow quotes Hsu Teh-Lih as saying that in northwest China, "Virtually nobody but a few landlords, officials, and merchants could read before we (i.e., the communist regime) arrived. The illiteracy rate seemed to be about 95 percent."[51]

The other explanation—the family-influence hypothesis—takes two forms. One is that there is a reciprocal obligatory relationship between parents and the male child that enhances school success. In China, parents, according to this view, support and encourage their children to grow up as successful adults who will later support them in their old age. Children have a moral obligation to repay the labor of their parents by being successful and providing for aging parents. In America, parents encourage their children's schooling for the same reason. Children reciprocate by working hard to succeed in school in order to obtain good jobs and fulfill their filial obligations. The other aspect of the family-influence hypothesis is that the authority structure of the Chinese family, especially the parent-child relationship, is congruent with the teacher-pupil relationship in the public school. Thus Chinese children socialized at home into subordination and obedience and into respect and submission to elders and other authority figures easily transfer their attitudes and behaviors to their relationship with teachers and other school personnel. The latter respond by rewarding Chinese students with good grades, etc., not only for their academic performance but also for their good behavior, obedience, and responsibility.[52]

The explanation of Chinese school success in terms of family structure and socialization sounds plausible. But one has yet to explain why it is generalized to other groups like Mexican Americans. Furthermore, this hypothesis does not account for the failure of the same variable to enhance the school success of immigrants and their peers in China. It is true, of course, that the socialization of the immigrants' children in an authority relationship that stresses submission, obedience, and respect for authority enables them to achieve positive educational stereotypes that enhance their school success: teachers generally perceive Chinese students as well behaved, intelligent, and hardworking, and teachers and counselors convey these perceptions and their expectations to the students in many ways. The students, in turn, respond by trying to conform to the "model students" role in order to get good grades.[53] The Chinese achieved this positive educational identity of model students quite early, as shown by different studies during various historical periods and in different parts of the country.[54]

Kim and Wong have suggested other factors that have made Chinese students docile in school.[55] Among these was a language barrier that prevented them from participating actively in class; another was fear of white antagonism. Wong notes also that in the earlier years many Chinese students entering the public school might, in fact, have been repeating what they had already learned in mission or other schools in China. Many of them were brought to America by their real or "paper" parents after they had already had considerable schooling. But when they arrived in the United States they were usually placed several grades behind, partly because of language difficulties and partly because local school officials considered their education in China inferior to what they had to offer them. Wong was told by one informant that a 15-year-old immigrant student would be placed in a third-grade class where he was taught skills he already had learned in China. Of course, he excelled, especially in those subjects requiring little use of English. Many immigrant children arriving after the repeal of the exclusion laws were also likely to have attended the best schools on Mainland China, Taiwan, or Hong Kong because they came from families of professional, technical, or other better-educated classes who were favored by the immigration quota and other arrangements. However, the children of the sojourners, the laborers, or peasant immigrants have also been successful in the public school. This is evident in interviews with some members of the Chinese community in Stockton and in the findings of current research in the Chinese community of Cherrywood, California.[56] Although the factors considered above are important, the things that have helped children of the sojourners and other Chinese immigrants succeed in the public schools are more rooted in the immigrants' perceptions of their status and objectives in the United States and the resulting responses they made to American education.

Immigrants' objectives and responses to the job ceiling

To understand Chinese responses to the job ceiling and other discriminatory barriers, as well as their responses to schooling in America, it is necessary to ask why they came to America. The main objective of the Chinese immigrants was to make money with which to return to China to improve their status as defined by Chinese culture. The laborers, for example, came to make money with which to buy land upon return—a traditional strategy for gaining entry into the gentry class. They also intended to use some for other purposes: to build a family house, provide dowry for a daughter's marriage, arrange a suitable marriage for a son, and so forth.[57] Evidence that the immigrants intended to return to China lies in the fact that they were mostly single males or husbands who left their wives and children behind. They used members of their families as collateral for passage money advanced by Chinese merchants; they explicitly said they were temporary immigrants or sojourners; and, before the communist takeover of Mainland China, the immigrants had their bones sent back to China for burial if they died in the United States.[58] Returning to China was not merely wishful thinking on the part of the laborers, merchants, shopkeepers, and their children: many reemigrated both before and after the passage of the exclusion laws. What determined one's return included making enough money to repay loans advanced by merchants for previous passage, to pay for return passage with enough left to improve one's status in China; for some it included having obtained a good education to enable one to compete successfully in the civil service examination in China.[59]

Under these circumstances, Chinese immigrants responded to the job ceiling and other barriers somewhat differently than black Americans. Distasteful as the barriers were, the immigrants tried to make the best of the situation in order to achieve their main objective of making enough money to return to China. They were not discouraged, therefore, by their lack of "civil rights." As Shibutani and Kwan sum it up, "Before the Communist Revolution, a Chinese sojourner was not concerned with civil rights; he took it for granted that he was an alien and did not even consider the possibility of gaining equal status."[60] Because their main objective was to accumulate wealth or other resources with which to achieve higher status in China, the immigrants were pragmatic and accommodative in civil rights, housing, and employment. They did not accept the white definition of their objective menial positions or their racial identity as inferior, nor did they define themselves by the kind of jobs they did, which they regarded as temporary and a means to achieve higher positions in China. Consequently, they not only did their menial jobs well, but set up language schools beginning in 1886—with the help of the Imperial Government of China—to teach their children Chinese language, history, civilization, and important contributions they believed the Chinese had made to the world. Such teachings both countered any white assertions about Chinese inferiority and reinforced their alien identity.

Responses to schooling

Chinese immigrants initially desired American education as a means of achieving self-advancement back in China. Despite employment discrimination in the United States against educated Chinese, increasing use of Western-type education for civil service examinations and for political and economic advancement in China made school success in America a more and more attractive means to achieve a good position in China. The motivation to use American education to improve one's status in China was particularly strong before the repeal of the exclusion laws. There was very little educational payoff for the Chinese in America before World War II. For example, Sung reports that the Second California Constitutional Convention of 1879 prohibited the hiring of Chinese in all corporations in the state, and the Stanford University placement service noted in 1928 that it was almost impossible for a first- or second-generation Chinese or Japanese to find any jobs in engineering, manufacturing, or business. Some educated Chinese responded to these barriers by withdrawing into the Chinese sector of the economy—self- or family employment in a laundry, restaurant, or grocery store.[61] But many others chose to return to China, where they were more fully rewarded for their American education. The immigrants wanted to educate their children in America for opportunities in China. Sung put it this way: "Though his own life in the United States was wretched, he had hopes for the future. If by 'serving a term' in the United States he could save enough money to buy several parcels of land in China, he could raise himself to the gentry class. His sons would have a chance to get an education that would open doors to other opportunities. If his sons were in this country, they were urged and prodded into getting as much education as possible, for though the occupational outlook for them was bleak, they could always go back to China to practice as doctors, engineers, or scientists."[62] There are no statistics on the number of American-Chinese doctors, engineers, scientists, and others who returned to China because of employment barriers in the United States. But we do know that American education was highly valued in China during that period.

Moreover, the immigrants sought Western-type education not only for themselves and their children but also for their home communities in China. They remitted large sums of money to be used in building American-type schools. Thus we find that investment of remittance money in school building in Toishan district, from which most immigrants came, made it by 1940 the most educationally endowed district in China, with seven high schools, two normal schools, two trade schools, 167 consolidated schools, and 834 grade schools.[63]

Changes in U.S.-China relations since World War II expanded the Chinese-American opportunity structure and reinforced the motivation to pursue education as a route to self-betterment. As noted earlier, high-level professional and technical jobs were opened to both American-born and immigrant Chinese, resulting in the proportion of Chinese working in such jobs rising from 2.9 percent in 1940 to 26 percent in 1970. The absorption of the Chinese into visible high-level jobs not only acted favorably on children's perceptions of opportunity structure but also provided them with models of success.

The instrumental attitudes and approaches of the immigrants toward American education became a part of Chinese-American folklore; American criteria for success and the instrumental behaviors enhancing school success were accepted and became culturally sanctioned. These are passed on to generations of Chinese-American children. As Ong reports, "The immigrants viewed free public education of their children as the hope of the future. Education became the chief means to raise their economic status and social conditions and to get out of Chinatown ghetto. The Chinese were motivated to use education to advance themselves."[64] She goes on to add that, "As a matter of fact, one of the major reasons for immigration was the quest for a better life for their children through American free public education." Consequently, the immigrants exerted a considerable pressure on their children to study hard and succeed according to American criteria or standards of school success.

A survey of Chinese and other Asian students at the University of California, Berkeley, in the mid-1970s found that they experienced considerable parental pressure to do well in school for the same reasons that the earlier immigrants wanted their children to succeed. The four reasons most frequently given by the students for attending college, in rank order, are to make money, to get a better job (than parents have), because it is difficult to find menial jobs, and because other avenues for advancement (in the United States) are closed to Asians.[65] This pragmatic attitude extends to choices of fields of study. A number of Chinese informants have explained that the disproportionate representation of Chinese students in the fields of science and mathematics is a kind of insurance against employment discrimination. They point out that even a white employer prejudiced against Chinese will hire one with the technical skills the employer needs. This disproportionate representation is borne out by data from Berkeley. One survey found that between 1961 and 1968, 74.3 percent of the Chinese males enrolled majored in engineering and physical sciences; a random-sample survey in 1971 found that 75 percent were in engineering or the physical and biological sciences, and in 1976 about 73.6 percent of males and 51.13 percent of females were in the same three fields.[66]

The Chinese, in summary, brought with them certain cultural resources that encouraged school success in America, especially traditional respect for and value of education as a means for social mobility, and their family structure and authority relationships. But they also brought other cultural resources that might have discouraged school success: a learning style that emphasizes external forms and rote memorization rather than observation, analysis, and comprehension; their language, which is so different from English; and their authority structure, which discourages socialization of children for independence and autonomy. All of these are qualities that psychologists find essential for development of achievement motivation and school success.[67] Whatever positive or negative cultural resources the Chinese immigrants brought, situational factors associated with their immigrant status appear largely to have influenced their perceptions and efforts to do well in school.

Conclusion

In this paper we have stressed the importance of distinguishing between types of minorities. Autonomous, immigrant, and castelike minority statuses appear to have different educational implications. We have also suggested a conceptual framework—the status-mobility system—for a comparative analysis of the education of various minority types. And we have used it to show why castelike minorities (e.g., black Americans), but not immigrant minorities (e.g., Chinese Americans), disproportionately experience persistent school failure under relatively similar structural conditions. Elsewhere,[68] we have pointed out that this approach might be useful in studying the school experiences of the same minority group in two different settings. For example, the Buraku outcastes in Japan (where they constitute a castelike minority) experience persistent disproportionate school failure, but the same Burakus in the United States (where they are an immigrant minority group) are doing as well as other Japanese-Americans in school.

Notes

1 John U. Ogbu, *Minority Education and Caste: The American System in Cross-cultural Perspective* (New York: Academic Press, 1978), and "Equalization of Educational Opportunity and Racial/Ethnic Inequality," in *Comparative Education*, ed. Philip G. Altbach, Robert F. Arnove, and Gail P. Kelly (New York: Macmillan, 1982).
2 Ogbu, *Minority Education and Caste*, pp. 21–25.
3 Arthur R. Jensen, "Statement of Dr. Arthur R. Jensen, Senate Select Committee on Education" (unpublished manuscript).
4 Akim L. Mabogunje, *Regional Mobility and Resource Development in West Africa*

(Montreal and London: McGill–Queens University Press, 1972); Tamotsu Shibutani and Kian M. Kwan, *Ethnic Stratification: A Comparative Approach* (New York: Macmillan, 1965).

5 Shibutani and Kwan, p. 119.

6 Ibid., p. 517.

7 Gerald D. Berreman, "Concomitants of Caste Organization," in *Japan's Invisible Race: Caste in Culture and Personality*, ed. George A. DeVos and Hiroshi Wagatsuma (Berkeley: University of California Press, 1967), pp. 308–24, and "Caste in India and the United States," *American Journal of Sociology* 66 (1960): 120–27; Allison Davis, Burleigh B. Gardner, and Mary R. Gardner, *Deep South: A Social Anthropological Study of Caste and Class*, abridged ed. (Chicago: University of Chicago Press, 1965); Gunnar Myrdal, *An American Dilemma: The Negro Problem and Modern Democracy* (New York: Harper, 1944).

8 Fred H. Schmidt, *Spanish Surname American Employment in the Southwest* (Washington, D.C.: Government Printing Office, 1972).

9 Julian Nava, "Cultural Backgrounds and Barriers That Affect Learning by Spanish-speaking Children," in *Mexican-Americans in the United States: A Reader*, ed. John H. Burma (New York: Schenkman, 1970); Clarence Senior, "Puerto Ricans on the Mainland," in *The Puerto Rican Community and Its Children on the Mainland: A Source Book for Teachers, Social Workers and Others Professionals*, ed. Francisco Cordasco and Eugene Buccioni (Metuchen, N.J.: Scarecrow, 1972); U.S. Department of Interior, Bureau of Indian Affairs, *Statistics concerning Indian Education* (Washington, D.C.: Government Printing Office, 1974).

10 Nava, pp. 131–32.

11 Berreman, "Concomitants of Caste Organization," p. 314; Arthur Tuden and Leonard Plotnicov, "Introduction," in *Social Stratification in Africa*, ed. Tuden and Plotnicov (New York: Free Press, 1970).

12 Robert A. Levine, *Dreams and Deeds: Achievement Motivation in Nigeria* (Chicago: University of Chicago Press, 1967).

13 Alex Inkeles, "Society, Social Structure and Child Socialization," in *Socialization and Society*, ed. J. A. Clausen (Boston: Little, Brown, 1968).

14 Everett C. Hughes, *Men and Their Work* (Glenco: Free Press, 1950); L. Berg, *Education and Jobs: The Great Training Robbery* (New York: Praeger, 1969); Elliot Liebow, *Tally's Corner: A Study of Negro Streetcorner Men* (Boston: Little, Brown, 1966); Herman P. Miller, *Rich Man, Poor Man* (New York: Crowell, 1971).

15 Miller, p. 18.

16 Inkeles; Otis D. Duncan and Robert W. Hodge, "Educational and Occupational Mobility: A Regression Analysis," *American Journal of Sociology* 68 (1963) 629–44; T. Fox and S. M. Miller, "Intra-Country Variations: Occupational Stratification and Mobility," in *Class, Status and Power*, 2d ed., ed. R. Bendix and S. M. Lipsett (New York: Free Press, 1966); Celia S. Heller, *Structured Social Inequality: A Reader in Comparative Social Stratification* (New York: Macmillan, 1969); Irving Kraus, *Stratification, Class and Conflict* (New York: Free Press, 1976).

17 George D. Spindler, "The Transmission of Culture," in *Education and Culture: Toward an Anthropology of Education*, ed. George D. Spindler (New York: Holt, Rinehart & Winston, 1974), and "From Omnibus to Linkages: Cultural Transmission Models," in *Educational Patterns and Cultural Configurations: The Anthropology of Education*, ed. Joan I. Robers and Sherry K. Akinsanya (New York: McKay, 1976); Christopher Jencks, *Inequality* (New York: Basic, 1972); LeVine.

18 John U. Ogbu, *The Next Generation: An Ethnography of Education in an Urban Neighborhood* (New York: Academic Press, 1974); Arnold Lewis, "Minority Education in Sharonia, Israel, and Stockton, California: A Comparative Analysis," *Anthropology and Education Quarterly* 12 (1981): 30–50.

19 John U. Ogbu, "Education, Clientage, and Social Mobility: Caste and Social Change in the United States and Nigeria," in *Social Inequality: Comparative and Developmental Approaches*, ed. Gerald D. Berreman (New York: Academic Press, 1981).

20 Myrdal (n. 7 above), p. 671.

21 Otis D. Duncan and Peter M. Blau, *The American Occupational Structure* (New York: Wiley, 1967); Jencks.

22 William B. Gould, *Black Workers in White Unions: Job Discrimination in the United States* (Ithaca, N.Y.: Cornell University Press, 1977); Myrdal (n. 7 above); Paul H. Norgren and Samuel E. Hill, *Toward Fair Employment* (New York: Columbia University Press, 1964); Dorothy K. Newman et al., *Protest, Politics and Prosperity: Black Americans and White Institutions 1940–1975* (New York: Pantheon, 1978); Ray F. Marshall, *The Negro Worker* (New York: Random House, 1978).

23 John Dollard, *Caste and Class in a Southern Town*, 3d ed. (Garden City, N.Y.: Doubleday, 1957); St. Claire Drake and Horace R. Cayton, *Black Metropolis: A Study of Negro Life in a Northern City*, vols. 1 and 2 (New York: Harcourt, Brace & World, 1970); J. Farmer, "Stereotypes of the Negro and Their Relationship to His Self-Image," in *Urban Schooling*, ed. H. C. Rudman and R. L. Featherstone (New York: Harcourt, Brace & World, 1968).

24 J. Kaufman, "Black Executives Say Prejudice Still Impedes Their Path to the Top," *Wall Street Journal* (July 9, 1980), p. 1.

25 John U. Ogbu, "A Review of *Caste and Class Controversy*," *Harvard Educational Review* 51 (1981): 205–9.

26 Ogbu, *Minority Education and Caste*, chap. 6 and p. 177.

27 Myrdal (n. 7 above), pp. 897–99.

28 W. Curtis Banks and Gregory V. McQuarter, "Achievement Motivation and Black Children," *IRCD Bulletin* 11 (1976): 1–8; Bernard C. Rosen, "Race, Ethnicity and the Achievement Syndrome," in *Achievement in American Society*, ed. Bernard C. Rosen, Harry J. Crocket, and Clyde Z. Nunn (Cambridge, Mass: Schenkman, 1969).

29 D. K. Newman et al., *Protest, Politics and Prosperity: Black Americans and White Institutions, 1940–1975* (New York: Pantheon, 1978); Joseph W. Scott, *The Black Power Revolt: Racial Stratification in the USA* (Cambridge, Mass: Schenkman, 1976); Ogbu, "Education, Clientage, and Social Mobility: Caste and Social Change in the United States and Nigeria."

30 Ralph H. Turner, "Sponsored and Contest Mobility and the School Systems," *American Sociological Review* 35 (1960): 121–39.

31 Paul Bullock, *Aspirations vs. Opportunity: "Careers" in the Inner City* (Ann Arbor: University of Michigan Press, 1973); Herbert L. Foster, *Ribbin', Jivin' and Playin' the Dozens: The Unrecognized Dilemma of Inner City Schools* (Cambridge, Mass.: Ballinger, 1974); N. C. Heard, *Howard Street* (New York: Dial, 1968); Christina A. Milner, "Black Pimps and Their Prostitutes: Social Organization and Value Systems of a Ghetto Occupational Subculture" (Ph.D. diss., Department of Anthropology, University of California at Berkeley, 1970); Betty Valentine, *Hustling and Other Hardwork: Lifestyles in the Ghetto* (New York: Free Press, 1979); Tom Wolfe, *Radical Chic and Mau-Mauing the Flack Catchers* (New York: Strauss & Giroux, 1970).

32 Barry Silverstein and Ronald Krate, *Children of the Dark Ghetto: A Developmental Psychology* (New York: Praeger, 1975), pp. 185, 235.

33 William A. Shack, "On Black American Values in White America: Some Perspectives on the Cultural Aspects of Learning Behavior and Compensatory Education" (paper prepared for the Social Science Research Council, Sub-Committee on Values and Compensatory Education, 1970–71).

34 I. Katz, "The Socialization of Academic Motivation in Minority Group Children," in *Nebraska Symposium on Motivation*, ed. D. Levine (Lincoln: University of Nebraska Press, 1967).

35 U.S. Department of Commerce, Census Bureau, *Special Tabulation, Public Use Sample Data* (Washington, D.C.: Government Printing Office, 1970).

36 Betty L. Sung, *Mountain of Gold: The Story of the Chinese in America* (New York: Macmillan, 1967).

37 Betty L. Sung, *Chinese American Manpower and Employment* (Washington, D.C.: Department of Labor, Manpower Administration, 1975).

38 Sung, *Mountain of Gold*, pp. 253–55.

39 H. Brett Melendy, *The Oriental Americans* (New York: Twayne, 1972).

40 Helen Cather, "History of San Francisco's Chinatown" (unpublished manuscript, n.d.); M.R. Coolidge, *Chinese Immigration* (New York: Arno, 1969), p. 411.

41 Coolidge, p. 366; Sung, *Mountain of Gold*; P. Chiu, "Chinese Labor in California" (M.A. thesis, University of Wisconsin, 1967), pp. 23, 105.

42   Stanley M. Lyman, *The Asian in the West* (Reno and Las Vegas: Western Studies Center, Desert Research Institute, University of Nevada, 1970), p. 124.
43   Sung, *Chinese American Manpower and Employment*, p. 112.
44   Sung, *Mountain of Gold*; Coolidge, pp. 435–36; Charles C. Dobbie, *San Francisco's Chinatown* (New York: Appleton-Century, 1936).
45   Ogbu, *The Next Generation* (n. 18 above).
46   Pamela Ow, "The Chinese and the American Educational System" (Master's thesis, Department of Sociology, University of California, Berkeley, 1976), pp. 18–19.
47   Sung, *Mountain of Gold*, p. 125.
48   U.S. Department of Commerce, Census Bureau (n. 35 above), p. 68.
49   Sung, *Mountain of Gold*, pp. 124–25.
50   Buck is quoted in Suzzane Pepper, "Education and Political Development in Communist China," *Studies in Comparative Communism* 3 (1971): 199.
51   Edgar Snow, *Red Star over China* (New York: Grove, 1961), p. 253.
52   Coolidge, pp. 343–47; Stanley L. M. Fong, "Assimilation and Changing Social Roles of Chinese Americans," *Journal of Social Issues* 29 (1973): 115–27; J. S. Tow, *The Real Chinese in America* (New York: Academic Press, 1923), p. 77.
53   Stanley Sue and Harry H. L. Kitano, "Stereotypes as a Measure of Success," *Journal of Social Issues* 29 (1973): 95; Tow, p. 77.
54   Coolidge, p. 437; Fong; p. 117; Sue and Kitano, p. 88; Tow, p. 77.
55   E. H. Kim, "Yellow English," *Asian American Review* 2 (1975): 44–63; Karen Wong, "An Investigation of the Reasons for the Changing Political Mood in San Francisco Chinatown" (unpublished research project paper, Department of Anthropology, University of California, Berkeley, 1972).
56   Ogbu, *The Next Generation*; Grace P. Guthrie, "An Ethnography of Bilingual Education in a Chinese Community" (Ph.D. diss., Graduate College of Education, University of Illinois at Urbana-Champaign, 1982).
57   Sung, *Mountain of Gold*, p. 240; Shibutani and Kwan (n. 4 above), p. 517.
58   G. Barth and G. Gunther, *Bitter Strength* (Cambridge, Mass.: Harvard University Press, 1964), p. 77; Cather (n. 40 above), p. 1; Lyman (n. 42 above), pp. 21, x.
59   Sung, *Mountain of Gold*, pp. 83–84.
60   Shubtani and Kwan, p. 517.
61   Sung, *Mountain of Gold*, pp. 236, 240.
62   Ibid., p. 240.
63   Ibid., p. 17.
64   Cindy Ong, "The Educational Attainment of the Chinese in America" (unpublished research project manuscript, Department of Anthropology, University of California, Berkeley, 1976), p. 8.
65   Ibid., pp. 11–12.
66   Ow (n. 46 above), pp. 17–18.
67   David McClelland, *The Achieving Society* (Princeton, N.J.: Van Nostrand, 1961); Rosen (n. 28 above), pp. 131–54.
68   Ogbu, *Minority Education and Caste* (n. 1 above).

CHAPTER 4

MOTIVATING THE CULTURALLY DIFFERENT STUDENT (1983)

Gwendolyn C. Baker

Motivating children to learn continues to be one of the greatest challenges facing teachers. Few students approach the learning environment with enthusiasm and interest, and even those who do, require encouragement and reinforcement to perpetuate their eagerness for learning. Similarly, not all students who lack motivation are culturally different, but these children frequently are not successful in school. Some sit immobile and unresponsive in classrooms, while others are so disruptive that discipline becomes a problem. Many minority children are performing below grade level, require remedial work, and are not promoted. If they graduate from high school, they often find work only in menial jobs.

Whether or not the school is responsible for the problems that confront these low achievers is not the question; the real issue is that schools can do much to alleviate this condition. There are possible solutions to the problem, and one answer may be found through involving a multicultural approach in the teaching and learning process.

Multicultural education is a process that builds on the cultural back-grounds and experiences of the learner and fosters growth and development in that which is familiar to the student. It is a process that helps to expose the individual to diversity and encourages an understanding and appreciation for differences.

Generally, schools and curricula are structured around the assumption that all children need to learn the same content in the same manner. Rarely do schools give serious attention to the different needs of all the students it serves. Curricula, instructional materials, and teaching strategies in most learning environments are geared to serve students from white, middle class backgrounds. Content that is not relevant and familiar to students will not encourage the desire for involvement, nor will instructional strategies which do not take into account what the students bring to the classroom and what they need as a result of their cultural backgrounds. Instruction that is multicultural does provide what is needed and can serve as a motivational force for all students.

For the culturally different student, this approach can enhance the worth of self, motivating and encouraging academic achievement. Culturally different students need to know that they are a legitimate part of the society. It is also important for the non-minority child to know of the involvement of other people in the building of this nation.[1]

Once differences and needs have been acknowledged and the desire to meet these needs has been established, the culturally different child presents an interesting challenge for the school and the teacher. They are then ready to plan and organize for multicultural instruction. This process requires, first, a knowledge of the ethnic and cultural background of the students being served. A commitment to the importance of providing relevant and meaningful instruction is also mandatory, as are necessary changes in curricula and instructional modes if full implementation is to be achieved. At first glance, the task may appear to be difficult, even overwhelming. However, if planned systematically and carefully, it can be achieved.

It is essential to involve the teacher in the overall design in planning for multicultural instruction. Generally, the needs of teachers will fall into two categories: background information and assistance in planning for classroom instruction. Establishing a knowledge base about culture and ethnic groups is crucial if teachers are to understand what they are going to teach. It is also necessary for them to understand why their cultural awareness is important for the student. Not all teachers who become involved in multicultural education are fully committed at the onset. However, once they begin to learn about culture and its importance to the individuals in the learning process, their interest and commitment is usually established and they become involved in developing a rationale and philosophy of multicultural education.

An effective way of approaching classroom instruction is to stress the importance of integrating ethnic/cultural content throughout the curriculum. Teaching about specific ethnic groups and/or exploring issues relevant to these groups through separate units and activities are often not effective. Multicultural content can be integrated into larger units of study so that it becomes a natural part of the unit.

For example, studying the history and lifestyle of Vietnamese Americans in a separate social studies unit is not as effective, from a multicultural standpoint, as presenting the same content in appropriate areas of exploration such as housing, neighborhoods, geography, food. Children who are culturally different should not be made to feel that their differences are negative, but rather, that they are understandable, acceptable and appreciated. On the other hand, non-minority children need to learn that there are many different kinds of responses to and types of involvement in most of the areas and topics that are studied.

The selection and development of appropriate instructional materials are also important for the successful implementation of a multicultural approach to teaching. Too often what is needed is not available through commercial sources, and teachers must design and create materials. Textbooks, tradebooks, filmstrips, films, and bulletin boards that do not adequately include and represent the minority child do little to enhance the motivational process. Because pictorial representation is an effective way to make the culturally different student feel included and important, teachers should be sensitive in preparing bulletin boards and selecting books and stories that reflect diversity.

Although relevant content and instructional materials are crucial to multicultural education, the value of the attitudes and expectations held by teachers cannot be overlooked. In a study of how children perceive their teachers' attitudes toward them, Davidson and Lang concluded that "the more positive the children's perceptions of their teachers' feelings, the better was their academic achievement, and the more desirable their classroom behavior as rated by the teachers."[2] Many teachers, because they do not perceive differences—and particularly cultural differences—as positive attributes, tend to respond to minority children in negative ways and to expect less of them. This kind of behavior does not serve to enhance the motivational level of the student who is culturally different. Gollnick and Chinn suggest the following:

> Unless teachers can critically examine their treatment of different students in the classroom, they will not know whether they treat students inequitably because of ethnic differences. Once that step has been taken, changes can be initiated to ensure that ethnicity is not a factor for automatically relating differently to students. Teachers may have to become more proactive in initiating interaction and providing encouragement, praise, and reinforcement to students from cultural backgrounds different from their own.[3]

If multicultural education is to serve as a motivating force for the culturally different student, the involvement of the teacher is crucial. The teacher will need to acquire a knowledge base about ethnic and cultural groups, develop a rationale and/or philosophy for teaching a multicultural curriculum, and provide appropriate and supportive classroom instruction. When the above is achieved and coupled with the desire of the teacher to improve the academic achievement of the minority student, success is imminent.

Multicultural education will not solve all of the problems facing the teacher and the school with regard to stimulating the minority child to learn. However, if planned and approached carefully and sincerely, this approach will improve the motivation of the culturally different student.

Notes

1   G.C. Baker, "The Teachers and Multiethnic Education," *Education of the 80s: Multiethnic Education*, edited by James A. Banks, Washington, D.C., National Education Association, 1981, p. 35.
2   H.H. Davidson and G. Lang, "Children's Perceptions of Their Teachers' Feelings Toward Those Related to Self Perception, School Achievement, and Behavior," *Teaching Social Studies to Culturally Different Children*, edited by James A. Banks and William W. Joyce, Reading, Mass., Addison-Wesley Publishing Company, 1971.
3   M. Gollnick and P.C. Chinn, *Multicultural Education in a Pluralistic Society*, St. Louis, C.V. Mosby, 1983.

Teachers' bibliography

Baker, Gwendolyn C., *Planning and Organizing the Multicultural Instruction*, Reading, Mass., Addison-Wesley, 1983.
Banks, James A., *Teaching Strategies for Ethnic Studies*, Second Edition, Boston, Allyn and Bacon, 1979.
Carlson, Ruth Kearney, *Emerging Humanity: Multi-ethnic Literature for Children and Adolescents*, Dubuqu, Iowa, Wm. C. Brown, 1972.
Cheyney, Arnold B., *Teaching Children of Different Cultures in the Classroom: A Language Approach*, Columbus, Ohio, C.E. Merrill, 1976.
Garcia, Ricardo L., *Teaching in a Pluralistic Society*, New York, Harper & Row, 1982.
Gold, M.J., C.A. Grant and H.N. Rivlin, *In Praise of Diversity: A Resource Book for Multicultural Education*, and *In Praise of Diversity: Multicultural Classroom Applications*, and *Multicultural Education: A Functional Bibliography for Teachers*, Center for Urban Education, The University of Nebraska at Omaha, 3805 North 16th Street, Omaha, Neb. 68110.
Gollnick, Donna M. and Philip C. Chinn, *Multicultural Education in a Pluralistic Society*, St. Louis, C.V. Mosby & Co., 1983.
Grant, Carl, ed., *Sifting and Winnowing: An Exploration of the Relationship Between*

Multi-Cultural Education and CBTE, Madison, Wisconsin, Teacher Corps Associates, University of Wisconsin-Madison, 1975.

Longstreet, Wilma, *Aspects of Ethnicity*, New York, Teachers College Press, 1978.

Ramirez, Manuel and Alfredo Castaneds, *Cultural Democracy, Bicognitive Development and Education*, New York, Academic Press, 1974.

Schuman, Jo Miles, *Art From Many Hands: Multicultural Art Projects For Home and School*, Englewood Cliffs, N.Y., Prentice Hall, Inc., 1981.

Tiedt, Pamela L. and Iris M. Tiedt, *Multicultural Teaching: A Handbook of Activities, Information and Resources*, Boston, Allyn and Bacon, 1979.

CHAPTER 5

MULTICULTURAL EDUCATION (1991)
A vital investment strategy for culturally diverse youth groups

Patricia J. Larke

Demographic changes in the youth population across this nation show a substantial increase in the number of minority youth who are less than 20 years of age (Hodgkinson, 1989; Quality Education for Minorities Project [QEMP], 1990). However, minority (African American, Hispanic American, Asian American and Native American [AHANA]) group membership in formal organizations is not reflective of this demographic change. This lack of cultural diversity in many historically monocultural youth groups has captured national, state and local attention. Concerns about the recruitment and retention of minority youth in organizations that have been historically dominated by Anglo youth and advised by Anglo youth leaders have been reflected by the agendas of many special conferences and symposia. In addition, organizations, such as 4-H groups, are making concerted efforts to change the "Anglo youth image" and are beginning to sensitize youth leaders about the interests and concerns of minority student members (Wessel & Wessel, 1982). Two questions often asked about the emergence of cultural diversity in youth groups are: (1) How do organizations become reflective of multicultural education as a strategy to implement change? and (2) How can one work effectively with youth whose culture is different from that of youth leaders?

Multicultural education and multiculturalism are possible responses to the aforementioned questions. The purpose of this paper is to explore the components of multicultural education that will enable leaders to work more effectively with culturally diverse youth groups within their organizations. Such an approach is designed to increase minority participation in youth organizations. An overview of the demographic changes in one state highlights the need to understand better why the involvement of minority youth in youth organizations is crucial to the education and economic stability of many of our states.

Youth in Texas: an overview

Like California and Florida, Texas is experiencing a majority/minority reversal in its youth population (less than 20 years of age). In 1980, minority youth represented 46 percent of the total youth population in Texas. Demographic projections suggest that by the year 2010, minority youth will be more than 50 percent of the total youth population (Hodgkinson, 1986). Since 1987, the majority of Texas' first graders have been minority students (Texas Education Agency, 1988). If this trend continues, and all evidence suggests that it will, then by 1998, the majority of the school-age population will be Hispanic American, African American, Asian American and Native American students. Clearly, this changing population should be found not only in schools but in youth organizations as well.

A substantial number of Texas youth (many of whom are racial/ethnic minorities) live in urban areas. In fact, eighty percent of the people in Texas live in 26 metropolitan areas (Hodgkinson, 1986). Therefore, youth groups which historically have served a non-minority rural youth population will need to accommodate the present urban population of minority youth.

Texas is ranked 42nd nationally in the percentage of high school graduates. The average dropout rate in 1986 was 35.7% (Johnson, 1988), and a recent report indicates that the percentage is increasing ("State's Dropout," 1989). The Intercultural Development Research Association (1986) reported that in Texas: (1) about 152,000 young people had completed fewer than nine years of schooling before leaving school; (2) of 500,000 dropouts, 52% were males; (3) for females, the dropout range is 26% for Anglos to 43% for Hispanics; (4) dropout rates differ for racial/ethnic groups: Anglos—27%; African Americans—34%; Hispanics—45%; (5) African American male dropouts were less likely to be employed than either Hispanic or Anglo male dropouts; and (6) the dropout problem is costing the State of Texas $17.12 billion in advance income and lost tax revenues and has increased costs in welfare, crime and incarceration, unemployment insurance and placement, and adult training education. Every dollar invested in the education of a potential dropout is estimated to result in a return of nine dollars.

According to Hahn's (1987) comprehensive study of dropouts, students reported many reasons for dropping out of school such as: (1) being behind in grade level and being older than classmates; (2) poor academic performance; (3) dislike of school; (4) detention and suspension; (5) pregnancy; (6) being welfare recipients; (7) attractiveness of work; (8) attractiveness of the military; (9) undiagnosed learning disabilities and/or emotional problems; and (10) language difficulties. However, research suggests that students who are least likely to drop out are those who are involved in school activities and organizations, who are able "to fit" in the dynamics of school, and who have a support system of peers who share similar academic interests (Shainline, 1987; Valverde, 1987).

It appears then that youth organizations can be instrumental in helping at risk youth develop academic skills and raise their self-esteem. Improvement in these two areas will help them form more positive feelings about school and society. Additionally, youth organizations can provide youth and adults who can serve as support systems for at risk students both in and out of school settings.

Multicultural education in youth groups

As student populations became more diverse because of desegregation and legal mandates, educators began to employ strategies of multicultural education to meet the needs of all students, regardless of their racial/ethnic identity. Today, this educational strategy enables educators to become more cognizant of, and sensitive to, the cultural and academic concerns of minority and non-minority students. In addition, this strategy enables excellence and equity to be viewed not as competing dichotomies but as enhancers of each other.

The conceptual framework for this strategy was conceived in cultural pluralism which provided the impetus for promoting acceptance and respect for human diversity. Cultural pluralism, a term coined by Horrace Kallen (1924), has three basic principles: (1) people do not choose their ancestry; (2) each racial/ethnic minority culture has something positive to contribute to American society; and (3) the ideas of democracy and equality carry the implicit assumption that there are differences between individuals and groups that can be viewed as "equal" (Gollnick & Chinn, 1986). From this framework, multicultural education was developed. For the purpose of this paper, the following definition will be used. Multicultural education is defined as:

> ... a philosophy, a process and [an education reform movement] by which [educational institutions] demonstrate in [such areas as] staffing patterns, curricula, [institutional practices and policies] an acceptance and respect for human diversity as a means of providing all students an equitable quality education in preparing for living in a culturally pluralistic society. It means that an education system is cognizant of more than skin colors, backgrounds and religious beliefs ... [but] to educate to eliminate classism, racism, sexism, ageism, handicappism and the more recently recognized uglyism (Mills, 1983).

A multicultural organization is defined as:

> ... an organization which is genuinely committed to diverse representation of its membership; is sensitive to maintaining an open, supportive and responsive environment; is working toward and purposefully including elements of diverse cultures in its ongoing operations and ... is authentic in its response to issues confronting it (Barr & Strong, 1989).

Components of multicultural education

To implement and integrate effectively the tenets of multicultural education into an organization, several factors are required: commitment, cultural sensitization, role models, parental/significant other involvement and modification of youth activities/projects. Discussion of these factors will be expounded upon in this section. Youth organizations that reflect cultural diversity often incorporate these strategies.

Commitment

For an organization to display commitment several support systems must be established. These systems involve: (1) investing financial resources, (2) developing and implementing policies and programs and (3) hiring personnel. Implementing effective programs to include more minority youth means having financial resources to (a) hire and promote minority youth leaders, (b) develop programs that are culturally sensitive and interesting to minority youths and (c) provide staff development programs for present and prospective employees in order to sensitize them to the cultural differences associated with the youth whom the organization will serve. Expressing a desire to involve more minority youth and to make it an organizational priority without monetary commitment only reinforces "lip service" or a verbal commitment.

Policy development and implementation involve the governing structure of an organization to request that issues about minority youth be included on their agendas, to design policies to implement programs and to matriculate program goals with realistic timelines. Program goals with monitoring systems are most progressive. Accountability and reward systems should be built into programs to provide checking systems and incentives for members to achieve the goals of the organization. One-shot, quick fix programs do not work. Such programs only serve to exacerbate, mask or displace problems and impede problem resolution.

Hiring effective and sensitive personnel is important because successful programs cannot operate without people who are genuinely concerned and culturally sensitive and knowledgeable about minority youth. Finding people who demonstrate these characteristics frequently requires funds with which to attract them. Many organizations rely exclusively on volunteers to work with their youth groups. Organizations must consider the fact that minorities and poor people cannot afford to volunteer because of financial conditions that often require parents to work several low paying jobs to support their families. Therefore, finding people with the aforementioned characteristics become extremely difficult without financial support.

Cultural sensitization

Cultural sensitization is moving from ethnocentric behavior (an emotional attitude that one's own ethnic group, nation and/or culture is superior to all others) to cultural relativism (the ability to understand other ethnic groups or cultures from the perspective of that particular culture. Many find this process different and difficult. It becomes different and difficult because, in many instances, a person much accept and respect a new value system. For example, the value of sharing in the dominant culture will not be interpreted as stealing in another culture when people use or remove objects without asking, or the value of "being on time" should not be interpreted as lazy or uncaring when the person does not arrive "on time."

Leaders of youth organizations must ask themselves, "How does it feel to be a minority youth in the organization?" To understand this question truly, youth leaders must be empathetic with the experiences of racism and discrimination that are often displayed in subtle forms of attitudes and behaviors. When this is acknowledged within the organization, then members of that organization are becoming culturally relative. That is, they are able to understand the experiences of minority youth who are able to make and those who are unable to make the necessary adjustments to "fit" into the organization.

The ongoing process of cultural sensitization begins in two areas, knowledge of self and knowledge of others to create the culturally sensitive person (see Figure 5.1). The process of increasing self awareness must begin with people. This model presents areas that are needed to become a culturally sensitive person. Such areas can be explored through staff development and training programs wherein staff members can learn more about themselves. The process of critically examining one's self is often painful which is a significant area of exploring the knowledge of self. Using fictional characters and objects which remove the person from the situation is one approach to initiate the process. Through this type of relaxed atmosphere, many other sensitive issues may be discussed without having participants feel that they are being attacked.

At some point in the staff development and training program, and at some appropriate comfort level, issues such as (1) one's attitudes and beliefs regarding stereotypes about minority youth should be examined; (2) how stereotypes affect one's interactions with minority youth; and (3) one's nonverbal communication

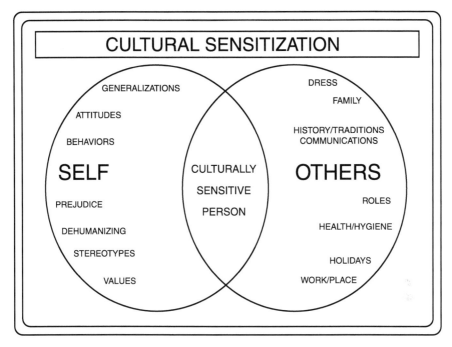

CULTURAL SENSITIZATION

GENERALIZATIONS

ATTITUDES

BEHAVIORS

SELF

PREJUDICE

DEHUMANIZING

STEREOTYPES

VALUES

CULTURALLY
SENSITIVE
PERSON

DRESS

FAMILY

HISTORY/TRADITIONS
COMMUNICATIONS

OTHERS

ROLES

HEALTH/HYGIENE

HOLIDAYS

WORK/PLACE

Figure 5.1

and silence about controversial issues which may subtly reinforce and promote discriminatory practices. In addition, some specific negative practices that should be explored involve staying one-up, generalizing, disempowering, self-protection, dehumanizing, easing the presence, White solidarity and expecting to be taught (Hardiman, 1988). To capture the impact of these negative practices a brief description is necessary.

Staying one up. This belief system assumes that minorities are in their position or a member of the organization because of their race and not because they are qualified or eligible. Persons of this mindset send to view cultural differences such as speech, dress, music and mannerisms as cultural deficiencies and/or lower socioeconomic status characteristics. They demand that minorities have a higher level of performance than everyone else before giving them equal respect.

Generalizing. This is assuming that mistakes made by one member of a minority group is indicative of the entire race/ethnic group. Inappropriately, it is assumed that one member or several members of the minority group can speak for the entire group or for all minority groups. It is also expected that the minority person will take care of all of the racial concerns for the organization.

Disempowering. Many who hold this belief assume that Anglos can determine the needs for all minorities. As such, Anglos are hired to design and administer social services for minorities. Often these administrators impose their help on others, especially "help" that is not respectful of the values or culture of minority recipients.

Self-protection. This attitude is characterized by not giving honest, especially negative, feedback to a minority person. For example, if a person's work is unacceptable, give specific reasons why and suggestions for improvement rather than say it's "okay" when it's not. In addition, this attitude means that there is a need to make the point that, "I'm not prejudiced or my upbringing was different" of which the expectation is to receive credit for being identified as liberal.

Dehumanizing. Some minority groups are seen as objects and are deprived of the character of humanity. For example, comparing people with objects such as "a is for apple and I is for Indian", using product symbols to refer to people such as "Big Chief" writing tablet and people as mascots, the "Cleveland Indians."

Easing the presence. Some practices are designed to neutralize the presence or impact of minorities. These include using materials (books, handouts, posters, pictures, magazines) which give no indication of the ethnicity of the authors. Such lack of information injects that minorities did not make historical or educational contributions because of the lack of an experiential or knowledge base. It's not surprising then, that non-minorities are given credit for the material. This further exacerbates that everybody in a "real" social or educational situation is non-minority and ignoring the ethnic background of authors, speakers and teachers as if it does not affect their perspective.

White solidarity. Group solidarity often supersedes normally appropriate behavior. For example, Anglos supporting another Anglo person when he/she does or says something racist and trying to minimize the behavior by telling the minority person that "He/she is really nice, he/she is just a little prejudiced." Such persons frequently laugh at racist jokes and do not take racist behavior seriously. They may tell the racially oppressed victim of these incidents that they are overreacting or being too "sensitive" when they get upset.

Expecting to be taught. Frequently minorities are called upon to be the conscience or teachers of Anglos with whom they interact. Anglos often use minorities to teach them about racism. This is usually done by asking minorities to keep nonminorities on their toes about their language and their actions that may be viewed as racist without taking the responsibility for their own racist behaviors.

In staff development and training programs, the second ongoing process of cultural sensitization provides experiences to learn more about people from culturally diverse backgrounds (see Figure 5.1). It is important to assess one's knowledge base about components of culture other than food and clothing, such as history, traditions, lifestyles, home environment and the roles of males and females. Books and articles, as well as audio visuals such as videos, films, records and tapes can provide valuable insight. An experiential component that includes interaction with minority youth and visitation within the neighborhood and community organizations (community centers and churches) can contribute much to increasing the knowledge base. However, one must become more than a spectator for the experiences to have an impact. For example, visiting a Native American reservation once and saying "it is really a beautiful place" without understanding the Native American culture and historical significance of the reservation only reinforces stereotypical attitudes and beliefs about Native Americans.

Saville-Troike (1978) provides some guidelines for better understanding the history and culture of other cultural groups. These guidelines include questions about many cultural aspects: general stereotypes, the family, the life cycle, roles, interpersonal relationships, communication, decorum and discipline, religion, health and hygiene, food, dress and personal appearance, history and traditions, holidays and celebrations, education, work and play, time and space, natural phenomena, pets and other animals, art and music and expectations and aspirations.

Cultural sensitivity is more than a "quick-fix" one afternoon in a multicultural education workshop. It is an ongoing process that involves changing the attitudes, values, beliefs, and actions of people to work effectively with people who share a different culture. As noted, a high level of commitment is necessary to increase cultural sensitivity. Increased self-awareness and increased knowledge about others are complementary dichotomies that raise the level of cultural sensitivity. Organizational policies and procedures related to minority youth participants must be inclusive of these issues and not exclusive.

Minority role models

Role models are very significant in shaping the lives of young people. Youth model their behavior after the behavior of available and significant adults. However, the number of minority role models is limited at a time when minority students are increasing. For example, there is a well-noted decrease in the number of minority teachers and a shortage of minority professionals such as doctors and engineers (Larke, 1990; Arbieter, 1987; Thomas, 1987). This is particularly true for African Americans, Hispanic Americans and Native Americans.

The visibility of role models has much significance for minority youth. These role models provide stability, aspirations, hope, career awareness, cultural understanding and the opportunity for personal contact. Role models often encourage youth to persevere by using education as a means to upward mobility while providing a feeling of "I can become a successful person like . . ." instead of "I can't." This person dwindles hopelessness and increases hopefulness by emphasizing the point that life can be meaningful and students can exhibit much autonomy and personal control over their own lives.

Career awareness is one of many areas that role models assist youth. Many role models increase the choices of career opportunities for youth by informing the youth about their careers and the careers of others whom they know in different areas. Role models provide youth with cultural understanding. This person knows how it feels to be a minority person in that particular career and has much empathy and can share experiences with youths who find it necessary to explain to others why they act, think, or behave in a particular way. Lastly, role models become a personal acquaintance or contact person who shares the minority youth's own ethnic identity and cultural experience and, most importantly, is seen as having succeeded despite many negative circumstances.

Parental/significant other involvement

Parents, guardians and significant others (extended family members—grandparents, siblings, and aunts/uncles and non-relatives—teachers, family friends and other interested adults) are instrumental in setting educational goals and encouraging children to become involved in youth organizations. Too often in the popular media, minority parents/guardians/significant others (MPGSOs) have been stereotyped as uncaring. Most parents, guardians and significant others of all races and classes *do* care about the education of children within their charge and/or protection and want the very best for them.

Many youth leaders are unaware of the obstacles that prevent MPGSOs from actively participating in youth organizations. For example, people who had negative experiences during their youth in various organizations or those who had youth leaders who possessed the "missionary attitude". That is, "I must help these poor people by assimilating them in the dominant culture." Such adults are cautious and find a need to protect their children from these kinds of youth leaders who have exploited them. Many lack finances for projects and trips, and others may experience a feeling of tokenism in a situation in which they are not serving a "real" function in the governance of the organization. Also, minority participants sometimes have little contact or personal identification with people who traditionally have been a part of the organization.

Youth organizations can begin to work around these obstacles if MPGSOs are to be involved actively. In deciding the level of MPGSOs involvement, one should consider MPGSOs as an audience, as advocates, as helpers, as learners, as partners, as experts, and as "just people" (Swap, 1987).

To facilitate the recruitment of MPGSOs, youth leaders could use churches, community organizations and schools to assist in the identification process. They could then develop a list of MPGSOs who can provide the experiences and have the appropriate background to serve as role models, volunteers or youth leaders. It is also essential to provide training for MPGSOs to learn about the goals/objectives/programs of the youth organizations and to provide the cultural awareness information about the youth whom they will be serving.

Modification of activities/projects

Traditionally, many nationally recognizable youth organizations: (a) did not meet the needs of minority students; (b) were sexist in nature; and (c) were designed for "Anglo" youth in rural farm areas. For example, historically, 4-H organizations required students to live in rural areas or have access to farms where youth could raise animals. In addition, youth projects were designated as male or female. However, if youth organizations are to involve culturally diverse youth, then those organizations must reflect activities/projects that could be developed in urban and suburban areas, meet the interest level of minority youth and must be non-sexist and culturally sensitive. Projects dealing with human resources education (e.g., sex, drugs, suicide, teenage pregnancy), poverty, homeless children/families, technology, cultural awareness, limited English proficiency and career education are many of the issues confronting youth today and should be included as projects. Organizations that assist youth in project development in these areas are responding to concerns that are significant to the lives of youth and the society at large.

Conclusion/summary

The demographic trends indicate that Texas and other southwestern and southeastern states will soon witness a 50 percent (and more) minority youth population in which many will be identified as at risk. No longer can this large segment of the youth population be ignored. This population is a state's educational and economic force that needs to be nurtured and directed. Youth organizations and youth leaders have a challenge to include this group; most importantly, they face the challenge of making the necessary adaptations within their organizations through "genuine" commitment.

There is no doubt that multicultural education, when integrated effectively, will sensitize youth organizations and leaders about the needs of minority youths. This ideology is needed if there is a serious commitment to increasing the number of minority youth in traditional non-minority groups. Moreover, multicultural education emphasizes respect and acceptance for human diversity and provides opportunities to remove the ignorance of stereotypes. The bureaucracy of organizations such as policies, procedures, objectives and rules makes it difficult to institute real commitment (money, programs and policies and personnel) to include minority youth. However, bureaucracy must not be used as an excuse for excluding minority youth from participating in youth organizations.

As indicated from the cultural sensitization model, the changing and accepting of other cultures, attitudes, values and beliefs are ongoing processes involving two dichotomies—knowledge of self and knowledge of others. These dichotomies are essential to preparing cultural sensitive leaders to meet the needs minority youths.

A continued commitment by those in leadership and decision making positions to increase the number of minority youth leaders who can serve as role models must become a priority issue. It is projected that the absence of role models will be devastating in the lives of minority youth. The absence of minority teachers is one visible example. In addition, careful examination of ways to include more MPGSOs is necessary as they are significant to the educational levels and career goals of minority youth.

Having activities/projects that are interesting and culturally sensitive are necessary adaptations for youth organizations prior to including minority youth, and such adaptations should be clearly visible. In summary, the issues discussed in this paper must be reflected in youth organizations if organizations expect to include the "new majority youth" in the states that are reflecting increases in the minority youth population.

References

Heser, S. (1987). Black enrollments: The cases of the missing students. *Change 19*, 14–19.
Barr, D., & Strong, L. (1989). Embracing multiculturalism: The existing contradictions. *NASPA Journal, 26*(2), 85–90.
Gollnick, D. & Chinn, P. (1986). *Multicultural education in pluralistic society*. Columbus, OH: Charles E. Merrill.
Hahn, A. (1987). Reaching out to America's dropouts: What to do? *Phi Delta Kappan, 69*(4), 256–263.
Hardiman, R. (1988). Overcoming racism in the group. Unpublished manuscript.
Hodgkinson, H. L. (1986). *Texas: The state and its educational system*. Washington, DC: The Institute for Educational Leadership.
Hodgkinson, H. L. (1989). *The same client; The demographics of education and service delivery systems*. Washington, DC: The Institute for Educational Leadership.
Intercultural Development Research Association. (1986). *Texas school dropout survey project: A summary of findings*. San Antonio, TX. Intercultural Development Research Association.
Johnson, H. (Feb. 26, 1988) States' progress in public education slows down. *USA Today.* 5d.
Larke, P. J. (1990). Black teachers: An endangered species in the 1990s. In G. Thomas (Ed.), *U.S. Race Relations in the 1980s and 1990s: Challenges and Alternatives* (pp. 79–94). New York: Hemisphere Publishing.
Mills, J. (1983). Multicultural education: Where do we go from here? *Journal of Social and Behavioral Sciences 9*, 45–51.
Quality Education for Minorities Project. (1990). *Education that works: An action plan for the education of minorities*. Cambridge, MA: Massachusetts Institute of Technology.
Saville-Torike, M. (1978). *A guide to culture in the classroom*. Rosslyn, VA: National Clearing House for Bilingual Education.
Shainline, M. (1987). *Albuquerque Public Schools dropout follow-up study findings and conclusions*. Albuquerque, NM: Albuquerque Public Schools.

74   *Patricia J. Larke*

State's dropout strategy failing to help minorities, study reveals. (1989, November). *The Sunday Express-News*, p. 20–A.

Swap, S. M. (1987). *Enhancing parent involvement in schools.* New York: Teachers College Press.

Texas Education Agency (1988). *Texas public school fall membership by ethnic group.* Austin, TX: Texas Education Agency.

Thomas, G. (1987). Black students in U.S. graduate and professional schools in the 1980s: A national and institutional assessment. *Harvard Educational Review 57*, 261–282.

Valverde, S. (May 1987). A comparative study of Hispanic high school dropouts and graduates—Why do some leave school early and some finish? *Education and Urban Society, 19*(3), 320–329.

Wessel, T., & Wessel, M. (1982). *4-H: An American idea 1900–1980.* Chevy Chase, MD: National 4-H Council.

PART 2

SINGLE GROUP STUDIES

CHAPTER 6

ASIAN PACIFIC AMERICAN STUDENTS (1995)
A rainbow of dreams
Russell L. Young and Valerie Ooka Pang

Asian Pacific American students are like a brilliant rainbow of colors. They represent a large diversity of cultural groups and each individual students has her or his own dreams. However, Asian Pacific Americans are sometimes seen as a homogenous group. The purpose of this article is to challenge teachers to examine over-generalized and unsubstantiated beliefs which they may hold about Asian Pacific American students. Over-generalized conceptions of Asian Pacific American youth can act as barriers—barriers to the creation of affirming and effective classrooms where students can begin to reach for their dreams.

How does labeling impact the perceptions of Asian Pacific American students?

Americans have long divided people into ethnic categories. These categories have been based on assumptions of geographical, linguistic, and racial backgrounds. The macrosociety often uses the label of "Oriental" when categorizing Asian Pacific Americans. We believe this label distances Asian Pacific Americans away from the mainstream as being foreign, exotic, and strange. Labeling, in this case, is part of the process of dehumanizing a group as being less than desirable.

In the case of Asian Pacific American students, the label of "Oriental" acts as a smokescreen to their identity as Americans and to the vast diversity within the group. Why do teachers use a large category to identify students? As humans, people naturally generalize about others that are not part of their group. Group membership provides a sense of personal security, and solidarity can be strengthened with hostility and alienation toward out-groups (Allport, 1979).

Members of the macroculture may feel a sense of community as part of a group which is different from Asian Pacific Americans. In addition, stereotypes develop to confirm beliefs that Asian and Pacific Islanders are from an out-group. Women may be assumed to be submissive and exotically beautiful (*i.e.* Suzie Wong), while males are martial arts experts (*i.e.* Bruce Lee).

The Asian label may also include "positive" stereotypes such as being smart, family-oriented, humble, and hard-working. Pacific Islander "positive" stereotypes include traits like fun-loving, friendly, and musically-inclined. Ironically, "positive" stereotypes are dehumanizing because they, like negative images, act as inaccurate filters of individual characteristics. They also create barriers between peoples.

Stereotypes serve many purposes. They may arise from a lack of knowledge about a group. They may be used as a barrier to interact from fear of the unknown. Also, stereotypes give a person generalized knowledge needed to make it easier to understand and behave towards Asians and Pacific Islanders.

Ultimately, stereotypes and ethnic categorizations are racist acts. Barriers can be built to justify discrimination. For example, people react differently to various accents. While a person with a European accent is often thought of as cosmopolitan, romantic, and refined, an Asian accent may elicit images of nerdy, wimpy, and simple-mindedness. Having an accent can limit a person's success in society. For example, Chang-lin Tien was encouraged to get coaching to eliminate his accent during his first few months as chancellor of the University of California, Berkeley (Tien, 1995).

Smart students are suddenly labeled old fashioned, nerds, or weird in dress and behaviors. These labels are often used to alienate and isolate Asian Pacific American students because they are seen as not fitting in. Pacific Islanders may be seen as too fun-loving to academically compete. The model minority myth also has a heavy cost; teachers who hold that belief may disregard the academic, psychological, financial, and social needs of students.

Though research indicates that Asian Pacific Americans have lower self-concepts, are most test-anxious, face continual discrimination, and have grave linguistic problems (Chang, 1975; Pang, 1991; Pang, Mizokawa, Morishima, & Olstad, 1985; Sue & Okazaki, 1990; Trueba, Cheng & Ima, 1993), many teachers are unaware of these needs. The labels of "Oriental," "model minority," and other stereotypes devalue the diversity among Asian Pacific Americans and the complexity of the cultures along with their rich stories of life.

To many educators, Asian Pacific American students seem to look and to be alike. To some teachers, unfamiliar Asian names and different accents and customs seem to reinforce in their minds that Asian Pacific American students are foreigners with limited allegiance to the United States. We hope that teachers will examine their beliefs and understand that though it may be natural for humans to generalize, looking at a cultural group from gross categories can act to deny the individualism of a child.

Knowing a child's culture can provide important keys to understanding him or her; however, each child as an individual will interpret that culture in his or her own way. Over-generalizing is dangerous. It is likewise dangerous to feign colorblindness and ignore the richness of culture.

How do Asian Pacific American students differ?

Asian Pacific American children encompass a number of different groups, including those who are Bangladeshi, Bhutanese, Bornean, Burmese, Cambodian, Celbesian, Cernan, Chamorro, Chinese, East Indian, Filipino, Hawaiian, Hmong, Indonesian, Japanese, Korean, Laotian, Okinawan, Samoan, Sikkimese, Singaporean, Sir Lankan, and Vietnamese. They constitute the fastest growing population in the United States; Asian Pacific Americans increased almost 100 percent from 1980 to 1990 (Ong & Hee, 1993). Due to immigration and high birth rates, Asian Pacific Americans could number about 20 million by the year 2020.

Another important variable is place of birth—American born or immigrant. The experiences of the two groups may differ greatly, and so does the manner in which they identify themselves. Though it is dangerous to over-generalize across individuals within a group, American-born students are likely to be more highly assimilated into the mainstream, especially those who do not reside in ethnic communities (Cabezas, 1981; Sue, Sue, & Sue, 1983). For example, many Japanese-American students who live in middle-class suburban neighborhoods may not choose to identify themselves along ethnic lines (Kitano, 1976; Matute-Bianchi, 1986).

In contrast, many American-born students may readily identify themselves through ethnic lines, and even boast, "I can be President of the United States." These children may come to school unable to speak English because they have spoken their ancestral languages all their lives. Kindergarten could be the first setting requiring them to speak English.

On the other hand, many American-born students only speak English. They can be categorized as being bicultural, look positively at ethnic membership, and live in an environment that blends mainstream and traditional Asian values (Sue & Sue, 1971). These children may be family oriented, respect elders, and value education, while at the same time participate in mainstream, after-school activities like football or ballet. They may not choose to take part in Asian Pacific American activities at school, but are active, for example, in their local Buddhist temple.

Like their American-born peers, immigrant students clearly demonstrate a wide range of beliefs about their ethnicity. Some are highly assimilated and feel compelled to blend into American society and so relinquish ancestral values, behaviors, and traditions. They may, for example, refuse to speak their ancestral language at home and see their ethnicity as an obstacle to being accepted into the mainstream. Others may be extremely proud of their cultures. Some children proudly speak their ancestral language and attend special Saturday or after-school language schools conducted to ensure that the values, beliefs, customs, and language of the home culture remain in the community (Guthrie, 1985; Kim, 1980).

The history of each group in the United States will differ. Chinese-American, Filipino-American, Japanese-American, and Korean-American communities had long American roots prior to 1965. Immigration had been severely curtailed by Acts to prohibit the Chinese after 1882, Koreans, and Japanese after 1924, and the Filipinos after 1934 (Kim, 1978). With the Immigration Act of 1965, the numbers of Chinese, Korean, and Filipino immigrants dramatically rose.

More recently, after the governments of South Vietnam, Cambodia, and Laos fell in 1975, thousands of Vietnamese, Chinese, Cambodians, Laotians, and other Asian refugees fled Southeast Asia because of political upheaval and war (Hune, 1979). They represented a large diversity in socioeconomic and educational levels. Some were fluent English speakers while others had little or no English language skills. With this influx, difficulties have sometimes developed between immigrant and American-born Asian students.

Students from various cultural groups also show diverse academic needs. When test scores of all Asians are placed in one large group, it is impossible to see the individual and cultural needs of different students. Recently, large school districts have been gathering data on specific Asian and Pacific cultural groups. This provides teachers with more specific information on how groups may differ.

For example, in the 1985–1986 school year in the San Diego School District, Samoans and Guamanians had the highest high school dropout rates of any group at 17.1 percent (Rumbaut & Ima, 1988). This was even greater than Latinos who dropped out of school at a rate of 14.1 percent. In comparison, 10.7 percent of the Vietnamese and 8.6 percent of the Filipinos dropped out of school, while only 6.2 percent of Asians (Chinese, Japanese, and Korean) students did not attend school. Differing patterns within the Asian Pacific American population are also seen in their academic scores.

For example, in the Seattle School District in 1986–1987, only 12.8 percent of the Japanese American students scored below the 50th percentile on the reading portion of the California Achievement Test, while 76.9 percent of the Samoan American children, 29.2 percent of the Chinese American youth, and 55.7 percent of the Vietnamese did not score well on this measure (Pang, 1995). The differences in scores demonstrate how each group has differing language expertise, value orientations, and acculturation levels.

How will intergroup differences appear in class?

Intergroup differences can account for cultural conflict within the classroom. Teachers need to understand that Asian Pacific American students may not associate with other Asian Pacific Americans because they are from another community. Historically, many Asians have been enemies for years. For example, the Japanese occupied China during World War II and killed 35 million Chinese. They tortured, raped, and massacred many children and adults. Some Chinese Americans may feel hostility toward Japanese Americans due to this historical event.

Historical hostility can also be actively brought into the classroom. For example, there was a teacher who had a Vietnamese American pupil and a Cambodian American student in the class. The Vietnamese American student had lived in the United States for about seven years and spoke English well; the Cambodian American student had been in the United States for only three years and was having some difficulties understanding the material. The teacher mistakenly assumed that they would be happy to work with each other, since they had similar refugee experiences. He asked the Vietnamese youth to help the Cambodian.

Since such students generally have a high regard for teachers, they were reluctant to speak out, but the Vietnamese student explained diplomatically that he did not think the other student would accept his help. This greatly surprised the teacher, but the prediction of the student was confirmed when the Cambodian student said, "I do not want to accept help from a Vietnamese." These feelings were worked through, but even then it was difficult for students who had been in adversary roles to view situations in a new light. Teachers need to know that historical differences can impact dynamics within the classroom and to understand where the conflict may stem from.

How does prejudice impact Asian American students?

Prejudice and discrimination are two disturbing aspects Asian Pacific American students cope with continuously in schools. Both authors remember many times being confronted by teachers and peers with the question "Are you Chinese or Japanese?" The assumption was that Chinese people could not be distinguished from Japanese individuals. There were even the jokes about looking at the difference in the slant of the eyes to tell the difference. This is an example of a lack of understanding about distinct cultural groups (Chinese and Japanese). Even the use of the term "slant" to separate Asian Americans from other Americans was offensive. The assumption is that Asians have eyes which "slant" while other people's eyes have shape or form.

Secondly, one must become aware of the diversity within cultural groups. An example of prejudice can be found in assuming most Asian Pacific Americans are born in another country and are not native Americans. Teachers may, with good intentions, compliment students on how well they learned to speak English when English is their native tongue.

One of the authors recalls taking an essay test in junior high school that had a question that made reference to the biblical Job. When asking the teacher for clarification of who Job was, he pronounced the name incorrectly (like working on a job). The teacher's response was "Oh, I would expect you not to know who he was." The implication was that she still held the stereotype that someone who is Chinese could not be Christian (the "Heathen Chinee"). In reality, there are many Americans of Chinese descent who are Lutheran, Baptist, Presbyterian, Unitarian, and Catholic.

Lastly, people may fear balkanization or tribalism when they see Asian Pacific Americans associate with others of the same cultural group. Others may feel threatened because they see this as being too clannish or cliquish (they must be talking about them behind their back when they speak a non-English language). Asians or Pacific Islanders are seen as difficult to get to know or become friends with. Congregations are seen as being inhospitable and justification that they are not easy to assimilate.

For example, other faculty began referring to three Asian Pacific American teachers as "the yellow peril" when they were seen together at lunch. However, when several European American educators met for lunch, no references were made to their ethnicity.

For children, associating with other Asians may create a feeling of belonging. Perceived similarity brings a sense of trust and security; students may associate with others from the same ethnic group as a survival strategy. Communication may be facilitated in a non-English language thus also facilitating resource sharing.

We hope teachers create learning environments which affirm and celebrate Asian Pacific American students. Each group brings a different historical background, set of cultural values, language, and needs to schools which can contribute a richness and excitement to the classroom. Asian Pacific American students are a brilliant rainbow of dreams, cultures, and possibilities. As teachers, our job is to bring out that brilliance.

Recommendations

Asian Pacific American students are a complex rainbow of groups. We hope teachers do not believe in the "model minority" myth and truly address the needs of Asian Pacific students. There are many Asian Pacific students who are "at risk" and not achieving in school. We suggest the following:

- *Stop name-calling* or any other kind of discrimination immediately and discuss why these acts are not tolerated in class.
- *Ask students to write about their experiences* traveling with family, celebrating customs, and their dreams.
- *Do not assume all Asian Pacific American children are excellent math and science students.* Encourage students to look into a variety of occupations like journalism, acting, politics, economics, and painting.
- *Provide Asian Pacific American students with specific feedback about their writing.* This may include errors in subject-verb agreement or may point to the need for a topic sentence.

- *Give Asian Pacific American students opportunities to develop leadership skills.* This may begin by appointing students to lead discussion groups.
- *Keep a journal about the needs of your Asian Pacific American students.* Maybe you notice they do not know how to ask for help. Maybe you notice that they would like to be better at speaking in front of the class. Create instructional activities which address those needs.
- *Bring in guest speakers* from the community who are positive role models. You may invite an engineer, librarian, minister, historian, professor, architect, judge, or carpenter.
- *Integrate information about Asian Pacific Americans who have made contributions* to society like: Mary Kawena Pukui—writer, editor; Philip Vera Cruz—Vice President of the United Farm Workers; Eduardo San Juan—conceptual designer of Lunar Rover; Younghill Kang—writer; James Wong Howe—cinematographer; Ah Bing—developed and grew Bing cherries; Daniel Inouye—U.S. Senator; Dorothy and Frederick Cordova—historians; Dalip Singh Saund—member of U.S. House of Representatives; Chien Shiung Wu—nuclear physicist; An Wang—computer developer (Wang Computer); Patsy Takemoto Mink—member of the U.S. House of Representatives; Alan Lau—poet and painter; Kristi Yamaguchi—Olympic gold medal figure skater; Jose Aruego—artist, children's book illustrator; Ellison S. Onizuka—astronaut, aerospace engineer; Greg Louganis—Olympic diving champion; Janice Mirikitani—poet, writer; Laurence Yep—screenwriter and children's book author; Maya Ying Lin—architect, sculptor; Lance Ito—judge, lawyer.

References

Allport, G. (1979). *The nature of prejudice.* Reading, MA.: Addison-Wesley.

Cabazas, A. (1981). *Early childhood development in Asian and Pacific American families: Families in transition.* San Francisco, CA: Asian Inc.

Chang, T. (1975). The self-concept of children in ethnic groups: Black American and Korean American. *Elementary School Journal,* 76, 52–58.

Guthrie, G.P. (1985). *A school divided.* Hillsdale, NJ: Lawrence Erlbaum Associates.

Hune, S. (1979). U.S. immigration policy and Asian and Pacific Americans: Aspects and consequences. In S. Hune (Ed.), *Civil rights issues of Asian and Pacific Americans: Myths and realities* (pp. 283–291). Washington, DC: U.S. Commission on Civil Rights.

Kim, B. (1978). *The Asian Americans: Changing patterns, changing needs.* Montclair, NJ: Association of Korean Christian Scholars in North America.

Kim, B. (1980). *The Korean-American child at school and at home.* Washington, DC: U.S. Department of Health, Education, and Welfare.

Kitano, H. (1976). *Japanese Americans: The evolution of a subculture* (2nd ed). Englewood Cliffs, NJ: Prentice-Hall.

Matute-Bianchi, M. (1986). Ethnic identities and patterns of school success and failure among Mexican-descent and Japanese-Americans students in a California high school: An ethnographic analysis. *American Journal of Education,* 94, 233–255.

Ong, P. & Hee, S. (1993). The growth of the Asian Pacific American population: Twenty million in 2020. In *The state of Asian Pacific America: A public policy report: Policy issues to the 2020.* Los Angeles, CA: LEAP Asian Pacific Americans Public Policy Institute and UCLA Asian American Studies Center.

Pang, V.O. (1991). The relationship of test anxiety and math achievement to parental values in Asian-American and European-American middle school students. *Journal of Research and Development in Education,* 24(4), 1–10.

Pang, V.O., Mizokawa, D., Morishima, J., & Olstad, R. (1985). Self concepts of Japanese American children. *Journal of Cross-Cultural Psychology, 16*, 99–109.

Pang, V.O. (1995). Asian Pacific American students: A diverse and complex population. In J. Banks & C. Banks (Eds.), *Handbook of research on multicultural education* (pp. 412–424). New York: Macmillan Publishing.

Rumbaut, R. & Ima, K. (1988). *The adaptation of Southeast Asian refugee youth: A comparative study*. Washington, DC: U.S. Department of Health and Human Services, Family Support Administration. Office of Refugee Resettlement.

Sue, S. & Okazaki, S. (1990). Asian-American educational achievements: A phenomenon in search of an explanation. *American Psychologist, 45*(8), 913–920.

Sue, D., & Sue, S. (1971). Chinese American personality and mental health. *Amerasia Journal, 1*, 95–98.

Sue, S., Sue, D., & Sue, D. (1983). Psychological development of Chinese-American children. In G. Powell (Ed.), *The psychological development of minority group children* (pp. 159–166). New York: Brunner/Mazal Publishers.

Tien, C.L. (1995, July 18). A tool for a colorblind America. *L.A. Times*, B9.

Trueba, H., Cheng, L., & Ima, K. (1993). *Myth or reality: Adaptive strategies of Asian Americans in California*. Washington, DC: Falmer Press.

CHAPTER 7

ASIAN AMERICANS AS MODEL MINORITIES? (1995)

A look at their academic performance

Grace Kao

Introduction

Recent years have witnessed increasing speculation about the academic success of Asian-American students. The relatively high socioeconomic standing of Asian-Americans (compared with blacks and Hispanics), low rates of marital disruption, and the relative success of Asian-American students suggests an almost problem-free home environment (Takaki 1989; Hurh and Kim 1989). The phenomenon of academic success is part of a broader discussion of Asian[1] success in the United States that has prompted the media to coin the term "model minority" for this population.

Support for the model minority image of Asians ranges from full acceptance to complete dismissal. In favor of the model minority image, Sowell writes, "Groups that arrived in America financially destitute have rapidly risen to affluence, when their cultures stressed the values and behavior required in an industrial and commercial economy. Even when color and racial prejudice confronted them—as in the case of the Chinese and Japanese—this proved to be an impediment but was ultimately unable to stop them" (Sowell 1981, p. 284). Other scholars have criticized the homogeneous characterizing of Asians, arguing that this image is just another phase in the evolution of stereotypes of Asian-Americans (Hurh and Kim 1989; Takaki 1989; Steinberg 1989). Yet another group has offered conditional support for Asian-American success in some arenas of life but notes that Asian-Americans are still not on a par with whites in other realms (Hirschman and Wong 1981; Barringer et al. 1990). Barringer et al. (1990), for instance, found that while Asians have higher levels of education than whites, economic returns to education are lower for Asians than whites.

Despite the attention Asian academic success and achievement has received from the media, there has been little research on the mechanisms responsible for this phenomenon. The relative neglect of Asians' educational experience can be explained in two ways. First, the success of Asians is not a problem in need of a solution. Second, until recently, a nationally representative survey of students with adequate samples of Asian-Americans has been lacking; hence researchers have been unable to examine on a national level whether and how academic achievement of Asians differs from that of the white population.

The motivation for the few studies of Asians' school performance stems from a desire to decode the "secrets of their success." Indeed, if Asian students are academically successful because of certain parental practices in the home environment, there may be lessons to policymakers that can benefit others. In the words of Mike Wallace of CBS's *60 Minutes,* "They must be doing something right. Let's bottle it" (from Takaki 1989, p. 474). Implicit in this view is that cultural differences between Asians and whites hold the secret to understanding their success. An alternative interpretation of the high educational performance of Asians students is that it merely reflects socioeconomic differences between Asians and whites. That is, because the average Asian parent has completed more schooling than the average white parent and because parental schooling is a critical determinant of their children's academic success, differences between Asian and white children simply mirror these differences. I hope to clarify the relative merits of both interpretations.

This article has several aims: (1) to examine whether Asian eighth graders overall and students from eight Asian ethnic groups (specifically, Chinese, Filipino, Japanese, Korean, Southeast Asian, Pacific Islander, South Asian, and West Asian)[2] perform better in school than their white counterparts as measured by their grades, math test scores, and reading test scores; (2) to characterize the features of students' home and school environments that affect their academic outcomes; and finally (3) to analyze the diversity of educational performance and the home environment among the eight Asian ethnic groups.

The analyses proceed as follows. First, I present a literature review to formulate the theoretical issues and substantive concerns in the area of educational performance among ethnic minorities. The empirical analysis begins with comparisons between Asians overall, Asian ethnic groups, and whites on a variety of background measures and outcome variables. Subsequently, I compare math and reading scores to consider whether Asians, whites, and Asian subgroups differ in their skill development, and I examine how background variables, family context, home educational resources, and student characteristics affect grades. The concluding section considers why Asians overall receive higher grades than white students and examines the pattern of differentiation within the Asian population, emphasizing the different parent-child relationship among Asians and the higher expectations some Asian parents have for their children, by using insight gained from focus-group discussions.

In most of the descriptive and analytic tables, I examine Asians as a group and Asian ethnic groups separately. Although the category "Asian" incorporates many heterogeneous groups, there is reason to evaluate how Asians fare relative to whites. That is, in order to properly evaluate the model minority thesis, which implicitly lumps all Asian groups together, it is critical that I measure how Asians as a group differ from whites. If Asians as a group perform at comparable or lower levels than whites, then that alone provides evidence against the caricature of Asians as model minorities. However, as we will see, the heterogeneity of family educational resources within the Asian population makes any single characterization of this group inadequate.

Ethnicity and academic performance

There are several approaches to understanding ethnic differentials in educational performance. One approach links academic performance to the meanings attached to ethnic labels (Fordham and Ogbu 1986; Matute-Bianchi 1986; Ogbu 1991; Gibson and Ogbu 1991). Matute-Bianchi found that in a California school, Japanese-American identity was compatible with academic success, but that being a good student was less consistent with being Mexican (Matute-Bianchi 1986).

Some minority students who succeed in school are criticized by their peers as "trying to act white," so that a positive identification with black peers, for instance, may include not doing well in school. Ogbu also finds that blacks identify largely in opposition to whites; so if success in school is labeled as a "white" activity, this may discourage blacks from pursuing academic goals (Clark 1983; Ogbu 1991).

Another type of explanation for differential academic performance focuses on culture. For instance, Schneider and Lee (1990) argue that the cultural components that benefit East Asian children's school performances include "(1) the East Asian cultural tradition which places a high value on education for self-improvement, self-esteem, and family honor, and (2) the determination by some East Asian families to overcome occupational discrimination by investing in education" (Schneider and Lee 1990). However, their research does not directly provide evidence that East Asians value education more than whites, blacks, Hispanics, or other Asian groups.

Schneider and Lee (1990) conducted in-depth interviews to illustrate how academic achievement is inextricably linked to children's perception of what makes their parents happy. Their insights suggest a working hypothesis, namely, that white parents, on average, express satisfaction with their children if they are successful in one of the many realms of youths' lives (school, sports, music, or other hobbies), but Asian parents express satisfaction only when their children have near perfect academic performance (i.e., straight A's). This difference comes not only from differential expectations, but also from differences in the expressiveness of Asian and white parents (Stevenson and Stigler 1992).

Another explanation comes from Ogbu's (1991) analysis of blacks. He argues that although black parents value schooling, they warn their children that American society does not reward blacks and whites equally for such credentials. On the basis of their concrete experiences, black parents offer their children ambivalent and perhaps contradictory values toward education (Ogbu 1991). Although Asian-Americans also receive returns for education unequal to those of whites (Barringer et al. 1990), their higher levels of education partly compensate for this inequity. Asian parents may be promoting higher levels of educational attainment for their children to compensate for anticipated discrimination in the job market. Nonetheless, it is interesting that the experience of discrimination, according to different scholars, accounts for the relative failure of blacks and the success of Asians in educational achievement (Sue and Okazaki 1990; Schneider and Lee 1990; Ogbu 1991).

Finally, Sue and Okazaki (1990) attempt to identify the parental behaviors among Asian and white parents that can clarify the differences found in school achievement. They argue against cultural explanations of Asian achievement and instead propose that, aware of the obstacles (discrimination) in the labor market, Asian parents and children learn to value education, which is related to but not entirely synonymous with career success. Their review of prior research also revealed difficulties in linking the average behavior of Asian parents to their children's performance. As a group, Asian parents were more likely to insist on unquestioned obedience to parents and to believe in minimal parental involvement, and they were less likely to have expectations for mature behavior and to encourage two-way communication between their children and themselves compared to the average behavior of white parents. The average behavior of Asian parents would have predicted low academic achievement for the sample as a whole, yet the mean grade point average of Asian children was the highest of any group (Dornbusch 1989; Sue and Okazaki 1990).

These results suggest that systematic group differences in parental behavior exists between Asians and whites. It may be that, on average, Asian parents may not only have higher expectations of their children, but also are unwilling to negotiate these terms. Children understand this message and are obligated to their parents to do well in school. For the children who are able to attain academic success, their parents' high expectations may further their own educational aspirations, but for those who cannot, the effects of such pressure are potentially harmful.

Parental resources and academic achievement

Much of the research about what promotes academic success has concentrated on three general domains of the students' social environment that influence academic achievement, namely, parental involvement, home resources, and peer influences (Murnane et al. 1981; Baker and Stevenson 1986; Fehrman et al. 1987; Rumberger et al. 1990; Astone and McLanahan 1991).

First, some emphasize the importance of parental involvement (Baker and Stevenson 1986; Fehrman et al. 1987). Baker and Stevenson (1986) argue that to be effective managers of their children's educational careers, parents must know the demands of the school, their children's performance, and when to use their managerial skills. They found that mothers with higher socioeconomic standing had more accurate information about their children's performance and contact with the school. Mothers with at least a college education were more likely to choose college-preparatory classes for their children, regardless of their children's grade point average (Baker and Stevenson 1986). High levels of parental involvement, measured by knowledge of the child's activities in school and frequent contact with the school, have positive effects on children's academic achievement (Baker and Stevenson 1986; Fehrman et al. 1987; Hoover-Dempsey et al. 1987; Sue and Okazaki 1990; Astone and McLanahan 1991).

Some researchers have focused on home resources, which can include the presence of books, a home computer, or newspapers (Teachman 1987; Stevenson and Stigler 1992). Teachman (1987) argues that the availability of home resources creates an environment conducive to studying by displaying a positive orientation toward schooling. He also points out that parents with more education and income are probably more motivated to provide home resources for education.

Finally, others have examined the effect of peer groups on academic achievement. Although there is some disagreement about whether peers are generally a positive or negative influence on educational performance, researchers recognize the importance of peers in affecting educational achievement. Hallinan (1988) argues that much of the evidence suggests that peer group culture usually hinders learning. On the other hand, Corsaro and Eder (1990) find that older adolescents select friends who have similar attitudes toward school, college plans, and achievement outcomes. Their findings suggest that peers only reinforce the adolescent's own educational plans and performance. The National Education Longitudinal Study of 1988 (NELS:88) measures of peer evaluation allow us to examine the respondents' self-perceptions of how others think of him/herself, thus allowing us to examine group differences in self-perception.

Conceptual model

Sue and Okazaki (1990) claim that there are two general hypotheses to explain Asian-American academic achievement. One hypothesis invokes the idea that

Asians are better equipped for schooling or more skilled than their white counterparts, while the second argues that there is something distinctive in the value system or the behavior of Asians that promotes successful outcomes in school.

The first set of analyses addresses whether Asians and whites differ in the assessment of their achievement. Here I use reading and math scores from the test developed for the NELS:88 respondents as a proxy for an objective evaluation of their achievement level.

Then I examine the second hypothesis using their self-reported grade point averages as a measure of academic performance that is more sensitive to behavioral differences. Fehrman et al. (1987) argue that "grades are given more frequently in schools than are achievement tests and can therefore give a more continuous indication of a student's academic performance. Grades are also more readily understood by parents and students due to their frequency and universal use. Furthermore, grades are likely to be more sensitive than achievement test scores to student effort" (p. 331).[3]

Figure 7.1 presents the conceptual model. Our model includes measures of family background and structure, educational resources, and student characteristics. Parent's education[4] and family income[5] measure socioeconomic status. Parent's education has consistently been shown to be associated with higher achievement (grades, test scores), as well as greater levels of parental involvement (Murnane

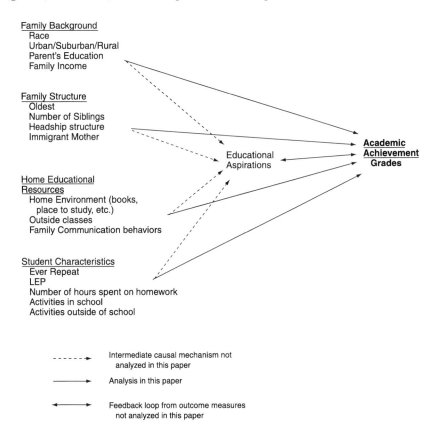

Figure 7.1 Conceptual model

et al. 1981; Baker and Stevenson 1986; Fehrman et al. 1987; Rumberger et al. 1990; Astone and McLanahan 1991).

Measures of family structure include whether the respondent is the oldest child, the number of siblings of the student, and the headship structure of the household. Being the oldest child should have a positive effect on grades, because of the greater sense of responsibility placed on the oldest. We would expect the number of siblings to have a negative effect on grades, because of increased competition for material and psychological resources. However, Caplan et al. (1992) found that among Indochinese youth, siblings benefit from doing homework together. When older siblings tutor their younger siblings, younger siblings benefit from the help they get, while older siblings gain an opportunity to review educational materials.

Measures for household headship include variables for living with both parents and living with mother only. Preliminary analyses suggested that these two types of headship characterize the difference between Asians and whites in the relationship between headship and scholastic performance. Since these are compared with other headship structures, living with both parents is hypothesized to have positive influences on grades while living with mother only should have no effect (Astone and McLanahan 1991).

Prior studies indirectly suggest that having an immigrant mother may raise grade performance because first-generation parents may be more optimistic than those who have been subjected to disparate treatment for many generations (Ogbu 1991). Mother's immigrant status also proxies for the effect of not becoming "Americanized" (i.e., living and adopting the culture and values of the United States) and being able to exert more control over their adolescents since traditional (Asian) values promote more authoritarian behavior from parents (Sue and Okazaki 1990; Schneider and Lee 1990). Finally, if cultural influences benefit Asian students' performance, then the manifestation of cultural distinctiveness should be more apparent among those who are less acculturated.

Building on Teachman's (1987) idea of home resources, I expanded the definition to include not only items such as having more than 50 books, having regularly received a magazine or newspaper, or having a typewriter, but also whether or not respondents have a personal computer at home and a specific place to study. In addition, we examine the effects of family communication about academic concerns on grade performance. Recent studies suggest that the greater the interaction between parent and child, the greater the positive effects of communication (Baker and Stevenson 1986; Fehrman et al. 1987).[6]

The conceptual model also allows for individual differences that influence educational achievement. Having ever repeated a grade between fifth and eighth grades should lower current grades because these experiences may act as negative signals to teachers as well as to decrease attachment to school. A variable indexing "limited English proficiency" (LEP)[7] is included as a control because lack of English fluency may lower grades. Limited English proficiency status also differentially affects the Asian population, with Southeast Asians suffering most from LEP status because of their more recent arrival, while LEP status does not significantly affect the lives of most South Asians since they tend to have excellent English skills.

Other behavioral indicators that influence academic achievement include the number of hours spent on homework per week,[8] whether the child participates in any activities in school, and whether the child participates in any activities outside of school. Extracurricular activities signal an attachment to school and hence should be associated with higher grades. Furthermore, activities outside of school (such as Boy Scouts or Girl Scouts, religious clubs, summer institutes) may heighten interest in school by broadening the child's experiences.

Data and methods

The primary data used for this study come from NELS:88. The NELS:88 used a two-stage stratified probability design to select a nationally representative sample of schools and students. The first stage resulted in 1,052 participating schools, and the second stage produced a random sample of 26,435 students, of which 24,599 participated. The NELS:88 includes oversamples of Asian-American and Hispanic students, resulting in 1,527 Asian students. The NELS:88 also surveyed the respondents' parents, two of each student's teachers (one from English or history and the other from mathematics or science), and a school administrator. These analyses are restricted to base year survey data.

The NELS:88 is unique in other ways as well, namely, in that it provides information directly from the parents, teachers, and schools. It allows, for instance, a comparison of answers between the student's expected educational attainment and the parent's aspiration for their child's educational attainment. Student respondents also took a series of cognitive tests that provide a standardized assessment of skill development.[9]

The secondary source of data are three focus groups conducted during the Spring of 1992 (see app. C for a more detailed description). Each of these focus groups (one with Asian, one with black, and one with Hispanic students) consisted of open-ended responses from a group of university students on a series of questions regarding the salience of their ethnic identity and how their identification plays out in everyday life. These discussions will be used primarily to illuminate the statistical analysis and to further suggest the mechanisms in educational performance.

Population comparisons

Since higher levels of parental education are associated with academic success (Baker and Stevenson 1986), table 7.1 presents the distribution of parent's education. The relative edge Asian parents have is particularly evident at the highest educational levels, as 49 percent of the Asian parents are college graduates compared with only 35 percent of the white parents. Nonetheless, the educational advantage of Asian over white parents must be qualified. More than 8 percent of the Asian parents had less than high school education compared to less than 6 percent of the white parents. In addition, there are striking differences within the Asian population. Overall, South Asian parents are overwhelmingly better educated than their other Asian counterparts. Over 80 percent of South Asian parents have at least a college degree as compared to 35 percent of white parents. On the other hand, South-east Asian parents have much lower levels of education than white parents. Almost 20 percent of Southeast Asian parents have less than high school education while only about 6 percent of white parents have similarly low levels of education. Chinese parents are more heterogeneous than white parents, with a larger proportion falling in both the lowest and highest educational levels—specifically, about 13 percent have less than a high school education while about 43 percent have at least a college degree. When comparing the mean levels of education, we see that only Southeast Asian parents have lower levels of education than white parents.

Table 7.1 Parent's education

	Whites	Asians (all)	Asian subgroups							
			Chinese	Filipino	Japanese	Korean	Southeast Asian	Pacific Islander	South Asian	West Asian
Less than high school (%)	5.5	8.4	12.6	1.1	3.3	2.2	19.6	12.4	1.6	7.1
High school graduate (%)	19.5	11.4	15.3	8.7	4.4	10.4	14.7	12.4	2.5	16.1
Some college (%)	40.0	30.9	28.6	30.5	29.7	23.0	43.6	48.3	14.8	29.0
College graduate (%)	17.4	24.0	15.6	41.8	40.7	32.2	11.1	15.7	17.2	19.4
Master's degree (%)	10.9	12.4	13.9	7.6	13.2	19.1	6.2	7.9	27.9	10.3
M.D. or Ph.D. (%)	6.7	12.9	13.9	10.2	8.8	13.1	4.9	3.4	36.1	18.1
Mean educational level	14.6	15.2***	14.90*	15.53***	15.65***	15.90***	13.69***	14.09	17.51***	15.28**
	(2.49)	(2.83)	(3.12)	(2.18)	(2.22)	(2.50)	(2.62)	(2.37)	(2.50)	(3.02)
N	16,116	1,453	294	275	91	183	225	89	122	155

SOURCE.—NELS:88.

NOTE.—Numbers in parentheses are standard deviations.
* Significantly different from whites at $p < .05$ level.
** Significantly different from whites at $p < .01$ level.
*** Significantly different from whites at $p < .001$ level.

A mechanism through which parent's education leads to academic success is educational aspirations. Educational aspirations deserve special attention because they help to explain why some students are more motivated than others to achieve high grades. At the same time, the level of grades one receives shapes one's educational aspirations, so that educational goals and grades are mutually reinforcing. Table 7.2 presents two measures of educational aspirations: parents' expectation and child's own expectation. The means reveal that, overall, Asians rank higher than whites on both of these measures. Asian parents were almost two and a half times as likely as white parents to expect their children to complete postgraduate degrees—47 percent versus 20 percent. South Asian parents also have extraordinary expectations; about 92 percent of the South Asian parents expect their children to graduate from college while 72 percent expect their children to earn graduate degrees. Even though Southeast Asian parents have lower levels of education than white parents, they have *higher* expectations for their children's eventual educational attainment than white parents. However, Asians are not uniformly high in their aspirations. Note that almost 20 percent of Pacific Island students do not plan to go beyond high school, while 15 percent of their parents also have such low aspirations. Only 45 percent of Pacific Islander parents expect their children to graduate from college, compared to over 60 percent of white parents. Nonetheless, over three-quarters of parents and students from all other Asian groups aspire to graduate from college. In fact, with the exception of Pacific Islanders, both parents and children from each Asian ethnic group have *higher* educational aspirations than white parents and eighth graders. From these results, it would be reasonable to hypothesize that Asians achieve higher grades than whites simply because they have higher educational aspirations.

Table 7.3 examines whether having high aspirations is the key to success for Asian youth by comparing grades, math, and reading test scores of Asian and white students at each level of educational aspirations. Overall, we find that Asians have slightly higher math scores but comparable reading scores relative to whites. With respect to grades, Asians average 3.24 grade points compared to 2.96 for whites. If Asians earn higher grades simply because they have higher educational aspirations, then we should expect to find no difference in grades between whites and Asians with comparable educational aspirations. Instead, we find that at each level of aspirations, Asian students still perform better than white students in terms of grades. It appears that Asians overestimate the level of grades needed to realize their level of educational aspirations, regardless of the amount of education they plan to accumulate. However, we do not find a clear "Asian advantage" in test scores. The general pattern regarding test scores, once educational aspirations are controlled for, reveals no differences in math scores except among those with the highest aspirations. With respect to reading scores, however, Asians score comparable to or *lower* than whites, with white students who aspire to graduate from college or attend graduate school earning higher scores than Asian students with comparable aspirations. Thus, Asians outperform whites in terms of grades rather than test scores.

Table 7.4 compares Asian and white youth on various background measures, including those used in the regression analysis. Financial resources increase the likelihood that students will be able to pursue college plans. Although the average incomes of white and Asian families do not significantly differ, more Asian parents reported having begun to save money for their children's college expenses. Moreover, of those who have set aside money for college, Asian parents had saved significantly more, and planned to save significantly more by the time their

Table 7.2 Parents' and children's educational aspirations: Whites, Asians, and Asian ethnic groups

	Whites	Asians (all)	Chinese	Filipino	Japanese	Korean	Southeast Asian	Pacific Islander	South Asian	West Asian
Parents' aspirations:										
High school or less (%)	11.5	6.5	3.8	7.5	3.5	5.9	7.8	15.9	3.5	6.5
Some college (%)	26.7	13.2	12.0	11.5	10.6	5.3	16.1	39.0	4.3	13.8
College graduate (%)	41.4	33.8	32.0	45.2	41.2	31.4	30.4	24.4	20.0	37.7
Beyond college (%)	20.4	46.5	52.3	35.7	44.7	57.4	45.6	20.7	72.2	42.0
Mean level of aspirations	15.41	16.41***	16.65***	16.18***	16.54***	16.81***	16.28***	15.0*	17.22***	16.30***
	(1.84)	(1.81)	(1.66)	(1.75)	(1.59)	(1.68)	(1.91)	(1.99)	(1.47)	(1.79)
N	15,254	1,341	266	252	85	169	217	82	115	138
Eighth grader's aspirations:										
High school or less (%)	10.5	5.1	3.6	4.9	6.7	1.6	5.9	18.6	0.8	4.9
Some college (%)	19.7	15.0	12.7	18.5	5.6	5.9	18.9	32.0	6.3	16.0
College graduate (%)	45.1	37.1	37.7	43.0	45.6	33.7	39.1	28.9	30.2	33.3
Beyond college (%)	24.7	42.8	46.1	33.6	42.2	58.8	36.1	20.6	62.7	45.7
Mean level of aspirations	15.68	16.35***	16.53***	16.10***	16.47***	16.99***	16.11***	15.03***	17.10***	16.40***
	(1.83)	(1.73)	(1.63)	(1.69)	(1.67)	(1.37)	(1.77)	(2.04)	(1.30)	(1.77)
N	16,236	1,515	308	286	90	187	238	97	126	162

SOURCE.—NELS:88.

NOTE.—Numbers in parentheses are standard deviations.
* Significantly different from whites at $p < .05$ level.
*** Significantly different from whites at $p < .001$ level.

Table 7.3 Comparison of grades, math test scores, and reading test scores overall and within educational aspirations levels: Asians and whites

	Grades	Math scores	Reading scores	N
Overall mean achievement:				
Whites	2.96	52.50	52.32	15,750
	(.75)	(9.90)	(9.78)	
Asians	3.24***	54.91***	51.95	1,477
	(.72)	(10.46)	(9.99)	
Within levels of educational aspirations:				
High school or less:				
Whites	2.23	43.96	44.04	1,693
	(.75)	(7.55)	(8.66)	
Asians	2.46*	44.58	43.85	72
	(.83)	(8.69)	(9.06)	
Some college:				
Whites	2.60	47.63	48.10	3,088
	(.69)	(8.53)	(9.11)	
Asians	2.80***	48.61	45.91	219
	(.76)	(8.72)	(8.66)	
College graduate:				
Whites	3.07	53.68	53.37	7,082
	(.66)	(9.15)	(9.00)	
Asians	3.20***	53.94	51.28***	544
	(.67)	(9.95)	(9.22)	
Beyond college:				
Whites	3.36	57.86	57.29	3,901
	(.62)	(8.96)	(8.41)	
Asians	3.53***	59.20**	55.62***	635
	(.55)	(9.38)	(9.44)	

SOURCE.—NELS:88.

NOTE.—Values in parentheses are standard deviations.
* Significantly different from whites at $p < .01$ level.
** Significantly different from whites at $p < .05$ level.
*** Significantly different from whites at $p < .001$ level.

children graduated from high school, than white parents. We stress that this behavior does not reflect greater financial resources but rather a greater commitment of resources for education among Asian parents than among white parents.

Home resources are important in creating an environment conducive to good study habits and strong academic achievement. Again, differences between Asians and whites are apparent. While more Asian students have a place to study, more white students report having their own room. This reinforces the notion that even where differences in material resources are minimal, as between Asians and whites, the stronger commitment to education among Asian parents is evident in their emphasis on study over privacy for their children. Asians are also more likely than whites to have a personal computer in the home. Other differences reflecting

Table 7.4 Background characteristics of students by race

	Asians	Whites
Financial resource:[a]		
Mean family income ($)	48,676	46,964
	(43,937)	(39,579)
Have money for post-high-school education	.62***	.53
Of those who have money saved up, how much now ($)	6,959***	5,845
	(5,739)	(5,303)
How much by time child finishes high school ($)	10,532***	9,640
	(5,005)	(4,948)
Home resources:[b]		
Place to study	.59***	.40
Own room	.73***	.86
Personal computer	.52***	.48
Outside classes:[a]		
Art	.11*	.09
Music	.34***	.29
Ethnic history	.11***	.04
Computer	.16***	.12
Household rules:[a]		
Rules about TV programs	.61***	.70
Rules about how late can watch TV	.75***	.85
Rules about how many hours TV daily	.50***	.40
Rules about maintaining grades	.74***	.68
Rules about doing homework	.90	.91
Rules about doing chores	.80***	.88
Parent-child interaction:[a]		
How often talk to child about school experiences[c]	3.49***	3.81
	(.73)	(.45)
How often talk about high school plans[c]	3.21***	3.37
	(.79)	(.68)
How often talk about post-high-school plans[c]	3.10***	3.20
	(.83)	(.72)
How often help child with homework[d]	2.05***	2.26
	(1.02)	(.96)
Characteristics of student:[b]		
Ever repeat	.02***	.05
Limited English proficiency	.08***	.78
Number of hours worked for pay	3.03***	4.91
	(5.09)	(5.97)
Peer evaluation:[b,e]		
Popular	.91***	.99
	(.59)	(.57)
Athletic	.95***	1.03
	(.73)	(.71)

(*Continued*)

Table 7.4 (Continued)

	Asians	Whites
Good student	1.47***	1.26
	(.58)	(.61)
Troublemaker	.26***	.35
	(.51)	(.57)

Source.—NELS:88.

Note.—Values in parentheses are standard deviations.

[a] The number of respondents varies from about 1,300 for Asians to 15,000 for whites (parent questionnaire items).

[b] The number of respondents varies from about 1,500 for Asians to 16,000 for whites (student questionnaire items).

[c] Answer categories are 1 = not at all to 4 = regularly.

[d] Answer categories are 1 = seldom or never to 4 = almost every day.

[e] 0 = not at all (popular, athletic, a good student, etc.), 1 = somewhat, 2 = very.

* Significantly different from whites at $p < .05$ level.

*** Significantly different from whites at $p < .001$ level.

academic priorities are discernible in NELS:88. For instance, Asian parents are more likely to enroll their children in art, music, ethnic history, and computer classes.

Asians also differ from whites in their parenting behavior. For instance, Asian parents are more likely to restrict the number of hours watching television, while white parents are more likely to restrict the types of programs and how late the child may stay up to watch television. Asian parents' interest in limiting the number of hours spent watching television is probably driven by the desire to protect the amount of time available for homework. Asian parents are also more likely to have rules about maintaining grades (74 percent vs. 68 percent) but are less likely to have rules about doing chores around the house (80 percent vs. 88 percent). This pattern of rules is also consistent with a slightly greater emphasis on the importance of schoolwork over all other responsibilities the child may have at home.

Asian parents are less likely than white parents to talk to their children about school experiences or their plans for high school and beyond, and they are less likely to help with homework. Overall, parents who help with their children's homework have lower achieving children. Recall that Sue and Okazaki (1990) also found that Asian parents scored lowest on parental involvement measures yet their children had the highest grades. For many Asian parents, a sense of duty clearly marks the boundaries of responsibility. In an ideal world, parents are responsible for the economic support of their children and providing the material resources for their children's education. In turn, children are responsible for performing well in school, and, if they do so, they have fulfilled their most important duty to their parents.

Asians are less likely than whites to have ever repeated fifth, sixth, seventh, or eighth grade (2 percent vs. 5 percent) but are more likely to be labeled LEP. Grade repetition and LEP status are hypothesized to lower grades. Finally, students' impression of their peers' evaluations indicate that Asians are more often considered to be good students but whites are more likely to be considered popular, athletic, or troublemakers. Being considered a good student reinforces the identity of doing well in school.

Table 7.5 presents the background characteristics of the Asian ethnic groups. Although Asians and whites do not differ with regard to income, these tabulations show that there are substantial differences in material resources within the Asian population. South Asians are the most economically advantaged, while Southeast Asians are the least. Pacific Islanders also have lower family incomes, although their small number in the sample makes it more difficult for us to distinguish them from whites statistically. In addition to South Asians, Koreans and Japanese families also have higher incomes than whites, while Chinese, Filipino, and West Asian families have comparable family incomes. Nonetheless, despite the lower socioeconomic status of the Southeast Asians (and Pacific Islanders), the share of those who have begun to save money for postsecondary education is comparable to that of whites. In addition, Southeast Asians manage to provide a place to study in proportions comparable to those of their other Asian counterparts even though they have fewer economic resources.

A greater share of South Asian, Japanese, Korean, and West Asian students take outside classes than white youth. South Asian households have more rules about watching television, maintaining grades, and homework than all other groups. With the exception of South Asians, other Asian ethnic groups generally have fewer rules about permissible kinds of programs or how late they may watch television, but more rules about how many hours they can watch daily than white eighth graders.

With respect to parent-child interaction about school, Chinese and Southeast Asian parents seem to have the least amount of interaction. Koreans also do not interact with their children as much as white parents, except in terms of how often they talked about post-high-school plans. With the sole exception of South Asians, whose parents spoke about plans for high school more often than white parents, parents from all Asian ethnic groups generally interact with their children less about school experiences and were less likely to help their children with their homework.

In terms of student characteristics, Southeast Asians are most likely to be classified as limited English proficient, and all Asian ethnic groups had greater proportions of LEP students than whites. Pacific Islanders appear to have higher rates of grade repetition than whites, but their small numbers in the sample make this observed difference not statistically significant. Chinese, Filipinos, Koreans, Southeast Asians, South Asians, and West Asians are all more likely to be considered a good student than their white counterparts.

To sum up, the Asian population is heterogeneous but some behavioral similarities remain. No matter what the level of income (Southeast Asians report an income about half of that of whites), greater shares of Asians than whites report that they have a place to study in their homes. Other material resources, however, are harder to obtain. South Asians outrank all other Asian groups in parental socioeconomic status, educational aspirations, home educational resources, outside classes, and in the number of rules about homework and so forth. Southeast Asians, despite their lack of education and income, perform well. Pacific Islanders are the least different from whites, although they also provide children with a specific place to study in proportions comparable to other Asian groups: yet, they have the lowest educational aspirations. The upcoming analysis reveals how groups with comparable social and economic resources perform academically.

Table 7.5 Background characteristics of students: Whites and Asian ethnic groups

	White	Chinese	Filipino	Japanese	Korean	Southeast Asian	Pacific Islander	South Asian	West Asian
Financial resources:[a]									
Mean family income ($)	46,964	45,714	47,169	60,104**	56,401**	28,789***	38,765	77,983***	52,920
	(39,579)	(41,702)	(36,413)	(38,825)	(46,019)	(32,744)	(39,751)	(55,244)	(50,462)
Have money for post-high-school education	.53	.73***	.63**	.62	.58	.52	.55	.72***	.53
Of those who have money saved, how much now	5,845	7,443***	5,837	5,804	7,106*	4,417*	5,324	10,412***	8,375***
	(5,303)	(5,792)	(5,419)	(4,823)	(5,727)	(4,996)	(5,811)	(5,252)	(6,069)
How much by time child finished high school	9,640	10,688*	9,790	9,723	11,094**	8,329*	9,242	12,911***	11,590**
	(4,948)	(5,066)	(4,929)	(4,872)	(4,788)	(5,112)	(5,758)	(3,976)	(4,975)
Home resources:[b]									
Place to study	.40	.56***	.60***	.63***	.62***	.60***	.56**	.71***	.54**
Own room	.86	.63***	.76***	.88	.83	.60***	.71***	.82	.82
Computer	.48	.54*	.50	.62**	.61**	.34***	.37*	.71***	.58*
Outside classes:[a]									
Art	.09	.13	.07	.13	.15**	.07	.13	.17**	.09
Music	.29	.33	.34	.42*	.52***	.14***	.35	.38*	.37*
Ethnic history	.04	.09***	.03	.09*	.15***	.10***	.12***	.20***	.16***
Computer	.12	.15	.14	.18	.18*	.12	.13	.28***	.16
Household rules:[a]									
Rules about TV programs	.70	.50***	.64	.54**	.60**	.60**	.73	.83***	.64
Rules about how late child can watch TV	.85	.68***	.78**	.77*	.69***	.71***	.83	.91	.81

Rules about how many hours TV daily	.40	.44	.51***	.51*	.45	.43	.53*	.78***	.51**
Rules about maintaining grades	.68	.71	.73	.72	.72	.75*	.73	.84***	.74
Rules about doing homework	.91	.87*	.91	.86	.88	.88	.96	.98***	.91
Rules about doing chores	.88	.73***	.88	.80*	.78***	.82**	.89	.83	.73***
Parent-child interaction:[a]									
How often talk to child about school experiences[c]	3.81 (.45)	3.27*** (.85)	3.68 (.50)	3.74 (.56)	3.42** (.70)	3.23*** (.82)	3.61*** (.62)	3.68** (.55)	3.67*** (.68)
How often talk about high school plans[c]	3.37 (.68)	2.99*** (.85)	3.39 (.68)	3.36 (.70)	3.09*** (.77)	3.02*** (.83)	3.22 (.78)	3.49* (.68)	3.38 (.73)
How often talk about post-high-school plans[c]	3.20 (.72)	2.90*** (.86)	3.24 (.70)	3.28 (.69)	3.15 (.77)	2.96*** (.93)	3.14 (.90)	3.27 (.73)	3.17 (.87)
How often help child with homework[d]	2.26 (.96)	1.91*** (.98)	2.11* (1.00)	2.09 (.98)	1.92*** (.97)	1.89*** (1.06)	2.43 (1.08)	2.36 (1.00)	2.09* (1.01)
Characteristics of student:[b]									
Ever repeat	.05	.02*	.02**	.02	.02*	.02	.09	.01*	.05
LEP	.01	.11***	.07***	.07***	.04***	.17***	.06***	.04***	.07***
Number of hours worked for pay	4.91 (5.97)	2.78*** (4.91)	2.72*** (4.43)	2.91** (4.91)	2.94*** (4.32)	3.06 (5.32)	3.82 (5.63)	1.78*** (4.17)	4.47 (6.59)

(Continued)

Table 7.5 (*Continued*)

	White	Chinese	Filipino	Japanese	Korean	Southeast Asian	Pacific Islander	South Asian	West Asian
Peer evaluations:[b,c]									
Popular	.99	.78***	.96	.96	.97	.85***	1.02	.88*	1.02
	(.57)	(.59)	(.60)	(.53)	(.55)	(.62)	(.57)	(.55)	(.61)
Athletic	1.03	.82***	.99	.96	.90*	.96	1.15	.88*	1.07
	(.71)	(.71)	(.74)	(.69)	(.69)	(.74)	(.74)	(.69)	(.75)
Good student	1.26	1.52***	1.43***	1.26	1.51***	1.57***	1.31	1.66***	1.38**
	(.61)	(.54)	(.58)	(.62)	(.54)	(.56)	(.69)	(.48)	(.60)
Troublemaker	.35	.22***	.26*	.34	.29	.18***	.42	.15***	.31
	(.57)	(.49)	(.51)	(.56)	(.53)	(.43)	(.63)	(.36)	(.35)

SOURCE.—NELS:88.

NOTE.—Values in parentheses are standard deviations.

[a] The number of respondents varies: about 15,000 for whites, 227 for Chinese, 250 for Filipinos, 84 for Japanese, 165 for Koreans, 211 for Southeast Asians, 83 for Pacific Islanders, 114 for South Asians, and 134 for West Asians (parent questionnaire items).

[b] The number of respondents varies: about 16,000 for whites, 307 for Chinese, 280 for Filipinos, 93 for Japanese, 187 for Koreans, 238 for Southeast Asians, 96 for Pacific Islanders, 126 for South Asians, and 160 for West Asians (student questionnaire items).

[c] Answer categories are 1 = not at all to 4 = regularly.

[d] Answer categories are 1 = seldom or never to 4 = almost every day.

[e] 0 = not at all (popular, athletic, a good student, etc.), 2 = somewhat, 3 = very.

* Significantly different from whites at $p < .05$ level.

** Significantly different from whites at $p < .01$ level.

*** Significantly different from whites at $p < .001$ level.

Results

Appendix A describes the variables used in the multivariate analysis and their operational definitions.[10] To evaluate the hypothesis that Asians and whites differ in their levels of skill development, I analyze the background characteristics that affect math and reading test scores. Subsequently, to evaluate the hypothesis that Asians and whites differ in behavior, I examine the determinants of grades among Asians and whites. I also analyze how the achievement of Chinese, Filipino, Japanese, Korean, Southeast Asian, Pacific Islander, South Asian, and West Asian students compares to that of white students.

Test scores

Table 7.6 presents the estimates of multivariate regression analyses using math and reading scores separately as the outcome variables of interest. We present two versions of each model—the first includes a dummy variable for Asians, which allows us to examine the mean effect of "Asian" ancestry, while the second model incorporates each ethnic group separately in order to examine ethnic differences. Results show that even after holding the effects of sex and parental socioeconomic status constant, Asians as a group earn higher math test scores but comparable reading scores relative to whites. But, when we expand the definition of material resources to include household structure, having an immigrant mother, and other resources, Asians and whites no longer differ in either math or reading test scores. Among the Asian ethnic groups, Chinese, Koreans, and Southeast Asian students earn higher math scores than whites from similar family backgrounds. Filipinos, Japanese, South Asians, and West Asians earn comparable math and reading scores, while Pacific Islanders score much lower than whites from comparable socioeconomic backgrounds. With the exception of Pacific Islanders, all Asian ethnic groups earn comparable reading scores.

It is striking that Pacific Islanders are less successful than the remaining Asian subgroups. What sets this group apart from their Asian counterparts may be their greater acculturation to the American mainstream. Our finding is consistent with recent literature that suggests that immigrant minorities are best positioned to achieve academically (Rumbaut 1990; Gibson 1993) because they have not yet adopted American peer norms. During a recent presentation, Margaret Gibson (1993) stated that many teachers like recent immigrant youth best as students. One teacher stated, "They're great when they first arrive, but after a few years, they get corrupted" (Gibson 1993).

Results from the expanded model produce substantively interesting results. Despite taking into account socioeconomic status, home resources and outside classes increased test scores while patterns of family interaction have no effect. This is expected, as the former two factors have to do with fostering intellectual activities, while the latter has more to do with encouraging enthusiasm for academic performance. Also, experiences of grade repetition and limited proficiency in English lowers test scores by three to four points.

Overall, our analysis finds no difference between Asian and white youth from comparable family backgrounds and home resources in the assessment of their skill development. But, subgroup differences within the Asian population were present, with Chinese, Korean, and Southeast Asians earning higher math scores than whites from comparable family backgrounds and home resources while Pacific Islanders consistently earned lower math and reading scores than whites, even after controlling for the effects of differential home resources.

Table 7.6 Effects of background characteristics on standardized math and reading test scores: Asians and whites

| | Model 1 | | | | Model 2 | | | |
| | With Asians | | With Asian subgroups | | With Asians | | With Asian subgroups | |
	Math	Reading	Math	Reading	Math	Reading	Math	Reading
Asian	1.394**	−.780			1.104	−.885		
	(.498)	(.499)			(.679)	(.681)		
Chinese			4.970***	.632			5.100***	.724
			(1.161)	(1.165)			(1.365)	(1.375)
Filipino			−1.114	−1.137			−.515	−.761
			(1.089)	(1.095)			(1.352)	(1.358)
Japanese			2.102	−1.106			2.595	−1.088
			(2.032)	(2.004)			(2.132)	(2.104)
Korean			4.900***	2.346			4.006*	1.711
			(1.462)	(1.467)			(1.723)	(1.735)
Southeast Asian			3.669**	.370			4.280**	2.050
			(1.376)	(1.380)			(1.603)	(1.615)
Pacific Islander			−5.728***	−7.258***			−5.538**	−6.156***
			(1.639)	(1.649)			(1.816)	(1.837)
South Asian			2.098	.758			1.300	.738
			(1.598)	(1.604)			(1.870)	(1.884)
West Asian			.470	−1.668			.395	−1.693
			(1.279)	(1.276)			(1.448)	(1.447)
Female	−.054	2.431***	−.071	2.421***	−.695**	1.933***	−.715**	1.920***
	(.212)	(.212)	(.211)	(.212)	(.235)	(.237)	(.235)	(.237)

Oldest					.644** (.246)	1.147*** (.248)	.634** (.246)	1.144*** (.248)
Number of siblings					-.095 (.081)	-.322*** (.081)	-.088 (.081)	-.317*** (.082)
Adult guardians:								
Mother and father					.507 (.308)	-.187 (.310)	.493 (.308)	-.189 (.310)
Mother only					2.046*** (.434)	1.087* (.437)	2.039*** (.433)	1.091* (.436)
Immigrant mother					1.774** (.560)	1.336* (.563)	1.198* (.576)	.776 (.580)
Family communication factor					-.096 (.139)	.172 (.140)	-.065 (.139)	.191 (.140)
Home resources factor					1.253*** (.187)	.996*** (.189)	1.257*** (.187)	1.005*** (.189)
Specialized classes factor					1.532*** (.168)	1.308*** (.168)	1.540*** (.167)	1.317*** (.168)
Ever repeat					-4.497*** (.545)	-4.261*** (.547)	-4.460*** (.544)	-4.229*** (.547)
LEP					-3.153* (1.239)	-4.348*** (1.246)	-3.526** (1.242)	-4.569*** (1.251)
Constant	43.003*** (.588)	43.032*** (.589)	43.013*** (.587)	43.049*** (.589)	45.067*** (.804)	46.032*** (.808)	45.101*** (.803)	46.043*** (.808)
Adjusted R^2	.159	.140	.163	.142	.196	.173	.200	.174

SOURCE.—NELS:88.

NOTE.—Numbers in parentheses are standard errors.

* $p < .05$.

** $p < .01$.

*** $p < .001$.

Grades

Table 7.7 presents the effects of background variables on grades with separate models for Asian (both as a single group and as eight subgroups) and whites. Model 1 only includes measures of urbanicity, parental education, and family income, while model 2 adds measures of family structure, home resources, and student characteristics. I present separate models, as preliminary analyses suggested significant interactions between "Asian" and several independent variables. Pooled models were also examined, and I will discuss these results in table 7.8 in order to compare Asians and whites from similar backgrounds. Please note that because these regression analyses are weighted to account for the sampling scheme and varying response rates, the effective sample of Asians (and whites) is greatly reduced. This makes it extremely difficult for the effects of independent variables in the Asian models to reach statistical significance.

Overall, we can see that Chinese, Koreans, Southeast Asians, and South Asians earn significantly higher grades than West Asians (the baseline group) from similar family socioeconomic backgrounds. Filipinos, Japanese, and Pacific Islanders, on the other hand, earn grades similar to those of their West Asian counterparts. However, when we add measures of family structure, home resources, and student characteristics, differences between the Asian ethnic groups are no longer statistically significant.

However, differences remain in the effects of background characteristics on grade performance of Asians and whites. Specifically, sibship order seems to have no effect on the grades of Asians, while it has significant influence on the grades of whites. There are also racial differences with respect to household structure. For whites, living with both mother and father is associated with higher grades (as compared to all other types of headship besides living with mother only) while no comparable effect is found among Asians. For Asians, however, there is a greater cost incurred by living with a single mother. As hypothesized earlier, having an immigrant mother is associated with higher grades. This result supports the hypothesis that cultural differences between immigrant and native-born parents play an important role in determining educational achievement.

Consistent with numerous other studies (Fehrman et al. 1987; Hoover-Dempsey et al. 1987), we also find that talking to parents about school experiences has a positive impact on grades among whites. However, family communication about school has no discernible effect on the grades of Asians. It may be that Asian parents stress educational activities more abstractly instead of giving daily reminders about doing homework and so forth. Home resources are associated with higher grades among whites, but not Asians, in this model.[11] Taking specialized classes outside of school also tends to raise grades among whites, but not Asians. These three factors together form a home environment conducive to education, although Asian parents convey their valuation of school differently than white parents.

Having ever repeated fifth to eighth grade has the single largest negative effect on grades for both Asians and whites—about 0.5–0.6 grade points. More hours spent on homework is associated with higher grades among whites, as is participating in school or extracurricular activities, which suggests that these activities promote a sense of belonging in school.

We can better gauge the difference between Asians and whites (i.e., estimate an "Asian effect") when we estimate pooled models. Table 7.8 presents pooled models with Asian and white students. Because our primary concern here is to compare Asian and white students from comparable backgrounds, we only

Table 7.7 Effects of background characteristics on grades: Separate models for Asians and whites

	Model 1			Model 2		
	Whites	Asians	Asian subgroups	Whites	Asians	Asian subgroups
Ethnicity:						
Chinese			.294*			.104
			(.129)			(.186)
Filipino			.140			-.117
			(.128)			(.188)
Japanese			-.014			-.140
			(.178)			(.235)
Korean			.360*			.119
			(.148)			(.203)
Southeast Asian			.410**			.258
			(.143)			(.213)
Pacific Islander			-.151			-.009
			(.158)			(.229)
South Asian			.433**			.265
			(.158)			(.235)
Female	.175***	.134	.109	.099***	.121	.092
	(.017)	(.076)	(.075)	(.021)	(.098)	(.100)
Oldest				.066**	.014	.024
				(.022)	(.105)	(.106)
Number of siblings				-.014*	-.040	-.046
				(.007)	(.036)	(.037)
Adult guardians:						
Mother and father				-.080**	-.046	-.059
				(.027)	(.144)	(.145)
Mother only				.029	-.479	-.501*
				(.038)	(.247)	(.248)

(Continued)

Table 7.7 (Continued)

	Model 1			Model 2		
	Whites	Asians	Asian subgroups	Whites	Asians	Asian subgroups
Immigrant mother				.123*	.419***	.329*
				(.053)	(.119)	(.140)
Family communication factor				.039**	−.026	−.019
				(.012)	(.045)	(.046)
Home resources factor				.073***	.030	.041
				(.017)	(.080)	(.081)
Outside classes factor				.077***	.045	.046
				(.015)	(.071)	(.071)
Ever repeat				−.545***	−.638*	−.638*
				(.047)	(.299)	(.302)
LEP				−.115	−.157	−.193
				(.130)	(.227)	(.230)
Hours of homework				.048***	.058	.055
				(.007)	(.033)	(.033)
Activities in school				.302***	.293	.312
				(.034)	(.164)	(.165)
Activities outside school				.123***	.151	.139
				(.026)	(.115)	(.116)
Constant	2.122***	2.963***	2.754***	1.910***	2.444***	2.475***
	(.047)	(.194)	(.208)	(.081)	(.382)	(.390)
Adjusted R^2	.124	.060	.106	.215	.174	.173

Source.—NELS:88.

Note.—Numbers in parentheses are standard errors. All models include controls for urban/rural/suburban residence, family income, and parental education.

* $p < .05$.   ** $p < .01$.   *** $p < .001$.

Table 7.8 Effects of background characteristics on grades: Asians and whites

	Model 1[a]		Model 2[b]	
	With Asians	With Asian subgroups	With Asians	With Asian subgroups
Asian	.228***		.120*	
	(.039)		(.061)	
Chinese		.343***		.210
		(.092)		(.119)
Filipino		.135		−.024
		(.085)		(.118)
Japanese		−.065		−.164
		(.151)		(.194)
Korean		.357**		.214
		(.117)		(.143)
Southeast Asian		.533***		.457**
		(.107)		(.139)
Pacific Islander		−.051		.053
		(.129)		(.187)
South Asian		.425***		.330
		(.126)		(.180)
West Asian		.078		.019
		(.101)		(.141)
Adjusted R^2	.125	.127	.218	.219

Source.—NELS:88.

Note.—Numbers in parentheses are standard errors.
[a] Model 1 includes controls for urban/rural/suburban residence, family income, and parental education.
[b] Model 2 adds measures of family structure, home educational resources, and student characteristics identical to those of model 2 in table 7.7.
* $p < .05$.
** $p < .01$.
*** $p < .001$.

present the effects of ethnicity in these models. The "with Asians" model in models 1 and 2 includes a dummy variable for the effect of Asian ancestry. The models marked with "with Asian subgroups" includes dummy variables for Chinese, Filipino, Japanese, Korean, Southeast Asian, Pacific Islander, South Asian, and West Asian ancestry. Controlling for the effects of parental socio-economic status, we can see that Asians, as a group, earn higher grades than whites. However, when we examine ethnic group differences, we can see that only Chinese, Koreans, Southeast Asians, and South Asians earn higher grades than whites from comparable family backgrounds. Filipinos, Japanese, Pacific Islanders, and West Asians earn grades similar to those of whites from statistically equivalent family backgrounds.

In model 2, we add measures of family structure, immigrant mother, home resources, and student characteristics. Here, Asians still earn slightly higher grades than their white counterparts with similar family characteristics and home resources. However, ethnic effects reveal that the advantage of "Asians" in this expanded model is perceivably driven by Southeast Asians, the only group that still earns higher grades than whites even after these expanded control measures. Caution should be taken when interpreting this result because analyses in Table 7.7 found that the grades of all eight Asian ethnic groups could not be statistically distinguished from one another. Thus, it is unclear that Southeast Asians are the only group driving the "Asian" effect in the pooled model.

Summary and conclusion

The main question this article addressed is how well Asian-American youth fit the model minority image. Our findings support the hypothesis that the higher grades earned by Asian youth stem from cultural and behavioral as well as compositional differences. A crucial cultural difference is that Asian parents invest more in educational resources than their white counterparts despite comparable family incomes. Hence, the availability of educational resources is driven, in part, by cultural values. With respect to math and reading test scores, parental socio-economic status and educational resources do account for the average difference between Asians and whites. However, our model finds that Chinese, Korean, and Southeast Asian youth earn higher math test scores than comparable white youth. Our model also finds that Asians overall have a slight edge in grades, and, while some of their relative success can be attributed to family background and educational resources, their achievement is also a result of cultural practices that cause some Asian subgroups to overachieve.

For instance, Asian and white youth differ in the relationship between their educational aspirations and their grades. The results indicate that at every level of educational aspirations, Asian children outperform their white counterparts in terms of grades.[12] Sue and Okazaki (1990) report that Ritter and Dornbusch (1989) found that on a variety of items regarding why one should work hard in school, only one item yielded a significant difference between Asians and other racial groups. Specifically, Asian Americans were more likely to believe that success in life depended on the things studied in school (Sue and Okazaki 1990).

One person in our Asian focus group discussion revealed how his brother's success on the track team was not a source of pride for the parents; in fact, they refused to attend any of his track meets. Only straight A's and getting into an Ivy League school would completely satisfy the parents, and this sentiment was echoed in the other Asian students' own experiences. Another respondent wanted to take an acting class but had to plead with his mother for permission to do so. The fear from his mother came from the respondent's cousin who was attending Yale (which is a source of satisfaction for the parents) but had changed his major to drama (which signals a "major disaster"). So, not only is there a greater ambivalence toward success in nonacademic realms, there is the fear that adolescents may be distracted from their schoolwork or later choose a career deemed "unsafe." As one person from the focus group stated, "There's a real fear that life is really unstable, and that's why there's such an emphasis on getting in the safe professions, being a doctor, lawyer [someone else: 'fixed income']. Yeah, fixed income, finding a good home in the suburbs with a good school."

But why is this the case? Perhaps Asians, as Sue and Okazaki (1990) argue, see other avenues of success closed to them. Asian-American parents push their children to get good grades and enter "safe" professions, such as becoming a physician, an engineer, a physical science researcher, or an accountant. It is likely that this results from a worldview that places Asians in technical (vs. creative) fields and may serve to protect youth from perceived future discrimination in occupations that are deemed unsafe. Despite being relatively successful, many Asian-Americans also believe in the "glass ceiling" effect, which keeps a cap on just how high Asians can rise in the ranks. Thus, it is conceivable that parents encourage their children to overachieve to offset the effects of perceived discrimination.

However, the results also challenge the model minority image by demonstrating that Asians are not uniformly advantaged educationally and economically, but that compositional differences account for differences in skill development and most of the variation in grades. Indeed, South Asians seemed to be especially well equipped to succeed while Southeast Asians have very little education and relatively low incomes. Not only do family backgrounds differ among these regional groups, but they also differ in their utilization of their resources in promoting school performance. Pacific Islanders seem to be educationally disadvantaged, as we found them to have low grades, test scores, and educational aspirations relative to whites and all other Asian ethnic groups. This finding should prompt researchers to investigate the wide variation in outcomes within the Asian population. It may be that acculturation to the American mainstream negatively affects academic achievement, since we found higher achievement among children of immigrant parents. More research into these areas would heighten our understanding of educational processes, more generally, but would also clarify the ways race and ethnicity shape one's educational performance.

In contrast to the Pacific Islanders, Southeast Asians are recent arrivals whose parents are disadvantaged educationally and economically. Nonetheless, they outperform their Asian counterparts with comparable family backgrounds. Caplan et al. (1992) have also explored the extraordinary educational achievements of the Indochinese youth despite limited material resources and limited proficiency in English. They suggest that siblings benefit from having to tutor younger siblings or by being tutored by older siblings since both groups benefit from repetition of school lessons. But, even the Southeast Asians are composed of many different ethnic groups (Vietnamese, Laotians, Cambodians, Hmong, etc.) that may differ in their propensity for academic success. Unfortunately, NELS:88 does not allow us to separate these distinct groups from each other.

This article has revealed many more questions about the role race and ethnicity plays in effecting educational outcomes. It is unclear just what Asian parents do (or do not do) which accounts for the disparate academic performance of Asian and white youth. It may be that Asian parents are just more authoritarian in their demands of their children's academic performance (which would be consient with the low scores in family communication and previous research). Why does family communication influence grades among white students but not Asian youth? Indeed, our results suggest that the nature of communication of their expectations for their children differs between Asian and white parents. If anything, our results suggest that researchers should not expect the forms of parental involvement documented by studies of white parents and children to necessarily be valid for other racial and ethnic groups. Indeed, it is not that Asian parents score lower on measures of parental involvement because they are less concerned with their children's academic outcomes, but that their styles of involvement differ from that of the mainstream. Future research about Asian-Americans should examine the concept of "safe" professions and why Asian youth with similar goals as white youth earn higher grades.

Appendix A: Definitions of variables used in multivariate analysis

Asian	Equals 1 if Asian, 0 if white. The subdivisions for Asian/Pacific Islanders as given on the NELS:88 student questionnaire are worded exactly as follows: (1) Chinese; (2) Filipino; (3) Japanese; (4) Korean; (5) Southeast Asian (Vietnamese, Laotian, Cambodian/Kampuchean, Thai, etc.); (6) Pacific Islander (Samoan, Guamanian, etc.); (7) South Asian (Asian Indian, Pakistani, Bangladeshi, Sri Lankan, etc.); (8) West Asian (Iranian, Afghan, Turkish, etc.); (9) Middle Eastern (Iraqi, Israeli, Lebanese, etc.); and (10) Other Asian. Because the sample contained only 35 West Asians, and 45 Middle Eastern Asians, I combined these groups with the other Asians to form a group "West Asians."
Chinese	Equals 1 if Chinese, otherwise 0. (All other ethnic dummy variables are coded similarly.)
Female	Equals 1 if female, 0 if male.
Parent's education:	
Less than high school	Equals 1 if parent with highest level of education has less than high school education, otherwise 0.
High school graduate	Equals 1 if parent with highest level of education is a high school graduate, otherwise 0. This is the basis of comparison in the multivariate analysis. (Note that the other parent's education variables follow the same configuration.)
Family income	Family income as reported by the parents. These were categorical variables recorded by taking the value of the midpoint of each category. The categories are as follows: none, less than $1,000, $1,000–$2,999, $3,000–$4,999, $5,000–$7,499, $7,500–$9,999, $10,000–$14,999, $15,000–$19,999, $20,000–$24,999, $25,000–$34,999, $35,000–$49,999, $50,000–$74,999, $75,000–$99,999, $100,000–$199,999, and $200,000 or more.
Oldest child	Equals 1 if respondent is oldest, otherwise 0.
Number of siblings	This is the number of siblings as reported by the eighth grader. It ranges from 0 to 10 in value.
Adult guardians:	
Mother and father	Equals 1 if respondent lives with both natural or adopted mother and father (excluding stepparents), otherwise 0.
Mother only	Equals 1 if respondent lives with mother only, otherwise 0.
Immigrant mother	Equals 1 if respondent's mother immigrated into the United States (e.g., foreign-born), otherwise 0.
Family communication factor	Factor computed using items on the parent questionnaire about how often parent and child discuss school-related issues and how often parent helps child with homework.

Home resources factor	Factor computer using items regarding whether there is a specific place to study, computer, more than 50 books, etc., in the home environment.
Specialized classes factor	Factor computed using items about what kinds of educational classes eighth grader takes outside of school, such as music, art, dance, and foreign language classes.
LEP	Equals 1 if any of the two teachers report or if the respondent self-reports having limited English proficiency, otherwise 0.
Ever repeat	Equals 1 if eighth grader repeated fifth, sixth, seventh, or eighth grades, otherwise 0.
Hours of homework	Number of hours eighth grader spends on homework. This was a categorical variable recoded using the midpoint value of each category.
Activities in school	Equals 1 if respondent takes part in school activities, such as being a member of any clubs, otherwise 0.
Activities outside school	Equals 1 if respondent takes part in activities outside of school. This includes Boy Scouts or Girl Scouts, religious activities, etc., otherwise 0.

SOURCE.—NELS:88.

Appendix B

Table B1 Survey items and factor loadings for home resources, family communication, and outside classes factors*

Factor	Factor loading
Home resources (0 = no; 1 = yes):	
Family has a specific place to study	.215
Family receives daily newspaper	.362
Family regularly receives magazine	.480
Family has an encyclopedia	.379
Family has a typewriter	.403
Family has a computer	.425
Family has more than 50 books	.470
Student has his/her own bedroom	.245
Family communication (1 = not at all; 4 = regularly):	
How often parent talks to child about school experiences	.468
How often parent talks to child about high school plans	.787
How often parent talks to child about post-high-school plans	.576
Outside classes (0 = no; 1 = yes):	
Art	.415
Music	.540
Dance	.430
Foreign language	.355
Religion	.412
	(*Continued*)

Table B1 (Continued)

Factor	Factor loading
Ethnic history	.336
Computer	.390
Other	.428

Source.—NELS:88.
* These items were grouped according to theoretical considerations and ease of interpretations.

Appendix C: Description of focus groups on being Asian, Black, and Hispanic

The focus groups mentioned throughout this article were conducted between May and July, 1992, under the auspices of the MacArthur Foundation's Successful Adolescent Development Network. These discussions focused on the ways ethnic identities shape conceptions of self, success, and family relationships. Each of these focus groups lasted between 1.5 and 2 hours. All participants were undergraduate students. Each of these discussions were prompted by a set of questions (which follows this brief description). We encouraged open-ended answers from the respondents and allowed respondents to talk about related areas.

Despite the selection bias of this sample, racial and ethnic differences in values and behavior were readily apparent. These focus groups serve to clarify the mechanisms through which race and ethnicity affects schooling outcomes of ethnic youth. The following is the outline used for leading the focus group discussion with Asian students. The other outlines (used in the black and Hispanic groups) are similar in structure and use the labels appropriate for that ethnic group.

The ethnic groups represented among the participants of the Asian focus group include Chinese, Korean, Indian, and Japanese students.

Focus group: On being Asian

Goals:

I. To help understand the cultural content of being Asian from a developmental perspective.
II. To highlight and compare personal life experiences linked to being Asian that shaped relections of the self as an ethnic being.
III. To provide insight into the cultural content of being Asian which ramifies on belief systems.

Guiding Questions:

1 Do you identify with being Asian, Asian-American, (nationality)-American, or do the labels not matter to you? Otherwise, how do you distinguish between these labels? Has your identification changed over your lifetime?
2 What does being Asian mean to you? How important is it? Has the importance of this changed over your lifetime? If so, in what way has it changed?

3   Has being Asian affected the goals you or your parents set for yourself? How so?
4   How are Asians similar to other people of color, say Latinos or blacks or other groups? How are Asians different from these groups? When did you first realize that you were different from these other groups? How important are these differences and how has these changed over time?
5   Over your lifetime, how often have you been treated differently (either positively or negatively) because you were Asian? In what ways were you treated differently? Who treated you differently?
6   Do you think it will be easier or harder to get ahead because you are Asian? Are your friends mostly Asian or mostly non-Asian? Do your non-Asian friends share similar ideas as you about what it means to be successful? What about your Asian friends?
7   What does it mean to "act Asian" to to "act White"?
8   What is your most important life goal?
9   Who is your hero?

Notes

An earlier draft of this article was presented at the 1994 Meetings of the American Educational Research Association, New Orleans, and the 1993 Meetings of the Southwestern Social Science Association, New Orleans. Special thanks go to Marta Tienda for her numerous insights throughout the writing of this article. I also thank Julie Brines and Barbara Schneider for their comments. I am grateful to Jeffrey Rubidge for his technical assistance and support. This research was supported by a grant from the Spencer Foundation.

1   The labels "Asian-American" and "Asian" will be used interchangeably throughout this article.
2   Please refer to appendix A for a definition of these eight Asian ethnic groups.
3   NELS:88 provides only self-reported grades. While self-reported grades are likely to be higher than actual grades, our usage of these measures for comparative purpose renders these items to be appropriate.
4   This variable takes on the highest value of either the mother's or father's education from the parent questionnaire. If there was no parent questionnaire available, then the information was taken from the student's questionnaire using the same principle.
5   The family income item contained categorical responses, which ranged from none (less than $1,000, $1,000–$2,999, and so on) to $200,000 or more. These answer categories were recoded by using the midpoint of the range in each category. Preliminary analyses using dummies for each of these categories (except for one) resulted in nonsignificance for almost all of these dummies; thus the method described above was used. This was also the case for some other variables which do not have a series of dummies for the answer categories in the final regression models.
6   See app. B for the factor loading coefficients for these factors.
7   This is a liberal definition of having limited English proficiency in that it is coded 1 if the student answered "not very well" to how well s/he understands, speaks, reads, and writes English or if either one of the two teachers interviewed identified the respondent as LEP. Nonetheless, this is an underestimate of the extent of the phenomenon since students who were thought to have very limited English skills did not participate in the survey.
8   This variable had categorical answers such as none, 0.5–1.00, 2–2.99, and so on up to 21.00 and above hours per week. These were recoded as the value of the midpoint of each category.
9   The base year sample does, however, exclude many language minority students who were unable to complete the questionnaire and tests in English, thus underestimating the numbers of recent immigrants and the effects of lacking proficiency in English (National Center for Education Statistics 1990).

10 To construct indices representing home resources (conducive to education), specialized classes, and family communication behavior, I used factor analysis as a data reduction technique. A single factor for each of these domains emerged from the analysis. Questions regarding whether the family has a specific place to study, receives a daily newspaper, regularly receives a magazine, has an encyclopedia, has a typewriter, has a computer, has more than 50 books, and whether students have their own bedrooms were used to construct the home resources factor. For the family communication factor, items about how often parents talk to their children about school experiences, high school plans, and post-high-school plans were utilized. Finally, the factor for specialized classes outside of school includes whether the respondent takes art, music, dance, foreign language, religion, ethnic history, computer, or other classes.

11 By itself, home resources is associated with higher grades among Asians. In this model, however, there is no additional effect from having home educational resources. It is possible that home resources explains some of the variance between Asian-white differences but cannot account for the variance within the Asian population.

12 This may be because of the unmeasured fact that more Asian children are aspiring to go to prestigious high schools and colleges than white children, something this survey does not allow us to measure.

References

Astone, Nan Marie, and Sara S. McLanahan. "Family Structure, Parental Practices and High School Completion." *American Sociological Review* 56 (1991): 309–20.

Baker, David P., and David L. Stevenson. "Mothers' Strategies for Children's School Achievement: Managing the Transition to High School." *Sociology of Education* 59 (1986): 156–66.

Barringer, H. D., D. Takeuchi, and P. Xenos. "Education, Occupational Prestige, and Income of Asian-Americans." *Sociology of Education* 63 (1990): 27–43.

Caplan, Nathan, Marcella H. Choy, and John K. Whitmore. *Children of the Boat People: A Study of Educational Success.* Ann Arbor: University of Michigan Press, 1992.

Clark, Reginald M. *Family Life and School Achievement: Why Poor Black Children Succeed or Fail.* Chicago: University of Chicago Press, 1983.

Corsaro, William A., and Donna Eder. "Children's Peer Cultures." *Annual Review of Sociology* 16 (1990): 197–220.

Dornbusch, Sanford M. "The Sociology of Adolescence." *Annual Review of Sociology* 15 (1989): 233–59.

Farkas, George, Daniel Sheehan, Robert P. Grobe, and Yuan Shuan. "Cultural Resources and School Success: Gender, Ethnicity, and Poverty Groups within an Urban School District." *American Sociological Review* 55 (1990): 127–42.

Fehrman, P. G., T. Z. Keith, and T. M. Reimer. "Home Influence on School Learning: Direct and Indirect Effects of Parental Involvement on High School Grades." *Journal of Educational Research* 80 (1987): 330–37.

Fordham, Signthia, and John Ogbu. "Black Students' School Success: Coping with the Burden of 'Acting White.'" *Urban Review* 18 (1986): 176–206.

Gibson, Margaret. "Accommodation without Assimilation." Paper presented at the Conference on Immigrant Students in California, Center for U.S.-Mexican Studies, University of California, San Diego, 1993.

Gibson, Margaret, and John Ogbu. *Minority Status and Schooling: A Comparative Study of Immigrant and Involuntary Minorities.* New York: Garland, 1991.

Hallinan, M. T. "Equality of Educational Opportunity." *Annual Review of Sociology* 14 (1988): 249–68.

Hirschman, Charles, and Morrison Wong. "Trends in Socioeconomic Achievement among Immigrant and Native-Born Asian Americans, 1960–1976." *Sociological Quarterly* 22 (1981): 495–513.

Hoover-Dempsey, V., O. C. Bassler, and J. S. Brissie. "Parent Involvement: Contributions of Teacher Efficacy, School Socio-Economic Status, and Other School Characteristics." *American Educational Research Journal* 24 (1987): 417–35.

Hurh, Won Moo, and Kwang Chung Kim. "The 'Success' Image of Asian Americans: Its

Validity and Its Practical and Theoretical Implications." *Ethnic and Racial Studies* 12 (1989): 512–38.

Matute-Bianchi, Maria Eugenia. "Ethnic Identities and Patterns of School Success and Failure among Mexican-Descent and Japanese-American Students in a California High School: An Ethnographic Analysis." *American Journal of Education* 94 (1986): 233–55.

Murnane, R. J., R. A. Maynard, and J. C. Ohls. "Home Resources and Children's Achievement." *Review of Economics and Statistics* 63 (1981): 369–77.

National Center for Education Statistics. *The National Education Longitudinal Study of 1988, Base Year: Student Component Data File User's Manual*. Washington, D.C.: U.S. Department of Education, March 1990.

Ogbu, John. "Minority Coping Responses and School Experience." *Journal of Psychohistory* 18 (1991): 433–56.

Ritter, P. L., and S. M. Dornbusch. "Ethnic Variation in Family Influences on Academic Achievement." Paper presented at the annual meeting of the American Educational Research Association, March 1989.

Rumbaut, Ruben G. *Immigrant Students in California Public Schools: A Summary of Current Knowledge*. Report for Center for Research on Effective Schooling for Disadvantaged Students, Johns Hopkins University, 1990.

Rumberger, Russell W., Rita Ghatak, Gary Poulos, Philip L. Ritter, and Sanford M. Dornbusch. "Family Influences on Dropout Behavior in One California High School." *Sociology of Education* 63 (1990): 283–99.

Schneider, Barbara, and Yongsook Lee. "A Model for Academic Success: The School and Home Environment of East Asian Students." *Anthropology and Education Quarterly* 21 (1990): 358–77.

Sowell, Thomas. *Ethnic America: A History*. New York: Basic, 1981.

Steinberg, Stephen. *The Ethnic Myth: Race, Ethnicity, and Class in America*. 2d ed. Boston: Beacon, 1989.

Stevenson, Harold W., and James W. Stigler. *The Learning Gap: Why Our Schools Are Failing and What We Can Learn from Japanese and Chinese Education*. New York: Summit, 1992.

Sue, Stanley, and Sumie Okazaki. "Asian-American Educational Achievements: A Phenomenon in Search of an Explanation." *American Psychologist* 45 (1990): 913–20.

Takaki, Ronald. *Strangers from a Different Shore: A History of Asian-Americans*. New York: Penguin, 1989.

Teachman, J. "Family Background, Educational Resources, and Educational Attainment." *American Sociological Review* 52 (1987): 548–57.

CHAPTER 8

MAKING EDUCATION WORK FOR THE AMERICAN INDIAN (1981)

Robert K. Chiago

In order to discuss American Indian education with some degree of intelligence, we must first have some idea of what we are talking about with respect to the definition of Indian. Unfortunately, most articles on the topic of Indian education have made the all too common mistake of assuming too much. We assume that everyone knows how an Indian looks, how an Indian behaves, how Indians live, and even how Indians think. We also assume that there is such a thing as an Indian language. As a step toward dispelling the myth of the stereotype Indian, we will briefly examine some of the complexities involved with attempting to understand "Indian." We will then proceed to review Indian education.

What is an American Indian?

There is no universally accepted single description or definition of American Indian.[1] The 1980 Census assumes that a person who is an American Indian can identify with a specific tribe. The Indian Self-Determination and Indian Education Assistance Act defines Indian as a person who is a member of a federally recognized Indian tribe. The Indian Education Act is somewhat more elaborate and confusing in its definition of Indian. Section 453 of the Act defines Indian as follows:

> For purposes of this title, the term "Indian" means any individual who (1) is a member of a tribe, band, or other organized group of Indians, including those tribes, bands, or groups terminated since 1940 and those recognized now or in the future by the state in which they reside, or who is a descendant, in the first or second degree, of any such member, or (2) is considered by the Secretary of the Interior to be an Indian for any purpose, or (3) is an Eskimo or Aleut or other Alaska Native, or (4) is determined to be an Indian under regulations promulgated by the Commissioner, after consultation with the National Advisory Council on Indian Education, which regulations shall further define the term "Indian."

Since there are so many different definitions of Indian and since almost every definition is contingent on a tribal relationship, for purposes of this article *Indian* will be defined as a person who is identified by the community in which he or she resides as an Indian, identifies himself or herself as an Indian, and who has some relationship with an Indian tribe as a member or descendant.

There are more than 500 different Indian tribes in the United States today. These tribes vary in size of population from less than 100 to over 150,000. Over 90 percent of the Indian tribes are recognized by the federal government and thus have a special relationship with the federal government. Other tribes are recognized only by the states in which they are located and do not have a relationship with the federal government. A few "tribes" which are sometimes groups of people claiming to be an Indian tribe are not recognized by the federal government or by the states in which they are located.

Indian tribes also vary in custom, history, economy, wealth, location, tribal language, government, religion, and degree of acculturation. No two tribes are identical in all respects even though there does exist some commonalities and close relationship between some of the tribes. In addition to the differences between Indian tribes, it should be understood that there are also individual differences within each tribe. These differences include differences in degree of acculturation (usually from the least acculturated to those who might be classified as the most acculturated even to the point of being completely assimilated), and differences in wealth, social standing, religion and educational attainment. There are no laws which prohibit tribal members from moving off their reservations and, in fact, we find that in many cases several generations of Indians have been raised off their Indian reservations. These Indians would have a tendency to be more acculturated than their counterparts who remain on the reservation.

Off-reservation Indians who reside in urban areas are often called "urban Indians" as opposed to their reservation counterparts who are usually labeled "reservation Indians." There are numerous exceptions to this rule with regard to where Indians live and their degree of acculturation. Due to a multitude of reasons, with one of the most important being employment, many Indians live in urban centers, including some who might be recent immigrants from their reservations. The degree of difficulty in coping with off-reservation living is generally inversely proportioned to the length of time one lives off the reservation, but also may include numerous other variables such as education, religion, and degree of acculturation.

Since Indian tribes have the right to establish their own membership critera, it is conceivable that a person who genetically possesses what is termed as four-fourths degree Indian blood may not be able to obtain tribal membership while on the other hand a person who possesses one-sixteenth degree Indian blood or less can be a member of a particular Indian tribe. Thus, a person who possesses the racial characteristics of one of several groups can by law and by personal identity be an Indian. This means that what might appear to be a black or white child can really be an Indian child.

Education for Indians

Contrary to the democratic ideology of cultural pluralism, education has been used as the primary weapon in the white man's arsenal toward changing Indian tribal cultures. Beginning in 1568, when a mission school was established for Florida Indians, the white man has been using education in an unrelenting effort to assimilate Indians. Some historians believe that assimilation through education was not an end in itself, but rather a means by which Indians would need and use less land, thereby releasing more land for occupation and settlement by the Europeans and their descendants.[2]

For whatever the reasons, a vast number of treaties between the government and the various Indian tribes, which ceded nearly a billion acres of Indian lands to the United States, contained provisions which entitled and guaranteed an education to Indians.[3] Thus, through treaties, Indians were separated from their land and, subject to the success of the government's educational programs, and through these educational programs, Indians were also separated from their culture.

Federal education

Since 1802 when the federal government first became involved in educating Indian children, federal responsibility for the education of Indians as measured in dollars and cents has evolved from a fifteen thousand dollar annual program into nearly a half-billion dollar annual program in 1977.[4] More than two-thirds of the federal expenditure for Indian education is administered by the Bureau of Indian Affairs, most of which is used to provide an education for approximately 50,000 Indian children in the following kinds of elementary and secondary schools:

1   107 Bureau of Indian Affairs (BIA) Day Schools:
2   68 BIA Boarding Schools
3   15 BIA Dormitories
4   19 Contract Day Schools
5   8 Contract Boarding Schools[5]

In addition to the above, the BIA operates or supports a number of post-secondary schools. The BIA also administers monies which provide post-secondary vocational training and/or a higher education for Indians.

The Bureau of Indian Affairs is a federal program located within the United States Department of Interior. The educational component of the BIA is one of the few federal educational programs not presently in the new United States Department of Education, even though the justification for the establishment of the new Department of Education was to promote efficiency within the federal government by consolidating the numerous and often identical educational programs spread out in the various departments of the federal bureaucracy.

As has previously been mentioned, the BIA operates or funds the operation of several kinds of elementary and secondary schools. The BIA day school is usually located on an Indian reservation and includes grades K-12. The operation of a BIA day school is almost identical to that of a public school. The Indian children attend day school by commuting to school from home and vice versa each day. BIA boarding schools are located either on or off Indian reservations and may include grades K-12. Some of the Indian children attending boarding schools, in particular those boarding schools located off an Indian reservation, board at the school during the school year. These children live in dormitories, eat meals prepared by the government, and receive their instruction at the boarding school. BIA dormitories are not schools but rather exclusively dormitories. Indian children in grades K-12 may reside in a BIA dormitory, but BIA dormitories primarily serve Indian children in grades 9–12. The difference between a BIA dormitory and BIA boarding school is that students in a BIA dormitory attend public schools while Indian children in a boarding school attend BIA schools.

Contract schools are funded by the BIA but are operated by a "middle man" such as an Indian tribe, Indian organization, or public school district. An advantage of a contract school is that Indians can have more flexibility in the operation of the school. The function of contract day schools and contract boarding schools correspond with those of BIA day and boarding schools.

BIA schools have traditionally been the center of much controversy. This controversy has most often been focused on the BIA boarding school, especially since the boarding school has been blamed as the primary means short of genocide by which the federal government has attempted to eradicate "Indian culture." Today, while the stated purpose of boarding schools is not to eradicate Indian culture, they have been perceived as an institution of the federal government which has perpetuated a dependency relationship of Indians on the government. This means that while many Indian parents have the resources to send their children to day schools or public schools, they prefer to send them to BIA boarding schools so that they would not have to assume the additional responsibility of housing and feeding their children. Such excuses as family economic condition, the distance from home to school, the road conditions, or the racist curriculum used in the public schools are offered as partial justification for the continued existence of boarding schools. It must be understood that some of the above listed excuses have some validity, meaning that public schools are located further from the homes of Indians than others, that the attitude of those working in public schools are perceived as racist, and that many Indian families are not economically well off.

A multitude of reports, some of which are based on sound research, have suggested that BIA schools are inferior to public schools in that Indian children who attend BIA schools are on the whole several years behind their public school counterparts as indicated by achievement tests. The BIA has also been criticized for being unable to effectively and efficiently manage their schools as reported on numerous occasions by the General Accounting Office of the United States.

In an attempt to make some needed reforms in the BIA's educational programs, the United States Congress recently passed the Basic Indian Education Act. This act, passed in 1978, is expected to provide for the establishment of educational standards, equalize BIA school funding, provide school boards with some responsibility, and make other changes in the BIA's educational system. At present, it is too early to evaluate the effect of this act. Initial reports, however, indicate that the BIA is not implementing the law with any precision.

Public education

It is estimated that nearly 85 percent of all Indian children attend public schools. Some of these public schools are located on or near Indian reservations while others are located far from Indian reservations. Indian children attend public schools in every state of the Union. Public school districts located on or near Indian reservations are entitled to Impact Aid monies in the same manner as those public school districts located on or near military bases or other federally impacted areas. Public school districts are also entitled to receive other monies from the federal government by virtue of their Indian enrollment for either basic support, supplemental programs, or for both. The Indian Education Act, otherwise known as Title IV of Public Law 92-318, and the Johnson-O'Malley Act, are the primary laws by which public school districts receive assistance.

Even though Indians are citizens of the states in which they reside, some state boards of education have been intentionally negligent in providing an equally accessible education to Indian children who reside on Indian reservations. This negligence has contributed to the justification for the continued existence of BIA schools. This racist attitude of certain state officials, in particular those located in some western states with relatively large numbers of Indians, is not only reflected by the location of schools but also reflected by what happens in the classroom, the results of which are a continued indictment of the American system of education.

Symptoms and problems

Studies using nonverbal tests have indicated that Indian children are at least as intelligent as American European children.[6] Even so, they consistently under-achieve and, according to school statistics, exemplify other problems.[7] It must be understood that Indian children are not problems, but rather they may demonstrate symptoms of society's ills including racism, cultural ethnocentrism, greed, stereotyping, and bureaucratic bungling. The notorious Senate committee report of November 1969 entitled "Indian Education: A National Tragedy—A National Challenge"[8] dramatically portrays the extent to which Indian children have been victimized in the United States. The following are highlights of that report:

1   Approximately 16,000 Indian children are not in school.
2   Dropout rates of Indian children are twice the national average.
3   The level of formal education is half the national average.
4   Indian children, more than any other group, believe themselves to be "below average" in intelligence.
5   Indian children in the twelfth grade have the poorest self concept of all minority groups tested.
6   The average Indian income is $1,500.
7   Indian unemployment is ten times the national average.

Eleven years have lapsed since this report was made without any substantial evidence of improvement in the lives and education of Indian children. We can only hope that several laws passed by Congress, aimed at improving the education of Indians, will have a positive effect.

American Indians, as one of the many minority groups in the United States, encounter a multitude of adverse and sometimes hostile conditions in life. Racism in America has had a devastating effect on many aspects of Indian life. In the more extreme cases, the effects have been total cultural genocide. To the extent that racism is exhibited in the schools, teachers and administrators can have an influence in reducing it by being aware that it does exist and by bringing it out in the open and dealing with it.

Teacher-child relationships

Sometimes teachers make the mistake of treating Indian children differently from other children in the classroom without any justification for this dual standard. Unless a teacher knows why s/he is using a different technique with an Indian child, it is best to treat an Indian child like any other child. Teachers are not the only people who have a great influence on the child in the school. We know that attitudes affect performance and thus a child's attitude toward the total school setting can have an impact on how well the child will do in the classroom. Special treatment by a teacher toward a seemingly different child can sometimes focus the attention of other children in the classroom on certain differences they otherwise would not care about, serving to complicate situations which might already be difficult for the child. Imagine a teacher introducing Johnny to the class. Johnny is a new student who has recently moved from an Indian reservation to a large, metropolitan area. Johnny is shy, self-conscious, uncomfortable, and possibly in a state of cultural shock. The teacher tells the class that Johnny is an Indian and suggests that Johnny bring some Indian artifacts such as rugs, baskets, or Indian jewelry to class.

In the first place, the teacher does not usually introduce other students to the class in this manner. S/he does not say that Jack is Jewish, Ron is black or Bill is German-Irish. Such behavior creates additional pressures on the student including certain expectations by other students. In the second place, not all Indians weave rugs or make baskets. In fact, specific traditional skills, if retained, are to a great extent determined by tribal culture. Even so, a person does not necessarily have to be an Indian to learn a traditional tribal craft, and not all Indians are traditional. Thus, the teacher can very easily make a mistake based on a stereotype of Indians. A good rule to remember is if you don't know why you would be doing what you are planning on doing, then don't do it!

Since most teachers are trained to recognize the needs of their students, the teacher should use his or her training and experience in teaching an Indian child and attempting to meet the child's educational needs. If an Indian child exhibits what appears to be an unusual behavior, the teacher should realize that this could be for a multitude of reasons which may or may not be associated with the fact that the child is an Indian. When discussing teacher-child relationships, it is important to remember the elusive nature of the definition of Indian including the fact that every Indian child is a unique person.

Curriculum

Teachers have traditionally taken the opportunity to develop some attention to Indians when studying about Thanksgiving, the Pilgrims, and turkeys. Children are taught that Indians say "how" and raise their right hand when greeting each other, that Indians have long black braided hair, that very often they wear headbands, that Indians wear beaded vests, and that Indians live in tepees. Children are also taught that Indians make "tom-toms" and sit with their legs crossed and their arms folded. Indians are often treated in the classroom as some mythical group of people such as Amazons or leprechauns. In fact, what children are taught about Indians is often closer to mythology than fact. A number of studies have indicated that textbooks and other instructional materials used in classrooms are not only incorrect and tend to perpetuate false stereotypes of Indians, but are nothing less than libelous.[9,10] Such materials have a tendency to cause some Indian children to develop negative perceptions of themselves.[11] This problem is intensified by the fact that this kind of misinformation also helps shape the attitudes which other children are developing toward Indians. These children, some of whom are likely to be classroom peers of Indian children, can potentially treat their Indian classmates in a condescending manner as reflected by their learned attitude. Inaccurate textbooks, reinforced by teachers and other students, can cause Indians to develop and adopt harmful fallacies about themselves which in turn may be reflected by poor performance in the classroom, high dropout rates, and other behaviors demonstrating a negative attitude toward school.

Recognizing that many teachers will not have feasible access to resources necessary to evaluate the content of material for use in the classroom and also recognizing that most universities are not geared toward preparing teachers to meet the special educational needs of Indian children, it becomes necessary for teachers to take special care in the determination of methods and materials to be used in the classroom. This can be accomplished by being conscientious and attempting to predict what effect certain approaches and materials might have on students. When teaching a unit about Indians, teachers should use books which portray Indians as real people, and which do not neglect to provide information about Indian contributions to the world. Such products as corn, potatoes, tomatoes, beans, peanuts, pumpkins, chocolate, tobacco, American cotton, and rubber are some of the agricultural contributions of Indians.[12] Political, medical, recreational, and other Indian contributions that are often overlooked also should be included in any classroom discussion of Indians. In some cases, Indian parents or Indian educators can be useful as a resource to the teacher. Many large metropolitan areas have "Indian Centers" usually staffed by Indians who are knowledgeable of the Indians in their particular area and who can be a resource in a variety of ways to the teacher, to the Indian child, or the child's family. In addition there are a number of Indian organizations which can provide information potentially useful to teachers. The following are two of these organizations:

1   The American Indian Historical Society
    1451 Masonic Avenue
    San Francisco, Calif. 94117
2   National Indian Education Association
    1115 2nd Avenue South
    Minneapolis, Minn. 55403

Summary

Every Indian child is a unique person with most of the same educational needs as other children. Likewise as with other children, Indian children have many of the same educational non-needs. Both the needs and the non-needs should be viewed from a relative perspective. An approach that would be degrading to a non-Indian student should not be considered appropriate for an Indian student. Teachers and administrators need to increase their awareness of issues regarding Indian students if they are to begin to move toward serving the best educational interests of their students.

Notes

1   Wax, Murray L. *Indian Americans? Unity and diversity.* New Jersey: Prentice-Hall, 1971, 4.
2   United States Congress, Senate Committee on Labor and Public Welfare. *Indian education: A national tragedy—A national challenge, 1969 report by the special subcommittee on Indian education.* 91st Congress, 1st session, 1969. Washington, D.C.: U.S. Government Printing Office, 1969, 9.
3   U.S. Department of Health, Education, and Welfare, Office of Education. *A brief history of the federal responsibility to the American Indian* (based on report by Vine Deloria, Jr.). Washington, D.C.: U.S. Government Printing Office, 1979, 6.
4   Odden, Alan, Funding schools financed by the Bureau of Indian Affairs—1974 to 1977. (an unpublished study conducted under the direction of the Education Commission of the States, August 1978), 10.
5   Ibid, 12.
6   Havighurst, Robert J. *The education of Indian children and youth: Summary report*

and recommendations. *National study of American Indian education. Summary report and recommendations.* Washington, D.C.: U.S. Department of Health, Education and Welfare, Office of Education, 7–8.

7 Ibid, 22–26
8 U.S. Congress. *Indian Education: A National Tragedy* . . .
9 Cahn, Edgar S. and Hearne, David W. (Eds.), *Our brother's keeper: The Indian in white America.* Washington, D.C.: New Community Press, 1972, 35–36.
10 U.S. Congress. *Indian Education: A National Tragedy* . . ., 22–24.
11 Soares, Anthony T. and Soares, Louise M. Self-perceptions of culturally disadvantaged children, *American Educational Research Journal, 6,* January 1969, 31.
12 Cohen, Felix. Americanizing the white man, *Indian Education, 7,* September 1976, 3.

CHAPTER 9

NAVAJO YOUTH AND ANGLO RACISM (1995)

Cultural integrity and resistance

Donna Deyhle

Graduation day was near at Navajo High School.[1] Young Navajo men wearing blue jeans, T-shirts, and Nikes stood in the hall talking to the shop teacher. "You learned lots of skills in my class. Try the job services office in town. They can help you find jobs," he told them. One student disagreed. "I haven't really seen any Navajo people working, like in convenience stores or grocery stores. So, the job outlook is pretty slim. Unless you figure out something else to do. Like shoveling snow or something. But the job outlook isn't really great. For Indians, you know."

Several of the students nodded in agreement. The teacher continued, "There are lots of jobs out there. You just have to look for them." As I passed them, I remembered a Navajo parent's comment: "It's the way it has always been. The Anglos keep the jobs for themselves, they don't hire real Navajo. That's the way it is."[2]

I continued down the hall to the library to interview one of the graduating seniors. She was in the top 10 percent of her class and had turned down two college scholarships to stay home with her family on the reservation. "I've always wanted to do things but it's like I couldn't because of school. That's what has held me back. I feel that." Going to college away from the reservation would cause her to miss opportunities to participate in, for example, traditional Navajo ceremonies. She explained her decision: "If I go to college, I will get a job in the city and then I won't come back very often. When am I going to have time to spend with my grandmother learning about my culture? I feel that kind of resentment towards school. I feel cheated out of my own culture."

This article is about the lives, in and out of school, of young Navajo men and women in a border reservation community.[3] Here, school success and failure are best understood as one part of the larger process of racial conflict, which I have seen fought out in the workplace and in schools in this polarized community. This article will illustrate how Anglos maneuver to acquire the best jobs (some of which are teaching jobs) and how they systematically prepare Navajos for the lowest level jobs. These Navajo people are subject to racial discrimination in the workplace and at school. Young Navajos may respond to the vocational, assimilationist curriculum in their schools by withdrawing or resisting "education." For Navajo students, one of the most life-affirming strategies is to embrace reservation life and traditional Navajo culture. Indeed, the students in my study who were able to maintain Navajo/reservation connections gained a solid place in Navajo society and were also more successful in the Anglo world of school and workplace.

As an anthropologist interested in issues related to American Indian education, I discovered an absence of ethnographic research on American Indian adolescents' lives in and out of school since Murray Wax, Rosalie Wax, and Robert Dumont published *Formal Education in an American Indian Community* in 1964.[4] No such studies existed on the Navajo. In the early 1980s, a doctoral student, who at the time was an elementary school principal in the local school district, invited me to conduct a similar study in his community. District administrators and Navajo parents were concerned with the high dropout rate of Navajo youth, and requested a study that would examine the reasons for the school success and failure of these students. In the fall of 1984, I moved to the community as an ethnographer to start this study. Over the next ten years, I listened to Navajo youth talk about their lives and watched them grow up and have families of their own. I attended their high schools, joining them in over three hundred classes, watching their struggles, successes, and failures. With field notes of observations and casual conversations, audiotapes of meetings and interviews, and ethnohistorical archival data, I documented their lives over the past decade.

Border High School (BHS) is located in a small town of 3,500 people about twenty miles from the Navajo reservation. Almost half of the student population is Navajo. Navajo High School (NHS) is located on the Navajo reservation, and almost 99 percent of the student population is Navajo. Both high schools, as part of one large public school district in one county, are administered from a central district office. They use both state and local standardized curricula.

For this study, I developed a main database that tracked by name all Navajo students who attended BHS and NHS during the school years from 1980–1981 to 1988–1989. This master list contained attendance data, grade point averages, standardized test scores, dropout and graduation rates, community locations, current employment situations, post-high school training, and General Education Diploma (GED) or regular high school graduation diploma received for 1,489 youth. Formal interviews took place with 168 youth who had left school and another one hundred who were either still in school or had successfully graduated. Teachers, administrators, political leaders, parents, and community members also answered my endless questions within the context of formal and casual conversations over the past ten years. During this time, I became involved in extracurricular school activities, including athletic games, plays, dances, and carnivals, and "hanging out" on Main Street and at local fast food restaurants. I attended school and community meetings with Navajo parents. After several years, I was invited to participate in discussions with Navajo parents and to help develop strategies to intervene in school district decisions, such as disciplinary codes, attendance regulations, busing schedules, equal band equipment, and bilingual education. I watched and participated as parents fought for local political control over their children's education and struggled through racist treatment by the Anglo community. These parents were clearly aware of racist practices that occurred, and which I observed, on a daily basis.

I lived for two summers with a Navajo family on the reservation, herding sheep and cooking with children and adolescents. Over the years, as I continually returned to their community, they decided it was worth their time and energy to "educate" me about their cultural norms and values. The oldest daughter, Jan, was a student I had come to know from my initial observations at BHS. She explained her family's decision: "That first year, my Dad said you wouldn't come back. Most people come and study Navajos and leave. He was surprised you came back the next year. And every year you came back. So he said we could trust you."

This family introduced me to others, who in turn introduced me to still other families. My hosts graciously explained their perceptions of life, school, and education. I was invited to attend traditional ceremonies as "part of the family." From the ceremony I describe in this article, I have chosen to reveal only dialogue that is relevant to education in order to avoid disclosing any confidential religious beliefs. I have shared drafts of this article over the years with Navajos in the community who have confirmed my observations and who have helped me represent their experiences and concerns more accurately. They have agreed that this article should be published, in order to share with others both the concerns Navajos have for their children's education and the importance of having their children remain faithful to their Navajo traditions.

Anglos living in the community on the border of the reservation also patiently answered my endless questions in over one hundred informal interviews. Approximately 85 percent of the Anglos are members of the Church of Latter Day Saints (LDS), commonly called Mormons. I attended religious meetings at the Indian Ward (a local unit of the LDS Church), seminary classes (religious training) at the two high schools, and interviewed several religion teachers who were bishops in the LDS Church. My research with Navajo youth was a frequent topic of conversations at picnics, dinners, and socials, where Anglos carefully explained their personal understanding, as well as the LDS Church's views, of American Indians. The Anglo voices in this community do not represent a definitive Mormon perspective, but they do illustrate a cultural view that is influenced, in part, by religious beliefs. In the context of this community, Mormon and non-Mormon Anglo voices are consistent in opposition to their Navajo neighbors.[5] As an outsider to both the Navajo and Anglo communities, I was supported, tolerated, and educated by many local people in my efforts to understand the contemporary lives of Navajo people.[6]

Theoretical framework

Educational anthropologists and sociologists who attempt to explain minority youths' responses to school primarily present either a cultural difference theory or a sociostructural theory.[7] Cultural difference theorists such as Cummins argue that cultural conflicts and other problems develop in minority classrooms because of the differences between students' home and school cultures.[8] Sociostructural theorists such as Ogbu argue that the explanations for minority school failure lie outside of the school itself, specifically in the racial stratification of U.S. society and the economy.[9] Both of these positions provide a useful perspective and have contributed to our understanding of cultural conflict. In particular, I find Ogbu's[10] structural analysis of castelike or involuntary minorities and the job ceiling they face and Cummins's analysis of cultural differences and cultural integrity useful in understanding the situation faced by these Navajo youth.[11]

My research represents a more traditional anthropological approach. I am not attempting to create a general theory of castelike minorities, but rather to represent the specific Navajo experience. In so doing, I take a different position than Ogbu. This ethnographic study speaks to some general claims made by Ogbu, but it does not replace his theory. Specifically, I speak about "racial warfare" to capture two points on which my interpretation and Ogbu's theory diverge: First, Navajos and Anglos conflict economically, politically, and culturally in both the schools and workplace. While Ogbu views the schools as a relatively neutral terrain, I portray the ways in which teachers and students play out this racial conflict. Second, Navajos have substantive ethical disagreements with the Anglo values manifested in the schools and the greater economy. The concept of racial warfare is intended to represent the integrity of Navajo culture and to avoid reducing this culture to a reinterpretation of traditional values in reaction to denial of opportunity in the Anglo-dominated schools and businesses, as I believe Ogbu does.

Young Navajo men and women face a racially polarized landscape, in which historically defined racial conflicts between Navajos and Anglos continue to engulf their lives. As a result, political and economic power remains in the hands of local Anglos who maintain a limited "place" for Navajos. This discrimination is basic to Navajos' attitudes towards schools. As Ogbu has pointed out, any comprehensive understanding of minority students' responses to school must include the power and status relations between minority and majority groups, as well as the variability among different minority groups.

According to Ogbu, the main factor differentiating the more successful from the less successful minorities appears to be the nature of the history of subordination and exploitation of the minorities, and the nature of the minorities' own instrumental and expressive responses to their treatment. In Ogbu's analysis, immigrant groups who came to this county more or less voluntarily arrived with an intact culture developed *before* contact with the dominant group. They viewed schooling as a means for increased opportunity and economic mobility, not as a threat to their cultural identity. In contrast, castelike minorities, which include African Americans, Mexican Americans, and American Indians, have been historically positioned as involuntary subordinates through slavery, conquest, or colonization. Ogbu argues that castelike minorities face schooling with a set of secondary cultural characteristics—a reinterpretation of traditional culture that is developed *after* contact with the dominant White group—to help them cope with the social, economic, political, and psychological history of rejection by the dominant group and its institutions. Schools, as sites of conflict with the dominant group, are seen as a threat to their cultural identity. These castelike minorities have developed oppositional cultural responses to schooling as they reject a system that has rejected them. Ogbu sees this resistance, which takes the form of truancy, lack of serious effort in and negative attitudes toward school, refusal to do classwork or assignments, and delinquency, as an adaptation to their lower social and occupational positions, which do not require high educational qualifications. This, in turn, has been counterproductive to school success. Specifically, pressure from the minority community not to "act White," coupled with feelings that they will not get jobs anyway, further decreases students' school efforts because they struggle with the fear of being estranged from their community if they are successful. The dominant group maintains this "adaptation" by providing inferior education and by channeling the students to inferior jobs after they finish high school.

Although Ogbu's general framework, which combines structural barriers and culturally based reactions, generally "fits" the Navajo situation, there are also striking differences between Navajos and other "castelike" minorities. Navajos have not played the same role in the national economy as other castelike minorities. African Americans, for example, have historically played a central role in the White-dominated economy. Navajos, in contrast, have never been an essential part of the White-dominated economy, except in regard to land procurement. Navajos accurately perceive that they are shut out of the job market, and that their school success is not linked to their economic prosperity.

Whereas Ogbu views the cultures of castelike minorities as a reaction to the dominant White group, I believe that Navajo practices and culture represent a distinct and independent tradition. Navajos do occupy a castelike, subordinate position in the larger social context. However, only a small part of Navajo cultural characteristics can appropriately be called "secondary" or "oppositional." Navajos face and resist the domination of their Anglo neighbors from an intact cultural base that was not developed in reaction to Anglo subordination. An oppositional description of Navajo culture ignores the integrity of Navajo culture and neglects the substantive value disagreements between Navajos and Anglos.

Navajo success is closely tied to family and reservation economic and cultural networks. It is these traditional values that parents seek to pass on to their children. For example, traditional Anglo notions of "success"—school credentials, individual careers, and individual economic prosperity—do not reflect those of the Navajo. The successful Navajo is judged on intact extended familial relations, where individual jobs and educational success are used to enhance the family and the community and aggressive individualism is suppressed for the cooperation of the group. These Navajo values—the communal nature of success and the primacy of the family—exist in well-developed institutional structures on the reservation independent of Anglo culture, and during social and economic crises, help secure the Navajos' identity as a people.

These cultural characteristics in themselves do not necessarily result in school failure, although they contribute to the tension and misunderstanding between Navajos and Anglos. Youth who have little identity as Navajos and who are not accepted by Anglos because they are not White face the greatest risk of school failure and unemployment. To understand this position more fully, it is necessary to turn to Cummins, who argues that the strength of one's cultural identity is a vital factor in the expressive responses to the schooling experience. Cummins states that "widespread school failure does not occur in minority groups that are positively oriented towards both their own and the dominant culture, that do not perceive themselves as inferior to the dominant group, and that are not alienated from their own cultural values."[12] This position suggests that Navajo youth who are better integrated into their home culture will be more successful students, regardless of the structural barriers they face. In other words, the more Navajo students resist assimilation while simultaneously maintaining their culture, the more successful they are in school.

In this article, I draw upon three events—a racial fight, a meeting of the Native American Church, and a high school career day—to portray the race struggle between Navajos and Anglos and the way that struggle manifests itself in schools. My position captures, but also moves beyond, central insights from both cultural difference theory and structural theory. Like cultural difference theorists, I believe that differences in culture play a role in the divisions between Anglo teachers and Navajo students. Anglos do not understand Navajo values, and thus manufacture deficit explanations to account for behavior they assume is unguided by specific beliefs. When Navajo students act on their beliefs, they act in contrast to existing institutional values.

Furthermore, like Ogbu, I believe that these cultural differences become barriers because of the power relations involved. However, Ogbu implies that castelike minority students withdraw from academic effort not only because of the power relations in schools, but also because of the job ceiling and their own communities' social realities or folk theories that undermine the importance of school success. As a result, he takes the accommodationist position that castelike minorities would do better to adopt the strategies of immigrant groups, accept the school's regime, and succeed by its standards. Ogbu does not see culture as a terrain of conflict, nor does he perceive the significance of race as contributing to racial warfare, as I do; rather, he believes it is possible for the culture of the student to be left "safely" at home so that his or her cultural identity can be disconnected from what occurs in school.

This is not possible for Navajo youth. My data supports Navajo students' perception that Anglos discriminate against them and that they have no reason to believe that their cooperation with the educational regime would bring advantages in either schools or in the workplace. The issue for Navajo students is not that doing well in school is to "act White," but that playing by the rules of the classroom represents a "stacked deck." Educational compliance, or succeeding in the *kind* of schooling available to them, does not result in economic and social equality in the Anglo-dominated community. I argue, in this article, that the Navajos' experiences of racial and cultural warfare must be placed at the center of an explanatory model of their education and work experiences.

The fight: racial conflict

Racial polarization is a fact of life in this border community. In 1989, a fight broke out between a Navajo and an Anglo student at BHS. Claiming his younger cousin had been verbally and physically assaulted, a Navajo junior struck an Anglo student across the face in the school hallway during lunch. Navajo and Anglo students quickly gathered at the scene as the principal and the football coach pulled the boys apart. Police were called to the school; the Anglo student was released to his parents, while the Navajo student was taken to jail. The Navajo community demanded a meeting with school officials to discuss the incident, which more than seventy-five Navajo parents attended. The superintendent, the two high school principals, and several teachers also attended, along with the school district lawyer, the DNA lawyer, the local sheriff, and myself.[13] The tension felt in the meeting was a reflection of the larger battles lived out between Navajos and Anglos in the community each day.

The president of the parent association, who served as the meeting translator, spoke first in Navajo and then in English. His son-in-law was the Navajo youth involved in the incident:

> It kinda hurts to hear this information. The parents hurt over this. The parents have come to me with the problem. It hurts the parents and the students. We have to get over this problem. When kids come home and say they have been thrown around, they can't concentrate on their work. It hurts. Word gets around that the Indians are having an uprising. No. It is not true. We want our kids to go to school and do well. They are far behind. We want them to do well in academics. I hope we can talk about this. It gets worse every time we talk. I hear the police came into school and took him away. This is not fair, to knock around youth. If this is happening in school, I want to know about it.

As he sat down, the principal from the high school where the fight occurred stood up. He glanced at notes on a yellow pad, cleared his throat, and spoke:

> Let me express very strongly that there are a lot of things that cannot occur in

a school for students to succeed. One thing is that they must feel safe. One of our goals is that it be a safe place. A week ago, following a school dance, a group of Anglos and Navajos got into a fight. They have a history of not getting along. The following week there was a fight in school, only one blow. I didn't talk to the Anglo boy because the police did.

The Navajo student accused of starting the fight interrupted the principal. "You have a problem. The Anglo started it. He was picking on a little kid and I told him to stop. Then he fought me."

The vice principal shook his head in disagreement. Several Navajo students shouted that Anglo students were always picking on and making fun of Navajos.

The principal, still standing, responded, "This is the first time I have heard this. I didn't know the Indian students were being picked on."

Sharon, a Navajo senior who witnessed the fight, stood and faced the principal. "We are never asked. I was not asked. I never get anything from Anglos." Her mother asked, "Why is it so hard for the kids to go to you with their problems?" Sharon persisted in questioning the principal. "I don't like the way Whites treat Indians. Why do you believe what the Anglo students say only? It's one side in this case. Can you guarantee that they won't continue?" The Navajo crowd clapped.

The principal responded, "We can talk about it. No, I can't guarantee. That's what you have to do as an individual. You have to take it." Murmurs of discontent echoed throughout the room. The principal continued, "Rumors of a fight were all around the school on Thursday, so I called in the police. There was no fight that day. Because of the tension we invited the police in to investigate. On Friday morning there was a fight. Both the students were taken in and charged."

The DNA lawyer stood and asked the principal, "Is it true that the Anglo student was not charged and the Navajo student was?" The principal uttered softly, "Yes." Again the crowd muttered their disapproval.

"That cop tried to get me to fight him," shouted the Navajo youth involved in the fight. "He said, 'Come and fight me.' They told me not to step a foot in the school. Not to ever come back."

After a pause for a translation into Navajo, the principal urged parents to come to him with their problems. "If you feel your kids have been made fun of, you should come up to the school. You must come up to the school. We will do everything we can to help. If I can't help, you can go to the superintendent and say, 'That crazy principal can't help us.' That is the avenue we have in the district. We will do everything to help." At this point the superintendent stood and moved to the front of the room to stand by the principal:

I want to say two things. We expect a lot of our principals, but not to be policemen. We don't expect them to do that. We have a good relationship with the police, so we turn problems over to the police. And then the school gives up jurisdiction. The world is a great place. I hope that the students we turn out have great opportunities. Our schools are good schools, but not perfect.

An elderly Navajo woman brought the discussion back to the issue of discrimination. "Why is it so hard for us to understand that we have this problem? It has been this way for years. I think the problem is that we have the police treating people differently. So you see, the policeman is the problem." A mother added, "I used to go to that high school. I bear the tragedy with the students now. The higher I went, the greater pressure I got. So I left and went to another high school to graduate." An elderly medicine man spoke last:

> We are just telling stories about each other now. Who was in the incident should be up front talking. When my kids were in school it was the same. And we are still trying to solve this problem. These kids who were talking tonight were in elementary school when my kids had this problem in high school. And I think the kids who are in elementary school now will also have this problem. We need to talk about it. Each time we talk about it the problem continues.

The meeting ended shortly before midnight. The school officials quickly left the building. Many of the Navajo parents and children continued to talk in small groups. Although charges against the youth had been dropped, he was not allowed to return to school. "They told me I was eighteen so I could not go to high school any more. I was told to go to adult education to finish."

As I sat with his family, his mother-in-law bitterly complained she should have said the following to the vice-principal, with whom she had gone to school twenty years before: "You know what it is like for the high school kids. You used to do the same things the kids are doing now against Indians. You remember when you put the pins in my seat? All the things that you used to do to Indians, it is still going on here and now. You did it, and now your kids are doing it."

I left with Sharon, the senior who spoke during the meeting, and her mother. We went to my house and continued talking about the incident. Sharon spoke of her own experiences in the racially mixed school. "They always give us trouble. Like there is this one group of guys. I told one, 'Shut up you pale face, or you red neck!' When they are rude to me I call them everything I know. They think Indians stink. I tell them, if you don't like Indians, why did you move here!"

Important public officials, like those who attended the meeting, are Anglos, and their ability to ignore Navajo concerns speaks to the security of their power base. All public institutions in the county are controlled by Anglos and by members of the Mormon Church.[14] The school superintendent, all four high school principals, four out of five elementary school principals, and the administration of the local community college are all LDS members. Over half of the county's population is Navajo, but Navajos account for only 15 percent of the teaching staff, and more than half of those have converted to Mormonism. The few Navajos in power have been sponsored for upward mobility since they joined the LDS church.[15] Locally, these converted Navajos are described by Anglos as "responsible," "good," and the "right kind" of Navajo. Anglo-controlled political and economic networks open slightly for these few individuals. Even for Navajos who hold middle-class jobs, racial stratification limits their place in the community. Navajos and Anglos do not socialize, and they pass each other without acknowledgment in stores, banks, and restaurants. As the meeting revealed, even when Navajos speak they are seldom heard, contributing to a strong sense of disempowerment.

Over the last one hundred years, the Anglo population has expanded and prospered.[16] The Navajo population has also expanded, now comprising 54 percent of the country's population, but they have not prospered. Their life conditions speak loudly of discrimination. A colonized form of government exists in the county where the Anglo population benefits disproportionately from Navajo resources: 60 percent of the county's economic resources comes from the reservation, but only 40 percent is returned in goods and services. Almost 50 percent of the Navajo in the county live without running water or utilities. Their per capita income is $3,572, compared to $11,029 for Anglos. Almost 60 percent of Navajo families have incomes below the poverty level, compared to less than 10 percent of Anglo families. Nearly 90 percent of those in the county on public assistance are American Indian—Navajos or Utes. The unemployment rate of Indians is over 40 percent, four times the unemployment rate for Anglos. Navajo youth and their families are well aware of this economic marginalization. Shoveling snow, envisioned as a job possibility by a young Navajo student at the beginning of this article, speaks powerfully of the job ceiling in this arid, high desert community.

Racial conflict in the schools

Racism and cultural beliefs, particularly the issues of assimilation and resistance, are at the heart of the interactions between Navajos and Anglos. The Anglo perspective is informed by a century-old model of assimilation that views Navajo culture and language as a problem to be eradicated. During this period, the Navajo have resisted assimilation and successfully struggled to maintain a Navajo way of life. Faced with continued colonization and discrimination, few Navajos remain silent.

The antagonisms apparent at the meeting also produce tensions in schools. Discrimination takes different forms between teachers and students in classes and in the hallways. Some racism is overt: Anglo students and teachers speak openly about disliking Navajos. Other interactions are more subtle, disguising racism in ostensibly well-intentioned actions, such as teachers lowering their academic expectations to "accommodate" the culture of their Navajo students. Some paternalistic racism exists, such as when teachers assume Navajos are "childlike" and that educators know what is best for "their Navajos." Still other racism is based on superficial stereotypes of Navajo culture, which assume that because Navajo families do not share middle-class Anglo values they hinder their children's success in schools. This section depicts the cultural and racial warfare that comes as a result of dismissing Navajos as being culturally inferior.

Daily encounters with Anglo peers and teachers demonstrate the power of the racial and cultural struggle occurring in schools. Shortly after the meeting, Sharon spoke of her embarrassment and the anger she had towards the science teacher:

> He is prejudiced. He talks about Navajos and welfare. "You all listen, you aren't going to be on welfare like all the other Navajos." He shouldn't talk like that! And then the White students say things like that to us. Like all Navajo are on welfare. I'm not like that. We work for what we have. He shouldn't say things like that. It makes us feel bad.

Some youth use subtle counterattacks when put down by their non-Indian peers. One day in class, two Anglo students teased a young Navajo studying to be a medicine man about his hair bun, lice, and the length of his hair: "Hey, how long did it take you to grow that?" The Navajo boy replied with a soft smile, "Ten minutes." Other confrontations are not so subtle. One young woman, whose last name was Cantsee, explained why she was no longer in math class: "When I came into class late, that teacher said, 'Oh, here is another Indian who can't see how to get to class.' I told him to go to hell and left class."

Teachers' lack of experience in the Navajo community and stereotyping of

Navajos results in both the distortion and the dismissal of Navajo culture. During an English class I attended, a teacher was discussing the romantic and realist periods in literature:

> Have you ever dreamed about something that you can't get? That is romanticism, when you dreamed that everything would work out. But then there is the realism period. Some people during this time in your literature text, they lived together six to a room with fleas and lice and everything. They had dreams but they weren't coming true. I hope all of you have bigger dreams than that.

A Navajo student whispered to a friend, "It sounds like he is describing a *hogan* [the traditional Navajo one-room round home]!" In a reading class I observed, the teacher said, "We are studying tall tales. This is something that cannot be true. Like Pecos Bill. They said he lived with the coyotes. You see, it can't be true." Two Navajo students look at each other and in unison said, "But us Navajo, we live on the reservation with the coyotes." The teacher replied, "Well, I don't know anything about that. Let's talk about parables now."

Although some teachers' actions may be seen as "innocent" or "ignorant," others clearly reveal a hostile edge. Some teachers do know that coyotes are a fact of life on the reservation and still dismiss and mock students' lives. For example, during Sharon's senior year, her career education teacher lectured the class on the importance of filling out job applications. "You must put your address. When you are born, you are born into a community. You are not isolated. You are part of a community at birth. So you have an address." To which a student replied, "But I was born waaaaaaay out on the reservation! Not in a community." "I don't care if you were born out there with the coyotes. You have an address," argued the teacher. Students hooted, groaned, and laughed as several shouted, "Yessss, lady!" to which the teacher shouted back, "You sound like you are all on peyote. Let's go to the occupations quiz in your books."

Just as all Navajo youth are not dropouts, all Anglo teachers are not racist. Some teachers care deeply about their Navajo students. However, continued resistance to their educational efforts frustrates even the best teachers. I shared the frustration of Sharon's English teacher, who urged her Navajo students to perform in class: "You guys all speak two languages. Research shows that bilinguals are twice as smart. Language is not your problem. It's your attitude. You have given up because Whites intimidate you. Don't you want to be a top student?" "No!" the class responded loudly, "we don't care." This teacher, who had expressed a great deal of concern and empathy for her Navajo students three years earlier, recently told me, "You are not going to like what I say about Indians now. I am a racist! I'm not kidding. Working with these Indian kids makes you a racist. They just sit here and do nothing." Throughout the district, at both elementary and high school levels, administrators and teachers believe Navajo students have difficulties in school because of their language and culture.

Equally damaging to Navajo students' school experiences are teachers who refuse to acknowledge the racial discrimination in the community. By reducing racial conflict to "others' problems" or a thing of the past, the local power struggle is kept out of the classroom. During the last week of studying *To Kill a Mockingbird* in a twelfth-grade English class, the teacher focused on racial conflict between Whites and Blacks, and summarized the discussion of the book by saying:

It used to be that Whites treated Blacks badly. Remember, this is racial discrimination, when one group treats another badly just because of the color of their skin, and it is against the law. It was a sad part of history and I'm glad it doesn't happen any more.

A Navajo student turned to me and said, "But it happens to us! Why didn't he say that? What about what happens to us?"

Navajo student's attempts to make racial discrimination visible within the school have been silenced by the Anglo students and school administrators. Shortly after the fight and community meeting, Sharon's journalism class called a "press conference" to discuss Navajo education and racial prejudice for an article in the school paper. The journalism teacher, who was also the faculty advisor for the school paper, suggested the conflict between Navajo and Anglo students was an important topic to be covered by the newspaper. The students, fourteen Anglos and two Navajos, voted to invite Navajo parents, the high school principal, the Indian advisor, and myself to be interviewed. We had all attended the community meeting following the fight. At the press conference, an Anglo student who was new to the district spoke first:

When I came I didn't know about Indians. The kids here tried to scare me, told me about Indian witches and evil spirits. It made me afraid of Indians, that they were weird or gross and they were out to scalp Whites!

The principal suggested that when students hear discriminatory comments they should correct them. Another Anglo student replied, "What do we do when teachers say bad things about Indians? Like the AP [advanced placement] history teacher. We don't have any Indians in there, and he says really awful things about Indians." The principal shook his head, "I'm sure most teachers don't do that. If they do you kids can tell us." He continued, "All students, Anglo and Navajo, are just the same. I don't see the difference. Kids are just kids. The fight between the Anglo and Navajo boy was an isolated incident. We have taken care of the problem." A Navajo parent, who had been silent, then stood and said:

I hear that there was this Anglo kid who was caught stealing a little radio. But then the teacher found out the boy was from an important family here, so the teacher did nothing to the boy. So, you see, we still have this problem.

The bell rang. The press conference was concluded. The students, concerned that discussions of racial prejudice would both demoralize Navajo students and embarrass Anglo students, decided not to print the story.

Racial attitudes are also evident in teachers' and administrators' expectations of Navajo students. These attitudes include assumptions about the "academic place" for Navajos. The sixth-graders from an elementary school feeding into Border High School all scored above the national norm in mathematics on the Stanford Achievement Test. Yet upon entering high school, Navajo children were systematically placed in the lowest level mathematics class. When asked about the placement the principal explained, "I didn't look at the scores, and elementary grades are always inflated. Our Navajo students always do better in the basic classes." These attitudes about race and culture place a ceiling on learners; in a school-administered survey, 85 percent of the teachers in one school indicated that Navajo students had learned "almost all they can learn." Standardized test scores showed an average seventh percentile for the school, the lowest in the state, which the principal explained, saying, "Our district level scores are low and dropout rate high because we have Navajo students."

Racism surfaces not only in ill-intentioned treatment of Navajo students, but also when well-intentioned educators make demeaning assumptions about them, representing a cultural mismatch. Anglos frequently distort Navajo values and view them as inadequate compared to their own cultural values. For example, Navajos are viewed as present oriented and practical minded. "I've never met a Navajo that planned far in the future, to like go to college. It's more [about] what to do tomorrow and the day after," said an Anglo school counselor. Another explained, "The Navajo are very practical minded. They think, 'What value is it to me in my everyday life?' A lot of abstract ideas in education just don't mean anything." Anglo stereotypes of Navajos also include the perception that they work well with their hands. A career education teacher said, "Well, I mean, they are good in spatial things. Working hands-on. They don't learn theoretically. You can talk until you are blue in the face. It's much better if there is practical hands-on application." Anglos intertwine such "descriptions" of Navajo culture with the belief that the Navajo family does not teach children school-appropriate values. A counselor explained:

> We [Anglos] were brought up every day with the question, "What are you going to be when you grow up?" And that is something that the Navajo parents never ask. And then I bring them in the counseling office and I ask, "What are you going to be when you finish high school?" That is the first time they have even heard the question. It's just not done at home. And it's my values. The importance of an education and a job. They don't think to the future.

Embedded in this cultural distortion of Navajo values is the assumption that the closeness of Navajo family ties (i.e., "cultural pressure") is problematic for "progress" and that it "causes" school failure. One of the teachers explained it graphically with a story about lobsters:

> You know what they say about lobsters? You can put them in water this high [indicating a depth of a few inches] and they won't get out. As soon as one tries to climb out the others pull him back in. [Laughter] That's what it is like with the Indians. As soon as one of their kind tries to better himself, the others pull him back in.

The owner of a local pottery factory, who employs work-study students from the high school, also saw the problem not as a lack of individual skills, but of the demands of family responsibilities:

> Many of them have been through all sorts of training programs. Take Tom. He is a graduate from technical school. A welder. But he came back here and is working here painting pottery. . . . They come back here to live with their families. There is a good and a bad side to that. Over there on the reservation they are getting strangled. It really strangles them over there with families. They can't make it on their own and their families strangle them with responsibilities.

It is within this racially divided community that Navajo youth must navigate the school system. Over the past ten years, in a district with 48 percent Navajos, one out of every three Navajo students left school before graduation; almost 80 percent of the district's dropouts are Navajos.[17] During a district-wide meeting, administrators identified the following as the causes of these youths' school failure: lack of self-esteem; inadequate homes; inadequate preparation for school; lack of parenting skills; poor communication between home and school; poor student attendance; limited vocabulary and language development; limited cultural enrichment opportunities; too academic a curriculum; poor attitude and motivation; and fetal alcohol syndrome. All of these place the blame on deficits of the students and their families. In contrast, only three causes listed found fault with the schools: questionable teacher support, lack of counseling, and non-relevant curriculum.

Navajo students paint a different picture. Acknowledging racism (i.e., citing it as one of the central reasons they leave school), over half of the 168 students I interviewed who had left school said simply, "I was not wanted in school." Over 40 percent of those who left school saw the curriculum as having little relevance for their lives. Although they acknowledge home difficulties, over half of the Navajo youth who left school complained of problems with administrators and uncaring teachers who would not help them with their work.

Assimilation: "Navajoness" as the problem

Navajos became wards of the federal government in 1868. In accordance with treaty provisions signed at that time, the federal government was to provide schooling for all Navajos. Ever since, schooling has been used by policymakers and educators at the district and federal levels as a vehicle for cultural assimilation. Because public officials considered Navajo culture and language problematic and superfluous, education became a way to eliminate the "Indian problem."

In 1976, the district lost a suit filed by Navajo parents. As a result of the court's decision, the district was required to build two high schools on the reservation and to develop a bilingual and bicultural program for all grades. Construction of the high schools took eight years. The bilingual and bicultural program sat unused, gathering dust in the district's materials center for fifteen years. In 1991, after an investigation by the Office for Civil Rights in the Department of Education, the district was again found out of compliance with federal requirements concerning English as a Second Language (ESL).[18]

The district then created a new bilingual plan, which the newly appointed director of bilingual education presented at a parent meeting at the beginning of the 1993 school year. The district's latest plan calls for a total immersion of Navajo students in the English language to eradicate the Navajo language "problem." It requires that all Navajo students be tested for English-language proficiency, after which, the proposal states, "All Limited English Proficient (LEP) (ESL) [the two terms are used interchangeably] students are placed in the regular classroom with fluent English proficient students to insure optimal modeling of language." This plan will operate even in schools with a 99 percent Navajo population. No special ESL classes will be provided for students who are Navajo-language dominant.

Navajo parents expressed disbelief that the new program would be implemented, and questioned whether Navajo would actually be used for instruction in their children's classrooms. The parents had reason to be concerned. The district had agreed to such a program seventeen years earlier and it still did not exist. The bilingual project director responded, "Trust us. We are now sincere."

The Office for Civil Rights rejected the most recent plan, issuing a citation of non-compliance to the district and turning the investigation over to the Education Litigation Division of the Justice Department. During the summer of 1994, U.S. Attorney General Janet Reno authorized the Justice Department to intervene in this case as "party-plaintiff." Based on a preliminary investigation, the Justice Department believes the school district has discriminated against American Indian students, violating federal law and the Fourteenth Amendment, by failing to adopt and implement an alternative language program for Limited English Proficient students. The district is accused of denying American Indian students the same educational opportunities and services, such as equal access to certain academic programs, provided to Anglo students, and of denying qualified American Indians employment opportunities equal to those provided to Anglos.

Throughout the district (at both Navajo and Border High Schools), administrators and teachers believe Navajo students have difficulties in school because of their language and culture. This explains, in part, why the district refuses to implement a bilingual program that uses Navajo as a language of instruction. "These kids we get are learning disabled with their reading. Because they speak Navajo, you know." The ESL teacher explained, "The Indian students need to learn English and basic skills to survive in the Anglo world. That bilingual and bicultural stuff is not important for them. The jobs are off the reservation, so they need to learn how to work in the Anglo world." Another teacher, in a letter to the editor of the local newspaper, argued, "Bilingual education will become the greatest obstacle a Navajo student has to overcome and an impediment to the education of all other students."

English language difficulties are acknowledged by Navajo parents; over a two-year period, the topic was brought up at eighteen parent meetings. "Our kids speak Navajo, they need more of those ESL classes to help them learn." But at the same time, they speak of the importance of Navajo culture. "Our kids learn White history. When are you going to have Navajo language and culture, too?" At each meeting, school administrators and teachers assured the parents that their children were getting the help they need to learn English, and that Navajo language and culture were part of the school's curriculum. Over the past ten years of my fieldwork, only four semester-long classes were offered in Navajo language, history, or culture. All ESL classes have been eliminated in the high schools and replaced with general reading classes, even though few teachers in the district are certified in reading education.

This model of assimilation, which views native culture and language as a barrier to be overcome, has always framed educational policy in schools for American Indians.[19] Various programs have attempted to eliminate native cultures, measuring success in part by how many students do not return to their homes and families on the reservation. In the late 1890s, the superintendent of the Carlisle Indian School, the first boarding school for American Indian students, informed a congressional committee that between 25 percent and 30 percent of their students found a job and earned a livelihood away from their home; the remainder returned to the reservation. Even a year or two at school, he said, gave the youth a new life, and only a small percentage go "back to the blanket" and "do nothing."[20]

While the structure has changed somewhat, this educational practice has changed very little in the past one hundred years. In 1990, Sharon's counselor explained, "Most of the kids want to stay right here. On the reservation. It's kinda like, we say, they have 'gone back to the blanket.' They will sit in their *hogan* and do nothing." Counselors cannot comprehend that a youth does not want to leave the reservation. Their typical comments include: "He said he wanted to be a medicine man![21] He can't really mean it. His card [counselor's student aspiration list] says the military," and "It's real progress when they want to get off the reservation. There is nothing for them to do out there." Today, as throughout history, American Indians who resist assimilation by maintaining their culture and remaining on the reservation are described as failures. Such was the case with Sharon. Upon her return to the reservation after college in 1992, I was told by her counselor, "It's too bad. She didn't make it away from here. And I had so much hope for her succeeding." The college graduate is viewed positively, but those who "come home" are labeled "failures" by the Anglo community.

Racial beliefs about Navajos, embedded in a model of assimilation, guide Anglos' "understandings" of how to teach or interact with Navajos. For Anglos, these assimilationist beliefs are generally used to frame either the need to "change" Navajos to fit into the outside world or to adjust educational and economic opportunities downward to be "appropriate" for Navajo culture. Either way, Navajo culture is seen as undesirable. Teachers and administrators believe students fail because of their impoverished homes, culture, and language. Counselors assume Navajo students are not bound for college, and that they therefore should receive practical, vocation-oriented instruction; additionally, they should be encouraged to leave their families for jobs off the reservation. The educational assimilation policies described in this section are part of the larger race war in the community. Within this context, the school curriculum is not "neutral." Navajo youth who resist school are in fact resisting the district's educational goal of taking the "Navajoness" out of their Navajo students.

As Cummins points out, virtually all the evidence indicates that, at the very least, incorporating minority students' culture and language into the school curriculum does not impede academic progress. He argues that Anglos' resistance to recognize and incorporate the minority group's language and culture into school programs represents a resistance to confer status and power (with jobs, for example) on the minority group.[22]

From this angle, Navajo culture is considered *the* reason for academic failure. To accept Navajo culture and language would be to confer equal status, which is unacceptable to the Anglo community. Navajo culture and students' lives are effectively silenced by the surrounding Anglo community. Navajo language and traditions are absent from the school curriculum. Teachers' ignorance of Navajo student's lives results in the dismissal of the credibility of Navajo life. Racial conflict is silenced, either on the premise that it does not exist or that to acknowledge racism is to "cause problems." This "silencing" is a clear denial of the value of the Navajo people's way of life.

Navajoness and school success

The Anglo community views assimilation as a necessary path to school success. In this view, the less "Indian" one is, the more academically "successful" one will become. Anglos perceive living in town, off the reservation, to be a socially progressive, economically advantageous move for Navajos. In fact, the opposite is true. The more academically successful Navajo students are more likely to be those who are firmly rooted in their Navajo community. This is consistent with

Cummins's position that school failure is *less* likely for minority youth who are not alienated from their own cultural values and who do not perceive themselves as inferior to the dominant group. Failure rates are *more* likely for youth who feel disenfranchised from their culture and at the same time experience racial conflict. Rather than viewing the Navajo culture as a barrier, as does an assimilation model, "culturally intact" youth are, in fact, more successful students.

Located on the Navajo reservation, Navajo High School (NHS) is more "successful" than Border High School in retaining and graduating Navajo students. The dropout rate from this school, 28 percent, is slightly less than the national average.[23] These students come from some of the most traditional parts of the reservation. Navajo is the dominant language in most of the homes, and 90 percent of them qualify for subsidized school meals. NHS has four certified Navajo teachers, a group of Anglo teachers with an average of five years' experience, and a school curriculum that is identical to other schools in the district. The differences in Navajo students' performance between BHS and NHS indicate the importance not only of the student's cultural identity, but also of the sympathetic connection between the community and its school. Where there are fewer Anglo students and more Navajo teachers, racial conflict is minimal and youth move through their school careers in a more secure and supportive community context. Nevertheless, even NHS students experience "well-intentioned" racism from some teachers and a vocationalized curriculum.

This pattern—reservation youth succeeding academically more than Navajo town youth—is also repeated *within* the Navajo student population at Border High School (BHS). Almost half the Navajos who attended BHS are bused to school from the reservation. Among Navajos living in town, only 55 percent graduate from BHS, whereas almost 70 percent of the Navajo students living on the reservation graduate from Border High School.[24] In other words, Navajo students who live in town and attend BHS are less successful than those who live on the reservation and attend NHS. Also, within the BHS Navajo population, the Navajos that are bused from the reservation do better than those who live in town. The most successful students, like Sharon, are from one of the most traditional areas of the reservation. In contrast, those who are not academically successful are both estranged from the reservation community and bitterly resent the racially polarized school context they face daily.

Many of the Navajo BHS students who live in town take a confrontational stance toward school: many of their teachers express fear and discomfort with them in their classrooms. Over three-fourths of the school's disciplinary actions involve these Navajo youth. These students' resistance is clear: the schools don't want them and they don't want the schools. The racial conflict in this school is highly charged, with each side blaming the other for the problem.

Faced with a school and community that refuse to acknowledge their "Navajoness" positively, and coming from homes that transmit little of "traditional" Navajo life, these youth clearly are living on a sociocultural border, with little hope of succeeding in either cultural context. Only 15 percent are employed, and fewer than 10 percent of those who leave school attempt educational training later on.

Navajo youth respond in a variety of ways to the racial treatment they experience. Many leave school, while others simply fade into the background of their classrooms. Most report suffering racial discrimination. Sharon's experiences mirror those of many high school graduates. Although Sharon felt unwanted in school, she persisted, and graduated in 1991. Of her six elementary school girl-friends, Sharon was the only one to finish school. Her persistence was framed by her experience growing up on the reservation. Sharon's ability to speak at the meeting and her school success reflect her own sense of confidence—a confidence supported by traditional influences. Her early years were spent with her grandparents in a *hogan* on the reservation. As she explains:

> After I was born my mom was working. My grandma and grandpa, they were the ones that raised me until I started going to school. He was a traditional, a medicine man, so he was strict with us. And he made us go to school all the time. I am thankful to him. His influence is all around me now. . . . I'm modern. I guess I'm kind of old-fashioned, too. I keep all those traditions. I really respect them. I really respect those old people. Like they tell me not to do something. I listen to them. I go to all kinds of ceremonies. I'm proud to be a Navajo.

Sharon places her traditional beliefs alongside those of the dominant culture and honors both. Her grandfather's advice supports her decision. "He told me that it was okay for me to go to both. He said, 'take what was good from both and just make it your life.' So that's what I did. If some old medicine man or somebody told me I needed some kind of ceremony, I'd do it. I'd do it both ways. I'd go for the blessing, too."

Sharon was an academically successful high school and college student. She completed her freshman year at the state university with a 2.8 grade point average, and then decided to return home. This choice securely embedded Sharon within her family and the Navajo community. She reflects on her decision:

> I used to think those people that go to college never come back. They always promise to come back to the reservation, but they never do. And now I understand why, because all the jobs are up there [in the city] and I mean, if I major in physical therapy, there is nothing I can do with that down here at home. I thought I could do it without Indians. I thought I could do it by myself, but it does make a difference. It makes me feel more at home. It is good to see some Indian people once in awhile. It really motivates me.

Sharon now lives with her mother on the reservation. She took community college classes for one year to certify as an Licensed Practical Nurse, but left after deciding the classes were boring. "You see, they make the classes easy because most of the students were Navajo. It was too easy and I got tired of it." She occasionally works as a medic on the county's ambulance. With a characteristically broad smile, she said:

> Maybe I'll go back [to the university] someday. I sometimes feel sucked in here. Like I'm stuck here. It's so hard to get out. But it feels good to be at my home with Navajo people, even though those Whites sometimes give us trouble. [Reflecting back on the racial fight and community meeting, she said little had changed.] . . . My brother, he is still at that school. And he is fighting back. You just have to keep doing it. Otherwise they just treat you like a dumb Indian. I will always fight. And someday my children will also go to school and fight and get jobs and be Indian.

Despite their treatment by a racist Anglo community that continues to dismiss the values and viability of Navajo life, the Navajo remain a culturally distinct and unified group of people. The continuity of Navajo culture provides a supportive framework or network of family and community for young Navajos, which increases their chances of academic success. This insistence on cultural integrity is visible in life on and near the reservation—where 70 percent of the Navajo youth will choose to live their lives.

The Native American Church: Cultural integrity

The Native American Church (NAC) and traditional Navajo ceremonies have a central place in the lives of almost of all these Navajo youth. Embedded in Navajo ceremonies are beliefs about the communal nature of success and the primacy of the family. Jobs and educational success are means to enhance the group, not just the individual. Jobs are seen as a means of earning necessary money, not as "good" in and of themselves. This contrasts sharply with Anglo values of hard work for individual mobility, agency, and economic success. To understand the Navajo perspective, it is necessary to experience Navajo life on the reservation, to see the goals and vitality of the Navajo community.

One ceremony I was invited to attend reveals a glimpse into this life. I had been invited by Joe, the father of the family with whom I had lived on the reservation:

> We are going to have a Peyote meeting for the girls.[25] For Jan's birthday, too. To help pray for them to finish school. Jan is trying to graduate this year. If you could come it would help to have an educated person like yourself, a professor.

I was asked to "go in," joining the family and friends for the all-night ceremony in a *tipi* [a traditional Plains Indian structure used for most Native American Church meetings]. Of the twenty-eight participants, I was the only *bilagaana* [Navajo for White person]. We sat around a central fire and a half-moon shaped altar that represented the path of life—from birth to death. The fire and altar were attended to by the Fire Chief. Songs and prayers started with the passing of prayer sticks and a drum, and continued over the next four hours until holy water was brought into the *tipi* at midnight. I spoke and offered prayers during the meeting when I was invited to do so by the Fire Chief, who spoke to Jan and her sister first in Navajo, and then for my benefit in English:

> You are young still. You do not know what will happen to you in ten years. It is important that you take this path, and finish school. Your parents love you very much. You must get your education. I pray for you, it is so important.

He spoke passionately for twenty minutes. Tears were rolling down his face as he pleaded with his kin to succeed in school. As the singing resumed, more participants spoke of their own problems and offered prayers for the hosts' daughters. An uncle spoke:

> I want you to have the good in life. It is hard. It is like a job. You are in school and you must work hard, like a job. We want you to get a good education, and then someday you might have a job like a secretary or something like that, in an office. I can see that. Your parents try hard, but it is up to you to get an education. We know it is hard, but it is important.

The meeting ended at dawn, with a second pail of holy water and ceremonial food. Afterwards, the men remained in the *tipi*, stretched out comfortably as they smoked and told stories. They allowed me to remain and took the opportunity to educate me. The Fire Chief spoke seriously about the general concerns Navajo parents had for their children:

> The things our grandparents knew, we do not know now, and our children will never know. There is a new life, forward, to live in this here dominant culture. This is what I think. Our children need to go out and get the best they can. Go to school and college and get everything they want, and then come back here, to their homes, here between the four sacred mountains. In the past Navajo parents told their children to go out and get an education. Go to college. And they did and they stayed in Albuquerque, in the towns, and then the parents were sad because they said they never saw their children again. But Navajo parents now have to tell their children to go out and get their education. To college. And graduate school. And then to come back home, where they belong. Here on this land. This is where they belong. They need to bring their education back here to the reservation, their home. Then we can be a whole people. This is what I think.

The Native American Church meeting captures the solidarity of the Navajo community and the cultural vitality of its people. Although often invisible to their Anglo neighbors, who view Navajo youths' lives as a "cultural vacuum," ceremonies and family gatherings cloak and support these Navajo youth.[26] The Enemy Way, a five-day ceremony for the purpose of curing illness caused by a ghost, an alien, or an enemy, occurs frequently during the summer months. Additional ceremonial dances occur in the area at least monthly, and a strong Native American Church is active weekly on the reservation. All but one of the young women in the study had their *Kinaalda*, a Navajo puberty ceremony that marks the beginning of Navajo womanhood.[27] Ceremonies are frequently used to bless and support youths' life paths, including their progress in schools and at jobs. In all ceremonies and events, the group serves to support and bond the individual to the Navajo community. Individual economic success becomes a part of the Navajo community's larger economic network.

As was expressed in the NAC meeting, Navajo parents want their children to succeed in both the Anglo and Navajo worlds. However, it is clear that the family and community are of paramount importance, and that educational success brings community and family responsibility. There is a dual side to this message. Navajos are not trying to "get away" from Anglo culture, just from assimilation. Thus, they do want certain material goods and school success, but not at the expense of their cultural identity. As Jan said shortly after her NAC ceremony, "They [parents] tell us to do good in school, but that we will always be Navajo."

Cultural integrity and resistance

Traditional Navajo cultural values still frame, shape, and guide appropriate behavior in the Navajo community. Navajo youths' choice to remain a part of the community assures them economic support through local kinship networks unavailable off the reservation. This choice also puts these youth in opposition to the goals set for them by school officials. Specifically, the choice to remain on the reservation and the insistence on maintaining culturally different values are central to the power struggle in the larger community, because these choices are defined as impoverished by Anglos. However, if one understands the viability of the Navajo community, resistance to assimilation is seen as a rational and appropriate choice.

The Navajos are a conquered and colonized people who have successfully resisted assimilation. They have survived over four hundred years of Anglo subjugation and exploitation with a culture that, although changed, has remained distinct in its values, beliefs, and practices. These Navajos have remained on their ancestral land; Anglos are the immigrants. The Navajos Nation, the largest American Indian reservation in the United States, comprises 26,897 square miles, an area approximately the size of West Virginia. Treaty rights recognize sovereignty status, a separate "nation within the nation," for the 210,000-strong Navajo Nation. John David reports that the total personal income in 1991, including wages and salaries, transfer payments, livestock, and crops, was $900,032,754, with a per capita income of $4,106.[28] Accurate portraits of reservation poverty, however, leave non-reservation residents unprepared to understand that there are viable economic and social institutions on the reservation. The Navajo Nation's budget supports an infrastructure of education, law enforcement, and health and human social services with revenues from oil, gas, mining, timber, taxes, and federal and state funds.

Unique to this governmental structure is the infusion of Navajo culture. Traditional home sites that are determined by sheep and cattle grazing rights are maintained by a Land Permit Office; a tribal court system relies on a Navajo legal code, as well as a federal legal code; the Navajo Medicine Men's Association is housed in the complex of the tribal headquarters, with an office at the local hospital; all significant tribal meetings are prefaced with a traditional prayer from a Medicine Man; and the Navajo Nation publishes its own newspaper to provide a Navajo perspective on local and national matters. In 1986, 286 retail businesses, ninety-four of them Navajo owned, operated on the reservation. The Navajo Communication Company provides cable television and telephones to homes with electricity, and the Native American Public Broadcasting Consortium provides local news to radio listeners. The Navajo Community College, a multi-campus institution with seven branches, serves over two thousand students.[29] In 1992, a total of three thousand students were awarded tribal scholarships totaling $3,320,377. This insistence on tribal autonomy and resistance to "blending in" has assured their youth their continuity as Navajos. Specifically, Navajo choices cannot be compared, as in Ogbu's theories, to other minorities, because Navajos only stand to lose by integration into the larger society. The U.S. Commission on Civil Rights explains this unique position:

> Politically, other minorities started with nothing and attempted to obtain a voice in the existing economic and political structure. Indians started with everything and have gradually lost much of what they had to an advancing alien civilization. . . . Indian tribes have always been separate political entities interested in maintaining their own institutions and beliefs. . . . So while other minorities have sought integration into the larger society, much of Indian society is motivated to retain its political and cultural separateness.[30]

It is important to realize that Navajo individuals do not monolithically represent "the" Navajo culture. There are hundreds of different ways of "being" Navajo. However, within this cultural constellation, specific values are maintained. These

Navajo beliefs and values surround the young as they learn how and what it
means to be Navajo. Although the autonomy of the individual regarding posses-
sions and actions is strongly maintained, consensus and cooperation for the good
of the group is emphasized over aggressive individualism.[31]

The insistence on recognizing Navajo cultural allegiance begins at an early age
and continues throughout life. Children learn to support and be supported by
families. "Like there are all these things we do differently," explained Jan, "but I
don't know them all. You learn them when you do something wrong. Then they
show you what to do right." These lessons are learned and challenged against a
backdrop of an Anglo world. Sometimes these worlds successfully coexist. Matt,
Jan's youngest brother, explained how a Navajo ceremony made things "right."
Lightning, which is a powerfully negative force in Navajo beliefs, hit the trans-
former at the trading post. He continued, "We were afraid we could never drink
a coke or get candy from there again! But then they had a medicine man do
something and it was okay to eat there again."

Other situations provide challenges to the adherence of Navajo values. Navajos
feel it is arrogant to try to control nature by planning every detail in the future.
After a counseling session during her senior year, Jan explained, "It's dangerous.
You can't change things that happen. That's the way it is. But my counselor said I
could change everything by planning on a career. I don't think that would work."
Navajos have a more humble view of "individual choice," which acknowledges
both the dependence of the individual on the group and the importance of the
extended family. When receiving sharply negative comments from an Anglo
friend about the crowded living conditions at her home, Jan "turned the lens" and
expressed disapproval of the Anglo nuclear family: "The way Whites live seems to
be lonely. To live alone is kind of like poverty."

The Navajo depend upon extended family networks of economic and social
support, critical factors in their lifestyle. On the reservation, the extended family
relies on multiple (often minimum wage) incomes to provide support for the
group. Joe's 1990 tax forms claimed twelve dependents supported on a $26,000
salary from a uranium plant. Their new pink, double-wide, three-bedroom trailer
houses four daughters, two sons, five grandchildren, and the husbands of two of
their daughters. Over the past several years, family members supplemented Joe's
income with work in the uranium plant and on road construction crews, and as
clerks, waitresses, cooks, motel maids, pottery painters, and temporary tribal
employees. Sons and daughters move off the reservation in search of employment,
and return when temporary employment ends. The family makes "kneel-down
bread" with corn from the garden and sells it at fairs and in town.[32] All who can,
work at jobs or at home. Pooled resources buy food, clothing, and necessities, and
pay for car and insurance bills.

Along with the economic stability the extended family supplies, there is pressure to place the family ahead of individual prosperity and careers. As an elderly
Navajo man said, "You can't get rich if you look after your relatives right. You
can't get rich without cheating some people."[33] And as Jan said, "In the traditional way and now, the family is the most important thing you can do. Life is too
short to worry about jobs. The family is needed for all those cermonies." Jobs are
seen as a way of earning necessary money, not as a way of life in and of itself.

Navajo families struggle with racial and economic discrimination imposed by
their Anglo neighbors at the same time they speak with pride of their "freedom" on
the reservation. As Jan's father explained, "We don't have electricity, and we don't
have electric bills. We haul water, and we don't have water bills. And out here we

don't have to pay for a [trailer] space." Nightly television watching, lights, and the vacuum cleaner only require an adapter and a car battery. Jan's aunt added,

> A medicine man warned us about what happens when you leave. He said, "They educate us to be pawns. We are educated to do a thing, and then we become pawns. Must work for money to pay for the water bills, the electricity. We become pawns." So you see, we have our water, even though we haul it from sixteen miles away, we have our warm house, and our meat, and food from the land. In town we have to pay for these things, and then we become dependent.

A move to the city does not necessarily mean an increase in standard of living or "success." For example, in 1992, Jan and her husband moved to a large city to stay with his relatives and seek employment. After three months with only sporadic employment, they returned to her family. "It was lonely in the city," Jan said. "My mother needed us, her daughters, so we moved back. The family is real important. That is the main thing. You depend on the family to teach each other, and to be brought up right. If it is not the whole family being involved in it, then it is like lack of communication." Jan reminded me of a Navajo insult: "She acts as if she doesn't have any relatives." The individual without family is an isolated and unsatisfied person. This echoes the Fire Chief's plea at the Native American Church meeting: ". . . and then come back home. Then we can be a whole people." Jan has successfully followed this life path. She has settled into rearing her own children in the home of her mother on the Navajo reservation.

Submerged in an Anglo-controlled social landscape that restricts employment opportunities for Navajos, over half of the youth who remain on the reservation try, like Jan, to continue their schooling to enhance their chances for employment. After graduating from high school, almost all of them attend the local community college, their last chance to learn job skills to qualify for local employment. This path, starting with the traditional "Career Day" experienced by most U.S. high school seniors, appears egalitarian in that a multitude of opportunities and choices are "open" to youth after high school. For these Navajo youth, however, the Anglo belief of "equal educational opportunity for all" leading to "equal employment opportunities" is racially restricted. Anglos construct educational "choices" or paths for Navajo youth that lead through a vocationalized curriculum in both high school and college. This path dead ends, however, in the secondary labor market.

Post-high school options offered Navajo youth include a combination of local job ceilings, impersonal universities, and the local community college. Navajo students face a world segmented by unattractive choices with which schools and career counselors never come to grips. Although Navajo youth enter high school with high aspirations about their future opportunities, their future aspirations are thwarted by the racism they experience in school. After high school, Navajo youth face a choice between a university-city route that works against their cultural beliefs, and a local job and school market that is totally subject to the racial struggle in the community.

High School Career Day: Racially defined choices

On one of my days of observation, I pulled into the small paved parking lot in front of Navajo High School five minutes before school began. The green athletic field stood in sharp contrast to the red dirt and sandstone bluffs. Sheep grazed on the lush lawn, rubbing against the chain-link fence that separated the school from the surrounding Navajo reservation. As I entered the windowless, one-story, red brick school for another day of fieldwork, I was joined by Vangie, a Navajo friend. "It's career day, so you can come with me, Professor, while I learn about schools!" she exclaimed. The juniors and seniors were excused from classes to attend presentations from seven regional colleges and universities, two vocational or technical schools, and the Job Corps. The Navajo Nation's Education Office had a representative to explain tribal scholarships. Students were to attend four information sessions located throughout the school.

Vangie and I attended two regional college presentations. "Some classes are outside and are so much fun. Then there is the choir. You should take that your first year, it is really fun. And you meet all sorts of nice people," a recruiter said. A professionally developed video accompanied the presentation. The second recruiter also showed a polished, upbeat video with smiling faces, a brief glimpse of a professor lecturing in a large amphitheater, shots of athletic events, tennis courts, and leisurely images of students reading books on rolling campus greens. The recruiter said:

> If you want to be a policeman don't come here. But if you want to go into the computer field, or nursing, or in-flight training, come here. It is beautiful and the campus is lots of fun. You can do all sorts of things while you are in school.

Students talked excitedly about which college would be more fun.

The representative from a local vocational training school slowly went through a slide presentation as he explained the school's program:

> And that girl there, she is working at a real good job in a TV station. And that one, she is underemployed. She could get a real good job if she would leave here! See, in all these pictures we have the old and the totally up-to-date equipment. You never know when you will be working in a small place that has old equipment. So we teach with the old and the new.

Looking at a student audience of only seven Navajo females, he backed up to a previous slide:

> See that computer on that slide. If you are going to work in a big office, you have to learn about computers. And then we have a heavy equipment program. We could use more girls. Because of the Equal Opportunity Program, we could place forty girls a year if they completed the program.

The students were quiet and attentive.

We stopped in the library to look at the literature brought by the local community college. District school staff were discussing with the dean of the college their success in sending many of the Navajo youth away to school after graduation. One of the counselors said, "Over 60 percent of the graduating class got accepted to college. Some went to the Job Corps. One year later they are all back. Every one of them!" The Dean of the local community college explained:

> We don't recruit our students. They come to us. Many of the Indian students

go to large universities and they fail. Then they come to us. After they have been with us, they all—100 percent who go to larger colleges—will succeed. If we recruited them to start with us, they might think they have missed something. They can get what they need here.

The booth was full of pictures of Navajo students sitting at computers, building houses, working in hospitals, and sitting in lectures. The recruiter was the only Navajo on the professional staff at the college. Raised by a Mormon family, he had recently returned to work at the college.[34] He spoke softly to several Navajo students. "You can get a good education here. And your Pell Grant will pay for everything. It's close to home so your parents can watch you girls!" They laughed and moved on to examine the pamphlets in the Job Corps booth.

The last presentation was by the state's largest university, my employer. Two student recruiters stood in front of the small group and emphasized the importance of filling out the applications correctly and getting financial aid forms into the university on time. "It is very important that you do things on time and correctly. It is a huge university. But we also have support for minority students and we want you to seriously consider coming to the university." The presentation continued with a list of the academic fields offered by the university and the statement, "The classes may be hard, but they are real interesting. And you can get a good education at our university." The presentation was dry, the "fun" of college life was presented as "getting an education," and the recruiters did not smile.

After these presentations, students moved into the auditorium for two films by the College Board on financial aid. Students filled the room, talking about the sessions they had attended, graduation plans, their personal relationships, and after-school activities. The first film pictured an African American man, one of several individuals interviewed who had "made it." He urged others to attend college. "Anyone can go to college. It is worth it. A small sacrifice now to have the money to go to college. But it is worth it. I am glad I went." The second film, a cartoon on how to correctly fill out financial aid forms, covered topics from estimating summer earnings to who in the household was the legal "provider." Students were bored and restless with the films and cheered when the lights came on, and then left for lunch. A counselor spoke to me as we were leaving the auditorium:

> We are the ones that fill out the forms. The students don't do it. About half will go on to some kind of school and almost all of them will be on financial aid grants. And the other half will sit out on the reservation and do nothing.

We left school early. As I was driving Vangie, her brother Sam, and several of their friends home, the conversation turned to what they were going to do after graduation. "I'm thinking about going to Dartmouth. They have a special Indian program. But I don't know if I want to be so far away from home. I might go into the Army. They will pay for my college." Another said, "I'll probably end up with a baby and be stuck here." She laughed, "I really want a baby of my own. I would be really happy, then, at home with my baby. That's what us Navajo do." Vangie jumped into the conversation. "There are a lot of girls that get pregnant. I'm just not going to do it. It will ruin your life if you have a baby. I want to go to college and get away from here so I can get a good job!" One said, "My parents tell me to do what I feel I want to do. I want to go to college. I hear college is a lot of fun. I want to have a business or something and come back to the reservation to live and help my people. I go crazy about thinking about taking care of my parents in the future." Another, who had been silent, softly spoke, "I want to be a race car driver. But my mom thinks it's too dangerous. So I guess I can be a secretary or nurse. She wants me to have a good job like a secretary or something and live at home." Vangie and Sam's home was the last stop. As they climbed out of my car, Sam teased his sister, "I'm not going to have a baby either! At least till I get married and have a job."

Educational and economic marginalization

The images shown during Career Day of youth lounging on green fields, smiling faces in a choir, a class, using computers, and laboratories, filled the picture window of opportunities facing youth beyond high school. Few Navajo youth will realize the life depicted in these tableaux. Their dreams of a wide range of occupational choices and jobs in distant big cities dim with the reality of their limited academic skills, which relegate them to semi-skilled jobs. High school career days present hollow images for Sam and most of his peers, who do not face "unlimited" opportunities dependent only on individual achievement, but rather a set of political, economic, and social constraints that intertwine in schools and communities to limit their possibilities. Economic disparity is maintained by the continued role of vocational education in local schools and colleges as one aspect of an ongoing racist strategy to limit the opportunities of Navajo and secure opportunities for Anglos. Navajo youth are trained to remain below the job ceiling.

Sam's experiences, which follow in this section, mirror that of many Navajo youth. Sam and Vangie have ten brothers and sisters. They live on the reservation ten miles from the bus stop in a complex that includes eighteen relatives, a new government home, an older stone home, traditional *hogans*, and a satellite dish. They haul their water from a well six miles away, but have electricity from a nearby oil rig. Shortly before graduation in 1989, while flying kites near their home, Sam talked about what he wanted to do with his life: "I want to go into business or finance. Or maybe electronic engineering. Or maybe the military. I would like to go to Berkeley, in California, but I will need a tribal scholarship. I am working on getting my grades up." He had a 2.1 grade point average. Navajo tribal scholarships require a 3.5, a goal he did not reach. The rhythmic whishing of the oil pump was the only sound on the mesa. Sam proudly pointed out the canyon where their livestock grazed and to the far mountains where his father was born. "I have relatives up there that I don't even know. I would like to come back here to live on the reservation. It would be all right. But they say that it is better to get off the reservation to get jobs." His brother was an example. "My brother, he travels all over the world with his job. He works with computers." But there remains the pull of home. "There are not many jobs here. But I like it here. It is home for us Navajo."

Students' experiences in and out of school modify their expectations about future job possibilities. For the Anglo students, future possibilities increase as students approach graduation. Navajo youths' aspirations, on the other hand, are greater than the future envisioned for them by the schools. After four years in high school, their aspirations often match the vocational orientation constructed by their schools. Even though Sam intended to go to college, with the help of a counselor, he filled his senior year schedule with basic and vocational level classes. The counselor explained:

We are not supposed to track kids, it is against the law. But by the time these kids are in high school they know what they are going to do. So we have most of our Indian students in vocational classes. After all, most won't go to college anyway.

The assumption that Navajo youth knew they wanted a future in vocational jobs early in high school was not supported by my data. During the 1987–1988 school year, 132 Anglo and Navajo students in grades nine through twelve completed the JOBO, a career inventory test that translated student "interest" into job fields. Although 20 percent of the Navajo ninth-graders indicated interest in professional careers requiring college, twice as many Anglo ninth-graders saw their future jobs as being in professional fields. The reverse was true regarding vocational, semi-skilled jobs. Almost half, 47 percent, of the Navajo ninth-graders were interested in such jobs, whereas only 30 percent of the Anglo students saw vocational jobs as part of their desired future. This pattern changed by the twelfth grade. The Anglo students desiring vocational jobs dropped by half, from 30 percent to 15 percent, and over 60 percent now desired professional careers. Just the opposite occurred with the Navajo seniors: 62 percent of these students had readjusted their goals downward, towards vocational jobs, and only 15 percent remained determined to achieve professional careers. These figures must be viewed against the backdrop of the dropout rate: by their senior year, close to 40 percent of Navajo youth had already left school—leaving behind the most academically successful Navajo youth.

Navajo culture and local employment opportunities are used by the Anglo educators as a rationale to limit Navajo students' educational opportunities, while, in reality, a vocational curriculum assures the continuity of the local job ceiling for Navajos. The principal at Sam's high school explained the school's vocational orientation:

I'm interested in equal educational opportunity. I have been here for ten years. We used to be 75 percent academic and 25 percent vocational. Now we have 75 percent vocational and 25 percent academic. We need to recognize the needs of the people in this local area. I'm not saying we should ignore the academic classes. But the vocational training is where the jobs are for the local Navajo people.

His vice principal added:

Academics are very important in this world, but we've got to realize that half the kids or more out of this high school are not going into academic jobs. They are going to go into vocational. In fact, the majority of jobs in the future are still going to be vocational. They're not going to be in the white-collar type job. But how do you tell them that?

In 1990, the district received a $3.5 million grant to construct a vocational career center. In an open letter to the community, an administrator explained the new thrust of the school district into technology and job preparation. Citing a state statistic that 40 percent of youth finish college or university training when only 20 percent of the available jobs require a four-year degree, he told of the shock facing graduates who have to be retrained in vocational and technical areas. "Since only 20 percent of the jobs in Utah will require a college degree, the secondary schools must take a more active role in preparing students for employment." He explained the necessity for the curriculum to be responsive to employers' needs:

> This concept does not mean a lowering of academic standards; to the contrary, most technical jobs now require a strong background in math, physics, and language. Nor does this concept infer that all student should know a specific vocational skill prior to leaving high school. The jobs in our society are changing so rapidly that students will be much better served if they develop certain basic skills and attitudes toward work. Most employers now prefer to train their own employees in specific skill areas. What they want from high schools are students with basic understandings of technology, good basic academic skills, and the flexibility to be retrained as often as the job market requires.

This emphasis in high schools sets the stage for focusing the educational careers of Navajo youth onto vocational paths. The districts' "state of the art" vocational school is Navajo High School; the predominantly Anglo high school in the northern part of the district remains college preparatory. This assures college-educated Anglo youth a brighter job future in the community.[35] The administrator's state statistic that 40 percent of youth finish college or university reflects the 97 percent Anglo population of the state, not the local Navajo population served by the district. Almost half of the Navajo youth from the local school district attempt some kind of post-high school education. Out of one thousand youth, one-third eventually attend the local community college, 6 percent attend universities, and 7 percent attend vocational institutions. Regardless of these efforts, less than one-half of one percent complete a four-year degree, only 2 percent complete two-year degrees, and 5 percent receive a vocational certificate. None of the youth who attend the community college go on to finish a four-year degree. Over 90 percent of the Navajo youth do not receive a degree higher than their high school diploma. Sam and his friends are in this group.

Sam graduated in 1989 from Navajo High School. During his senior year, he fluctuated among wanting to study business or finance, join the military, or wanting to go to technical school to learn electronics. He decided to go to the city to hunt for a job. Off the reservation, Navajo family networks are utilized for economic support—both for the family left behind and the person moving to the city. Youth who leave for the city do so only if there is a relative who can assist with housing and the location of a job. The housing tends to be low-income and jobs are usually minimum-wage labor in fast food restaurants, motels, and factories. During the two years following high school, Sam worked at an airplane parts factory in Salt Lake City and did construction work in Phoenix. He lived with relatives in both cities. Back on the reservation to visit his family, he stopped by my house:

> It has been two years since I graduated and I haven't gotten it together to go to college. And now my younger brother is already up at the university ahead of me! I would like to come back here to live on the reservation. It would be all right. But they say that it is better to get off the reservation to get jobs. That's what I did. There are not many jobs here. But I like it here. It is my home. And the air is clear.

Sam stayed on the reservation. He enrolled in the community college in a program that promised good local employment. "It's for electronics. Job Services and the college are running it. I will be able to get a good job with the certificate."

The two-year community college Sam attended is where most Navajos finish their time in higher education. The creation of this community college ten years ago has been an economic boom for the local Anglo community, whose members occupy all of the teaching positions and 99 percent of the administrative and support staff. The college is supported, due to its two-thirds Navajo student population, by federal tuition grants targeted for "disadvantaged" youth and from the Navajos' own oil royalties money.[36]

One Navajo high school counselor explained, "The college comes with scholarship money and says they [youth] can come to the college free. Many don't know about other places. And they need the money to go. And the college needs them to survive." Last year the community college established a scholarship fund for all county residents, using $500,000 from Navajo royalty money to establish matching funds from the state.[37] Prior to this, Navajo students could use their scholarships to attend the college of their choice. Now, under the guidelines of the new scholarship fund, all scholarships are limited to attendance at the local college. By putting these stipulations on the funding, the community college has insured middle-class jobs for the Anglos and vocational training for jobs that do not exist for Navajos.

As in high school, Navajo youth at the community college are encouraged to seek terminal degrees in vocational areas. As the academic dean explained, "We have looked into the economic development of the next decade and it is in the service industry. Our students want to stay in this community and these are where the jobs will be." I argued for encouraging more students to go for four-year professional degrees, reminding him that the better jobs in the county required a college degree. He argued, "Most of the jobs here are in the service industry. We are happy if we can keep a Navajo student for a one-year program. That is success." The mission statement of the college supported his emphasis. Only its concluding goal mentioned preparing students to go on to four-year institutions.[38]

The college has a large vocational program. During the 1992 winter quarter, out of almost one hundred courses offered, two-thirds were in vocational or technical areas. Certificates of Completion, requiring one year of study, are offered in accounting, auto mechanics, general clerical, secretarial occupations, office systems, practical nursing (LPN), stenography, and welding. In addition to these specialties available to all its students, the college offers special vocational programs for Navajo students that are cosponsored by the Navajo tribe. Designed to fill immediate job needs, these latter certificates are offered in marina hospitality training, needle trades (sewing), building trades, sales personnel training for supermarket employment, security officers, building maintenance training, pottery trades, modern office occupations, restaurant management, and truck driving. These latter "Navajo only" certificates are designed to prepare students for local employment. An instructor explained, "These programs are designed to prepare the student for good jobs that are out there. They are extensive, lasting for three quarters. One quarter they are prepared with communication skills. And then how to get along with their bosses. It is the general social skills, work skills, and the particular skills for the job."[39] These programs are not without criticism. Another instructor explained:

We trained forty or fifty people at a time to run cash registers. That's good. But how many stores around here are going to hire all those people? They're training for limited jobs. Why send everybody to carpenter's school? In this small area we have tons of carpenters. Why teach them all welding? You can do it at home, but how many welders are there in this area? Probably every other person is a welder.

During the last decade at this community college, 95 percent of the vocational certificates were earned by Navajo youth and adults. Even this training, however, did not necessarily result in a job. The Dean of the college explained: "Our marina hospitality program was a good one. And it was going to get a lot of Navajo jobs. The tribe had built a new marina and the tourist dollars were going to be good. But then they had the flood. It wiped out the marina. It hasn't been built again. So all those people, almost one hundred, were trained for jobs that never happened." And then there was the needle trades program. "We trained twenty-four women, but there weren't many jobs. The one sewing factory closed down. The other only hired a few." The employment results from the truck driver program were minimal. "We trained over thirty for that program. The uranium tailings over on the reservation were supposed to be hauled away, so we trained truck drivers. It's still in the courts and so no one was hired. We could have gotten them good jobs in other states, like Oklahoma, but they didn't want to leave the reservation." And the largest program, sales personnel, a joint effort of business, the tribe, and the college, placed students in local supermarkets for "on-the-job training" with the understanding that they would receive employment after completing the program. The supermarkets supervised the student trainees for three months while they learned job-required skills, such as boxing, shelf stocking, and check-out packing:

> We had a real good success with this one. A lot of our students were working in the supermarkets in towns. But then there were problems with the supermarkets not hiring them after the training. Cutbacks, you know. But some people thought they were just using the Navajo students for cheap labor. And then they didn't hire them.

Some vocational training programs lead to jobs. Most do not.

After completing the one-year certificate in electronics, Sam found a job—at a factory in the city. Again, he left the reservation. After eighteen months, he was laid off. In 1993, he returned to his home, this time with a wife and child. Sam said, "I'll find something around here, or we will try the city again. Right now I have things to do at home. My parents need help, after my sister died in the car accident, so I need to be here. I have things to do, you know. My younger sister is going to have her *Kinaalda* and the wood has to be gathered. I can get a job around here." After six months without a job, he enrolled at the community college again. He is studying building trades in a community that saw a 9 percent reduction in the construction industry in 1992.

The only successful job networks Navajo youth have are through their parents or relatives, which are for low-level jobs. Mothers grew up working in the local restaurants and school cafeterias, or as maids in the three local motels. Fathers worked at temporary construction jobs, and in the local oil and uranium fields. Sons and daughters have access into the same lines of employment, especially when the training paths available to them in high school and at the community college limit them to these kinds of jobs.[40] If they remain in their home community (as most do), even Navajo youth with a high school diploma face a future of semi-skilled jobs, training programs, and seasonal work, mirroring the lives of their parents.

High school graduates are twice as likely to have jobs as those who do not finish school.[41] On the surface, this seems like an incentive for youth to finish high school. However, there is little difference in the *kinds* of jobs held by graduates and non-graduates. With rare exceptions, both groups of employed youth work at the same kinds of service industry jobs characterized by low pay with few or no benefits, seasonal employment, and a highly transitional work force: cooks, motel maids, school aides, bus drivers, tour guides, making or painting pottery, clerical workers, electrical assistants, janitors, waitresses, seamstresses, the military, uranium and oil workers, and construction. Working at the same job alongside peers who dropped out of school, many Navajo youths question the relevance of their high school and college diplomas. At the very least, Navajo youth see a successful academic effort paying off less for them than for their Anglo peers. On the one hand, leaving school is not the route most youth choose, as it affects their chances for employment, and completing school is a goal encouraged by their families and the community. On the other hand, they are acutely aware that completing school does not guarantee employment at other than menial jobs. The Navajo youths mentioned at the beginning of this article who disagreed with their shop teacher about the limited job opportunities facing them after high school clearly understood this dilemma.

Regardless of school success or failure, after high school, all of these youth face the same structural barriers in the community because they are Navajo. Here, Ogbu's model partly explains this situation. He argues that the existence of a "job ceiling," intertwined with a "rejection" of the Anglo world, mediates against school success for some castelike minorities. Ogbu states:

> Members of a castelike minority group generally have limited access to the social goods of society by virtue of their group membership and not because they lack training and ability or education. In particular, they face a job ceiling—that is highly consistent pressures and obstacles that selectively assign blacks and similar minority groups to jobs at the lowest level of status, power, dignity, and income while allowing members of the dominant white group to compete more easily for more desirable jobs above that ceiling.[42]

Ogbu implies that the job ceiling affects student attitudes towards school and that vocational tracking is the school's adaptation to the job market. A picture of the economic landscape of the community illustrates the racial stratification that frames the employment possibilities of Navajo youth like Sharon, Jan, and Sam. Although American Indians comprise over half of the local population, they are marginalized to either low-paying jobs or no jobs.[43] The unemployment rate for Indians, 41 percent, is over four times the unemployment rate for Anglos. A breakdown of the jobs in the county by occupation illustrates the different opportunity structures faced by Anglo and American Indian workers. Over 90 percent of official and management jobs are held by Anglos. Only 8 percent of these top-level jobs are held by American Indians. In other professional positions, Anglos hold over two-thirds of the jobs. Twenty-five percent of all jobs in the county are classified in these two management and professional categories, but few American Indians make it into these powerful positions. In other areas, Anglos occupy almost 90 percent of the jobs as technicians, 91 percent of the sales workers, 80 percent of office and clerical workers, and 63 percent of the skilled craft workers. American Indians are employed in the service-maintenance and the construction trades, and as laborers and para-professionals. All of the assemblers and hand-working jobs, 75 percent of non-precision machine operators, 50 percent of construction, 61 percent of cleaning and building services, 50 percent of laborers, and 47 percent of food preparation and service jobs are held by American Indians. This job ceiling is faced by all Navajo youth—dropouts, graduates, and community college students.

The Navajo in this community experience a racially defined job ceiling, but student attitudes toward the job ceiling do not result in the rejection of schooling or of the Anglo world. Rather, Navajo reject assimilation as a path they must follow in order to be defined as "successful." Navajo students on the reservation, where there are fewer jobs than in town, are more successful in school, even though they are acutely aware of their limited economic opportunities in the community. Historical experiences and the job ceiling, by themselves, do not explain how Navajo youth respond to school: rather, their response to school is mediated by culture, especially the cultural integrity of the group.

Regardless of students' "cultural stance" (degree of acculturation or assimilation), a key factor in the relationship between schools and students seems to be what schools *do* to students—successful students are still limited by the *quality* of their schooling experience. In viewing schools as sites of conflict, vocational tracking is one part of the racial struggle in this community.

Navajo students are counseled into vocational classes in high school, limiting their access to college preparatory classes. By the time these youth leave high school, their "academic fate" is assured. Almost half of them try schools away from the area, but with minimal academic skills and limited economic resources, they drop out and return home. They then move into the "arms" of the community college to complete the education they will "need" to live, training locally for semi-skilled jobs.[44] Ironically, Navajo youths' failure to succeed educationally "outside" actually enhances the local Anglo economic power base by assuring the continuity of the community college.

Navajo youth are encouraged to leave the area for "good" jobs, which in turn also fits with the Anglos' interest in maintaining good local jobs for their group. Many Navajos work in factories in cities for a while, but, separated from their families, they remain detached, isolated, and poor. Most return home and seek whatever paying job they can find. Unlike middle-class youth, who attach their self-image to the kinds of job they strive for, these Navajo youth view a job as a means of making money, which is necessary for survival. The kind of job they work at does not define their "goodness." That is defined by their family relationships. As Paul Willis argues, the concept of "job choice," from semi-skilled to professional jobs, is a middle-class construct.[45] Some people get "jobs," others have "careers." Structural and economic determinants restrict individual alternatives, but choices are made among the remaining possible choices. Navajo youth seek whatever jobs are available to them in their community. In doing so, they support their families with an income and secure the continuity of Navajo culture.

Regardless of the dismal job ceiling, Navajos are persistent in their schooling efforts to enhance their employability. Navajo men and women who do hold the credentials necessary for better jobs are increasingly competitive for these positions. Almost without exception, these educational credentials are earned at schools outside of the county. These few hold positions as teachers, social workers, health care providers, and administrators for tribal and county programs. Without these credentials, however, Navajo people are guaranteed to lack qualifications for positions of leadership and power in the community—a community that has always been their "home" and where most of them will live their lives.

Navajo lives: Cultural integrity

Navajos are treated differently from Anglos in this community's educational and economic institutions. However, as John Ogbu, Margaret Eisenhart and M. Elizabeth Grauer, and Margaret Gibson have pointed out, there is intra-group variability in responses to schooling within each minority group.[46] The Navajos are no exception. Clearly, Navajo youth are not homogeneous in their responses to schooling. Some, like Sharon, Jan, and Sam, follow paths that Gibson calls "accommodation without assimilation" and that Ogbu calls an "alternative strategy or the immigrant strategy," even though they are from a "castelike" group. They are successful in the educational system, even though this does not necessarily translate into economic stability. At the same time, they insist on maintaining their place as Navajos within the community. By refusing to accept either assimilation or rejection, these youth force us to look at new ways of viewing success. The school success of these Navajo students, with strong traditions intact, is explained, in part, by a model of "cultural integrity." Supported by a solid cultural foundation, they resist by moving through high school as a short "interruption" in their progression to lives as adult Navajo men and women. For them, high school is something one tolerates and sometimes enjoys; school success does not pose a serious threat to their cultural identity. What is clear from the lives of these Navajo youth, however, is that rather than attempting to erase Native culture and language, schools should do everything in their power to use, affirm, and maintain these if they truly want to achieve equity and promote Navajo students' academic success.

Even though Navajo youth develop a variety of responses to their schooling experiences, what is significant is that the school system issues a homogeneous institutional response to the Navajo youth, regardless of their "good" or "bad" student status. Focusing on student behaviors and their values towards school must be coupled with what schools *do* to these students, such as subjecting them to racial humiliation and vocational tracking. As I have illustrated in this article, the school context and curriculum are not neutral. Racism frames the stage and remains a barrier for all Navajo youth, regardless of their academic success or social compliance. Ironically, academic achievement under these conditions is questionable because of the watered-down curriculum and the persistent discrimination in the job market. This suggests that school reform and changes in the job market must be connected in order to talk about educational success in a meaningful way.

In looking at the variability of Navajo youths' responses to education and the homogeneity of Anglo responses, "cultural identity" is used by both to establish cultural boundaries and borders.[47] Cultural boundaries can be thought of as behavioral evidence of different cultural standards of appropriateness. These can be manifested in different speech patterns, child-rearing practices, and learning styles. The presence of these cultural differences, by themselves, is a politically neutral phenomenon. Navajo youth, securely rooted in their culture, move back and forth between their community and the surrounding Anglo community. The cultural framework surrounding Navajo youth, unlike secondary cultural differences, did not initially arise to maintain boundaries and to provide the ability to cope with Anglo subordination. Cultural boundaries, however, are often turned into cultural borders or barriers during inter-group conflict. In this situation, cultural differences become politically charged when rights and obligations are allocated differently. The Anglo community uses Navajo culture as a border, a reason to deny equality by claiming the privilege of one kind of knowledge over another. Navajo families are judged by what they don't have – money, middle-class Anglo values, higher education, and professional jobs – rather than by what they do have – extended families, permanent homes, strong Navajo values and religious beliefs.

Remaining Navajo is a desired goal, not one settled on by default. Life in homes on the reservation, surrounded by family, friends, and similar "others," is a sound choice for youth, with or without school credentials. The choice to remain on the reservation represents failed attempts to find security and happiness in towns and cities amid racial isolation and under- or unemployment. This choice also represents an ethical commitment and valuing of families and Navajo traditions. The Navajo community provides a place of social acceptance and economic survival unavailable in Anglo-dominated communities off the reservation. This choice, however, situates Navajo youth within a local Anglo community structure that dismisses their lives and limits their educational and economic opportunities.

Cultural and racial differences serve both as reasons used by the Anglo community to deny equal educational or economic opportunity to Navajos and as a means Navajos use to resist cultural homogeneity. Jan, Sharon, and Sam chose a "boundary" strategy, resisting assimilation by maintaining pride in their culture and language, which led them successfully through school. They followed the "rules of the game," even though they knew they faced a "stacked deck." This path, fraught with conflict, uncertainty, and pain, was not easy. For some Navajo youth, however, boundaries become borders. A few cross over and leave their families and lives on the reservation. Most, however, choose their families and Navajo traditions over the illusory promises of wealth in the larger society. As Jan said earlier in this article, "They [parents] tell us to do good in school, but that we will always be Navajo." This choice assures the continuity of the Navajo people, and answers the plea expressed in the NAC meeting: "They need to bring their education back here to the reservation, their home. Then we can be a whole people."

Acknowledgments

Although they must remain unnamed, I wish to thank the hundreds of Navajo and Anglo women, men, children, and young adults who have patiently listened to my questions, tirelessly corrected my misconceptions, and honestly tried to teach me about their lives. Without their help this research would not have been possible. I would like to thank Frank Margonis, John Ogbu, Harvey Kanter, Laurence Parker, Beth King, Audrey Thompson, and the members of the Cultural, Critical, and Curriculum Group in the Department of Educational Studies at the University of Utah for their insightful critiques on numerous drafts of this article. I bear sole responsibility, however, for the interpretations presented. I would also like to acknowledge the financial support for this research from the Spencer Foundation and the University of Utah.

Notes

1   In this article, I use pseudonyms for the schools and the individuals who participated in my research.
2   Although somewhat contested as a term that attempts to represent all majority people, I use the term "Anglo" as it is used by the Navajos in this community, as a political category that unifies all White people.

3 "Border" refers to the economic, social, and political marginalization of the Navajo. It also describes the literal "border" of the reservation community, which is divided geographically by a river. Most of the Anglos live in the North and almost all Navajo live in the South.

4 Murray Wax, Rosalie Wax, and Robert Dumont, *Formal Education in an American Indian Community* (Prospect Heights, IL: Waveland Press, 1989). The original study was published in 1964 by another publisher.

5 I shared my research with LDS and non-LDS Anglos. They also helped me correct my understandings of the Mormon Church.

6 For a more detailed analysis of my fieldwork relations, see D. Deyhle, G. A. Hess, and M. LeCompte, "Approaching Ethical Issues for Qualitative Researchers in Education," in *Handbook of Qualitative Research*, ed. M. LeCompte, W. Millroy, and J. Preissle (San Diego: Academic Press, 1992); Donna Deyhle, "The Role of the Applied Educational Anthropologist: Between Schools and the Navajo Nation," in Kathleen Bennett deMarrais, *Inside Stories: Reflections on Our Methods and Ethics in Qualitative Research* (New York: St. Martin's Press [in press]).

7 See Frederick Erickson, "Transformation and School Success: The Politics and Culture of Educational Achievement," *Anthropology & Education Quarterly, 18* (1987), 335–356; John Ogbu, "Variability in Minority School Performance: A Problem in Search of an Explanation," *Anthropology & Educational Quarterly, 18* (1987), 312–334; and Henry T. Trueba, "Culturally Based Explanations of Minority Students' Academic Achievement," *Anthropology & Education Quarterly, 19* (1988), 270–287, for debates on these positions.

8 Jim Cummins, "Empowering Minority Students: A Framework for Intervention," *Harvard Educational Review, 56* (1986), 18–36.

9 John Ogbu, *Minority Education and Caste: The American System in Cross-Cultural Perspective* (New York: Academic Press, 1978).

10 Ogbu, *Minority Education and Caste.*

11 Cummins, "Empowering Minority Students," p. 22.

12 Cummins, "Empowering Minority Students," p. 22.

13 DNA is short for *Dinebeiina Nahiilna be Agadithe*, which translates to English as "people who talk fast to help people out." The DNA is a legal service that provides free legal counsel to low-income Navajos.

14 Racial issues in the county are made more complex by the relationship between the dominant religion, The Church of Latter Day Saints (LDS), or Mormons, and non-Mormons. A majority of the Anglos in the county are Mormons. A majority of the Navajos were either traditionalists or members of the Native American Church. The LDS church teaches that American Indians are "Lamanites," descendants of Laman, Lemuel, and others who, having emigrated to the Americas, rejected the gospel. Righteous groups are White, while those who had rejected the covenants they had made with God received a "sore cursing," even "a skin of blackness . . . that their seed might be distinguished from the seed of their brethren" (*Book of Mormon, 2*, Nephi. 5:21; Alma 3:14). Converting back to the gospel results in the "scales of darkness" falling from Lamanite's eyes and a return to a "white and delightsome" being.

15 For an analysis of the relationship between Mormons and American Indians, see Mark P. Leone, *Roots of Modern Mormonism* (Cambridge: Harvard University Press, 1979); Dan Vogel, *Indian Origins and the Book of Mormon* (Signature Books, 1986); and Wallace Stegner, *Mormon Country* (Lincoln: University of Nebraska Press, 1970).

16 The Anglo population in this county arrived in the 1800s as pioneers from the Church of Jesus Christ of Latter-day Saints (Mormons). Sent by Brigham Young, the 236 settlers were to start a colonizing mission among Navajos and to increase the land base and religious influence of the LDS church throughout the region. From the beginning, cloaked within the assimilationist philosophy of the LDS church, the Mormons dismissed Indians' claims to political and cultural sovereignty.

17 I determined the graduation and dropout rates in this community by following "cohorts" of Navajo youth throughout their school careers. A total of 629 students forming six different cohorts from two schools, from the class of 1984 to the class of 1989, are represented with complete four-year high school records. Combining the data from both schools revealed that 59 percent graduated through either traditional or

nontraditional means, 34 percent left school, and 7 percent remained "unknown." The graduation rate of 59 percent is lowered to 49 percent when reporting only students who graduated on time in the traditional high school program. Over half, 55 percent, of the youth that dropped out did so during the twelfth grade.

18 This was based on the *Lau v. Nichols* court decision, which mandated that school districts test and provide special English instruction to non-native English speakers. See, for example, Courtney B. Cazden and Ellen L. Leggett, "Culturally Responsive Education: Recommendations for Achieving Lau Remedies II," in *Culture and the Bilingual Classroom*, ed. Henry T. Trueba, Grace Pung Guthrie, and Kathryn Hu-Pei Au (Rowley, MA: Newbury House, 1981), pp. 69–86, for the educational implications of this court decision.

19 See, for example, Margaret C. Szasz, *Education and the American Indian: The Road to Self-Determination Since 1928* (Albuquerque: University of New Mexico Press, 1977); Gloria Emerson, "Navajo Education," in *Handbook of North American Indians, 10*, ed. Alfonso Ortiz (Washington, DC: Smithsonian Institution, 1983), pp. 659–671; and Estelle Fuch and Robert Havighurst, *To Live On This Earth: American Indian Education* (Albuquerque: University of New Mexico Press, 1972).

20 Robert A. Trennert Jr., *The Phoenix Indian School: Forced Assimilation in Arizona, 1891–1935* (Norman: University of Oklahoma Press, 1988).

21 Navajo medicine men and women are regarded as the most powerful people within Navajo culture. One studies to obtain the knowledge and practices throughout a lifetime, as all of Navajo beliefs about their origin, and reasons and ways to live one's life are intertwined with ceremonies to "balance" and guide themselves for a healthy life. The medicine men and women are the mediators between the beliefs of a tradition and personal health. In addition to conducting large-scale religious ceremonies, such as the Enemy Way, Navajo medicine men and women perform traditional weddings and *Kinaaldas*, as well as being called upon by families for curing illnesses that range from headaches and nightmares to cancer and diabetes. Most Navajo use the services of both traditional medicine men and women and Western trained medical doctors. See, for an example, Clyde Kluckhohn and Dorothea Leighton, *The Navajo* (Cambridge: Harvard University Press, 1974); Gladys Reichard, *Navaho Religion* (Tucson: University of Arizona Press, 1983); and Leland C. Wyman, "Navajo Ceremonial System," in *Handbook of North American Indians, 10*, ed. Alfonso Ortiz (Washington, DC: Smithsonian Institution, 1983), pp. 536–557.

22 Cummins, "Empowering Minority Students," p. 25.

23 U.S. Department of Education, *State Education Statistics* (Washington, DC: U.S. Department of Education, January 1984 and January 1986).

24 The situation has worsened. The dropout rate among Navajo students has increased over the past five years. Although the combined cohort rate at BHS shows only a dropout average of 41 percent, 75 percent of the 1991 class at Border High School did not graduate. In 1991, the district reported that the dropout rate for Navajo students was five times higher than for Anglo students; 80 percent of the dropouts were Navajos.

25 The Native American Church, commonly referred to as the Peyote religion, is a pan-Indian, semi-Christian, nativistic religious movement in the course of whose ritual believers eat the Peyote cactus, a substance containing more than 10 alkaloids, the best known of which is mescaline. It is pan-Indian in the sense that its ideology emphasizes the unity of Indians and their distinctness from Whites. Its origins are traced to the Plains Indian nativistic religious movements at the turn of the century. It was introduced to the Navajo by the Ute, their neighbors to the north of the reservation. See David Aberle, *The Peyote Religion among the Navajo* (Chicago: University of Chicago Press, 1982). Peyote meetings are jointly conducted by a Fire Chief and a Roadman.

26 This ideology asserts that the Indian home and the mind of the Indian child is meager, empty, or lacking in pattern. See Wax, Wax, and Dumont, *Formal Education*, for an excellent examination of this ideology. This study of a Sioux community and its school was conducted over thirty years ago; many of these researchers' results were mirrored in this Navajo community.

27 With a Navajo girl's first menses, she becomes a young woman and has a "coming of age" ceremony to usher her into adult society. The chief aim of the four-day ceremony is to impart the physical, moral, and intellectual strength she will need to carry out the

duties of a Navajo woman, following the example set by Changing Woman in the creation story. Details of the ceremony are reported by Shirley M. Begay, *Kinaalda: A Navajo Puberty Ceremony* (Rough Rock, AZ: Rough Rock Demonstration School, Navajo Curriculum Center, 1983), and Charlotte J. Frisbe, *Kinaalda: A Study of the Navaho Girl's Puberty Ceremony* (Middletown, CT: Wesleyan University Press, 1964).

28 David L. John, *Navajo Nation Overall Economic Development Plan 1992–93* (Window Rock, AZ: The Navajo Nation, 1992).

29 Both Anglos and Navajos teach at the College. The President and Board are Navajo – this is a strong, Navajo-controlled organization. Navajo philosophy, language, and culture are part of the curriculum. The school is currently working on developing a Navajo teacher-training program.

30 U.S. Commission on Civil Rights, *Indian Tribes: A Continuing Quest for Survival* (Washington, DC: U.S. Government Printing House, 1981), pp. 32–33.

31 Louise Lamphere, *To Run After Them: Cultural and Social Bases of Cooperation in a Navajo Community* (Tucson: University of Arizona Press, 1977).

32 "Kneel-down" bread is a traditional food of the Navajo. A fist-sized ball of ground corn is wrapped in fresh corn leaves and buried in an underground pit oven. The name comes from the process of having to "kneel down" when putting the bread into the pit.

33 Kluckhohn and Leighton, *The Navajo*, p. 300.

34 In 1954, the LDS Church officially adopted, as part of their missionary activities, the Indian Student Placement Program, in which American Indian children were "adopted" by a Mormon family. American Indian youth lived with foster families during the year, went to public schools, and were educated into the LDS Church. Home visits occurred for a few weeks or months during the summer. By 1980, approximately 20,000 Indian students from various tribes had been placed in LDS foster homes. The program is no longer expanding, placing only 1,968 in 1980, and in the future will be focusing on high-school-age children. This program had touched almost all of the Navajo families in this area. In every family, close or distant clan members have experienced LDS foster homes. For some, the experience was positive; for others it was disastrous. See the following for a discussion of this program: J. Neil Birch, "Helen John: The Beginnings of Indian Placement," *Dialogue: A Journal of Mormon Thought, 18* (Winter 1985), 119–129; Lacee A. Harris, "To Be Native American—and Mormon," *Dialogue: A Journal of Mormon Thought, 18* (Winter 1985), 143–152; and M. D. Topper, "Mormon Placement: The Effects of Missionary Foster Families on Navajo Adolescents," *Ethos, 7*, No. 2 (1979), 142–160. There were many reasons for parents to put their children in this program, including the chance for better educational opportunities in the cities, more economic security in White families, and, in situations of extreme poverty, better food.

35 A local county report revealed that two-thirds of the jobs in the county were located in the northern portion of the county, where almost 75 percent of the Anglo population lived. The government ranked as the number one employer, the school district the second, and the county the third. These three provided a total of 750 jobs, or 23 percent of the county's employment. A majority of these jobs required either a college degree or some college education. Specifically, 20 percent of jobs in the state of Utah will require a college degree, 40 percent will require six months to four years post-high school training, and 40 percent will require less than six months of training.

36 In 1933, Congress passed a bill that added this area to the Navajo reservation located in Utah. The bill gave the Navajo people in these areas the right to 37.5 percent of any gas or oil royalties, to be used for tuition for Navajo children, for building or maintaining roads on the lands added to the reservation, and for other benefits for these residents. The state of Utah was the trustee of this trust. In 1956, great quantities of oil were discovered in this area. In lawsuits filed in 1961, 1963, 1977, 1984, and 1987, the Court found in favor of Navajos who claimed the Utah Division of Indian Affairs had failed to comply with the terms of the 1933 Act by using the money for the benefit of non-Navajos. In the most recent lawsuit, in 1992, the Navajos accused the state of breach of trust and breach of fiduciary duties, and are suing to recover millions of dollars lost through this mismanagement. Estimates of how much could be awarded in the case run to more than 50 million dollars.

37   After Navajo complaints of mismanagement, the state attorney general's office audited the trust fund. The audit found a questionable use of funds, including $146,000 to finance the administration building, science building, and dormitories; $35,000 for nursing faculty; and $43,500 for a counselor who administered the scholarship program. The audit questioned using Navajo monies to defray the costs of a state institution.

38   "... the curriculum includes associate degree programs, vocational-technical programs, developmental programs, adult and community education programs and courses which are transferable towards four year degrees."

39   During the 1992 Winter Quarter, this instructor taught twenty-four one- to six-credit cooperative education classes. Each class covered a different subject area, such as anthropology, auto mechanics, geology, drafting, and secretarial work, with a title that included, "Work Experience."

40   Out of two hundred employed graduates from my database, 25 percent of the males were in the military, the National Guard, or the Marines, and 75 percent were in trade types of occupations, particularly construction, welding, electrical, and oilfield work. Most of the women were in traditional low-paying pink collar jobs, such as LPN, office worker, seamstress, pottery painter, and clerk. One woman had a bachelor's degree and was teaching; one other was a supervisor at K-Mart.

41   All the Navajo youth, from the high school classes of 1982 to 1989 in two different schools, were tracked in my database over the past eight years to determine what happened to them after they had graduated or left school. Two-thirds of these youth were successfully located. The percentages given are based on these youth. Out of 732 youth, both graduates and non-graduates, 32 percent were employed, 39 percent were unemployed, and 29 percent were students. Higher employment, lower unemployment, and more student status were revealed by examining the high school graduates separately. Out of 499 graduates, 39 percent were employed, 26 percent unemployed, and 35 percent were students. The image is bleaker when looking at the youth who left school prior to graduation. Of these 233 youth, only 19 percent were employed, 66 percent were unemployed, and 15 percent were students. There were slight gender differences. More men were employed, 37 percent, compared to 27 percent of the women. Close to half, 47 percent, of the women were unemployed, compared to 34 percent of the men. An equal number of men and women were students. The label "student" is one that needs to be viewed cautiously. Over 80 percent of these were enrolled in the local community college. Many of these youth attended school on a part-time basis, lived at home, and were otherwise unemployed.

42   John Ogbu, "Societal Forces as a Context of Ghetto Children's School Failure," in *The Language of Children Reared in Poverty*, ed. Lynne Feagans and Dale C. Farren (San Diego: Academic Press, 1982), p. 124.

43   In this rural county, existing jobs are limited. The services industry sector (lodging, personal, business, repair, health, and educational services) was the largest contributor of jobs in the country, accounting for 21 percent in 1986. The largest occupational group, representing 36 percent of all jobs in 1986 and 37 percent in 1991, was in production, operations, and maintenance—basically in the blue collar group of occupations. These jobs were concentrated primarily in the goods-producing industries of agriculture, mining, construction, and manufacturing. Second in the number of jobs hierarchy are the professional, paraprofessional, and technical groups, followed by service and clerical occupations. The Utah Department of Employment Security published a projected occupations outlook from 1986 to 1991 specific for this county. The occupations listed as being in demand included: blue collar workers, supervisors, cashiers, combined food preparation and service workers, continuous mining machine operators, conveyor operators and tenders, electricians, underground mining machinery mechanics, maintenance repairers (general utility), roof bolters, secretaries, sewing machine operators, and shuttle car operators. This local profile mirrors that of the state in general. The services and trade industry will account for half of all jobs in Utah by 1991 and will claim 58 percent of all new job growth over the same period. Brad M. McGarry, "Utah's Affirmative Action Information 1987: A Blueprint for Hiring," Utah Department of Employment Security Labour Market Information Services, May 1988; John T. Matthews and Michael B. Sylvester, "Utah Job Outlook: Statewide and Service

Delivery Areas 1990–1995," Utah Department of Employment Security Labour Market Information Services, January 1990.

44 For a discussion of how community colleges function to "cool out" students, limiting rather than leading them to professional degrees, see Steven Brint and Jerome Karabel, *The Diverted Dream* (New York: Oxford University Press, 1989); Burton Clark, "The 'Cooling-Out' Function in Higher Education," *American Journal of Sociology, 45* (1960), 569–576; Kevin J. Dougherty, "The Community College at the Crossroads: The Need for Structural Reform," *Harvard Educational Review, 61* (August 1991), 311–336; and W. Norton Grubb, "The Decline of Community College Transfer Rates," *Journal of Higher Education, 62* (March/April 1991), 194–222.

45 Paul Wills, *Learning to Labour* (Westmead, Eng.: Saxon House, 1977).

46 Ogbu, *Minority Education and Caste*; John Ogbu, "Variability in Minority School Performance: A Problem in Search of an Explanation," *Anthropology & Education Quarterly, 18* (1987) 312–334; John Ogbu, "Understanding Cultural Diversity and Learning," *Educational Researcher, 21* (November 1992), 5–14; Margaret A. Eisenhart and M. Elizabeth Grauer, "Constructing Cultural Differences and Educational Achievement in Schools," in *Minority Education: Anthropological Perspectives*, ed. Evelyn Jacob and Cathie Jordan (Norwood, NJ: Ablex, 1993); and Margaret A. Gibson, *Accommodation Without Assimilation: Sikh Immigrants in an American High School* (Ithaca: Cornell University Press, 1988).

47 Erickson, "Transformation and School Success," p. 346.

CHAPTER 10

DO BLACK AND WHITE STUDENTS LOOK FOR THE SAME CHARACTERISTICS IN TEACHERS? (1981)

Robert W. Sizemore

Few educators would deny that teachers' efforts to create a classroom atmosphere conducive to learning are at times unsuccessful. The results of this failure are evidenced in decreased academic achievement, increased behavioral problems and a high degree of emotional stress for administrators, teachers, and students. Secondary school teachers often acknowledge particular difficulty in establishing and maintaining pleasant classroom environments for junior high school-age students. Many teachers contend that such problems are magnified in interracial junior high school classrooms. In 1978–79, a study was conducted in an eastern Virginia city school system, which operates under a federal court ordered busing plan, to investigate the possibility that teachers may have difficulty working with junior high school-age and black students because these groups perceive as important a set of teacher behaviors and characteristics different from their senior high school-age and white counterparts. This article reports on one aspect of that study.

The study was undertaken on the assumption that impressions of others are formed in terms of characteristics the perceiver feels are important. Friedman, Carlsmith and Sears stated that at times perception of other persons is influenced as much by what the rater is like as by what the person being rated is like.[1] Brown defined this perceptual discrimination as one's ability to sort out individuals according to some important criterion, noting general differences between persons along certain dimensions characteristic of the perceiver.[2] Tetenbaum contended that the evaluation of teachers by students would depend at least in part on "the extent to which teacher behaviors were congruent, dissonant, or irrelevant to student needs."[3] Other researchers[4] have reported findings on race or grade level perceptual differences in students' evaluations of teachers.

The population of this study was drawn from an urban school system that includes approximately 11,600 secondary school students in four intermediate schools (grades 8 and 9), and four high schools (grades 10–12). Approximately 60 percent of the students are white and 40 percent are black. Thirty white and 30 black students from each school were randomly selected from the alphabetical listings of ninth and twelfth grade enrollments. Thus, the sample was comprised of a total of 480 secondary students, equally distributed by race and grade.

The students were administered a modified version of the Personnel Decision Analysis developed by Alan Brown. The research instrument required students to select their three best and three worst teachers during the past two years. The students were asked to state what they considered to be the most important difference between each good and bad teacher. Each student identified 18 differentiating teacher characteristics or behaviors that were perceived as important. Students could identify behaviors associated with what good teachers did well or what bad teachers did poorly. The identified behaviors were stated, therefore, in terms of bipolar pairs of descriptive adjectives. Because the test is projective in nature and student responses were limited only by their own imagination and vocabulary, the data revealed a valid indication of students' perceptions of teachers.

The 8,640 identified behaviors were then categorized according to the three general dimensions of teacher behaviors identified by Ryans as warmth, organization, and stimulation.[5] Warmth behaviors included such factors as the teacher's being nice, friendly, caring, and fair. Organization behaviors included such factors as the teacher's preparation and organization, and the teacher's ability to explain the material and control the class. Stimulation behaviors included such factors as the teacher's ability to vary instructional techniques, to have an interesting class, and to be stimulating and enthusiastic.

Analyses of variance of general dimensions of teacher behaviors revealed that black and white secondary students in the school system surveyed perceived different teacher behaviors as important. Race differences in the perception of warm teacher behaviors ($p < .001$), well-organized teacher behaviors ($p < .016$), and stimulating teacher behaviors ($p < .001$) were highly significant. Perceptual differences by grade level were even more pronounced. Ninth graders and twelfth graders differed at the .001 level on warmth, organization, and stimulation.

The 20 specific behaviors most frequently perceived as important by students were also identified. Chi square analysis revealed that of these 20 specific behaviors, 18 differed significantly by race or grade level. These 20 specific bipolar behaviors are listed in Table 10.1.

A particularly interesting and noteworthy finding was that the perception of racial prejudice in teachers differed according to the grade level of students, but not the race of students. Black and white ninth graders were more sensitive to and conscious of racial prejudice in teachers than were either black or white twelfth graders. It should be added that it is indicative of the school system's successful efforts in promoting racial harmony and understanding that only 93 out of 8,640 responses pertained to racial prejudice at all.

It was difficult to construct a profile of a good teacher as perceived by black and white secondary students because perceptions differed more significantly according to grade level than to race. Greater differences existed between the same race at different grade levels than between different races at the same grade level. Twelfth grade students were more concerned with organization and stimulation and less concerned with warmth. Of the 20 most frequently identified behaviors, chi square analysis revealed that 14 differed significantly according to grade level. The data revealed that twelfth graders were particularly conscious of the teacher not covering assignments too fast, being fair in grading and testing, and varying instructional techniques. Ninth graders were particularly conscious of the teacher being nice, not losing temper, having a reluctance to yell, and not being prejudiced.

It is obvious, however, that analyses of both general dimensions of teacher behaviors and the most frequently identified specific teacher behaviors revealed that black and white students differed in their perception of which teacher characteristics are important. White students at the ninth and twelfth grade levels perceived as important well-organized, systematic teacher behavior, and stimulating,

Table 10.1 Specific teacher behaviors identified by students

| Behaviors | Ninth grade | | Twelfth grade | | |
	Whites	Blacks	Whites	Blacks	Totals
1. Explains material/does not explain material (o)	191	132	182	182	687*
2. Nice/mean (w)	98	164	32	64	358***
3. Interesting/boring (s)	87	41	129	100	357***
4. Helps students with work/does not help students with work (instructionally) (o)	78	62	98	101	339***
5. Cares/does not care (w)	64	62	75	86	287**
6. Goes too fast/does not go too fast (s)	50	34	77	81	242**
7. Makes sure students understand/ does not make sure students understand (o)	52	31	56	85	224**
8. Tries to teach/does not try to teach (o)	61	32	60	43	196*
9. Controls class/does not control class (o)	42	28	84	41	195***
10. Understanding/not understanding (w)	51	37	43	39	170
11. Uses different instructional techniques/does not use different instructional techniques (s)	20	8	87	40	155***
12. Fair/not fair (in grades and tests) (w)	38	9	47	53	147**
13. Helpful/is not helpful (in personal matters) (w)	29	44	23	48	144*
14. Yells/does not yell (w)	51	40	20	19	130**
15. Listens to students/does not listen to students (w)	27	31	29	40	127
16. Mad, has bad temper/not mad, good temper (w)	53	35	21	13	122***
17. Gives too much work/does not give too much work (s)	27	54	15	20	116***
18. Racially prejudiced/not racially prejudiced (w)	21	38	18	16	93**
19. Is not at school, late/present, on time (o)	15	12	39	27	93**
20. Talks too much/does not talk too much (s)	16	36	11	29	92*

Key:
(w) Warmth, (o) Organization, (s) Stimulation.
* Race Difference; **Grade Level Difference; ***Race and Grade Level.
Difference at 0.5% level of significance.
Vergule indicates bipolar behaviors.

interesting behaviors more frequently than black students at the same level. The black students more frequently perceived warm teacher behaviors as important. Specifically, white students perceived as important the teacher controlling the class and really trying to teach. Black students more frequently identified as important the teacher being nice and helpful.

Of the 20 specific behaviors, 18 differed significantly by race or grade level. Yet, when analyzed in terms of rank order listings for the four groups, 4 of the top 5 behaviors for each group were identical. Thus, the most revealing (and encouraging) finding of the study may not have been the identification of differences among groups, but the identification of a few fundamental, critically significant teacher behaviors perceived as important by all secondary groups. The behaviors thus identified were (1) the teacher's ability or willingness to explain the material adequately, (2) the ability of teachers to present the material in an interesting way, (3) the teachers' willingness "to help students with the work" after it has been presented, and (4) the teacher's caring attitude.

While each student group perceived certain basic characteristics as important, the secondary students clearly differed in their perceptions of most teacher characteristics according to race and grade level. What do these differences mean? What do they reveal about the students who hold these perceptions and the teachers whose behaviors were perceived as important?

Each student is particularly sensitive to certain characteristics of teachers. Brown[6] described these important characteristics as constructs—"personal, bipolar abstractions, used to structure a person's world." The students who participated in this survey are apparently structuring their worlds according to different abstractions. Blacks and ninth graders apparently have a greater need for warm, understanding and friendly behavior because they are to a greater extent structuring their worlds according to these dimensions.

Teachers are to a significant degree perceived as bad if they are weak in the construct behaviors through which groups of students structure their world for meaning and need satisfaction, and are perceived as good if they are strong in the constructs through which meaning and need satisfaction are derived. These perceptions may have no relationship to the fact that a student is actually learning anything in a particular teacher's class, but they have a positive relationship to the creation of teacher-student interpersonal harmony and the establishment of a classroom atmosphere conducive to learning. Obviously, if students who have a strong need for warmth or stimulation do not perceive it in their teachers, their behavior will reflect tension or boredom to the extent that neither the student's nor the teacher's needs will be met.

Do black and white students look for the same characteristics in teachers? The results of this study indicate "yes and no." All secondary students, regardless of race or grade level, apparently look for teachers who care, who explain the material in a thorough and interesting way, and who help students master the material after it has been presented. Yet, blacks seem to differ on their sensitivity and responsiveness to nice, friendly, and helpful teachers. Thus, we might conclude that when working with black students teachers must be particularly conscious not only of demonstrating sound instructional skills but of developing warm personal relationships. The data indicate that without this personal relationship, many black students, particularly those who are younger, will not benefit fully from even the most sophisticated instructional techniques.

It is hoped that teachers and students will change as they become aware of students' perceptions. Teachers can adjust their behaviors and instructional methods to accommodate student needs. Students can become more conscious of instructionally related teacher skills and less concerned with personality variables as an awareness of their perceptions develops maturity in their expectations of teachers. Yet neither teachers nor students can be expected to become what they are not. Both groups will continue to see things through lenses colored by their experiences, attitudes, and needs. It is the inescapable task of school administrators to develop instructional programs and to train instructional staff members with an awareness and acceptance of perceptual differences as important factors in decision-making.

Notes

1   J. Friendman, J. M. Carlsmith and D.O. Sears, *Social Psychology* (Englewood Cliffs, N.J.: Prentice-Hall Inc., 1974), p. 41.
2   Alan F. Brown, "Exploring Personnel Judgments with Discriminant Perception Analysis" (Paper presented at the Third Canadian Conference on Educational Research, MacDonald College, 1964), p. 229.
3   Toby Tetenbaum, "The Role of Student Needs and Teacher Orientations in Student Ratings of Teachers," *American Educational Research Journal*, 12 (Fall, 1975), 417–428.
4   See S. Bowles and H.M. Levin, "More on Multicollinearity and the Effectiveness of Schools," *Journal of Human Resources*, 3 (1968), 3–24; Robert Heath, "Ability of White Teachers to Relate to Black Students and White Students," *American Educational Research Journal*, 8 (1971), 635–648; Nancy St. John, "Thirty-six Teachers: Their Characteristics and Outcomes for Black and White Pupils," *American Educational Research Journal*, 8 (1971), 1–10; and Alexander Tolor, "Evaluation of Perceived Teacher Effectiveness," *Journal of Educational Psychology*, 64 (1973), 98–103.
5   D.G. Ryans, *Characteristics of Teachers; Their Description, Comparison and Appraisal* (Washington: American Council on Education, 1960).
6   Alan F. Brown, "Changing Promotion Criteria" (Paper presented at the Canadian Educational Researchers Association, Fredericton, New Brunswick, 1977), p. 20.

CHAPTER 11

THE SCHOOL EXPERIENCES OF BLACK GIRLS (1986)
The interaction of gender, race, and socioeconomic status

Diane Scott-Jones and Maxine L. Clark

We intend to examine in this article the academic, social, and motivational experiences of black females in the schools. Clearly, girls who belong to caste-like minorities experience discrimination at several levels. Since black males also experience discrimination, the relationship of black females to their male counterparts is not the same as the relationship of white females to white males. Likewise, the pattern of sex differences among blacks may differ from that among whites.

Few research studies have focused on both race and gender; moreover, researchers have frequently confounded socioeconomic status with minority-group membership. Though hampered by these realities, we will review in this article the findings that are available on the achievement of black females in science and mathematics and in verbal skills. We will discuss the educational expectations, aspirations, and motivations of black females and examine their educational and occupational attainments. We will describe the ways in which parental methods of socialization, teacher/student interactions, and peer inter-actions correlate with academic achievement. We will also suggest the directions in which research and practice ought to be moving.

Space does not permit us to examine the school experiences of females who belong to other minority groups. Moreover, less data are available on many of these groups than on blacks. We do know that, with the exception of a few Asian-American groups that achieve well in school, minorities share somewhat similar patterns of low school achievement. We know, as well, that minorities differ. It is important that we consider the school experiences of all minority groups; therefore, future research—especially major national studies—should focus on collecting adequate data from which to draw conclusions about such groups.

Math/science achievement

High achievement in mathematics and science is a prerequisite for lucrative careers that have traditionally been closed to women and minorities. General agreement exists that blacks, females, and disadvantaged students achieve less well in science and mathematics than do white middle-class male students. However, information is not readily available on how the variables of race, gender, and socioeconomic status might interact to produce this outcome.

Herbert Ginsburg and Robert Russell found few social-class or racial differences in the mathematical thinking of preschoolers and kindergartners, as measured by a variety of tasks. The sample for their study included both boys and girls, but they reported no analyses for sex differences.[1] Meanwhile, a review of the research on sex differences found that differences in mathematical thinking that favor males do not appear consistently until 10th grade; even then, the differences are usually not large, and they are not found invariably.[2]

A study of black eighth-graders in an inner-city school found no sex differences in mathematics and science achievement. However, boys scored significantly higher than girls on a measure of science self-concept, and, when forced to choose between paired occupations, they were significantly more likely than girls to choose a science-related occupation over a non-science-related occupation.[3]

A meta-analysis of the characteristics and science performance of kindergartners through 12th-graders indicated that, of all the variables considered, gender had the weakest relationship to the three performance measures employed.[4] Males scored slightly higher than females on cognitive and achievement measures, and the difference was greater in middle school than in elementary school or in high school. Gender differences in attitudes toward science showed the opposite pattern: in elementary school and in high school, males had more positive attitudes toward science than females, but the reverse was true in middle school. On cognitive and achievement measures, the effects attributable to race were almost three times as great as those attributable to gender. Whites scored higher than blacks across grade levels. Whites in elementary school also had more favorable attitudes toward science than blacks, but this difference disappeared at the middle school and high school levels.

Socioeconomic status correlated significantly with the three performance measures. The relationship of socioeconomic status to cognitive measures was constant across grade levels. The effect of socioeconomic status on achievement increased with grade level. The relationship of socioeconomic status to attitudes toward science was relatively small, disappearing by high school. However, Lynette Fleming and Mark Malone, who conducted the meta-analysis, pointed out that the variables of socioeconomic status and race are likely to be confounded, since the studies that they included in the racial comparisons generally failed to report the subjects' socioeconomic status. Thus, as is true in much psychological and educational research, the findings that Fleming and Malone labeled racial differences may actually be differences related to socioeconomic status instead. Although sex differences for blacks were not analyzed, the findings of this meta-analysis suggest that the science performance of black females is more likely to resemble the science performance of black males than that of white females.

Meanwhile, the National Assessment of Educational Progress (NAEP) showed that, at age 13, black females and black males did not differ in their mathematics achievement. The NAEP also found no sex differences for white 13-year-olds. However, the performance of white youngsters was substantially higher than that of blacks. Socioeconomic factors, such as parents' educational and occupational status, were related to students' performance.

By age 17, significant sex differences favoring males showed up for both blacks and whites. But the difference between the two racial groups was five times as large as the sex differences within the races. For males and females of both races combined, the best predictor of mathematics achievement at age 17 was the number of mathematics courses completed. On the average, students who had taken two years of algebra and a year of geometry answered 82% of the test items correctly, whereas students who had taken none of these courses answered only 47% of the items correctly.[5]

When the groups are equated for the number of mathematics courses completed, black females (and black males and white females, as well) may equal the mathematics performance of white males. The High School and Beyond Project, sponsored by the National Center for Education Statistics, found no race or sex differences in the mathematics achievement test scores of high school seniors, when two variables—sophomore achievement test scores and number of math courses completed—were controlled.[6] The mathematics achievements tests assessed a variety of skills, including computation, arithmetic, reasoning, graph reading, algebra, and geometry. Some research has found that girls outperform boys in certain areas, such as computation, and that boys outperform girls in other areas, such as reasoning.[7] Thus the breadth of these tests is important. The findings of the High School and Beyond Project suggest that race and sex differences in mathematics achievement could be eliminated by encouraging black females, black males, and white females to enroll in appropriate math courses.

Although the performance of blacks of both sexes in mathematics and science remains below that of whites (especially white males), the performance gap appears to be decreasing somewhat.[8] The mathematics performance of black 9-, 13-, and 17-year-olds on the NAEP improved between 1978 and 1982—and, for 13-year-olds, the gain of 6.5 percentage points was statistically significant. During the same interval, the science achievement of black females increased among 9-year-olds, remained approximately the same among 13-year-olds, and declined slightly among 17-year-olds. The scores of the black females were approximately equal to those of black males except among 17-year-olds, where males performed slightly better. In the part of the NAEP science assessment that covered inquiry, the performance of blacks of both sexes declined only slightly, while the performance of whites of both sexes declined significantly.

Computer literacy is a related area of concern. Although studies have been conducted to assess the availability of computers in schools and the extent to which students use them, this research has not focused on the situation of black students per se. Linnda Caporael and Warren Thorngate have suggested that computer technology may intensify existing social roles.[9] Clearly, there is a need for research that examines the computer literacy of black females, black males, and children of the poor.

Verbal skills

The general belief is that females outperform males in verbal skills, but research suggests instead a complex pattern of differential performance. Sex differences in verbal skills are rarely found among children younger than 10. However, males are more often identified as problem readers in the elementary grades. Among older children, females perform better than males on many verbal measures, but males outperform females in vocabulary and some higher-level verbal skills. When sex differences are found, they are often small, with much overlap in performance between males and females. Sex differences in verbal skills may be larger for low-ability students than for others.[10] Black children score lower on reading skills in the NAEP than do white children, but the gap has decreased steadily.[11]

Expectations, aspirations, and motivations

A study of fourth- through eighth-graders showed that black children were no more likely than whites or Hispanics to attribute their successes or failures in mathematics to external factors, such as luck or low ability. However, those black children who did behave in this fashion were predominantly female and were not achieving well in mathematics.[12]

A study of male and female adolescents in rural schools in the South, which examined both blacks and whites, found that black males and females have high educational and career aspirations.[13] Moreover, the sex differences that the investigators found among white adolescents with regard to aspirations did not show up among blacks. The researchers suggested two possible explanations for this finding: 1) the experience of being black may be more salient than gender to black adolescents themselves and to others, and 2) similar labor market opportunities for black adults of both sexes may cause black adolescents and their parents to devalue traditional definitions of females work roles.

Research conducted in the 1970s[14] produced similar findings: at the high school level, black females have educational and occupational aspirations as high as or higher than those of black males or white females. But this research also showed that, at the college level, the aspirations of black females drop below those of black males. Like their white counterparts, black females of college age tend to adhere to sex-role stereotypes in their educational and occupational goals and choices. Indeed, gender influences such things as the expectation of obtaining a doctorate (rather than a master's degree), grade-point average, and score on the Graduate Record Examination. However, black females differ from white females in their motivations for working outside the home. Black females tend to be concerned about contributing to the economic support of their families, while the motivations of white females focus on self-fulfillment.

Educational and occupational attainment

Both educational and occupational attainment are gauges by which to measure the success of earlier school experiences. Moreover, the level of education and the level of occupation typically attained by adult black females may influence the aspirations and expectations of young black females.

The proportion of blacks who did not graduate from high school declined substantially between 1970 and 1982. The number of black females who left school without graduating dropped from 65.2% to 45.7% during that interval, while the number of black males who dropped out fell from 67.5% to 44.3%. For whites of both sexes, the comparable decline was from about 42% to about 27%. Among all races and genders, older individuals are now more likely than younger ones to have ended their schooling before graduation.[15]

In the High School and Beyond study of 1980 high school sophomores, the dropout rate was 14.1% for black females, 20.3% for black males, 13% for white males, and 11.5% for white females. The reasons that students gave for dropping out varied somewhat by race and gender. Male and female blacks, Hispanics, and American Indians as a group cited poor grades most frequently (30%). Among minority females, the reasons most often given were pregnancy (29.2%), dislike of school (24.9%), and marriage (19.2%). White females most often mentioned marriage (36.4%), dislike of school (34.1%), poor grades (30%), and pregnancy (20.5%). White males cited dislike of school (45.6%), and minority males cited poor grades (31.2%).[16] Because students could give more than one reason for dropping out, these findings are difficult to interpret.

Census Bureau data for 1981 show lower dropout rates than those reported in the High School and Beyond study. According to the Census Bureau, the dropout rates among 16- and 17-year-olds were 7.2% for black males, 8.7% for black females, 8.1% for white males, and 7.5% for white females. Once again, the dropout rates were lower for younger teens and higher for older teens.[17] However, some urban areas report dropout rates much higher than those found by the Census Bureau.

In higher education, female enrollment has increased and male enrollment has remained stable. Thus by 1982 a majority of college students (52%) were female. That same year, females earned a majority of the bachelor's and master's degrees, one-third of all doctoral degrees, and more than one-fourth of all professional degrees. By contrast, the enrollment of blacks and other minorities and the proportion of all degrees granted to them have remained stable or have shown only slight gains.[18]

In 1980 black females made up 5.3% of the total enrollment in higher education; that same year, black males accounted for only 3.8% of the total. During the 1980–81 school year 3.9% of all bachelor's degrees went to black females, and 2.6% of all bachelor's degrees went to black males. Black females received 6.4% of all bachelor's degrees awarded in education, but only .5% of all bachelor's degrees awarded in engineering. Black males, by contrast, received 2.4% of all education degrees and 2.7% of all engineering degrees.

Black females received 3.7% of all master's degrees awarded during the 1980–81 school year, while black males received 2.1%. Once again, black females received 6.7% of all master's degrees awarded in education but only .2% of all master's degrees awarded in engineering. Black males, by contrast, received 2.1% of all master's degrees in education and 1.4% of all master's degrees in engineering.

Black females earned 1.7% of all doctorates awarded during the 1980–81 school year, while black males earned 2.1%. Black females earned 4.1% of all doctorates awarded in education; black males earned 3.7%. In engineering, black males received .9% of all doctoral degrees, and black women received .03%.[19]

In a study of black eighth-graders in an inner city, sex proved to be a better predictor of preference for a career in science than mathematics achievement, science achievement, or children's perceptions of their ability in science. (However, the other three variables were also significantly linked to such a career preference.[20]) In this particular study, career preference was assessed by forced choices between science-related and non-science-related occupations that may not have reflected students' actual career goals accurately. In other words, students may not have wanted – or expected – to work toward either of the careers in the pairs presented to them. If none of the careers that were presented (e.g., biochemist, aerospace engineer, lawyer, city planner) seemed personally appropriate to the inner-city students in this sample, they may have allowed sex-role stereotypes, rather than their own abilities and interests, to determine their choices.

Academic achievement is dependent on more than individual abilities and aspirations. The social environment in which learning takes place can enhance or diminish the behaviors that lead to achievement.

The school is a microcosm of the society. Therefore, the racial and sex-role stereotypes and biases prevalent in the society find their way into the school. The school environment reflects the fact that the society values males over females and whites over nonwhites. Thus students who are members of minority groups must adjust to teachers and peers as well as to schoolwork; in other words, they must live a bicultural existence.[21]

Socialization by parents

Families influence their children's cognitive development and school achievement in a variety of ways.[22] The widely accepted perception of black families as matriarchal and thus emasculating is not supported by contemporary theory or research. Indeed, the socialization practices of black families are relatively egalitarian.[23]

The myth that black mothers encourage their daughters' academic achievement at the expense of their sons' achievement may persist, but it is not supported by research.[24] The myth may have arisen because of the strong sex-role stereotypes regarding educational and occupational attainment to which white families adhered until recently. Whites may have interpreted the lack of strict differentiation by gender of educational and occupational roles among blacks as inappropriate encouragement of black females.

In black families, a great deal of overlap exists between the characteristics that are considered appropriate for males and those that are considered appropriate for females. Black children of both sexes are socialized to be independent and to achieve.[25]

In a study of second-graders, by contrast, middle-class white parents expected their sons to earn higher grades than their daughters in mathematics (even though actual grades for the two groups did not differ). Working-class parents, both white and black, expected higher grades for their daughters than for their sons in both mathematics and reading, however.[26]

Teacher/student interactions

Research has solidly established the fact that teachers' expectations of students vary as a function of the students' race. Teachers look for and reinforce achievement-oriented behaviors in white students more often than in black students. Teachers also attribute the achievement-oriented behaviors of white students to such internal factors as effort or motivation, while they attribute the achievement-oriented behaviors of black students to factors that students cannot control, such as parental encouragement or heredity.[27] Teachers are more likely to give white students praise and attention, and they have higher performance standards for white students than for black students. When teachers praise black students for their academic performance, the praise is often qualified: "This is a good paper; it is better than yesterday's." Teachers tend to praise white students who have been labeled as gifted but to criticize black students who have been similarly labeled. This differential treatment may occur because teachers do not expect intellectual competence in black students.[28]

The data supporting the fact that teachers treat boys and girls differently are just as solid as those supporting the fact that teacher expectations vary according to the race of a student. Male students receive more attention, praise, encouragement, and criticism from teachers than do their female counterparts.[29] Boys have more contacts with teachers overall than do girls, and those contacts are more likely to relate to their academic work or classroom behavior.[30] Teachers have more contacts with female students during reading periods and more contacts with male students during math classes.[31]

However, the relationship between teacher expectations and gender of students is not clear and depends on a variety of factors, such as grade level and content area. Elementary teachers have higher expectations for females than for males.[32] This pattern is rarely duplicated in high school, however.[33] With regard to expectations for abstract or mathematical reasoning skills, Barbara Simmons failed to find a bias among teachers in favor of male students.[34] Some researchers have concluded that teacher expectations for academic achievement are not related to the gender of students, although teacher expectations for students' behavior and adjustment are weakly related to students' gender.[35]

Several studies have investigated the degree to which teacher expectations for achievement vary as a function of the students' social class. When significant differences were found, the teachers expected higher achievement from middle-class students than from lower-class students.[36]

A few studies have also tried to determine whether race and social class interact in determining teacher expectations. However, the results of these studies have been inconclusive.[37]

Two questions arise regarding the teacher's role in the achievement of black females: Do teachers encourage black females to achieve academically? And what is the nature of the interaction between black females and their teachers?

In response to the first question, research suggests that black females do not receive – at least, in the early grades – the same kind of academic encouragement that whites of both sexes experience. In an ethnographic study of first-graders, Linda Grant found that teachers were more likely to perceive black female students as socially mature and white female students as intellectually competent. Teachers encouraged the social competence of black girls by seeking their help in nonacademic matters. Black females often served as "rule enforcers" and as "go-betweens," bringing messages from other students to the teacher. Meanwhile, teachers gave white girls intellectual encouragement and sought their help in academic matters. They assigned tasks involving high degrees of responsibility to white girls more often than to black girls or to boys of either race. This increased the likelihood that white girls would be perceived by their peers as intellectually competent.[38]

Most teachers praised academic performance more often than they praised social behavior. However, black females received more praise for behavior than any other subgroup of students. Black males received the least praise for, and the most criticism of, their behavior. White males received the largest number of teacher comments related to academics, and black females received the largest number of teacher comments related to nonacademic matters. These findings show that black children of both sexes were denied the degree of intellectual encouragement given to their white counterparts.[39] Further research is needed to determine whether these patterns remain consistent throughout the school years.

With regard to the *quality* of student/teacher interactions, Grant found that black girls approached the teacher only when necessary. Their contacts were usually brief, task-oriented, and conducted on behalf of a peer. White girls, by contrast, had more prolonged contact with teachers and were likely to converse about personal matters in addition to school-related issues. Black males had the fewest contacts with teachers and the most contacts with peers of all the subgroups studied.[40]

Peter Woolridge and Charles Richman[41] studied teachers' responses to hypothetical descriptions of student misbehaviors. For fighting, teachers were just as likely to prescribe severe punishments for black females as for black males. There were significant differences in their treatments of white males and white females, however. The teachers were less likely to prescribe severe punishments for white females than for white males. (They prescribed severe punishments slightly more often for white males than for blacks.)

Teachers' perceptions of students are presumed to be the factors determining the quality of teacher/student interactions. Valora Washington found that both black teachers and white teachers evaluated white girls more positively than they evaluated black girls or boys of either race. The teachers evaluated black males and black females similarly, but they evaluated white males more negatively than white females.[42] Similarly, Diane Pollard found that teachers rated white females higher than white males or blacks of either sex in the areas of responsibility, compliance, persistence, performance/ability, and relations with peers and teachers.[43] In other words, in evaluating their students, teachers make gender distinctions among white children more often than among black children.

Black teachers may be more inclined than white teachers to criticize black students, however. Robert Byalick and Donald Bersoff found that teachers reinforce children of other races more frequently than they reinforce children of their own race. In their study, black females were the group of students who received the least reinforcement – especially in the classrooms of black female teachers, who reinforced males of both races more frequently than they reinforced girls of either race.[44] Washington found that black teachers in integrated classrooms were most critical of black girls, whereas white teachers in integrated settings were most critical of white boys.[45]

Peer interactions

The influence of peer interactions is more variable than that of teacher/student interactions on academic achievement. In some studies, academic performance has correlated positively with acceptance by peers and positive peer interactions.[46] Ralph Lewis and Nancy St. John found that popularity with white girls was a significant predictor of black girls' grade-point averages.[47] However, Martin Patchen and his colleagues found that interracial contact had little impact on the academic performance of black students.[48]

Are black females more likely than black males to experience peer acceptance in ethnically mixed classes? The answer is not clear. Some researchers have described black females in biracial junior high and high school classrooms as social isolates. Black females also tend to be more ethnocentric than black males in their friendship choices and peer interactions. In predominantly white classrooms, however, black students of both sexes make more cross-race friendship choices than do white students (though these choices are rarely reciprocated).[49]

A different pattern of peer interactions seems to exist among first-graders. Linda Grant found that black female first-graders had more extensive peer interactions than any other racial or gender-based subgroup. In their interactions, they crossed race and gender lines more often than other children. But these peer relationships were generally weak and one-sided, not strong and reciprocal. Meanwhile, black girls and black boys helped one another in both academic and nonacademic matters, while white girls gave white boys more help than they received in return.[50]

Sometimes black females must cope with a disproportionate number of racist remarks. In Grant's study, the racist remarks, which were generally made by white males, tended to come after the teacher praised a black girl's academic performance. Grant suggested that white males may have used the racist remarks for self-enhancement, since the remarks were intended to emphasize the lower status of black females.

When it comes to schooling, black males do not enjoy a "male advantage." Blacks of both sexes – especially those from low-income families – tend to achieve at lower levels than whites. For black females, then, attending to inequities caused by race and social class is at least as important as attending to inequities fostered by sex bias. However, blacks do encounter some sex-role stereotyping. Therefore, attending to sex equity would probably enhance the educational attainment of blacks of both sexes.

Where appropriate, future research studies should cover all three variables of race, gender, and socioeconomic status. Researchers should adequately describe their subjects in terms of these three characteristics. And finally, researchers must seek to avoid confounding the variables of race and socioeconomic status.

Notes

1 Herbert P. Ginsburg and Robert L. Russell, "Social Class and Racial Influences on Early Mathematical Thinking," *Monographs of the Society for Research in Child Development*, vol. 46, no. 6, 1981.
2 Elizabeth K. Stage et al., "Increasing the Participation and Achievement of Girls and Women in Mathematics, Science, and Engineering," in S. Klein, ed., *Handbook for Achieving Sex Equity Through Education* (Baltimore: Johns Hopkins University Press, 1985), pp. 237–68.
3 Tina Jacobowitz, "Relationship of Sex, Achievement, and Science Self-Concept to the Science Career Preferences of Black Students," *Journal of Research in Science Teaching*, vol. 20, 1983, pp. 621–28.
4 M. Lynette Fleming and Mark R. Malone, "The Relationship of Student Characteristics and Student Performance in Science as Viewed by Meta-Analysis Research," *Journal of Research in Science Teaching*, vol. 20, 1983, pp. 481–95.
5 Lyle V. Jones, "White-Black Achievement Differences: The Narrowing Gap," *American Psychologist*, vol. 39, 1984, pp. 1207–13; Lyle V. Jones, Nancy W. Burton, and Ernest C. Davenport, "Monitoring the Mathematics Achievement of Black Students," *Journal for Research in Mathematics Education*, vol. 15, 1984, pp. 154–64; and Westina Matthews et al., "The Third National Assessment: Minorities and Mathematics," *Journal for Research in Mathematics Education*, vol. 15, 1984, pp. 165–71.
6 Lyle V. Jones, "Black-White Differences in Mathematics: Research Findings and Direction for Research," paper presented at the annual meeting of the American Educational Research Association, Chicago, April 1985.
7 Stage et al., "Increasing the Participation. . . ."
8 Jones, Burton, and Davenport, "Monitoring . . ."; Matthews et al., "The Third National Assessment . . ."; and Audrey Weinberg and Debra Gerald, "Elementary/Secondary Education," in V. Plisko, ed., *The Condition of Education* (Washington, D.C.: U.S. Government Printing Office, 1984), pp. 3–60.
9 Linnda R. Caporael and Warren Thorngate, "Introduction: Towards the Social Psychology of Computing," *Journal of Social Issues*, vol. 40, 1984, pp. 1–13.
10 Kathryn P. Scott, Carol Anne Dwyer, and Barbara Lieb-Brilhart, "Sex Equity in Reading and Communication Skills," in Klein, pp. 269–79.
11 Jones, "White-Black Achievement. . . ."
12 Ann C. Willig et al., "Sociocultural and Educational Correlates of Success-Failure Attributions and Evaluation Anxiety in the School Setting for Black, Hispanic,

and Anglo Children," *American Educational Research Journal*, vol. 20, 1983, pp. 385–410.

13 Larry W. DeBord, Larry J. Griffin, and Melissa Clark, "Race and Sex Influences in the Schooling Processes of Rural and Small Town Youth," *Sociology of Education*, vol. 42, 1977, pp. 85–102.

14 John A. Centra, "Graduate Degree Aspirations of Ethnic Student Groups," *American Educational Research Journal*, vol. 17, 1980, pp. 459–78; and Elsie J. Smith, "The Black Female Adolescent: A Review of the Educational, Career, and Psychological Literature," *Psychology of Women Quarterly*, vol. 6, 1982, pp. 261–88.

15 Larry Suter and Valena Plisko, "Educationally Disadvantaged Adults," in Plisko, pp. 129–48.

16 Richard E. Whalen, "Secondary Education: Student Flows, Course Participation, and State Requirements," in Plisko, pp. 149–82.

17 W. Vance Grant and Thomas D. Snyder, *Digest of Education Statistics* (Washington, D.C.: U.S. Government Printing Office, 1983), p. 71.

18 Debra Gerald and Audrey Weinberg, "Higher Education," in Plisko, pp. 149–82.

19 Grant and Snyder, pp. 85–103.

20 Jacobowitz, pp. 621–28.

21 Diane Pollard, "Patterns of Coping in Black Schoolchildren," in A. W. Boykin, A. Franklin, and F. Yates, eds., *Research Directions of Black Psychologists* (New York: Russell Sage, 1979), pp. 188–209; and Bertha Holliday, "Towards a Model of Teacher-Child Transactional Processes Affecting Black Children's Academic Achievement," in M. Spencer, G. Brookins, and W. Allen, eds., *Beginnings: The Social and Affective Development of Black Children* (Hillsdale, N.J.: Erlbaum, 1985), pp. 117–30.

22 Diane Scott-Jones, "Family Influences on Cognitive Development and School Achievement," *Review of Research in Education*, vol. 11, 1984, pp. 259–304.

23 Pamela Reid, "Socialization of Black Female Children," in P. Berman and E. Ramey, eds., *Women: A Developmental Perspective* (Washington, D.C.: U.S. Department of Health and Human Services, 1982), pp. 137–55; and Diane Scott-Jones and Sharon Nelson-Le Gall, "Defining Black Families: Past and Present," in E. Seidman and J. Rappaport, eds., *Redefining Social Problems* (New York: Plenum, forthcoming).

24 Smith, "The Black Female Adolescent. . . ."

25 Scott-Jones and Nelson-Le Gall, "Defining Black Families. . . ."

26 Doris R. Entwisle and D.P. Baker, "Gender and Young Children's Expectations for Performance in Arithmetic," *Developmental Psychology*, vol. 19, 1983, pp. 200–9.

27 Mary Wiley and Arlene Eskilson, "Why Did You Learn in School Today? Teachers' Perceptions of Causality," *Sociology of Education*, October 1978, pp. 261–69.

28 Reuben Baron, David Tom, and Harris Cooper, "Social Class, Race, and Teacher Expectations," in J. Dusek and G. Joseph, eds., *Teacher Expectancies* (Hillsdale, N.J.: Erlbaum, 1985), pp. 251–69; Wiley and Eskilson, "Why Did You Learn in School Today? . . ."; Linda Grant, "Black Females' Place in Desegregated Classrooms," *Sociology of Education*, April 1984, pp. 98–110; Pamela Rubovits and Martin Maehr, "Pygmalion Black and White," *Journal of Personality and Social Psychology*, vol. 25, 1953, pp. 210–18; and Reid, "Socialization of Black Female Children."

29 Jere Brophy, "Teacher Praise: A Functional Analysis," *Review of Educational Research*, Spring 1981, pp. 5–32; and Robert Byalick and Donald Bersoff, "Reinforcement Practices of Black and White Teachers in Integrated Classrooms," *Journal of Educational Psychology*, vol. 66, 1974, pp. 473–80.

30 Jere Brophy and Carolyn Evertson, *Student Characteristics and Teaching* (New York: Longman, 1981).

31 Gaea Leinhardt, Andrea Seewald, and Mary Engel, "Learning What's Taught: Sex Differences in Interaction," *Journal of Educational Psychology*, vol. 71, 1979, pp. 432–39.

32 Barbara Bank, Bruce Biddle, and Thomas Good, "Sex Roles, Classroom Instruction, and Reading Achievement," *Journal of Educational Psychology*, vol. 72, 1980, pp. 119–32.

33 Thomas Good and Maureen Findley, "Sex Role Expectations and Achievement," in Dusek and Joseph, *Teacher Expectancies*, pp. 271–300.

34 Barbara Simmons, "Sex Role Expectations of Classroom Teachers," *Education*, Spring 1980, pp. 249–59.

35 Jerome Dusek and Gail Joseph, "The Bases of Teacher Expectancies," in Dusek and Joseph, *Teacher Expectancies*, pp. 229–50.

36 Ibid.

37 Baron, Tom, and Cooper, "Social Class, Race, and Teacher Expectations."

38 Linda Grant, "Black Females' Place. . . ."

39 Ibid.; and idem, "Uneasy Alliances: Black Males, Teachers, and Peers in Desegregated Classrooms," paper presented at the annual meeting of the American Educational Research Association, Chicago, 1985.

40 Linda Grant, "Uneasy Alliances. . . ."

41 Peter Woolridge and Charles Richman, "Teachers' Choice of Punishment as a Function of a Student's Gender, Age, Race, and I.Q. Level, *Journal of School Psychology*, vol. 23, 1985, pp. 19–29.

42 Valora Washington, "Racial Differences in Teacher Perceptions of First and Fourth Grade Pupils on Selected Characteristics," *Journal of Negro Education*, vol. 51, 1982, pp. 60–72.

43 Pollard, "Patterns of Coping. . . ."

44 Byalick and Bersoff, "Reinforcement Practices. . . ."

45 Valora Washington, "Teachers in Integrated Classrooms: Profiles of Attitudes, Perceptions, and Behavior," *Elementary School Journal*, vol. 80, 1980, pp. 193–201.

46 Kenneth Green et al., "An Assessment of the Relationship Among Measures of Children's Social Competence and Children's Academic Achievement," *Child Development*, vol. 51, 1980, pp. 1149–56.

47 Ralph Lewis and Nancy St. John, "Contributions of Cross-Racial Friendship to Minority Group Achievement in Desegregated Classrooms," *Sociometry*, vol. 37, 1974, pp. 79–91.

48 Martin Patchen, Gerald Hofmann, and William Brown, "Academic Performance of Black High School Students Under Different Conditions of Contact with White Peers," *Sociology of Education*, January 1980, pp. 33–51.

49 Martin Patchen, *Black-White Contact in School: Its Social and Academic Effect* (West Lafayette, Ind.: Purdue University Press, 1982), David De Vries and Keith Edwards, "Student Teams and Learning Games: Their Effect on Cross-Race and Cross-Sex Interaction," *Journal of Educational Psychology*, vol. 66, 1974, pp. 741–49; and Maureen Hallinan, "Classroom Racial Composition and Children's Friendship," *Social Forces*, vol. 61, 1982, pp. 56–72.

50 Linda Grant, "Black Females' Place. . . ."

CHAPTER 12

OPENING THE CLOSET (1997)
Multiculturalism that is fully inclusive
Cathy A. Pohan and Norma J. Bailey

> I have learned that oppression and the intolerance of difference come in all shapes and sexes and colors and sexualities; and that among those of us who share the goals of liberation and a workable future for our children, there is no hierarchy of oppression.
>
> —Audre Lorde (Lorde, 1983, 9)

Recognizing that too many children in this country were not receiving an equal educational opportunity, many voices rose up demanding that schools address the needs of those groups who had traditionally been denied access and representation in the educational process. Yet, "with few exceptions, most school districts still fail to acknowledge or serve the needs of gay, lesbian, bisexual students, parents, and staff" (Goodman, 1996, 10). Coupled with the homophobia[1] and heterosexism[2] in society, the lack of recognition, resources, and support for gay and lesbian[3] youth makes these youngsters perhaps one of the most at-risk of all student populations.

It is encouraging to see The National Association for Multicultural Education (NAME) add its name to a growing list of professional organizations that are addressing the needs of gay and lesbian youth today. Yet, while several scholars leading the field of multicultural education (*e.g.*, executive committee of NAME; Nieto, 1996; Sleeter & Grant, 1993) have broadened the umbrella of multiculturalism to be inclusive of sexual orientation, many educators may still feel unable to articulate why such inclusion is imperative. In this article, we seek to build a rationale for inclusion by reviewing: (a) the experiences of gay and lesbian youth that place them at-risk in society and school; (b) how homophobia and heterosexism hurts both gay and non-gay individuals; and (c) the goals and role of multicultural education in helping to create a more just and equitable society.

Gay and lesbian youth: an at-risk population

Adolescence can be a difficult, if not tumultuous, developmental period for youngsters to navigate. In addition to the challenge of integrating increasing biological, psychological, and social demands, adolescents are also becoming aware of their sexuality. The reluctance of parents and "educators to deal candidly with teenage sexual orientation issues, particularly if that orientation is homosexual, places a significant number of adolescents at risk, not only of school failure, but of personal and social crises—even death" (Walling, 1993, 7). The following words illustrate the intense struggles faced by many adolescents in our schools today:

> I hear homophobic comments all the time in my classes. Sometimes I think teachers don't hear what goes on in their classrooms. I want teachers to remember that I can't block out the homophobia. I hear it even when I don't want to listen. I hear it every day that I am in this school. And it hurts a lot. (A 16-year-old lesbian, Jennings, 1996, 258)

> I was very different from other students and they picked up on it. Immediately the words "faggot" and "queer" were used to describe me. Freshman year of high school was hard enough; but with the big seniors pushing you around because the rumor is you're a faggot, it's ten times worse. I knew I was gay. But who could I talk to? I was spit upon, pushed, and ridiculed. My school life was hell. I decided to leave school because I couldn't handle it. (An 18-year-old gay male, Jennings, 1996, 259)

> I felt as though I was the only gay person my age in the world. I felt as though I had nowhere to go to talk to anybody. Throughout eighth grade, I went to bed every night praying that I would not be able to wake up in the morning, and every morning waking up and being disappointed. And so finally I decided that if I was going to die, it would have to be at my own hands. (An 18-year-old gay male, The Governor's Commission on Gay and Lesbian Youth, 1993, 12)

In addition to such testimonies, there is mounting evidence suggesting that gay and lesbian youth are believed to be at greater risk than their heterosexual counterparts for substance abuse, poor mental health, running away, dropping out of school, suicide, risky sexual behavior, and hate violence (Denver Area Alliance for Hate Free Schools, 1995; The Governor's Commission on Gay and Lesbian Youth, 1993). Indeed, the most disturbing fact is that young lives are being needlessly lost. It is estimated that 30 percent of the completed teen suicides are committed by gay or lesbian youth or those struggling with their sexual identity. Further, gay and lesbian youth are two to three times more likely to attempt suicide than their heterosexual counterparts (The Governor's Commission on Gay and Lesbian Youth, 1993; Remafedi, 1994).

Even if suicide is not chosen as an avenue of escape, gay and lesbian youth face many other problems which put them at high risk. Because of the negative self-images they buy into as a result of living in a homophobic society and the pain of the internal conflicts, gay and lesbian youth are three times more likely than their heterosexual peers to abuse substances (Gibson, 1989). Twenty-six percent of those who "come out" to their families are "thrown out" of their homes because of conflicts with moral and religious values (Gibson, 1989). Further, it is estimated that between 30 percent and 40 percent of the homeless youth in large cities are gay and lesbian youth. Tragically, many often engage in prostitution to survive (Denver Area Alliance for Hate Free Schools, 1995).

In addition to the previously mentioned risk behaviors, it is not uncommon for youth who are struggling with their sexual identity to increase their sexual experimentation. Some increase sexual activity with heterosexuals just to "prove" that they are not gay or lesbian. Still others may experiment with the same gender to determine if they really are gay or lesbian. Unfortunately, participation in risky and unprotected sexual activity increases the likelihood of contracting sexually transmitted diseases or HIV (Gibson, 1989; Remafedi, 1994).

Still further, while members of many minority groups are the victims of hate violence, gays and lesbians are increasingly the most frequent victims, particularly of brutal crimes. According to the *Klanwatch Intelligence Report* of the Southern Poverty Law Center, gays and lesbians bore the brunt of hate violence in 1994. Among the assault victims documented in their report, over 25 percent were gay or lesbian, and of the 18 murders Klanwatch verified, 11 were motivated by anti-gay bias (*Klanwatch Intelligence Report*, 1995).

It is tragic that adolescents struggling with their sexual orientation find themselves in an often hostile society with little (if any) support even at home. It is even more tragic that while school is the other primary social institution where all young people should be able to feel safe, this is often not the case. Harassment, threats, and/or violence against gay and lesbian youth (and those perceived to be gay or lesbian) continues to increase on high school, middle school, and junior high school campuses acros our nation (The Governor's Commission on Gay and Lesbian Youth, 1993).

The school experiences of gay and lesbian youth

Of 289 secondary school counselors surveyed nationally, 54 percent strongly agreed that "students are very degrading toward fellow students whom they discover are homosexual," and 67 percent strongly agreed that "homosexual students are more likely to feel isolated and rejected" (Price & Telljohann, 1991). As well, "45 percent of the males and 20 percent of the females [surveyed] reported having experienced verbal or physical assaults in secondary school because they were perceived to be gay or lesbian" (The Governor's Commission on Gay and Lesbian Youth, 1993, 9).

While some teachers and administrators harass, ridicule, and unfairly punish gay students, or those "suspected" or "accused" of being gay, the predominant feature of the discriminatory school environment for gay youth is the failure of school officials to provide protection from peer harassment and violence (Dennis & Harlow, 1986; Governor's Commission on Gay and Lesbian Youth, 1993). Counselors, who should provide confidential and supportive counseling to gay and lesbian youth, often do not do so for a number of reasons: too busy; themselves uncomfortable with the issue of homosexuality; not trained to deal with the issue; afraid of controversy; or, worse yet, strongly homophobic themselves (Gibson, 1989).

Another school practice that needs to be addressed in order to provide a more equitable education for gay and lesbian youth is the "conspiracy of silence" that envelops most schools (Sears, 1991). In the majority of schools, neither curriculum—including sex education classes—nor library resources provide students, gay or non-gay, with accurate and positive information about homosexuality. As with people of color or women 30 to 40 years ago, this leaves gay and lesbian youth with no sense of history and historical role models with whom to identify. Nor do these students have role models in their schools because the majority of gay and lesbian teachers are not "out" because of fears for their job security, etc.

In addition, the vast majority of schools do not have anti-slur or anti-discrimination policies in place which include sexual orientation. This means that gay and lesbian students have no recourse when harassed, nor have teachers been trained to ensure their safety. As well, there are virtually no support groups for gay and lesbian students, at the very time when they are desperate for support and someone to talk to in order to alleviate their feelings of difference and aloneness and when acceptance from a peer group is so important (Woog, 1995). What makes this void so devastating is that while students of different ethnicities, races, and religions can go home for emotional support from the family, students who are gay or lesbian often have no place to go for the much needed support.

Much of the school situation for gay and lesbian youth today is similar to the situation for students of color, the poor, women, and students with disabilities, before the efforts of multicultural educators began to create environments which were more supportive and inclusive of the lives and needs of these individuals. Thirty to 40 years ago (and still sometimes today), individuals from these groups experienced verbal and physical harassment, lack of protection, counselors untrained regarding their needs, curriculum which did not include their history and role models, libraries/media centers which did not have adequate holdings reflecting their existence, no teachers as role models, and school policies that did not offer protections. Much progress has been made for many of these minority groups, but the situation for gay and lesbian youth is still shamefully bleak.

Homophobia and heterosexism hurt everyone

Homophobia, and these often unspoken, and/or unrecognized, practices of ignorance, denial, repression and discrimination toward homosexuality on the part of the educational community, have an enormous effect on all the youth in the American public school system—both gay and non-gay. In elementary school, children quickly learn that one of the worst insults is to call someone a **queer** or a **sissy**. By the time students are in middle schools and high schools, this name-calling becomes a powerful weapon when directed against gay and lesbian youth and also has an enormous power to keep all others from expressing any emotions or actions that deviate from the accepted gender-role expectations. In its 1993 report on sexual harassment in America's schools, the American Association of University Women (AAUW) Educational Foundation found that when students were asked to what degree they would be upset if they were the targets of the 14 different types of sexual harassment outlined in the survey, 85 percent of the boys and 87 percent of the girls surveyed said they would be "very upset" if they were called gay or lesbian. No other type of harassment—including actual physical abuse—provoked a reaction this strong among boys (Louis Harris & Associates, 1993).

Thus, it is clear that homophobic attitudes are powerful and pervasive, also limiting the potential of heterosexual youth. Fearing being called gay or lesbian, many heterosexual adolescents change their behaviors in order to accommodate this fear. For example, heterosexual youth may: become sexually active earlier than they might normally in order to prove their heterosexuality; choose classes, activities, and/or career goals which are not expressions of what they really want to be doing; engage in anti-gay harassment which diminishes their humanity; or limit themselves from the development of emotional intimacy between same-sex friends. As Elze (1992) summarizes:

> Homophobia serves to squeeze young men and women into rigid gender roles, limiting their aspirations, squelching their dreams of what they can be,

isolating those youths whose behaviors defy traditional ideals of "masculine" and "feminine," and fostering violence against gay and lesbian youths and those perceived to be gay or lesbian. (p. 101)

Another group of young people who are also the victims of homophobia are those students whose parents are gay or lesbian or who have other family members who are homosexual. "Schools are often the first place children from gay and lesbian families learn the insults that describe their mothers and fathers. They learn that one of the worst accusations someone can make about you is to say you are gay" (Walling, 1996, 12). Thus, children are torn between positive and negative images about their family and soon realize that it may be unsafe to defend those whom they love. Even the more benign heterosexism (the presumption of heterosexuality as the norm in society) plays a part with these children in that children of gays and lesbians receive a mixed message about family. At home, these children learn that their family is "natural, acceptable, and loving, but at school, only heterosexual families are validated in the stories/books/movies children are exposed to or in the assumptions made by their teachers/peers" (Walling, 1996, 12).

In light of the data outlining the unique challenges facing gays and lesbians and the impact of homophobia and heterosexism on society at large, it is imperative that we, as multicultural educators, take seriously our obligation to understand the role multicultural education can (and should) play in making schools and society a safer, more accepting place for all individuals. Therefore, it is important that we review the goals of multicultural education in continuing to build a rationale for making multicultural education fully inclusive.

The goals of multicultural education

Growing out of the civil rights movement which was grounded in the democratic ideals of freedom, justice, and equality, multicultural education seeks to extend to all people the ideals and rights that were originally meant for only an elite few (Banks, 1993b). In *Affirming Diversity: The Sociopolitical Context for Multicultural Education*, Sonia Nieto (1996) poignantly reminds us that "multicultural education is for everyone, regardless of ethnicity, race, language, social class, religion, gender, sexual orientation, ability, and any differences." Few would disagree that multicultural education aims to create a more just society and schools that are more inclusive and representative of the diversity in our nation (Banks, 1993a; Nieto, 1996; Sleeter & Grant, 1993). Though programs implementing a multicultural approach come in many shapes and sizes (Banks, 1993a; Sleeter & Grant, 1993), some common purposes and goals which would clearly apply to gays and lesbians can be readily identified. These include:

1   Combating a narrow and/or mono-dimensional curriculum; affirming and legitimizing the presence and contributions of diverse groups;
2   Creating a climate that promotes an appreciation of diverse peoples, values, perspectives, and ways of life;
3   Reducing prejudice and working toward the elimination of discrimination in teaching and in society;
4   Working toward equality and justice for all;
5   Respecting the rights and dignity of all individuals;
6   Supporting pluralism within the educational system;

7   Broadening and/or diversifying the values schools promote. (Cushner, McClelland, & Safford, 1992; Miller-Lachmann & Taylor, 1995)

In essence, teachers who align themselves with multicultural education believe that schools and classrooms are to be "places of hope, where students and teachers gain glimpses of the kind of society we could live in and where students learn the academic and critical skills needed to make it a reality" (Bigelow, Christensen, Karp, Miner, & Peterson, 1994, 4). Certainly, these goals and hope should be inclusive of gays and lesbians.

Multicultural education's role and responsibility

Schools are often reluctant to support the implementation of policies and practices that prohibit discrimination on the basis of sexual orientation and to make the curriculum and social structure more inclusive and representative of gays and lesbians. This reluctance is usually a result of inaccurate or misguided assumptions about homosexuality and/or pressure from special interest groups (*e.g.*, the Religious Right). For example, many educators feel that since we have made "great strides" in dealing with racism and sexism, that is enough. But the reality is that schools will not be safe for all students until we eliminate all forms of discrimination. Further, the notion that this commitment is "too controversial" fails to acknowledge the fact that human rights issues are always controversial. Still further, many want educators to steer clear of gay and lesbian issues because they believe that this is a moral issue. However, what these individuals fail to recognize is that it is a moral issue when any student population is systematically denied support, representation, and/or resources within the educational system (Walling, 1996).

If those of us who adhere to the tenets of multicultural education are committed to creating more inclusive and democratic schools, then we must confront even the most controversial social justice issues. Clearly, the most recent challenges facing gays and lesbians (*e.g.*, recognition/acknowledgment as contributing individuals; discrimination policies in housing and employment; domestic partnership benefits; etc.) are directly related to civil rights and social justice in a democratic society. In *Democratic Schools*, Beane and Apple (1995) propose several conditions on which a democracy depends. Four of these conditions are relevant to making multicultural education inclusive of sexual orientation:

1   Concern for the welfare of others and for "the common good";
2   Concern for the dignity and rights of individuals and minorities [those not belonging to the dominant group];
3   The open flow of ideas, regardless of their popularity, that enables people to be as fully informed as possible; and
4   The organization of social institutions to promote and extend the democratic way of life. (Beane & Apple, 1995, 6–7)

"Xenophobia, discrimination, ethnocentrism, racism, classism, sexism, and homophobia are societal phenomena that are inconsistent with the principles of democracy and lead to the counterproductive reasoning that differences are deficiencies" (NAME brochure, 1996). As educators, we have an obligation to confront such counterproductive thinking. Further, since we must work toward the elimination of all forms of oppression, it is impossible to ignore gays and lesbians as a group that continues to experience oppression and discrimination (Gordon, 1995). To do so would be shortsighted. In the words of Audre Lorde (1983), a Black, lesbian, feminist, and member of an interracial couple, we are reminded that what affects one group affects all other groups:

> I cannot afford the luxury of fighting one form of oppression only. I cannot afford to believe that freedom from intolerance is the right of only one particular group. And I cannot afford to choose between the fronts upon which I must battle these forces of discrimination, wherever they appear to destroy me. And when they appear to destroy me, it will not be long before they appear to destroy you. (Lorde, 1983, 9)

Indeed, issues facing individuals who are gay or lesbian will eventually affect all who have historically been oppressed. As educators who believe so passionately in the promise and practice of multicultural education, may we challenge ourselves once again to come to a fuller understanding of Lorde's words "there is no hierarchy of oppression" and strengthen our commitment to fight for the dignity and rights of all individuals, including our sisters and brothers who are gay.

Notes

1   Homophobia: The irrational fear, dislike, anger, or intolerance of homosexuality, bisexuality, gay men, lesbians, or bisexuals which can be both personal or institutional prejudice and often results in acts of discrimination. (A composite of several popular definitions. See Bailey, 1996).
2   Heterosexism: The institutional and societal reinforcement of the belief that heterosexuality is better and more natural than homosexuality or bisexuality. The presumption that everyone is heterosexual. (A composite of several popular definitions. See Bailey, 1996).
3   Gay and Lesbian: In order not to be too cumbersome, the authors will use the phrase "gay and lesbian" to describe all people who are homosexual, bisexual, or transgendered.

References

Bailey, N.J. (1996). Attitudes/Feelings, knowledge, and anticipated professional behaviors of middle level teachers regarding homosexuality and gay and lesbian issues as they relate to middle level students. Greeley, CO: Unpublished dissertation, The University of Northern Colorado.
Banks, J. (1993a). Multicultural education: Characteristics and goals. In J. Banks & C.A.M. Banks (Eds.), *Multicultural education: Issues and perspectives* (2nd ed.) (pp. 3–28). Boston, MA: Allyn & Bacon.
Banks, J. (1993b). Multicultural education: Development, dimensions, and challenges. *Phi Delta Kappan*, 75(1), 22–28.
Beane, J. & Apple, M. (1995). The case for democratic schools. In J. Beane & M. Apple, *Democratic Schools* (pp. 1–25). Alexandria, VA: Association for Supervision and Curriculum Development.
Bigelow, B., Christensen, L., Karp, S., Miner, B., & Peterson, B. (Eds.). (1994). *Rethinking our classrooms: Teaching for equity and justice*. Milwaukee, WI: Rethinking Schools.
Cushner, K., McClelland, A., & Safford, P. (1992). *Human diversity in education: An integrated study*. New York: McGraw-Hill.
Dennis, D.I. & Harlow, R.E. (1986). Gay youth and the right to education. *Yale Law and Policy Review*, 4, 445–455.
Denver Area Alliance for Hate Free Schools. (1995). *Youth at risk*. Denver, CO: Denver Area Alliance for Hate Free Schools.

Elze, D. (1992). It has nothing to do with me. In W. J. Blumenfeld (Ed.), *Homophobia: How we all pay the price* (pp. 95–113). Boston, MA: Beacon Press.

Gibson, P. (1989). Gay male and lesbian youth suicide. In *Report of the Secretary's Task Force on Youth Suicide. Volume 3: Prevention and interventions in youth suicide.* Washington, DC: U.S. Department of Health and Human Services.

Goodman, J.M. (1996). Lesbian, gay, and bisexual issues in education: A personal view. In D.R. Walling (Ed.), *Open lives, safe schools* (pp. 9–27). Bloomington, IN: Phi Delta Kappa Educational Foundation.

Gordon, L. (1994). What do we say when we hear "faggot"? In D. Levine, R. Lowe, B. Peterson, & R. Tenorio (Eds.), *Rethinking schools: An agenda for change* (pp. 40–44). New York: The New Press.

The Governor's Commission on Gay and Lesbian Youth. (1993). *Making schools safe for gay and lesbian youth: Breaking the silence in schools and in families.* (Publication No. 17296–60–500–2/93-C.R.). Boston, MA: The Governor's Commission on Gay and Lesbian Youth.

Jennings, K. (1996). Together, for a change: Lessons from organizing the Gay, Lesbian, and Straight Teachers Network (GLSTN). In D.R. Walling (Ed.), *Open lives, safe schools* (pp. 251–260). Bloomington, IN: Phi Delta Kappa Educational Foundation.

Klanwatch Intelligence Report. (1995, March). 1994 hate crime recap: A year of close calls. (Special Year-End Edition: 1994). Montgomery, AL: Southern Poverty Law Center.

Lorde, A. (1983). There is no hierarchy of oppressions. *Council on Interracial Books for Children*, 14(3/4), 9.

Louis Harris & Associates (1993, June). *Hostile hallways: The AAUW survey on sexual harassment in America's schools* [Study number 923012]. Washington, D.C.: American Association of University Women Educational Foundation.

Miller-Lachmann, L. & Taylor, L. (1995). *Schools for all: Educating children in a diverse society.* Albany, NY: Delmar.

Nieto, S. (1996). *Affirming diversity: The sociopolitical context for multicultural education* (2nd ed.). New York: Longman.

Price, J.H. & Telljohann, S.K. (1991). School counselors' perceptions of adolescent homosexuals. *Journal of School Health*, 61(10), 433–438.

Remafedi, G. (1994). *Death by denial: Studies of suicide in gay and lesbian teenagers.* Boston, MA: Alyson.

Sears, J.T. (1991). Helping students understand and accept sexual diversity. *Educational Leadership*, 49 (11), 54–56.

Sleeter, C. & Grant, C. (1993). *Making choices for multicultural education: Five approaches to race, class, and gender* (2nd Ed.). New York: Macmillan.

Snowder, F. (1996). Preventing gay teen suicide. In D.R. Walling (Ed.), *Open lives, safe schools* (pp. 261–268). Bloomington, IN: Phi Delta Kappa Educational Foundation.

Walling, D.R. (Ed.) (1996). *Open lives, safe schools.* Bloomington, IN: Phi Delta Kappa Educational Foundation.

Walling, D.R. (1993). *Gay teens at risk* (Fastback 357). Bloomington, IL: Phi Delta Kappa Educational Foundation.

Woog, D. (1995). *School's out: The impact of gay and lesbian issues on America's schools.* Boston, MA: Alyson.

CHAPTER 13

IN THE TRIANGLE/OUT OF THE CIRCLE (1999)
Gay and lesbian students facing the heterosexual paradigm
Roberta W. Ginsberg

> Every time an inferior class emerges from enslavement and degradation, the
> human race again perfects itself.
> —Germain de Staël, French novelist and literary critic, 1766–1817

In a multicultural society, schools have the opportunity to expose children to the
pluralistic richness of the world they inhabit. As Ellis (1998, 237) noted,

> All students—regardless of social class, gender, ethnic, racial, cultural char-
> acteristics or exceptionality—should have equal opportunities to learn in
> school. In addition . . . some institutional characteristics of schools inhibit the
> progress of some groups of students, while others have better chances to
> achieve academically. Therefore, an important thrust of multicultural educa-
> tion is to reform the schools and other educational institutions so that all
> students have equal access to knowledge.

Apparently, however, the word *all* is subject to interpretation. In New York City,
a survey indicated that residents were willing to permit gay people to become
doctors, though nearly half of respondents would feel uncomfortable going to a
gay doctor. Living next door to a gay couple was okay, but they should not hold
hands or kiss in public.

Prejudice against gays is twice as frequent among students than against African
Americans, Hispanics, or Asian Americans (Savin-Williams and Cohen 1996). Of
the 25 million gay men and lesbians living in the United States, more than 7,000
reported hate crimes in a year (O'Connor 1991). Evidence suggests a resurgence
of heinous crimes directed at gays (National Broadcasting Corporation 1999).
Matthew Shepard met his terror-filled fate tied to a fence in Wyoming, and Henry
Edward Northington was beheaded in Virginia (Dunning 1999). The latest gay
victim, Billy Jack Gaither, a 39-year-old computer operator, was lured into a car
by his killers, who beat him with an ax handle, then disposed of his body in the
soaring flames of burning car tires. Ironically, these men will not be convicted
under the laws applying to hate crimes—a Hate Crime Bill including sexual orientation as a category has twice been defeated in Alabama.

Genesis of the research

The United States likely has about 2,610,000 gay/lesbian students (Ginsberg 1998). Parents, Families and Friends of Lesbians and Gays (PFLAG 1995) has suggested that, among those who attend our country's public schools, about one in 20 is likely to be gay or lesbian. Thus, each time a middle or high school teacher addresses a class, he or she is likely to be addressing one or more gay/lesbian students and is just as likely contributing to their pain through ignorance or inadequate training. Though violence against gays and lesbians has received some media attention, less commonly reported are high suicide rates and alcohol and drug abuse (Roane 1994; O'Conor 1993/94).

Official acknowledgement of the special problems of gay and lesbian students and their right to the same protections offered other minorities has occurred in only two states. Massachusetts enacted the Gay and Lesbian Student Rights Bill (1993), and the Austin Human Rights Commission (1995) in Texas held the first public hearings to address the needs of its lesbian, gay, and bisexual youth. These steps, if largely symbolic, are important because the bias against gays and lesbians is so ingrained in our society that it has become the last "acceptable" prejudice. What young gays and lesbians learn instinctively is that most people perceive them as "different."

Identity issues

Unlike members of physically identifiable minorities, the "invisible" gay remains unprotected by his or her minority status. In addition, most minorities benefit from constitutional protections and legislation. Gays and lesbians, on the other hand, largely have been left to fend for themselves. As a result, gay and lesbian students seem destined to remain a sociological minority, which Allport (1958) defined as any segment of the population suffering negative acts by the rest of society. These acts—ranging from mild discrimination to scapegoating (Besner and Spungin 1995)—send messages that undermine the development of a healthy self-concept.

D'Emilio (1992, 55–56) has argued that homosexual oppression stems from a system of heterosexual supremacy founded on the myth of nuclear family primacy: "Raised as we were in heterosexual families, we grew up and discovered our gayness deprived of gay ancestors, without a sense of our roots. . . . We need to affirm and appreciate our past, not in some abstract way, but as it is embodied in living human beings."

In a similar vein, Unks (1995, 5–6) observed that repressing "valid information about homosexuality cuts both ways; heterosexual students are given no reasons not to hate homosexuals, while homosexual students are given no reason not to hate themselves. . . . Both groups suffer a loss, for they are denied important information about a significant group of human beings."

To deal effectively with a problem seemingly so intractable, enduring, and amorphous, educators and students would benefit by framing the problem. Doing so may help them discover how—individually or collectively, consciously or unconsciously—they contribute to the dilemma's continuance.

Significance of the study

Beginning this process of discovery required a return to the secondary school, where all students—gay, lesbian, and straight—spend the greater part of their formative years. Students in gay/lesbian support groups in two high schools told me their stories. Delivered in their own voices, these stories provided a new basis for understanding gay/lesbian students and their school experience. Their voices are vital; before one may interpret and/or understand the "other," one must listen.

These support groups gave me that listening opportunity. As the young people spoke, a recurring question reverberated: How can a multicultural nation ensure a cultural democracy of schooling without expanding curricula to include diversity? As Ward and Taylor (1992) cautioned, answering that question requires that we first ask whose needs are being met. A dialogue among students and educators seems essential if schools are to include individuals previously left out of the conversation.

Prospects

Once gay and lesbian students answer fundamental questions regarding what they need and seek from others in the school community, educators can begin to design a school environment in which all students may learn—and teachers may teach—free from intimidation and released from "fear of attack" (Whatley 1992, 6). Perhaps then, educators can fulfill the nation's mission of providing educational opportunity for all youth and begin to seek "coalitions against injustice and the ideologies underlying it" (Rhode 1990, 9). In such an environment, relationships of acceptance rather than anger, shame, or fear may become the norm (Savin-Williams and Cohen 1996). Educators and students alike—regardless of sexual orientation—should benefit from such an inclusive school environment.

One important reason why homosexual adolescents continue to feel isolated, fearful, and confused is that there remains a paucity of reliable information concerning gays, either in the public domain or within our schools (Ginsberg 1998). The foremost objective of this study was to identify and understand the difficulties expressed by gay and lesbian students in school. With that knowledge, improvements in curricula that address these difficulties could be implemented.

Findings

Educators, often unaware of the unintended impact of their actions or heterosexual presumptions, are as much a part of the problem as the solution. A focus on curriculum, literature, student population, and setting is essential to finding a solution.

Curriculum

Some schools have responded to gay/lesbian adjustment issues through special programs (Ginsberg 1998). Yet even in schools that recognize gay and lesbian students and staff members, little progress has been made in changing curricular content. Ultimately, society must choose either to unite itself around humanity's inherent similarities or divide along lines of superficial differentiation.

In this regard, teachers must learn to critique "the ways of thinking and behaving characteristic of the culture into which they were born" (Greene 1973, 3). Humans tend to take for granted, noted Greene (1973, 9–10), that each "culture has its recognizable identity; and each is ordered by particular constructs—myths, fictions, patterns of belief. The *meaning* of each culture is a function of the way its members think about reality, symbolize it, describe it; and people exist within and by means of the codifications that develop over time." Words are intrinsic to such codification, and educators have long understood the maxim "words have power" in stimulating some of the essential questions regarding curriculum, educational theory, and pedagogy. In part, these questions inspired me to investigate how we might make the curriculum inclusive of all diversity and how education might transform knowledge to secure a place for gay and lesbian students.

Literature

Investigating human diversity and issues faced by sexual minorities, Savin-Williams and Cohen (1996, 218) noted, "Homosexuality is seldom covered in the social sciences, education, the humanities, or the arts." Their work has attempted to move readers from introspection to assessment of an individual's inherent bias, to betterment of the lives of sexual minorities through education. As Savin-Williams and Cohen (1996, 5) suggested, "The path to acceptance is knowledge and understanding."

The emergence of homosexuality as a subject of scholarly study appears relatively recent; the earliest academic work found for this study was published 65 years ago (Benedict 1934). The literature that does exist highlights several important, seemingly enduring gay/lesbian issues with regard to adolescents, which is why a qualitative methodology emerged as the most potentially productive approach to exploring them.

The complex process of gay/lesbian adolescent identity formation seems characterized by confusion, danger, and pain. All are inherently subjective concepts. One person's confusion is another's clarity; danger is as much a matter of individual perception as of objective reality; and pain has more to do with personal thresholds than empirical measurement. Thus, quantification might determine how many gays and lesbians are confused, frightened, and in pain, yet this information would do little to advance our understanding of these emotions and their impact.

Similarly, though educators and educational institutions may have important roles to play in supporting gays and lesbians and in shaping inclusive curricula, the form and dimensions of that support and specific curricular changes required remain muddy. By eliciting opinions and experiences of those affected by such programs, this research may inform the discussion and refocus its approach on gay/lesbian adolescent needs rather than with institutional process.

Homosexuality, noted Unks (1993/94, 1), "has become the acceptable stuff of public discourse, but there is little to suggest that the subjects of the topic, homosexuals, are much better off than they were a generation ago." Indeed, the high school "stands staunchly aloof and rigidly resistant to even a suggestion that any of its faculty or student body might be homosexual or that homosexuals deserve anything but derision and scorn within its walls" (Unks 1993/94, 1). Furthermore, "high schools may be the most homophobic institutions in American society, and woe be to anyone who would challenge the heterosexist premises on which they operate" (Unks 1993/94, 2).

Finally, because the literature comprises a cacophony of agenda-driven viewpoints, some means of striking a common chord must be found if progress is to be made. Again, that chord will most likely emerge by adding to the chorus the voices of gay and lesbian young people.

Student population

Research-study groups were chosen in conjunction with school counselors, who in turn sought consensus from students regarding my attendance at their meetings.

The groups comprised students between 15 and 18 years of age. Neither class nor ethnicity was considered in selecting subjects. The single qualifying criterion was their professed gay or lesbian orientation.

The setting

Student observations and interviews were conducted in two mainstream high schools located in a mid-sized southwestern U.S. city. The setting comprised student-requested, school-responsive support groups in their second year of operation. During the course of the semester, both groups expanded as more gay and lesbian students, as well as several teachers, gained the courage to attend meetings.

Typically, the schools' head counselors led the meetings, frequently accompanied by a co-facilitator or guest speaker. Meetings consisted of a single class period at a designated time and day each week. Doors were locked at the beginning of each support-group discussion meeting, because students feared repercussion if others realized the nature of the meetings.

From rosters of 15, 6 to 8 students typically attended. The relatively small research population represents student success in obtaining written parental permission to participate. Due to the promise of anonymity, all documented conversations come under the domain of data reported through personal conversation. Pseudonyms used for narrative purposes are not included in the list of references. Subsequent interviews were conducted with one parent, a father of a bisexual daughter, ten administrators (five each, male and female), and ten gay or lesbian students: four males and six females, in grade levels 9 through 12, for a total sample of 21 volunteer participants.

Two problems quickly emerged. First, much of the language, concerns, and behavior of gay and lesbian adolescents, at least superficially, is indistinguishable from those of other adolescents. Second, like other oppressed groups, these students found it easy to criticize or suspect my motives (Alcoff 1991/92).

To counteract any potential ambiguity, findings from various sessions have been grouped within three general categories that encompass the specific concerns of gay/lesbian adolescents: coming to terms and coming out; family, values, and religion; and the school experience and the support group. To blunt Alcoff's criticism, findings are, for the most part, presented in the voices and words of the participants themselves. This approach fosters a focus on the messages rather than the messengers and conveys important dimensions of the personalities and passions of the participants. Insofar as these quotations reflect a particular gay/lesbian adolescent sensibility, they infuse the findings with a visceral impact at least as instructive as the language and locutions themselves, which is why findings are presented in the students' voices and words, unless otherwise indicated.

Coming to terms and coming out

One similarity in the findings is the relatively young age at which these adolescent students began to sense their sexual preferences. As Benjamin related, "In third grade, I had an experience with some guy. We just started playing a little game. I didn't know about the gay/bisexual thing. . . . I liked it, so we did it a couple more times." Jonathan recalled, "I was five years old. I remember because I was attracted to this little boy in day care. I knew I was different and stuff, but I knew that this was bad at the same time."

These accounts of early sexual awareness—the settings, guilt, and experimentation—are in every way, except the gender of the peer to whom they are attracted, like those of heterosexuals. The similarities between the students' stories and those of their heterosexual peers appear to support the argument that sexuality is genetically determined. As Patricia, a straight school psychologist, expressed, "This is not a choice. I think the gods or goddesses of medicine will laugh at us one day because we actually thought we could ask questions like that."

As Jason noted, "I think I was born with it; it may be hormones or whatever, but in my case I think it is genetic. I had no idea until eighth grade; I didn't have an attraction for men before that. I didn't have an attraction for women either, but then I thought being attracted to women is natural; being gay is something on *Geraldo*."

Marcy, a straight student, added, "It could be environment or maybe experience. You decide. Maybe some people are born with it. I don't really know statistics or anything, but unless someone tells you something different, I think you are what you think you are."

Participants' confusion about the origins of homosexuality seems unrelated either to their early awareness experiences or to specific events. Their confusions ran the gamut from homosexual to bisexual to transsexual.

As Karla, a teacher, noted, "I remember going behind the curtain in elementary school with Paul and learning how to kiss. I dated boys in high school, and I'm still very attracted to men. But I identify as a lesbian. I love having men in my life, but sex with them is like being with an alien."

Nathan's case illustrates how badly these students need peer support and counseling. As Nathan related:

> At times I feel that I'm not gay—that I may be a girl trapped in a man's body. But then, I'm not gonna lie, I have tried changing, tried to go straight. But I can't. It makes me sick to my stomach when I think of being with a woman. It's like a man who is straight thinking about being with a man. I think this is the way God wanted me to be. I think I'm a guy/lesbian: a man who thinks he's a woman trapped in a man's body.

If the notion of a sexual continuum has any currency, with heterosexuality representing one extreme, Nathan may represent the opposite end. In fact, regardless of knowing the inherent risk, Nathan has begun taking hormones in hopes of transforming himself physically into Toni (the student has already developed breasts). Significantly, however, these students' stated sexual identities, including Nathan's, are often determined with little or no sexual experience.

Despite the presumption of promiscuity that colors much public debate about homosexuality, these adolescents' sexual experiences were similar to those of their heterosexual peers. Like their early childhood awakenings, their intimate attractions to members of the same sex tended to be emotional rather than sexual.

As Jonathan related, "I love Steve a lot. We've been together for a month. We haven't had a sexual relationship or anything—I just love him and he loves me. We're waiting until prom. We want to show that a gay relationship is not all about sex. It's just like a normal—not a normal, a straight relationship."

As Jason explained, "I don't know what it was, but it's strange, emotionally, I get along very, very well with women. I don't know why, me and women just click. But, I feel *secure* with a man. Being in a man's arms I feel secure and sexually attracted."

Finally, Amy noted:

It was my sophomore year here, that summer, and my family was going on a trip, so I invited her to go along. She didn't know I was gay; she had a crush on my brother and I was like, oh darn. Then, like eight months later, Kate tells me: "Well, I had a crush on you not your brother," and "came out" to me and I was like, "Well, I had a crush on you too, but it's too late now," and so we've been best friends ever since then.

Ultimately, these adolescent romantic encounters would eventually be followed with others of a more explicit sexual nature. Here too, the gay/lesbian adolescent experiences were similar to heterosexuals' experiences, as Jonathan's case illustrates:

First was my next door neighbor; he's married and has two kids and, while his wife was gone, that happened. He was probably like 30 or 29, 28—I'm not sure. He told me once that I looked like a faggot; that I walked like a faggot and talked like a faggot, like that. I didn't say anything. First he asked me if I had had sex with a girl, and I said, "No! I was a virgin." So he says, "Do you want me to show you how . . . show you some things?" I'm like, "Yeah, OK," 'cause I did want to have sex with a girl, you know. But I was scared. I really just wanted to get out of there.

Except for their sexual difference, the process of sexual awakening and self-awareness for gay and lesbian adolescents mirrors those of most adolescents. Though the similarities are striking, a single element defines the difference: the gay adolescent's fear of having his or her sexual preference revealed. This fear was virtually universal among the adolescents in this study.

Coming out

Most adolescents benefit from the universal presumption of heterosexuality and consequently have no need to announce their sexual preference. For gay adolescents, however, coming out is an all-consuming issue. Indeed, for many, the coming-out process continues well beyond their adolescent years.

The steps involved in coming out to others become increasingly difficult. Most often, coming out is rooted in an overwhelming need for emotional support rather than from a passion to disclose. First telling a trusted friend appears logical, yet the risk of destroying an important friendship through revelation remains fearsome. This tension keeps these adolescents perpetually suspended between two worlds: the world that "knows" and the one that does not.

Rationalization and guilt also inform the coming-out process. Of course, not all come out to their friends first. Some rely on teachers, counselors, or coaches who are gay or are in some way perceived as likely to be accepting. In most cases, the tension between desire for acceptance and fear of rejection is exacerbated by the decision to come out to a parent or sibling.

As Maya said, "My sister's gay, and my parents found out. They threatened to disown her if she continued with this lifestyle; told her she was going to hell; told her she was a disgrace to them."

As Amy related, "I came out to my mom first. I told them both in the car. If they didn't accept it, I would jump out and kill myself. My dad is funny. We really don't talk about it at all."

As Jonathan recalled:

I told my dad about me. I was crying, and he was like, "What's wrong?" I said, "I can't tell you 'cause I'm scared." He's like, "You can tell me anything," and I said, "No, I can't." Then he says, "You're not turning on me, Son, are you?" I didn't say anything. I was just quiet for a minute. So he says, "You like boys? You're like that?" I say, "Just half-way." Then my dad's quiet for awhile, and he says, "You're going to die you know, from AIDS or something like that." Because his brother—my uncle—he died of AIDS last year. He was gay.

These excerpts highlight two themes repeated during the course of these students' narratives. First, a gay/lesbian orientation tends to "run in families." The majority of those interviewed referred to having a relative who was similarly disposed sexually. Second, whether male or female, these students came out to their mothers far more often than to their fathers. They believed that their mothers would be more accepting and supportive than their fathers, and they were proven correct in their assumptions. Although fathers were similar in terms of their reluctance to accept a child's gay/lesbian orientation, they manifested their reluctance in very different ways. The previous examples reveal both passive and aggressive psychological responses.

Family, religion, and values

To a large extent, churches and other institutions—including the family—define themselves as much by what they oppose as by what they favor. Our societal values in general, and religion in particular, categorize homosexuality as deviant, sinful, or both, and our schools are populated by adolescent peers and adult educators who share these heterosexual values.

The issue of acceptable roles affects both males and females. Many of the females interviewed told of their families' expectations regarding the age at which daughters were expected to marry and bear children, for example—even after they came out. The presumption of the heterosexual paradigm is so firmly engrained that parents "closet" themselves rather than deal with the reality of their child's existence. The so-called "lifestyle" issue implies that being gay or lesbian is a matter of choice. Indeed, many study participants indicated that their parents—and others—continue to cling tenaciously to this belief. As Jonathan noted,

My mom's like, "You're hanging around those people, and they're influencing you to do this." I'm like, "No, they're not." She tells me, "You have to fall in love with a girl, a woman, whatever. You have to change; you have to avoid being like that." I'm like, "Mom, I can't. I already tried." She told me that God punished her, that it was her fault.

Confusion and denial are common responses to gay and lesbian children. Some parents even forbade their children to participate in gay/lesbian support groups for fear of their detrimental influence.

The lack of acceptance, the insistence that being gay is an alterable condition, and the reluctance to sanction support-group involvement all reflect conflicting values. They represent manifestations of the overwhelmingly negative attitudes toward gays from many U.S. institutions. If there is a single source for this pervasive attitude, it may be religion. Each person related feelings of guilt, exclusion, and suffering they said resulted from their religious beliefs or those of their parents. The impact of religion with respect to gays and lesbians can produce internal conflict between religious beliefs and administrative responsibility, as illustrated by Peter, a school administrator:

> As a Christian, I believe homosexuality is a sin, and I don't want people teaching my son it is okay. It is society that is putting the seal of approval on homosexuality. There are support groups and advocates saying we have to accept it. I don't believe that. I guess, if a guy thinks he loves another guy, long as they don't have sex, then it's not sinful. A person can love somebody. There are a number of people nowadays who lead celibate lives. Priests do. Nuns do.

This administrator, torn between religious beliefs and professional commitment, supported the establishment of the gay support group in his school. Nevertheless, his conflict personifies the difficulties faced by school-age gays and lesbians. The same values that pervade their families are present in their schools. Greater inclusion is vital, and the lack of support groups is particularly difficult for gays and lesbians. These groups provide one of the few forums in which adolescents can safely discuss the significant problems associated with their sexual orientation. Members become passionate about the group's value.

Students generally drive the establishment of such groups rather than counselors or educators, indicating the general "benign neglect" policies toward gays and lesbians most schools follow. Even when groups have been established, educators involved in their approval and oversight were far from unanimous in their favorable judgment of them. Unless educators first agree that the school should play a role, a debate about its dimensions is fruitless. Furthermore, how effective in dealing with these subjects would educators be?

Besieged by difficulty and danger, suffering feelings of despair and humiliation, gay and lesbian adolescents who sought sanctuary in the wisdom of their elders or through a more enlightened public often found wisdom lacking and enlightenment elusive. Here, perhaps, lies the crux of their dilemma: The families to whom they have been taught to turn, the values they have been trained to cherish, and the religions they were schooled to worship do not provide the support or guidance these kids seek. Though typical adolescents in most respects, they find themselves defined, defiled, or excluded by these institutions for the one aspect of their beings that is not typical—their sexuality. These children need help. Whether or not and to what extent schools should shoulder responsibility for providing it remains less clear.

Recommendations

The overall national education objective of inclusion of a multicultural perspective should extend to gay and lesbian students. They should be integrated into the school population, and the prevailing heterosexual bias must be eliminated. Schools must implement programs that increase awareness and sensitivity of gay/lesbian issues among educators, administrators, students, parents, and the community. Teachers and counselors must include gay/lesbian issues in curriculum materials and discussions, become familiar with gay/lesbian resources and organizations, and promote use of inclusive language.

The education of teachers and students is vital, but growth should not be limited. It must be expanded "outside the circle" to include parents, community members, and other institutions. Back to school forums could provide opportunities to learn, discuss, and debate gay/lesbian issues.

Not knowing is a luxury that some may cherish but which society can no longer tolerate. Students have brought the issue to educators' attention. The community and its children may derive benefit in having initiated institutional support for such groups in the schools and having all students understand that not everyone is heterosexual. Many of the nation's gay, lesbian, and bisexual students are at risk; breaking the silence in the school systems concerning homosexuality is essential to preventing suicide, alcohol and drug abuse, AIDS, violence, poor academic achievement, loss of human potential, and violation of human rights (Besner and Spungin 1995).

This study illustrates that further research can only enhance knowledge of how gay and lesbian students understand their school experience. A yearlong study on a high school campus that focuses on student interactions could yield insight. On-site researchers and practitioners who establish long-term rapport with students and faculty could highlight student perceptions that lead to curricular and policy changes. An in-depth study of faculty and administrators who are "out of the closet" could offer substantial insight into human nature, prejudice, and discrimination with specific attention to the school situation. A study of homosexual behavior, speech patterns, and personal habits may provide additional insights into the nature/nurture aspects of gay/lesbian developmental patterns. Replication of this study following implementation of anti-homophobic workshops could help determine their effects on students of all orientations. Finally, a follow-up study for this particular group of participants could illustrate the long-term academic, familial, and social effects of an on-site support group.

It is unlikely that such research recommendations will lead to definitive answers regarding the complex issues associated with being a gay or lesbian adolescent. Yet progress can be made in learning about the problems and motivations of these students. Continued investigation by researchers with a facility for relating well to adolescents and employing the naturalistic tools necessary to elicit relevant data would seem to be the most productive approach to expanding understanding and framing solutions. The students in this study confirm the value of pursuing such results.

References

Alcoff, L. 1991/92. The problem of speaking for others. *Cultural Critique* 20(Winter): 5–32.
Allport, G. W. 1958. *The nature of prejudice*, abridged ed. Garden City, N.Y.: Doubleday.
Austin Human Rights Commission. 1995. Report on lesbian, gay, and bisexual youth. Austin, Tex.: *Executive Summary* (26 June): 1–28.
Benedict, R. 1934. *Patterns of culture*. Boston: Houghton Mifflin.
Besner, H. F., and C. I. Spungin. 1995. *Gay and lesbian students: Understanding their needs*. Washington, D.C.: Taylor & Francis.
D'Emilio, J. 1992. *Making trouble: Essays on gay history, politics, and the university*. New York: Routledge.
Dunning, J. 1999. Arts & ideas: A tribute to a gay student who was slain. *New York Times*, 3 April, B15.
Ellis, A. K. 1998. *Teaching and learning elementary social studies*, 6th ed. Boston: Allyn & Bacon.
Ginsberg, R. W. 1998. Silenced voices inside our schools. *Initiatives: The Journal of NAWE* 58(3): 1–15.

Governor's Commission of Gay and Lesbian Youth. 1993. The gay and lesbian student rights bill: Executive summary. Boston: Commonwealth of Massachusetts.

Greene, M. 1973. *Teacher as stranger: Educational philosophy for the modern age.* Belmont, Calif.: Wadsworth.

National Broadcasting Corporation. 1999. *Dateline*, 10 March.

O'Connor, J. J. 1991. Gay images: TV's mixed signals. *New York Times*, 10 May, 1H.

O'Conor, A. 1993/94. Who gets called queer in school? Lesbian, gay and bisexual teenagers, homophobia and high school. *High School Journal* 77(1/2): 7–12.

Parents, Families and Friends of Lesbians and Gays. 1995. *Act out '95.* Austin, Tex.: PFLAG Youth Summit.

Roane, K. R. 1994. Two white sport coats, two pink carnations: One couple for a prom. *New York Times*, 22 May, Y12.

Rhode, D. 1990. *Theoretical perspectives on sexual difference.* New Haven, Conn.: Yale University Press.

Savin-Williams, R. C., and K. M. Cohen. 1996. *The lives of lesbians, gays, and bisexuals: Children to adults.* Orlando, Fla.: Harcourt Brace.

Unks, G. 1993/94. Thinking about the homosexual adolescents. In *The High School Journal* 77(1/2): 1–6.

Unks, G., ed. 1995. *The gay teen: Educational practice and theory for lesbian, gay, and bisexual adolescents.* New York: Routledge.

Ward, J. V., and J. M. Taylor. 1992. Sexuality education for immigrant and minority students: Developing a culturally appropriate curriculum. In *Sexuality and the curriculum: The politics and practices of sexuality education*, ed. J. T. Sears, 183–202. New York: Teachers College Press.

Whatley, M. H. 1992. Commentary: Whose sexuality is it anyway? In *Sexuality and the curriculum: The politics and practice of sexuality education*, ed. J. T. Sears, 78–84. New York: Teachers College Press.

PART 3

INTERSECTIONS OF RACE, CLASS, AND GENDER

CHAPTER 14

MIXED-RACE CHILDREN (1999)
Building bridges to new identities
Carlos Cortés

In April 1997, a charismatic young golfer named Tiger Woods stunned the sports world when he outplayed a star-studded field to win the prestigious Masters Golf Tournament. That victory also set off a scramble to ascertain and communicate Woods' ethnic identity. Sports commentators have variously referred to him as black, as having a Thai mother, or as being multiracial. Nike has marketed him as an African American in the United States and as an Asian American in Asia. Woods has kept the pot boiling by occasionally, with tongue in cheek, identifying himself as a Cablinasian (Caucasian, American Indian, African American, and Asian American).

While this label helps clarify Woods' family tree, which includes all of these ancestries, it does little to illuminate his *personal racial identity*. With all due respect, I doubt that his identity is really Cablinasian, but rather surmise that it reflects his having been raised by a father with a deep sense of African-American tradition and a mother with a strong attachment to the Thai culture. I suspect that Woods has a firm combination of racial and ethnic identities. In using the term "race," I am not arguing for its scientific validity, which is under widespread scholarly assault (Omi & Winant, 1994; Webster, 1992). Rather, I am using it as it has become part of the U.S. English vernacular as the result of America's long historical love-hate relationship with diversity.

While unique as a sports figure. Woods is not unique racially. Instead, he is part of, perhaps the epitome of, a dramatic national phenomenon—the rapidly growing number of Americans with racially diverse parentage (Root, 1992).

Miscegenation in America

This phenomenon is no historical accident. Mingling of racial bloodlines has been a part of American tradition ever since Europeans first cohabited with Native Americans and plantation owners had sexual relations with slaves. However, the offspring of those unions were almost always arbitrarily assigned to a single racial category. Put another way, to "qualify" as white in the United States generally required possessing—or being viewed as possessing—a sufficiently high percentage of "white blood" that was often defined by state laws with excruciating attempts to achieve mathematical precision.

In an effort to preserve racial "purity," 36 states (at one point) adopted some form of anti-miscegenation law prohibiting interracial marriage. Most such laws banned black-white marriages, but others barred various combinations—and often bizarrely, as in laws banning white-Chinese but not white-Asian marriages (Spickard, 1989).

If this sounds un-American (as in "all men are created equal"), it certainly sounded that way to the 1967 U.S. Supreme Court, which overturned those laws in the case of *Loving v. Virginia* (regarding the marriage between a Caucasian man and an African-American woman). That decision made it possible, for the first time, for Americans in every state to marry across racial lines. Finally given the opportunity to legally marry persons whom they loved, regardless of racial designation, growing numbers of Americans have done exactly that.

Today, in the late 1990s, nearly one third of U.S.-born Latinos are out-marrying (that is, marrying someone who is not Latino). More than one out of every 10 African Americans now out-marries. There is a huge variation among Asian Americans. According to some estimates, more than 80% of Japanese Americans now out-marry, compared with about 10% of Chinese Americans and less than 5% of Korean Americans. As the result of such unions, the United States now has a growing number of Tiger Woods-style Americans.

The multiracializing of schools

This strong trend is increasingly evident in schools, as each year more students of racially mixed marriages enroll. During back-to-school nights or parent-teacher conferences the teacher may be surprised when a parent does not conform to the educator's perceptions of a student's "race." Because such students do not fall into neat single-race categories, they also complicate district efforts to compile racial records necessary to comply with funding requirements and help determine school district programs.

In my multicultural education workshops, no topic has elicited a greater response than when I raise the theme of interracial marriage and its ramifications. Many teachers and administrators seem eager to talk about, or are at least relieved that they can discuss, their own personal situations—ancestors, spouse, or children. Others who view themselves as monoracial are looking for suggestions about how to address the special needs, desires, and circumstances of students who come from mixed backgrounds.

Likewise, educators must also grapple with negative student interpersonal perceptions, as mixed-race students are sometimes rejected by student groups or cliques because of their lack of racial or ethnic "purity." Mixed-race students also can be pressured by other students to ally themselves with a single racial or ethnic identity (and therefore reject other strands of their backgrounds).

There are numerous youth-related dimensions to the growing mixed-race reality. I will briefly discuss four of them: differentiating heritage from identity; supporting the self-determination of individual identity; facilitating student organizations; and developing valid curricula.

Heritage vs. identity

All students have an ethnic heritage. With diligence and luck, most can trace their family trees back far enough to discover at least some of their roots, even though there may be complications due to such factors as adoption, single-parent families, and remarriage.

In the process of studying their own heritages, students may also gain greater insight into their personal identities. However, the recognition and construction of individual heritage does not automatically translate into a sense of personal ethnic identity. Educators should avoid making the unwarranted leap from heritage to identity, as these are distinct though related concepts. While heritage influences identity, the latter also involves a deeper, more visceral sense of connection and psychic belonging, often with ramifications for values and behavior (Zack, 1993).

The relationship between heritage and identity becomes even more complex when a student's heritage is not just ethnically but also racially diverse. Most European-American students do not come from a single European background. (In one of my recent multicultural in-service workshops, only three of the 24 European-American teachers had parents who were both of the same Euro-ethnic background.) In fact, some students have so many European national branches in their family trees that they do not have, and may never develop, any sense of specific ethnic identity. They are simply non-ethnic Americans (or as some refer to themselves, "Heinz 57 Americans").

While educators have long recognized European American blending, even after three decades of the post-Loving era, many are still unprepared or unwilling to grapple with the personal and societal significance of mixed racial—not just ethnic—heritages. For students and others who come from racially mixed homes, the study of heritage and the issue of identity may be far more complex than for monoracial students, including monoracial students with multiple ethnic heritages (O'Hearn, 1998). This leads to the second dimension of addressing this new reality—supporting the right of students to determine their own racial identities.

Identity self-determination

If educators truly believe in freedom, individuality, and human dignity in the area of personal identity, they need to drop two questions often included in educational materials and used in the classroom. To what ethnic group (singular) do you belong? What race (singular) are you? These questions may work for some students, but for others they amount to demanding the rejection of either Mom or Dad and of more distant relatives.

Today many students simply do not belong to an ethnic group. And in the post-Loving era, many do not even belong to a racial group (once again, as used in U.S. parlance). Educators need to recognize and respond to this new reality. They should at least support such students as they assert or contemplate their individual identities. At the same time, teachers must avoid the knee-jerk tendency of trying to cram mixed-race students into inappropriate single-race categories. Based on my work and reading in this area, I have developed the following tentative typology for examining and categorizing the variety of identity routes taken by students and others who enjoy multiple racial heritages:

Single Racial Identity. Some gravitate toward one of their racial heritages, developing strong monoracial identities even while recognizing their multiple (two or more) racial heritages.

Multiple Racial Identity. Some students develop multiple racial identities, honoring the role that each plays in shaping their personal sense of being, rather than choosing one as their dominant identity. (This has even become a part of popular culture. For example, the powerful TV series, *Homicide: Life on the Streets* now features an American policeman who is part black and part Italian, played by the intense Giancarlo Esposito, who himself has an Italian-born father and an African-American mother.)

Multiple Racial/Multiracial Identity. In addition to feeling a strong sense of identity involving each of their racial heritages taken individually (multiple racial), some students additionally feel the special identity of being racially mixed (multiracial), irrespective of the combination.

Multiracial Identity. For some students, this latter multiracial status becomes their racial identity, superseding any sense of individual racial connection. They may not have a name for it, like Tiger Woods' "Cablinasian," but their sense of mixed-race specialness provides them with a unique identity shared with other mixed-race students.

Non-Racial Identity. Finally, I have encountered some students, as well as adults, who assert that they have no sense of racial identity (somewhat analogous to non-ethnic European-Americans with multiple national ancestries). I find this non-racial identity most common among immigrants from cultures that view race quite differently than U.S. Americans. (While some sports pundits have labeled Sammy Sosa as black, I have yet to hear the Dominican home-run-hitting sensation actually state his racial identity, if he has one. He may simply have a Dominican identity.)

Even as I investigate the identity and experiences of racially mixed students, I feel the burden of language's poverty. The very labeling of the previous categories has a cumbersome, somewhat artificial quality. Even without a common, satisfying terminology, educators cannot avoid this growing reality. In particular, they cannot retreat into such clichéd posturing as simply stating "we ought to stop categorizing and labeling people."

Categories provide the very basis for developing generalizations, while labels enable us to communicate about categories of items, including people. Try teaching U.S. history without categories and labels—Puritans, Confederates, Cherokees, African Americans, and Mormons. Without using such categories and labels, the stories of the Massachusetts Bay Colony, the Civil War, the Trail of Tears, slavery, and the state of Utah would not make much sense.

One complication of the post-Loving era is that old monoracial labels do not apply to all students with racially mixed backgrounds. Although we do not yet have an agreed-upon set of terms for talking about this new reality, teachers should refrain from imposing monoracial categories on students who come from racially mixed heritages. Instead, they should support, respect, and, if necessary, defend students' rights to assert their own racial identities.

Student organizations

This new assertiveness has sometimes been expressed through the formation of organizations of mixed-race students. These students find associational common ground based on the shared fact that they all have complex racial backgrounds and, as a result, have some commonality of experience.

One of the most pervasive experiential commonalities is the sense of being misrepresented and misunderstood by other students and even by educators. Many mixed-race students face the organically American peer pressure to choose a race: "Either you are one of us—and only us—or you are one of them (meaning the 'not-us'). You can't be both." Multiracial student organizations provide an alternative—a "nest" in which to discover connections, a forum in which to share experiences, and a "think tank" in which to develop more constructive responses to such external pressures.

These organizations deserve the support and encouragement of educators. Unfortunately, problems sometimes are caused by the very individuals who should be providing assistance when educators try to foist their rigid racial categorization ideologies on their students. An example of this occurred during one of my multicultural education workshops at a high school with a thriving organization of mixed-race students. Commenting on that organization, one administrator lamented that so many of its members seemed to have confused personal identities. As evidence, he pointed out that some students belonged not only to that organization, but also to single-group organizations of African Americans, Asian Americans, Latinos, and the like. I responded that possibly the real problem was his confused perceptions. Those students might have had very healthy multiple identities, both racial and multiracial. Unfortunately, I have heard such comments from many teachers who, possibly with good intentions, have tried to help mixed-race students clarify their identities by inappropriately encouraging them to choose one race.

Curriculum

One principal purpose of the study of history is to address two basic questions: who am I, and what about the past has contributed to my becoming who I am? In a collective sense, that is one of the reasons that schools require U.S. history, so that we as Americans will develop a better understanding of who we are as a nation and what about our country's heritage has made our nation what it is. Likewise, this is one role of single-group ethnic studies courses—fostering an understanding of the unique heritages, experiences, and cultures of different groups of Americans.

Beginning at the elementary level, school curricula should provide opportunities for students to investigate their individual heritages and to develop an understanding of the relationship of their unique pasts to U.S. and global history. This pedagogical process may include creating family trees, conducting oral history interviews with relatives, collecting family artifacts, perusing family records, writing family histories, and studying local communities. It should also include learning about the experiences of various racial, ethnic, and religious groups to which members of their families belong. These are not soft, "feel-good" activities designed to foster better self-concepts, although that may be a result. They should be addressed as good academic activities: good history, good research, good skill development, and good writing.

Yet the contemporary K-12 curriculum provides almost no illumination of the historical process that brought about racially mixed people in the United States. The solution is not simply to include a discussion of *Loving v. Virginia* as part of U.S. history courses. The curriculum should also involve the history of interracial contact and exclusion, the development and use of U.S. racial categories, the ways in which people have been assigned to those categories, the rise and fall of anti-miscegenation laws, and the ramifications of all of these developments for American life.

Literature should include stories (including biographies and autobiographies) of racially mixed Americans (Williams, 1995) because their lives are a critical and revealing part of the American story. Schools that examine racial and ethnic diversity, yet avoid the theme of racial mixture, distort the American experience. Moreover, such schools do serious if unintended injustice to students of all backgrounds who need to be weaned from their rigid reliance on old categories when grappling with changing realities.

Call to response

Race American-style has been a long-standing part of our nation's history, has pervaded American cultural consciousness (Cortés, 1991), and continues into the present, even as scholars debunk its scientific validity. Schools need to address it both in its traditional single-race and inchoate mixed-raced dimensions.

The issues of identity and self-identification are becoming an increasingly contentious part of our nation's multicultural landscape. Consider the extended battle over whether or not to include a multiracial category in the year 2000 Census. While that category was rejected, respondents will be given the option of marking more than one racial category (based on the federal Office of Management and Budget's October 1997, guidelines for collecting racial and ethnic data).

Certainly the need to address the mixed-race issue raises complications. The topic may be unsettling for educators who are uncomfortable moving beyond America's traditional racial categories and labels. Moreover, we lack a common language and agreed-upon set of concepts for addressing this complex area. Even current, widely used scholarly paradigms of ethnic identity formation fail to deal adequately with this issue.

Yet schools cannot wait for the languid process of scholarly debate and clarification. They must grapple now with the growing race-mixed reality, spurred by *Loving v. Virginia*. The time for recognizing, honoring, and responding to racial mixture has arrived.

References

Cortés, C. E. (1991). Hollywood interracial love: Social taboo as screen titillation. In P. Loukides and L. K. Fuller (Eds.), *Plot conventions in American popular film* (pp. 21–35). Bowling Green, OH: Bowling Green State University Popular Press.

O'Hearn, C. C. (Ed.) (1998). *Half and half: Writers on growing up biracial and bicultural*. New York: Pantheon.

Omi, M., & Winant, H. (1994). *Racial formation in the United States: From the 1960s to the 1990s*. 2nd ed. New York: Routledge.

Root, M. P. P.(Ed.) (1992). *Racially mixed people in America*. Newbury Park, CA: Sage.

Spickard, P. R. (1989). *Mixed blood: Intermarriage and ethnic identity in twentieth-century America*. Madison: University of Wisconsin Press.

Webster, Y. O. (1992). *The racialization of America*. New York: St. Martin's Press.

Williams, G. H. (1995). *Life on the color line: The true story of a white boy who discovered he was black*. New York: Dutton.

Zack, N. (1993). *Race and mixed race*. Philadelphia: Temple University Press.

CHAPTER 15

RACE, SOCIO-ECONOMIC SITUATION, ACHIEVEMENT, IQ, AND TEACHER RATINGS OF STUDENTS' BEHAVIOR AS FACTORS RELATING TO ANXIETY IN UPPER ELEMENTARY SCHOOL CHILDREN (1971)

Thomas H. Hawkes and Norma F. Furst

Hawkes and Koff (1970) reported the results of a normative study which examined the effects of racial and socioeconomic background (indexed by school attended), sex, and grade on the responses of upper elementary school children to a general anxiety questionnaire. Through a content analysis of the test items, the investigators also explored theoretical and practical issues relevant to the manifestation of anxiety in "culturally disadvantaged" children.

The Hawkes and Koff data showed that fifth and sixth grade children in an inner city school had significantly higher scores (p < .001), indicative of higher levels of anxiety, than did private school children of the same sex and school grade. At the same time, "lie" scores derived from responses to the anxiety questionnaire were uniformly low for both groups. An analysis of the types of anxiety—for example, real fear, school achievement, and anxiety symptomatology—revealed that the average inner city child was as high or higher on all types of anxiety as his private school counterpart.

Hawkes and Koff collected their data in a black inner city school and in a predominantly white, university laboratory school. Both schools were located in the same large midwestern city. A considerable proportion of the inner city school children came from families that were receiving welfare benefits; the private school population came mostly from upper-middle class professional homes.

This paper reports a replication of the original study, expanded to include 45 fifth and sixth grade classrooms in eight elementary schools representing various public–private, urban–suburban, inner and outer city school situations. These schools were located in a large, eastern metropolitan area. Where possible, anxiety and lie scores were supplemented by IQ scores, achievement scores, and teacher ratings of student behavior.

The present study sought to determine whether or not the same relationship between anxiety and school situation as revealed in the earlier study (Hawkes and Koff, 1970) would be found for a much larger population in another geographical location. The data on IQ, achievement, and teacher ratings of pupil behavior were collected to discover relationships which might exist between these measures and manifest anxiety.

Method

Subjects and schools

1201 children, comprising the entire fifth and sixth grades in eight elementary schools, were examined in this study. Only children absent from class on the day of testing were excluded from the sample population. Table 15.1 contains the number of subjects by grade, sex, and race in each of the eight schools used in this study.

Although permission to collect the data was granted by each of the school systems involved, final approval rested with each principal. The investigators personally contacted each school principal and also collected all of the data. The investigators are unaware of any undue effect in the selection of schools that would invalidate generalization from the results to other schools of similar characteristics.

School A is a private, non-sectarian, suburban school serving children from primarily middle and upper-middle class professional homes. There are a few scholarship students. The school is located in a country-like setting. The school has small classes and an experimental philosophy which includes some non-graded instructional periods during the school day.

Table 15.1 Distribution of total sample of 1201 upper elementary school children by grade, sex, race, and school

School	Sex	Fifth Grade		Sixth Grade	
		White	*Black*	*White*	*Black*
Private-Suburban					
School A	Boys	6	0	3	2
	Girls	3	1	3	0
School B	Boys	9	2	9	2
	Girls	3	1	12	1
Public-Suburban					
School C	Boys	23	3	19	0
	Girls	23	2	17	0
School D	Boys	53	0	56	0
	Girls	54	0	58	0
Public-Outer City					
School E	Boys	35	12	27	14
	Girls	28	17	27	16
School F	Boys	6	34	7	28
	Girls	5	25	8	26
Public-Inner City					
School G	Boys	0	52	0	73
	Girls	0	52	0	69
School H	Boys	0	62	0	64
	Girls	0	67	0	82
Total	Boys	132	165	121	183
	Girls	116	165	125	194

School B is a private school which also serves children from middle and upper-middle class professional families. It, too, is located in a suburb with rural surroundings. There are few overt differences between schools A and B in aims, methods, or clientele.

Both schools have parent bodies that display a high level of interest in school affairs; in each school some mothers work as teachers' aids.

School C is one of three public elementary schools serving a small city thirty miles from the center of the metropolitan area. The children in this school come from white families representing all but the lowest level of socioeconomic status. During the year of the study, some fifth grade black children were bussed to School C from another township area as an initial attempt at district racial integration.

School D serves a middle class suburban community which is one district removed from the city itself. The children in this school are all white and come from lower-middle and middle class families. Available occupational and educational data on parents of these children indicate that the great majority had one to four years of education beyond high school and were in service or lower management positions.

School E, an outer city school, is located two miles from the city center. It is in an upper-lower and lower-middle class community predominantly composed of second and third generation Italian Americans. Most of these families have lived in the area for some time. Also included in this school is a sizable (30%) minority of black children who are bussed into the school from a "ghetto" area closer to the center of the city.

School F serves an upper-lower and lower-middle class community and also is an outer city school about two miles removed from the inner city. This school has experienced rapid turnover in student population during the past five years. Prior to that time, the school served a predominantly white, middle class, Jewish population. Presently, the community is undergoing a very rapid change in racial and ethnic composition. The school reflects this change. The present student population consists of about 80 per cent black children newly moved into the area from the inner city and 20 per cent white children representing those older families that have remained in the community.

Schools G and H are in the heart of the inner city. Both schools have entirely non-white student populations. Black, lower SES families are predominant in the attendance areas of these schools. A sizable proportion (about 60%) of the students in each school come from homes in which the average annual income is below $3,000.

Instruments

1. *Anxiety*. The "General Anxiety Questionnaire" (GAQ) was derived by Hawkes and Koff (1970). The GAQ contains two scales, an anxiety scale and a lie scale. The anxiety scale is composed of 31 items taken from the Children's Manifest Anxiety Scale (Castaneda, et al., 1955) and eight items taken from the General Anxiety Scale for Children (Sarason, et al., 1960). The items of the GAQ and the serial position in which they occur are found in Table 15.10. In addition, interspersed among the anxiety items are the eleven items of the lie scale of the General Anxiety Scale for Children. (See Table 15.11.) Hawkes and Koff (1970) report the rationale used for the inclusion of the various items in the GAQ.

An answer of "yes" to any anxiety item on the GAQ indicates anxiety. An answer of "no" on any "lie" item is interpreted as indicating lying.

2. *Intelligence.* An attempt was made to obtain individual IQ scores from the personal school records of each student in the study. For schools E, F, G, and H this was the Lorge-Thorndike General Intelligence score, for school C, the Kuhlman-Anderson total IQ score. For School D, California Test of Mental Maturity scores were obtained, and school B provided scores from the Stanford-Binet Intelligence Test. No IQ scores were available at school A.

3. *Achievement.* For all of the schools used in this study, Iowa Test of Basic Skills (ITBS) scores were included in the subjects' personal records. The composite achievement score for each student for the year of the study was used. However, school D did not have achievement scores for its fifth grades.

4. *Teacher Ratings of Behavior.* In schools E, F, and H, it was possible to obtain from the subjects' records a score which indicated current teachers' ratings of student deportment. On a five point scale, a score of 5 indicated a superior rating by the teacher, a score of 1 that the teacher viewed the child's behavior in unsatisfactory terms.

Procedure

The principal investigators administered the GAQ, labelled the "Student Questionnaire," to the students in these subjects' regular classrooms. The testing procedure was preceded by an introduction in which the researchers explained to the children that they were collecting information about the cares, concerns, and aspirations of fifth and sixth grade boys and girls in order to help university students who were preparing to be teachers to understand the children they would be teaching.

The investigators, after requesting that the subjects follow along with them, read these instructions, printed on the face sheet of each questionnaire:

> This questionnaire covers items 1–50 on your answer sheet. These questions are about how you think and feel, and have no right or wrong answers. People think and feel differently. The person next to you may very well answer each question differently. If you were asked if you like school, you might answer *yes* while someone else might answer *no*. For questions 1 to 50, you are to mark your answer sheet as follows.
>
> If you would answer *Yes* to the question, put an *X* in the space by yes. If you would answer *No* to the question, put an *X* in the space by no. For each question, put an *X* next to yes if your answer is *Yes*, or put an *X* by no if your answer is *No*.

The subjects also were told that if they could not answer an item, or did not feel like answering an item, they could leave the item blank. Thirteen children exercised this option to some degree. Data for these children were not included in the analysis.

Each question then was read aloud by the researchers and was repeated. The children were allowed thirty seconds to check "yes" or "no" on the answer sheet. Reading each question aloud permitted all subjects, regardless of reading ability, the opportunity to respond.

Results

Descriptive statistics

Tables 15.2–15.6 report the Ns, means, and standard deviations for the scores on the anxiety and lie scales, and on intelligence, achievement, and teacher ratings of behavior by grade and by sex for each school.

Grade, sex, and race differences

Table 15.6 is a summary table which allows statistical comparisons to be made for the total boy and girl subsamples, the total fifth grade and sixth grade subsamples, and the total white and black subsamples—the latter a comparison, given the locations of the eight schools, of socioeconomic situations as well as of race. t-test comparisons were made for the anxiety, lie, behavior rating, and IQ scores by sex, grade, and race.

The authors chose this summary form because they felt that these three factors represented the major effects in the sample. It is apparent from the description of the total sample that most of the black children, irrespective of school, were either residents of the inner city "ghetto" or just recently had moved from the inner city; most of the white children were residents of urban or suburban lower-middle and middle class communities.

Table 15.2 Anxiety scores: Ns, means, and standard deviations by grade and sex for eight schools

School	Sex	Fifth Grade			Sixth Grade		
		N	Mean	S.D.	N	Mean	S.D.
Private-Suburban							
School A	Boys	6	19.16	4.53	5	8.20	3.27
	Girls	4	19.00	10.09	3	9.00	3.05
School B	Boys	11	15.18	7.15	11	15.54	7.65
	Girls	4	22.60	5.16	12	17.41	5.29
Public-Suburban							
School C	Boys	26	19.30	6.23	19	14.78	5.36
	Girls	25	16.96	8.22	17	16.47	6.12
School D	Boys	53	15.03	7.25	56	17.16	6.32
	Girls	54	19.62	7.59	58	20.48	6.76
Public-Outer City							
School E	Boys	47	19.92	6.23	40	17.47	6.91
	Girls	45	21.64	6.58	43	21.60	5.45
School F	Boys	40	19.82	5.66	33	20.78	5.43
	Girls	30	22.70	5.83	34	22.79	5.92
Public-Inner City							
School G	Boys	52	22.50	5.88	72	21.41	5.92
	Girls	51	24.45	6.23	69	24.85	5.99
School H	Boys	60	22.71	5.53	63	21.30	5.69
	Girls	65	25.67	5.65	81	23.24	5.97

Table 15.3 Lie scores: Ns, means, and standard deviations by grade and sex for eight schools

School	Sex	Fifth Grade			Sixth Grade		
		N	Mean	S.D.	N	Mean	S1.D.
Private-Suburban							
School A	Boys	6	2.33	1.86	5	4.00	2.82
	Girls	4	.75	1.15	3	4.66	1.52
School B	Boys	11	2.27	1.48	11	3.09	1.86
	Girls	4	1.00	2.00	12	1.75	1.21
Public-Suburban							
School C	Boys	26	2.53	1.92	19	2.31	1.24
	Girls	25	3.20	2.53	17	2.00	1.62
School D	Boys	53	3.43	1.88	55	2.20	1.95
	Girls	54	2.44	1.80	58	2.03	1.42
Public-Outer City							
School E	Boys	47	2.52	1.61	40	3.27	2.25
	Girls	45	2.06	1.82	43	2.11	1.76
School F	Boys	40	3.10	2.19	34	2.58	1.74
	Girls	30	2.43	1.86	34	2.32	1.53
Public-Inner City							
School G	Boys	52	2.47	2.02	72	3.54	2.33
	Girls	51	2.65	1.78	69	1.95	1.52
School H	Boys	60	2.70	2.10	63	3.17	1.90
	Girls	65	2.60	1.78	81	2.53	1.94

An examination of the data in Table 15.7 reveals several areas in which significant differences are well beyond the p = .001 level. The results of the analyses show that girls are higher on anxiety, teacher behavior ratings, and IQ scores. Boys, however, are significantly higher than girls on the "lie" scores. The black respondents from predominantly lower socioeconomic situations had both anxiety and "lie" scores that were significantly higher than those of the white respondents from predominantly lower-middle and upper-middle socioeconomic situations. The white respondents had significantly more positive teachers' ratings on behavior than had the black students. The white, higher socioeconomic respondents also had higher IQ scores than did their black peers from lower socioeconomic situations.

None of the analyses reached statistical significance for differences between the two grade levels.

The findings of sex differences on the anxiety and "lie" scales are consistent with the Hawkes and Koff (1970) data and with previous findings (Ruebush, 1963; Sarason, et al., 1960) regarding the manifestation of anxiety and lying as between the sexes. The finding of significant black vs. white differences on anxiety also is consistent with the Hawkes and Koff study.

The finding that the black children from predominantly lower income homes scored higher on the "lie" factor is not consistent with the previous study. However, in both studies the average lie scores are exceedingly low, an average of less

Table 15.4 IQ scores: Ns, means, and standard deviations by grade and sex for seven schools[a]

School	Sex	Fifth Grade			Sixth Grade		
		N	Mean	S.D.	N	Mean	S.D.
Private-Suburban							
School B	Boys	10	115.30	13.16	8	116.75	20.09
	Girls	3	124.33	14.04	12	115.16	18.01
Public-Suburban							
School C	Boys	15	98.13	12.51	13	104.92	16.97
	Girls	21	106.23	11.74	11	113.09	16.29
School D	Boys	49	108.83	16.28	53	112.50	14.47
	Girls	50	113.34	17.38	58	114.86	11.30
Public-Outer City							
School E	Boys	42	98.04	17.57	34	96.85	14.68
	Girls	42	101.94	14.12	37	100.89	10.01
School F	Boys	37	91.45	12.12	25	97.44	19.32
	Girls	27	95.74	12.10	27	92.11	12.81
Public-Inner City							
School G	Boys	43	84.67	12.63	59	84.77	9.62
	Girls	39	87.66	9.23	57	90.15	11.04
School H	Boys	55	82.72	14.84	53	83.07	16.57
	Girls	60	88.40	8.98	70	86.54	12.31

[a] These data were not available for School A.

than 3 of 11 items, with the differences between the racial-socioeconomic groups being less than 1 item. Statistical significance in this case may not accompany substantive significance.

Although the data from the present study suggest slightly higher anxiety scores for the younger children (fifth grade) than for the older group (sixth grade), the analysis did not prove significant. This finding also is congruent with the Hawkes and Koff findings.

Subsample comparisons

The data in Tables 15.2–15.6 permit some interesting comparisons between sub-samples of the population. t-tests for uncorrelated measures were computed on the anxiety, lie, intelligence, achievement, and behavioral rating scores between the following pairs of subsamples:

(a) total private-suburban subsample vs. total public-suburban subsample,
(b) total public-suburban subsample vs. total public outer city subsample, and
(c) total public outer city subsample vs. total public inner city subsample. (See Table 15.8.)

In each case, statistically significant differences were found, showing higher

Table 15.5 Current achievement: Ns, means, and standard deviations by grade and sex for eight schools

School	Sex	Fifth Grade			Sixth Grade		
		N	Mean	S.D.	N	Mean	S.D.
Private-Suburban							
School A	Boys	6	6.25	1.27	5	6.70	1.38
	Girls	4	7.40	.21	3	6.53	.70
School B	Boys	11	7.50	1.37	12	8.82	1.57
	Girls	3	5.26	.61	11	7.10	1.52
Public-Suburban							
School C	Boys	16	5.86	1.18	15	7.21	1.05
	Girls	22	6.30	.98	11	8.01	.80
School D	Boys	. .[a]	. . . .[a]	. . . .[a]	54	7.30	1.25
	Girls	. .[a]	. . . .[a]	. . . .[a]	58	7.59	1.06
Public-Outer City							
School E	Boys	47	4.87	1.38	40	5.49	1.31
	Girls	44	5.19	1.22	43	5.73	1.02
School F	Boys	37	4.25	1.10	33	5.49	1.65
	Girls	30	4.75	1.09	34	5.51	1.18
Public-Inner City							
School G	Boys	49	3.70	.86	66	4.43	.87
	Girls	47	3.90	.79	64	4.85	1.03
School H	Boys	49	4.03	.76	48	4.72	1.16
	Girls	50	4.00	.70	74	4.91	1.01

[a] These data were not available.

Table 15.6 Teacher behavior ratings: Ns, means, and standard deviations by grade and sex for schools E, F, and H[a]

School	Sex	Fifth Grade			Sixth Grade		
		N	Mean	S.D.	N	Mean	S.D.
Public-Outer City							
School E	Boys	45	3.41	1.23	36	3.25	.99
	Girls	42	4.19	.96	40	4.12	.85
School F	Boys	39	3.05	1.00	34	3.32	1.19
	Girls	27	4.07	1.00	34	3.87	.85
Public-Inner City							
School H	Boys	60	2.46	1.17	62	2.69	1.32
	Girls	61	3.36	.91	79	3.45	1.22

[a] Behavior ratings were available only for these schools.

Table 15.7 Summary comparison: anxiety, lie, behavior rating, and IQ scores for boys and girls, fifth and sixth grades, blacks and whites

Scores	N	Mean	S.D.	N	Mean	S.D.	t ratio[a]
			Sex				
		Boys			*Girls*		
Anxiety	593	19.47	6.64	595	22.31	6.83	7.23
Lie	594	2.90	2.00	596	2.31	1.80	4.90
Behavior Ratings	276	2.97	1.20	282	3.74	1.05	8.19
IQ Scores	496	94.84	18.44	514	98.37	16.45	3.38
			Grades				
		Fifth Grade			*Sixth Grade*		
Anxiety	573	21.14	7.08	615	20.66	6.69	1.20
Lie	574	2.65	1.94	616	2.56	1.91	.81
Behavior Ratings	247	2.65	1.17	284	3.39	1.21	.60
IQ Scores	491	96.30	17.32	519	96.95	17.75	.58
			Race				
		White			*Black*		
Anxiety	489	18.10	6.96	699	22.84	6.12	12.12
Lie	490	2.45	1.85	700	2.71	1.97	2.38
Behavior Ratings	135	3.96	1.85	423	3.71	1.16	2.13
IQ Scores	416	108.68	15.44	595	88.20	13.54	22.02

[a] p < .001 = 3.29
p < .01 = 2.57
p < .05 = 1.96

anxiety scores for those students closer to the inner city situation. The intelligence and achievement scores (with one exception) also showed statistically significant differences. Not surprisingly, the further away from the private suburban situation, the lower were the IQ scores and achievement scores. However, the lie score comparisons revealed no significant differences. There was a significant difference in the teacher ratings of behavior. Inner city children received lower teacher ratings than did outer city school children. In sum, as we went further away from the inner city school situation we found lower student anxiety scores and higher intelligence, achievement, and behavioral rating scores.

Relationships between variables

Table 15.9 presents by grade and sex Pearson Product Moment Correlations among scores on five variables: the anxiety and lie scales, achievement, IQ and teacher ratings of behavior. Several patterns are readily observable. In each grade

Table 15.8 Summary comparison: anxiety, lie, IQ, achievement, and behavior rating scores by type of school

Scores	N	Mean	S.D.	N	Mean	S.D.	t ratio[a]
	Total Suburban, Private			*Total Suburban, Public*			
Anxiety	56	16.00	6.07	308	17.82	6.86	2.04
Lie	56	2.40	1.24	307	2.52	1.79	.70
IQ	33	116.42	16.68	270	110.86	14.52	1.83
Achievement (5th grade)	24	6.88	1.05	38	6.11	1.06	2.84
Achievement (6th grade)	31	7.64	1.43	138	7.46	1.11	.66
	Total Suburban, Public			*Total Outer City*			
Anxiety	308	17.82	6.86	312	20.74	6.03	5.72
Lie	307	2.52	1.79	313	2.52	1.50	0.00
IQ	270	110.86	14.52	271	97.10	14.03	11.28
Achievement (5th grade)	38	6.11	1.06	158	4.79	1.21	6.94
Achievement (6th grade)	138	7.46	1.11	150	5.56	1.27	18.11
	Total Outer City			*Total Inner City*			
Anxiety	312	20.74	6.03	513	23.25	5.86	5.99
Lie	313	2.52	1.50	513	2.70	1.92	1.63
IQ	270	97.10	14.03	436	86.04	11.91	9.78
Achievement (5th grade)	158	4.79	1.21	195	3.93	.77	7.52
Achievement (6th grade)	150	5.56	1.27	252	4.73	1.00	7.01
Behavior Ratings[b]	297	3.65	1.01	262	3.02	1.16	7.07

[a] $p < .05 = 1.96$
$p < .01 = 2.57$
$p < .001 = 3.29$
$p < .0001 = 3.89$
[b] These data were available only for the two public outer and one of the public inner city schools (E, F, H).

and for each sex there are significant negative relationships between scores on the anxiety and lie scales, IQ, and achievement. Anxiety and teacher ratings of behavior show significant negative relationships for fifth grade boys and girls and sixth grade girls, but for sixth grade boys this relationship is small and in a positive direction.

Lie scores have significant negative relationships with IQ for fifth grade girls and sixth grade boys. For fifth grade boys and sixth grade girls this relationship is either nil or slightly negative. Lie scores and achievement are related negatively and significantly for fifth grade girls and sixth grade boys, while the other two groups show small negative trends. Lie scores relate significantly and negatively to teacher ratings of behavior for fifth grade girls and sixth grade boys. IQ scores relate positively and highly significantly with achievement and teacher behavior ratings for each group.

Table 15.9 Intercorrelations among scores on anxiety and lie scales, IQ, achievement, and teachers' behavior ratings by grade and sex[a]

	Total Fifth Grade Boys (N = 297)			
	Lie	*IQ*	*Achievement*	*Behavior Rating*
Anxiety	− .41(295)**	− .40(248)**	− .37(213)**	− .22(142)**
Lie		.00(248)	− .07(213)	− .03(142)
IQ			.78(187)**	.34(136)**
Achievement				.47(131)**

	Total Fifth Grade Girls (N = 281)			
	Lie	*IQ*	*Achievement*	*Behavior Rating*
Anxiety	− .42(278)**	− .31(240)**	− .40(171)**	− .21(127)*
Lie		− .14(241)*	− .15(199)**	− .18(129)*
IQ			.83(176)**	.45(128)**
Achievement				.51(115)**

	Total Sixth Grade Boys (N = 304)			
	Lie	*IQ*	*Achievement*	*Behavior Rating*
Anxiety	− .36(298)**	− .40(242)**	− .36(268)**	.11(128)
Lie		− .14(243)*	− .17(269)*	− .20(129)*
IQ			.85(228)**	.49(108)**
Achievement				.41(115)**

	Total Sixth Grade Girls (N = 319)			
	Lie	*IQ*	*Achievement*	*Behavior Rating*
Anxiety	− .32(316)**	− .36(270)**	− .39(299)**	− .23(151)**
Lie		− .11(270)	− .11(299)	− .10(151)
IQ			.83(265)**	.45(133)**
Achievement				.49(145)**

* p < .05
** p < .001
[a] Number in parenthesis represents available pairs of scores for correlations.

Anxiety and lie item analysis by race

Table 15.10 presents an analysis of "yes" answers to the anxiety items for the white and black respondents. Chi-square analyses indicate that the black children from predominantly lower socioeconomic backgrounds were significantly more likely to answer "yes" on 31 of the 39 items, with no significant differences between the blacks and whites on 7 items. Only one question resulted in significantly more "yes" answers by the white children than by the black pupils.

These findings are consistent with a similar analysis of items in the Hawkes and Koff study (1970). With the larger population of the present study, many more of the items attained significance at or beyond the .05 level. Again, the type of anxiety, indicated by inspection of the content of the items, shows that the black children from lower socioeconomic backgrounds manifest greater

Table 15.10 Analysis of anxiety items: "yes" answers by race

Anxiety Item	Black (N = 704) % Yes	White (N = 495) % Yes	Chi-square[a]
10. Do you worry that you might get hurt in some accident?	78	52	89.60
50. I often worry about something bad happening to me.	73	47	83.27
26. I worry most of the time.	43	18	82.94
39. My feelings get hurt easily when I am scolded.	65	40	73.64
13. Do you get scared when you have to go into a dark room?	49	25	70.30
18. I wish I could be very far from here.	51	27	68.70
40. I feel someone will tell me I do things the wrong way.	65	42	63.26
1. It is hard for me to keep my mind on anything.	41	20	60.05
28. I worry about what my parents will say to me.	74	54	51.94
6. Are you sometimes frightened when looking down from a high place?	71	51	49.32
36. I worry about what is going to happen.	71	52	45.57
29. I get angry easily.	55	37	37.76
47. I often worry about what could happen to my parents.	94	84	31.99
49. I have bad dreams.	55	39	29.72
41. I am afraid of the dark.	28	15	28.22
14. Do you sometimes get the feeling that something bad is going to happen to you?	77	63	27.63
43. It is hard for me to keep my mind on school work.	48	33	27.17
7. Do some of the stories on radio or television scare you?	63	48	26.61
34. My feelings get hurt easily.	53	38	26.27
24. I have trouble making up my mind.	73	59	25.99
38. I worry about how well I am doing in school.	88	78	24.70
44. I worry when I go to bed at night.	44	30	24.59
48. I get tired easily.	31	19	21.65
3. I feel I have to be best in everything.	38	26	18.92
20. I am secretly afraid of a lot of things.	43	31	18.28
30. Other children are happier than I am.	40	31	18.28
21. I feel that others do not like the way I do things.	58	47	13.83
12. Without knowing why, do you sometimes get a funny feeling in your stomach?	76	69	7.08

35. I worry about doing the right things.	75	68	6.72
25. I get nervous when things do not go the right way for me.	63	56	6.12
9. Do you think you worry more than other boys and girls?	30	24	5.12
23. I feel alone even when there are people around me.	30	27	1.19
45. I often do things I wish I had never done.	85	84	0.00
5. When you are in bed at night trying to go to sleep, do you often find that you are worrying about something?	71	70	0.00
31. I worry about what other people think of me.	46	46	0.00
2. I get nervous when someone watches me work.	47	48	0.13
17. At times I feel like shouting.	72	73	0.12
19. Others seem to do things easier than I can.	64	65	0.12
33. I have worried about things that did not really make any difference later.	55	64	9.86

[a] Chi-square of 3.84 significant at p < .05 with 1 df.
Chi-square of 6.63 significant at p < .01 with 1 df.
Chi-square of 10.82 significant at p < .001 with 1 df.

degrees of real fear, concern for school achievement, general anxiety, and specific symptomatology of anxiety than do their white peers from more affluent socioeconomic levels.

The exception to this conclusion involves an interesting item. To the question, "I have worried about things that did not really make any difference later," more white children answered "yes" than did their black counterparts. Perhaps the concerns or worries manifested by the black ghetto child are not of a kind that is likely to disappear or to warrant only passing concern.

Table 15.11 presents a similar analysis for the lie items.

Summary of results

1. This study, using a much larger population located in a different geographical region, replicated the findings of a previous study (Hawkes and Koff, 1970) on the relationship between anxiety and sex, anxiety and race and socioeconomic situation, and anxiety and grade level among upper elementary school children.

(a) Girls manifest significantly more anxiety than do boys.
(b) Black pupils from predominantly lower socioeconomic home situations manifest significantly more anxiety than do white students from higher socioeconomic situations.
(c) There is no statistically significant difference in the amount of anxiety manifested by fifth and sixth graders.

Table 15.11 Analysis of lie items: "yes" answers by race

Lie Item	Black % Yes	White % Yes	Chi-Square[a]
4. Do you ever worry about knowing your lessons?	82	86	3.98
8. Do you ever worry about what other people think of you?	45	60	25.93
15. Have you ever had a scary dream?	85	90	6.89
16. When you were younger, were you ever scared of anything?	62	33	66.72
22. Have you ever been afraid of getting hurt?	69	57	18.14
42. Do you ever worry about what is going to happen?	71	59	18.02
32. Do you ever worry about something bad happening to someone you know?	85	80	5.09
37. Are you ever unhappy?	84	91	14.39
11. Do you ever worry that you won't be able to do something you want to do?	78	75	1.05
46. Do you ever worry?	89	92	3.04
27. Has anyone been able to scare you?	78	80	0.69

[a] Chi-square of 3.84 significant at $p < .05$ with 1 df.
  Chi-square of 6.63 significant at $p < .01$ with 1 df.
  Chi-square of 10.82 significant at $p < .001$ with 1 df.

2. Although there was a statistically significant difference between white and black respondents on the lie scale, the absolute scores on that scale were low, and there was a less than one item difference between the two sets of respondents.

3. It was deduced from analysis of the types of race and socioeconomic situations of schools that the further away from the inner city one goes in school situations, the lower the anxiety and the higher the intelligence, achievement, and teacher ratings of student behavior.

4. The present study also computed correlations among the students' anxiety, lie, achievement, IQ, and teacher behavioral rating scores. Of particular interest are the significant negative relationships between anxiety and the lie scale, IQ, and achievement scores for the fifth grade boys, fifth grade girls, sixth grade boys, and sixth grade girls. Teacher behavior ratings and anxiety also were significantly and negatively related in three of the four subsamples with only the sixth grade boys showing an insignificant relationship between these two variables.

5. An item analysis of the anxiety questionnaire yielded results similar to those of the Hawkes and Koff study. In 31 of 39 items, the black students from predominantly lower socioeconomic backgrounds evidenced significantly higher anxiety than did the white population from higher socioeconomic levels. These black children evidenced more concern for school achievement, greater degrees of real fear, general anxiety, and specific symptomatology of anxiety than did their white counterparts from higher socioeconomic levels.

Discussion

What does it mean that more of the black children in the inner city schools answer the anxiety items with a "yes" than do their white middle class peers? One might speculate that the "yes" answers by the black children indicate a social naïveté concerning what it is socially desirable to reveal of one's feelings, aspirations, or concerns (Edwards, 1957). If such is the case, then one must dismiss any child scoring high on a "manifest" anxiety questionnaire as being naive and dismiss any of the work demonstrating the relationship between anxiety and performance as fallacious. One also must dismiss the face validity of the items. One could speculate that inner city children who may be slower intellectually than their middle class peers (at least as measured by standard IQ tests) respond automatically to complex stimulus questions with a "yes" rather than a "no." One then would have to consider what is complex, and why a "yes" rather than a "no" is more likely.

One also could argue that the inner city school child uses a different language code than his middle class peers and that when he says "yes" to the same words that his middle class peer says "no" to he is saying it to words which have a different meaning for him. Hawkes and Koff during the construction of the GAQ talked with their subjects about the words used and could not discern any differences in meaning.

Each of these interpretations would maintain the assumption that there are no differences in anxiety in children from different racial-socioeconomic situations. However, a more plausible assumption is that there are differences in anxiety, or social-emotional mediating structures, of children from different racial-socioeconomic situations. If so, then one might infer that the more frequent "yes" answers by the black children represent or reflect the harsh realities of the world of the inner city child compared with the realities of his middle class peers (Deutsch, 1967; Hawkes and Koff, 1970; and Long, 1969). When one surveys the items in Table 15.10, it is apparent that the most differentiating items refer to situations of real fear, for example, concern about something happening to oneself, a friend, or a parent.

Obviously, this finding does not mean that there are no highly anxious middle class children, nor does it mean that all children in the inner city are highly anxious. It only means that environmental factors predisposing to anxiety are more likely to be present for the inner city child than for his counterpart in the suburb. It suggests that anxiety, or the social-emotional mediating structures tapped by this questionnaire, are not only the result of particular types of interaction between parent and child (Ruebush, 1963), but are rooted directly or indirectly in unmet physical and security needs. There is ample support for such an idea both in modern popular black literature and in educational literature concerning the ghetto.

If one does accept the existence of anxiety differences between different racial or socioeconomic situations, the "yes" answers in Table 15.10 cast serious doubts on certain prevalent stereotypes characteristic of U.S. society. For example, when we look at the items concerned with school achievement, we see that both the suburban school children and the inner city school children worry about how they are doing in school; the inner city school children, however, worry more. If one sees as the genesis of worry an individual's inability (either through his own efforts or because of external conditions which are overpowering) to cope with the world, then our findings make sense. When we look at the differences between the white children and the black children on achievement and teachers' ratings of behavior, it is obvious that the white children are much more successful in their school efforts than are their black counterparts.

We will not speculate concerning causation; we would only emphasize that the observed relationships with children's anxiety scores are negative and strong. These relationships are not consistent with the view of anxiety as a middle class phenomenon. This view implies that anxiety is a motivational force which results from middle-class parents' training their children to achieve and excel. Thus, it is said, their children do well in school and eventually in life. But this view also implies that lower class parents and children are uncaring about achievement, school, or other life circumstances. The findings in this study flatly contradict this implication.

Acknowledgments

The authors gratefully acknowledge financial support for the project provided by the Division of Educational Psychology and the College of Education at Temple University.

References

Ausubel, D., and P. Ausubel.
   1967   "Ego development among segregated Negro children." Pp. 231–260 in Joan Roberts (ed.), School Children in the Urban Slum. New York: The Free Press.
Castaneda, A., B. R. McCandless, and D. S. Palermo.
   1965   "The children's form of the manifest anxiety scale." Child Development 27:317–326.
Deutsch, Martin, et al.
   1967   The Disadvantaged Child: Selected Papers of Martin Deutsch and his Associates. New York: Basic Books.
Edwards, Allen L.
   1957   The Social Desirability Variable in Personality Research. New York: Dryden.
Hawkes, T. H., and R. H. Koff.
   1970   "Differences in anxiety of private school and inner city public elementary school children." Psychology in the Schools 7 (July):250–259.
Langnear, T. S.
   1966   "Socio-economic status and personality characteristics." Pp. 180–214 in Joan Roberts (ed.), School Children in the Urban Slum. New York: The Free Press.
Long, Barbara H.
   1969   "Critique of Soares and Soares: self-perception of culturally disadvantaged children." American Educational Research Journal 6:710–711.
Ruebush, B.
   1963   "Anxiety." Pp. 460–516 in H. W. Stevenson, J. Kagan, and C. Spiker (ed.), Child Psychology: The Sixty-Second Yearbook of the National Society for the Study of Education. Part I. Chicago: The University of Chicago Press.
Sarason, S. B., et al.
   1960   Anxiety in Elementary School Children. New York: Wiley and Sons.

CHAPTER 16

RACE, CLASS, AND GENDER IN EDUCATION RESEARCH (1986)

An argument for integrative analysis

Carl A. Grant and Christine E. Sleeter

Race, social class, and gender as issues related to schooling have received major attention from educators and social scientists over the last two decades. Although social scientists and educators employ various approaches to conceptualize educational equity (see, for example, Bennison, Wilkinson, Fennema, Masemann, & Peterson, 1984; Grant & Sleeter, 1985, for typologies of approaches), the common aim has been to understand how education can be constructed and distributed so it does not discriminate against major social groups. This education literature includes case studies, experimental studies, and survey studies of what occurs in schools; it also includes reviews of studies, issue, historical, and theoretical analyses, and analyses of litigation.

We applaud the attention directed toward race, social class, and gender, but we are concerned about education literature's failure to conceptualize these as integrated issues. We therefore argue that more attention needs to be paid to the integration of race, class, and gender. We mean, for example, that if one integrates race and gender, one recognizes each sex within racial groups, and different racial groups within each gender. This is different from treating race and gender as separate groups or issues, as if individuals had membership in only a racial group or a gender group. We will first briefly discuss the integration of these three status groups in American society, then examine a sample of the education literature to determine the extent of integration. Then we will offer examples of research that has integrated at least two of these status groups, to illustrate how integration can help our understanding of schooling.

Integration of race, class, and gender in American society

Race, social class, and gender are used to construct major groups of people in society. Some members of these groups—people of color, women, and poor people—historically have enjoyed less power, status, and wealth. Struggle against oppression by these status groups has been a feature of the history of this country. Although such struggles are often interpreted separately (e.g., the women's movement as distinct from the Black Power movement), theorists are beginning to see them as inextricably related, and are recognizing that failure to understand their interrelatedness ultimately weakens the power of these struggles to effect social change.

For example, Aronowitz (1981) has pointed out that many black freedom movement participants have adopted a Marxist perspective because of its analysis of the economic circumstances of most blacks. He stated, "Having succeeded in wresting important concessions in social and political rights, blacks have been obliged to face the reality that economic equality is no closer to realization twenty-five years after the historic Supreme Court decision barring segregation in education" (p. 96). He argued that struggles of people of color must include attention to class because most people of color are oppressed on the basis of class as well as race. At the same time, he argued, racism cannot be reduced to a class analysis. Similarly, the oppression of women pre-dates capitalism and is based on biological rather than material factors, but it is connected with oppression based on race and class, particularly for poor women of color. Aronowitz warned that, "Unless these questions [related to racism] are raised simultaneously with those of class and sex, the abolition of conditions for the reproduction of capitalist relations of production is beyond realization" (p. 97).

Davis (1981) has offered a similar analysis of the history of emancipation movements in the U.S. Her analysis reveals divisions based on status groups within movements that eventually weakened the movements. Unlike Aronowitz's example of blacks who have recognized a connection between race and social class, she pointed out the failure of white middle-class women to recognize concerns of lower-class women and women of color, that ultimately weakened their efforts to combat sexism. She noted that "the convenient omission of household workers' problems from the programs of 'middle class' feminists past and present has often turned out to be a veiled justification—at least on the part of the affluent women—of their own exploitative treatment of their maids" (p. 98).

What writers such as these point out is that all people are members of not just one status group, but of all three, and these simultaneous memberships influence perceptions and actions. An example is a child in the classroom who is not just Hispanic, but also male and middle class. Thus he is linked with an oppressed ethnic group, but also with a gender group and a social class that historically have oppressed others. Therefore, his view of reality and his actions based on that view will differ from those of a middle-class Hispanic girl or a lower-class Hispanic boy.

There is compelling evidence that young people construct views of reality within the material and cultural contexts of their lives, and that these contexts are shaped partly by the status groups to which they belong. For example, Willis's (1977) "lads" constructed a view of their opportunities by observing working-class men in their community, and drew on working-class male cultural themes to define a value structure that made sense of them within the limitations of those opportunities. What Willis explored only slightly was how the lads' race affected their views and actions. The black students studied by Ogbu (1978) constructed beliefs about their job opportunities by observing what jobs were held by blacks in their communities. Ogbu argued that the behavior of black students depends in part on their perceptions of the opportunity structure, that is shaped in part by the caste-like position of people of color. What Ogbu did not examine was the role gender played in shaping the realities of male and female black students and how students perceived the opportunities open to their race, social class, and gender groups.

The education literature tells us little about how and when the integration of these status groups is important. Race, social class, and gender tend to be examined separately. As a result, Davis's distinction, for example, between affluent women and their maids, becomes lost. Connections Aronowitz cited between black and white members of the lower class are blurred when students are examined only by race, and racial distinctions are blurred or lost when students are examined only by social class. A failure to consider the integration of race, social class, and gender leads at times to an oversimplification or inaccurate understanding of what occurs in schools, and therefore to inappropriate or simplistic prescriptions for educational equity.

Race, class, and gender in education literature

To determine to what extent race, social class, and gender are integrated in the education literature, we examined a sample of literature published over a ten-year period (1973–1983), during which these issues received considerable attention. This sample included all issues of the following journals: *American Educational Research Journal, Harvard Educational Review, Review of Educational Research*, and *Teachers College Record*. We included all articles that focused directly on race, social class, equal opportunity, and/or gender in U.S. schools, grades kindergarten–12; articles that did not directly relate to schooling were not included. We excluded articles focusing on methods for evaluating intervention programs, articles on legal or funding issues that did not discuss programs, and articles reporting studies in which race, social class, or gender were variables but were not discussed substantively.

A total of 71 articles were analyzed. Thirty clearly focused primarily on race, 15 on social class, and 18 on gender; five articles focused equally on two of these, and three focused on all three. We will briefly describe how the articles treated or failed to treat the intersection of race, social class, and gender, the area of study (e.g., desegregation), and the kind of article (e.g., experimental study).

Race

Thirty articles focused primarily on race, or on school issues related directly to race, such as desegregation. As Table 16.1 shows, few of these articles gave substantive attention to gender or social class, although class received more attention than gender. Twenty-four of the articles made little or no reference to the social class membership of the racial group(s) being discussed. We classified an article as giving little attention to class if class was only mentioned but not discussed. For example, Harber and Bryen (1976) occasionally referred to speakers of black English as low-income blacks, and Otheguy (1982) included a few statements such as "For Hispanics who are poor . . ." (p. 314); neither author explored ramifications social class may have for their discussions.

Five of the 30 articles on race mentioned social class as a variable but did not discuss it much. For example, Bradley and Bradley (1977) mentioned social class as a variable that can affect desegregation programs; Kennedy and Suzuki (1977) used it as a control variable but did not discuss in much depth how it might effect their results; and Scott and McPartland (1982) reported data in tables by social class levels within racial groups but did not discuss these data in the article. One article implicitly equated race and social class: in their review of desegregation studies, Kirk and Goon (1975) referred to the mixing of black and white students and the mixing of lower-class and middle-class students as if the two were the same.

Five of the 30 articles gave fairly substantive attention to social class. Two of these (Beady & Hansel, 1981; Willig, Harnish, Hill, & Maehr, 1983) reported studies in which subjects of various racial groups were divided by social class;

Table 16.1 Articles with primary focus on race

Article	Kind of article	Area of study	Attention to gender		Attention to social class	
			Amount	Integrated?	Amount	Integrated?
Abrams (1975)	Case study	Desegregation	None		None	
Banks, McQuater, and Hubbard (1978)	Review of research	Black achievement motivation	Little	Yes	None	
Beady and Hansel (1981)	Survey study	Teacher expectations	None		Moderate	Yes
Bradley and Bradley (1977)	Review of research	Black achievement and desegregation	None		Little	No
Cummins (1979)	Review of research	Bilingual education	None		None	
Engle (1975)	Review of research	Bilingual education	None		None	
Foster (1973)	Issue analysis	Desegregation	None		None	
Hall and Turner (1974)	Review of research	Black English	None		Great	Yes
Hannafin (1983)	Experimental study	Math concept attainment in Anglos and Hispanics	Moderate	Yes	None	
Harber and Bryen (1976)	Review of research	Black English	None		Little	Yes
Hernandez (1973)	Review of research	Mexican-American student achievement	Little	Yes	Moderate	Yes
Jackson and Cosca (1974)	Survey study	Teacher behavior toward Mexican and Anglo students	None		Little	Yes
Kennedy and Suzuki (1977)	Experimental study	Verbal behavior of Anglo and Mexican-Americans	None		Little	Yes
Kirk and Goon (1975)	Review of research	Desegregation	None		Moderate	No
Kirp (1976)	Case study	Desegregation	None		None	
Kirp (1981)	Analysis of litigation	Desegregation	None		None	
Kleinfield (1973)	Review of research	Eskimo learning style	None		None	

Study	Method	Topic				
Maruyama and Miller (1979)	Reanalysis of survey data	Desegregation	None		Little	Yes
Otheguy (1982)	Issue analysis	Bilingual education	None		Little	Yes
Pettigrew and Green (1976)	Review of research	Desegregation	None		None	
Ravitch (1976)	Historical analysis	Education of minority groups	None		None	
Ryan (1982)	Analysis of legislation	Indian education	None		Little	Yes
Schlossman (1983)	Historical analysis	Bilingual education	None		Little	Yes
Scott and McPartland (1982)	Survey study	Desegregation	Moderate	Yes	Little	Yes
Shade (1982)	Review of research	Afro-American cognitive style	None		None	
Sharan (1980)	Review of research	Cooperative learning and student relationships	Little	No	None	
Slavin and Madden (1979)	Survey study	Student relationships	Little	Yes	Little	Yes
Sowell (1981)	Issue analysis	Ethnic education	None		Great	Yes
Teitelbaum and Hiller (1977)	Analysis of litigation	Bilingual education	None		None	
Willig et al. (1983)	Survey study	Achievement attributions and math performance	Moderate	Yes	Moderate	Yes

both found some significant differences between, for example, middle-class and lower-class Hispanics, and middle-class blacks and whites. Three articles included sections that discussed relationships between race and class. Hall and Turner (1974) discussed standard and nonstandard English usage by middle- and lower-class blacks and whites; Hernandez (1973) discussed social class as an important variable affecting the achievement of Mexican-American students; and Sowell (1981) discussed class as an important variable affecting the use various ethnic groups have made of education.

Gender received less notice than class in the articles focusing on race. Twenty-seven of the 30 articles gave little or no attention to it. Some of these mentioned it as a variable without providing much discussion; for example, Sharan (1980) noted that cooperative learning improves student relationships across gender and race, thus treating gender as a parallel but independent variable. Three articles reported studies in which gender was a variable integrated with race (but not with race and social class). Hannafin (1983) found gender to have no effect on math achievement in any of the racial groups of his sample (he surmised that this was because they were younger than the age at which gender normally begins to matter), although Willig et al. (1983) found an interaction of gender and race to affect math achievement attributions. Finally, Scott and McPartland (1982) found an interaction of race and gender to affect students' perceptions about some racial integration issues.

Social class

Fifteen articles focused primarily on social class. We included articles in this section if the author(s) said the article was about social class or class-related issues. Articles varied widely in their definition of class, ranging from no definition to income, education, and occupation-based definitions. As Table 16.2 shows, articles gave little attention to race or gender. Thirteen of the social class articles made little or no mention of race. Two of these, on the "disadvantaged," implicitly equated race and social class: the sample in Becker's (1977) study was lower-class and predominantly of color, results were discussed mainly in terms of poverty, and very little attention was given to the students' racial backgrounds. The other article on the "disadvantaged" (Hodges, 1978) reviewed research studies, discussing them in terms of social class variables and failing to describe the racial composition of samples, which were likely predominantly of color.

Three social class articles gave some attention to race, mostly discussing it as a variable related to school achievement or school processes (Duncan, 1973; Giroux, 1983; Walberg & Marjoribanks, 1976). One article offered a substantive discussion of race in relationship to social class: Edmonds and colleagues (1973) critiqued racist biases in research methodology and result interpretations in Jencks et al.'s *Inequality: A Reassessment of the Effect of Family and Schooling in America* (1972). They argued that, by failing to consider race and culture seriously, the book assumed black children to be culturally deprived rather than culturally different and institutionally oppressed.

Gender was given moderate attention in only one of the 16 social class articles. In critiquing theories of social reproduction and resistance, Giroux (1983) cited some problems that have remained unexamined when gender has been ignored. Of neo-Marxist works as a whole, he argued that, "The failure to include women and racial minorities in such studies has resulted in a rather uncritical theoretical

Table 16.2 Articles with primary focus on social class

Article	Kind of article	Area of study	Attention to race		Attention to gender	
			Amount	Integrated?	Amount	Integrated?
Anyon (1979)	Content analysis of textbooks	Ideology of school history books	Little	No	None	
Becker (1977)	Experimental study	"Disadvantaged"	Little	Yes	None	
Coleman (1973)	Critique of previous survey study	Jencks et al.'s *Inequality*	None		None	
Duncan (1973)	Critique of previous survey study	Jencks et al.'s *Inequality*	Moderate	Yes	Little	Yes
Dwyer (1977)	Historical analysis	Worker/labor studies	None		None	
Edmonds et al. (1973)	Critique of previous survey study	Jencks et al.'s *Inequality*	Great	Yes	None	
Giroux (1983)	Theory critique	Social reproduction theory	Little	Yes	Moderate	Yes
Haller and Davis (1980)	Survey study	Ability grouping	None		None	
Hodges (1978)	Review of research	"Disadvantaged"	None		None	
Michelson (1973)	Critique of previous survey study	Jencks et al.'s *Inequality*	Little		None	
Rivlin (1973)	Critique of previous survey study	Jencks et al.'s *Inequality*	None		None	
Schultz and Sherman (1976)	Review of research	Effectiveness of forms of reinforcement	None		None	
Snow (1983)	Case study	Literacy	None		None	
Steinitz, King, Soloman, and Shapiro (1973)	Survey study	Ideological development of working class youth	None		None	
Wallberg and Marjoribanks (1976)	Review of research	Cognitive development	Little	No	None	

tendency to romanticize modes of resistance even when they contain reactionary racial and gender views" (p. 287). He went on to point out that ironically much of this work, "although allegedly committed to emancipatory concerns, ends up contributing to the reproduction of sexist and racist attitudes and practices" (p. 287).

Social class and race

Only one article gave equal attention to race and social class. Freijo and Jaeger (1976) examined teacher evaluations of students, integrating the race and social class of students in their analysis. They found that teachers respond somewhat differently to students of different racial groups but of the same social class background, and that they respond differently to students of different social class backgrounds but the same race. Gender was not a variable, although it was in a larger study that included this study. The authors did not say why they omitted gender here.

Gender

Eighteen articles focused primarily on gender; these are summarized on Table 16.3. Fourteen of these articles gave little or no attention to social class and sixteen gave little or no attention to race. Several of these were survey studies comparing male and female students or teacher attitudes toward male and female students. In most of the studies, the reader is not informed of the race or social class backgrounds of the students, although some authors stated that the sample was predominantly white (e.g., Sherman & Fennema, 1977) or middle- to upper-class (e.g., Benbow & Stanley, 1982).

Social class was treated as a variable in three gender articles, and race was a variable in two. Fennema and Sherman (1977) and Haertel, Walberg, Junker, and Pascarella (1981) found middle-class boys to have higher achievement motivation than middle-class girls in math and science, but this pattern did not hold for lower-class girls and boys. In addition, Haertel and colleagues (1981) found an interaction between race and gender in some aspects of science learning. Pallas and Alexander (1983) included race and social class as independent variables in regression equations. They found a greater gender effect than race or class effect on math achievement, until they factored in coursework students had completed, when the race effect became greater than the gender effect. However, race and class were not discussed, nor was any possible interaction between variables.

Substantive discussions of the intersection of gender and social class were offered in two articles, and of gender and race in one article. Biklen (1978) discussed women's education during the Progressive movement, pointing out some differences in affluent versus working class women's education. Marini and Greenberger (1978) found significant differences in educational aspirations of middle-class and lower-class girls and boys. Finally, Adkison (1981) reviewed literature on women in administration, and included a section on career paths of black and Hispanic women.

Race and gender

Three of the 71 articles focused equally on race and gender. As Table 16.4 shows, all three articles integrated these two status variables; two, however, gave no

Table 16.3 Articles with primary focus on gender

Article	Kind of article	Area of study	Attention to social class		Attention to race	
			Amount	Integrated?	Amount	Integrated?
Adkison (1981)	Review of research	School administration	None		Great	Yes
Agre and Finkelstein (1978)	Issue analysis	Feminist school reform	Little	Yes	None	
Benbow and Stanley (1982)	Longitudinal study	Math achievement	None		None	
Benz, Pfeiffer, and Newman (1981)	Survey study	Teacher sex-role expectations	None		None	
Biklen (1978)	Historical analysis	Progressive education	Moderate	Yes	None	
Dwyer (1973)	Review of research	Reading achievement	None		None	
Fennema and Sherman (1977)	Survey study	Math achievement	Moderate	Yes	None	
Haertel et al. (1981)	Survey study	Science achievement	Moderate	Yes	Moderate	Yes
Kedar-Voivodas (1983)	Review of research	Teacher attitudes	None		None	
Lee and Gropper (1974)	Theory critique	Sex roles	None		Little	
Lyman and Speizer (1980)	Survey study	School administration	None		None	
Marini and Greenberger (1978)	Survey study	Educational aspirations	Great	Yes	None	
Pallas and Alexander (1983)	Survey study	Math achievement	Little	Yes	Little	Yes
Pedro, Wolleat, Fennema, and Becker (1981)	Survey study	Math course selection	None		None	
Saario, Jacklin, and Tittle (1973)	Survey study	Content of textbooks, achievement tests, and vocational education tracks	None		None	
Sherman and Fennema (1977)	Survey study	Math achievement	None		None	
Stake and Katz (1982)	Survey study	Teacher attitudes and behavior	None		None	
Tobias and Weissbrod (1980)	Research review	Math anxiety	None		None	

Table 16.4 Articles with equal focus on race and gender

Article	Kind of article	Area of study	Race and gender integrated?	Attention to social class	
				Amount	Integrated?
Hennessy and Merrifield (1978)	Survey study	Cognitive attitudes	Yes	None	
Lightfoot (1976)	Research review	Black girls	Yes	None	
Simpson and Erickson (1983)	Survey study	Teacher behavior	Yes	Little	Yes

attention to social class, and Simpson and Erickson (1983) used it as a control variable but did not discuss it. Both survey studies found statistically significant results by integrating race and gender. Simpson and Erickson (1983) found that teachers praised as well as criticized male students more than female students, and criticized black males more than any other group. Hennessy and Merrifield (1978) found a few cognitive aptitude differences between race-gender groups. The third article, by Lightfoot (1976), reviewed literature on sexism, and criticized its failure to discuss race. Lightfoot pointed out that in most writings, "almost automatically, sexism becomes synonymous with the experiences of white middle class girls" (p. 257).

Gender and social class

The only article to focus equally on gender and social class was by Apple (1983). He analyzed teaching as a profession, arguing that expectations placed on teachers and their responses to those expectations can be understood best by examining teaching as a proletarian profession for women, who usually must contend with domestic responsibilities in addition to teaching.

Race, social class, and gender

Three articles focused equally on all three status groupings, but only one integrated them (see Table 16.5). Kirp (1977) and Tollett (1982) discussed litigation and legislation at the federal level for equal opportunity programs. They discussed demands for equal educational opportunity made by women, blacks, bilinguals, and the handicapped, in a way that suggested these are discrete, parallel groups. The third article (Rumberger, 1983) examined factors related to dropping out of school. By integrating race, social class, and gender, Rumberger was able to describe a complex pattern of factors associated with those who drop out (or are pushed out). For example, he found that the higher their mother's level of education, the more likely black and white females and black males were to stay in school, but the mother's education level had little effect on white males or Hispanic youths. Rumberger suggested that mothers are important educational role models for black youths and white females, that fathers are more important role models

Table 16.5 Articles with equal focus on race, social class, and gender

Article	Kind of article	Area of study	Race, social class, gender integrated?
Kirp (1977)	Issue analysis	Equal opportunity litigation	No
Rumberger (1983)	Survey study	Dropouts	Yes
Tollett (1982)	Issue analysis	Litigation and legislation for equal opportunity	No

for white males, and that for Hispanic youths, other factors are more important in determining whether or not to stay in school. For lower-class Hispanic males, the main reason for dropping out was the need to work to help support the family. Economic reasons were important to members of other groups, but family responsibilities were particularly important to the lower-class Hispanic male.

Analysis of relevant literature

Our analysis shows that most of the literature in our sample treated race, social class, and gender separately. To illustrate how this may oversimplify equity issues and mislead researchers, we examined an area of study in two of the articles. Slavin and Madden (1979) and Sharan (1980) wrote articles on school practices for improving race relationships among students. Both articles focused primarily on race, and both concluded that group work is an effective strategy for improving race relations in school. We will summarize their main arguments, then question them on the basis of studies that have looked at race and gender together, and race and class together.

Slavin and Madden (1979) reported findings from a survey of 51 schools regarding practices for improving race relations among students. Questionnaires were sent to teachers and students. Students were asked about behaviors with peers of another race, attitudes about other races, and participation in school activities attempting to improve race relations; teachers were asked about their use of different activities to improve race relations and their participation in workshops designed to change teacher attitudes. The strongest finding was that activities in which students work with members of other races correlated with positive interracial attitudes and behavior for both blacks and whites. In analyzing the data, gender and SES were two control variables. However, the article did not mention whether there might be an interaction of race and gender, or of race and social class, leaving the reader to assume that there is not.

Sharan (1980) reviewed studies on the use in desegregated schools of various forms of cooperative learning designed to improve ethnic relations, achievement, and attitudes toward self and school. This article was similar to the Slavin and Madden article in that it concluded that cooperative learning does tend to improve ethnic relationships, and that racial groups are discussed as if they were internally homogeneous. Sharan criticized these studies on several grounds: most investigators, he stated, did not report data separately on each ethnic group, so it is not known whether only one group changed its attitudes and behavior; some investigators reported changes made by one ethnic group only; several investigators did not use measures that would indicate whether improved relationships transferred to situations outside the intervention; and most conclusions about improved relationships were derived from sociometric questions alone.

Sharan pointed out that most of the studies did not help clarify which features of cooperative learning actually make a difference. In Sharan's reporting and discussing of the studies, students were consistently aggregated by race. Sharan noted that "most investigators reported increased cross-racial selections without indicating . . . whether the change was evenly distributed among members of both ethnic groups named in the selections" (p. 259). He followed this with a discussion of the pitfalls of assuming that both or all ethnic groups changed equally as groups, but he did not discuss the pitfalls of assuming that change was evenly distributed *within* groups.

These two articles do not tell us some things that would be helpful. We do not know whether boys and girls within racial groups experience cooperative learning in the same way. It is possible, for example, that reported gains are modest because white girls and boys of color develop more positive interracial relationships than girls of color and white boys, but that these differences are not evident when data are aggregated. Further, we do not know whether cooperative learning affects boys and girls of different racial groups (e.g., black girls vs. Mexican girls) differently. We also do not know whether it affects members of different social classes within racial groups differently. For example, in a black and white student population, do middle-class blacks respond more favorably to cooperative learning than lower-class blacks? Finally, we do not know whether there might be an interaction of race, class, and gender. We now provide evidence from other studies to suggest that questions such as these should be investigated.

Many desegregated schools attempt to mix minority students, who on the average are from lower or working class backgrounds, with white students who on the average are of middle-class backgrounds. Confounding race with class makes the development of positive race relations more difficult. This was certainly a problem in the school studied by Rist (1978), in which there was little overt attempt to improve race relations once the school was desegregated. It was also a factor in the school studied by Schofield (1982). The school did attempt to equalize status differences by reducing or eliminating tracking and ability grouping; many teachers did not deliberately use cooperative learning techniques reviewed by Sharan, but some features of cooperative learning were incorporated into school practices. These was some improvement of race relations, but a fair amount of social segregation and tension persisted among students. Schofield was unable to ferret out the role played by social class due to inaccessibility of school records on individual students' backgrounds, but she recognized that students were aware of differences in their economic status outside school. How cooperative learning might affect students in schools in which one racial group is of a higher social class is an important issue that is not addressed when class is ignored.

Do students of different social class backgrounds perceive and interact with ethnically different peers of the same social class in different ways? An ethnographic study of a desegregated high school suggests that they do (Sullivan, 1979). The school had a multiracial student body, and most racial groups contained members of more than one social class background. Sullivan found that middleclass students interacted across racial lines much more readily than the lower-class students. He suggested that this was due to two factors. One was that the middleclass students had more in common culturally with their ethnically different but same-class peers than lower-class students did with ethnically different peers, because the lower-class students were more strongly influenced by their ethnic cultures. A second factor was that the middle-class students saw the advantage of learning to interact with those of different ethnic backgrounds. They were thrown together in some of the more prestigious classes and activities in the school, and thus felt they received higher status and benefits by making use of these opportunities. The lower-class students tended to be placed in lower status classes that were less racially mixed, and they participated less in activities.

There is evidence from other studies that middle-class people of color see themselves as having much in common with middle-class whites (e.g. Banks, 1984), but that lower-class racial groups are often antagonistic toward one another because they feel they are competing for a limited share of rewards (Hill, 1982). These social class dynamics may be very important to understand when working with race relations in a school. It may well be that in many schools cooperative learning would have less impact on race relations among lower-class than middle-class students because of the cultural perceptions and experiences of students. By failing to examine relationships between race and social class, the literature cited earlier does not even suggest this as a possibility.

There is evidence that boys and girls within racial groups experience somewhat different social relationships in desegregated schools, and this may affect their responses to cooperative learning interventions. We will cite findings from three recent case studies, which do not suggest a coherent pattern as much as they raise questions. L. Grant (1984) found that black girls in six first grade classrooms played a much more active social role among their classmates than any other race-gender group, and crossed race and gender lines more than any other group. She also found some tension between the black girls and white boys, who put black girls down with racist remarks if they felt threatened by the girls' accomplishments. Schofield (1982) found friction between black and white middle-school girls from competition over black boys; she also found that white boys felt somewhat threatened by black boys and acted defensively toward them. Both researchers noted that white girls were somewhat passive and acquiescent in social relationships. Fuller (1980) found that a sample of lower-class black girls in Britain distanced themselves from black boys and white students because of their high aspirations for themselves, their concern about not wanting their peers to ridicule them or try to hold them back, and their desire not to be viewed as acquiescing to whites.

It could be that the black girls in Grant's study developed an interracial social network more than girls in the Schofield and Fuller studies because they were in the distinct minority in the classroom (2 to 3 in four of the six sample classrooms), and felt they needed to cultivate relationships to survive. Nevertheless, these three studies suggest that different race-gender groups may react differently to cooperative learning. The black girls in Grant's study could react very favorably to it, but it may pose a threat to the white boys attempting to prove their superiority. Tensions could continue to erupt among students such as those in the Schofield study, in spite of cooperative learning interventions, with tensions among girls relating primarily to racial competition over boys, and tensions among boys relating to attempts to prove masculinity. The black girls in the Fuller study could well resist efforts to build interracial relationships if placed in a cooperative learning situation, seeing such relationships as useless and possibly a hinderance to their future goals and sense of identity. The point is that the cooperative learning literature reviewed earlier does not hint of such dynamics because it ignores gender.

Conclusion

Of the sample of 71 articles we reviewed that addressed equity issues related to race, social class, or gender, most treated racial, class, and gender groups as if they were homogeneous. For some purposes, this may be appropriate. But there seems to be a tendency to do this even when not appropriate. We suspect this is due in part to myopia of educators and researchers. Concern with one status group can lead to neglect of people's multiple group memberships that may relate to an issue. This seems to have been the case with our example of the two articles on cooperative learning. One could find additional examples, although attempts to do so would be hindered by the paucity of literature that integrates race, social class, and gender substantively.

There needs to be more dialogue among those interested in race, social class, and gender. For example, those concerned with student social relationships in school across racial lines might work with those interested in social relationships across gender and class lines, because there is evidence that simultaneous memberships in these groups do affect social behavior in school. Very likely the same is true for achievement in math and science, for instance, decisions about higher education, teacher expectations of students, or achievement in learning a second language. Until integrations of these three status groups are investigated, we cannot argue that they are not all important in any issue or research question. We may oversimplify theory and perpetuate biases by failing to integrate them.

References

Abrams, R. I. (1975). Not one judge's opinion: Morgan v. Hennigan and the Boston schools. *Harvard Educational Review, 45*, 5–16.

Adkison, J. A. (1981). Women in school administration: A review of the research. *Review of Educational Research, 51*, 311–344.

Agre, G. P., & Finkelstein, B. (1978). Feminism and school reform: The last fifteen years. *Teachers College Record, 80*, 305–315.

Anyon, J. (1979). Ideology and United States history textbooks. *Harvard Educational Review, 49*, 361–386.

Apple, M. W. (1983). Work, gender, and teaching. *Teachers College Record, 84*, 611–628.

Aronowitz, S. (1981). *The crisis in historical materialism.* New York: Praeger.

Banks, C. W., McQuater, G. V., & Hubbard, J. L. (1978). Toward a reconceptualization of the social-cognitive basis of achievement orientations in blacks. *Harvard Educational Review, 48*, 381–397.

Banks, J. A. (1984). Black youths in predominantly white suburbs: An exploratory study of their attitudes and self-concepts. *Journal of Negro Education, 53*, 3–17.

Beady, C. H., Jr., & Hansell, S. (1981). Teacher race and expectations for student achievement. *American Educational Research Journal, 18*, 191–206.

Becker, W. C. (1977). Teaching reading and language to the disadvantaged—What have we learned from field research? *Harvard Educational Review, 47*, 518–543.

Benbow, C. P., & Stanley, J. C. (1982). Consequences in high school and college of sex differences in mathematical reasoning ability: A longitudinal perspective. *American Educational Research Journal, 19*, 598–622.

Bennison, A., Wilkinson, L. C., Fennema, E., Masemann, V., & Peterson, P. (1984). Equity or equality: What shall it be? In E. Fennema & M. J. Ayer (Eds.), *Women and education* (pp. 1–18). Berkeley: McCutchan.

Benz, C. R., Pfeiffer, I., & Newman, I. (1981). Sex role expectations of classroom teachers, grades 1–12. *American Educational Research Journal, 18*, 289–302.

Biklen, S. K. (1978). The progressive education movement and the question of women. *Teachers College Record, 80*, 316–335.

Bradley, L. A., & Bradley, G. W. (1977). The academic achievement of black students in desegregated schools: A critical review. *Review of Educational Research, 47,* 399–449.

Coleman, J. A. (1973). Equality of opportunity and equality of results. *Harvard Educational Review, 43,* 129–137.

Cummins, J. (1979). Linguistic interdependence and the educational development of bilingual children. *Review of Educational Research, 49,* 222–251.

Davis, A. Y. (1981). *Women, race, and class.* New York: Random House.

Duncan, B. (1973). Comments on inequality. *Harvard Educational Review, 43,* 122–128.

Dwyer, C. A. (1973). Sex differences in reading: An evaluation and critique of current theories. *Review of Educational Research, 43,* 455–468.

Dwyer, R. (1977). Workers' education, labor education, labor studies: An historical delineation. *Review of Educational Research, 47,* 179–207.

Edmonds, R., Billingsley, A., Comer, J., Deyer, J. M., Hall, W., Hill, R., McGehee, N., Reddick, L., Taylor, H. F., & Wright, S. (1973). A black response to Christopher Jencks' *Inequality* and certain other issues. *Harvard Educational Review, 43,* 76–91.

Engle, P. L. (1975). Language medium in early school years for language groups. *Review of Educational Research, 45,* 283–325.

Fennema, E., & Sherman, J. (1977). Sex-related differences in mathematics achievement, spatial visualization, and affective factors. *American Educational Research Journal, 14,* 51–71.

Foster, G. (1973). Desegregating urban schools: A review of techniques. *Harvard Educational Review, 43,* 3–36.

Freijo, T. D., & Jaeger, R. M. (1976). Social class and race as concomitants of composite halo in teachers' evaluative rating of pupils. *American Educational Research Journal, 13,* 1–14.

Fuller, M. (1980). Black girls in a London comprehensive school. In R. Deem (Ed.), *Schooling for women's work* (pp. 52–65). London: Routledge and Kegan Paul.

Giroux, H. (1983). Theories of reproduction and resistance in the new sociology of education: A critical analysis. *Harvard Educational Review, 53,* 257–293.

Grant, C. A., & Sleeter, C. E. (1985). The literature on multicultural education: Review and analysis. *Educational Review, 37,* 97–118.

Grant, L. (1984). Black females' "place" in desegregated classrooms. *Sociology of Education, 57,* 98–111.

Haertel, G. D., Walberg, H. J., Junker, L., & Pascarella, E. T. (1981). Early adolescent sex differences in science learning: Evidence from the National Assessment of Educational Progress. *American Educational Research Journal, 18,* 329–341.

Hall, V. C., & Turner, R. R. (1974). The validity of the "different language explanation" for poor scholastic performance by black students. *Review of Educational Research, 44,* 69–82.

Haller, E. J., & Davis, S. A. (1980). Does socioeconomic status bias the assignment of elementary school students to reading groups? *American Educational Research Journal, 17,* 409–418.

Hannafin, M. J. (1983). Fruits and fallacies of instructional systems: Effects of an instructional system approach on the concept attainment of Anglo and Hispanic students. *American Educational Research Journal, 20,* 237–250.

Harber, J. R., & Bryen, D. N. (1976). Black English and the task of reading. *Review of Educational Research, 46,* 387–405.

Hennessy, I. J., & Merrifield, P. R. (1978). Ethnicity and sex distinctions in patterns of aptitude factor scores in a sample of urban high school seniors. *American Educational Research Journal, 15,* 385–389.

Hernandez, N. G. (1973). Variables affecting achievement of middle school Mexican-American students. *Review of Educational Research, 43,* 1–39.

Hill, H. (1982). The AFL-CIO and the black worker: Twenty-five years after the merger. *Journal of Intergroup Relations, 10.*

Hodges, W. L. (1978). The worth of the follow through experience. *Harvard Educational Review, 48,* 186–192.

Jackson, G., & Cosca, C. (1974). The inequality of educational opportunity in the Southwest: An observational study of ethnically mixed classrooms. *American Educational Research Journal, 11,* 219–229.

Jencks, C., Smith, M., Acland, H., Bane, M. J., Cohen, D., Gintis, H., Heynes, B., & Michelson, S. (1972). *Inequality: A reassessment of the effect of family and schooling in America*. New York: Basic Books.

Kedar-Voivodas, G. (1983). The impact of elementary children's school roles and sex roles on teacher attitudes: An interactional analysis. *Review of Educational Research, 53*, 415–437.

Kennedy, S. P., & Suzuki, S. N. (1977). Spontaneous elaboration in Mexican-American and Anglo-American high school seniors. *American Educational Research Journal, 14*, 383–388.

Kirk, D. H., & Goon, S. (1975). Desegregation and the cultural deficit model: An examination of the literature. *Review of Educational Research, 45*, 599–611.

Kirp, D. L. (1976). Race, politics, and the courts: School desegregation in San Francisco. *Harvard Educational Review, 46*, 572–611.

Kirp, D. L. (1977). Law, politics, and equal educational opportunity: The limits of judicial involvement. *Harvard Educational Review, 47*, 117–137.

Kirp, D. L. (1981). The bounded politics of school desegregation and litigation. *Harvard Educational Review, 51*, 395–414.

Kleinfield, J. (1973). Intellectual strengths in culturally different groups: An Eskimo illustration. *Review of Educational Research, 43*, 341–360.

Lee, P. C., & Gropper, N. B. (1974). Sex-role culture and educational practice. *Harvard Educational Review, 44*, 369–410.

Lightfoot, S. L. (1976). Socialization and education of young black girls in school. *Teachers College Record, 78*, 239–262.

Lyman, K. D., & Speizer, J. J. (1980). Advancing in school administration: A pilot project for women. *Harvard Educational Review, 50*, 25–35.

Marini, M. M., & Greenberger, E. (1978). Sex differences in educational aspirations and expectations. *American Educational Research Journal, 15*, 67–79.

Maruyama, G., & Miller, N. (1979). Reexamination of normative influences processes in desegregated classrooms. *American Educational Research Journal, 16*, 273–283.

Michelson, S. (1973). The further responsibility of intellectuals. *Harvard Educational Review, 43*, 92–103.

Ogbu, J. U. (1978). *Minority education and caste*. New York: Academic Press.

Otheguy, R. (1982). Thinking about bilingual education: A critical appraisal. *Harvard Educational Review, 52*, 301–314.

Pallas, A. M., & Alexander, K. L. (1983). Sex differences in quantitative SAT performance: New evidence on the differential coursework hypothesis. *American Educational Research Journal, 20*, 165–182.

Pedro, J. D., Wolleat, P., Fennema, E., & Becker, A. D. (1981). Election of high school mathematics by females and males: Attributions and attitudes. *American Educational Research Journal, 18*, 207–218.

Pettigrew, T. I., & Green, R. L. (1976). School desegregation in large cities: A critique of the Coleman "White flight" thesis. *Harvard Educational Review, 46*, 1–53.

Ravitch, D. (1976). On the history of minority group education in the United States. *Teacher College Record, 78*, 213–228.

Rist, R. C. (1978). *The invisible children*. Cambridge, MA: Harvard University Press.

Rivlin, A. M. (1973). Forensic social science. *Harvard Educational Review, 43*, 61–75.

Rumberger, R. W. (1983). Dropping out of high school: The influence of race, sex, and family background. *American Educational Research Journal, 20*, 119–220.

Ryan, F. A. (1982). The federal role in American Indian education. *Harvard Educational Review, 52*, 419–471.

Saario, T. N., Jacklin, C. N., & Tittle, C. K. (1973). Sex role stereotyping in the public schools. *Harvard Educational Review, 43*, 386–416.

Schlossman, S. (1983). Self-evident remedy? George I. Sanchez, segregation, and enduring dilemmas in bilingual education. *Teachers College Record, 84*, 871–907.

Schofield, J. W. (1982). *Black and white in school*. New York: Praeger.

Schultz, C. B., & Sherman, R. H. (1976). Social class development and difference in reinforcement effectiveness. *Review of Educational Research, 46*, 25–59.

Scott, R. R., & McPartland, J. M. (1982). Desegregation as national policy: Correlates of racial attitudes. *American Educational Research Journal, 19*, 397–414.

Shade, B. J. (1982). Afro-American cognitive style: A variable in school success. *Review of Educational Research, 52,* 219–244.

Sharan, S. (1980). Cooperative learning in small groups: Recent methods and effects on achievement, attitudes, and ethnic relations. *Review of Educational Research, 50,* 241–271.

Sherman, J., & Fennema, E. (1977). The study of mathematics by high school girls and boys: Related variables. *American Educational Research Journal, 14,* 159–168.

Simpson, A. W., & Erickson, M. T. (1983). Teachers' verbal and nonverbal communication patterns as a function of teacher race, student gender, and student race. *American Educational Research Journal, 10,* 183–198.

Slavin, R. E., & Madden, N. A. (1979). School practices that improve race relations. *American Educational Research Journal, 16,* 169–180.

Snow, C. E. (1983). Literacy and language: Relationships during preschool years. *Harvard Educational Review, 53,* 165–189.

Sowell, T. (1981). Assumptions vs. history in ethnic education. *Teachers College Record, 83,* 37–71.

Stake, J. E., & Katz, J. F. (1982). Teacher-pupil relationships in the elementary school classroom: Teacher-gender and pupil-gender differences. *American Educational Research Journal, 19,* 465–471.

Steinitz, V. A., King, P., Solomon, E., & Shapiro, E. (1973). Ideological development in working-class youth. *Harvard Educational Review, 43,* 333–361.

Sullivan, M. L. (1979). Contacts among cultures: School desegregation in a polyethnic New York City high school. In R. C. Rist (Ed.), *Desegregated schools: Appraisals of an American experiment* (pp. 201–240). New York: Academic Press.

Teitelbaum, H., & Hiller, R. J. (1977). Bilingual education: The legal mandate. *Harvard Educational Review, 47,* 138–170.

Tobias, S., & Weissbrod, S. (1980). Anxiety and mathematics: An update. *Harvard Educational Review, 50,* 63–70.

Tollett, K. S. (1982). The propriety of the federal role in expanding equal educational opportunity. *Harvard Educational Review, 52,* 431–443.

Walberg, H. S., & Marjoribanks, K. (1976). Family environment and cognitive development: Twelve analytic models. *Review of Educational Research, 46,* 527–551.

Willig, A. G., Harnish, D. L., Hill, T., & Maehr, M. L. (1983). Sociocultural and educational correlates of success-failure attributions and evaluation anxiety in the school setting for Blacks, Hispanics and Anglo-children. *American Educational Research Journal, 20,* 385–410.

Willis, P. (1977). *Learning to labour.* Westmead, England: Saxon House.

CHAPTER 17

RACE, CLASS, AND GENDER AND ABANDONED DREAMS (1988)

Carl A. Grant and Christine E. Sleeter

Theoretical background

School plays a major role in the culture students develop. Like the family and neighborhood, school affects how students understand and pursue their life chances. It provides an institutional ideology, socializing agents, and an experiential context within which students define and shape the way they think about their personal dreams. The school context, containing social relations defined by race, social class, and gender, can produce a student culture in which young people accept and live out their parents' place in a stratified society, in spite of the school's espoused mission as equalizer and escalator to a better life. This happened in our study.

The study examines student culture as it is produced and lived in a particular community. We wanted to understand why students of color, lower-class white students, and female students, both white and of color, tend not to succeed in school and out, and tend to assume subordinate roles in society in spite of the fact that school is supposed to serve as an equalizer. We did *not* assume that schools serve all children equally, since there is abundant evidence that they do not.[1] We did believe it would be insufficient to study the school apart from the lives of students, since students are not passive automatons that are simply molded and shaped. Valli points out that too often, in studies of socialization and studies of unequal school processes, process "becomes little more than work upon the raw, inanimate materials of nature; people are objects transformed by processes to which they fall prey and become content enough to fit into the social slots that need to be filled."[2] We saw it as both naive and inaccurate to assume that students do not think about their world and resist attempts to fit them for subordinate social roles.

Student success, or lack of success, can best be understood as a result of interaction between students and the world in which they live, of which the school is a part. One understands how students perceive and act within their world by examining their culture, and also linking it with social-structural inequality as it is manifested in the students' daily experience. Weis describes student cultures as "semi-autonomous," and argues that they "arise in relation to structural conditions mediated by both the experience of schooling and the lived experiences of youth in their own communities."[3]

Relatively few studies have examined student culture in the way we have, and fewer have integrated race, social class, and gender relationships in their analyses.

For example, Ogbu, Payne, and Weis studied black lower-class student culture, examining its relationship to very poor quality schooling and the job structure in the community.[4] Everhart and Willis studied working-class white male student culture, analyzing it primarily in terms of social class relations.[5] Valli, Connelly, and McRobbie examined white female student culture in relationship to gender and social class relations, showing how schooling contributes partially to the subordination of women.[6] Fuller studied eight black girls in a London school, describing their resistance to triple subordination based on race, social class, and gender.[7] What all these studies show is that schooling itself is not equal in quality, and students themselves sometimes recognize and resist this. However, students also perceive and think about opportunities for themselves in the wider society, based on experiences in their own community. Sometimes they shape their behavior in ways that maximize success, often they do not, and often they redefine success to fit the opportunities and roles they believe are open to them.

Exactly what role schools play in this process is not thoroughly understood, particularly for racially mixed schools, and for male-female student cultures in interaction with each other. What also has not been investigated much is how student culture develops and changes over time: At what points do students become aware of, question, and even reject subordinate roles? How do they deal with their own questions, how do they sustain resistance, or how do they reshape their culture to accept eventually their own subordination? Are there critical points when educators could intervene to promote and sustain their success? These are questions this study addresses.

Context and method

The study of these twenty-four students began as a part of a three-year ethnographic study of a multiracial junior high school in a midwestern city in the United States.[8] The community that served as the attendance area for the school was located along a river, and historically served as an immigration site for low-income people, particularly people of color, who could not afford to live elsewhere and had often been rejected in other parts of the city. Over the years, as successive waves of Jewish, Lebanese, Syrian, black, Scandinavian, Native American, and Mexican immigrants moved into the area, an integrated housing pattern developed. In 1980 the mean family income of the community was about $16,000. Residents held such jobs as factory worker, janitor, postoffice worker, secretary, and auto mechanic; very few of the twenty-four students' parents had completed college.

The junior high served grades seven through nine. On completion of the ninth grade, students attended the high school that was physically connected to the junior high school. A school lunch room was shared by both schools and served as the architectural connection. Thus, these twenty-four students only had to go out of the other exit of their lunchroom to enter their high school. At the time we began this study, school statistics for the racial mix of the 580 junior high students were: white, 67.5 percent; Hispanic, 28.0 percent; Native American, 2.0 percent; black, 2.0 percent; and Asian, 0.5 percent.

The racial composition and the gender count of the twenty-four students we followed was: Mexican: nine (4 male, 5 female); white: eight (5 male, 3 female); black: two (1 male, 1 female); Puerto Rican: two (2 female); Native American: one (1 male); Southeast Asian: one (1 female); Arab-American: one (1 female).

Data for this phase of the study were collected over a seven-year period.

During the first three years a team of three researchers made one two-week visit, and twenty-three visits lasting two to three days each. Several methods of data collection were used: observations (including shadowing of students), interviews, and questionnaires. A total of 160 hours were spent observing in twenty-three junior high classrooms. During the last four years, two of the three original researchers maintained the vigil on the student population, periodically visiting the school and interviewing the students and a counselor. Phone calls were also made to the counselor in order to keep up with the students' actions. Interview data were recorded and transcribed for analysis. Research bias was controlled by rotating interviewers, having all researchers participate in data analysis, and re-asking the same questions in subsequent interviews.

Student culture and the abandonment of dreams

Our title suggests that the students once had optimistic dreams of making it—finishing high school and possibly further education, getting a good job, making their families proud, and achieving personal satisfaction—and they slowly abandoned those dreams. To a large extent, this is true. What the title does not delineate, however, is what their dreams were, and why they were abandoned. First we will examine the students' dreams for education and work beyond high school. Then we will examine the effect of the school, the family, and the economy on their dreams. Finally their personal identities, and their view of the world in which they lived, will be considered before making a summary assessment.

High school and further education

(9th grade, April 1981)

ANNA: All the kids in our family who have graduated went on to vocational schools and I want to go to college.
R: What do you want to be?
ANNA: A lawyer.

(11th grade, May 1983)

R: What do you plan to do when you graduate?
ANNA: Go to the technical vocational institute.
R: What influenced you to make these plans?
ANNA: Well, I work at _____ Publishing, and they have word processing, so I'll take up that.
R: Is that what you would like to do most?
ANNA: Not really. I'd rather be a lawyer, but right now I can't afford to go to school.

(9th grade, March 1979)

R: You still want to be a lawyer, right?
HAZEL: Yeah, but I'm not sure, it's kind of one of my dreams. [It was a dream she talked about with us all year.]

(12th grade, May 1982)

R: What do you think about doing [next month when you graduate]?
HAZEL: Well, I think about dancing. I don't know if I should go to college right

away and start that, or take dramatic arts and communication. . . . And
I just kinda want to dance for a year or something . . .

R: You've changed your mind since I talked to you last.

HAZEL: Yeah. That's true, it was law. I kinda gave up on law, I didn't think I had
the brains for it.

The students voiced a variety of career goals over the time they were interviewed.
Goals they discussed with interest included: lawyer (3 students), teacher (1), professional athlete (2), medical technologist (1), doctor (3), veterinarian (1), computer scientist (1), military (6), mechanic (4), truck driver (1), disc jockey (1),
model (2), secretary (2), stewardess (3), beautician (1), and police officer (1). The
numbers add up to more than twenty-four because most students changed their
minds at least once, or toyed with alternatives. Their degree of conviction about
these goals varied, but none of the twenty-four was without some goal.

College was a more immediate concern to many, since their career goals
would require college. We asked the students in every interview about career goals
and college. Since college is increasingly the "one important escalator" on the
"elevation of a people,"[9] we will discuss their responses in detail.

While in junior high (eighth and ninth grades), thirteen of the twenty-four
students said they definitely planned to attend college. Only one said definitely no
to college; the rest (10) were undecided. The white students tended to voice about
the same assurance as others about college: five of the eight white students definitely planned to attend college, and six of the eleven Hispanic students were
definite, with two more discussing professional career goals without specifically
discussing college. Of these thirteen, seven were girls and six were boys.

By the end of their senior year, however, only three of the thirteen who said
they definitely had college plans were heading for a four-year college, and one
dropped out his freshman year. What happened to the other twenty-one students?
Three entered a community college and five planned to enroll in a vocational-
technical institute; two of these were part of the thirteen who earlier planned on
college, and two more had considered college rather briefly in high school. Three
were flirting with the military, one viewing it as a possible career and two hoping
to earn money for college. Four more graduated, but were still unsure of plans and
talked of taking a "year off." Six did not graduate. Two of these took jobs as
mechanics, a goal both had discussed with some interest since junior high; one is
now working in a restaurant, a few credits shy of his diploma; one is working and
living with her boyfriend; we lost track of one; and one dropped out of a school to
which he was transferred, was shot on a city street, and now is a quadriplegic in a
wheelchair.

What did students say about reasons for their decisions? This can best be
answered by providing two representative examples.

Carmen's goals in junior high were very indefinite, although college was a
possibility. For Christmas in ninth grade, her father gave her a typewriter. Her
parents, both from Puerto Rico, had not graduated from high school, and saw
secretarial work as a good employment opportunity for Carmen. In tenth grade
she started taking clerical courses, receiving encouragement from her business
teacher and talking about becoming a legal secretary. By eleventh grade she was
thinking about community college to take legal secretarial courses, and reported
that her accounting and shorthand teachers were very supportive. By her senior
year, Carmen was sick of school—boy problems and boring classwork. She
wanted just to work for a while—"business, they always need people like clerical

workers and stuff." She felt her summer job in a company plus her business courses in high school had prepared her well enough to be a secretary. She simply wanted to be away from the hassles of school.

Larry's four older brothers were in the military, and while in junior high he figured he would follow suit, although he had not yet given it much thought. In tenth grade he was trying to take some of the harder courses because counselors had said these would help for college, although he was not too sure about college. Money was the main obstacle:

> I know college will be maybe third [choice], after the service and going to a voc. tech.—'cause it's a lot of money. And I ain't got a lot of money. . . . Money just keeps going up and up! So a lot of people find different ways to get around it. Through the service you can get the same schooling for, you know, free.

During his senior year, Larry said he wanted to be a disk jockey. He knew people who had tried and one who made it. If that failed, he did not know; he felt his opportunities to be restricted by his lack of money for college, the unemployment rate, and the poor quality of his secondary schooling. We quote at length because he articulated well the frustration most of our sample felt:

LARRY: Every year there's a scarcity of finding jobs. All over the place. . . . If you go to college and have, like, four years, when you get out, there's gotta be something. . . . If you can't get a job, you just wasted a lot of time and a lot of money.
R: But many colleges say they usually place 60, 70, 80 percent of their people.
LARRY: Yeah, but there's always a chance that you ain't that 70, 80 percent that's gonna get a job. . . . If you're not a part of that percentage that *does* get placed, say like me—I'm not a top quality guy in school. I don't think I could handle college right now. I mean, you get a lot of homework, and I haven't had homework for three years now in this school!

Most of the students felt that they were freely making their own choices about their futures. However, they were making choices within a particular set of social institutions: the school, the family, and the local economy in the community.

The school

The school can best be described as taking a laissez-faire stand—some resources for college preparation were there, but it was left up to the individual, for the most part, to take advantage of them. In junior high, the academic demand made of students was fairly light; we have described this in detail elsewhere.[10] Most classes gave easy work and no homework; the main person to talk seriously with students about their futures was a counselor who had grown up in the community. When students entered tenth grade, most said that the work was much harder. They were taking academic courses required for graduation (typically English, social studies, math, science, and two electives), and many were receiving homework (typically two or three times per week in math and science). Students also said that teachers explained or helped students with the work less, and expected them to figure it out more on their own. Students did not complain much about any of this—they described the high school as treating them more "grown up."

After tenth grade, things changed. We will describe the changes in relationship to three different categories of students. One category consisted of those who entered college or community college after graduation—six students. These students continued to take demanding courses until they graduated (except one who had a half day of work/study his senior year), and continued to have some homework. These might be thought of as the college-bound, in that their teachers treated them as if they were bound for college. However, it was often not the school that advised them which courses to take; it was often friends and family who had been to college and knew what preparation was needed. These students made the following kinds of comments about the counseling they received in high school:

(Senior Year)

R: What did [the counselors] tell you that made you take Chemistry and Physics?
Lin-Su: They didn't tell me anything. I just decided.
R: Did you know that those kinds of things are good for you to have if you're going to go to college?
Lin-Su: Yeah, that's why I took them.
R: Who told you you should be taking them in order to go to college?
Lin-Su: Some of my teachers. My mom and dad. And my older sister—she's going to college and she took those classes.

(Junior Year)

R: Why are you taking so many academic courses?
Rakia: Mm, I don't know. I don't really like gym. I just like classes where you can sit and do your work [History, French, Algebra, Trig., Computers, Biology] . . .
R: Has anyone told you that you need the math and the algebra and science courses in order to go to college and become a doctor?
Rakia: Yeah, my advisor. They usually ask you, "What do you plan to do after high school?" I said, "Go to college." And they said, "O.K., you need a lot of math and English and stuff like science."
R: Are most of your friends planning to go to college?
Rakia: . . . Sandra, she wants to be a veterinarian.
R: Is she taking courses like yours?
Rakia: Not at all. . . . I don't think she really talks to people about what she's going to do.

(Senior Year)

Rakia: I don't like the counselor. 'Cause instead of boosting up, he'll kinda put you down. He said that I wouldn't get in _____ College with my test scores. But I did. . . . I just got the letter back [from the college] that just proved him wrong.

The picture that emerged was that around tenth grade, counselors asked students what they planned to do after graduation. If they said "college," they were advised to take more math and science; three girls told us counselors "made" them stick with math and science at that point. After that, students seemed to be on their own. Some of their teachers told them which classes to take, and they got advice from counselors if they purposely sought it, but most of the advice they got came from outside the school.

A second group of five students consisted of those who were fairly certain they would become secretaries or mechanics. Little academic demand was placed on them in school. They were advised into secretarial or autoshop courses, and felt the school was helping them in that sense. These students reported getting advice and being made to work and think in their vocational classes. The other thirteen—the largest group—floated through with only minimal demands made on them after tenth grade. Several thought they were going to college, others were unsure. Either way, it appeared that no one in the school seriously thought they were headed for college; the school took steps mainly to help them fit into the blue-collar labor market. These students reported having little or no homework. Their senior English class was aimed, in one student's words, at "trying to make sure that our grammar's right." Their course schedules were filled with electives such as ceramics, office helper, bookstore worker, chorus, and gym; during their senior year several participated in half-day on-the-job-training programs. They reported that virtually no one in the school talked to them about the future; they were free to select their own courses, and counselors did not talk to them unless they sought the counselors out. There was not even much attempt to let students know what information might be available through the counselors, so few students voluntarily went to ask; one pointed out that counselors "gotta let you know that it's there [information about a college], for you to come and see, you know."

By their senior year, many of these students were bitter, and many were simply bored with school. For example, one who took the easy way through told us the following, one month before graduating:

R: You went through easy.
PABLO: Yeah.
R: Do you ever regret that now?
PABLO: Yeah, 'cause—I feel like I coulda learned more if I went, if I took some harder classes. . . . There's a lot of kids that just, they're smart, but they just take easy classes and not, you know, they're not learning nothing. Once you get into senior high, you don't even have to take math, you know, not at all.

Their experience with school, and particularly the last two years, left many ambivalent about any future schooling: On the one hand, it would help them, but on the other hand it would probably be boring and they were not prepared for it. Some blamed the school for being too lax, others blamed themselves.

We wondered whether the school offered any other kinds of opportunities for learning how to "make it" in society, such as leadership development. We looked for this in our study of the junior high, and examined interviews from the senior high for comments. We found very little. The student council was one avenue for developing leadership skills; one of our sample had been president of the junior high student body, another was senior class president. Even here, however, student leadership did not seem to be taken seriously. The student council did not have authority over anything very important or consequential, and the senior class president spent half of her senior year in on-the-job-training. One social studies teacher made a concerted effort to involve his students in school and community political events, but his singular effort did not seem to make a great impact on the students. The only other comment we found related to leadership development—and it is a weak one at that—was a shy student commenting that English classes that require students to make speeches had helped her learn to speak up more.

The family

The family was a second institution within which students constructed perceptions of their futures.

R: How do your parents feel about you going to school in general?
ALVIN: They want me to finish school and get a good education and get good grades, too.

This comment illustrates the way these students' parents felt about school achievement. Discussions with counselors, teachers, administrators, and students on this topic were of one kind: Parents sent their kids to school to learn and expected them not to fool around while learning was going on. Parents were very supportive of the school and left their children's education, guidance, and course selection almost solely in school's hands. We have reason to assume that because most of the parents had not attended college, and were familiar mostly with traditional blue- and pink-collar jobs, they were reluctant to give career advice or to lobby strongly for a certain course selection if they believed the school had endorsed their child's program. There were a few exceptions. For example, Ron's father and uncle were mechanics and encouraged him to follow suit. During the study his goal did not change. Notice his comment in his sophomore year.

R: What do you want to do when you graduate?
RON: My Dad tells me I should be a mechanic 'cause he is.

Ron left school in his junior year and is now working as a mechanic.

Juan, who early in the study said he wanted to be a doctor, often spoke of receiving advice from his uncle, who was a doctor, as to which courses to take and the need to work really hard in school in order to achieve the goal.

Since most of the students did not have homework on a regular basis, parents did not set up home study hours or have identifiable opportunities to discuss schoolwork with their children. The role that the parents played in helping their children fulfill their academic expectations was very small. Besides helping with homework, several ways to help children in academics include providing them with experiences such as museums, plays, and travel, and reading books, magazines, and newspapers. Most students when asked reported doing very little of the above either with parents or alone.

The economy

The local economy was a third institution within which the students constructed beliefs about their future. One important characteristic of the local economy was that neither the students nor their parents had extra money for things like college. This was, in fact, the main barrier to college cited by students. Many also discussed ways of dealing with it. The students' perception of reality may have been limited and even inaccurate, but it was based on available information and guided their behavior.

"Taking a year off" to work was an alternative several mentioned. None laid out a specific plan for doing this, but several felt they needed to work to save some money before they could go to college. Six students were more specific about how they would finance further education: They would join the military and either save their pay for college later, or receive their education "free" while in the military. They based this plan on talks given by military recruiters who came to the senior high school. Few students mentioned loans or scholarships for college. We asked them about this in interviews, and they had very little knowledge of this option—it was as if the option did not exist; no one had talked to most of them about it.

Another feature of the local economy that students perceived was the relatively high unemployment rate. It made students feel uncertain about the future, and caused several to view four years of college with some skepticism. Although Rakia, for example, enrolled in a community college, she said about the unemployment situation: "I'm kinda worried about it. I don't have a job right now, but that doesn't bother me. But it does worry me because when I get out of college I don't know what the situation's gonna be like." Other students were more worried about having a job right now, and felt some sense of security if they had at least their summer job or were involved in on-the-job-training. The unemployment situation made it risky to give up a job, expect financial support from parents, or incur debt to secure further schooling.

Students' career goals were wide-ranging, but their knowledge of the job market was based on jobs they or their parents actually held. Several distinguished between dreams and reality: One could dream of what one would like to do, but one would have to settle for a job that is really there, and that one can really get. Students commented about their own job experience:

R: What do you plan to do when you graduate? [Earlier goal had been veterinarian.]
LINDA: I'm going on to the technical-vocational institute. I'm either gonna take computers, or data processing, office fields, general accounting, or accounting.
R: What influenced you to do that?
LINDA: I work in 3M, in general accounting, so I'd like to get a job there.
R: Oh. How'd you get the job at 3M?
LINDA: Through on-the-job-training.
R: Do you think about the current unemployment rate at all?
LINDA: Yes! I'll probably end up being one of them if I don't get some training to keep my job.

Finally, we must consider the peer group itself. When we met the students in junior high school, we were struck by the strong division in their lives between school and the rest of the day. Most of their classwork was boring, but school could be tolerated from 8:00 A.M. to 2:30 P.M. After that, it could be forgotten, especially since few had homework. Students spent their free time either at home, playing sports, or "hanging around" with each other. They cared about passing their classes, but few cared which passing grade they received. It was considered neither "in" nor "out" to be smart—this was viewed in the peer group as irrelevant. Since high school did not offer much change, the peer group did not change much. Students spent less time playing and more time in jobs, but no more time with schoolwork. They became used to investing a prescribed number of hours in a work-type setting, and enjoying the rest of the day in social activities. This life-style fit the demands placed on them. The students also used each other as sources of information about future plans, quite possibly more than they used the counselors. Thus, their perceptions were widely shared, both because students encountered similar experiences and because they helped each other make sense of their futures.

Personal identities and view of the world

We wondered how the students viewed their identities as members of particular racial, social-class, and gender groups, and how they viewed the position of those groups in society. We were interested in the extent to which the students embraced the strengths offered by group membership without being constrained by social stereotypes or stigmas, and the extent to which their understanding of oppression developed, if at all. We also wondered what effect views of race, class, and gender had on their dreams. We learned about their personal and group identities by asking about their neighborhood, their views of each other, their views about cultural practices within the home, and their views about choices they made for themselves. We learned about their understanding of racism, classism, and sexism by asking them directly about these things.

Race and ethnicity

The students identified culturally with their community. The community was composed of working-class people of varied ethnic backgrounds, but the students viewed them as culturally all "the same." Households varied somewhat in menu, religion, strictness, and so forth, but the students did not see the various ethnic groups in the community as culturally distinct from one another. To the students, a distinguishing feature of their community was the fact that the people were different colors—this was positive, and students talked openly and eagerly about it. Culturally, however, they were not different from one another. Over the time of this study, we saw no change in this pattern.

What fascinated us was the extent to which many students disagreed with their parents on this. Several of their parents had moved from elsewhere (such as Puerto Rico, Egypt, Texas, Mexico), and saw different ethnic groups as culturally differ-ent. Some of the parents who had lived in the community a long time also saw them as different. These parents tended to want their children to date and marry members of their own ethnic group and some tried to discourage them from associating in any way with a particular ethnic group. The students did not see it this way, for the most part, and some argued with their parents about it. To the students, interracial dating and marriage were completely acceptable because color did not matter.

A few students commented on their parents' wanting them to retain their ethnic culture. Some saw this as important, but also saw no conflict between it and marrying someone of another ethnic group. Others did not see it as particu-larly important. For example, two Mexican-American students whose parents were from Texas told us they were not interested in learning Spanish, even though their parents wanted them to do so.

The students' acceptance of racial diversity seemed almost to interfere with their developing an understanding of racism. Only about half of the students believed any form of racism exists in society, and examples they described were, with two exceptions, individual prejudice. For example, a Mexican-American girl said that the students in an all-white school had said they were having an "invasion" when she visited there; a white girl said some of the police were racially prejudiced. A few students described their parents as racially prejudiced, but the only generalization they offered was that times have changed and younger people are not prejudiced any more. Students saw most prejudice away from the community; the main examples of prejudice in the community were offered by a Puerto Rican and an Arab-American (both of whom said people lumped them together with Mexicans, which they resented), and a Vietnamese-American, who commented on prejudice against newly arrived Hmongs.

Only two students attempted to describe institutional racism. One Mexican-American boy said that "just about everything is for white people," explaining that television, for example, is all white. A white boy explained that whites are upper class and Mexicans are lower class because Mexicans have not been able to afford college and therefore do not get good jobs.

The students of color had, as a group, no more understanding of racism than the white students. Nine of the sixteen students of color believed some racial prejudice exists in society, as did four of the eight white students, but the explanations or understanding of prejudice offered by the students of color were no more informed than were those of the white students. Since most students had not experienced overt discrimination in the community and many of the students had not ventured very far outside the community, they assumed race relations in society are similar to race relations in that community. Neither school nor parents taught them much about racism beyond what they experienced. One teacher in the junior high taught about it and a few students mentioned this while in junior high, but seemed to forget it in high school since the race relations where they lived were positive. We did not study their parents directly to find out what they taught about race relations, but the main thing students ever said about their parents was whether parents were prejudiced against their friends.

Social class

Students defined themselves as middle class (with the exception of one who said her family was poor, and one who said his was upper middle class). They said they were middle class because, in the words of one student, "We don't make a lot, but then we still have enough to make ends meet." Earlier we described the community as working class but as having two neighborhoods differentiated by racial composition and somewhat by income level; to most of the students, it was all one middle-class community.

The students generated this common self-definition on the basis of several interrelated factors. Geographically, the community was cut off by a river from most of the rest of the city, and residents tended not to venture out. The range of incomes in the community was not great, and the schools served the entire community from kindergarten through graduation. Thus, the students grew up together, and associated with others who shared their economic circumstances, their neighborhood, their school. Lacking much firsthand contact with people of diverse social classes, they figured they were middle class since few lived in poverty but none had much money for luxuries.

Their knowledge of the social class structure in society was very thin, even after taking Sociology in high school, in which social class was a topic they studied. When we asked students about social class, we often had to explain what we meant, and even then students sometimes did not know how to respond. Students believed anyone could achieve upward mobility by hard work, getting a good education, and—two girls said—marriage. Most students did not want to move up; a white boy said he would like more money but wanted to stay in the same community, and a few others suggested this.

Gender and sexism

Students' gender self-definitions were more complex and less shared. The patterns we will describe only very roughly follow ethnic group membership, with the Hispanic students tending slightly more than whites to adhere to traditional gender identities. All students saw themselves as potential job-holders regardless of sex. Students believed both sexes could hold almost any job, although several ruled out construction for women (they lack the strength) and child care for men (men lack patience). Their aspirations tended to follow sex-stereotypic patterns, particularly as they approached graduation. The aspiring mechanics, truck drivers, and professional football players were male; the aspiring secretaries, stewardesses, and models were female—but the girls also envisioned themselves as lawyers, doctors, and computer technologists, at least until they confronted the problem of paying for college.

Students identified males more than females as providers, and this increased as they got older. Before they started dating, providing was not an issue—when same-sex groups went out, sex did not determine who initiated or paid. Dating changed this. Six of the boys from the time they started dating expected to initiate dates and pay for them, although most were flexible about who could initiate phone calls. By their senior year, the three who graduated, plus a fourth who had not dated much, saw themselves as providers for their future families—their wives *could* work but would not have to, especially if there were children. One boy initially advocated flexible roles, but by his senior year he was paying for all his dates, and referred to a wife's paycheck as "extra money." Interestingly, only two of these eight boys had a firm career goal in mind all during the study; the rest were unsure what they would do. Five of the girls, by high school, also saw the male as the main provider: Their boyfriends initiated and paid for dates, and they expected the man to be the main family breadwinner. This was a relationship they seemed to learn partly through dating; one had offered to pay for dates but the offer was turned down; others thought hypothetically that girls could pay but knew boys preferred it the other way around. Two of these five girls earlier expressed a strong career orientation, but by their senior year were uncertain about their futures. One of them entertained the idea of herself as provider and her husband staying at home, but did not expect this. A sixth girl saw the male as the main provider but was also preparing for a good career in computer science.

On the other hand, three girls and one boy definitely saw initiating and providing as shared responsibilities, and had worked this out in date relationships. Two more girls expressed ambivalence about providing: They questioned but did not reject outright traditional dating roles, and saw themselves as career-bound. The remaining four students did not address this issue.

All students but one saw themselves as present and future workers in the home. Most divided chores by sex; the girls wrestled with this more than the boys. Eleven of the twenty-four students expected and preferred to divide domestic chores by sex, and did not debate or question this during the study; four were girls, seven were boys. These tended to be the same students who saw males as providers. Most engaged in these roles at home, although in one boy's home chores were not divided by sex and he thought they should be. Only one boy and two girls completely rejected sex roles at home throughout the study. The two girls were rejecting roles learned at home, and one felt very strongly about this, saying she *hated* it that guys want women to stay in the house.

The other nine students were less certain. Three (1 boy, 2 girls) simply said it depended on whether the wife holds a job; if she does, they would expect to divide chores fifty-fifty. Four more students (1 boy, 3 girls) questioned domestic roles while in junior high, two girls, having been angry about how chores were divided at home; but by their senior year all three of these girls seemed content to adopt traditional sex roles. Two more girls wanted to divide things fifty-fifty, but did not expect a man to go along with that.

Students justified role definition primarily based on masculine strength. Eleven students maintained that boys are the stronger sex, and therefore better in sports and heavy work; five disagreed, and two girls changed their minds on this during the study. What was particularly interesting was that approximately equal proportions of both sexes defined themselves as athletic, but many boys, and the girls as they got older, defined boys as naturally stronger and more athletic than girls.

With respect to sexism in society, students knew very little. They saw equal opportunity in the work place as an accomplished fact, with the exception of one girl who knew a woman who had filed a sex-discrimination grievance. The fact that many jobs are not sex-balanced was attributed mainly to individual choice or to ability to do the job. Several girls wrestled for a short period with sexism at home, but they saw this as a personal rather than a collective struggle, or as something women simply have to put up with. For example, one girl complained that men like to be outside until mealtime, and expect to come in and find dinner ready; this was an inconvenient male characteristic more than an arena for struggle. In fact, as students matured, they tended more and more to accept rather than resist sex-divided domestic work roles and supporting sex stereotypes. The only social issue any of the students discussed was whether women should fight in the military. Three boys brought this up, arguing that if women want equal rights they should be willing to fight in combat. This issue was being debated in the news, and seemed to be one of concern to boys who had considered entering the military.

The students generated gender self-definitions and their understandings of social relations between the sexes on the basis of several factors. A major one was observation. For example, a boy commented that girls must prefer sewing to cars because he had never seen roles switched, although another said girls in his autoshop class demonstrated that girls could be mechanical. As another example, a girl commented that she had seen traditional sex roles at home all her life. A related factor was doing: All but one student had chores at home, and most became used to and comfortable with those they were assigned, although a few rebelled against them. The local economy seemed to reinforce students' observations—girls were hired as babysitters and typists, boys as outdoor laborers, paper carriers, janitors, and mechanics. The school was a laissez-faire factor. It made available all courses and activities to both sexes, enabling many girls to develop an interest in sports, but hardly anyone in school (or at home), with the exception of one or two teachers, discussed gender or sexism. So students who questioned or rebelled against roles or expectations had to work these through themselves, and they tended to resolve them in favor of the status quo. A final, very important factor was the peer group itself. When students began to think about courtship, they began to shape their behavior and expectations in a way that would complement expectations of the opposite sex. The boys had fewer questions about role and gender-identity, and the girls tended to resolve their own questions by accepting the boys' definition. This facilitated courtship, although it also tended to help reproduce existing gender relations.

Discussion

This study has shown, particularly because it was longitudinal, that race, class, and gender relations in society are not reproduced simply because the young absorb and inherit the status and beliefs of their parents. It is a more complex process than this. As the young work through their dreams and questions in a particular context, the range of possibilities that seem open and real to them gradually narrows and tends to mirror the lives of their parents. The culture the young construct from the fabric of everyday life provides a set of answers and a sense of certainty for their questions and dreams. To the extent that everyday life embodies unequal social relationships, the culture students generate and regenerate over time gradually accepts and "explains" existing social relationships. The process may appear inevitable, but it is not. We will argue that at least part of the context within which the young grow up can be changed (the school), and can propel them in directions that diverge from the status quo. The school can be the key catalyst in this process. Unfortunately, in our study it did not perform this function well.

Let us review the students' dreams, particularly while they were in junior high and saw their futures as relatively open. In junior high, the students visualized themselves in a wide variety of career roles, unrestricted by race, social class, or, for the girls, gender. Over half aspired to college and only one rejected it. Their dreams of careers and college were, in fact, quite different from the lives of their parents. Elsewhere we have noted that this was particularly true for the girls, whose career goals tended to be more ambitious than those of the boys. In junior high, students seemed to adopt portions of the lives of adults around them that they liked (such as mechanical arts for those who liked working with their hands) and reject that which they did not like (such as housework for those girls who had become fed up with it).

The culture students generated out of everyday life, however, tended to hold them in their community and return them to lives very much like their parents'. One feature of everyday life they discussed often was their racial diversity. The students generated a common culture among themselves that transcended race. Many of their parents had also done this; others, particularly those who had grown up elsewhere, had not. Rather than adopting their parents' racism, however, the students resisted it. Their own daily experience with each other convinced them that racism was incorrect. It also tended to convince them that their own community was the best place to live. They frequently told us that schools or neighborhoods of one race would be dull, uninteresting. The students' common culture that transcended race was like a magnet keeping them in their community, and also keeping them somewhat ignorant of race relations in the broader society. The student culture did not recognize institutional racism; individual prejudice was the main manifestation of racism that the students saw in their daily lives.

The culture students generated out of everyday life was also nonacademic. Students believed in school and valued education, seeing it as a route to their dreams, but on a day-to-day basis, they invested minimal effort in it. Unwittingly, in fact, they played a role in limiting their academic empowerment, in that they never actively resisted the school's low demand of them. In junior high, for example, they recognized that homework demands were light, and several said they thought they should get more homework, but they did nothing about this. We found it interesting to contrast this with students' active resistance toward parents' racism. Why did the students resist their parents' racism but not the school's low expectations of them? Their everyday experience taught them that their parents were wrong, and that racism would interfere with enjoyment of daily life. (Mexicans aren't lazy because my friend Diego isn't lazy, and if I avoided Diego, I'd lose a good buddy.) Students' everyday experience with school taught them that it was boring and that the content was irrelevant to daily life. It may be important for attaining a career goal, but if the medicine is bitter, why ask for more than the doctor prescribes, especially if more time devoted to school would lessen time with friends? So the students accepted minimal homework and a low involvement with classwork, and developed other interests and behavior patterns, centering largely around sports, that filled their time and probably would have caused them to resist a sudden increase in school work (a "what if" they never faced).

The students generated a distorted version of social class, which they used to help answer questions about college as well as goals in general. The inaccuracies and distortions in their beliefs were striking. They believed themselves to be middle class, and when asked many said they did not want to move up in the class structure, particularly if it meant moving away from the community. A white male student put it as follows: "I'd like to probably move upward in money, but not out of the neighborhood." Students seemed to believe middle-class people cannot afford college these days, and since jobs are limited, it is better to get a job now than take a chance that one will find a job after college. They did not seem to see college as improving their chance of obtaining a job, only as opening doors to certain kinds of jobs. The students did not seem to see a great difference in the pay and power that accrue from different occupations. They believed hard work was the best route to upward mobility; the role capital plays in the economy seemed completely unknown. Finally, they seemed to believe that race and gender have nothing to do with one's place in the economic structure. While this belief encouraged them to aspire to any career, it also produced false insights into opportunities available to them. Ultimately, the main beneficiaries of students' beliefs would be local employers: The student culture helped produce workers who were fairly content with their lot and willing to work hard to maintain their lives.

Everyday life with friends and family provided considerable material for generating an understanding of gender. Most homes placed the young in a sex-divided domestic work role from an early age. This was a role that few of the boys seriously questioned, probably because they grew up in it and it provided routes to attaining some status: being strong, supporting a family, taking a lead in courtship. The boys had experienced only part of this role; supporting a family, which eventually could be difficult for them, was not yet a reality. The girls raised more questions about the female role, mainly when they found themselves working while their brothers played outside. Regardless of ethnic background, at one time or another most girls believed it to be unfair and demeaning. There were rewards to adhering to a traditional female role: dates, especially with the popular boys; harmonious relationships at home; and admiration achievable through fashion. Students' questions about gender were never used to help them understand sexism. Thus, they answered their own questions by generating stereotypes (boys are just stronger than girls), accepting things as inevitable (men are just like that, nothing you can do about it), and interpreting conflicts as individual rather than collective. Many resolved the question of dividing labor by sex by insisting that both partners in a marriage should do as much work, even though the work is different. We stress that there appeared to be little or no relationship between ethnicity and the questions the girls raised. The Hispanic homes were more likely to adhere to traditional sex roles than the white homes, but Hispanic girls were just as likely to question their role—temporarily, at any rate—as were white girls raised in traditional homes.

That portion of the context of students' lives that could be changed most readily was the school. In fact, the school had a very important role to play in students' abandonment of their dreams. The school staff, much more so than the parents or the students themselves, knew how the education system works—what kind of preparation is needed for college, how to obtain scholarships and loans, what the differences are between a four-year college degree and job training in the military, and so forth. They also knew more than the students about social class, race relations, and gender. Let us first consider their abdication of the job for which they were hired: promoting academic learning.

In spite of students' interest in further education, in spite of their good behavior in school, and in spite of the fact that the majority had normal learning ability, both the junior and senior high school faculty (with the exception of a very few individuals) accepted students' failure to empower themselves through education, and in so doing, ensured that they would fail. This was particularly true after the tenth grade. Prior to the tenth grade students were required to take academic courses to meet graduation requirements. While few of these courses rigorously challenged them, at least to a limited degree students were receiving an education. After tenth grade two things happened: The students started raising serious questions about their futures (a major one being whether they could afford college) and the school pulled out of their lives as much as it could, expending its academic energies on only those few who for one reason or another continued to take the more difficult classes. For the majority of the students, advising virtually ceased once graduation requirements had been met, and any homework they might have had in the tenth grade came to an end. The school's main effort became equipping them to take a minimum-wage job after graduation. The school staff may have viewed it as inevitable that these students would not continue schooling—interviews with the junior high teachers found strong acceptance of this belief—but there was no inevitability here; the school actively helped it to happen.

The school could also have taught more explicitly about race, class, and gender. What the school did was to treat all students as much alike as possible, while teaching a watered-down version of the traditional white, male-dominated curriculum. Students' racial backgrounds were acknowledged mainly through festivals and special programs at certain times during the year, the main one being Cinco de Mayo. One elective course in the junior high—Multicultural Education—taught about racism, and a few teachers taught isolated lessons about race or sexism, more in the junior than the senior high school. Courses that would have lent themselves particularly well to examining social inequality—Money and Banking, Law and Justice, and Sociology—were not used for this purpose. To some extent courses affirmed sex roles, in that home economics and industrial arts courses were dominated by one sex, home economics taught girls how to work with their appearance, and girls' and boys' sports were somewhat different. The main thing we noticed was that the school did not provide much knowledge about the social structure or the students' location in it. Yet the teachers had some knowledge, even without doing research; for example, the junior high teachers were well aware of the socioeconomic status of the community, and many were also aware of how sexism affects one's life because they discussed this with respect to their own lives.

The families also played a role in the abandonment of students' dreams, although the family's role interacted with that of the school. Research consistently finds a strong relationship between level of educational attainment and parent occupation.[11] It is often believed that home background limits aspirations and ability to learn in school. We did not find home background to limit students' aspirations or parental interest in school—it limited, rather, the school's aspirations for its clients. What the home background did limit was the help parents could give. They told their children to "get a good education," to do what the teacher says; most did not know that they should have been telling their children which courses to take, and demanding that teachers do more teaching. There is, in fact, a paradox here that works against parents of color and lower-class backgrounds.

Students who are white and middle or upper class tend to be taught better and challenged more,[12] regardless, we suspect, of what role the parents might be playing. The higher the social class, the more actively demanding of the school the parents tend to become, but the more likely it is that the school will be trying to empower the students academically anyway. It is those parents who know least about how the education system works, and who are most likely to feel intimidated by educators, who have most to gain by involving themselves actively with the school. We are reminded of conversations we had recently with black middle-class parents of children attending an upper-class desegregated school. They told us they needed to initiate and maintain contact with the school to let teachers know they, the parents, were educated themselves, and to make sure their children were placed in demanding classes and taught well. The teachers were reluctant to contact them, and many of the teachers expected less of the black than the white students. The problem was magnified at the school in this study: There was little home-school communication; the parents gave their children what advice they knew how to give, and assumed incorrectly that the school was doing the rest. This is a problem that may well grow as teaching staffs become increasingly white and professionalized and, in the process, increasingly removed from lower-class and minority communities.

The students achieved success primarily in their own ethnic self-definitions, in that they learned to embrace their racial diversity while developing a sense of community. Beyond that, they were dismally unsuccessful. What this study has shown is that their lack of success was due in a large part to the very inactive role the school played in their lives. It allowed them to dream and wonder, and allowed them to abandon their dreams on their own by failing to provide a strong academic thrust, and knowledge about their place in the world. One might accuse their homes and the community in general of the same thing, but this does not excuse the school. The students' culture was not simply a mirror reflection of their parents and neighbors—it was created as much in the school as elsewhere, and represented an attempt to understand family and community life, as much as it was a perpetuation of it. It is in the school where educators can affect students: by recognizing their dreams, acknowledging their very real attempt to make sense of the immediate world in which they live, and then teaching them accordingly.

Notes

1 Jean Anyon, "Elementary Schooling and Distinctions of Social Class," *Interchange* 12 (1981): 118–32; and Jeannie Oakes, *Keeping Track* (New Haven, Conn.: Yale University Press, 1985).
2 Linda Valli, *Becoming Clerical Workers* (Boston: Routledge & Kegan Paul, 1986), p. 15.
3 Lois Weis, *Between Two Worlds* (Boston: Routledge & Kegan Paul, 1985), p. 219.
4 John Ogbu, *The Next Generation* (New York: Academic Press, 1974); Charles N. Payne, *Getting What We Ask For* (Westport, Conn.: Greenwood Press, 1984); and Weis, *Between Two Worlds*.
5 Robert Everhart, *Reading, Writing, and Resistance* (Boston: Routledge & Kegan Paul, 1983); and Paul Willis, *Learning to Labour* (Westmead, England: Saxon House Press, 1977).
6 Valli, *Becoming Clerical Workers*; R.M. Connelly, *Making the Difference: Schools, Families and Social Division* (Sydney, Australia: Allen and Unwin, 1982); and Angela McRobbie, "Working Class Girls and the Culture of Feminity," in *Women Take Issue*, ed. Women's Studies Group (London: Hutchinson, 1978), pp. 96–108.
7 Mary Fuller, "Black Girls in a London Comprehensive School," in *Schooling for Women's Work*, ed. R. Deem (London: Routledge & Kegan Paul, 1981), pp. 52–65.
8 Carl A. Grant and Christine E. Sleeter, *After the School Bell Rings* (Lewes, England: Falmer Press, 1986).
9 Nathan Hare, "What Should Be the Role of Afro-American Education in the Undergraduate Curriculum?" in *New Perspectives on Black Studies*, ed. J.W. Blassingame (Urbana: University of Illinois Press, 1971), p. 12.
10 Grant and Sleeter, *After the School Bell Rings*.
11 J. Coleman et al., *Equality of Educational Opportunity*, 2 vols. (Washington, D.C.: Office of Education, U.S. Department of Health, Education, and Welfare, U.S. Government Printing Office, 1966).
12 Anyon, "Elementary-Schooling and Distinctions of Social Class"; and Oakes, *Keeping Track*.

CHAPTER 18

LESSONS FROM STUDENTS ON CREATING A CHANCE TO DREAM (1994)

Sonia Nieto

> How does it come about that the one institution that is said to be the gateway to opportunity, the school, is the very one that is most effective in perpetuating an oppressed and impoverished status in society?
>
> —Stein, 1971, p. 178

The poignant question above was posed in this very journal almost a quarter of a century ago by Annie Stein, a consistent critic of the schools and a relentless advocate for social justice. This question shall serve as the central motif of this article because, in many ways, it remains to be answered and continues to be a fundamental dilemma standing in the way of our society's stated ideals of equity and equal educational opportunity. Annie Stein's observations about the New York City public schools ring true today in too many school systems throughout the country and can be used to examine some of the same policies and practices she decried in her 1971 article.

It is my purpose in this article to suggest that successfully educating all students in U.S. schools must begin by challenging school policies and practices that place roadblocks in the way of academic achievement for too many young people. Educating students today is, of course, a far different and more complex proposition than it has been in the past. Young people face innumerable personal, social, and political challenges, not to mention massive economic structural changes not even dreamed about by other generations of youth in the twentieth century. In spite of the tensions that such challenges may pose, U.S. society has nevertheless historically had a social contract to educate *all* youngsters, not simply those who happen to be European American, English speaking, economically privileged, and, in the current educational reform jargon, "ready to learn."[1] Yet, our schools have traditionally failed some youngsters, especially those from racially and culturally dominated and economically oppressed backgrounds. Research over the past half century has documented a disheartening legacy of failure for many students of all backgrounds, but especially children of Latino, African American, and Native American families, as well as poor European American families and, more recently, Asian and Pacific American immigrant students. Responding to the wholesale failure of so many youngsters within our public schools, educational theorists, sociologists, and psychologists devised elaborate theories of genetic inferiority, cultural deprivation, and the limits of "throwing money" at educational problems. Such theories held sway in particular during the 1960s and 1970s, but their influence is still apparent in educational policies and practices today.[2]

The fact that many youngsters live in difficult, sometimes oppressive conditions is not at issue here. Some may live in ruthless poverty and face the challenges of dilapidated housing, inadequate health care, and even abuse and neglect. They and their families may be subject to racism and other oppressive institutional barriers. They may have difficult personal, psychological, medical, or other kinds of problems. These are real concerns that should not be discounted. But, despite what may seem to be insurmountable obstacles to learning and teaching, some schools are nevertheless successful with young people who live in these situations. In addition, many children who live in otherwise onerous situations also have loving families willing to sacrifice what it takes to give their children the chance they never had during their own childhoods. Thus, poverty, single-parent households, and even homelessness, while they may be tremendous hardships, do not in and of themselves doom children to academic failure (see, among others, Clark, 1983; Lucas, Henze, & Donato, 1990; Mehan & Villanueva, 1993; Moll, 1992; Taylor & Dorsey-Gaines, 1988). These and similar studies point out that schools that have made up their minds that their students deserve the chance to learn do find the ways to educate them successfully in spite of what may seem to be overwhelming odds.

Educators may consider students difficult to teach simply because they come from families that do not fit neatly into what has been defined as "the mainstream." Some of them speak no English; many come from cultures that seem to be at odds with the dominant culture of U.S. society that is inevitably reflected in the school; others begin their schooling without the benefit of early experiences that could help prepare them for the cognitive demands they will face. Assumptions are often made about how such situations may negatively affect student achievement and, as a consequence, some children are condemned to failure before they begin. In a study by Nitza Hidalgo, a teacher's description of the students at an urban high school speaks to this condemnation: "Students are generally poor, uneducated and come from broken families who do not value school. Those conditions that produce achievers are somewhere else, not here. We get street people" (Hidalgo, 1991, p. 58). When such viewpoints guide teachers' and schools' behaviors and expectations, little progress can be expected in student achievement.

On the other hand, a growing number of studies suggest that teachers and schools need to build on rather than tear down what students bring to school. That is, they need to understand and incorporate cultural, linguistic, and experiential differences, as well as differences in social class, into the learning process (Abi-Nader, 1993; Hollins, King, & Hayman, 1994; Lucas et al., 1990; Moll & Díaz, 1993). The results of such efforts often provide inspiring examples of success because they begin with a belief that all students deserve a chance to learn. In this article, I will highlight these efforts by exploring the stories of some academically successful young people in order to suggest how the policies and practices of schools can be transformed to create environments in which all children are capable of learning.

It is too convenient to fall back on deficit theories and continue the practice of blaming students, their families, and their communities for educational failure. Instead, schools need to focus on where they *can* make a difference, namely, their own instructional policies and practices. A number of recent studies, for example, have concluded that a combination of factors, including characteristics of schools as opposed to only student background and actions, can explain differences between high- and low-achieving students. School characteristics that have been found to make a positive difference in these studies include an enriched and more demanding curriculum, respect for students' languages and cultures, high expectations for all students, and encouragement for parental involvement in their children's education (Lee, Winfield, & Wilson, 1991; Lucas et al., 1990; Moll, 1992). This would suggest that we need to shift from a single-minded focus on low- or high-achieving students to the conditions that create low- or high-achieving schools. If we understand school policies and practices as being enmeshed in societal values, we can better understand the manifestations of these values in schools as well. Thus, for example, "tracked" schools, rather than reflecting a school practice that exists in isolation from society, reflect a society that is itself tracked along racial, gender, and social-class lines. In the same way, "teacher expectations" do not come from thin air, but reflect and support expectations of students that are deeply ingrained in societal and ideological values.

Reforming school structures alone will not lead to substantive differences in student achievement, however, if such changes are not also accompanied by profound changes in how we as educators think about our students; that is, in what we believe they deserve and are capable of achieving. Put another way, changing policies and practices is a necessary but insufficient condition for total school transformation. For example, in a study of six high schools in which Latino students have been successful, Tamara Lucas, Rosemary Henze, and Rubén Donato (1990) found that the most crucial element is a shared belief among teachers, counselors, and administrators that all students are capable of learning. This means that concomitant changes are needed in policies and practices *and* in our individual and collective will to educate all students. Fred Newmann (1993), in an important analysis of educational restructuring, underlines this point by emphasizing that reform efforts will fail unless they are accompanied by a set of particular commitments and competencies to guide them, including a commitment to the success of all students, the creation of new roles for teachers, and the development of schools as caring communities.

Another crucial consideration in undertaking educational change is a focus on what Jim Cummins (1994) has called the "relations of power" in schools. In proposing a shift from coercive to collaborative relations of power, Cummins argues that traditional teacher-centered transmission models can limit the potential for critical thinking on the part of both teachers and students, but especially for students from dominated communities whose cultures and languages have been devalued by the dominant canon.[3] By encouraging collaborative relations of power, schools and teachers can begin to recognize other sources of legitimate knowledge that have been overlooked, negated, or minimized because they are not part of the dominant discourse in schools.

Focusing on concerns such as the limits of school reform without concomitant changes in educators' attitudes towards students and their families, and the crucial role of power relationships in schools may help rescue current reform efforts from simplistic technical responses to what are essentially moral and political dilemmas. That is, such technical changes as tinkering with the length of the school day, substituting one textbook for another, or adding curricular requirements may do little to change student outcomes unless these changes are part and parcel of a more comprehensive conceptualization of school reform. When such issues are considered fundamental to the changes that must be made in schools, we might more precisely speak about *transformation* rather than simply about reform. But educational transformation cannot take place without the inclusion of the voices of students, among others, in the dialogue.

Why listen to students?

One way to begin the process of changing school policies and practices is to listen to students' views about them; however, research that focuses on student voices is relatively recent and scarce. For example, student perspectives are for the most part missing in discussions concerning strategies for confronting educational problems. In addition, the voices of students are rarely heard in the debates about school failure and success, and the perspectives of students from disempowered and dominated communities are even more invisible. In this article, I will draw primarily on the words of students I interviewed for a previous research study (Nieto, 1992). I used the interviews to develop case studies of young people from a wide variety of ethnic, racial, linguistic, and social-class backgrounds who were at the time students in junior or senior high school. These ten young people lived in communities as diverse as large urban areas and small rural hamlets, and belonged to families ranging from single-parent households to large, extended families. The one common element in all of their experiences turned out to be something we as researchers had neither planned nor expected: they were all successful students.[4]

The students were selected in a number of ways, but primarily through community contacts. Most were interviewed at home or in another setting of their choice outside of school. The only requirement that my colleagues and I determined for selecting students was that they reflect a variety of ethnic and racial backgrounds, in order to give us the diversity for which we were looking. The students selected self-identified as Black, African American, Mexican, Native American, Black and White American (biracial), Vietnamese, Jewish, Lebanese, Puerto Rican, and Cape Verdean. The one European American was the only student who had a hard time defining herself, other than as "American" (for a further analysis of this issue, see Nieto, 1992). That these particular students were academically successful was quite serendipitous. We defined them as such for the following reasons: they were all either still in school or just graduating; they all planned to complete at least high school, and most hoped to go to college; they had good grades, although they were not all at the top of their class; they had thought about their future and had made some plans for it; they generally enjoyed school and felt engaged in it (but they were also critical of their own school experiences and that of their peers, as we shall see); and most described themselves as successful. Although it had not been our initial intention to focus exclusively on academically successful students, on closer reflection it seemed logical that such students would be more likely to want to talk about their experiences than those who were not successful. It was at that point that I decided to explore what it was about these students' specific experiences that helped them succeed in school.

Therefore, the fact that these students saw themselves as successful helped further define the study, whose original purpose was to determine the benefits of multicultural education for students of diverse backgrounds. I was particularly interested in developing a way of looking at multicultural education that went beyond the typical "Holidays and Heroes" approach, which is too superficial to have any lasting impact in schools (Banks, 1991; Sleeter, 1991).[5] By exploring such issues as racism and low expectations of student achievement, as well as school policies and practices such as curriculum, pedagogy, testing, and tracking, I set about developing an understanding of multicultural education as antiracist, comprehensive, pervasive, and rooted in social justice. Students were interviewed to find out what it meant to be from a particular background, how this influenced their school experience, and what about that experience they would change if they could. Although they were not asked specifically about the policies and practices in their schools, they nevertheless reflected on them in their answers to questions ranging from identifying their favorite subjects to describing the importance of getting an education. In this article, I will revisit the interviews to focus on students' thoughts about a number of school policies and practices and on the effects of racism and other forms of discrimination on their education.

The insights provided by the students were far richer than we had first thought. Although we expected numerous criticisms of schools and some concrete suggestions, we were surprised at the depth of awareness and analysis the students shared with us. They had a lot to say about the teachers they liked, as well as those they disliked, and they were able to explain the differences between them; they talked about grades and how these had become overly important in determining curriculum and pedagogy; they discussed their parents' lack of involvement, in most cases, in traditional school activities such as P.T.O. membership and bake sales, but otherwise passionate support for their children's academic success; they mused about what schools could do to encourage more students to learn; they spoke with feeling about their cultures, languages, and communities, and what schools could do to capitalize on these factors; and they gave us concrete suggestions for improving schools for young people of all backgrounds. This experience confirmed my belief that educators can benefit from hearing students' critical perspectives, which might cause them to modify how they approach curriculum, pedagogy, and other school practices. Since doing this research, I have come across other studies that also focus on young people's perspectives and provide additional powerful examples of the lessons we can learn from them. This article thus begins with "lessons from students," an approach that takes the perspective proposed by Paulo Freire, that teachers need to become students just as students need to become teachers in order for education to become reciprocal and empowering for both (Freire, 1970).

This focus on students is not meant to suggest that their ideas should be the final and conclusive word in how schools need to change. Nobody has all the answers, and suggesting that students' views should be adopted wholesale is to accept a romantic view of students that is just as partial and condescending as excluding them completely from the discussion. I am instead suggesting that if we believe schools must provide an equal and quality education for all, students need to be included in the dialogue, and that their views, just as those of others, should be problematized and used to reflect critically on school reform.

Selected policies and practices and students' views about them

School policies and practices need to be understood within the sociopolitical context of our society in general, rather than simply within individual schools' or teachers' attitudes and practices. This is important to remember for a number of reasons. First, although "teacher bashing" provides an easy target for complex problems, it fails to take into account the fact that teachers function within particular societal and institutional structures. In addition, it results in placing an inordinate amount of blame on some of those who care most deeply about students and who struggle every day to help them learn. That some teachers are racist, classist, and mean-spirited and that others have lost all creativity and caring is not in question here, and I begin with the assumption that the majority of teachers are not consciously so. I do suggest, however, that although many teachers are hardworking, supportive of their students, and talented educators, many of these same teachers are also burned out, frustrated, and negatively influenced by societal views about the students they teach. Teachers could benefit from knowing more about their students' families and experiences, as well as about students' views on school and how it could be improved.

How do students feel about the curriculum they must learn? What do they think about the pedagogical strategies their teachers use? Is student involvement a meaningful issue for them? Are their own identities important considerations in how they view school? What about tracking and testing and disciplinary policies? These are crucial questions to consider when reflecting on what teachers and schools can learn from students, but we know very little about students' responses. When asked, students seem surprised and excited about being included in the conversation, and what they have to say is often compelling and eloquent. In fact, Patricia Phelan, Ann Locke Davidson, and Hanh Thanh Cao (1992), in a two-year research project designed to identify students' thoughts about school, discovered that students' views on teaching and learning were remarkably consistent with those of current theorists concerned with learning theory, cognitive science, and the sociology of work. This should come as no surprise when we consider that students spend more time in schools than anybody else except teachers (who are also omitted in most discussions of school reform, but that is a topic for another article). In the following sections, I will focus on students' perceptions concerning the curriculum, pedagogy, tracking, and grades in their schools. I will also discuss their attitudes about racism and other biases, how these are manifested in their schools and classrooms, and what effect they may have on students' learning and participation in school.

Curriculum

The curriculum in schools is at odds with the experiences, backgrounds, hopes, and wishes of many students. This is true of both the tangible curriculum as expressed through books, other materials, and the actual written curriculum as guides, as well as in the less tangible and "hidden" curriculum as seen in the bulletin boards, extracurricular activities, and messages given to students about their abilities and talents. For instance, Christine Sleeter and Carl Grant (1991) found that a third of the students in a desegregated junior high school they studied said that *none* of the class content related to their lives outside class. Those who indicated some relevancy cited only current events, oral history, money and banking, and multicultural content (because it dealt with prejudice) as being relevant. The same was true in a study by Mary Poplin and Joseph Weeres (1992), who found that students frequently reported being bored in school and seeing little relevance in what was taught for their lives or their futures. The authors concluded that students became more disengaged as the curriculum, texts, and assignments became more standardized. Thus, in contrast to Ira Shor's (1992) suggestion that "What students bring to class is where learning begins. It starts there and goes places" (p. 44), there is often a tremendous mismatch between students' cultures and the culture of the school. In many schools, learning starts not with what students bring to class, but with what is considered high-status knowledge; that is, the "canon," with its overemphasis on European and European American history, arts, and values. This seldom includes the backgrounds, experiences, and talents of the majority of students in U.S. schools. Rather than "going elsewhere," their learning therefore often goes nowhere.

That students' backgrounds and experiences are missing in many schools is particularly evident where the native language of most of the students is not English. In such settings, it is not unusual to see little or no representation of those students' language in the curriculum. In fact, there is often an insistence that students "speak only English" in these schools, which sends a powerful message to young people struggling to maintain an identity in the face of overpowering messages that they must assimilate. This was certainly the case for Marisol, a Puerto Rican girl of sixteen participating in my research, who said:

> I used to have a lot of problems with one of my teachers 'cause she didn't want us to talk Spanish in class and I thought that was like an insult to us, you know? Just telling us not to talk Spanish, 'cause they were Puerto Ricans and, you know, we're free to talk whatever we want, ... I could never stay quiet and talk only English, 'cause sometimes ... words slip in Spanish. You know, I think they should understand that.

Practices such as not allowing students to speak their native tongue are certain to influence negatively students' identities and their views of what constitutes important knowledge. For example, when asked if she would be interested in taking a course on Puerto Rican history, Marisol was quick to answer: "I don't think [it's] important. . . . I'm proud of myself and my culture, but I think I know what I should know about the culture already, so I wouldn't take the course." Ironically, it was evident to me after speaking with her on several occasions that Marisol knew virtually nothing about Puerto Rican history. However, she had already learned another lesson well: given what she said about the courses she needed to take, she made it clear that "important" history is U.S. history, which rarely includes anything about Puerto Rico.

Messages about culture and language and how they are valued or devalued in society are communicated not only or even primarily by schools, but by the media and community as a whole. The sociopolitical context of the particular city where Marisol lived, and of its school system, is important to understand: there had been an attempt to pass an ordinance restricting the number of Puerto Ricans coming into town based on the argument that they placed an undue burden on the welfare rolls and other social services. In addition, the "English Only" debate had become an issue when the mayor had ordered all municipal workers to speak only English on the job. Furthermore, although the school system had a student body that was 65 percent Puerto Rican, there was only a one-semester course on Puerto Rican history that had just recently been approved for the bilingual program. In contrast, there were two courses, which although rarely taught were on the books, that focused on apartheid and the Holocaust, despite the fact that both the African American and Jewish communities in the town were quite small. That such courses should be part of a comprehensive multicultural program is not being questioned; however, it is ironic that the largest population in the school was ignored in the general curriculum.

In a similar vein, Nancy Commins's (1989) research with four first-generation Mexican American fifth-grade students focused on how these students made decisions about their education, both consciously and unconsciously, based on their determination of what counted as important knowledge. Her research suggests that the classroom setting and curriculum can support or hinder students' perceptions of themselves as learners based on the languages they speak and their cultural backgrounds. She found that although the homes of these four students provided rich environments for a variety of language uses and literacy, the school did little to capitalize on these strengths. In their classroom, for instance, these children rarely used Spanish, commenting that it was the language of the "dumb kids." As a result, Commins states: "Their reluctance to use Spanish in an academic context also limited their opportunities to practice talking about abstract ideas and to use higher level cognitive skills in Spanish" (p. 35). She also found that the content of the curriculum was almost completely divorced from the experiences of these youngsters, since the problems of poverty, racism, and discrimination, which were prominent in their lives, were not addressed in the curriculum.

In spite of teachers' reluctance to address such concerns, they are often compelling to students, particularly those who are otherwise invisible in the curriculum. Vinh, an 18-year-old Vietnamese student attending a high school in a culturally heterogeneous town, lived with his uncle and younger brothers and sisters. Although grateful for the education he was receiving, Vinh expressed concern about what he saw as insensitivity on the part of some of his teachers to the difficulties of adjusting to a new culture and learning English:

> [Teachers] have to know about our culture. . . . From the second language, it is very difficult for me and for other people.

Vinh's concern was echoed by Manuel, a nineteen-year-old Cape Verdean senior who, at the time of the interviews, was just getting ready to graduate, the first in his family of eleven children to do so:

> I was kind of afraid of school, you know, 'cause it's different when you're learning the language. . . . It's kind of scary at first, especially if you don't know the language and like if you don't have friends here.

In Manuel's case, the Cape Verdean Crioulo bilingual program served as a linguistic and cultural mediator, negotiating difficult experiences that he faced in school so that, by the time he reached high school, he had learned enough English to "speak up." Another positive curricular experience was the theater workshop he took as a sophomore. There, students created and acted in skits focusing on their lived experiences. He recalled with great enthusiasm, for example, a monologue he did about a student going to a new school, because it was based on his personal experience.

Sometimes a school's curriculum is unconsciously disrespectful of students' cultures and experiences. James, a student who proudly identified himself as Lebanese American, found that he was invisible in the curriculum, even in supposedly multicultural curricular and extracurricular activities. He mentioned a language fair, a multicultural festival, and a school cookbook, all of which omitted references to the Arabic language and to Lebanese people. About the cookbook, he said:

> They made this cookbook of all these different recipes from all over the world. And I would've brought in some Lebanese recipes if somebody'd let me know. And I didn't hear about it until the week before they started selling them. . . . I asked one of the teachers to look at it and there was nothing Lebanese in there.

James made an effort to dismiss this oversight, and although he said that it didn't matter, he seemed to be struggling with the growing realization that it mattered very much indeed:

> I don't know, I guess there's not that many Lebanese people in ... I don't know; you don't hear really that much ... Well, you hear it in the news a lot, but I mean, I don't know, there's not a lot of Lebanese kids in our school. . . . I don't mind, 'cause I mean, I don't know, just I don't mind it. . . . It's not really important. It *is* important for me. It would be important for me to see a Lebanese flag.

Lebanese people were mentioned in the media, although usually in negative ways, and these were the only images of James's ethnic group that made their way into the school. He spoke, for example, about how the Lebanese were characterized by his peers:

> Some people call me, you know, 'cause I'm Lebanese, so people say, "Look out for the terrorist! Don't mess with him or he'll blow up your house!" or some stuff like that. . . . But they're just joking around, though. . . . I don't think anybody's serious 'cause I wouldn't blow up anybody's house—and they know that. . . . I don't care. It doesn't matter what people say. . . . I just want everybody to know that, you know, it's not true.

Cultural ambivalence, both pride and shame, were evident in the responses of many of the students. Although almost all of them were quite clear that their culture was important to them, they were also confronted with debilitating messages about it from society in general. How to make sense of these contradictions was a dilemma for many of these young people.

Fern, who identified herself as Native American, was, at thirteen, one of the youngest students interviewed. She reflected on the constant challenges she faced in the history curriculum in her junior high school. Her father was active in their school and community and he gave her a great deal of support for defending her position, but she was the only Native American student in her entire school in this mid-size city in Iowa. She said:

> If there's something in the history book that's wrong, my dad always taught me that if it's wrong, I should tell them that it is wrong. And the only time I ever do is if I know it's *exactly* wrong. Like we were reading about Native Americans and scalping. Well, the French are really the ones that made them do it so they could get money. And my teacher would not believe me. I finally just shut up because he just would not believe me.

Fern also mentioned that her sister had come home angry one day because somebody in school had said "Geronimo was a stupid chief riding that stupid horse." The connection between an unresponsive curriculum and dropping out of school was not lost on Fern, and she talked about this incident as she wondered aloud why other Native Americans had dropped out of the town's schools. Similar sentiments were reported by students in Virginia Vogel Zanger's (1994) study of twenty Latinos from a Boston high school who took part in a panel discussion in which they reflected on their experiences in school. Some of the students who decided to stay in school claimed that dropping out among their peers was a direct consequence of the school's attempts to "monoculture" them.

Fern was self-confident and strong in expressing her views, despite her young age. Yet she too was silenced by the way the curriculum was presented in class. This is because schools often avoid bringing up difficult, contentious, or conflicting issues in the curriculum, especially when these contradict the sanctioned views of the standard curriculum, resulting in what Michelle Fine has called "silencing." According to Fine: "Silencing is about who can speak, what can and cannot be spoken, and whose discourse must be controlled" (1991, p. 33). Two topics in particular that appear to have great saliency for many students, regardless of their backgrounds, are bias and discrimination, yet these are among the issues most avoided in classrooms. Perhaps this is because the majority of teachers are European Americans who are unaccustomed, afraid, or uncomfortable in discussing these issues (Sleeter, 1994); perhaps it is due to the pressure teachers feel to "cover the material"; maybe it has to do with the tradition of presenting information in schools as if it were free of conflict and controversy (Kohl, 1993); or, most likely, it is a combination of all these things. In any event, both students and teachers soon pick up the message that racism, discrimination, and other dangerous topics are not supposed to be discussed in school. We also need to keep in mind that these issues have disparate meanings for people of different backgrounds, and are often perceived as particularly threatening to those from dominant cultural and racial groups. Deidre, one of the young African American women in Fine's 1991 study of an urban high school, explained it this way: "White people might feel like everything's over and OK, but we remember" (p. 33).

Another reason that teachers may avoid bringing up potentially contentious issues in the curriculum is their feeling that doing so may create or exacerbate animosity and hostility among students. They may even believe, as did the reading teacher in Jonathan Kozol's 1967 classic book on the Boston Public Schools, *Death at an Early Age*, that discussing slavery in the context of U.S. history was just too complicated for children to understand, not to mention uncomfortable for teachers to explain. Kozol writes of the reading teacher:

> She said, with the very opposite of malice but only with an expression of the most intense and honest affection for the children in the class: "I don't want these children to have to think back on this year later on and to have to remember that we were the ones who told them they were Negro. (p. 68)

More than a quarter of a century later, the same kinds of disclaimers are being made for the failure to include in the curriculum the very issues that would engage students in learning. Fine (1991) found that although over half of the students in the urban high school she interviewed described experiences with racism, teachers were reluctant to discuss it in class, explaining, in the words of one teacher, "It would demoralize the students, they need to feel positive and optimistic—like they have a chance. Racism is just an excuse they use to not try harder" (p. 37). Some of these concerns may be sincere expressions of protectiveness towards students, but others are merely self-serving and manifest teachers' discomfort with discussing racism.

The few relevant studies I have found concerning the inclusion of issues of racism and discrimination in the curriculum suggest that discussions about these topics can be immensely constructive if they are approached with sensitivity and understanding. This was the case in Melinda Fine's description of the "Facing History and Ourselves" (FHAO) curriculum, a project that started in the Brookline (Massachusetts) Public Schools almost two decades ago (Fine, 1993). FHAO provides a model for teaching history that encourages students to reflect critically on a variety of contemporary social, moral, and political issues. Using the Holocaust as a case study, students learn to think critically about such issues as scapegoating, racism, and personal and collective responsibility. Fine suggests that moral dilemmas do not disappear simply because teachers refuse to bring them into the schools. On the contrary, when these realities are separated from the curriculum, young people learn that school knowledge is unrelated to their lives, and once again, they are poorly prepared to face the challenges that society has in store for them.

A good case in point is Vanessa, a young European American woman in my study who was intrigued by "difference" yet was uncomfortable and reluctant to discuss it; although she was active in a peer education group that focused on such concerns as peer pressure, discrimination, and exclusion, these were rarely discussed in the formal curriculum. Vanessa, therefore, had no language with which to talk about these issues. In thinking about U.S. history, she mused about some of the contradictions that were rarely addressed in school:

> It seems weird . . . because people came from Europe and they wanted to get away from all the stuff that was over there. And then they came here and set up all the stuff like slavery, and I don't know, it seems the opposite of what they would have done.

The curriculum, then, can act to either enable or handicap students in their learning. Given the kind of curriculum that draws on their experiences and energizes them because it focuses precisely on those things that are most important in their lives, students can either soar or sink in our schools. Curriculum can provide what María Torres-Guzmán (1992) refers to as "cognitive empowerment," encouraging students to become confident, active critical thinkers who learn that their background experiences are important tools for further learning. The connection of the curriculum to real life and their future was mentioned by several of the students interviewed in my study. Avi, a Jewish boy of sixteen who often felt a schism between his school and home lives, for instance, spoke about the importance of school: "If you don't go to school, then you can't learn about life, or you can't learn about things that you need to progress [in] your life." And Vanessa, who seemed to yearn for a more socially conscious curriculum in her school, summed up why education was important to her: "A good education is like when you personally learn something . . . like growing, expanding your mind and your views."

Pedagogy

If curriculum is primarily the *what* of education, then pedagogy concerns the *why* and *how*. No matter how interesting and relevant the curriculum may be, the way in which it is presented is what will make it engaging or dull to students. Students' views echo those of educational researchers who have found that teaching methods in most classrooms, and particularly those in secondary schools, vary little from traditional "chalk and talk" methods; that textbooks are the dominant teaching materials used; that routine and rote learning are generally favored over creativity and critical thinking; and that teacher-centered transmission models prevail (Cummins, 1994; Goodlad, 1984; McNeil, 1986). Martin Haberman is especially critical of what he calls "the pedagogy of poverty," that is, a basic urban pedagogy used with children who live in poverty and which consists primarily of giving instructions, asking questions, giving directions, making assignments, and monitoring seat work. Such pedagogy is based on the assumption that before students can be engaged in creative or critical work, they must first master "the basics." Nevertheless, Haberman asserts that this pedagogy does not work and, furthermore, that it actually gets in the way of real teaching and learning. He suggests instead that we look at exemplary pedagogy in urban schools that actively involves students in real-life situations, which allows them to reflect on their own lives. He finds that good teaching is taking place when teachers welcome difficult issues and events and use human difference as the basis for the curriculum; design collaborative activities for heterogeneous groups; and help students apply ideals of fairness, equity, and justice to their world (Haberman, 1991).

Students in my study had more to say about pedagogy than about anything else, and they were especially critical of the lack of imagination that led to boring classes. Linda, who was just graduating as the valedictorian of her class in an urban high school, is a case in point. Her academic experiences had not always been smooth sailing. For example, she had failed both seventh and eighth grade twice, for a combination of reasons, including academic and medical problems. Consequently, she had experienced both exhilarating and devastating educational experiences. Linda had this to say about pedagogy:

> I think you have to be creative to be a teacher; you have to make it interesting. You can't just go in and say, "Yeah, I'm going to teach the kids just that; I'm gonna teach them right out of the book and that's the way it is, and don't ask questions." Because I know there were plenty of classes where I lost complete interest. But those were all because the teachers just, "Open the books to this page." They never made up problems out of their head. Everything came out of the book. You didn't ask questions. If you asked them questions, then the answer was "in the book." And if you asked the question and the answer *wasn't* in the book, then you shouldn't have asked that question!

Rich, a young Black man, planned to attend pharmacy school after graduation, primarily because of the interest he had developed in chemistry. He too talked about the importance of making classes "interesting":

> I believe a teacher, by the way he introduces different things to you, can make a class interesting. Not like a normal teacher that gets up, gives you a lecture, or there's teachers that just pass out the work, you do the work, pass it in, get a grade, good-bye!

Students were especially critical of teachers' reliance on textbooks and blackboards, a sad indictment of much of the teaching that encourages student passivity. Avi, for instance, felt that some teachers get along better when they teach from the point of view of the students: "They don't just come out and say, 'All right, do this, blah, blah, blah.' . . . They're not so *one-tone voice*." Yolanda said that her English teacher didn't get along with the students. In her words, "She just does the things and sits down." James mentioned that some teachers just don't seem to care: "They just teach the stuff. 'Here,' write a couple of things on the board, 'see, that's how you do it. Go ahead, page 25.' " And Vinh added his voice to those of the students who clearly saw the connection between pedagogy and caring: "Some teachers, they just go inside and go to the blackboard. . . . They don't care."

Students did more than criticize teachers' pedagogy, however; they also praised teachers who were interesting, creative, and caring. Linda, in a particularly moving testimony to her first-grade teacher, whom she called her mentor, mentioned that she would be "following in her footsteps" and studying elementary education. She added:

> She's always been there for me. After the first or second grade, if I had a problem, I could always go back to her. Through the whole rest of my life, I've been able to go back and talk to her. . . . She's a Golden Apple Award winner, which is a very high award for elementary school teachers. . . . She keeps me on my toes. . . . When I start getting down . . . she peps me back up and I get on my feet.

Vinh talked with feeling about teachers who allowed him to speak Vietnamese with other students in class. Vinh loved working in groups. He particularly remembered a teacher who always asked students to discuss important issues, rather than focusing only on learning what he called "the word's meaning" by writing and memorizing lists of words. The important issues concerned U.S. history, the students' histories and cultures, and other engaging topics that were central to their lives. Students' preference for group work has been mentioned by other educators as well. Phelan et al. (1992), in their research on students' perspectives concerning school, found that both high- and low-achieving students of all backgrounds expressed a strong preference for working in groups because it helped them generate ideas and participate actively in class.

James also appreciated teachers who explained things and let everybody ask questions because, as he said, "There could be someone sitting in the back of the class that has the same question you have. Might as well bring it out." Fern contrasted classes where she felt like falling asleep because they're just "blah," to chorus, where the teacher used a "rap song" to teach history and involve all the students. And Avi, who liked most of his teachers, singled out a particular math teacher he had had in ninth grade for praise:

> 'Cause I never really did good in math until I had him. And he showed me that it wasn't so bad, and after that I've been doing pretty good in math and I enjoy it.

Yolanda had been particularly fortunate to have many teachers she felt understood and supported her, whether they commented on her bilingual ability, or referred to her membership in a folkloric Mexican dance group, or simply talked with her and the other students about their lives. She added:

> I really got along with the teachers a lot. . . . Actually, 'cause I had some teachers, and they were always calling my mom, like I did a great job. Or they would start talking to me, or they kinda like pulled me up some grades, or moved me to other classes, or took me somewhere. And they were always congratulating me.

Such support, however, rarely represented only individual effort on the part of some teachers, but rather was often manifested by the school as a whole; that is, it was integral to the school's practices and policies. For instance, Yolanda had recently been selected "Student of the Month" and her picture had been prominently displayed in her school's main hall. In addition, she received a certificate and was taken out to dinner by the principal. Although Linda's first-grade teacher was her special favorite, she had others who also created an educational context in which all students felt welcomed and connected. The entire Tremont Elementary School had been special for Linda, and thus the context of the school, including its leadership and commitment, were the major ingredients that made it successful:

> All of my teachers were wonderful. I don't think there's a teacher at the whole Tremont School that I didn't like. . . . It's just a feeling you have. You know that they really care for you. You just know it; you can tell. Teachers who don't have you in any of their classes or haven't ever had you, they still know who you are. . . . The Tremont School in itself is a community. . . . I love that school! I want to teach there.

Vanessa talked about how teachers used their students' lives and experiences in their teaching. For her, this made them especially good teachers:

> [Most teachers] are really caring and supportive and are willing to share their lives and are willing to listen to mine. They don't just want to talk about what they're teaching you; they also want to know you.

Aside from criticism and praise, students in this study also offered their teachers many thoughtful suggestions for making their classrooms more engaging places. Rich, for instance, said that he would "put more activities into the day that can make it interesting." Fern recommended that teachers involve students more actively in learning: "More like making the whole class be involved, not making only the two smartest people up here do the whole work for the whole class." Vanessa added, "You could have games that could teach anything that they're trying to teach through notes or lectures." She suggested that in learning Spanish, for instance, students could act out the words, making them easier to remember. She also thought that other books should be required "just to show some points of view," a response no doubt to the bland quality of so many of the textbooks and other teaching materials available in schools. Avi thought that teachers who make themselves available to students ("You know, I'm here after school. Come and get help.") were most helpful.

Vinh was very specific in his suggestions, and he touched on important cultural issues. Because he came from Vietnam when he was fifteen, learning English was a difficult challenge for Vinh, and he tended to be very hard on himself, saying such things as "I'm not really good, but I'm trying" when asked to describe himself as a student. Although he had considered himself smart in Vietnam, he felt that because his English was not perfect, he wasn't smart anymore. His teachers often showered him with praise for his efforts, but Vinh criticized this approach:

> Sometimes, the English teachers, they don't understand about us. Because something we not do good, like my English is not good. And she say, "Oh, your English is great!" But that's the way the American culture is. But my culture is not like that. . . . If my English is not good, she has to say, "Your English is not good. So you have to go home and study." And she tell me what to study and how to study and get better. But some Americans, you know, they don't understand about myself. So they just say, "Oh! You're doing a

good job! You're doing great! Everything is great!" Teachers talk like that, but my culture is different. . . . They say, "You have to do better."

This is an important lesson not only because it challenges the overuse of praise, a practice among those that María de la Luz Reyes (1992) has called "venerable assumptions," but also because it cautions teachers to take into account both cultural and individual differences. In this case, the practice of praising was perceived by Vinh as hollow, and therefore insincere. Linda referred to the lesson she learned when she failed seventh and eighth grade and "blew two years":

> I learned a lot from it. As a matter of fact, one of my college essays was on the fact that from that experience, I learned that I don't need to hear other people's praise to get by. . . . All I need to know is in here [pointing to her heart] whether I tried or not.

Students have important messages for teachers about what works and what doesn't. It is important, however, not to fall back on what Lilia Bartolomé (1994) has aptly termed the "methods fetish," that is, a simplistic belief that particular methods will automatically resolve complex problems of underachievement. According to Bartolomé, such a myopic approach results in teachers avoiding the central issue of why some students succeed and others fail in school and how political inequality is at the heart of this dilemma. Rather than using this or that method, Bartolomé suggests that teachers develop what she calls a "humanizing pedagogy" in which students' languages and cultures are central. There is also the problem that Reyes (1992) has called a "one-size-fits all" approach, where students' cultural and other differences may be denied even if teachers' methods are based on well-meaning and progressive pedagogy. The point here is that no method can become a sacred cow uncritically accepted and used simply because it is the latest fad. It is probably fair to say that teachers who use more traditional methods but care about their students and believe they deserve the chance to dream may have more of a positive effect than those who know the latest methods but do not share these beliefs. Students need more than such innovations as heterogeneous grouping, peer tutoring, or cooperative groups. Although these may in fact be excellent and effective teaching methods, they will do little by themselves unless accompanied by changes in teachers' attitudes and behaviors.

The students quoted above are not looking for one magic solution or method. In fact, they have many, sometimes contradictory, suggestions to make about pedagogy. While rarely speaking with one voice, they nevertheless have similar overriding concerns: too many classrooms are boring, alienating, and disempowering. There is a complex interplay of policies, practices, and attitudes that cause such pedagogy to continue. Tracking and testing are two powerful forces implicated in this interplay.

Tracking/ability grouping/grades and expectations of student achievement

> It is not low income that matters but low status. And status is always created and imposed by the ones on top.
>
> —Stein, 1971, p. 158

In her 1971 article, Annie Stein cited a New York City study in which kindergarten teachers were asked to list in order of importance the things a child should learn in order to prepare for first grade. Their responses were coded according to whether they were primarily socialization or educational goals. In the schools with large Puerto Rican and African American student populations, the socialization goals were always predominant; in the mixed schools, the educational goals were first. Concluded Stein, "In fact, in a list of six or seven goals, several teachers in the minority-group kindergartens forgot to mention any educational goals at all" (p. 167). A kind of tracking, in which students' educational goals were being sacrificed for social aims, was taking place in these schools, and its effects were already evident in kindergarten.

Most recent research on tracking has found it to be problematic, especially among middle- and low-achieving students, and suggestions for detracking schools have gained growing support (Oakes, 1992; Wheelock, 1992). Nevertheless, although many tracking decisions are made on the most tenuous grounds, they are supported by ideological norms in our society about the nature of intelligence and the distribution of ability. The long-term effects of ability grouping can be devastating for the life chances of young people. John Goodlad (1984) found that first- or second-grade children tracked by teachers' judgments of their reading and math ability or by testing are likely to remain in their assigned track *for the rest of their schooling*. In addition, he found that poor children and children of color are more likely to face the negative effects of tracking than are other youngsters. For example, a recent research project by Hugh Mehan and Irene Villanueva (1993) found that when low-achieving high school students are detracked, they tend to benefit academically. The study focused on low-achieving students in the San Diego City Schools. When these students, mostly Latinos and African Americans, were removed from a low track and placed in college-bound courses with high-achieving students, they benefitted in a number of ways, including significantly higher college enrollment. The researchers concluded that a rigorous academic program serves the educational and social interests of such students more effectively than remedial and compensatory programs.

Most of the young people in my study did not mention tracking or ability grouping by name, but almost all referred to it circuitously, and usually in negative ways. Although by and large academically successful themselves, they were quick to point out that teachers' expectations often doomed their peers to failure. Yolanda, for instance, when asked what suggestions she would give teachers, said, "I'd say to teachers, 'Get along more with the kids that are not really into themselves. . . . Have more communication with them.' " When asked what she would like teachers to know about other Mexican American students, she quickly said, "They try real hard, that's one thing I know." She also criticized teachers for having low expectations of students, claiming that materials used in the classes were "too low." She added, "We are supposed to be doing higher things. And like they take us too slow, see, step by step. And that's why everybody takes it as a joke." Fern, although she enjoyed being at the "top of my class," did not like to be treated differently. She spoke about a school she attended previously where "you were all the same and you all got pushed the same and you were all helped the same. And one thing I've noticed in Springdale is they kind of teach 25 percent and they kinda leave 75 percent out." She added that, if students were receiving bad grades, teachers did not help them as much: "In Springdale, I've noticed if you're getting D's and F's, they don't look up to you; they look down. And you're always the last on the list for special activities, you know?"

These young people also referred to expectations teachers had of students based on cultural or class differences. Vanessa said that some teachers based their expectations of students on bad reputations, and found least helpful those teachers who "kind of just move really fast, just trying to get across to you what they're trying to teach you. Not willing to slow down because they need to get in what they want to get in." Rich, who attended a predominately Black school, felt that some teachers there did not expect as much as they should from the Black students: "Many of the White teachers there don't push. . . . Their expectations don't seem to be as high as they should be. . . . I know that some Black teachers, their expectations are higher than White teachers. . . . They just do it, because they know how it was for them. . . . Actually, I'd say, you have to be in Black shoes to know how it is." Little did Rich know that he was reaching the same conclusion as a major research study on fostering high achievement for African American students. In this study, Janine Bempechat determined that "across all schools, it seems that achievement is fostered by high expectations and standards" (Bempechat, 1992, p. 43).

Virginia Vogel Zanger's research with Latino and Latina students in a Boston high school focused on what can be called "social tracking." Although the students she interviewed were high-achieving and tracked in a college-bound course, they too felt the sting of alienation. In a linguistic analysis of their comments, she found that students conveyed a strong sense of marginalization, using terms such as "left out," "below," "under," and "not joined in" to reflect their feelings about school (Zanger, 1994). Although these were clearly academically successful students, they perceived tracking in the subordinate status they were assigned based on their cultural backgrounds and on the racist climate established in the school. Similarly, in a study on dropping out among Puerto Rican students, my colleague Manuel Frau-Ramos and I found some of the same kind of language. José, who had dropped out in eleventh grade, explained, "I was alone. . . . I was an outsider" (Frau-Ramos & Nieto, 1993, p. 156). Pedro, a young man who had actually graduated, nevertheless felt the same kind of alienation. When asked what the school could do to help Puerto Ricans stay in school, he said, *"Hacer algo para que los boricuas no se sientan aparte"* (Do something so that the Puerto Ricans wouldn't feel so separate) (p. 157).

Grading policies have also been mentioned in relation to tracking and expectations of achievement. One study, for example, found that when teachers deemphasized grades and standardized testing, the status of their African American and White students became more equal, and White students made more cross-race friendship choices (Hallinan & Teixeira, 1987). In my own research, I found a somewhat surprising revelation: although the students were achieving successfully in school, most did not feel that grades were very helpful. Of course, for the most part they enjoyed receiving good grades, but it was not always for the expected reason. Fern, for instance, wanted good grades because they were one guarantee that teachers would pay attention to her. Marisol talked about the "nice report cards" that she and her siblings in this family of eight children received, and said, "and, usually, we do this for my mother. We like to see her the way she wants to be, you know, to see her happy."

But they were also quick to downplay the importance of grades. Linda, for instance, gave as an example her computer teacher, who she felt had been the least helpful in her high school:

> I have no idea about computer literacy. I got A's in that course. Just because he saw that I had A's, and that my name was all around the school for all the

"wonderful things" I do, he just automatically assumed. He didn't really pay attention to who I was. The grade I think I deserved in that class was at least a C, but I got A just because everybody else gave me A's. . . . He didn't help me at all because he didn't challenge me.

She added,

To me, they're just something on a piece of paper. . . . [My parents] feel just about the same way. If they ask me, "Honestly, did you try your best?" and I tell them yes, then they'll look at the grades and say okay.

Rich stated that, although grades were important to his mother, "I'm comfortable setting my own standards." James said, without arrogance, that he was "probably the smartest kid in my class." Learning was important to him and, unlike other students who also did the assignments, he liked to "really get into the work and stuff." He added,

If you don't get involved with it, even if you do get, if you get perfect scores and stuff . . . it's not like really gonna sink in. . . . You can memorize the words, you know, on a test . . . but you know, if you memorize them, it's not going to do you any good. You have to *learn* them, you know?

Most of the students made similar comments, and their perceptions challenge schools to think more deeply about the real meaning of education. Linda was not alone when she said that the reason for going to school was to "make yourself a better person." She loved learning, and commented that "I just want to keep continuously learning, because when you stop learning, then you start dying." Yolanda used the metaphor of nutrition to talk about learning: "[Education] is good for you. . . . It's like when you eat. It's like if you don't eat in a whole day, you feel weird. That's the same thing for me." Vanessa, also an enthusiastic student, spoke pensively about success and happiness: "I'm happy. Success is being happy to me, it's not like having a job that gives you a zillion dollars. It's just having self-happiness."

Finally, Vinh spoke extensively about the meaning of education, contrasting the difference between what he felt it meant in the United States and what it meant in his home culture:

In Vietnam, we go to school because we want to become educated people. But in the United States, most people, they say, "Oh, we go to school because we want to get a good job." But my idea, I don't think so. I say, if we go to school, we want a good job *also*, but we want to become a good person.

[Grades] are not important to me. Important to me is education. . . . I not so concerned about [test scores] very much. . . . I just know I do my exam very good. But I don't need to know I got A or B. I have to learn more and more.

Some people, they got a good education. They go to school, they got master's, they got doctorate, but they're just helping *themselves*. So that's not good. I don't care much about money. So, I just want to have a normal job that I can take care of myself and my family. So that's enough. I don't want to climb up compared to other people.

Racism and discrimination

> The facts are clear to behold, but the BIG LIE of racism blinds all but its
> victims.
>
> —Stein, 1971, p. 179

An increasing number of formal research studies, as well as informal accounts and anecdotes, attest to the lasting legacy of various forms of institutional discrimination in the schools based on race, ethnicity, religion, gender, social class, language, and sexual orientation. Yet, as Annie Stein wrote in 1971, these are rarely addressed directly. The major reason for this may be that institutional discrimination flies in the face of our stated ideals of justice and fair play and of the philosophy that individual hard work is the road to success. Beverly Daniel Tatum, in discussing the myth of meritocracy, explains why racism is so often denied, downplayed, or dismissed: "An understanding of racism as a system of advantage presents a serious challenge to the notion of the United States as a just society where rewards are based solely on one's merits" (Tatum, 1992, p. 6).

Recent studies point out numerous ways in which racism and other forms of discrimination affect students and their learning. For instance, Angela Taylor found that, to the extent that teachers harbor negative racial stereotypes, the African American child's race *alone* is probably sufficient to place him or her at risk for negative school outcomes (Taylor, 1991). Many teachers, of course, see it differently, preferring to think instead that students' lack of academic achievement is due solely to conditions inside their homes or communities. But the occurrence of discriminatory actions in schools, both by other students and by teachers and other staff, has been widely documented. A 1990 study of Boston high school students found that while 57 percent had witnessed a racial attack and 47 percent would either join in or feel that the group being attacked deserved it, only a quarter of those interviewed said they would report a racial incident to school officials (Ribadeneira, 1990). It should not be surprising, then, that in a report about immigrant students in California, most believed that Americans felt negatively and unwelcoming toward them. In fact, almost every immigrant student interviewed reported that they had at one time or another been spat upon, and tricked, teased, and laughed at because of their race, accent, or the way they dressed. More than half also indicated that they had been the victims of teachers' prejudice, citing instances where they were punished, publicly embarrassed, or made fun of because of improper use of English. They also reported that teachers had made derogatory comments about immigrant groups in front of the class, or had avoided particular students because of the language difficulty (Olsen, 1988). Most of the middle and high school students interviewed by Mary Poplin and Joseph Weeres (1992) had also witnessed incidents of racism in school. In Karen Donaldson's study in an urban high school where students used the racism they experienced as the content of a peer education program, over 80 percent of students surveyed said that they had perceived racism to exist in school (Donaldson, 1994).

Marietta Saravia-Shore and Herminio Martínez found similar results in their ethnographic study of Puerto Rican young people who had dropped out of school and were currently participating in an alternative high school program. These adolescents felt that their former teachers were, in their words, "against Puerto Ricans and Blacks" and had openly discriminated against them. One reported that a teacher had said, "Do you want to be like the other Puerto Rican women who never got an education? Do you want to be like the rest of your family and never go to school?" (Saravia-Shore & Martínez, 1992, p. 242). In Virginia Vogel Zanger's study of high-achieving Latino and Latina Boston high school students, one young man described his shock when his teacher called him "spic" right in class; although the teacher was later suspended, this incident had left its mark on him (Zanger, 1994). Unfortunately, incidents such as these are more frequent than schools care to admit or acknowledge. Students, however, seem eager to address these issues, but are rarely given a forum in which such discussions can take place.

How do students feel about the racism and other aspects of discrimination that they see around them and experience? What effect does it have on them? In interviews with students, Karen Donaldson found three major ways in which they said they were affected: White students experienced guilt and embarrassment when they became aware of the racism to which their peers were subjected; students of color sometimes felt they needed to overcompensate and overachieve to prove they were equal to their White classmates; and students of color also mentioned that discrimination had a negative impact on their self-esteem (Donaldson, forthcoming). The issue of self-esteem is a complicated one and may include many variables. Children's self-esteem does not come fully formed out of the blue, but is *created* within particular contexts and responds to conditions that vary from situation to situation, and teachers' and schools' complicity in creating negative self-esteem certainly cannot be discounted. This was understood by Lillian, one of the young women in Nitza Hidalgo's study of an urban high school, who commented, "That's another problem I have, teachers, they are always talking about how we have no type of self-esteem or anything like that. . . . But they're the people that's putting us down. That's why our self-esteem is so low" (Hidalgo, 1991, p. 95).

The students in my research also mentioned examples of discrimination based on their race, ethnicity, culture, religion, and language. Some, like Manuel, felt it from fellow students. As an immigrant from Cape Verde who came to the United States at the age of eleven, he found the adjustment difficult:

> When American students see you, it's kinda hard [to] get along with them when you have a different culture, a different way of dressing and stuff like that. So kids really look at you and laugh, you know, at the beginning.

Avi spoke of anti-Semitism in his school. The majority of residents in his town were European American and Christian. The Jewish community had dwindled significantly over the years, and there were now very few Jewish students in his school. On one occasion, a student had walked by him saying, "Are you ready for the second Holocaust?" He described another incident in some detail:

> I was in a woods class, and there was another boy in there, my age, and he was in my grade. He's also Jewish and he used to come to the temple sometimes and went to Hebrew school. But then, of course, he started hanging around with the wrong people and some of these people were in my class, and I guess they were . . . making fun of him. And a few of them starting making swastikas out of wood. . . . So I saw one and I said to some kid, "What are you doing?" and the kid said to me, "Don't worry. It's not for you, it's for him." And I said to him, "What?!"

Other students talked about discrimination on the part of teachers. Both Marisol and Vinh specifically mentioned language discrimination as a problem.

For Marisol, it had happened when a particular teacher did not allow Spanish to be spoken in her room. For Vinh, it concerned teachers' attitudes about his language: "Some teachers don't understand about the language. So sometimes, my language, they say it sounds funny." Rich spoke of the differences between the expectations of White and Black teachers, and concluded that all teachers should teach the curriculum *as if they were in an all-White school*, meaning that then expectations would be high for everybody. Other students were the object of teasing, but some, including James, even welcomed it, perhaps because it at least made his culture visible. He spoke of Mr. Miller, an elementary teacher he had been particularly fond of, who had called him "Gonzo" because he had a big nose and "Klinger" after the *M.A.S.H.* character who was Lebanese. James said, "And then everybody called me Klinger from then on. . . . I liked it, kind of . . . everybody laughing at me."

It was Linda who had the most to say about racism. As a young woman who identified herself as mixed because her mother was White and her father Black, Linda had faced discrimination or confusion on the part of both students and teachers. For example, she resented the fact that when teachers had to indicate her race, they came to their own conclusions without bothering to ask her. She explained what it was like:

> [Teachers should not] try to make us one or the other. And God forbid you should make us something we're totally not. . . . Don't write down that I'm Hispanic when I'm not. Some people actually think I'm Chinese when I smile. . . . Find out. Don't just make your judgments. . . . If you're filling out someone's report card and you need to know, then ask.

She went on to say:

> I've had people tell me, "Well, you're Black." I'm not Black; I'm Black and White. I'm Black and White American. "Well, you're Black!" No, I'm not! I'm both. . . . I mean, I'm not ashamed of being Black, but I'm not ashamed of being White either, and if I'm both, I want to be part of both. And I think teachers need to be sensitive to that.

Linda did not restrict her criticisms to White teachers, but also spoke of a Black teacher in her high school. Besides Mr. Benson, her favorite teacher of all, there was another Black teacher in the school:

> The other Black teacher, he was a racist, and I didn't like him. I belonged to the Black Students Association, and he was the advisor. And he just made it so obvious: he was all for Black supremacy. . . . A lot of times, whether they deserved it or not, his Black students passed, and his White students, if they deserved an A, they got a B. . . . He was insistent that only Hispanics and Blacks be allowed in the club. He had a very hard time letting me in because I'm not all Black. . . . I just really wasn't that welcome there. . . . He never found out what I was about. He just made his judgments from afar.

It was clear that racism was a particularly compelling issue for Linda, and she thought and talked about it a great deal. The weight of racism on her mind was evident when she said, "It's hard. I look at history and I feel really bad for what some of my ancestors did to some of my other ancestors. Unless you're mixed, you don't know what it's like to be mixed." She even wrote a poem about it, which ended like this:

> But all that I wonder is who ever gave
> them the right to tell me
> What I can and can't do
> Who I can and can't be
> God made each one of us
> Just like the other
> the only difference is,
> I'm darker in color.

Implications of students' views for transformation of schools

Numerous lessons are contained within the narratives above. But what are the implications of these lessons for the school's curriculum, pedagogy, and tracking? How can we use what students have taught us about racism and discrimination? How can schools' policies and practices be informed through dialogue with students about what works and doesn't work? Although the students in my study never mentioned multicultural education by name, they were deeply concerned with whether and in what ways they and their families and communities were respected and represented in their schools. Two implications that are inherently multicultural come to mind, and I would suggest that both can have a major impact on school policies and practices. It is important that I first make explicit my own view of multicultural education: It is my understanding that multicultural education should be *basic for all students, pervasive in the curriculum and pedagogy, grounded in social justice, and based on critical pedagogy* (Nieto, 1992). Given this interpretation of multicultural education, we can see that it goes beyond the "tolerance" called for in numerous proclamations about diversity. It is also a far cry from the "cultural sensitivity" that is the focus of many professional development workshops (Nieto, 1994). In fact, "cultural sensitivity" can become little more than a condescending "bandaid" response to diversity, because it often does little to solve deep-seated problems of inequity. Thus, a focus on cultural sensitivity in and of itself can be superficial if it fails to take into account the structural and institutional barriers that reflect and reproduce power differentials in society. Rather than promoting cultural sensitivity, I would suggest that multicultural education needs to be understood as "arrogance reduction"; that is, as encompassing *both* individual *and* structural changes that squarely confront the individual biases, attitudes, and behaviors of educators, as well as the policies and practices in schools that emanate from them.

Affirming students' languages, cultures, and experiences

Over twenty years ago, Annie Stein reported asking a kindergarten teacher to explain why she had ranked four of her students at the bottom of her list, noting that they were "mute." " 'Yes,' she said, 'they have not said one word for six months and they don't appear to hear anything I say.' 'Do they ever talk to the other children?' we asked. 'Sure,' was her reply. 'They cackle to each other in Spanish all day.' " (Stein, 1971, p. 161). These young children, although quite vocal in their own language, were not heard by their teacher because the language they spoke was bereft of all significance in the school. The children were not, however, blank slates; on the contrary, they came to school with a language, culture, and experiences that could have been important in their learning. Thus, we need to look not only at the individual weaknesses or strengths of particular students, but also at the way in which schools assign status to entire groups of students based on the sociopolitical and linguistic context in which they live. Jim Cummins addressed this concern in relation to the kinds of superficial antidotes frequently proposed to solve the problem of functional illiteracy among students from culturally and economically dominated groups: "A remedial focus only on technical aspects of functional illiteracy is inadequate because the causes of educational underachievement and 'illiteracy' among subordinated groups are rooted in the systematic devaluation of culture and denial of access to power and resources by the dominant group" (1994, pp. 307–308). As we have seen in many of the examples cited throughout this article, when culture and language are acknowledged by the school, students are able to reclaim the voice they need to continue their education successfully.

Nevertheless, the situation is complicated by the competing messages that students pick up from their schools and society at large. The research that I have reviewed makes it clear that, although students' cultures are important to them personally and in their families, they are also problematic because they are rarely valued or acknowledged by schools. The decisions young people make about their identities are frequently contradictory and mired in the tensions and struggles concerning diversity that are reflected in our society. Schools are not immune to such debates. There are numerous ways in which students' languages and cultures are excluded in schools: they are invisible, as with James, denigrated, as in Marisol's case, or simply not known, as happened with Vinh. It is no wonder then that these young people had conflicted feelings about their backgrounds. In spite of this, all of them spoke about the strength they derived from family and culture, and the steps they took to maintain it. James and Marisol mentioned that they continued to speak their native languages at home; Fern discussed her father's many efforts to maintain their Native American heritage; Manuel made it clear that he would always consider himself first and foremost Cape Verdean. Vinh spoke movingly about what his culture meant to him, and said that only Vietnamese was allowed in the home and that his sisters and brothers wrote to their parents in Vietnamese weekly. Most of these young people also maintained solid ties with their religion and places of worship as an important link to their heritage.

Much of the recent literature on educating culturally diverse students is helping to provide a radically different paradigm that contests the equation *education = assimilation* (Trueba, 1989). This research challenges the old assumptions about the role of the school as primarily an assimilationist agent, and provides a foundation for policy recommendations that focus on using students' cultural background values to promote academic achievement. In the case of Asian Pacific American youth, Peter Kiang and Vivian Wai-Fun Lee state the following:

> It is ironic that strengths and cultural values of family support which are so often praised as explanations for the academic achievement of Asian Pacific American students are severely undercut by the lack of programmatic and policy support for broad-based bilingual instruction and native language development, particularly in early childhood education. (Kiang & Lee, 1993, p. 39)

A study by Jeannette Abi-Nader of a program for Hispanic youth provides an example of how this can work. In the large urban high school she studied, students' cultural values, especially those concerned with *familia*, were the basis of everyday classroom interactions. Unlike the dismal dropout statistics prevalent in so many other Hispanic communities, up to 65 percent of the high school graduates in this program went on to college. Furthermore, the youth attributed their academic success to the program, and made enthusiastic statements about it, including this one written on a survey: "The best thing I like about this class is that we all work together and we all participate and try to help each other. We're family!" (Abi-Nader, 1993, p. 213).

The students in my research also provided impassioned examples of the effect that affirming their languages and cultures had on them and, conversely, on how negating their languages and cultures negated a part of them as well. The attitudes and behaviors of the teachers in Yolanda's school, for example, were reflected in policies that seemed to be based on an appreciation for student diversity. Given the support of her teachers and their affirmation of her language and her culture, Yolanda concluded, "Actually, it's fun around here if you really get into learning. . . . I like learning. I like really getting my mind working." Manuel also commented on how crucial it was for teachers to become aware of students' cultural values and backgrounds. This was especially important for Manuel, since his parents were immigrants unfamiliar with U.S. schools and society, and although they gave him important moral support, they could do little to help him in school. He said of his teachers:

> If you don't know a student there's no way to influence him. If you don't know his background, there's no way you are going to get in touch with him. There's no way you're going to influence him if you don't know where he's been.

Fern, on the other hand, as the only Native American student in her school, spoke about how difficult it was to discuss values that were different from those of the majority. She specifically mentioned a discussion about abortion in which she was trying to express that for Native Americans, the fetus is alive: "And, so, when I try to tell them, they just, 'Oh, well, we're out of time.' They cut me off, and we've still got half an hour!" And Avi, although he felt that teachers tried to be understanding of his religion, also longed for more cultural affirmation. He would have welcomed, for example, the support of the one Jewish teacher at school who Avi felt was trying to hide his Jewishness.

On the contrary, in Linda's case, Mr. Benson, her English teacher, who was also her favorite teacher, provided just that kind of affirmation. Because he was racially mixed like Linda, she felt that he could relate to the kinds of problems she confronted. He became, in the words of Esteban Díaz and his colleagues, a "sociocultural mediator" for Linda by assigning her identity, language, and culture important roles in the learning environment (Díaz, Flores, Cousin, & Soo Hoo, 1992). Although Linda spoke English as her native language, she gave a wonderful example of how Mr. Benson encouraged her to be "bilingual," using what she referred to as her "street talk." Below is her description of Mr. Benson and the role he played in her education:

> I've enjoyed all my English teachers at Jefferson. But Mr. Benson, my English Honors teacher, he just threw me for a whirl! I wasn't going to college until I met this man. . . . He was one of the few teachers I could talk to . . . 'cause Mr. Benson, he says, I can go into Harvard and converse with those people, and

> I can go out in the street and "rap with y'all." It's that type of thing. I love it. I try and be like that myself. I have my street talk. I get out in the street and I say "ain't" this and "ain't" that and "your momma" or "wha's up?" But I get somewhere where I know the people aren't familiar with that language or aren't accepting that language, and I will talk properly. . . . I walk into a place and I listen to how people are talking and it just automatically comes to me.

Providing time in the curriculum for students and teachers to engage in discussions about how the language use of students from dominated groups is discriminated against would go a long way in affirming the legitimacy of the discourse of *all* students (Delpit, 1992). According to Margaret Gibson (1991), much recent research has confirmed that schooling may unintentionally contribute to the educational problems of students from culturally dominated groups by pressuring them to assimilate against their wishes. The conventional wisdom that assimilation is the answer to academic underachievement is thus severely challenged. One intriguing implication is that the more students are involved in resisting assimilation while maintaining their culture and language, the more successful they will be in school. That is, maintaining culture and language, although a conflicted decision, seems to have a positive impact on academic success. In any case, it seems to be a far healthier response than adopting an oppositional identity that effectively limits the possibility of academic success (Fordham & Ogbu, 1986; Skutnabb-Kangas, 1988). Although it is important not to overstate this conclusion, it is indeed a real possibility, one that tests the "melting pot" ideology that continues to dominate U.S. schools and society.

We know, of course, that cultural maintenance is not true in all cases of academic success, and everybody can come up with examples of students who felt they needed to assimilate to be successful in school. But the question remains whether this kind of assimilation is healthy or necessary. For instance, in one large-scale study, immigrant students clearly expressed a strong desire to maintain their native languages and cultures and to pass them on to their children (Olsen, 1988). Other research has found that bilingual students specifically appreciate hearing their native language in school, and want the opportunity to learn in that language (Poplin & Weeres, 1992). In addition, an intriguing study of Cambodian refugee children by the Metropolitan Indochinese Children and Adolescent Service found that the more successful they became at modeling their behavior to be like U.S. children, the more their emotional adjustment worsened (National Coalition, 1988). Furthermore, a study of Southeast Asian students found a significant connection between grades and culture: in this research, higher grade point averages correlated with the *maintenance* of traditional values, ethnic pride, and close social and cultural ties with members of the same ethnic group (Rumbaut & Ima, 1987).

All of the above suggests that it is time to look critically at policies and practices that encourage students to leave their cultures and languages at the schoolhouse door. It also suggests that schools and teachers need to affirm, maintain, and value the differences that students bring to school as a foundation for their learning. It is still too common to hear teachers urging parents to "speak only English," as my parents were encouraged to do with my sister and me (luckily, our parents never paid attention). The ample literature cited throughout this article concerning diverse student populations is calling such practices into question. What we are learning is that teachers instead need to encourage parents to speak their *native* language, not English, at home with their children. We are also learning that they should emphasize the importance of family values, not in the rigid and limiting way that this term has been used in the past to create a sense of superiority for those who are culturally dominant, but rather by accepting the strong ethical values that all cultural groups and all kinds of families cherish. As an initial step, however, teachers and schools must first learn more about their students. Vinh expressed powerfully what he wanted teachers to know about him by reflecting on how superficial their knowledge was:

> They understand something, just not all Vietnamese culture. Like they just understand something *outside*. . . . But they cannot understand something inside our hearts.

Listen to students

Although school is a place where a lot of talk goes on, it is not often student talk. Student voices sometimes reveal the great challenges and even the deep pain young people feel when schools are unresponsive, cold places. One of the students participating in a project focusing on those "inside the school," namely students, teachers, staff, and parents, said, "This place hurts my spirit" (Poplin & Weeres, 1992, p. 11). Ironically, those who spend the most time in schools and classrooms are often given the least opportunity to talk. Yet, as we saw in the many examples above, students have important lessons to teach educators and we need to begin to listen to them more carefully. Suzanne Soo Hoo captured the fact that educators are losing a compelling opportunity to learn from students while working on a project where students became coresearchers and worked on the question, "What are the obstacles to learning?" a question that, according to Soo Hoo, "electrified the group" (1993, p. 386). Including students in addressing such important issues places the focus where it rightfully belongs, said Soo Hoo: "Somehow educators have forgotten the important connection between teachers and students. We listen to outside experts to inform us, and consequently, we overlook the treasure in our very own backyards: our students" (p. 390). As Mike, one of the coresearchers in her project, stated, "They think just because we're kids, we don't know anything" (p. 391).

When they are treated as if they do know something, students can become energized and motivated. For the ten young people in my study, the very act of speaking about their schooling experiences seemed to act as a catalyst for more critical thinking about them. For example, I was surprised when I met Marisol's mother and she told me that Marisol had done nothing but speak about our interviews. Most of the students in the study felt this enthusiasm and these feelings are typical of other young people in similar studies. As Laurie Olsen (1988) concluded in an extensive research project in California in which hundreds of immigrant students were interviewed, most of the students were gratified simply to have the opportunity to speak about their experiences. These findings have several implications for practice, including using oral histories, peer interviews, interactive journals, and other such strategies. Simply providing students with time to talk with one another, including group work, seems particularly helpful.

The feeling that adults do not listen to them has been echoed by many young people over the years. But listening alone is not sufficient if it is not accompanied by profound changes in what we expect our students to accomplish in school. Even more important than simply *listening* is *assisting* students to become agents of their own learning and to use what they learn in productive and critical ways. This is where social action comes in, and there have been a number of eloquent accounts of critical pedagogy in action (Peterson, 1991; Torres-Guzmán, 1992). I will quote at length from two such examples that provide inspiring stories of how listening to students can help us move beyond the written curriculum.

Iris Santos Rivera wrote a moving account of how a Freirian "problem-posing" approach was used with K-6 Chicano students in a summer educational program of the San Diego Public Schools in 1975 (Santos Rivera, 1983–1984). The program started by having the students play what she called the "Complain, Moan, and Groan Game." Using this exercise, in which students dialogued about and identified problems in the school and community, the young people were asked to identify problems to study. One group selected the school lunch program. This did not seem like a "real" problem to the teacher, who tried to steer the children toward another problem. Santos Rivera writes: "The teacher found it hard to believe in the problem's validity as an issue, as the basis for an action project, or as an integrating theme for education" (p. 5). She let the children talk about it for awhile, convinced that they would come to realize that this was not a serious issue. However, when she returned, they said to her, "Who is responsible for the lunches we get?" (p. 6). Thus began a summer-long odyssey in which the students wrote letters, made phone calls, traced their lunches from the catering truck through the school contracts office, figured out taxpayers' cost per lunch, made records of actual services received from the subcontractors; counted sand-wiches and tested milk temperatures, and, finally, compared their findings with contract specifications, and found that there was a significant discrepancy. "We want to bring in the media," they told the teacher (p. 6). Both the local television station and the major networks responded to the press releases sent out by the students, who held a press conference to present the facts and answer reporters' questions. When a reporter asked who had told them all this, one nine-year old girl answered, "We found this stuff out. Nobody had to tell us anything. You know, you adults give yourselves too much credit" (p. 7). The postscript to this story is that state and federal laws had to be amended to change the kinds of lunches that students in California are served, and tapes from the students in this program were used in the state and federal hearings.

In a more recent example, Mary Ginley, a student in the doctoral program at the School of Education at the University of Massachusetts and a gifted teacher in the Longmeadow (Massachusetts) Public Schools, tries to help her second-graders develop critical skills by posing questions to them daily. Their responses are later discussed during class meeting time. Some of these questions are fairly straight-forward ("Did you have a good weekend?"), while others encourage deeper thinking; the question posed on Columbus Day, "Was Columbus a hero?" was the culmination of much reading and dialogue that had previously taken place. Another activity she did with her students this year was to keep a daily record of sunrise and sunset. The students discovered to their surprise that December 21 was *not* the shortest day of the year. Using the daily almanac in the local news-paper, the students verified their finding and wrote letters to the editor. One, signed by Kaolin, read (spelling in original):

Dear Editor,

Acorting to our chart December 21 was not the shotest day of the year. But acorting to your paper it is. Are teacher says it happens evry year! What's going on?

As a result of this letter, the newspaper called in experts from the National Weather

Service and a local planetarium. One of them said, "It's a fascinating question that [the pupils] have posed. . . . It's frustrating we don't have an adequate answer." (Kelly, 1994, p. 12). Katie, one of the students in Mary's class, compared her classmates to Galileo, who shook the scientific community by saying that the earth revolved around the sun rather than the other way around. Another, Ben, said, "You shouldn't always believe what you hear," and Lucy asserted, "Even if you're a grown-up, you can still learn from a second-grader!"

In the first part of this article, I posed the question, "Why listen to students?" I have attempted to answer this question using numerous comments that perceptive young people, both those from my study and others, have made concerning their education. In the final analysis, the question itself suggests that it is only by first listening *to* students that we will be able to learn to talk *with* them. If we believe that an important basis of education is dialogue and reflection about experience, then this is clearly the first step. Yolanda probably said it best when she commented, "'Cause you learn a lot from the students. That's what a lot of teachers tell me. They learn more from their students than from where they go study."

Conclusion

I have often been struck by how little young people believe they deserve, especially those who do not come from economically privileged backgrounds. Although they may work hard at learning, they somehow believe that they do not deserve a chance to dream. This article is based on the notion that all of our students deserve to dream and that teachers and schools are in the best position for "creating a chance" to do so, as referred to in the title. This means developing conditions in schools that let students know that they have a right to envision other possibilities beyond those imposed by traditional barriers of race, gender, or social class. It means, even more importantly, that those traditional barriers can no longer be viewed as impediments to learning.

The students in my study also showed how crucial extracurricular activities were in providing needed outlets for their energy and for teaching them important leadership skills. For some, it was their place of worship (this was especially true for Avi, Manuel, and Rich); for others, it was hobbies (Linda loved to sing); and for others, sports were a primary support (Fern mentioned how she confronted new problems by comparing them to the sports in which she excelled: "I compare it to stuff, like, when I can't get science, or like in sewing, I'll look at that machine and I'll say, 'This is a basketball; I can overcome it' "). The schools' responsibility to provide some of these activities becomes paramount for students such as Marisol, whose involvement in the Teen Clinic acted almost like a buffer against negative peer pressure.

These students can all be characterized by an indomitable resilience and a steely determination to succeed. However, expecting all students, particularly those from subordinated communities, to be resilient in this way is an unfair burden, because privileged students do not need this quality, as the schools generally reflect their backgrounds, experiences, language, and culture. Privileged students learn that they are the "norm," and although they may believe this is inherently unfair (as is the case with Vanessa), they still benefit from it.

Nevertheless, the students in this research provide another important lesson about the strength of human nature in the face of adversity. Although they represented all kinds of families and economic and social situations, the students were almost uniformly upbeat about their future and their lives, sometimes in spite of what might seem overwhelming odds. The positive features that have contributed to their academic success, namely, caring teachers, affirming school climates, and loving families, have helped them face such odds. "I don't think there's anything stopping me," said Marisol, whose large family lived on public assistance because both parents were disabled. She added, "If I know I can do it, I should just keep on trying." The determination to keep trying was evident also in Fern, whose two teenage sisters were undergoing treatment for alcohol and drug abuse, but who nevertheless asserted, "I succeed in everything I do. If I don't get it right the first time, I always go back and try to do it again," adding, "I've always wanted to be president of the United States!" And it was evident as well in the case of Manuel, whose father cleaned downtown offices in Boston while his mother raised the remaining children at home, and who was the first of the eleven children to graduate from high school: "I can do whatever I want to do in life. Whatever I want to do, I know I could make it. I believe that strongly." And, finally, it was also clear in the case of Rich, whose mother, a single parent, was putting all three of her children through college at the same time. Rich had clearly learned a valuable lesson about self-reliance from her, as we can see in this striking image: "But let's not look at life as a piece of cake, because eventually it'll dry up, it'll deteriorate, it'll fall, it'll crumble, or somebody will come gnawing at it." Later he added, "As they say, self-respect is one gift that you give yourself."

Our students have a lot to teach us about how pedagogy, curriculum, ability grouping, and expectations of ability need to change so that greater numbers of young people can be reached. In 1971, Annie Stein expressed the wishes and hopes of students she talked with, and they differ little from those we have heard through the voices of students today: "The demands of high school youth are painfully reasonable. They want a better education, a more 'relevant' curriculum, some voice in the subject matter to be taught and in the running of the school, and some respect for their constitutional and human rights" (1971, p. 177). Although the stories and voices I have used in this article are primarily those of individual students, they can help us to imagine what it might take to transform entire schools. The responsibility to do so cannot be placed only on the shoulders of individual teachers who, in spite of the profound impact they can have on the lives of particular students, are part of a system that continues to be unresponsive to too many young people. In the final analysis, students are asking us to look critically not only at structural conditions, but also at individual attitudes and behaviors. This implies that we need to undertake a total transformation not only of our schools, but also of our hearts and minds.

Notes

1   I recognize that overarching terms, such as "European American," "African American," "Latino," etc., are problematic. Nevertheless, "European American" is more explicit than "White" with regard to culture and ethnicity, and thus challenges Whites also to think of themselves in ethnic terms, something they usually reserve for those from more clearly identifiable groups (generally, people of color). I have a more in-depth discussion of this issue in chapter two of my book, *Affirming Diversity* (1992).

2   The early arguments for cultural deprivation are well expressed by Carl Bereiter and Siegfried Englemann (1966) and by Frank Reissman (1962). A thorough review of a range of deficit theories can be found in Herbert Ginsburg (1986).

3   "Critical thinking," as used here, is not meant in the sense that it has come to be used conventionally to imply, for example, higher order thinking skills in math and science as disconnected from a political awareness. Rather, it means developing, in the Freirian

(1970) sense, a consciousness of oneself as a critical agent in learning and transforming one's reality.

4   I was assisted in doing the interviews by a wonderful group of colleagues, most of whom contacted the students, interviewed them, and gave me much of the background information that helped me craft the case studies. I am grateful for the insights and help the following colleagues provided: Carlie Collins Tartakov, Paula Elliott, Haydée Font, Maya Gillingham, Mac Lee Morante, Diane Sweet, and Carol Shea.

5   "Holidays and Heroes" refers to an approach in which multicultural education is understood as consisting primarily of ethnic celebrations and the acknowledgment of "great men" in the history of particular cultures. Deeper structures of cultures, including values and lifestyle differences, and an explicit emphasis on power differentials as they affect particular cultural groups, are not addressed in this approach. Thus, this approach is correctly perceived as one that tends to romanticize culture and treat it in an artificial way. In contrast, multicultural education as empowering and liberating pedagogy confronts such structural issues and power differentials quite directly.

References

Abi-Nader, J. (1993). Meeting the needs of multicultural classrooms: Family values and the motivation of minority students. In M. J. O'Hair & S. Odell (Eds), *Diversity and teaching: Teacher education yearbook 1* (pp. 212–236). Fort Worth, TX: Harcourt Brace Jovanovich.

Banks, J. A. (1991). *Teaching strategies for ethnic studies* (6th ed.). Boston: Allyn & Bacon.

Bartolomé, L. (1994). Beyond the methods fetish: Toward a humanizing pedagogy. *Harvard Educational Review, 64*, 173–194.

Bempechat, J. (1992). *Fostering high achievement in African American children: Home, school, and public policy influences.* New York: ERIC Clearinghouse on Urban Education, Teachers College, Columbia University.

Bereiter, C., & Englemann, S. (1966). *Teaching disadvantaged children in the preschool.* Englewood Cliffs, NJ: Prentice Hall.

Clark, R. M. (1983). *Family life and school achievement: Why poor Black children succeed or fail.* Chicago: University of Chicago Press.

Commins, N. L. (1989). Language and affect: Bilingual students at home and at school. *Language Arts, 66*, 29–43.

Cummins, J. (1994). From coercive to collaborative relations of power in the teaching of literacy. In B. M. Ferdman, R-M. Weber, & A. G. Ramírez (Eds.), *Literacy across languages and cultures* (pp. 295–331). Albany: State University of New York Press.

Delpit, L. (1992). The politics of teaching literate discourse. *Theory into Practice, 31*, 285–295.

Díaz, E., Flores, B., Cousin, P. T., & Soo Hoo, S. (1992, April). *Teacher as sociocultural mediator.* Paper presented at the Annual Meeting of the AERA, San Francisco.

Donaldson, K. (1994). Through students' eyes. *Multicultural Education, 2*(2), 26–28.

Fine, M. (1991). *Framing dropouts: Notes on the politics of an urban public high school.* Albany: State University of New York Press.

Fine, M. (1993). "You can't just say that the only ones who can speak are those who agree with your position": Political discourse in the classroom. *Harvard Educational Review, 63*, 412–433.

Fordham, S., & Ogbu, J. (1986) Black students' school success: Coping with the "burden of acting White". *Urban Review, 18*, 176–206.

Frau-Ramos, M., & Nieto, S. (1993). "I was an outsider": Dropping out among Puerto Rican youths in Holyoke, Massachusetts. In R. Rivera & S. Nieto (Eds.), *The education of Latino students in Massachusetts: Research and policy considerations* (pp. 143–166). Boston: Gastón Institute.

Freire, P. (1970). *Pedagogy of the oppressed.* New York: Seabury Press.

Gibson, M. (1991). Minorities and schooling: Some implications. In M. A. Gibson & J. U. Ogbu (Eds.), *Minority status and schooling: A comparative study of immigrant and involuntary minorities* (pp. 357–381). New York: Garland.

Ginsburg, H. (1986). The myth of the deprived child: New thoughts on poor children. In

U. Neisser (Ed.), *The school achievement of minority children: New perspectives*. Hillsdale, NJ: Lawrence Erlbaum.

Goodlad, J. I. (1984). *A place called school*. New York: McGraw-Hill.

Haberman, M. (1991). The pedagogy of poverty versus good teaching. *Phi Delta Kappan, 73*, 290–294.

Hallinan, M., & Teixeira, R. (1987). Opportunities and constraints: Black-White differences in the formation of interracial friendships. *Child Development, 58*, 1358–1371.

Hidalgo, N. M. (1991). *"Free time, school is like a free time": Social relations in City High School classes*. Unpublished doctoral dissertation, Harvard University.

Hollins, E. R., King, J. E., & Hayman, W. C. (Eds.). (1994). *Teaching diverse populations: Formulating a knowledge base*. Albany: State University of New York Press.

Kelly, R. (1994, January 11). Class searches for solstice. *Union News*, p. 12.

Kiang, P. N., & Lee, V. W-F. (1993). Exclusion or contribution? Education K-12 policy. In *The State of Asian Pacific America: Policy Issues to the Year 2020* (pp. 25–48). Los Angeles: LEAP Asian Pacific American Public Policy Institute and UCLA Asian American Studies Center.

Kohl, H. (1993). The myth of "Rosa Parks, the tired." *Multicultural Education, 1*(2), 6–10.

Kozol, J. (1967). *Death at an early age: The destruction of the hearts and minds of Negro children in the Boston Public Schools*. New York: Houghton Mifflin.

Lee, V. E., Winfield, L. F., & Wilson, T. C. (1991). Academic behaviors among high-achieving African-American students. *Education and Urban Society, 24*(1), 65–86.

Lucas, T., Henze, R., & Donato, R. (1990). Promoting the success of Latino language-minority students: An exploratory study of six high schools. *Harvard Educational Review, 60*, 315–340.

McNeil, L. M. (1986). *Contradictions of control: School structure and school knowledge*. New York: Routledge & Kegan Paul.

Mehan, H., & Villanueva, I. (1993). Untracking low achieving students: Academic and social consequences. In *Focus on Diversity* (Newsletter available from the National Center for Research on Cultural Diversity and Second Language Learning, 399 Kerr Hall, University of California, Santa Cruz, CA 95064).

Moll, L. (1992). Bilingual classroom studies and community analysis: Some recent trends. *Educational Researcher, 21*(2), 20–24.

Moll, L., & Díaz, S. (1993). Change as the goal of educational research. In E. Jacob & C. Jordan (Eds.), *Minority education: Anthropological perspectives* (pp. 67–79). Norwood, NJ: Ablex.

National Coalition of Advocates for Students. (1988). *New voices: Immigrant students in U.S. public schools*. Boston: Author.

Newmann, F. M. (1993). Beyond common sense in educational restructuring: The issues of content and linkage. *Educational Researcher, 22*(2), 4–13, 22.

Nieto, S. (1992). *Affirming diversity: The sociopolitical context of multicultural education*. White Plains, NY: Longman.

Nieto, S. (1994). Affirmation, solidarity, and critique: Moving beyond tolerance in multi-cultural education. *Multicultural Education, 1*(4), 9–12, 35–38.

Oakes, J. (1992). Can tracking research inform practice? *Educational Researcher, 21*(4), 12–21.

Olsen, L. (1988). *Crossing the schoolhouse border: Immigrant students and the California public schools*. San Francisco: California Tomorrow.

Peterson, R. E. (1991). Teaching how to read the world and change it: Critical pedagogy in the intermediate grades. In C. E. Walsh (Ed.), *Literacy as praxis: Culture, language, and pedagogy* (pp. 156–182). New Jersey: Ablex.

Phelan, P., Davidson, A. L., & Cao, H. T. (1992). Speaking up: Students' perspectives on school. *Phi Delta Kappan, 73*, 695–704.

Poplin, M., & Weeres, J. (1992). *Voices from the inside: A report on schooling from inside the classroom*. Claremont, CA: Claremont Graduate School, Institute for Education in Transformation.

Reissman, F. (1962). *The culturally deprived child*. New York: Harper & Row.

Reyes, M. de la Luz (1992). Challenging venerable assumptions: Literacy instruction for linguistically different students. *Harvard Educational Review, 62*, 427–446.

Ribadeneira, D. (1990, October 18). Study says teen-agers' racism rampant. *Boston Globe*, p. 31.
Rumbaut, R. G., & Ima, K. (1987). *The adaptation of Southeast Asian refugee youth: A comparative study*. San Diego: Office of Refugee Resettlement.
Santos Rivera, I. (1983–1984, October-January). Liberating education for little children. In *Alternativas* (Freirian newsletter from Río Piedras, Puerto Rico, no longer published).
Saravia-Shore, M., & Martínez, H. (1992). An ethnographic study of home/school role conflicts of second generation Puerto Rican adolescents. In M. Saravia-Shore & S. F. Arvizu (Eds.), *Cross-cultural literacy: Ethnographies of communication in multiethnic classrooms* (pp. 227–251). New York: Garland.
Shor, I. (1992). *Empowering education: Critical teaching for social change*. Chicago: University of Chicago Press.
Skutnabb-Kangas, T. (1988). Resource power and autonomy through discourse in conflict: A Finnish migrant school strike in Sweden. In T. Skutnabb-Kangas & J. Cummins (Eds.), *Minority education: From shame to struggle* (pp. 251–277). Clevedon, England: Multilingual Matters.
Sleeter, C. E. (1991). *Empowerment through multicultural education*. Albany: State University of New York Press.
Sleeter, C. E. (1994). White racism. *Multicultural Education, 1*(4), 5–8, 39.
Sleeter, C. E., & Grant, C. A. (1991). Mapping terrains of power: Student cultural knowledge vs. classroom knowledge. In C. E. Sleeter (Ed.), *Empowerment through multicultural education* (pp. 49–67). Albany: State University of New York Press.
Soo Hoo, S. (1993). Students as partners in research and restructuring schools. *Educational Forum, 57*, 386–393.
Stein, A. (1971). Strategies for failure. *Harvard Educational Review, 41*, 133–179.
Tatum, B. D. (1992). Talking about race, learning about racism: The application of racial identity development theory in the classroom. *Harvard Educational Review, 62*, 1–24.
Taylor, A. R. (1991). Social competence and the early school transition: Risk and protective factors for African-American children. *Education and Urban Society, 24*(1), 15–26.
Taylor, D., & Dorsey-Gaines, C. (1988). *Growing up literate: Learning from inner-city families*. Portsmouth, NH: Heinemann.
Torres-Guzmán, M. (1992). Stories of hope in the midst of despair: Culturally responsive education for Latino students in an alternative high school in New York City. In M. Saravia-Shore & S. F. Arvizu (Eds.), *Cross-cultural literacy: Ethnographies of communication in multiethnic classrooms* (pp. 477–490). New York: Garland.
Trueba, H. T. (1989). *Raising silent voices: Educating the linguistic minorities for the twenty-first century*. Cambridge, MA: Newbury House.
Wheelock, A. (1992). *Crossing the tracks: How "untracking" can save America's schools*. New York: New Press.
Zanger, V. V. (1994). Academic costs of social marginalization: An analysis of Latino students' perceptions at a Boston high school. In R. Rivera & S. Nieto (Eds.), *The education of Latino students in Massachusetts: Research and policy considerations* (pp. 167–187). Boston: Gastón Institute.

PART 4

MATCHING THE NEEDS OF DIVERSE STUDENTS TO ELEMENTS OF SCHOOLING

CHAPTER 19

REPUTATION AND RESPECTABILITY (1982)
How competing cultural systems affect students' performance in school
Margaret A. Gibson

This paper, based on a larger case study of ethnicity and education in a Caribbean community,[1] examines the relationship between school performance and students' cultural identities. It contrasts the performance of girls and boys in the public schools in St. Croix and suggests how sex-specific avenues to social respect within Crucian society influence students' responses to school, including academic success. Reasons for this focus are threefold. First, only one out of every five Crucian boys finishes high school, while four out of five Crucian girls finish. The paper seeks to explain this discrepancy. Second, the case study provides opportunity to analyze how students' multiple roles and statuses interact to influence their performance in school. As will be demonstrated, the interrelation between ethnicity, social class, and sex role is complex. Each of these factors influences students' responses to schooling, but no one of them is determinant. Third, explanation of the contrasting performance patterns of Crucian girls and boys and the interplay between ethnic identity, sex, and class requires setting the schools within the larger societal context. This paper will examine the intersection between home, community, and school culture.

The St. Croix case study shows that students' performance in school is directly affected by the relationship between the cultural patterns supported by the school and those adhered to by the students. Where there is congruence and compatibility between the two, the probability for success in school is enhanced. On the other hand, where there is discontinuity and incompatibility between cultural systems, there is likelihood for competition and tension between school authorities and students. In turn, this tension may result in interpersonal conflict and performance dysfunction. Cultural miscommunication and conflict may arise not only between different ethnic groups, but from sex, age, and social class differences and tensions within a single ethnic group.

Cultural discontinuities alone, however, do not explain adequately why certain subgroups of students have problems in school. Many different factors work together to influence students' school response patterns. Within the school itself, we must look at both the formal and informal dynamics of the teaching-learning process. For an understanding of schooling, we must also explore the larger community context over time, the political, social, and economic processes at work within it, and the interrelation between the school, the home, the community, and the workplace. While this article cannot address each of these factors in detail, it will demonstrate both the importance of an historical perspective and the utility

of a multifaceted and macro-ethnographic approach to analyzing school success
and failure.

Setting

The history and development of St. Croix have been well documented, particularly in recent years (Dookhan 1974; Green 1972; G. Lewis 1972; Lewisohn
1970), and need not be repeated here except as they contribute to the present
analysis. Like other Afro-Caribbean societies, St. Croix is characterized by its
relatively small size, its colonial and slave experience, a population predominantly
African in descent, and continued dependence on a colonial power. From roughly
1733, when the island was purchased from France by Denmark, until the abolition of slavery in 1848, St. Croix was a plantation society, with sugar its principal
crop. Economic decline followed emancipation. The sale of St. Croix, along with
St. Thomas and St. John, to the United States in 1917 did little for the abysmal
economic situation. Efforts to Americanize the U.S. Virgin Islands and to bring
them economic relief proceeded slowly prior to the 1960s.

During the 1960s the old, agriculturally based economy of St. Croix was
replaced forever by an economy based on industry, tourists, tourist-related services, and local government. Tourism and industry together brought full employment but at a cost to the native population, which rapidly became a minority in its
own homeland. Between 1960 and 1975 the population grew from 14,943 (U.S.
Bureau of the Census 1973) to nearly 55,000, the major cause of the increase
being immigration to St. Croix by workers from neighboring Caribbean islands.[2]

St. Croix society, by the mid-1970s, was divided into four major ethnic groupings, as follows: (1) 27 percent Crucian (a person who was born in St. Croix, who
speaks Crucian English, and whose mother or father was also born in St. Croix);
(2) 22 percent Puerto Rican (a first- or second-generation immigrant to St. Croix
from Puerto Rico, Vieques, or Culebra); (3) 7 percent Continental (a person from
the mainland or continental United States who has made St. Croix his or her place
of residence); and (4) 44 percent Down Islander or "alien" (a West Indian living in
St. Croix who came there from a non-United States island of the Caribbean).

Within the public schools the population ratios were somewhat different.
Down Islanders were the largest group, accounting for at least 40 percent of the
public school enrollment. The remaining 60 percent was nearly equally divided
between Crucians and Puerto Ricans. Total public school enrollment in 1975 was
12,043 or 78 percent of the island's total school population (Virgin Islands
Department of Education 1975). Another 3,316 students were attending the
island's private schools, including about 30 percent of all Crucian children and
almost all Continental children, both black and white.

This paper focuses analysis on the public schools, a social setting in which class
and racial distinctions among students are minimal. Almost all students are from
the lower socioeconomic classes and are black. Students are "black" using the
social definition of race prevalent in the continental United States. In actuality
their pigmentation runs the gamut from very light to very dark. With few exceptions those students whose parents can afford the tuition attend private school.
The white population comes largely from the continental United States, but it
includes also a small number of native Crucians and foreigners. There is little
movement of students from public to private school, or vice versa.

School success findings

This article focuses on the striking difference between Crucian boys' and girls' performance in public school. Puerto Rican and Down Islander groups will be used for comparative purposes in illustrating the interrelation of sex roles and ethnicity. Within each ethnic group, there are boy–girl contrasts. The differences, however, are much greater within the Crucian group than within either the Down Islander or Puerto Rican groups.

School success findings are based on three separate studies of students' success in school carried out as part of the fieldwork reported in this paper. Study A included all students who were enrolled in seventh grade during May 1974 in one of the island's two junior high schools. Studies B and C are longitudinal, following random samples of students over a 7-year period, from 1969 to 1975. The samples were drawn from a 1969 ethnic census of St. Croix public school students (Bramson 1969). Both samples were stratified by students' sex and ethnic identity. The samples were not stratified by social class, but, as noted, almost all public school children in St. Croix come from the lower classes.

The research design included initially only studies B and C. In analyzing the preliminary findings from these longitudinal studies, it became apparent that many students, especially boys, were never promoted from seventh to eighth grade. Study C, beginning as it did with eighth graders, included, therefore, a select group of students. Second, the samples, as it turned out, were not representative of the total Down Islander population, even though they included 50 percent of all Down Islander students enrolled in the fourth and eighth grades of public school in April 1969. The Down Islander population in St. Croix increased rapidly during the early 1970s. Also, most Down Islander children were prevented from enrolling in public schools until 1970, when the courts ruled that noncitizen students whose parents were residing legally in the U.S. Virgin Islands had the right to receive public education. Study A was undertaken both to include a more representative sample of Down Islanders and to focus on students during their junior high years.

Table 19.1 presents the sample size for each of the three studies of school success. Study A, as noted, included the total population of seventh graders in one junior high school. Study B included 21 percent of all students attending fourth grade in April 1969. Study C included 23 percent of all students attending eighth grade that same spring.

Grade level

Using school-defined criteria for success—school persistence (remaining in school through high school graduation), grade level (not repeating a grade), and annual

Table 19.1 School success studies: Sample size

	Total	CR Girl	CR Boy	PR Girl	PR Boy	DI Girl	DI Boy
Study A	273	34	41	20	28	77	73
Study B	106	22	24	17	20	11	12
Study C	75	16	18	13	10	9	9

Note: CR, Crucian; PR, Puerto Rican; DI, Down Islander.

marks—three groups of students met with a fairly high degree of success and three other groups consistently succeeded less well. At the top were the Down Islander girls, the Crucian girls, and the Down Islander boys. Next came the Puerto Rican girls and boys. Doing least well were the Crucian boys.

Boys in all subgroups were more likely to have been retained than girls, but the greatest contrast was between Crucian boys and girls. In the total school population of 1974 island wide, K to 12, in which boys made up 51 percent, boys were 62 percent of those held back in the same grade. In many schools twice the number of boys were retained as girls (Virgin Islands Department of Education 1974). The pattern was the same in studies A, B, and C. Within the Crucian group (study B), 65 percent of the girls had never repeated a grade and were attending tenth grade at the time of fieldwork, compared with only 12 percent of the boys. The rest of the boys had been held back at least once, generally twice, and sometimes three times.

Study A revealed the same pattern for the junior high years. At the end of seventh grade, 82 percent of all girls were promoted and attended eighth grade compared with 56 percent of the boys. Within the Crucian group only 34 percent of the boys were attending eighth grade in 1974–1975, compared with 43 percent of the Puerto Rican boys, 73 percent of the Down Islander boys, 75 percent of the Puerto Rican girls, 82 percent of the Crucian girls, and 84 percent of the Down Islander girls.

Table 19.2 shows the distribution of students attending eighth grade, repeating seventh grade, and not attending school at all. Of the 27 boys who repeated seventh grade, at least 8 for the second time, only 9 were promoted in June 1975. Of the 12 girls who repeated, only 4 failed to be promoted the following June.

School persistence

Most Crucian boys did not complete high school; most Crucian girls did. Of the Crucian boys who were fourth graders in April 1969 (study B), only 46 percent were still in school six years later (April 1975), compared with 86 percent of the Crucian girls. Many of these boys were doing poorly academically, rarely attended school, and were several years behind their proper grade level. By the following December the number of boys in school had fallen to 20 percent. Two boys were in ninth grade, three in eleventh (two of whom had one Down Islander parent but were considered Crucian since they had been born in St. Croix and had one native parent). Of the Crucian boys who reached eighth grade, which less than half did, only 44 percent received a high school diploma or the equivalent (study C). Of girls reaching eighth grade, 75 percent graduated from high school. Others had plans to attend night school and finish later.

Table 19.2 Study A: Promotion from seventh to eighth grade (in percent)[a]

	DI Girl	CR Girl	DI Boy	PR Girl	PR Boy	CR Boy
Attending 8th	84	82	73	75	43	34
Repeating 7th	11	9	19	5	21	46
Out of school	5	9	8	20	36	20

Note: DI, Down Islander; CR, Crucian; PR, Puerto Rican.
[a] Proportion of seventh graders, class of 1973–1974, who were attending eighth grade, repeating seventh, or had dropped out altogether as of April 1975.

School persistence patterns differ for each ethnic group. Most Down Islander students completed high school, both boys and girls. The majority of Puerto Rican students, girls as well as boys, left school before completing 12 years.

Table 19.3 shows the highest grade attended by students in study B for each of the six student subgroups. The table includes both those students who were still in school at the time of fieldwork and those who already had dropped out.

School marks

Crucian girls consistently received better marks than Crucian boys. The contrast was most striking in seventh grade (study A). The average mark for Crucian boys in seventh grade, all subjects combined, was a D (0.7 on a 4-point scale); for girls the end-of-year average mark was a B– (2.5 on a 4-point scale).

Study B revealed the same pattern over a 7-year period, analyzing marks given in both English and mathematics from fourth through tenth grade (or the highest grade attained for each student). The overall mark point average for girls was 1.9 and for boys 1.4. It would have been even lower for boys had all school records been available. No marks at all could be located for 6 of the 24 Crucian boys in study B, all of whom had had difficulties in school and had dropped out by the time of the fieldwork.

In study C, marks were also analyzed for English and math from eighth grade onward, until a student either graduated from high school, dropped out of school, or left the island. Again, girls received the better marks, although the boys who persisted into high school tended to take somewhat more difficult math courses than the girls.

Table 19.4 presents summary findings for all three studies, for each of the school success criteria. Student subgroups are ranked from 1 to 6, where 1 represents the subgroup that demonstrated the highest degree of success. The table shows the great disparity between performance of Crucian boys and girls, but also indicates that sex identity alone does not determine success in school.

Crucian cultural patterns

The contrasting school-success patterns of Crucian boys and girls may be explained, in part, by examining sex, age, and class differences within Crucian culture and the impact of these differences on students' responses to schooling. Although class distinctions like sex roles play a role in determining student

Table 19.3 Study B: Highest grade attended (in percent)

Grade	DI Girl	CR Girl	DI Boy	PR Girl	PR Boy	CR Boy
10	82	73	58	41	40	21
9	9	27	17	35	20	21
8	9	0	8	12	5	25
7	0	0	8	0	30	25
6	0	0	8	12	5	8

Note: DI, Down Islander; CR, Crucian; PR, Puerto Rican.
Note: Students all had been fourth graders in April 1969 and would normally have been tenth graders in 1975.

Table 19.4 School success summary findings

	DI Girl		CR Girl		DI Boy		PR Girl		PR Boy		CR Boy	
	%	(rank)	%	(rank)	%	(rank)	%	(rank)	%	(rank)	%	(rank)
School Persistence												
Study A (enrolled 5/75)	95	(1)	91	(3)	92	(2)	80	(4)	64	(6)	80	(5)
Study B (enrolled 5/75)	91	(1)	86	(2)	75	(3)	59	(4)	50	(5)	46[a]	(6)
Study C (graduated)	78	(1)	75	(2)	67	(3)	46	(4)	0	(6)	44	(5)
On Grade Level												
Study A (attending 8th)	84	(1)	82	(2)	73	(4)	75	(3)	43	(5)	34	(6)
Study B (attending 10th)	82	(1)	65	(2)	58	(3)	35	(4)	35	(5)	12	(6)
Study C (graduated)	56	(2)	50	(3)	62	(1)	29	(4)	0	(6)	22	(5)
	Mean	(Rank)	Mean	(Rank)	Mean	(Rank)	Mean	(Rank)	Mean	(Rank)	Mean	(Rank)
School Marks[b]												
Study A (all subjects)	1.7	(2)	2.5	(1)	1.4	(3)	1.1	(4)	0.9	(5)	0.7	(6)
Study B (math and English)	2.2	(1)	1.9	(3)	2.1	(2)	1.6	(5)	1.7	(4)	1.4	(6)
Study C (math and English)	2.3	(1)	1.7	(4)	1.9	(3)	1.9	(2)	1.2	(6)	1.4	(5)

Note: DI, Down Islander; CR, Crucian; PR, Puerto Rican.

[a] By 12/75 only five Crucian boys were still attending school (21%), three in eleventh grade and two in ninth grade.

[b] A = 4, B = 3, C = 2, D = 1, and F = 0.

response patterns, social class alone does not explain why Crucian girls and boys, who come from the same class background, perform very differently.

To understand students' family and community background and the adult roles and employment niches to which students were headed, research was carried out on the community setting and the social, cultural, political, and economic processes at work within it. Community research was balanced with fieldwork involving firsthand contact with the schools and with students. Participant observation was carried out in one junior high school over a 14-month period (1974–1975). Interviews, both formal and informal, were conducted with students, former students, school personnel, parents, and other community members.

The analysis of Crucian society focuses attention on contrasts between the roles of males and females, children and adults, and higher and lower social classes. A later section of the paper suggests how these distinctions of sex, age, and class influence students' responses to schooling. The term "responses" includes students' behavior in school, attitudes and beliefs about school, truancy, school persistence, and academic achievement.

Within Crucian society a woman's personal status is derived independently of her husband's achievements. It is the woman's role to run the household and rear the children. A woman spends a great deal of time at home, and her success in domestic and kinship domains determines in large part the respect that others accord her. Women also earn and maintain respect by their achievements apart from domestic affairs, through community and employment-related activities. Most women have a strong sense of wanting to be able to take care of themselves and their families. Economic security is important to them, and self-reliance is the surest way to provide such security, since Crucian men cannot always be counted on for steady support. Many Crucian women choose to work, even if their husbands can provide economic security for them and their children.

In contrast to the women, Crucian men seldom are at home. They have little time or opportunity to provide children with daily guidance or discipline. Children are brought up largely by their mothers and other female relatives, although there is variation in child-rearing styles based on education, financial status, and, more importantly, the degree to which a man has adopted middleclass Euro-American values regarding the role of a father.

It is the mother's role, traditionally, to be the authority in the home. A mother will "beat" (spank) her children, especially the younger ones, for minor as well as major transgressions. The child's role is not to question but to obey. Being a child means having to mind, even if a demand is unreasonable. This changes as the child grows older. Becoming an adult means no longer having to take orders, to admit blame, or to apologize.

Opportunities for getting out of the house and mixing socially are much more limited for girls than for boys. "Formal" occasions for socializing are large family parties and church affairs. Girls generally attend such functions with their parents, whereas boys are free to come and go separately. On a more informal basis, both girls and boys hang around the shopping centers on a Saturday afternoon or go to the beach in the summer. But most of the time girls, when they are not in school, are supposed to be at home doing housework and looking after younger brothers and sisters. Parents usually are very strict with their daughters. And, as one young Crucian man observed:

> It bothers some girls that they can't do all the things boys do. They think boys have all the fun. Like with Boys Club, they [the boys] go to the beach or the

pool, play ball, make trips around the island, have special programs at the library. Girls can be members of Boys Club, but not many are. Their parents keep them at home.

Parents are much less strict with their sons. Boys are given freedom to roam around the island and, consequently, have ample opportunity to get in "trouble." Boys, in fact, are expected to be bad. It is not the ideal, just the reality, as the following comments suggest:

> All my grandsons have bad tempers, but not my granddaughters. [*older woman*]

> Boys all come to ru'nation. [*father, whose teenage son was in trouble with the police*]

> I know my boys aren't always good, that they get in trouble. [*mother, whose sons were following company, i.e., hanging around with a bad crowd of friends*]

The people making these comments are upset by their sons' and grandsons' behavior but, from their perspective, boys' getting in trouble is almost inevitable.

From the boys' perspective, being free to roam around the island is a must. According to one young man:

> Boys simply won't stay at home. They don't want to miss out on the action. By the age of eleven or twelve a boy wants to be with the other guys and he starts following company. Most of the guys I know don't pay much attention to girls. Women are always telling you how to dress, how to fix your hair, what you should do. It's too much hassle. [*man, age 20, a high school dropout*]

Another young man observed that boys don't want to be put in a routine.

> It builds up tension. They have to do things spontaneously. Being a man means making decisions for yourself and not having others tell you what to do. By sixteen boys simply won't stand for being treated like a child. Girls are more conservative. They may wait till they are eighteen or even nineteen [*man, age 20, a college student*]

Boys, like men, are rarely at home. They hang around with a group of male companions on the street corner, at the ball park, or, as they get older, in the neighborhood bar. As young Crucian men see it, they are establishing a reputation.

Two separate, interrelated, generally sex-specific value systems are at work within Crucian society, each with its own criteria and standards for judging a person's worth. Women earn respect within a system of values that we shall call "respectability." Men, by contrast, who start out in their mother's respectability system (and may draw back to respectability again as older, established men), must earn a place for themselves as young men in a value system we shall call "reputation."

Women achieve status and authority by having good manners, keeping an immaculate house, and wearing presentable clothes whenever out in public. This behavior is essential to maintaining or advancing the respectability of oneself or one's family. Attending church regularly, being married in church, and not having children outside of one's legal marriage are also important symbols of Crucian respectability.

Wilson (1973) has proposed that *respectability* and *reputation* are cultural systems characteristic of Afro-Caribbean societies. Others, such as Patterson (1975), have described similar systems at work historically. Respectability has derived, according to Wilson, from the cultural system of the native elite in Caribbean societies. It is a Creolized version of European values and behavior, epitomized by a European conception of Christian morality. Wilson describes respectability as the summation of colonial dependence. The lower classes adopt the values and behaviors of the higher classes (historically the white European landowners, today the native elite), but have little hope of gaining equal power and privilege in the process.

In St. Croix the Euro-West Indian Creole culture of the higher classes has given way somewhat to American culture. Nevertheless, a system of class stratification continues which requires that people behave respectably in order to climb the social ladder, but that reserves elite status for only a few. The system places the lower classes in a bind. The subordinate groups, to improve their position, are required to mimic the higher classes. Yet displaying the outward symbols of respectability is not enough. A subtler complex of factors is constantly at work ready to trip people up and keep them in their places.

It is this dialectic between the higher and lower classes that Wilson (1973) has labeled *crab antics*:

> You have a barrel of crab and they start to climb. The one that climbs highest, all the others are pulling him back. If he ever reached the top, he'd have to be a big, strong crab.

Crab antics give rise to a suspiciousness about others' intentions. This runs deep in St. Croix. Gossip is used effectively as a leveling device, to undermine a person's efforts to improve social status, thereby preserving existing class assignments.

Women of the lower classes nevertheless seek to behave respectably. Such behavior is expected of a woman, by other women and by men. Men, on the other hand, particularly in the lower classes, have evolved a cultural system within which a person's worth is measured by his peers, rather than by imposed Euro-American standards of respectability. Men are evaluated for their personal achievements and given recognition for the things they can do well—talking well, showing toughness and generosity, as well as loyalty and leadership.

Reputation, according to Wilson (1973), is a creative response to the elusiveness of high-class status. This system is largely male dominated, although women participate in certain aspects of it. You earn a reputation, one Crucian man commented,

> by how well you talk, by how tough you are, by your willingness to fight, even if you lose, by how successful you are with women, by the dollars in your pocket and your willingness to spend them, and by your ability to lead others, no matter the direction.

For grown men, neighborhood bars are like social clubs, where no class lines are drawn and all may compete for peer respect on an equal basis (Green 1972).

For example, everyone, regardless of job status or formal education, is entitled to express an opinion about politics or business. Of course, all boasting and tale telling are not accepted at face value. A person naturally shows himself off to best advantage, and the accuracy of his claims becomes the subject of endless debate.

Boys emulate men, although their "hangouts" differ. They, too, strive to gain practical experience and knowledge and to demonstrate to others what "big men" they are (i.e., how grown up they are). Boys are supposed to challenge authorities, disobey the wishes of adults, smoke "pot" or gamble, and keep their shirts untucked. Boyish behavior directly confronts the norms of respectability, and boys are critical of others who try to make it within the respectability system. A boy who abides by the standards of respectability has little hope of earning peer respect unless he has other superior qualities, such as being exceptionally quick with words, good at athletics, or talented in music.

In sum, boys and men earn respect and status within the reputation system and thus feel freer to reject or defy the values and behavior required within the respectability system. To be good in business and politics, a man must have the status and authority that can only be earned within the reputation system. As a boy grows into manhood and makes his reputation secure, however, he is drawn more into the respectability system. The most successful people in St. Croix, both men and women, are those who can compete within the institutionalized world dominated by Euro-American values, as well as within the informal networks dominated by a more indigenous value system.

Implications for schooling

This analysis of Crucian culture has important and direct implications for both girls' and boys' responses to schooling. From the beginning of free and compulsory education in 1839, the public schools in St. Croix, staffed initially by Europeans and today by the native elite and imported Continentals, have served as a strong acculturative force. The public schools continue to teach the values of the higher classes. While most public school girls come from the lower classes, they encounter little difficulty adhering to these values, since it is culturally appropriate for all women, regardless of class status, to guide their lives by the Euro-American canon of respectability.

Girls

Girls' home training carries over into the schools. Whether at home or at school, girls are expected to be "good," to stay out of trouble, and to accept responsibility. Crucian girls will say, "I love to do my housework and also my school work. I love to work because all women must work and be strong." Acceptable girl behavior is also acceptable school behavior. Parents, boys, and girls all expect girls to be good. Girls earn respect from others by catering to these expectations.

Girls enjoy school because it provides them a major social outlet. Girls have to stay at home until age 16 or 17. Going to school is a chance to get out of the house, see their friends, and have a good time. They complain about being bored and about various rules and regulations that they find restrictive. For example, girls like to wear slacks, but most of the schools require girls to wear skirts (each school has its own distinctive uniform). Also, many girls wear headties, but some of the Crucian teachers prohibit them as inappropriate school attire. Unlike boys, however, "girls will take the pressure" (comment by a Crucian girl).

Not all girls are well behaved in school, but most are, especially those placed in the faster sections. In seventh grade (1973–1974), 70 percent of all Crucian girls were in top sections, compared with 30 percent of the Crucian boys. Some of the girls in the bottom sections do cause problems. Because of students' misbehavior, several "slow" sections of seventh grade were separated by sex (1974–1975 school year). The all-girl section presented teachers with sufficient frustrations that they called an emergency meeting with the girls' parents to discuss discipline.

> The main problem is the uncontrolled behavior which prevents teaching and learning from taking place. The noise never stops. The girls simply won't get quiet, are always giggling, chatting among friends, speaking out at the same time. Also, they can't refrain from eating in class, always want a drink of water or to go to the bathroom. They have no self-control. [*summary notes from parent meeting*]

These comments were confirmed by observation in the classroom.

Most of the girls in this group attended their classes regularly, while most boys in similarly "slow" sections attended irregularly. In English class, girls responded to the teacher's request to copy the new vocabulary assignment from the chalkboard. At least five girls, however, never opened their notebooks, and one sat on the floor in the back of the class throughout the entire period. The teacher had difficulty making herself heard without shouting because of talking within the classroom and the loud voices of boys outside the room. Conditions in this classroom were difficult, but teaching and learning were going forward. Boys in similar sections not only prevented instruction in their own classrooms but impeded it in other classes as well.

Girls in other sections misbehaved, but usually discreetly. Girls could be observed mimicking teachers when the teachers were not looking. They ate in class, but usually made sure the teacher did not care or would not see them. Even deliberate demonstrations of disrespect for teachers tended not to be disruptive— a girl sat in class putting on fingernail polish.

Girls want to stay in school until graduation. As one female junior high student pointed out, the ideal woman is "a woman who is dependent on herself and does not depend on her man to support her always." Furthermore, girls would say, "you can't get a job without high school." A diploma helps a girl find work, particularly a clerical position with the Virgin Islands government, and thus the economic security she desires. The mothers of most Crucian public school students (71 percent) were employed in 1975. Of those working, 70 percent had government jobs.

Only if a girl becomes pregnant does she drop out of school, and even then regulations permit her to reenroll or attend night school after delivery. Quite a few girls have babies before they are married, often having their first at age 16 or 17, occasionally younger. Of the study B sample, 14 percent had children by age 16. For an unmarried girl to get pregnant does cause some loss of family respectability, but becoming a mother has certain advantages and few disadvantages from the girl's perspective. Having a baby does not really tie a girl down; her mother or a relative will generally help raise the child. Nor need it jeopardize her education. In fact, having a baby greatly increases a girl's freedom. After her first baby is born, a girl is treated as a grown woman. Becoming a mother symbolizes becoming an adult. No longer is she restricted. No longer must she take orders. Now she is able to get out of the house and to do things her own way.

Boys

The transition from childhood to adulthood, in most respects, has little discernable influence on a girl's response to schooling. Boys, on the other hand, present a very different picture. Until their upper elementary years, most boys are willing to go along with the demands of school. Like all Crucian children, they know it is their role to do as they are told and to follow adult directions without question. By fifth or sixth grade, however, they begin to interpret direct suggestions from teachers as commands or criticism, and many of the boys simply will not do as requested. Boys, by their early teens, believe they are adults, yet the schools, they feel, treat them as children.

The following is a partial listing of the instructions given at the beginning of the year to all students in junior high school:

> Show respect for all adults.
> Wear your uniforms properly.
> Be grateful for your free education, lunch, and transportation.
> If you are absent or come late to school, bring a note.
> Don't cut class; if you must be late, get a pass.
> No destruction of school property.
> Obey the rules; we're not willing to put up with students who are lazy or rude.

Not mentioned directly but tacitly understood are the additional rules of no fighting, smoking, cursing, drinking, gambling, or drugs, and no harrassing of girls on school property.

Every one of these rules was broken repeatedly in the observed junior high school during two different school years. School records, interview data, and observation at both the elementary and high school levels, as well as at the other junior high, indicate that the problems are not unique to any one school or grade level. From about fifth grade on, boys come into more and more open conflict with school authorities.

During any class period, on any school day at the junior high school boys could be seen cutting class. Many sat quietly, chatting with friends, or they played handball in the corridors, read comics, played marbles, or shot baskets by the gym. Less apparent were those behind the gym, or on the roof, gambling, drinking, smoking, and bothering girls. All these actions, although decried by school authorities, are expected and accepted boyish behavior and help boys earn status with other boys and with girls. Students comment:

> I like a man that's always going out to play ball, that does not stay home . . .
> A masculine man is a man that likes to kiss and trouble girls. [*female junior high student*]

> Guys earn status by doing the silliest things. They say "he bad mon." "He's goin' on bad," [which is to say good] because he broke the rules, or beat up a bigger boy, or played his radio, broke a window, lit a brush fire. [*male college student*]

Boys create problems in class, as well as outside, especially in the slower sections of junior high school.

Classroom discipline became such a problem for teachers of students in the two all-boy sections of seventh grade that their parents were called to school to meet with teachers, counselor, and principal. The discussion revolved around attendance, attitudes, and grades. Only one-quarter to one-half of the boys were attending classes. Only a handful were passing. Most were easily influenced, the teachers felt, by those who wished to disturb class. Teachers noted that the boys lacked discipline:

> They can't sit still; they come and go during class as they please. In class students put their feet on the desks and refuse to remove them when asked. When questioned about an assignment boys will say, "I lose my book, I lose my pencil, or I finish," when in fact they haven't begun. [*summary notes from parent meeting*]

These boys' teachers simply did not know how to turn the situation around.

Frustration among teachers was not limited to those at the junior high. Throughout the system many found it difficult to get boys into class and, once there, to motivate them. Boys, caught cutting, would say they had no teacher (i.e., the teacher was absent and no aide was covering the class), or they simply would laugh or run off. Not infrequently they would make some obscene comment. In class, teachers felt the students deliberately harrassed them. One Continental teacher reported that if he inquired about homework, boys would reply: "That slavery, Mr. X," or "slavery done, mon." If he asked them to help with some task, like moving the desks or chairs, they would say, "No suh, me 'n carry dem chair. Me stay here. Me wanta learn." Students also said teachers are not their parents and, therefore, cannot tell them what to do.

All Crucians are quick to react if they feel someone is bossing them around. All want to do things their own way. School aides, clerks, custodians, school guards, bus drivers, and lunchroom workers, even Crucian teachers, are as sensitive to bossing as the students. They simply do not want others giving them directions. They do not respond well to instruction. Any direct remark can be taken as a criticism, and no criticism is considered constructive. No criticism is taken well.

> You simply don't criticize. You don't tell someone what to do. You mustn't be direct or it might appear you are giving orders. [*Crucian woman, higher-class family*]

As a result, some teachers and administrators shy away from disciplining the students. They know it will lead to hassles with the student, and, quite possibly, with his or her family.

Most mothers are deeply insulted if someone criticizes their children's manners. It reflects poorly on the mother and on the family's respectability. Boys rarely misbehave at home. But boys aren't home much, and parents are not generally aware of what their sons are doing while roaming about or even at school. The school authorities blame the parents; the parents and students blame the schools. The case of Alex Brown will illustrate many of the problems.

The Alex Brown case

Alex is one of seven children, four brothers and three sisters. His father lives elsewhere. Mrs. Brown has never had a problem with one of her girls at school.

Two of the girls had dropped out of high school to have babies; both later returned to night school. The two older boys had been held back several times and all the boys, except the youngest, were having serious academic problems. Alex, age 13, was transferred into the same fifth grade classroom as his 11-year-old brother, Gregory, because of poor behavior in a faster section. The teacher was young, inexperienced, and new to St. Croix. Alex rapidly became a leader among the younger boys. His behavior worsened. Officials warned Mrs. Brown that they might have to place Alex in a juvenile detention school.

Mrs. Brown came to school to meet with a social worker, who had received the following written report on Alex and his family:

> The discipline problems, chronic lateness, cutting of classes, excessive absences and traveling with troubled peer group continues. Mother is both physically and emotionally unable to handle Alex. Gregory is beginning to follow in Alex's footsteps.

> We have tried with parent conferences, therapy with the guidance counselor, and a special work-study arrangement . . . The deterioration continues.

> Typical statements made by Alex: He threatened to "kill" his music teacher and to "shoot her ass." To one of the aides he said, "your ass think you gonna run me. Come put me out now!" When finally he left class, he roamed the campus for the balance of the day.

> [Several days later] after cutting class, Alex marched around campus with two older boys, junior high students, carrying sticks and shouting obscenities into classrooms. A teacher asked him to go to the Office and he said, "Report me and I'll bust your mouth."

To the school this offered clear evidence that Alex instigated outrageous disruptions, which prevented teaching and learning.

Mrs. Brown was furious. Her competence as a mother and her respectability had been challenged. "I know my son's not perfect," she admitted, "but it doesn't matter what he does, they say he's wrong." She introduced social class and race as an explanation: "We're just poor black people." (Except for two teachers, all parties involved were black.) Mrs. Brown also knew her son had a bad and quick temper, but felt the school authorities were at fault. They harrassed Alex for wearing a hat. They refused to give him a pass to enter his classes when he came late to school, but criticized him then for hanging around campus. When he ceased going to school altogether and was tutored at a neighbor's, they ordered him back, saying he was under age and must either attend school or be placed in the Insular Training Home. Alex had a reading problem, Mrs. Brown realized, but at no time in the last three years had he been sent to the special reading teacher for help.

Mrs. Brown suspected that school officials deliberately discriminated against her boys because of "who they were," and because she had dared to stand up to school principals, counselors, and teachers. An atmosphere of deep suspicion, backed by gossip, surrounded contacts between Mrs. Brown and school personnel. Crab antics came into play. Grudges had built up for years between Mrs. Brown's family and the counselor's family on issues such as these. Insults followed: Mrs. Brown called the counselor a "bowl of fungi [mush]." The counselor insulted the Brown family as "rude." "I'll tolerate a dumb child," she said, "but when it comes to rudeness, I just can't tolerate it." Alex's education seemed secondary. He himself was deriving a reputation for talking "bad" and being a leader.

Most Crucian parents, unlike Mrs. Brown, do not go directly to the school with their concerns. They fear, with good reason, that school people will develop even worse grudges against their children if parents speak their minds. Such is the power of grudge and gossip that some parents even fear for their jobs if they intervene for their sons with school authorities. One mother, who happened to work as a school guard, told an assistant principal that it was against the law to "bash a child" and that she would bash the principal if it happened again. She was instructed to apologize to the principal or receive a bad job report. By blaming parents, schools are sure to get a hostile reaction even if the parents do not come directly to the school authorities with their anger. Parents may even, tacitly, support and encourage their boys' rebellion. A West Indian woman, who earns esteem from how well mannered her children are, will attempt to pull down, with all the force of Crucian gossip, those who challenge her respectability and her family's good name.

Classroom observation

The Brown family example, although extreme, is not unusual. Observation in a slow section of eighth grade revealed similar problems. Boys would regularly "forget" to bring the necessary books and materials to class, would stand up, wander around the room, shout answers to the teacher or comments to friends, crack jokes to gain attention, deliberately untuck their shirts or leave their hats on in class, and be blatantly rude to those teachers for whom they had little respect. Three of the four Crucian boys in the class had more than 50 demerits and had each been suspended several times during the year.

One boy, Wendell, who had repeated both fourth and seventh grades for following company, explained that his demerits were mostly for cutting. He simply would not attend those classes where teachers insisted on late slips. Wendell described other boys causing problems for the teachers they disliked or those who had too many rules. Wendell said many boys think "school is like a jail," and "mash up school property" because it makes them feel like "a king [grown up, no longer a child]." This same young man felt an education was important. He generally attended his reading, English, and math classes. He also like P.E. and his industrial arts class, where he was building a shelf. Both of these classes provided boys the opportunity to demonstrate their physical skills and to learn from actual experience. Most boys want to learn a trade and say the schools do not provide the training they need. Except for one semester during eighth grade, no vocational training is provided by the schools until tenth grade.

Observation in the top section of eighth grade revealed few discipline problems, but even there boys generally arrived late to their classes. And classes were frequently disrupted by boys wandering about outside, talking in loud voices, banging on the metal walls of the temporary classrooms, and blaring their radios. Students and teachers, nevertheless, seemed generally well pleased with the teaching and learning that was occurring in this and other "fast" sections. Top students were reported to be reading on or above grade level and ready for first-year algebra.

Boys who stay out of trouble at school and do well academically must find other ways to demonstrate their manliness and earn a reputation. As one teacher observed:

> Boys in the top sections will answer me back in front of their peers from lower sections, out in the hallway, to show they're not goody-goodies. Or they'll say to others, "I didn't do my homework," when in fact they have. Or they'll curse in front of teachers who get upset by it. They'll curse in front of the door to the classroom. Kids must be good cursers.

Indeed, teachers complained about the students' obscenities and could be heard shouting at students down the corridors to watch their language.

It is difficult for boys to conform to school demands while at the same time gaining and maintaining peer respect. Boys earn respect for behavior that conflicts directly with the standards of the schools. Boys fight to prove their manliness, argue to display their verbal agility, confront adults to prove they themselves are adults, reject the societal dress code to prove their independence, tease girls to demonstrate their way with women, and drink, smoke, and gamble to prove they are no longer children.

Student comments

Students themselves are bothered by all the confusion and problems in school. Both at the high school and junior high, they cite poor teaching, too many unnecessary rules, the overcrowding, insufficient materials, and student misbehavior as cause for the problems. The major complaint at the junior high was boys hanging around on campus, not in class, both students and outsiders, bothering others.

The general pattern, they felt, was that boys do not like the routine, are bored, are not learning, and feel that authorities are picking on them rather than teaching them. Also, boys feel they no longer are children and, therefore, do not have to listen. Boys cut class to be with their friends and to avoid hassles with the teachers. As a result, they fall farther and farther behind in their studies, eventually leaving of their own accord or being put out for lack of satisfactory academic progress. Boys also are expelled for rudeness and fighting.

Boys cannot stand teachers who, from their point of view, pick on them or embarrass them in front of peers for the way they dress or because they have not done their work. To a boy whose hair is half braided a teacher will say, "Why do you have your hair like that? Forget to comb it!" Or to one who says he lost his pencil, "What do you expect me to do? Go to Barkers and buy one!" Students even complain that teachers "does cuss the student dem," one reporting a teacher who said to a group of students standing in the corridor that "he gon' ge we a kick in our ass with his shoes if we don't hurry up and get in class." Such comments greatly distress the students.

> In joking among friends it's OK to insult each other. That's different. But in front of a whole class! It's mainly the Crucian teachers. They think they are helping, but it's wrong. [*Crucian woman, age 20, an elementary school aide*]

The boys' response to rudeness and sarcasm is to talk back, which causes them to be put out of class. Teachers believe students instigate the problems. Students, in particular boys who have run into trouble, see teachers and administrators as the cause.

The most effective teachers are those who will take time with the students, are well prepared, explain the lessons in ways that even the slow students understand, play no favorites, and make no direct commands. Even with the most unruly boys, some teachers are successful. In one of the all-boy sections of seventh grade the large majority of students attended their English class. Even boys who were not assigned to this class would attend or stand by the window looking in. The teacher had the boys reading aloud stories about life in Ghana. Most read haltingly, but were anxious to have a turn. Those who were disrupting class were requested to pay attention or leave. The request was made indirectly: "Some want to read. Some want to disturb. So maybe those who want to disturb better leave." The teacher only called on those who sat quietly and raised their hands. The students sensed this teacher's interest in young people, her respect for their ideas, and her willingness to help them learn to read without criticizing them for their past failures.

The reason junior high students cannot read, one young man explained, is because "they think what's going on in town is more important than school, even in fourth or fifth grade." Also, he noted that labeling students "remedial" is a real problem and pulls the students down farther. Boys feel the system plays favorites and is more concerned with their shirttails than with their ideas. The system, they realize, rewards perfect attendance, passive behavior, and acceptable personal appearance, but penalizes for speaking one's mind, taking initiative, and thinking for oneself. Indeed, the top eighth grade student, a girl, was described as "a model student" because she "pays attention, does what she's told," but, as one teacher observed, "doesn't have too much initiative." Teachers admitted that "if students behave they are never flunked." Not surprisingly, boys are more often held back than girls.

Girls pay a price for their good behavior. One boy's appraisal, a dropout, was that "girls ain't too smart listening to them talk." His conclusion: "They get a diploma for never being absent." Another young man, a college student, said, "most girls are feeble-minded. Girls do all the work at CVI [the college] but they never speak up. Acceptance of this male society is a bad thing."

It is true that Crucian girls appeared to stay in school even if they were doing poorly academically. By contrast, many of the boys who had dropped out were characterized as "bright," "college material," "having brains, if he would use them." Boys say what matters to them is not the diploma but the learning. They leave school to gain experience, as they see it, for it is experience that they value and it is experience that earns them respect from friends. While in school, since they do not feel they are acquiring the knowledge and skills they want, they use school for other purposes.

Schools of the past

In the past boys could not get away with unruly behavior at school. It simply was not tolerated. Back in the 1950s, students completed at least 6 years in school; children from the high-class families remained through high school. Parents pushed children to do well in school and placed great value on education. The 1950s were also the period when the old apprenticeship system (on-the-job training for young people after school) faded away completely, in part because of American laws regarding children working. Schools in those days were very strict. Students were required to behave and to do their school work. Those who could not do their assignments correctly were detained after school or even whipped. There were no ungraded classes or "social promotions." Students who failed end-of-the-year examinations simply failed the grade and either repeated or left school. There was no particular stigma attached to leaving school at 13 or 14; it was the traditional break between childhood and adulthood. Those who finished high school, possibly no more than 10 percent of all students and only those from the elite families, were well educated. They were able to enter stateside colleges and to do well.

In the late 1940s less than 3,000 students were attending school, both public and private (Senior 1947:25) and, according to one report, there were then only 68 teachers island wide. Parents knew who all the teachers were. Teachers were highly respected and among the most visible members of the community. They served as surrogate parents and had absolute control of their classes.

Some increase in school enrollment occurred during the 1950s, but, paralleling the island's population growth, full employment, and expansion of local government, it was the 1960s and early 1970s that caused a sweeping change within the public school system. School enrollment swelled to 12,043 by 1975 from only 4,006 a decade earlier (Virgin Islands Department of Education, 1975). Native students no longer viewed schools as an avenue to stateside employment, as so many had in years past; there were ample opportunities at home. Attitudes about the value of schooling shifted. Teachers and principals recall boys in the 1960s asserting, "I don't need an education 'cause I can get a government job with a big title and earn more money than you do as a college graduate." A high school diploma was less useful to boys than to girls in seeking government jobs because women wanted clerical work requiring the diploma, and men wanted manual positions in which they could acquire skills and training on the job.

The education system of the 1970s, although still very much a sorting device, "credentialing" some and "pushing out" others, was more democratic than in years past. A higher percentage of students had an opportunity to finish 12 years of schooling and to earn a diploma. The influence of the traditional class structure on the public educational system had weakened. Students from the higher-class families had abandoned the public schools, by and large, leaving student affairs to be dominated by lower-class groups. Furthermore, with the influx of outside teachers, quite ignorant of the Crucian class structure, the more personalistic criteria for dealing with students had given way. Over half of the 587 teachers in 1975 were from the mainland United States. A few others were Puerto Ricans or Down Islanders.

The old authoritarian structure remained in certain respects, but it no longer worked as well. It was effective in years past because students physically were forced to obey school authorities. They learned and they behaved out of fear of a beating. By the 1970s the law required witnesses to any corporal punishment. Moreover, schools no longer could so easily suspend students, again because of stateside laws protecting students' rights. More important, the teachers no longer were known and, in general, had not earned the community's respect, which was the only secure way to personal authority in the St. Croix social system. Teachers, for the most part, were frustrated by all the changes but felt helpless to bring order and discouraged from taking initiative.

Students, in the midst of such sweeping change, had discovered license inconceivable in years past. When parents trusted and respected teachers and when teachers could expect support from parents, even for whipping their sons, no boy dared be rude at school. By the 1970s, boys realized that schools had no effective method for controlling them.

Boys in the 1970s also found more to interest them outside of school than in, and wished to leave school before they were of legal age at 16. Those who persisted in school worried that they were missing out on the action, hearing friends talk about fishing, ball games, and what happened at the beach. Boys, older Crucians would observe, do not want to worry about their future. Some even say they do not plan to work. Teenage years are a time for boys to take it easy, to relax, to have fun.

Jobs

When the day comes for a boy to look for work, he feels that family connections and his own reputation will prove more valuable than school credentials. The boys' fathers, without any high school diplomas, have jobs and, for the most part, so do their older brothers. Students in 1975 reported that Crucians get the better jobs, better than Puerto Ricans and Down Islanders, which to them means government jobs, because "people look out more for their own." Other typical student comments regarding jobs going first to natives were, "They are from here and have the preference," they were "born here," "Crucians get the easier jobs," and "they're supposed to, they're Crucian." Parents of most Crucian students in 1975 (studies B and C) were working and most of these (74 percent) had positions with the government. The government employed 25 percent of the Virgin Islands labor force.

If jobs do indeed open up for the younger boys, as they have for the older ones, the present system may continue for some years. But boys do not want low-level jobs where others will boss them around. With government positions, this is less a problem, since most civil servants are natives and know they must avoid criticizing another's performance or making a direct demand. An endless growth in government jobs, however, cannot realistically be expected. In fact, jobs by 1974 and 1975, including government jobs, had become quite scarce. Many Down Islanders were being laid off and forced to leave the island if they lacked permanent residence papers.

Of all the Crucian young people interviewed (girls and boys), 73 percent felt it was difficult to find work. Study C boys, whose median age was 20, cited their own personal experience in explaining their feelings. Boys in study B, age 16, had yet to look for work, but they, too, said jobs were hard to come by. Although most had had summer positions with the government, only one of those out of school was working.

Assuming that job opportunities in St. Croix continue to tighten, Crucian boys may wish, increasingly, to persist in school until graduation in order to earn the credentials demanded by nongovernment employers, and quite possibly by the Virgin Islands government as well. Those who have dropped out may feel a need to return to complete their course of study. Should this be the case, the school system may want to reassess the existing education program in terms of its compatability with West Indian sex-role behaviors and realistic employment expectations, seeking to channel peer-group pressure into a positive force within the classroom. Otherwise, both school and societal tension can be expected to mount, as boys see traditional avenues to employment disappearing and, at the same time, perceive the school unresponsive to their needs.

Boys frankly admit that they will turn to crime. Some say quite directly that they prefer to steal than work. Others, older Crucians, explain that boys steal because they "are hopelessly lost" and because they feel entitled to the fruits of the land. Outsiders, recent arrivals, have stolen their island, as they see it. They, the natives, deserve their share. At least 25 percent of the study B boys were known to have had some scrape with the law by age 16 or 17. By the mid-1970s, crime in general was on the rise, and not just petty theft. Major felonies became frequent. Most families kept a watchdog. Bars on doors and windows were increasingly common, while only a few years earlier people had never even locked their houses. It can be anticipated that the crime rate will worsen, unless boys find more constructive places for themselves within the community.

Conclusion

The St. Croix case study offers an unusual opportunity to analyze the effect of ethnicity on students' performance in public schools. Social class and race are here constants; all students are black and drawn from the lower socioeconomic groups. Although the three distinct ethnic groups that divide the school population differ in language and cultural background and in their status within Crucian society, the greatest contrast in school performance was found to be intraethnic not interethnic. Within the native Crucian group, girls were found to be among the best achievers and boys, in adolescence, the worst; for Crucians, sex and age distinctions are critical. Peer-group identification for boys was of major importance to this divergence between sexes. Social-class identification was also influential, as were economic and political developments across time. Performance in the St. Croix public schools demonstrates the significance of a complex interaction of multiple roles and statuses.

Ethnicity is an important variable in the St. Croix example. Each ethnic group must be seen in relation to the others and to the larger society. Crucian students' responses to schooling—both performance in school and beliefs about the function of school—differ from those of the Puerto Rican and Down Islander groups. From the Crucian students' perspective, many of the discipline-related problems at school are caused by teachers treating students as children when they no longer see themselves as children, but Puerto Rican and Down Islander youngsters rarely explain discipline problems in this way. Similarly, while Crucian boys see little value in the high school diploma, Down Islander boys, stereotyped by Crucians as overage and underprepared, persist in school in spite of prejudice and discrimination because they see schools as the major avenue to their employment and continued residence in the American Virgin Islands (Gibson 1978). In this respect, Down Islanders are like other immigrant minorities who have moved voluntarily into a host society and are able to accept hostility as the price of success in their newly chosen homeland (Gibson 1981; Ogbu 1978).

Of all the variables considered for the Crucian group, sex role is probably the most critical. Sex-specific avenues to social respect influence students' behavior in school, their attitudes about schooling, and their ultimate decision to drop out or persist until graduation. Female sex roles are compatible with the student role. The "close correspondence between sex and pupil roles for girls, and the poor correspondence between the roles for many boys" (Lee and Gropper 1974:390) has been observed also in schools within the continental United States. What Lee and Gropper and others who talk about "sex-role culture" generally overlook is the interaction between sex roles and the other roles and statuses important to a student's identity. More attention, as Goetz (1978) notes, must be given to the influence of sex role on students' performance in school; such analysis, however, must focus not only on sex roles, but on the interplay among the multiple variables influencing student performance.

In addition to other roles and statuses, an individual's reference group proved critical in the St. Croix context. For Crucian adolescent boys, the peer group had possibly even stronger effect on values and behavior than family. DeVos (1975:31–33) has noted that a peer group is an "exacting socializer." He points out that in some circumstances a peer group may issue "sanctions against ready compliance with the objectives of the school"; in other cases peers' "conforming attitudes" reinforce the "need to learn at school." While in most instances the Crucian peer group draws boys out of the education process in the "slow" junior high sections, at least one teacher of an all-boy section was observed to use the peer group to pull boys into English class, even those not assigned to her classroom. Schwartz (1981) has also commented upon the interrelation between classroom structure and peer-group performance. Girls generally, however, are less affected by peer pressure than boys and are more drawn than boys to an adult reference group (Maccoby and Jacklin 1974).

The problem of quality and equity in education

The Crucian case study directs attention to the critical issue of how to provide high-quality education and equity of educational opportunity for all students. We have suggested that where there is compatibility and congruence between student and school culture, as with Crucian girls, the likelihood for tension at school is small. On the other hand, considerable tension, even serious conflict, is likely to result where there is discontinuity and incompatibility between school and student culture, as is the case for Crucian boys. There boys have been judged deviant and penalized by those in authority—principals, teachers, counselors—who enforce the dominant school culture. This demonstrates not a case of minority-group subordination by a dominant ethnic group, which is the focus of most discussions of structural inequality and of studies linking cultural differences to deficits in school settings (Baratz and Baratz 1970; D. Lewis 1976; Ogbu 1979). Rather it shows that a similar situation may exist within a single ethnic group.

Unless teachers and students find constructive ways to negotiate cultural differences, both social and academic problems can be anticipated. If students feel uncomfortable at school and also do not see sufficient value in what they are receiving from school to compensate for their discomfort, they can be expected to find a way out of the system, whether by dropping out voluntarily or causing enough problems either to be pushed out by the school or placed in some special compensatory program.

A cultural compatibility-incompatibility framework is useful for both identifying and alleviating performance dysfunctions that have a cultural basis (Jordan and Tharp 1979; Tharp et al. 1979). It is not cultural incompatibilities per se, however, that cause students to perform poorly in school. Patterns of success in school, as noted, may be seen among immigrant groups, such as the Down Islanders, whose cultural backgrounds differ from that of the dominant host culture. Children will bridge cultural differences, even ignore prejudice and discrimination, if they perceive that their schooling is instrumental to attaining their goals.

The value of school ethnography

Ethnographic studies of schooling must, as Ogbu (1981) argues, employ a multilevel approach if they are to contribute to our "overall conception of schooling" and to aid in constructing a useful body of theory in educational anthropology. Researchers need look not only at teaching and learning as they occur at school, both in and out of the classroom, but also at the interrelation between school, home, community, and workplace. Too few ethnographic studies have investigated adequately how schools relate to the larger society of which they are a part and to the historical, political, social, and economic processes within it. The St. Croix case suggests the necessity of placing any analysis of success in school within a larger social context. The power of ethnography for informing school policy is enhanced where micro- and macroanalyses are combined.

Notes

1   I would like to thank all the students, teachers, and community members in St. Croix, quoted anonymously in this paper, who contributed to the research. Fieldwork was supported by grants from the National Science Foundation and the Graduate School of Education, University of Pittsburgh. An earlier version of the paper was read at the Council on Anthropology and Education annual meeting symposium on "Females and the Educative Process," Washington, D.C., November 1976. I gratefully acknowledge the valuable comments and editorial assistance provided by Lynn L. Marshall in the preparation of this revision.
2   The 55,000 estimate is based on a population of 100,000 for the three islands, St. Thomas, St. John, and St. Croix, for fiscal year 1975 (U.S. Department of the Interior 1976). Fuller explanation of this and other statistics used in the paper are found in Gibson (1976).

References cited

Baratz, Stephen S., and Joan C. Baratz
    1970   Early Childhood Intervention: The Social Science Base of Institutional Racism. Harvard Educational Review 40:29–50.
Bramson, Leon
    1969   An Ethnic Census of St. Croix Schools. Appendix to a Plan for Higher Education on St. Croix. R.O. Cornett. Report prepared for the College of the Virgin Islands. St. Croix, U.S. Virgin Islands. Unpublished manuscript.
DeVos, George
    1975   Ethnic Pluralism: Conflict and Accommodation. *In* Ethnic Identity: Cultural-Continuities and Change. G. DeVos and L. Romanucci-Ross, eds. Palo Alto, Calif.: Mayfield Publishing Co.
Dookhan, Isaac
    1974   A History of the Virgin Islands of the United States. Essex, England: Caribbean Universities Press for the College of the Virgin Islands.
Gibson, Margaret A.
    1976   Ethnicity and Schooling: A Caribbean Case Study. Ph.D. Dissertation. University of Pittsburgh.
    1978   Down Islander Responses to Schooling in the United States Virgin Islands. *In* Perspectives in West Indian Education, N. A. Miles and T. Gardner, eds. pp. 50–67. East Lansing, Mich.: West Indian Association, Michigan State University.
    1981   Punjabi Immigrants in a U.S. School System. Paper presented at the American Anthropological Association annual meeting, Los Angeles, December 5, 1981.
Goetz, Judith P.
    1978   Theoretical Approaches to the Study of Sex-Role Culture in Schools. Anthropology and Education Quarterly 9(1).
Green, James W.
    1972   Social Networks in St. Croix, United States Virgin Islands. Ph.D. Dissertation. University of Washington.
Jordan, C., and R. G. Tharp
    1979   Culture and Education. *In* Perspectives in Cross-Cultural Psychology. A. Marsalla, R. G. Tharp and T. C. Berowski, eds. New York: Academic Press.

Lee, Patrick C., and Nancy B. Gropper
1974   Sex-Role Culture and Educational Practice. Harvard Educational Review 44: 369–410.
Lewis, Diane K.
1976   The Multi-Cultural Education Model and Minorities: Some Reservations. Anthropology and Education Quarterly 8(4):32–37.
Lewis, Gordon K.
1972   The Virgin Islands. Evanston, Ill.: Northwestern University Press.
Lewisohn, Florence
1970   St. Croix under Seven Flags. Hollywood, Fla.: Dukane Press.
Maccoby, Eleanor E., and Carol N. Jacklin
1974   The Psychology of Sex Differences. Stanford, Calif.: Stanford University Press
Ogbu, John U.
1978   Minority Education and Caste: The American System in Cross-Cultural Perspective. New York: Academic Press.
1979   Social Stratification and the Socialization of Competence. Anthropology and Education Quarterly 10(1):3–20.
1981   School Ethnography: A Multilevel Approach. Anthropology and Education Quarterly 12(1):3–29.
Patterson, Orlando
1975   Context and Choice in Ethnic Allegiance: A Theoretical Framework and Caribbean Case Study. In Ethnicity: Theory and Experience. N. Glazer and D. Moynihan, eds. Cambridge: Harvard University.
Schwartz, Frances
1981   Supporting or Subverting Learning: Peer Group Patterns in Four Tracked Schools. Anthropology and Education Quarterly 12(2):99–121.
Senior, Clarence
1947   The Puerto Rican Migrant in St. Croix. Social Science Research Center, University of Puerto Rico (mimeographed).
Tharp, R. G., and C. Jordan, L. Baird, and L. Loganbill
1979   Coming Home to School. 16mm film and videotape cassette. Honolulu: Kamehameha Early Education Project.
U.S. Bureau of the Census
1973   1970 Census of Population. Vol. 1, Characteristics of the Population, Part 55, Virgin Islands. Washington, D.C.: U.S. Government Printing Office.
U.S. Department of the Interior
1976   Annual Report of the U.S. Government Comptroller for the Virgin Islands on the Government of the Virgin Islands, Fiscal Year Ended June 30, 1975. St. Thomas (mimeographed).
Virgin Islands Department of Education
1974   Virgin Islands Public School Retention Report for 1973–74 (mimeographed).
1975   School Enrollment Reports, June 13, 1975 (mimeographed).
Wilson, Peter J.
1973   Crab Antics: The Social Anthropology of English-Speaking Negro Societies of the Caribbean. New Haven, Conn.: Yale University Press.

CHAPTER 20

EMPOWERING MINORITY STUDENTS (1986)
A framework for intervention
Jim Cummins

During the past twenty years educators in the United States have implemented a series of costly reforms aimed at reversing the pattern of school failure among minority students. These have included compensatory programs at the preschool level, myriad forms of bilingual education programs, the hiring of additional aides and remedial personnel, and the institution of safeguards against discriminatory assessment procedures. Yet the dropout rate among Mexican-American and mainland Puerto Rican students remains between 40 and 50 percent compared to 14 percent for whites and 25 percent for blacks (Jusenius & Duarte, 1982). Similarly, almost a decade after the passage of the nondiscriminatory assessment provision of PL94–142,[1] we find Hispanic students in Texas overrepresented by a factor of 300 percent in the "learning disabilities" category (Ortiz & Yates, 1983).

I have suggested that a major reason previous attempts at educational reform have been unsuccessful is that the relationships between teachers and students and between schools and communities have remained essentially unchanged. The required changes involve *personal redefinitions* of the way classroom teachers interact with the children and communities they serve. In other words, legislative and policy reforms may be necessary conditions for effective change, but they are not sufficient. Implementation of change is dependent upon the extent to which educators, both collectively and individually, redefine their roles with respect to minority students and communities.

The purpose of this paper is to propose a theoretical framework for examining the types of personal and institutional redefinitions that are required to reverse the pattern of minority student failure. The framework is based on a series of hypotheses regarding the nature of minority students' educational difficulties. These hypotheses, in turn, lead to predictions regarding the probable effectiveness, or ineffectiveness, of various interventions directed at reversing minority students' school failure.

The framework assigns a central role to three inclusive sets of interactions or power relations: (1) the classroom interactions between teachers and students, (2) relationships between schools and minority communities, and (3) the intergroup power relations within the society as a whole. It assumes that the social organization and bureaucratic constraints within the school reflect not only broader policy and societal factors but also the extent to which *individual educators* accept or challenge the social organization of the school in relation to minority students and communities. Thus, this analysis sketches directions for change for policymakers at all levels of the educational hierarchy and, in particular, for those working directly with minority students and communities.

The policy context

Research data from the United States, Canada, and Europe vary on the extent to which minority students experience academic failure (for reviews, see Cummins, 1984; Ogbu, 1978). For example, in the United States, Hispanic (with the exception of some groups of Cuban students), Native American, and black students do poorly in school compared to most groups of Asian-American (and white) students. In Canada, Franco-Ontarian students in English language programs have tended to perform considerably less well academically than immigrant minority groups (Cummins, 1984), while the same pattern characterizes Finnish students in Sweden (Skutnabb-Kangas, 1984).

The major task of theory and policy is to explain the pattern of school success and failure among minority students. This task applies both to students whose home language and culture differ from those of the school and wider society (language minority students) and to students whose home language is a version of English but whose cultural background is significantly different from that of the school and wider society, such as many black and Hispanic students from English language backgrounds. With respect to language-minority students, recent policy changes in the United States have been based on the assumption that a major cause of students' educational difficulty is the switch between the language of the home and the language of the school. Thus, the apparently plausible assumption that students cannot learn in a language they do not understand gave rise in the late sixties and early seventies to bilingual education programs in which students' home language was used in addition to English as an initial medium of school instruction (Schneider, 1976).

Bilingual programs, however, have met with both strong support and vehement opposition. The debate regarding policy has revolved around two intuitively appealing assumptions. Those who favor bilingual education argue that children cannot learn in a language they do not understand, and, therefore, L1 (first language) instruction is necessary to counteract the negative effects of a home/school linguistic mismatch. The opposition contends that bilingual education is illogical in its implication that less English instruction will lead to more English achievement. It makes more sense, the opponents argue, to provide language-minority students with maximum exposure to English.

Despite the apparent plausibility of each assumption, these two conventional wisdoms (the "linguistic mismatch" and "insufficient exposure" hypotheses) are each patently inadequate. The argument that language minority students fail primarily as a result of a home/school language switch is refuted by the success of many minority students whose instruction has been totally through a second language. Similarly, research in Canada has documented the effectiveness of "French immersion programs" in which English background (majority language) students are instructed largely through French in the early grades as a means of developing fluent bilingualism. In spite of the home/school language switch, students' first language (English) skills develop as well as those of students whose instruction has been totally through English. The fact that the first language has high status and is strongly reinforced in the wider society is usually seen as an important factor in the success of these immersion programs.[2]

The opposing "insufficient exposure" hypothesis, however, fares no better with respect to the research evidence. In fact, the results of virtually every bilingual program that has been evaluated during the past fifty years show either no relationship or a negative relationship between amount of school exposure to the majority language and academic achievement in that language (Baker & de Kanter, 1981; Cummins, 1983a, 1984; Skutnabb-Kangas, 1984). Evaluations of immersion programs for majority students show that students perform as well in English academic skills as comparison groups despite considerably less exposure to English in school. Exactly the same result is obtained for minority students. Promotion of the minority language entails no loss in the development of English academic skills. In other words, language minority students instructed through the minority language (for example, Spanish) for all or part of the school day perform as well in English academic skills as comparable students instructed totally through English.

These results have been interpreted in terms of the "interdependence hypothesis," which proposes that to the extent that instruction through a minority language is effective in developing academic proficiency in the minority language, transfer of this proficiency to the majority language will occur given adequate exposure and motivation to learn the majority language (Cummins, 1979, 1983a, 1984). The interdependence hypothesis is supported by a large body of research from bilingual program evaluations, studies of language use in the home, immigrant student language learning, correlational studies of L1–L2 (second language) relationships, and experimental studies of bilingual information processing (for reviews, see Cummins, 1984; McLaughlin, 1985).

It is not surprising that the two conventional wisdoms inadequately account for the research data, since each involves only a one-dimensional linguistic explanation. The variability of minority students' academic performance under different social and educational conditions indicates that many complex, inter-related factors are at work (Ogbu, 1978; Wong-Fillmore, 1983). In particular, sociological and anthropological research suggests that status and power relations between groups are an important part of any comprehensive account of minority students' school failure (Fishman, 1976; Ogbu, 1978; Paulston, 1980). In addition, a variety of factors related to educational quality and cultural mismatch also appear to be important in mediating minority students' academic progress (Wong-Fillmore, 1983). These factors have been integrated into the design of a theoretical framework that suggests the changes required to reverse minority student failure.

A theoretical framework

The central tenet of the framework is that students from "dominated" societal groups are "empowered" or "disabled" as a direct result of their interactions with educators in the schools. These interactions are mediated by the implicit or explicit role definitions that educators assume in relation to four institutional characteristics of schools. These characteristics reflect the extent to which (1) minority students' language and culture are incorporated into the school program; (2) minority community participation is encouraged as an integral component of children's education; (3) the pedagogy promotes intrinsic motivation on the part of students to use language actively in order to generate their own knowledge; and (4) professionals involved in assessment become advocates for minority students rather than legitimizing the location of the "problem" in the students. For each of these dimensions of school organization the role definitions of educators can be described in terms of a continuum, with one end promoting the empowerment of students and the other contributing to the disabling of students.

The three sets of relationships analyzed in the present framework—majority/minority societal group relations, school/minority community relations, educator/minority student relations—are chosen on the basis of hypotheses regarding the relative ineffectiveness of previous educational reforms and the directions required to reverse minority group school failure. Each of these relationships will be discussed in detail.

Intergroup power relations

When the patterns of minority student school failure are examined from an international perspective, it becomes evident that power and status relations between minority and majority groups exert a major influence on school performance. An example frequently given is the academic failure of Finnish students in Sweden, where they are a low-status group, compared to their success in Australia, where they are regarded as a high-status group (Troike, 1978). Similarly, Ogbu (1978) reports that the outcast Burakumin perform poorly in Japan but as well as other Japanese students in the United States.

Theorists have explained these findings using several constructs. Cummins (1984), for example, discusses the "bicultural ambivalence" (or lack of cultural identification) of students in relation to both the home and school cultures. Ogbu (1978) discusses the "caste" status of minorities that fail academically and ascribes their failure to economic and social discrimination combined with the internalization of the inferior status attributed to them by the dominant group. Feuerstein (1979) attributes academic failure to the disruption of intergenerational transmission processes caused by the alienation of a group from its own culture. In all three conceptions, widespread school failure does not occur in minority groups that are positively oriented towards both their own and the dominant culture, that do not perceive themselves as inferior to the dominant group, and that are not alienated from their own cultural values.

Within the present framework, the *dominant* group controls the institutions and reward systems within society; the *dominated* group (Mullard, 1985) is regarded as inherently inferior by the dominant group and denied access to high-status positions within the institutional structure of the society. As described by Ogbu (1978), the dominated status of a minority group exposes them to conditions that predispose children to school failure even before they come to school. These conditions include limited parental access to economic and educational resources, ambivalence toward cultural transmission and primary language use in the home, and interactional styles that may not prepare students for typical teacher/student interaction patterns in school (Heath, 1983; Wong-Fillmore, 1983). Bicultural ambivalence and less effective cultural transmission among dominated groups are frequently associated with a historical pattern of colonization and subordination by the dominant group. This pattern, for example, characterizes Franco-Ontarian students in Canada, Finns in Sweden, and Hispanic, Native, and black groups in the United States.

Different patterns among other societal groups can clearly be distinguished (Ogbu & Matute-Bianchi, in press). Detailed analysis of patterns of intergroup relations go beyond the scope of this paper. However, it is important to note that the minority groups characterized by widespread school failure tend overwhelmingly to be in a dominated relationship to the majority group.[3]

Empowerment of students

Students who are empowered by their school experiences develop the ability, confidence, and motivation to succeed academically. They participate competently in instruction as a result of having developed a confident cultural identity as well as appropriate school-based knowledge and interactional structures (Cummins, 1983b; Tikunoff, 1983). Students who are disempowered or "disabled" by their school experiences do not develop this type of cognitive/academic and social/emotional foundation. Thus, student empowerment is regarded as both a mediating construct influencing academic performance and as an outcome variable itself.[4]

Although conceptually the cognitive/academic and social/emotional (identity-related) factors are distinct, the data suggest that they are extremely difficult to separate in the case of minority students who are "at risk" academically. For example, data from both Sweden and the United States suggest that minority students who immigrate relatively late (about ten years of age) often appear to have better academic prospects than students of similar socioeconomic status born in the host country (Cummins, 1984; Skutnabb-Kangas, 1984). Is this because their L1 cognitive/academic skills on arrival provide a better foundation for L2 cognitive/academic skills acquisition, or alternatively, because they have not experienced devaluation of their identity in the societal institutions, namely schools of the host country, as has been the case of students born in that setting?

Similarly, the most successful bilingual programs appear to be those that emphasize and use the students' L1 (for reviews, see Cummins 1983a, 1984). Is this success due to better promotion of L1 cognitive/academic skills or to the reinforcement of cultural identity provided by an intensive L1 program? By the same token, is the failure of many minority students in English-only immersion programs a function of cognitive/academic difficulties or of students' ambivalence about the value of their cultural identity (Cohen & Swain, 1976)?

These questions are clearly difficult to answer; the point to be made, however, is that for minority students who have traditionally experienced school failure, there is sufficient overlap in the impact of cognitive/academic and identity factors to justify incorporating these two dimensions within the notion of "student empowerment," while recognizing that under some conditions each dimension may be affected in different ways.

Schools and power

Minority students are disabled or disempowered by schools in very much the same way that their communities are disempowered by interactions with societal institutions. Since equality of opportunity is believed to be a given, it is assumed that individuals are responsible for their own failure and are, therefore, made to feel that they have failed because of their own inferiority, despite, the best efforts of dominant-group institutions and individuals to help them (Skutnabb-Kangas, 1984). This analysis implies that minority students will succeed educationally to the extent that the patterns of interaction in school reverse those that prevail in the society at large.

Four structural elements in the organization of schooling contribute to the extent to which minority students are empowered or disabled. As outlined in Figure 20.1, these elements include the incorporation of minority students' culture and language, inclusion of minority communities in the education of their children, pedagogical assumptions and practices operating in the classroom, and the assessment of minority students.

Cultural/linguistic incorporation

Considerable research data suggest that, for dominated minorities, the extent to which students' language and culture are incorporated into the school program constitutes a significant predictor of academic success (Campos & Keatinge, 1984; Cummins, 1983a; Rosier & Holm, 1980). As outlined earlier, students' school success appears to reflect both the more solid cognitive/academic foundation developed through intensive L1 instruction and the reinforcement of their cultural identity.

Included under incorporation of minority group cultural features is the adjustment of instructional patterns to take account of culturally conditioned learning styles. The Kamehameha Early Education Program in Hawaii provides strong evidence of the importance of this type of cultural incorporation. When reading instruction was changed to permit students to collaborate in discussing and interpreting texts, dramatic improvements were found in both reading and verbal intellectual abilities (Au & Jordan, 1981).

An important issue to consider at this point is why superficially plausible but

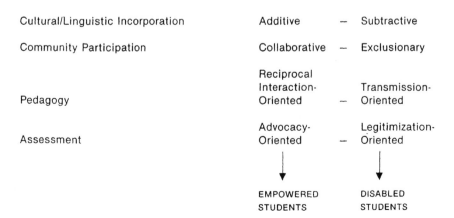

Figure 20.1 Empowerment of minority students: A theoretical framework

patently inadequate assumptions, such as the "insufficient exposure" hypothesis, continue to dominate the policy debate when virtually all the evidence suggests that incorporation of minority students' language and culture into the school program will at least not impede academic progress. In other words, what social function do such arguments serve? Within the context of the present framework, it is suggested that a major reason for the vehement resistance to bilingual programs is that the incorporation of minority languages and cultures into the school program confers status and power (jobs, for example) on the minority group. Consequently, such programs contravene the established pattern of dominant/dominated group relations. Within democratic societies, however, contradictions between the rhetoric of equality and the reality of domination must be obscured. Thus, conventional wisdoms such as the insufficient exposure hypothesis become immune from critical scrutiny, and incompatible evidence is either ignored or dismissed.

Educators' role definitions in relation to the incorporation of minority students' language and culture can be characterized along an "additive-subtractive" dimension.[5] Educators who see their role as adding a second language and cultural affiliation to their students' repertoire are likely to empower students more than those who see their role as replacing or subtracting students' primary language and culture. In addition to the personal and future employment advantages of proficiency in two languages, there is considerable, though not conclusive, evidence that subtle educational advantages result from continued development of both languages among bilingual students. Enhanced metalinguistic development, for example, is frequently found in association with additive bilingualism (Hakuta & Diaz, 1985; McLaughlin, 1984).

It should be noted that an additive orientation does not require the actual teaching of the minority language. In many cases a minority language class may not be possible for reasons such as low concentration of particular groups of minority students. Educators, however, communicate to students and parents in a variety of ways the extent to which the minority language and culture are valued within the context of the school. Even within a monolingual school context, powerful messages can be communicated to students regarding the validity and advantages of language development.

Community participation

Students from dominated communities will be empowered in the school context to the extent that the communities themselves are empowered through their interactions with the school. When educators involve minority parents as partners in their children's education, parents appear to develop a sense of efficacy that communicates itself to children, with positive academic consequences.

Although lip service is paid to community involvement through Parent Advisory Committees (PAC)[6] in many education programs, these committees are frequently manipulated through misinformation and intimidation (Curtis, 1984). The result is that parents from dominated groups retain their powerless status, and their internalized inferiority is reinforced. Children's school failure can then be attributed to the combined effects of parental illiteracy and lack of interest in their children's education. In reality, most parents of minority students have high aspirations for their children and want to be involved in promoting their academic progress (Wong-Fillmore, 1983). However, they often do not know how to help their children academically, and they are excluded from participation by the school. In fact, even their interaction through L1 with their children in the home is frequently regarded by educators as contributing to academic difficulties (Cummins, 1984).

Dramatic changes in children's academic progress can be realized when educators take the initiative to change this exclusionary pattern to one of collaboration. The Haringey project in Britain illustrates just how powerful the effects of simple interventions can be (Tizard, Schofield, & Hewison, 1982). In order to assess the effects of parental involvement in the teaching of reading, the researchers established a project in the London borough of Haringey whereby all children in two primary level experimental classes in two different schools read to their parents at home on a regular basis. The reading progress of these children was compared with that of children in two classes in two different schools who were given extra reading instruction in small groups by an experienced and qualified teacher who worked four half-days at each school every week for the two years of the intervention. Both groups were also compared with a control group that received no treatment.

All the schools were in multiethnic areas, and there were many parents who did not read English or use it at home. It was found, nevertheless, to be both feasible and practicable to involve nearly all the parents in educational activities such as listening to their children read, even when the parents were nonliterate and largely non-English-speaking. It was also found that, almost without exception, parents welcomed the project, agreed to hear their children read, and completed a record card showing what had been read.

The researchers report that parental involvement had a pronounced effect on the students' success in school. Children who read to their parents made significantly greater progress in reading than those who did not engage in this type of literacy sharing. Small-group instruction in reading, given by a highly competent specialist, did not produce improvements comparable to those obtained from the collaboration with parents. In contrast to the home collaboration program, the benefits of extra reading instruction were least apparent for initially low-achieving children.

In addition, the collaboration between teachers and parents was effective for children of all initial levels of performance, including those who, at the beginning of the study, were failing in learning to read. Teachers reported that the children showed an increased interest in school learning and were better behaved. Those teachers involved in the home collaboration found the work with parents worthwhile, and they continued to involve parents with subsequent classes after the experiment was concluded. It is interesting to note that teachers of the control classes also adopted the home collaboration program after the two-year experimental period.

The Haringey project is one example of school/community relations; there are others. The essential point, however, is that the teacher's role in such relations can be characterized along a *collaborative-exclusionary* dimension. Teachers operating at the collaborative end of the continuum actively encourage minority parents to participate in promoting their children's academic progress both in the home and through involvement in classroom activities. A collaborative orientation may require a willingness on the part of the teacher to work closely with mother-tongue teachers or aides in order to communicate effectively, in a noncondescending way, with minority parents. Teachers with an exclusionary orientation, on the other hand, tend to regard teaching as *their* job and are likely to view collaboration with minority parents as either irrelevant or detrimental to children's progress.

Pedagogy

Several investigators have suggested that many "learning disabilities" are pedagogically induced in that children designated "at risk" frequently receive intensive instruction which confines them to a passive role and induces a form of "learned helplessness" (Beers & Beers, 1980; Coles, 1978; Cummins, 1984). This process is illustrated in a microethnographic study of fourteen reading lessons given to West Indian Creole-speakers of English in Toronto, Canada (Ramphal, 1983). It was found that teachers' constant correction of students' miscues prevented students from focusing on the meaning of what they were reading. Moreover, the constant corrections fostered dependent behavior because students knew that whenever they paused at a word the teacher would automatically pronounce it for them. One student was interrupted so often in one of the lessons that he was able to read only one sentence, consisting of three words, uninterrupted. In contrast to a pattern of classroom interaction which promotes instructional dependence, teaching that empowers will aim to liberate students from instruction by encouraging them to become active generators of their knowledge. As Graves (1983) has demonstrated, this type of active knowledge generation can occur when, for example, children create and publish their own books within the classroom.

Two major pedagogical orientations can be distinguished. These differ in the extent to which the teacher retains exclusive control over classroom interaction as opposed to sharing some of this control with students. The dominant instructional model in North American schools has been termed a transmission model (Barnes, 1976; Wells, 1982). This model incorporates essentially the same assumptions about teaching and learning that Freire (1970, 1973) has termed a "banking" model of education. This transmission model will be contrasted with a "reciprocal interaction" model of pedagogy.

The basic premise of the transmission model is that the teacher's task is to impart knowledge or skills that she or he possesses to students who do not yet have these skills. This implies that the teacher initiates and controls the interaction, constantly orienting it towards the achievement of instructional objectives. For example, in first- and second-language programs that stress pattern repetition, the teacher presents the materials, models the language patterns, asks questions, and provides feedback to students about the correctness of their response. The curriculum in these types of programs focuses on the internal structure of the language or subject matter. Consequently, it frequently focuses predominantly on surface features of language or literacy such as handwriting, spelling, and decoding, and emphasizes correct recall of content taught by means of highly structured drills and workbook exercises. It has been argued that a transmission model of teaching contravenes central principles of language and literacy acquisition and that a model allowing for reciprocal interaction among students and teachers represents a more appropriate alternative (Cummins, 1984; Wells, 1982).[7]

A central tenet of the reciprocal interaction model is that "talking and writing are means to learning" (Bullock Report, 1975, p. 50). The use of this model in teaching requires a genuine dialogue between student and teacher in both oral and written modalities, guidance and facilitation rather than control of student learning by the teacher, and the encouragement of student/student talk in a collaborative learning context. This model emphasizes the development of higher level cognitive skills rather than just factual recall, and meaningful language use by students rather than the correction of surface forms. Language use and development are consciously integrated with all curricular content rather than taught as isolated subjects, and tasks are presented to students in ways that generate intrinsic rather than extrinsic motivation. In short, pedagogical approaches that empower students encourage them to assume greater control over setting their own learning goals and to collaborate actively with each other in achieving these goals.

The development of a sense of efficacy and inner direction in the classroom is especially important for students from dominated groups whose experiences so often orient them in the opposite direction. Wong-Fillmore (1983) has reported that Hispanic students learned considerably more English in classrooms that provided opportunities for reciprocal interaction with teachers and peers. Ample opportunities for expressive writing appear to be particularly significant in promoting a sense of academic efficacy among minority students (Cummins, Aguilar, Bascunan, Fiorucci, Sanaoui, & Basman, in press). As expressed by Daiute (1985):

> Children who learn early that writing is not simply an exercise gain a sense of power that gives them confidence to write—and write a lot. . . . Beginning writers who are confident that they have something to say or that they can find out what they need to know can even overcome some limits of training or development. Writers who don't feel that what they say matters have an additional burden that no skills training can help them overcome. (pp. 5–6)

The implications for students from dominated groups are obvious. Too often the instruction they receive convinces them that what they have to say is irrelevant or wrong. The failure of this method of instruction is then taken as an indication that the minority student is of low ability, a verdict frequently confirmed by subsequent assessment procedures.

Assessment

Historically, assessment has played the role of legitimizing the disabling of minority students. In some cases assessment itself may play the primary role, but more often it has been used to locate the "problem" within the minority student, thereby screening from critical scrutiny the subtractive nature of the school program, the exclusionary orientation of teachers towards minority communities, and transmission models of teaching that inhibit students from active participation in learning.

This process is virtually inevitable when the conceptual base for assessment is purely psychoeducational. If the psychologist's task is to discover the causes of a minority student's academic difficulties and the only tools at his or her disposal are psychological tests (in either L1 or L2), then it is hardly surprising that the child's difficulties will be attributed to psychological dysfunctions. The myth of bilingual handicaps that still influences educational policy was generated in exactly this way during the 1920s and 1930s.

Recent studies suggest that despite the appearance of change brought about by PL 94–142, the underlying structure of assessment processes has remained essentially intact. Mehan, Hertweck, and Meihls (in press), for example, report that psychologists continued to test children until they "found" the disability that could be invoked to "explain" the student's apparent academic difficulties. Diagnosis and placement were influenced frequently by factors related to bureaucratic procedures and funding requirements rather than to students' academic performance in the classroom. Rueda and Mercer (1985) have also shown that designation of minority students as "learning disabled" as compared to "language impaired" was strongly influenced by whether a psychologist or a speech pathologist was on the placement committee. In other words, with respect to students' actual behavior, the label was essentially arbitrary. An analysis of more than four hundred psychological assessments of minority students revealed that although no diagnostic conclusions were logically possible in the majority of assessments, psychologists were most reluctant to admit this fact to teachers and parents (Cummins, 1984). In short, the data suggest that the structure within which psychological assessment takes place orients the psychologist to locate the cause of the academic problem within the minority student.

An alternative role definition for psychologists or special educators can be termed an "advocacy" or "delegitimization" role.[8] In this case, their task must be to delegitimize the traditional function of psychological assessment in the educational disabling of minority students by becoming advocates for the child in scrutinizing critically the societal and educational context within which the child has developed (Cazden, 1985). This involves locating the pathology within the societal power relations between dominant and dominated groups, in the reflection of these power relations between school and communities, and in the mental and cultural disabling of minority students that takes place in classrooms. These conditions are a more probable cause of the 300 percent overrepresentation of Texas Hispanic students in the learning disabled category than any intrinsic processing deficit unique to Hispanic children. The training of psychologists and special educators does not prepare them for this advocacy or delegitimization role. From the present perspective, however, it must be emphasized that discriminatory assessment is carried out by well-intentioned individuals who, rather than challenging a socioeducational system that tends to disable minority students, have accepted a role definition and an educational structure that makes discriminatory assessment virtually inevitable.[9]

Empowering minority students: The Carpinteria example

The Spanish-only preschool program of the Carpenteria School District, near Santa Barbara, California, is one of the few programs in the United States that explicitly incorporates the major elements hypothesized in previous sections to empower minority students. Spanish is the exclusive language of instruction, there is a strong community involvement component, and the program is characterized by a coherent philosophy of promoting conceptual development through meaningful linguistic interaction.

The proposal to implement an intensive Spanish-only preschool program in this region was derived from district findings showing that a large majority of the Spanish-speaking students entering kindergarten each year lacked adequate skills to succeed in the kindergarten program. On the School Readiness Inventory, a districtwide screening measure administered to all incoming kindergarten students, Spanish-speaking students tended to average about eight points lower than English-speaking students (approximately 14.5 compared to 23.0, averaged over four years from 1979 to 1982) despite the fact that the test was administered in students' dominant language. A score of 20 or better was viewed by the district as predicting a successful kindergarten year for the child. Prior to the implementation of the experimental program, the Spanish-background children attended a bilingual preschool program—operated either by Head Start or the Community Day Care Center—in which both English and Spanish were used concurrently but with strong emphasis on the development of English skills. According to the district kindergarten teachers, children who had attended these programs often mixed English and Spanish into a "Spanglish."

The major goal of the experimental Spanish-only preschool program was to bring Spanish-dominant children entering kindergarten up to a level of readiness for school similar to that attained by English-speaking children in the community. The project also sought to make parents of the program participants aware of their role as the child's first teacher and to encourage them to provide specific types of experiences for their children in the home.

The preschool program itself involved the integration of language with a large variety of concrete and literacy-related experiences. As summarized in the evaluation report: "The development of language skills in Spanish was foremost in the planning and attention given to every facet of the pre-school day. Language was used constantly for conversing, learning new ideas, concepts and vocabulary, thinking creatively, and problem-solving to give the children the opportunity to develop their language skills in Spanish to as high a degree as possible within the structure of the pre-school day" (Campos & Keatinge, 1984, p. 17).

Participation in the program was on a voluntary basis and students were screened only for age and Spanish-language dominance. Family characteristics of students in the experimental program were typical of other Spanish-speaking families in the community; more than 90 percent were of low socioeconomic status, and the majority worked in agriculture and had an average educational level of about sixth grade.

The program proved to be highly successful in developing students' readiness skills, as evidenced by the average score of 21.6 obtained by the 1982–83 incoming kindergarten students who had been in the program, compared to the score of 23.2 obtained by English-speaking students. A score of 14.6 was obtained by Spanish-speaking students who experienced the regular bilingual preschool program. In 1983–84 the scores of these three groups were 23.3, 23.4, and 16.0, respectively. In other words, the gap between English-background and Spanish-background children in the Spanish-only preschool had disappeared; however, a considerable gap remained for Spanish-background students for whom English was the focus of preschool instruction.

Of special interest is the performance of the experimental program students on the English and Spanish versions of the Bilingual Syntax Measure (BSM), a test of oral syntactic development (Hernandez-Chavez, Burt, & Dulay, 1976). Despite the fact that they experienced an exclusively Spanish preschool program, these students performed better than the other Spanish-speaking students in English (and Spanish) on entry to kindergarten in 1982 and at a similar level in 1983. On entrance to grade one in 1983, the gap had widened considerably, with almost five times as many of the experimental-program students performing at level 5 (fluent English) compared to the other Spanish-background students (47 percent vs. 10 percent) (Campos & Keatinge, 1984).

The evaluation report suggests that

> although project participants were exposed to less *total* English, they, because of their enhanced first language skill and concept knowledge were better able to comprehend the English they were exposed to. This seems to be borne out by comments made by kindergarten teachers in the District about project participants. They are making comments like, "Project participants appear more aware of what is happening around them in the classroom," "They are able to focus on the task at hand better" and "They demonstrate

greater self-confidence in learning situations." All of these traits would tend to enhance the language acquisition process. (Campos & Keatinge, 1984, p. 41)

Campos and Keatinge (1984) also emphasize the consequences of the preschool program for parental participation in their children's education. They note that, according to the school officials, "the parents of project participants are much more aware of and involved in their child's school experience than non-participant parents of Spanish speakers. This is seen as having a positive impact on the future success of the project participants—the greater the involvement of parents, the greater the chances of success of the child" (p. 41).

The major relevance of these findings for educators and policymakers derives from their demonstration that educational programs *can* succeed in preventing the academic failure experienced by many minority students. The corollary is that failure to provide this type of program constitutes the disabling of minority students by the school system. For example, among the students who did not experience the experimental preschool program, the typical pattern of low levels of academic readiness and limited proficiency in both languages was observed. These are the students who are likely to be referred for psychological assessment early in their school careers. This assessment will typically legitimize the inadequate educational provision by attributing students' difficulties to some vacuous category, such as learning disability. By contrast, students who experienced a preschool program in which (a) their cultural identity was reinforced, (b) there was active collaboration with parents, and (c) meaningful use of language was integrated into every aspect of daily activities were developing high levels of conceptual and linguistic skills in *both* languages.

Conclusion

In this article I have proposed a theoretical framework for examining minority students' academic failure and for predicting the effects of educational interventions. Within this framework the educational failure of minority students is analyzed as a function of the extent to which schools reflect or counteract the power relations that exist within the broader society. Specifically, language-minority students' educational progress is strongly influenced by the extent to which individual educators become advocates for the promotion of students' linguistic talents, actively encourage community participation in developing students' academic and cultural resources, and implement pedagogical approaches that succeed in liberating students from instructional dependence.

The educator/student interactions characteristic of the disabling end of the proposed continua reflect the typical patterns of interaction that dominated societal groups have experienced in relation to dominant groups. The intrinsic value of the group is usually denied, and "objective" evidence is accumulated to demonstrate the group's "inferiority." This inferior status is then used as a justification for excluding the group from activities and occupations that entail societal rewards.

In a similar way, the disabling of students is frequently rationalized on the basis of students' "needs." For example, minority students need maximum exposure to English in both the school and home; thus, parents must be told not to interact with children in their mother tongue. Similarly, minority children need a highly structured drill-oriented program in order to maximize time spent on tasks to compensate for their deficient preschool experiences. Minority students also need a comprehensive diagnostic/prescriptive assessment in order to identify the nature of their "problem" and possible remedial interventions.

This analysis suggests a major reason for the relative lack of success of the various educational bandwagons that have characterized the North American crusade against underachievement during the past twenty years. The individual role definitions of educators and the institutional role definitions of schools have remained largely unchanged despite "new and improved" programs and policies. These programs and policies, despite their cost, have simply added a new veneer to the outward facade of the structure that disables minority students. The lip service paid to initial L1 instruction, community involvement, and nondiscriminatory assessment, together with the emphasis on improved teaching techniques, have succeeded primarily in deflecting attention from the attitudes and orientation of educators who interact on a daily basis with minority students. It is in these interactions that students are disabled. In the absence of individual and collective educator role redefinitions, schools will continue to reproduce, in these interactions, the power relations that characterize the wider society and make minority students' academic failure inevitable.

To educators genuinely concerned about alleviating the educational difficulties of minority students and responding to their needs, this conclusion may appear overly bleak. I believe, however, that it is realistic and optimistic, as directions for change are clearly indicated rather than obscured by the overlay of costly reforms that leave the underlying disabling structure essentially intact. Given the societal commitment to maintaining the dominant/dominated power relationships, we can predict that educational changes threatening this structure will be fiercely resisted. This is in fact the case for each of the four structural dimensions discussed earlier.[10]

In order to reverse the pattern of widespread minority group educational failure, educators and policymakers are faced with both a personal and a political challenge. Personally, they must redefine their roles within the classroom, the community, and the broader society so that these role definitions result in interactions that empower rather than disable students. Politically, they must attempt to persuade colleagues and decisionmakers—such as school boards and the public that elects them—of the importance of redefining institutional goals so that the schools transform society by empowering minority students rather than reflect society by disabling them.

Acknowledgments

Discussions at the Symposium on "Minority Languages in Academic Research and Educational Policy" held in Sandbjerg Slot, Denmark, April 1985, contributed to the ideas in the paper. I would like to express my appreciation to the participants at the Symposium and to Safder Alladina, Jan Curtis, David Dolson, Norm Gold, Monica Heller, Dennis Parker, Verity Saifullah Khan, and Tove Skutnabb-Kangas for comments on earlier drafts. I would also like to acknowledge the financial support of the Social Sciences and Humanities Research Council (Grant No. 431–79–0003) which made possible participation in the Sandbjerg Slot symposium.

Notes

1 The Education of All Handicapped Children Act of 1975 (Public Law 94–142) guarantees to all handicapped children in the United States the right to a free public education, to an individualized education program (IEP), to due process, to education in the least segregated environment, and to assessment procedures that are multidimensional and nonculturally discriminatory.

2 For a discussion of the implications of Canadian French immersion programs for the education of minority students, see California State Department of Education (1984).

3 Ogbu (1978), for example, has distinguished between "caste," "immigrant," and "autonomous" minority groups. Caste groups are similar to what has been termed "dominated" groups in the present framework and are the only category of minority groups that tends to fail academically. Immigrant groups have usually come voluntarily to the host society for economic reasons and, unlike caste minorities, have not internalized negative attributions of the dominant group. Ogbu gives Chinese and Japanese groups as examples of "immigrant" minorities. The cultural resources that permit some minority groups to resist discrimination and internalization of negative attributions are still a matter of debate and speculation (for a recent treatment, see Ogbu & Bianchi, in press). The final category distinguished by Ogbu is that of "autonomous" groups who hold a distinct cultural identity but who are not subordinated economically or politically to the dominant group (for example, Jews and Mormons in the United States).

     Failure to take account of these differences among minority groups both in patterns of academic performance and sociohistorical relationships to the dominant group has contributed to the confused state of policymaking with respect to language minority students. The bilingual education policy, for example, has been based on the implicit assumption that the linguistic mismatch hypothesis was valid for all language minority students, and, consequently, the same types of intervention were necessary and appropriate for all students. Clearly, this assumption is open to question.

4 There is no contradiction in postulating student empowerment as both a mediating and an outcome variable. For example, cognitive abilities clearly have the same status in that they contribute to students' school success and can also be regarded as an outcome of schooling.

5 The terms "additive" and "subtractive" bilingualism were coined by Lambert (1975) to refer to the proficient bilingualism associated with positive cognitive outcomes on the one hand, and the limited bilingualism often associated with negative outcomes on the other.

6 PACs were established in some states to provide an institutional structure for minority parent involvement in educational decision making with respect to bilingual programs. In California, for example, a majority of PAC members for any state-funded program was required to be from the program target group. The school plan for use of program funds required signed PAC approval.

7 This "reciprocal interaction" model incorporates proposals about the relation between language and learning made by a variety of investigators, most notably in the Bullock Report (1975), and by Barnes (1976), Lindfors (1980), and Wells (1982). Its application with respect to the promotion of literacy conforms closely to psycholinguistc approaches to reading (Goodman & Goodman, 1977; Holdaway, 1979; Smith 1978) and to the recent emphasis on encouraging expressive writing from the earliest grades (Chomsky, 1981; Giaccobe, 1982; Graves, 1983; Temple, Nathan, & Burris, 1982). Students' microcomputing networks such as the *Computer Chronicles Newswire* (Mehan, Miller-Souviney, & Riel, 1984) represent a particularly promising application of reciprocal interaction model of pedagogy.

8 See Mullard (1985) for a detailed discussion of delegitimization strategies in antiracist education.

9 Clearly, the presence of processing difficulties that are rooted in neurological causes is not being denied for either monolingual or bilingual children. However, in the case of children from dominated minorities, the proportion of disabilities that are neurological in origin is likely to represent only a small fraction of those that derive from educational and social conditions.

10 Although for pedagogy the resistance to sharing control with students goes beyond majority/minority group relations, the same elements are present. If the curriculum is

not predetermined and presequenced, and the students are generating their own knowledge in a critical and creative way, then the reproduction of the societal structure cannot be guaranteed—hence the reluctance to liberate students from instructional dependence.

References

Au, K. H., & Jordan, C. (1981). Teaching reading to Hawaiian children: Finding a culturally appropriate solution. In H. Trueba, G. P. Guthrie, & K. H. Au (Eds.) *Culture and the bilingual classroom: Studies in classroom ethnography* (pp. 139–152). Rowley, MA: Newbury House.

Baker, K. A., & de Kanter, A. A. (1981). *Effectiveness of bilingual education: A review of the literature.* Washington, DC: U.S. Department of Education, Office of Planning and Budget.

Barnes, D. (1976). *From communication to curriculum.* New York: Penguin.

Beers, C. S., & Beers, J. W. (1980). Early identification of learning disabilities: Facts and fallacies. *Elementary School Journal, 81,* 67–76.

Bethell, T. (1979, February). Against bilingual education. *Harper's,* pp. 30–33.

Bullock Report. (1975). *A language for life.* [Report of the Committee of Inquiry appointed by the Secretary of State for Education and Science under the Chairmanship of Sir Alan Bullock]. London: HMSO.

California State Department of Education. (1984). *Studies on immersion education: A collection for United States educators.* Sacramento: Author.

Campos, J., & Keatinge, B. (1984). *The Carpinteria preschool program: Title VII second year evaluation report.* Washington, DC: Department of Education.

Cazden, C. B. (1985, April). *The ESL teacher as advocate.* Plenary presentation to the TESOL Conference, New York.

Chomsky, C. (1981). Write now, read later. In C. Cazden (Ed.), *Language in Early Childhood Education* (2nd ed., pp. 141–149). Washington, DC: National Association for the Education of Young Children.

Cohen, A. D., & Swain, M. (1976). Bilingual education: The immersion model in the North American context. In J. E. Alatis & K. Twaddell (Eds.), *English as a second language in bilingual education* (pp. 55–64). Washington, DC: TESOL.

Coles, G. S. (1978). The learning disabilities test battery: Empirical and social issues. *Harvard Educational Review, 48,* 313–340.

Cummins, J. (1979). Linguistic interdependence and the educational development of bilingual children. *Review of Educational Research, 49,* 222–251.

Cummins, J. (1983a) *Heritage language education: A literature review.* Toronto: Ministry of Education.

Cummins, J. (1983b). Functional language proficiency in context: Classroom participation as an interactive process. In W. J. Tikunoff (Ed.), *Compatibility of the SBIS features with other research on instruction for LEP students* (pp. 109–131). San Francisco: Far West Laboratory.

Cummins, J. (1984). *Bilingualism and special education: Issues in assessment and pedagogy.* Clevedon, Eng.: Multilingual Matters, and San Diego: College Hill Press.

Cummins, J., Aguilar, M., Bascunan, L., Fiorucci, S., Sanaoui, R., & Basman, S. (in press). *Literacy development in heritage language programs.* Toronto: National Heritage Language Resource Unit.

Curtis, J. (1984). *Bilingual education in Calistoga: Not a happy ending.* Report submitted to the Instituto de Lengua y Cultura, Elmira, NY.

Daiute, C. (1985). *Writing and computers.* Reading, MA: Addison-Wesley.

Feuerstein, R. (1979). *The dynamic assessment of retarded performers: The learning potential assessment device, theory, instruments, and techniques.* Baltimore: University Park Press.

Fishman, J. (1976). *Bilingual education: An international sociological perspective.* Rowley, MA: Newbury House.

Freire, P. (1970). *Pedagogy of the oppressed.* New York: Seabury.

Freire, P. (1973). *Education for critical consciousness.* New York: Seabury.

Giacobbe, M. E. (1982). Who says children can't write the first week?, In R. D. Walshe (Ed.), *Donald Graves in Australia: "Children want to write"* (pp. 99–103). Exeter, NH: Heinemann Educational Books.

Goodman, K. S., & Goodman, Y. M. (1977). Learning about psycholinguistic processes by analyzing oral reading. *Harvard Educational Review, 47*, 317–333.

Graves, D. H. (1983). *Writing: Teachers and children at work*. Exeter, NH: Heinemann Educational Books.

Hakuta, K., & Diaz, R. M. (1985). The relationship between degree of bilingualism and cognitive ability: A critical discussion and some new longitudinal data. In K. E. Nelson (Ed.), *Children's language* (Vol. 5, pp. 319–345). Hillsdale, NJ: Erlbaum.

Heath, S. B. (1983). *Ways with words*. Cambridge: Cambridge University Press.

Hernandez-Chavez, E., Burt, M., & Dulay, H. (1976). *The bilingual syntax measure*. New York: The Psychological Corporation.

Holdaway, D. (1979). *The foundations of literacy*. Sydney, Australia: Ashton Scholastic.

Jusenius, C., & Duarte, V. L. (1982). *Hispanics and jobs. Barriers to progress*. Washington, DC: National Commission for Employment Policy.

Lambert, W. E. (1975). Culture and language as factors in learning and education. In A. Wolfgang (Ed.), *Education of immigrant students* (pp. 55–83). Toronto: O.I.S.E.

Lindfors, J. W. (1980). *Children's language and learning*. Englewood Cliffs, NJ: Prentice-Hall.

McLaughlin, B. (1984). Early bilingualism: Methodological and theoretical issues. In M. Paradis & Y. Lebrun (Eds.), *Early bilingualism and child development* (pp. 19–46). Lisse: Swets & Zeitlinger.

McLaughlin, B. (1985). *Second language acquisition in childhood: Vol. 2. School-age children*. Hillsdale, NJ: Erlbaum.

Mehan, H., Hertweck, A., & Meihls, J. L. (in press). *Handicapping the handicapped: Decision making in students' educational careers*. Palo Alto: Stanford University.

Mehan, H., Miller-Souviney, B., & Riel, M. M. (1984). Research currents: Knowledge of text editing and control of literacy skills. *Language Arts, 65*, 154–159.

Mullard, C. (1985, January). *The social dynamic of migrant groups: From progressive to transformative policy in education*. Paper presented at the OECD Conference on Educational Policies and the Minority Social Groups, Paris.

Ogbu, J. U. (1978). *Minority education and caste*. New York: Academic Press.

Ogbu, J. U., & Matute-Bianchi, M. E. (in press). Understanding sociocultural factors: Knowledge, identity and school adjustment. In California State Department of Education (Ed.), *Sociocultural factors and minority student achievement*. Sacramento: Author.

Ortiz, A. A., & Yates, J. R. (1983). Incidence of exceptionality among Hispanics: Implications for manpower planning. *NABE Journal, 7*, 41–54.

Paulston, C. B. (1980). *Bilingual education: Theories and issues*. Rowley, MA: Newbury House.

Ramphal, D. K. *An analysis of reading instruction of West Indian Creole-speaking students*. Unpublished doctoral dissertation, Ontario Institute for Studies in Education, 1983.

Rosier, P., & Holm, W. (1980). *The Rock Point experience: A longitudinal study of a Navajo school*. Washington, DC: Center for Applied Linguistics.

Rueda, R., & Mercer, J. R. (1985, June). *Predictive analysis of decision making with language-minority handicapped children*. Paper presented at the BUENO Center 3rd Annual Symposium on Bilingual Education, Denver.

Schneider, S. G. (1976). *Revolution, reaction or reform: The 1974 Bilingual Education Act*. New York: Las Americas.

Skutnabb-Kangas, T. (1984). *Bilingualism or not: The education of minorities*. Clevedon, Eng.: Multilingual Matters.

Smith, F. (1978). *Understanding reading* (2nd ed.). New York: Holt, Rinehart & Winston.

Temple, C. A., Nathan, R. G. & Burris, N. A. (1982). *The beginnings of writing*. Boston: Allyn & Bacon.

Tikunoff, W.J. (1983). Five significant bilingual instructional features. In W. J. Tikunoff (Ed.), *Compatibility of the SBIS features with other research on instruction for LEP students* (pp. 5–18). San Francisco: Far West Laboratory.

Tizard, J., Schofield, W. N., & Hewison, J. (1982). Collaboration between teachers and parents in assisting children's reading. *British Journal of Educational Psychology, 52,* 1–15.

Troike, R. (1978). Research evidence for the effectiveness of bilingual education. *NABE Journal, 3,* 13–24.

Wells, G. (1982). Language, learning and the curriculum. In G. Wells, (Ed.), *Language, learning and education* (pp. 205–226). Bristol: Centre for the Study of Language and Communication, University of Bristol.

Wong-Fillmore, L. (1983). The language learner as an individual: Implications of research on individual differences for the ESL teacher. In M. A. Clarke & J. Handscombe (Eds.), *On TESOL '82: Pacific perspectives on language learning and teaching* (pp. 157–171). Washington, DC: TESOL.

CHAPTER 21

MISMATCH (2001)
Historical perspectives on schools and students who don't fit them

Sarah Deschenes, Larry Cuban, and David Tyack

Compared to their predecessors, reformers in the standards movement have been making a rather radical argument: that all students can learn and that all students should be held to a high standard of performance. Though many educators have held these beliefs, never before has an educational movement incorporated these tenets so fully into its reform strategy. There have always been children in schools labeled as slow, delinquent, or incapable of learning. They have been held back, put in special classes, tracked, and expelled. Despite the beliefs of the standards movement, though, there will always be a number of children who do not or cannot accomplish what their schools expect them to accomplish.[1] In this way, the standards movement has and will have something in common with every American educational movement of the past century and a half: students who perform poorly and who fail. These students, we argue, are part of a mismatch between schools and groups of students who do not meet the "standards" of their day. We need to pay attention to the fate of the students in the present mismatch; understanding what has happened to these kinds of students in past educational movements can help us understand what might happen to the number of students who will end up failing in the standards movement.[2]

In the early part of the century, Helen Todd gained firsthand knowledge of what happened to students who were expected to fail. Her work as a child-labor inspector in Chicago required her to go into the factories of the city where boys and girls stripped tobacco leaves, made paper boxes, lacquered canes, and ran endless errands. Despite the boredom of repetitive work, long hours, and miserable working conditions, most of the young workers she talked with did not want to go back to school. In 1909, Todd asked 500 children between the ages of 14 and 16 this question: "If your father had a good job and you didn't have to go to work, which would you do—go to school or work in a factory?" More than 80 percent said that they preferred the factory over the school, the paycheck over the report card.[3]

"School ain't no good," said one. "When you works a whole month at school, the teacher she gives you a card to take home that says how you ain't any good. And yer folks hollers on yer an' hits yer." Another told Todd: "You never understands what they tells you in school, and you can learn right off to do things in a factory." Over and over again the young workers told her that teachers beat them for not learning, or not standing up or sitting down on command, or forgetting the correct page in recitation. "Would it not be possible," Todd asked, "to adapt this child of foreign peasants less to education, and adapt education more to the child? ... Nothing that a factory sets them to do is so hard, so terrifying, as learning. ... We do not make our education fit their psychology, their traditions, their environment or inheritance." The students Todd interviewed became labeled as misfits. They were the ones who could not do what their teachers wanted them to do, so their teachers expected them to fail and these students fulfilled their teachers' expectations by leaving schools for the factories.

Over time, educators have identified a number of groups of "problem" students like these: pupils who did not learn efficiently what educators sought to teach; who misbehaved or were truant and delinquent; or who fell behind, were not promoted, and dropped out. In Todd's day, the major targets of concern were the immigrant children, a majority of whom clustered in the lower grades because they failed the annual examinations for promotion from grade to grade. In his book *Laggards in Our Schools*, Leonard Ayres described such children as "thoroughly trained in failure."[4] These students did not fit the mainstream mold; they did not meet schools' expectations for success. As we see it, these differences between schools and students is based on a mismatch between the structure of schools and the social, cultural, or economic backgrounds of students identified as problems. It is not a problem of individual or cultural deficit, as many educators have argued, but this mismatch has had serious consequences for both individuals and groups of students.[5]

Reform movements have sometimes paid attention to these "laggards" and sometimes not, but when such labels are used to identify students, they are more often than not used to identify non-mainstream students. For example, *A Nation at Risk* (1983) stressed in its title and in its text a *nation* at risk but paid little attention to *children* at risk, assuming that what was needed was a return to academic basics, harder work, more of the same (in the shape of more hours of school, more homework, and longer school years), in the hope that intensifying standard schooling would lead to a more competitive economy. The report showed little awareness that schools as currently organized are much better calibrated to serve privileged groups than groups placed on the margin.[6]

The standards movement similarly uses schools and academic achievement as indicators of the country's health. Though it focuses on raising the bar for all groups of students, teachers, and administrators, it makes few provisions for those students who experience a mismatch with schools. Summer school, retention, and extra work are not going to solve the problems made apparent by the chasm between some students and the educational institutions that are failing to serve them. The push in many urban areas for an end to social promotion as part of the standards movement also punishes the student for failure, with little attention to the structures that might be contributing to student failure. In the words of a recent National Research Council report on high-stakes testing, "the lower achievement test scores of racial and ethnic minorities and students from low-income families reflect persistent inequalities in American society and its schools, not inalterable realities about those groups of students. The improper use of test scores can reinforce these inequalities."[7] The use of these test scores to label and categorize certain students as failures would ensure that the standards movement is a direct descendant of other educational movements that have structured failure, intentionally or not, into their goals.

These historical and current constructions of success and of failure as individual problems have legitimized inequalities by "teaching children to blame themselves for failure."[8] Several contemporary historians have grappled with this concern about the failure of distinct groups of students. Some have been concerned with the class-based nature of school structures and the methods schools have used to legitimize individual differences as a way to channel children of different classes into different types of jobs.[9] Others have focused on the effects of differentiated curricula and tracking, though these reforms have been some of the ways schools have tried to adapt their structures to different kinds of students.[10] Still others have looked at how schools took responsibility for and have treated students identified as having "learning difficulties."[11] Although these Progressive era structures and special arrangements were meant as an attempt at equal educational opportunity, in many ways they have provided less opportunity.[12] According to one student of these reforms, the educational structure that leads to failure "was made possible only by the genuine belief—arising from social Darwinism—that children of various social classes, those from native-born and long-established families and those of recent immigrants, differed in fundamental ways."[13] On the other hand, these reforms have also provided greater access to schools during periods of great change in the make-up of the student body, even when they did help to create a new underclass.[14] In either scenario, many students were bound to fail, which was usually predictable based on a student's social class or race.

Despite the persistent presence of students who fail, educators in different movements and at different times have framed the problem of this mismatch in sharply different ways. In turn, these diagnoses led to quite different solutions. We are convinced that unless practitioners, policy makers, and researchers question how problems are framed, including misconceptions and omissions, they may implement solutions, like the elimination of social promotion, that may hurt children rather than help them. This essay is an exploration of what has happened to the students who have not been able to do what educators wanted them to do and of what implications this history might have for students in the current standards-based reform movement. To understand how educators have framed these problems of failure and poor school performance, we first look at how educators have labeled poor school performers in different periods and how these labels reflected both attitudes and institutional conditions. We then summarize four major explanations for why children fail in school—who is to blame and why. We suggest that many of the earlier assumptions and explanations have persisted into modern reform periods, even though rhetoric has changed. Finally we argue that educators need to focus on adapting the school better to the child as the most feasible way to remedy the mismatch in public education and to prevent in the standards movement much of the labeling and stratification that has worked to the detriment of students in previous eras. Teaching children effectively will require a thorough rethinking of both the familiar structures of schooling, such as the graded school, and the gap between the culture of the school and the cultures of the communities they serve. Todd had it right, "We do not make our education fit their psychology, their traditions, their environment or inheritance."[15]

Naming the problem: labels, goals, and structure

Labels are telling. Contained in names, either explicitly or implicitly, are both explanations and prescriptions. The labels that educators and reformers have given to low-performing students contain important information about educators' and reformers' values about success, social diversity, and individual achievement.[16] They give us some insight in to the discrepancies between school-sanctioned values and the backgrounds of the waves of new groups of students attending school throughout the past two centuries and the changes in the types of mismatch over time. Labels also reveal just how embedded categorization and constructions of difference are in the structure of schooling. Over time, as the institutional structure of schools changed and as bureaucracies evolved and expanded, so did the way educators and reformers thought of the students they served. But the fact that there were students labeled as failures remained constant.[17]

In his illuminating study of "educational misfits," Stanley J. Zehm has compiled a list of the varied names given to children who failed to do well in school.[18] He breaks the categories down into four periods: 1800 to 1850, 1850 to 1900, 1900 to 1950, and 1950 to 1970. Although there is clearly an overlap between the periods in the labels and the explanations they pose or imply, there are, nonetheless, discernable changes in the ways the problem of poor performance is posed.

In the first half of the nineteenth century, when the common school was in its formative stage, writers spoke of the poor performer as *dunce, shirker, loafer, idle, vicious, reprobate, depraved, wayward, wrong-doer, sluggish, scapegrace, stupid,* and *incorrigible*. Although terms like *dunce* and *stupid* suggest that educators sometimes saw low achievement as the result of lack of brains, far more common was the belief that the child who did not do well in school was deficient in character. Underlying much of the rhetoric was a set of religious and moral convictions that placed responsibility for behavior and achievement in the sovereign individual.[19]

The primary goals of the common school of that period were to train the rising generation in morality, citizenship, and the basic skills represented by the three *Rs*. Crusaders for the common school shared what later generations might see as a utopian hope: that a relatively brief exposure to the same curriculum might mitigate the advantages enjoyed by the fortunate. In 1830, the workingmen's committee of Philadelphia put the aspiration this way: "Our main object is to secure the benefits of education for those who would otherwise be destitute, and to place them mentally on a level with the most favored in the world's gifts." The common school was to make real "the glorious principle and vivifying declaration that 'all men are born equal.' "[20] More conservative advocates of public education mostly shared the underlying conviction of the workingmen that a proper educational system—one that mixed together all the children of all the people in a free and public institution—could provide equality of educational opportunity that would lead in turn to fair competition in the quest for achievement in later life. If the young were exposed to this similar opportunity, then it was primarily the fault of individual pupils if they did not succeed academically.[21]

Since the United States was primarily a rural nation in this period, the major agency of pubic education was the one-room school in dispersed agricultural communities. One should not romanticize the old-time rural school. Children attended class only a few months a year; formal schooling was only a casual and occasional part of their lives. Often the one room school was a battleground of wills between teacher and students. The child who did not learn easily what the teacher taught or who acted up in the classroom might be whipped—in part because of the assumption that the reluctant learner lacked character. A boy or girl who did not do well in school, however, had many other ways of demonstrating competence and achieving recognition. And in the nongraded, informal structure of the rural school pupils could progress informally at their own pace, making "failure" more obscure.[22]

By contrast, failing and passing were defining features of bureaucratized urban education of the latter part of the nineteenth century. To a large degree failure became an artifact of the rigidity of a system that sought to process large batches of children in uniform ways. The age-graded school, a standardized curriculum, and annual testing programs to determine promotion to the next grade were all based on the notion that children could and should be taught the same subjects, in the same way and at the same pace. The graded school separated children into supposedly uniform groups by age and proficiency. Gradation of classes became popular in large part because it promised to emulate the efficiency that came from the division of labor that was appearing in factories and other modern forms of social organization. Educators arranged the curriculum into standardized parts that corresponded with the grades, year by year. At the end of the year pupils took a test to demonstrate that they were ready to move to the next level; success meant moving up the ladder, failure meant staying in place. At the top of the nineteenth century arch of urban schooling was the meritocratic and graded high school. Tests to enter the high school were often very difficult and flunking rates high. Far from defining failures in these examinations as a problem, many educators saw them instead as a sign that academic standards were being maintained.[23]

How did educators of the latter half of the nineteenth century describe those students who did not keep up with the factory-like pace of the elementary grades and the meritocratic competition of secondary schooling? Zehm finds these epithets emerging in this period: *born-late, sleepy-minded, wandering, overgrown, stubborn, immature, slow, dull.* The religious language of condemnation used in the early nineteenth century was diminishing, but the notion that academic failure came from defects of character or disposition continued. If pupils did not learn, it was largely their own fault. From her rich sample of accounts of nineteenth century classrooms Barbara Jean Finkelstein concluded that teachers believed that "the acquisition of knowledge represented a triumph of the will as well as the intellect. Consistently, . . . teachers treated academic failure, not as evidence of their own inabilities as instructors, but as evidence of the students' personal and moral recalcitrance."[24] Increasingly as the century progressed, educators came to associate the character defects of the pupils with the moral and social inadequacies of their families, especially in the case of immigrants.

But some of the terms that educators used to describe poor performers— *immature, born-late, overgrown*—also showed an emerging notion of the *normal* student that automatically made the *slow* student into a deviant category. The normal student was the one who proceeded at the regular pace demanded by the imperatives of a graded school—the batch processing of pupils by the school bureaucracy. The student who was held back was deviant, "retarded," a failure. By the turn of the twentieth century, careful studies of "retardation" showed that a very large minority of students—perhaps one-third—were denied promotion. The result was that the vast majority of pupils were lumped in the lower grades of the system. In Tennessee in 1906 about 150,000 entered the first grade, 10,000 the eighth, and only 575 graduated from high school. Nationwide the comparable average figures for city schools were 1,000 in first grade, 263 in the eighth grade, and 56 in the high school senior class. In Memphis, Tennessee, 75 percent of Black students were held back.[25] Though this system might have appeared efficient to the urban reformers who created and supported it, for vast numbers—especially immigrants, Blacks, and other groups—it was geared to produce failure.

During the Progressive era of the early twentieth century, educators began to question not the age-graded school but the premise embedded in it that in a democracy all students should have the same education. In the name of efficiency and a new concept of equal opportunity, differentiation became the watchword of the day. Educators believed that their new "science," especially the new technology of testing, provided the key to assigning students systematically to different classes and curricula. This took various forms: tracking pupils by "ability" (educators kept the notion that there were "normal" students but added sub-normal and above-normal categories); offering different curricular options like vocational classes and gender segregated courses; and creating a host of new programs for specific categories of students—retarded, physically handicapped, truants, and hard discipline cases, and groups like Blacks, newly arrived immigrants, and Mexican Americans.[26] Even though some of these attempts to adapt schools to a broader range of talents began as elite programs, like vocational education, most of them soon became educational channels for students who were failing or who were thought to be at risk of failing.

The labels educators used during the period from 1900 to 1950 indicate this shift in the way they conceptualized the "misfits" in the educational system: *pupils of low I.Q., low division pupils, ne'er-do-wells, sub-z group, limited, slow learner, laggards, overage, backward, occupational student, mental deviates,* and (bluntly) *inferior.*[27] The message of the labels was clear: There were students who simply did not have smarts, and the pedagogical answer was to teach them different things in a different way in a different place. Older views about poor performers persisted, however, even in an era when the language of science provided a rationale for discriminating on supposedly objective grounds. The notion that poor performers were morally weak died hard. Two experts on scientific approaches to teaching spelling lamented that bad spellers "do not have a spelling conscience. They must come to feel that to miss a word is to commit a real social offence."[28]

Even before the development of group intelligence testing some educators and lay people were beginning to think that there were students who were incapable of mastering the standard curriculum. When these tests were employed in massive numbers during the 1920s, they seemed to confirm the prejudice that there were not only incapable individuals but incapable groups (though even the most enthusiastic testers admitted that there might be talented persons in even the most unpromising ethnic or class groupings).[29] The superintendent of schools in Newark, New Jersey, argued in 1920 that the schools must adapt to provide "equal opportunity" to children who were genetically inferior:

> All children are not born with the same endowments or possibilities; they cannot be made equal in gifts or development or efficiency. The ultimate barriers are set by a power inexorable. There are in the schools tens of thousands of children over age physiologically, but only five, six, or seven years old mentally. The educational system must therefore be adjusted to meet this condition, so that the democratic theory of "equal opportunity" for all may be fully exemplified as well as preached.[30]

In practice, testing was used not so much to diagnose specific learning problems and to devise appropriate learning strategies (surely valuable uses of the new technology of assessment) as to isolate the *ne'er-do-wells* from the mainstream of the graded school for the *normal* students.

As a way of moving large numbers of "normal" students through a standardized curriculum in a fairly efficient manner, the age-graded school had been a stunning success, and few educators have wanted then or since to change its basic structure. It worked better, however, during an era when academic misfits could and did simply quit school and go to work than during the twentieth century, when compulsory schooling and child labor laws compelled hundreds of thousands of students to continue in schools that were mismatched to their class and ethnic cultures and often scornful about their abilities and aspirations. The administrative progressives used curricular differentiation to protect the pupils in the pedagogical mainstream—mostly middle class—from being "retarded" by the nonmainstreamers. In the process, they marginalized and segregated the misfits, sometimes in programs that were mere holding bins for "laggards" until they could be eliminated from school.[31]

For most of the twentieth century, educators themselves took the initiative in devising solutions to the mismatch of student and school. But beginning in the late 1950s, a new set of actors entered school politics and sought to redefine both the problem and the solutions. Starting with Blacks in the civil rights movement and spreading to other groups—Hispanics, women, advocates for the handicapped, Native Americans, and others—outsiders who had been ignored or underserved demanded new influence over education. These groups rejected earlier diagnoses of the problem of poor performers, especially those that located the trouble in the defects of individuals (whether of character or chromosomes). Instead, they demanded equality of access (as in integration); programs that would equalize resources or even compensate for past discrimination; a broadening of the curriculum to honor the cultural diversity of the society; and various other ways of attacking the obvious and hidden injuries of race, gender, class, and cultural difference. The protesters wanted to adapt the school better to the child and called for a halt in blaming the victim.[32]

Some of the new names reformers gave to children who were not performing well in school began to reflect new ways of seeing. Such terms as these, emerging in the period from 1950–1980, suggested that the blame lay more with the school than with the students: *the rejected, educationally handicapped, forgotten children, educationally deprived, culturally different*, and *pushouts*. But the older habits of thought remained embedded in labels like these: *socially maladjusted, terminal students, marginal children, immature learners, educationally difficult, unwilling learners*, and *dullards*. Such language still located the cause of the trouble largely with the student, though protest groups made educators generally more euphemistic, as in names like *bluebirds* and *less fortunate*.[33]

When educators responded to the demands of protest groups for greater social justice in education, they sometimes based their actions on old diagnoses. Some programs—like pull-out remedial help under Title I—appeared to respond to the need to adapt schools better to "different" children, but in practice they often continued to segregate and label children, as had differentiation in the Progressive era. Much of early compensatory education was based on a concept of deprivation and cultural deficit rather than honoring cultural difference and sharing power with dispossessed groups.[34] The outsiders in protest movements were not satisfied with such warmed-over solutions, and they raised fundamental questions not addressed by the old diagnoses. They called on federal and state governments and local districts to improve schooling for those who had been cheated in their education. They questioned the use of intelligence tests and the practice of tracking. They illuminated the bias and narrowness of the curriculum and the variety of forms of institutional racism and sexism. They asked why it was that groups like Blacks and Mexican Americans were so overrepresented in classes for the mentally retarded. They called for attention to linguistic and cultural differences and promoted bilingual and multicultural education. In raising such issues they were rejecting the labels that had denigrated their children. They were creating an agenda of change that went beyond efforts to intensify and make more efficient the traditional pattern of schooling and sought to fundamentally reexamine the institutional structures that led to these biases, similar to the kind of reexamination we discuss below.

In each era, educators have used these labels in part to explain away failure. There has always been a reason for failure that, for the most part, has been rooted in individual or cultural deficit. The institution of schooling has won out in each of these eras. Labels have created categories of individual failure and have left school structures largely intact. These labels create a powerful argument for what might happen to the standards movement: Which students will be labeled and how?

These labels also embody certain constructions of failure in different periods, which both reflect and influence the way educators have viewed students and their relationship to schools over time. Whether it was individual inability, "slowness," lack of motivation, or any other kind of implicit characterization in these labels, these judgements and their underlying notions of success and failure indicated to educators and reformers certain ways to explain why students were performing poorly. The next section investigates these explanations more in depth.

Assigning blame

Historically, students, families, inefficiency in schools, and cultural difference have been identified as the sources for failure. In different ways, each of these explanations points to the mismatch between certain groups of students and their schools. Each defines failure as a problem of fit, and the only reform period in which schools did change in response to students—the Progressive era—yielded less than desirable results for students who did poorly in traditional classroom structures. We first look at four ways educators and reformers have assigned blame for failure. We then propose a different historical explanation that locates this problem in a mismatch between students and the structure of schools and in schools' resistance to adapting to the changing needs of their student populations. We also consider how the current standards movement might reinforce existing age graded institutional structures.

> A. *Students who do poorly in school have character defects or are responsible for their own performance.* As the previous section demonstrated, locating responsibility in the individual—a response with deep roots in American ways of thinking—has been the dominant way of framing the problem.[35] In the educational system of the nineteenth and early twentieth centuries, this manifested itself in a focus first on character deficiencies, which reformers believed children could overcome, and later on students' low IQs, which students were thought to have no control over. Labels like *ne'er-do-well*, *sleepy-minded*, and *limited* exemplify this way of thinking about students.
>
> In the nineteenth century, when notions of "intelligence" and cultural differences were rudimentary, educators typically explained poor academic performance in terms of flawed character: The student was a *shirker* or was *depraved*. Individual-based solutions flowing from this explanation centered on the ability of teachers to exhort or coerce the lazy or immoral children to achieve at a higher level.

In the twentieth century, when the "science" of education informed professional decision making, educators leaned heavily on psychological interpretations for school failure, primarily low I.Q. and inadequate motivation. This science of individual differences led to new responses: using intelligence tests to segregate pupils into different tracks or curricula presumably adapted to their talents; altering expectations for performance and seeking to find different motivations and incentives for different kinds of pupils; and, when all else failed, eliminating misfits from the mainstream by assigning them to special classes or letting them drop out at the earliest opportunity.

The belief that the school system was basically sound and the individual was defective in character, genes, or motivation has persisted. Current proposals requiring students to attend summer school or other remedial programs as part of the elimination of social promotion is consistent with framing the problem as an individual student's responsibility.

B.   *Families from certain cultural backgrounds prepare children poorly for school and give them little support for achievement as they pass through the elementary and secondary grades.* Some of the moral complaints against children in the nineteenth century spilled over to their parents: Parents were intemperate, ignorant, undisciplined, and unfamiliar with American values and customs. In the twentieth century, with the rise of social science, finger pointing became less moralistic. But still families were the culprit in theories that stressed the culture of poverty or the supposed cultural deficits in parents who produced seemingly unteachable children.[36] Some of the labels used for students in these periods have some implications for families as well; if a child was *wayward* or was a *laggard*, why didn't the parents do anything to address these problems?

If families were to blame for the academic inadequacies of their children—and this was a popular theory—it was not entirely clear how schools could improve parents. One solution was to create in the school a counterculture that would overcome the defective socialization children received at home. An extreme example of this way of thinking can be found in the attempt of the Bureau of Indian Affairs to place the younger generation in boarding schools far from their communities.[37] A more common strategy was to "Americanize" the children of immigrants in the hope that some of their acquired learning would rub off at home. The kindergarten, in particular, targeted immigrant parents as much as five-year-olds.[38] Some city school systems sought to give adults special training, to work with settlement houses, and to use community schools as centers of "Americanization." Litigation to force parents to obey compulsory school attendance laws concentrated on urban immigrants.[39]

C.   *The structure of the school system is insufficiently differentiated to fit the range of intellectual abilities and different destinies in life of its heterogeneous student body.* In the Progressive era, many reformers argued that high rates of failure stemmed from the rigidity of the standardized curriculum and rigidity of age grading and promotion in schools. They did not frontally attack the graded school *per se*, for it had served their purposes well for the majority of students. Rather, they argued that a single, lockstep course of studies produced failures because not all students were capable of studying the same subjects at the same rate of progress.[40] Schools would have to adjust to accommodate the *low-division pupils, sub-z group*, and *occupational students*.

This interpretation of failure obviously was closely related to the first—the explanation of failure in terms of individual deficits. It focused, however, on institutional changes that would leave intact the basic system of age-graded schools while finding places where the "laggards" could proceed at a slower pace and often in a different direction from the "normal" students. The remedy, then, was a differentiation of curriculum, grouping, and methods of teaching. This search for organizational causes and solutions led to ability grouping in elementary schools and to specialized curricular tracks in high schools, coupled with an apparatus of testing and counseling. Only rarely did such administrative changes reveal an understanding of cultural differences or conflicts of value between different segments of society. Rather, as one phase of a top-down drive to make schools "socially efficient," it was a fundamentally conservative movement that took as a starting point the assumption that educational planners should find a place for the misfits and prepare them for their likely (subordinate) roles in later life.[41] It reified categories like "slow learner" or "hand-minded" or "ne'er-do-well" and attempted to find appropriate institutional niches for them. This differentiation often entailed watering down the standard curriculum for the "laggards" or assigning them to an inferior and segregated position within the system.[42]

D. *Children often fail academically because the culture of the school is so different from the cultural backgrounds of the communities they serve.* This interpretation places the responsibility for school failure not on culturally different families and individuals but rather on the schools themselves, arguing that it is the schools, not the clients, that should adapt to social diversity and the *forgotten children, culturally different*, and *pushouts*. Early advocates of this perspective, like Leonard Covello, Principal of New York City's Benjamin Franklin High School, argued that schools should be community-based and responsive to the different ethnic and class backgrounds of the students and families. Covello attacked the cultural bias in I.Q. tests, for example, objected to the assumption that Italian-American youth in East Harlem chiefly needed vocational education, and claimed that the curriculum should reflect the linguistic and cultural traditions represented in the community.[43] Covello's community-centered school is one example of an attempt to remedy the mismatch between school structures and students.

The social movements of the 1960s and 1970s heightened awareness of the multicultural character of American society and the culturally mono-chromatic environment of most schools. In this view, the standardized age-graded school was insensitive to low-income ethnic and racial minorities and largely unconsciously embodied the dominant ethos of middle-class, White, Anglo-Saxon values, attitudes, and behavior. Intent on imposing (through teachers, curriculum, and daily routines) mainstream culture on the children, such schools displayed little respect for differences in language, beliefs, and customs.[44] In this view, teachers were often unconscious of the ways in which they served as agents of a rigid cultural system geared to standardizing their pupils. Constantly correcting nonmainstream children's speech, as if to say that there was only one acceptable way to speak in any situation, is one example of this rigidity. The teachers unwittingly became active agents in creating student failure. As a result classrooms became cultural battlegrounds in which teachers communicated lower expectations, failed to connect with their culturally different students, and thus contributed to low academic performance and high dropout rates. The analysis of cultural bias and rigidity led to solutions that focused largely on making the curriculum more multicultural, increasing the cultural sensitivity and knowledge of teachers, and building school programs around values that reflected those of surrounding ethnic communities.[45]

Each of these different diagnoses of poor school performance led to different conclusions. Blaming the individual student or the family provided an alibi, not a solution. Blaming the rigidity of traditional education for its lack of proper niches for the "ne'er-do-well" exposed institutional faults, but it led to policies that all too often sequestered the misfits in an inferior and segregated corner of the system. Spot-lighting the gaps between the culture of the school and the cultural backgrounds of students provided a useful corrective to the earlier ethnocentric explanations that blamed the students and parents, but the cultural conflict explanation typically did not question the basic structure and processes of schooling. Focusing on the cultural biases of teachers ran the danger of personalizing the answer: What was needed was more sensitive instructors (but where were they to come from and what were they to do once in the classroom?). Enriching the curriculum by adding Black history or bilingual strategies of instruction was surely an improvement, but such attempts to make schools multicultural typically were just that: additions to a familiar age-graded pattern of instruction, not recasting the character of the institution.

The standards movement departs from these previous explanations in the way it frames students and performance, but not in the solutions it offers students who do not fit its structures. Note that almost all of these previous problem definitions and the solutions they generated left the core structure and assumptions of the institution—in particular the age-graded school as the chief building block—basically untouched. Although the administrative progressives did recognize the regimentation inherent in traditional graded instruction, they solved the problem of the misfits not by questioning the assumptions underlying the age-graded school but by making new niches for the unsuccessful. The standards movement, though, questions the assumptions if not the structure of schooling, arguing that all students can be held and should be held to high levels of performance. The contrast is striking between current reforms, in which all students would ideally get the same curriculum (though this is not always the case), and the nineteenth century, when individual students were judged on their character or individual ability, or the Progressive era, when reformers were proud of finding a different niche or a track for every student. The problem is now that the structure of schools still does not allow for the variety of students and the variety of areas in which they might excel. As a result, students who do not excel in the age-graded, narrowly academic world may once again be subject to the same kinds of labeling and failure that their predecessors were.

The pedagogical assumptions and practices embedded in the urban age-graded school—the scheduling of time, the segmentation of the curriculum, grouping according to notions of "ability," annual promotions, elaborate bureaucratic structures of control, and views of learning, teaching, and knowledge—remained largely unquestioned throughout the century. There were consequently not many options for solutions outside this structure. We see a continuation of this today with standards-based reforms focused on requiring low-performing students to do more during the school year and during the summer or repeat a year of school rather than questioning why these students are failing and what structures in their schooling lead to failure. The standards movement, admirable in its goal of raising the bar for the entire educational system, must ask how it can ensure that this mismatch does not continue to let success elude large groups of students, many of whom live in impoverished urban and rural districts. The focus must be on what happens to the students who do not fit the mainstream academic mold and how school structures can change to meet their needs.

Where do we go from here?

Thus far we have argued that American public schools have always included large numbers of children who do not meet schools' expectations for success. There never was a golden age when educators held the key to success for all pupils, and there will, we imagine, always be children who will not fit the educational structures of their day. As labels and diagnoses shifted over time and as the social constructions of success and failure changed, people fixed on partial solutions or were more concerned with excuses than with rethinking schooling for such students in a comprehensive way. They focused more on the student side of the school-student mismatch than on refashioning the school to fit the children. One reason is that for a majority of students—the middle-class mainstream—the standard form of schooling worked reasonably well, and the political power lay with them rather than with the outsiders.

Recent reforms around raising standards have maintained the structures that are working for the middle-class mainstream students and are still for the most part focused on the student side of the equation. These reforms include many high-stakes consequences for individual performance, most notably placing students in tracks, withholding promotion, or preventing graduation for failing grades.[46] California, Delaware, South Carolina, and Wisconsin have had current plans to end social promotion, but there are only thirteen states that require and fund programs to help low-achieving students meet state standards.[47] There is little evidence to support this strategy of eliminating social promotion. Studies have shown that children who are held back tend to drop out more often than those who are not held back and that students learn more if promoted than if retained.[48] Reformers and policy makers are pushing children further out of the mainstream by holding them back.

Policy makers' focus on promotion and retention in the standards movement is to some extent misguided. There is less thought given to who is failing, why they are failing, and what schools can do about this failure than there is to political strategy and accountability for accountability's sake. The students who are suffering are the same students who have felt the brunt of the school-student mismatch in the past: poor and minority children. It is not the White, middle-class students who are suffering from high-stakes strategies. Michelle Fine once wondered, though, what would happen if failure were the rule in schools that serve White, middle-class boys and girls: "How would federal and state governments respond if 50 percent of White, middle-class students dropped out of high school? Would they increase promotional standards, toughen testing and standardization, cut access to school lunches, reduce student options in coursework, and make it harder to graduate? Or would they reassess the policies, structures, and practices of educators?"[49]

We think it is important to ask what the legacy of this history of failure and of mismatches is: What will happen to the students who experience a mismatch in the standards movement and what will ultimately happen to the movement itself? What does it mean to say that all children can learn and at the same time create severe penalties for failure through high-stakes accountability? We don't see failure going away any time soon. We imagine that there will be new kinds of labels for the students who fail to meet high expectations in the standards movement. Maybe they will be similar to the individual deficit explanations of the nineteenth century or maybe we will revert to the cultural deficit arguments of the mid-twentieth century if ethnic or racial groups fail in large numbers. And what if we find that not all children can reach the same high standard? Will that mean the end of the movement or will it mean that students are punished even more for not performing?

The history of the education of students in this mismatch underscores three points relevant to the standards movement. One is that most efforts have concentrated on fitting the pupil to the school or on supplying alibis for the mismatch rather than looking to institutional factors to explain failure. The second is that broader social inequalities must be addressed in conjunction with failure and discrepancies in schools to give students their best shot at success. The third is that reforms have mostly been piecemeal and disconnected rather than comprehensive and coordinated. Standards-based reform has been assembled into a coherent design, but without alignment with other kinds of change that children need for success. In addition, proposals for reform have spilled forth from all sides of the political and pedagogical spectrum.

If our analysis is convincing, three policy implications might follow that would help the standards movement learn from the history of mismatches. One is that hard as it may be to change the school to match the student, it is a more promising strategy than trying to fit the student to the school. A second would be to acknowledge and address social inequality by tempering some of the high-stakes features of the reforms and to link up with other social reform movements, particularly in inner city neighborhoods. Poorer neighborhoods by definition have fewer resources than their wealthier suburban counterparts and in many cases have a harder time meeting standards because of this. The last implication is to undertake comprehensive changes that take no features of current schools for granted. Humans have created the structure of schools and humans can change them, however much the status quo seems to be etched in stone.

Fitting the school and the school system to the student

Consider features of urban education that have typically been taken for granted but which in the present time may be dysfunctional. One of these is the age-graded school itself, preserved amid almost all reform movements (true, there was a brief attempt to create "ungraded" classrooms in the 1960s, but this was largely unsuccessful).[50] From the age-graded school flowed many institutional arrangements: a self-contained classroom with one teacher and a group of students of comparable age and, supposedly, of academic attainment; the isolation of teachers from one another in their workplaces; a sequential curriculum, often cut up in distinct segments; an expandable structure in which classrooms could be added to one another in an "eggcrate" building that could reach a size so large that staff and students often knew only a fraction of the school "community"; the notion that there was a normal progression from grade to grade, sometimes enforced by competency testing for promotion.

Although such an organization for teaching was probably an improvement over the chaotic nonsystem it replaced, it is apparent that if one were to start anew in designing a school, some of these features would hardly recommend themselves, at least for nonmainstream children. For example, the 1988 Carnegie report *An Imperiled Generation* recommended that urban schools should be nongraded for children who now attend kindergarten through fourth grade and that a "transition school" of flexible years and schedule replace the current high school. In addition, Kentucky's reforms under the Kentucky Education Reform Act (KERA) use primary units (K-3) instead of grades. We have already suggested that the notion of "normal" progress from grade to grade was an invention that produced failure for some students as a necessary consequence of its own rigidity. Learning should be a series of personal benchmarks toward a larger set of goals, not a public display of passing and failing. If schools are really to be communities—an idea brilliantly described by John Dewey in *School and Society*—it is clear that they should be much smaller than most urban schools and offer much more opportunity for collaboration among teachers and continuity of instruction for teachers and the taught.[51] Specialization of high schools by curricular tracks puts the burden of integration of knowledge on students and divides curricula—and hence students—into hierarchies.

Like the age-graded school, bureaucratic governance of urban schools is an abiding legacy of the past. In its origins it represented a dream that experts could design and control a "one best system," free from input from local lay people. This separation of the planning of instruction from its execution—administration from teaching—led to the paperwork empires and fragmented centralization characteristic of many urban systems today in which accounting often takes the place of adaptive planning.[52] Again, few educators today would willingly recreate a system of control that produced such red tape and distractions from the real work of teaching (though vested interests protect the bureaucracy). Instead, those who would adapt schools to the urban communities they serve commonly argue for much greater school site control and input from parents. As school leaders like Leonard Covello have shown, really adapting the school to the cultural backgrounds and values of the communities they serve requires a high degree of self-determination and flexibility at the local level.[53] To put such "wisdom of practice" into effect demands freedom from the legacy of centralized control.

Examining broad social inequalities

As the National Research Council's report on high-stakes testing suggests, the use of these tests has the potential to reinforce social, racial, and ethnic inequalities. By forcing large numbers of urban youth to attend summer school or to repeat a year, and by placing these youth at risk of dropping out, high-stakes strategies in the standards movement are doing a disservice to many students. These reforms are anchored in narrow conceptions of how to understand success and failure. Students might flourish in one arena and not in another. For example, students who do not do well in academic settings might be great athletes or conscientious community members or outstanding artists. The standards movement does not have the capacity to capture all of these different ways of succeeding and, as a result, might contribute to the social inequalities already found in inner-city communities.

Promotion and retention are not the responsibility of individual students alone. There are whole systems involved in the fate of any one student, and the poorer urban students are the ones suffering at the hands of high-stakes measures.

Although all children can certainly learn, they have a harder time doing so in schools that are falling down and that have teachers teaching outside their specialty or in communities where there are empty lots and high crime rates. Failure is just as much a result of these conditions as it is of individual factors.

Some possibilities for addressing broader social inequalities in addition to educational inequalities include schools and community development groups working together to address neighborhood conditions or engaging in reforms like Beacon schools that bring schools and community organizations together in a shared governance structure to operate community centers after school and on weekends, focusing on comprehensive and healthy youth development as well as community-building work.[54] Schools could also engage students themselves in the work of their community, as Leonard Covello did, to get them to recognize and address inequalities in their own communities.

Undertaking comprehensive change

As suggested by the other two policy implications, change that is done in isolation—focused on the confines of the school campus or only on the changes that might occur within individual students—will fail for its short-sightedness. Whole schools, whole systems, whole neighborhoods must change to reap the benefits of educational reform. The characteristics of a reformulated, standards-based education we have been describing exist in scattered places where administrators, teachers, and parents work together to support all children. Such efforts alter what happens routinely in schools and demonstrate a willingness to question what is now taken for granted. But such successful programs typically lie at the periphery; the core urban school systems remain largely untouched by these efforts. The challenge is to develop a comprehensive vision of what effective schools could be and do and to win the political support that might transform them, over time, into reality.[55]

The standards movement does not have to be part of the legacy of this history of failure and mismatches. A reform like Covello's community-centered school suggests alternative ways to frame student success and failure and rethink how schools can fit the educational needs of students. Reflecting on his work in a public school for boys in East Harlem, Covello wrote,

> To me, failure at any age . . . is something the seriousness of which cannot be exaggerated. Forcing a boy who is an academic failure, or even a behavior problem, out of school solves nothing at all. In fact, it does irreparable harm to the student and merely shifts the responsibility from the school to a society which is ill-equipped to handle the problem. The solution must be found within the school itself and the stigma of failure must be placed in a boy as seldom as possible.[56]

He respected and attended to the cultural background of his students while maintaining high expectations for their academic achievement. He also went to great lengths to involve the community in the life of the school and involve the school in the life of the community by addressing housing concerns in the community, encouraging his students to work with community groups, creating a community center next to the school, and establishing an Old Friendship Club for boys who had already dropped out of school. Through these efforts, Covello demonstrated that it is possible to create a school structure that supports success rather than failure and brings together academic standards and nonmainstream students. With attention to the policy implications discussed above and with its worthy goals of getting all students to learn at high levels, we believe the standards movement might be able to achieve some of this success.

Notes

1   For a full treatment of arguments about the dilution of curriculum since the early twentieth century and the case for raising standards of performance, see David L. Angus and Jeffrey E. Mirel, *The Failed Promise of the American High School, 1890–1995* (New York; Teachers College Press, 1999); Diana Ravitch, *The Troubled Crusade: American Education, 1945–1980* (New York: Basic Books, 1983); Ravitch and Maris Vinovskis, eds., *Learning From the Past: What History Teaches Us About School Reform* (Baltimore: Johns Hopkins University Press, 1995).

2   For a discussion of current structures of failure in school systems, see Raymond P. McDermott, "Achieving School Failure 1972–1997," in George D. Spindler, ed., *Education and Cultural Process: Anthropological Approaches* (Prospect Heights, IL: Waveland Press, 1997).

3   Helen Todd, "Why Children Work: The Children's Answer," *McClure's Magazine* 40 (April 1913): 68–79.

4   Leonard Ayres, *Laggards in Our Schools: A Study of Retardation and Elimination in City School Systems* (New York: Survey Associates, 1913): 200.

5   Although it is clear that not all immigrants, working-class students, or students of ethnic and racial minority groups did poorly in school or were subject to this mismatch, the majority of the students who were labeled failures did come from these groups. This incongruity cannot be applied as a blanket explanation across the United States and across time, either. Local variation and significant differences between urban and rural schooling surely had an impact on how and whether this mismatch manifested itself in local communities. We think it is important nevertheless to take note of this inconsistency in an era when high standards, test scores, and strict accountability measures threaten the welfare of students who might still be feeling the impact of this mismatch.

6   National Commission on Excellence in Education, *A Nation at Risk: The Imperative for Educational Reform: A Report to the Nation and the Secretary of Education* (Washington, DC: Author, 1983).

7   National Research Council Committee on Appropriate Test Use, *High Stakes: Testing for Tracking, Promotion, and Graduation* (Washington, DC: National Academy Press, 1999).

8   Michael Katz, "Education and Inequality: A Historical Perspective," in *Social History and Social Policy*, David Rothman and Stanton Wheeler, eds. (New York: Academic Press, 1981): 91; David Tyack, "Constructing Difference: Historical Reflections on Schooling and Social Diversity," *Teachers College Record* 95 (Fall 1993): 9–34.

9   See, for example, Michael Katz, *Class, Bureaucracy, and Schools: The Illusion of Educational Change in America* (New York: Praeger, 1975).

10 For example, Jeannie Oakes, *Keeping Track: How Schools Structure Inequality* (New Haven: Yale University Press, 1985).

11 Barry Franklin, *From "Backwardness" to "At-Risk": Childhood Learning Difficulties and the Contradictions of Reform* (Albany: SUNY Press, 1994).

12 David Tyack, *The One Best System: A History of American Urban Education* (Cambridge: Harvard University Press, 1974).

13 Oakes, 35.

14 Barry Franklin, "Progressivism and Curriculum Differentiation: Special Classes in the Atlanta Public Schools, 1898–1923," *History of Education Quarterly* 29 (1989): 571–593.

15 Todd, 74, 76.

16 See Tyack, "Constructing Difference" on social diversity and values.

17 For another discussion of the impact of labels for low achieving students, see Franklin, *From "Backwardness" to "At-Risk."*

18 Stanley J. Zehm, *Educational Misfits: A Study of Poor Performers in the English Class, 1825–1925* (Unpublished Ph.D. dissertation, Stanford University, 1973).
19 Ibid., Appendix A.
20 Quoted in David B. Tyack, ed., *Turning Points in American Educational History* (Waltham, MA: Blaisdell Publishing Company, 1967): 145, 143.
21 Carl Kaestle, *Pillars of the Republic* (New York: Hill and Wang, 1983); David Tyack and Elisabeth Hansot, *Managers of Virtue: Public School Leadership in America, 1820–1980* (New York: Basic Books, 1982).
22 Zehm, *Educational Misfits*, chapter 2; Wayne Edison Fuller, *The Old Country School: The Story of Rural Education in the Middle West* (Chicago: University of Chicago Press, 1982).
23 David F. Labaree, *The Making of an American High School: The Credentials Market and the Central High School of Philadelphia, 1838–1939* (New Haven: Yale University Press, 1988); William Reese, *The Origins of the American High School* (New Haven; Yale University Press, 1995); Tyack, *The One Best System: A History of American Urban Education* (Cambridge: Harvard University Press, 1974); Maris Vinovskis, *History and Educational Policymaking* (New Haven: Yale University Press, 1999).
24 Barbara Jean Finkelstein, "Governing the Young: Teacher Behavior in American Primary Schools, 1820–1880: A Documentary History" (Unpublished dissertation, Teachers College, Columbia University, 1970): 134–35.
25 Ayres, *Laggards in Our Schools*, 3, 14, 72, 88.
26 Lewis Terman, *The Measurement of Intelligence* (Boston: Houghton Mifflin, 1916); Terman, *Intelligence Tests and School Reorganization* (Yonkers-on-Hudson: World Book, 1922); Paul Davis Chapman, *Schools as Sorters: Lewis M. Terman, Applied Psychology, and the Intelligence Testing Movement, 1890–1930* (New York: New York University Press, 1988).
27 Zehm, *Educational Misfits*.
28 Quoted in Zehm, *Educational Misfits*, 200.
29 Terman, *The Measure of Intelligence*; Terman, *Intelligence Tests and School Reorganization*; Joel Spring, *Education and the Rise of the Corporate State* (Boston: Beacon Press, 1972); Clarence J. Karier, Paul C. Violas, and Joel Spring, *Roots of Crisis: American Education in the Twentieth Century* (Chicago: Rand McNally, 1973).
30 Oscar T. Corson, *Our Public Schools, Their Teachers, Pupils, and Patrons* (New York: American Book Company, 1920).
31 Tyack, *The One Best System*.
32 William Ryan, *Blaming the Victim* (New York: Pantheon Books, 1971); Robert G. Newby and David Tyack, "Victims Without 'Crimes': Some Historical Perspectives on Black Education," *Journal of Negro Education* 40 (Summer 1971): 192–206.
33 Zehm, *Educational Misfits*.
34 Tyack and Hansot, *Managers of Virtue*, part 3.
35 See Tyack, "Constructing Difference" for discussion of individual versus group identity in the history of education and social diversity.
36 Ryan, *Blaming the Victim*; Terman, *Intelligence Tests and School Reorganization*; Karier, Violas, and Spring, *Roots of Crisis*.
37 See David Wallace Adams, *Education for Extinction: American Indians and the Boarding School Experience, 1875–1928* (Lawrence: University of Kansas Press, 1995).
38 Marvin Lazerson, *Origins of the Urban School: Public Education in Massachusetts, 1870–1915* (Cambridge: Harvard University Press, 1971).
39 David Tyack and Michael Berkowitz, "The Man Nobody Liked: Toward a Social History of the Truant Officer, 1840–1940," *American Quarterly* 26 (1977): 321–354.
40 Frank Forest Bunker, *Reorganization of the Public School System*, U.S. Bureau of Education, Bulletin No. 8 (Washington, DC: GPO, 1916); Lawrence A. Cremin, *The Transformation of the School: Progressivism in American Education, 1876–1957* (New York: Knopf, 1961).
41 Edward A. Krug, *The Shaping of the American High School* (New York: Harper & Row, 1964); Ellwood P. Cubberley, *Changing Conceptions of Education* (Boston: Houghton Mifflin, 1909).
42 William H. Dooley, *The Education of the Ne'er-Do-Well* (Cambridge: Houghton Mifflin, 1916).

43 Leonard Covello, *The Heart Is the Teacher* (New York: McGraw-Hill, 1958).

44 John Ogbu, *Minority Education and Caste* (New York: Academic Press, 1982); Kenneth Clark, *Dark Ghetto* (New York: Harper & Row, 1965); Elizabeth Eddy, *Walk the White Line: A Profile of Urban Education* (Garden City: Doubleday, 1967); William Labov, *The Social Stratification of English in New York City* (Washington, DC: Center for Applied Linguistics, 1982); Raymond P. McDermott, *Kids Make Sense*, Ph.D. dissertation, Stanford University, 1976.

45 James Banks, *Multicultural Education* (Boston: Allyn and Bacon, 1989); Ray C. Rist, *The Urban School: a Factory for Failure* (Cambridge, MA: MIT Press, 1973); Shirley Brice Heath, *Ways with Words: Language, Life, and Work in Communities and Classrooms* (New York: Cambridge University Press, 1983); K. Au, "Participation Structures in a Reading Lesson with Hawaiian Children: Analysis of a Culturally Appropriate Instructional Event," *Anthropology and Education Quarterly* 11, 1980.

46 National Research Council, *High Stakes*.

47 Robert C. Johnson, "Turning Up the Heat," *Education Week*, January 11, 1999; National Research Council, *High Stakes*.

48 Robert M. Hauser, "What If We Ended Social Promotion?" *Education Week*, April 7, 1999.

49 Quoted in M. Sandra Reeves, " 'Self-Interest and the Common Weal': Focusing on the Bottom Half," *Education Week*, April 27, 1988, 21.

50 John Goodlad, *The Non-Graded Elementary School* (New York: Teachers College Press, 1987).

51 Dewey, *The School and Society* (Chicago: University of Chicago Press, 1909).

52 John W. Meyer, *The Impact of the Centralization of Educational Funding and Control of State and Local Organizational Governance* (Stanford: Institute for Research on Educational Finance and Governance, 1980).

53 Covello, *The Heart Is the Teacher*.

54 See Lisbeth B. Schorr, *Common Purpose: Strengthening Families and Neighborhoods to Rebuild America* (New York: Anchor Books, 1997).

55 Carnegie Foundation for the Advancement of Teaching, *An Imperiled Generation: Saving Urban Schools* (Princeton, NJ: Carnegie Foundation for the Advancement of Teaching, 1988).

56 Covello, *The Heart Is the Teacher*, 124.

CHAPTER 22

ETHNICITY, CLASS, COGNITIVE, AND MOTIVATIONAL STYLES (1998)
Research and teaching implications
James A. Banks

Ethnic minorities and academic achievement

The low academic achievement of some ethnic minority youths, such as Afro-Americans, Mexican Americans, and Puerto Rican Americans, is a major national problem that warrants urgent action at the local, state, and national levels. The problem is complex and difficult to diagnose because there is substantial disagreement among educational researchers, practitioners, and the lay community about what causes the wide discrepancies in the academic achievement of groups such as Blacks and mainstream White youths, and between Mexican American and Japanese American students. The writer has reviewed and discussed elsewhere the conflicting explanations and paradigms that have emerged since the civil rights movement of the 1960s to explain the low academic achievement of ethnic youths.[1]

The cultural deprivation and cultural difference hypotheses

When national attention focused on the underachievement of poor and ethnic minority youths in the 1960s, cultural deprivation emerged as the dominant paradigm to explain their educational problems.[2] Cultural deprivation theorists stated that lower-income and minority students were not achieving well in school because of the culture of poverty in which they were socialized. The cultural deprivation paradigm was harshly attacked in the late 1960s and during the 1970s.[3] Its critics argued that it promoted assimilationism and violated the cultural integrity of students from diverse income and cultural groups.

Researchers who rejected the cultural deprivation paradigm created a conception of the cultures and educational problems of lower-income and minority youths based on a different set of assumptions. They argued that these students, far from being culturally deprived, have rich and elaborate cultures. Their rich cultural characteristics are evident in their languages and communication styles, behavioral styles, and values.[4] These theorists also contended that the cognitive, learning, and motivational styles of ethnic minorities such as Afro-Americans and Mexican Americans are different from those fostered in the schools.[5] These students, therefore, achieve less well in school because the school culture favors the culture of White mainstream students and places students from other backgrounds and cultures at a serious disadvantage. The school environment consequently needs to be reformed substantially so that it will be sensitive to diverse learning, cognitive, and motivational styles.

The social class hypothesis

While the cultural difference paradigm has provided rich insights with implications for practice, it has devoted little attention to variation within ethnic groups. Learning and other social science theories should accurately reflect the tremendous diversity within ethnic groups such as Afro-Americans and Mexican Americans. While these cultures share a number of overarching beliefs, values, and behavioral styles, there are enormous within-group differences caused by factors such as region, gender, and social class. Diversity within ethnic groups has received insufficient attention within the social science literature and in the popular imagination.

While variables such as region, religion, gender, and social class create intragroup variation within ethnic groups, social class is presumably one of the most important of these variables. Wilson's important and controversial book—in which he argues that the importance of race in the United States has declined and that class has created important divisions among Blacks—evoked a stimulating and acid debate about race and class in the United States.[6] Wilson believes that class is a major factor that stratifies the Afro-American community. Gordon also hypothesizes that class has a strong influence on ethnic behavior.[7] He writes, "With regard to cultural behavior, differences of social class are more important and decisive than differences of ethnic group. This means that people of the same social class tend to act alike and to have the same values even if they have different ethnic backgrounds."[8]

My aim in this article is to examine the social class hypothesis and to determine the extent to which ethnicity is class sensitive. I will do this by reviewing studies on cognitive styles, learning styles, and motivational styles which include social class as a variable. If social class is as powerful a variable as Wilson and Gordon state, then middle-class Black and White students should not differ significantly in their cognitive, learning, and motivational styles. However, middle-class and lower-class Blacks should differ significantly on these variables. Another, and perhaps more likely possibility, is that social class and ethnicity interact in complex ways to influence learning, motivation, and cognitive styles.

Problems in studying class and ethnicity

Several intractable problems confront the scholar who tries to determine the relationship between social class, ethnicity, and cognitive and motivational styles. Most of the literature that describes the cognitive and motivational styles of ethnic students includes little or no discussion of social class or other factors that might cause within-group variations, such as gender, age, or situational aspects. Social class is often conceptualized and measured differently in studies that include class as a variable; this makes it difficult to compare results from different studies. Researchers frequently use different scales and instruments to measure variables related to cognitive, learning, and motivational styles. To operationally define social class, especially across different ethnic and cultural groups, is one of the most difficult tasks facing social scientists today.

The nature of social class is changing in the United States. Behavior associated with the lower-class fifteen years ago—such as single-parent families—is now common among the middle class. Social class is a dynamic and changing concept. This makes it difficult to study social class over time and across different cultural and ethnic groups. Many of the studies reviewed in this article used

Warner's Index of Status Characteristics which was published almost forty years ago.[9]

Cognition and learning studies

Lesser, Fifer, and Clark studied the patterns of mental abilities in six- and seven-year-old children from different social-class and ethnic backgrounds.[10] They studied verbal ability, reasoning, number facility, and space conceptualization among Chinese, Jewish, Black, and Puerto Rican students in New York City. They found that the four ethnic groups were markedly different in both the level of each mental ability and the pattern among these abilities. In a replication study, Lesser, Fifer, and Clark studied middle- and lower-class Chinese, Black, and Irish Catholic first-grade students in Boston.[11] The replication data for Chinese and Black students were similar to the data on these groups from their earlier study. However, the data for the Irish Catholic students showed neither a distinctive ethnic-group pattern nor similarity of patterns for the two social classes.

Burnes studied the pattern of WISC (Wechsler Intelligence Scale for Children) scores of Black and White students who were upper-middle and lower class.[12] She found significant social-class differences in the scores of the students but no significant racial differences. No interaction effects were found for social class and race. The scores on the subtests for Blacks and Whites did not show a pattern by race or cultural group.

Backman studied six mental ability factors among 2,925 twelfth-grade students who had participated in Project TALENT.[13] She examined how the six mental abilities were related to ethnicity, social class, and sex. Sex accounted for a much larger proportion of the variance than did either ethnicity or social class. Sex was related significantly to both the shape and the level of the patterns of mental ability. It accounted for 69 percent of the total variance in the shape of the patterns. Ethnicity was the only other variable that showed a significant effect on the patterns. It accounted for 13 percent of the total variance: 9 percent associated with shape and 4 percent with level. The patterns of mental abilities of the social-class groups differed significantly in both shape and level. However, these differences accounted for only 2 percent of the variance and were considered by the investigator too small to be important.

A number of researchers have examined a variety of learning variables and cognitive functions related to ethnicity and social class. However, it is difficult to derive clear-cut generalizations from these studies. Siegel, Anderson, and Shapiro examined the categorization behavior of lower- and middle-class Black preschool children.[14] The children were presented with sorting objects, colored pictures, and black-and-white pictures. Lower-class and middle-class children differed in their ability to group only on the pictures. They used different types of categories. Lower-class children preferred to form groups based on use and interdependence of items. Middle-class children preferred to group items on the basis of common physical attributes.

Orasanu, Lee, and Scribner investigated the extent to which category clustering in recall is dependent on preferred organization of the to-be-recalled items and whether preferred organization or recall are related to ethnic or economic group membership.[15] Social-class status was related to the number of high-associate pairs the subjects produced in sorting. Middle-income children produced significantly more pairs than low-income children. Ethnicity was related to the number of taxonomic categories; White children sorted taxonomically more often than did Black children, who showed a preference for functional sorting. Ethnicity and social-class status were unrelated to amount recalled on the pairs-list tasks or to the amount of clustering. Although Black and White children showed differences in organizational preferences, there were no differences in recall.

Rychlak investigated the role of social class, race, and intelligence on the affective learning styles of 160 lower- and middle-income seventh-grade children who were equally divided by sex and race (White and Black).[16] The researchers hypothesized and found that, for all subjects, moving from positive to negative reinforcement value across lists resulted in less nonspecific transfer than does moving from negative to positive reinforcement across successive lists. They hypothesized that this general pattern would be more apparent for Blacks than for Whites and for lower-class than for middle-class subjects. Their hypotheses were confirmed. The White subjects reflected positive non-specific transfer across the lists regardless of whether they were moving from positive to negative or negative to positive levels of reinforcement value. However, Black subjects reflected a negative transfer when moving from positive to negative and a positive transfer when moving from negative to positive lists.

Family socialization

Some evidence indicates that the socialization and intellectual environment of the homes of different racial groups vary even when they are members of the same social class as determined by an index such as Warner's Index of Status Characteristics.[17] Trotman compared the home environment ratings of fifty Black and fifty White middle-class families of ninth-grade girls to the girls' Otis-Lennon Mental Ability Test results, Metropolitan Achievement Test scores, and grade point averages.[18] She found that the home environments of middle-class White families showed a significantly higher level of intellectuality than did those of middle-class Black families. There was an overall positive relationship between the family's home environment and the child's score on the Otis-Lennon Mental Ability Test. This relationship was stronger for Black than for White families. Trotman believes that there is a cultural difference in the home experience and parent-child interactions in Black and White families of the same social class, and that this difference may help to explain the variation in intelligence test performance by members of the two cultural groups.

Research by Moore supports the hypothesis that family socialization practices related to intelligence test performance is different within Black and White families of the same social class.[19] She compared the intelligence test performances of a sample of Black children adopted by Black and by White middle-class parents. She hypothesized that Black children adopted by Black families would achieve significantly lower WISC scores than Black children adopted by White families. Her hypothesis was confirmed. The children adopted by the White families scored significantly higher on the WISC than did those adopted by Black families. The 13.5-point difference in performance between the two groups is the level usually observed between Black and White children.

The studies by Trotman and by Moore support the hypothesis that the socialization practices of Black and White middle-class parents, at least as they relate to intelligence test performance, differ significantly. However, it cannot be inferred from these findings that family socialization practices do not vary within different social classes in the Black community. A study by Kamii and Radin indicates that the socialization practices of lower-lower and middle-class Black mothers differ in significant ways.[20] These researchers directly observed how the mothers interacted with their preschool children and conducted interviews with the mothers in their homes. While they found that lower-lower and middle-class mothers differed significantly in some socialization practices, "not all mothers demonstrated the characteristics of their strata. Social class is thus not a determinant of behavior but a statement of probability that a type of behavior is likely to occur."[21]

Cognitive styles

Theorists and researchers who support the cultural difference hypothesis, such as Ramírez and Castañeda, Hilliard, White, and Hale-Benson,[22] have been heavily influenced by the "cognitive style" concept pioneered by Witkin.[23] Witkin hypothesizes that the learning styles of individuals vary; some are field independent in their learning styles, while others are field dependent. Learners who are field independent easily perceive a hidden figure on the Embedded Figures Test, while field-dependent learners find it difficult to perceive because of the obscuring design.[24]

Ramírez and Castañeda used Witkin's concept in their work with Mexican American students. They substituted "field sensitive" for "field dependent," which they believe has negative connotations.[25] Field-independent and field-sensitive students differ in some significant ways in their learning styles and behaviors. Field independent learners prefer to work independently, while field-sensitive learners like to work with others to achieve a common goal. Field-independent learners tend to be task-oriented and inattentive to their social environment when working. Field-sensitive learners tend to be sensitive to the feelings and opinions of others.[26] Ramírez and Castañeda found that Mexican American children tend to be field sensitive in their learning styles, while teachers usually prefer field-independent students and assign them higher grades. The teaching styles of most teachers and the school curriculum also tend to reflect the characteristics of field-independent students. Mainstream Anglo students tend to be more field independent than ethnic minorities such as Mexican American and Black students. Although field-independent students tend to get higher grades than do field-dependent students, researchers have found that cognitive style is not related to measured intelligence or IQ.

Cohen,[27] who has influenced the works of Hale-Benson and Hilliard, has conceptualized learning styles similar to those formulated by Witkin. She identifies two conceptual styles, analytic and relational. The analytic style is related to Witkin's field-independent concept. The relational is similar to his field-dependent concept. Cohen found that these styles of thinking are produced by the kinds of families and groups into which students are socialized. Family and friendship groups in which functions are periodically performed or widely shared by all members of the group, which she calls "shared function" groups, tend to socialize students who are relational in their learning styles. Formal styles of group organization are associated with analytic styles of learning.

Several researchers have tested the hypothesis that ethnic minority students tend to be more field-dependent or relational in their learning styles than mainstream students, even when social-class status is held constant. Ramírez and Price-Williams studied 180 fourth-grade children to determine whether Mexican American and Black students were more field dependent than Anglo students.[28] Both the Black and the Mexican American students scored in a significantly more field-dependent direction than did the Anglo children. The social-class effect was not significant. Ramírez found that most teachers are significantly more field independent than are Mexican American students. However, their level of field independence does not differ significantly from that of Anglo students.[29]

Perney studied field dependence-independence among suburban Black and White sixth-grade students.[30] No information is given about the social-class status of the community. She found that the Black students were significantly more field dependent than were the White students. However, it was the scores of the Black females that accounted for most of the difference between the races. Black females were the most field-dependent subjects in the study. The females in the study, as a group, were significantly more field dependent than the males. Perney's study reveals that there are significant field-dependence differences between Black and White students and between males and females. However, it does not help us determine the extent to which field dependence is related or sensitive to social-class status.

Locus of control and motivation

Researchers have devoted considerable attention to locus of control and its influence on learning and motivation.[31] This psychological construct is related to how individuals perceive the relationship between their action and its consequences. Individuals who believe that consequences are a direct result of their actions are said to have internal locus of control or internality. Persons who believe that there is little or no relationship between their behavior and its consequences are said to have an external locus of control.

Researchers have found that internality is positively related to academic achievement.[32] Students who believe that their behavior can determine consequences tend to achieve at higher levels than students who believe that their behavior is determined by external forces such as luck, fate, or other individuals. Researchers have found that internality is related to social class and to socialization practices.[33] Higher-socioeconomic-status students tend to be more internal in their orientations than are lower-socioeconomic-status students.

Some researchers interested in minority education have devoted considerable attention to locus of control because of the percentage of ethnic minority students who are lower-class and consequently tend to be external in their psychological orientations.[34] Research rather consistently indicates a relationship between social-class status, internality, and academic achievement. A study by Garner and Cole indicates that while both field dependence and locus of control are related to academic achievement, field dependence is the more important factor; the achievers in their study were more field independent.[35] However, when locus of control and field dependence were combined, locus of control dominated. The achievement of the groups ranged from high to low as follows: internal and field independent, internal and field dependent, external and field independent, external and field dependent. A study by Battle and Rotter supports the well-established principle that locus of control is related primarily to social class rather than to race or ethnicity.[36]

The persistence of ethnicity

As the above review of research indicates, our knowledge of the effect of social-class status on cognitive and motivational styles among ethnic minorities is thin and fragmentary. My review of such studies is representative but not exhaustive.

This research does not give a clear and unmixed message about how sensitive ethnicity is to social-class status. Some researchers, such as Lesser, Fifer, and Clark, Trotman, and Moore, have found that ethnicity has a powerful effect on behavior related to learning and intellectual performance when social class is varied or controlled. Other researchers, such as Orasanu, Lee, and Scribner and Burnes, have derived findings that reveal the effects of social class on learning behavior or the effects of both class and ethnicity.

Collectively, the studies reviewed in this article provide more support for the cultural difference than for the social-class hypothesis. They indicate that ethnicity continues to have a significant influence on the learning behavior and styles of Afro-American and Mexican American students, even when these students are middle class. *In other words, the research reviewed in this article indicates that while ethnicity is to some extent class sensitive, its effects persist across social-class segments within an ethnic group.* However, the research also indicates that social class causes within-ethnic-group variation in behavior. Middle-class Afro-Americans and middle-class Whites differ in some significant ways, as do middle-class and lower-class Afro-Americans.

While the research reviewed herein indicates that cognitive and learning styles are influenced by ethnicity across social classes within ethnic groups, it suggests that locus of control is primarily a class variable. Whether students believe that they can exert control over their environment appears to be related more to their socioeconomic status than to their ethnic socialization or culture.

Why does ethnicity persist across social classes?

In his important and influential publication, Gordon hypothesizes that social-class differences are more important and decisive than ethnic-group differences.[37] He also states that people of the same social class will share behavioral similarities. Gordon emphasizes the importance of social class in shaping behavior. His "ethclass" hypotheses need to be revised and made more consistent with the research and thinking that have taken place during the last two decades.[38]

Gordon's hypotheses are not consistent with many of the studies reviewed in this paper. His ethclass hypotheses predict that social class has a stronger effect on behavior than ethnicity has on behavior. However, this does not seem to be the case for behavior related to the learning and cognitive styles of Afro-Americans and Mexican Americans. We need to examine why there is an inconsistency between Gordon's hypotheses and the research reviewed in this article.

I believe that this inconsistency results primarily from a major problem in social science research in the United States related to the conceptualization and study of social classes within non-White populations such as Afro-Americans and Mexican Americans. The tendency in social science is to use standard indices such as occupation, income, and educational level to identify lower-class and middle-class populations within these groups and to compare them with White populations with similar occupational, income, and educational characteristics. The assumption is made that social-class groups within the non-White populations and those within the White population are equivalent.

The comparative study of social classes across ethnic groups in the United States creates problems in both theory construction and in the formulation of valid generalizations because significant differences often exist between Blacks and Whites with similar income, educational, and occupational characteristics. The study of the Black middle class is a case in point. Most middle-class White families live in a middle-class community, have middle-class relatives and friends, and send their children to middle-class schools. This may or may not be true of a middle-class Black family. Approximately 55 percent of Blacks in the United States are members of the lower class.[39] Many Black middle-class families have relatives who are working class or lower class. Black middle-class families often live in mixed-class neighborhoods, participate in community organizations and institutions that have participants from all social-class groups, and often visit relatives who live in the inner city.[40]

Many Blacks are also members of an extended family, which often includes lower- and working-class relatives. Lower-class relatives often play an important role in the socialization of their children. These relatives may serve as babysitters for short and long periods for the middle-class family. There is a strong expectation within the Black extended family that the individual who becomes middle class will not forsake his or her family and should help it financially when necessary.[41] Unlike many middle-class White families, which tend to function highly independently within a largely middle-class world, the middle-class Black family is often a first-generation middle-class family that exists within an extended family and a community network that have definite group expectations for it and strongly influence its behaviors and options. Many of the generalizations made here about Black families are also true for Mexican American and Puerto Rican American middle-class families.[42]

The persistence of ethnicity: Theory and research implications

To reformulate Gordon's ethclass hypotheses to make them more consistent with research that has taken place in the last two decades, we need to recognize the persistence of ethnicity when social-class mobility takes place. This is especially the case when an ethnic group is non-White and is a part of a group that has a disproportionately large working-class or lower-class population. Significant differences exist for the individual who is middle class but functions within a community that is primarily working class or lower class, and for the individual who is middle class but who functions within a predominantly middle-class community. Taking these factors into account, we may reformulate one of Gordon's hypotheses to read: With regard to cultural behavior, ethnicity continues to influence the behavior of members of ethnic groups with certain characteristics when social mobility occurs. This means that while people of the same social class from different ethnic groups will exhibit some similar behaviors, they will have some significant behavioral differences caused by the persistence of ethnicity.

When studying race, class, and ethnicity, social scientists need to examine *generational middle-class status* as a variable. There are often important behavioral and attitudinal differences between a Black individual who grew up poor and became middle class within his or her adulthood and a Black who is fourth-generation middle class. Many of the middle-class Afro-Americans and Mexican Americans described in existing research studies are probably first-generation middle class. Such individuals are sometimes compared with Whites who have been middle class for several generations. Generational social-class status needs to be varied systematically in research studies so that we can learn more about the tenacity of ethnicity across generations.

Other research implications

We need more replications of studies related to race, class, and cognitive styles. One of the major problems with the research is that various researchers formulate different questions, study subjects of different ages who attend different kinds of schools, use different statistical analysis techniques, and use different instruments to measure the same variables. Important lines of inquiry on problems related to ethnic groups and cognitive styles are begun but not pursued until valid generalizations and theories have been formulated. Lesser, Fifer, and Clark published a pathbreaking study that described the patterns of mental abilities of ethnic minorities in 1967. However, we know little more about patterns of mental abilities in ethnic groups today than we knew in 1967. Neither the original researchers nor other students have pursued this line of inquiry in any systematic way. As a result, the research on learning patterns among ethnic minorities remains thin and fragmented, and provides few insights that can guide practice.

The persistence of ethnicity: Implications for practice

Teachers and other practitioners reading the review of research in this article are likely to be disappointed by the fragmentary nature of the research that exists on ethnicity, social class, and cognitive styles. It is difficult to find such studies. Nevertheless, we can glean some guidelines for practice from the research.

The research suggests that students will come to the classroom with many kinds of differences, some of which may be related to their ethnic group, their social-class status, or social class and ethnicity combined. Research suggests that Afro-American and Mexican American students tend to be more field sensitive in their learning styles than are mainstream Anglo-American students. This means that Mexican American and Afro-American students are more likely to be motivated by curriculum content that is presented in a humanized or story format than are mainstream Anglo students. The research also suggests that middle-class students tend to be more internal than are lower-class students. This suggests that teachers will need to work with many lower-class students to help them to see the relationship between their effort and their academic performance.

It is important for teachers to understand that the characteristics of ethnic groups and socioeconomic classes can help us to understand groups but not individual students. All types of learning and motivational styles are found within *all* ethnic groups and social classes. Many Afro-American students are field independent and analytic; many White students are field dependent and relational. The teacher cannot assume that every Mexican American student is field dependent and that every Anglo student is field independent. These kinds of assumptions result in new stereotypes and problems. There is a delicate and difficult balance between using generalizations about groups to better understand and interpret the behavior of groups, and using that knowledge to interpret the behavior of a particular student. Cox and Ramírez have described some of the difficulties that resulted when practitioners applied their research on cognitive styles:

> The dissemination of research information on cognitive styles has also had a negative effect in some cases, arising primarily from common problems associated with looking at mean differences; that is, by using averages to describe differences between groups, the dangers of stereotyping are more likely. The great diversity within any culture is ignored, and a construct

which should be used as a tool for individualization becomes yet another label for categorizing and evaluating.[43]

Teachers should recognize that students bring a variety of learning, cognitive, and motivational styles to the classroom, and that while certain characteristics are associated with specific ethnic and social-class groups, these characteristics are distributed throughout the total student population. This means that the teacher should use a variety of teaching styles and content that will appeal to diverse students. Concepts should be taught when possible with different strategies so that students who are relational in their learning styles as well as those who are analytic will have an equal opportunity to learn. Researchers such as Slavin and Cohen have documented that cooperative learning strategies appeal to ethnic-group students and foster positive intergroup attitudes and feelings.[44]

Teachers should also select content from diverse ethnic groups so that students from various cultures will see their images in the curriculum.[45] Educational equity will exist for all students when teachers become sensitive to the cultural diversity in their classrooms, vary their teaching styles so as to appeal to a diverse student population, and modify their curricula to include ethnic content. This is a tall but essential order in an ethnically and racially diverse nation that is wasting so much of its human potential.

Notes

1 J. A. Banks, "Multicultural Education: Developments, Paradigms, and Goals," in J. A. Banks and J. Lynch, eds., *Multicultural Education in Western Societies* (New York: Praeger, 1986), pp. 2–28.

2 F. Reissman, *The Culturally Deprived Child* (New York: Harper, 1962); B. S. Bloom, A. Davis, and R. Hess, *Compensatory Education for Cultural Deprivation* (New York: Holt, 1965).

3 C. A. Valentine, *Culture and Poverty: Critique and Counter-Proposals* (Chicago: University of Chicago Press, 1968); S. S. Baratz and J. C. Baratz, "Early Childhood Intervention: The Social Science Base of Institutional Racism," *Harvard Educational Review*, 40 (Winter 1970), 29–50.

4 G. Smitherman, *Talking and Testifying: The Language of Black America* (Boston: Houghton Mifflin, 1977); J. Hale, "Black Children: Their Roots, Culture and Learning Styles," *Young Children*, 36 (January 1981), 37–50; J. L. White, *The Psychology of Blacks* (Englewood Cliffs, N.J.: Prentice-Hall, 1984).

5 M. Ramírez and A. Castañeda, *Cultural Democracy, Bicognitive Development and Education* (New York: Academic Press, 1974); B. J. Shade, "Afro-American Cognitive Style: A Variable in School Success?" *Review of Educational Research*, 52 (Summer 1982), 219–244; J. Hale-Benson, *Black Children: Their Roots, Culture, and Learning Styles*, rev. ed. (Baltimore: The Johns Hopkins University Press, 1986).

6 W. J. Wilson, *The Declining Significance of Race: Blacks and Changing American Institutions* (Chicago: University of Chicago Press, 1978); A. Pinkney, *The Myth of Black Progress* (New York: Cambridge University Press, 1984).

7 M. Gordon, *Assimilation in American Life* (New York: Oxford University Press, 1964).

8 Ibid., p. 52.

9 W. L. Warner, *Social Class in America* (Chicago: Science Research Associates, 1949).

10 G. S. Lesser, G. Fifer, and D. H. Clark, "Mental Abilities of Children from Different Social-Class and Cultural Groups," *Monographs of the Society for Research in Child Development*, 30, No. 4 (1965).

11 Cited in S. S. Stodolsky and G. Lesser, "Learning Patterns in the Disadvantaged," *Harvard Educational Review*, 37 (Fall 1967), 546–593; reprinted Series No. 5, *Harvard Educational Review*, 1975, pp. 22–69.

12 K. Burnes, "Patterns of WISC Scores for Children of Two Socioeconomic Classes and Races," *Child Development*, 41 (1970), 493–499.
13 M. E. Backman, "Patterns of Mental Abilities: Ethnic, Socioeconomic, and Sex Differences," *American Educational Research Journal*, 9 (Winter 1972), 1–12.
14 I. Siegel, L. M. Anderson, and H. Shapiro, "Categorization Behavior in Lower- and Middle-Class Preschool Children: Differences in Dealing with Representation of Familar Objects," *Journal of Negro Education*, 35 (1966), 218–229.
15 J. Orasanu, C. Lee, and S. Scribner, "The Development of Category Organization and Free Recall: Ethnic and Economic Group Comparisons," *Child Development*, 50 (1979), 1100–1109.
16 J. F. Rychlak, "Affective Assessment, Intelligence, Social Class, and Racial Learning Style," *Journal of Personality and Social Psychology*, 32 (1975), 989–995.
17 Warner, *Social Class in America*.
18 F. K. Trotman, "Race, IQ, and the Middle Class," *Journal of Educational Psychology*, 69 (1977), 266–273.
19 E. G. J. Moore, "Ethnicity as a Variable in Child Development," in *The Social and Affective Development of Black Children*, ed. M. G. Spencer, G. K. Brookins, and W. R. Allen (Hillsdale, N.J.: Lawrence Erlbaum Associates, 1985), pp. 101–115.
20 C. K. Kamii and N. J. Radin, "Class Differences in Socialization Practices of Negro Mothers," *Journal of Marriage and the Family*, 29 (1967), 302–310; reprinted in *The Black Family: Essays and Studies*, ed. R. Staples (Belmont, Calif.: Wadsworth Publishing Co., 1971), pp. 235–247.
21 Ibid., p. 244.
22 Ramírez and Castañeda, *Cultural Democracy*; A. Hilliard, "Alternatives to IQ Testing: An Approach to the Identification of Gifted Minority Children" (Final report to the California State Department of Education, 1976); White, *The Psychology of Blacks*; and Hale-Benson, *Black Children*.
23 H. A. Witkin, *Psychological Differentiation* (New York: Wiley, 1962); H. A. Witkin and D. R. Goodenough, *Cognitive Styles: Essence and Origins* (New York: International Universities Press, Inc., 1981).
24 H. A. Witkin, "Individual Differences in Ease of Perception of Embedded Figures," *Journal of Personality*, 19 (1950), 1–15.
25 Ramírez and Castañeda, *Cultural Democracy*.
26 Ibid.
27 R. A. Cohen, "Conceptual Styles, Cultural Conflict, and Nonverbal Tests of Intelligence," *American Anthropologist*, 71 (1969), 828–856.
28 M. Ramírez and D. R. Price-Williams, "Cognitive Styles of Children of Three Ethnic Groups in the United States," *Journal of Cross-Cultural Psychology*, 5 (1974), 212–219.
29 M. Ramírez, "Cognitive Styles and Cultural Democracy in Education of Mexican Americans," *Social Science Quarterly*, 53 (1973), 895–904.
30 V. H. Perney, "Effects of Race and Sex on Field Dependence-Independence in Children," *Perceptual and Motor Skills*, 42 (1976), 975–980.
31 H. M. Leftcourt, *Locus of Control: Current Trends in Theory and Research*, 2nd ed. (Hillsdale, N.J.: Lawrence Erlbaum Associates, 1982).
32 Ibid.
33 Ibid.
34 J. A. Vasquez, "Bilingual Education's Needed Third Dimension," *Educational Leadership*, 37 (November 1979), 166–168.
35 C. W. Garner and E. G. Cole, "The Achievement of Students in Low-SES Settings: An Investigation of the Relationship Between Locus of Control and Field Dependence," *Urban Education*, 21 (July 1986), 189–206.
36 E. S. Battle and J. B. Rotter, "Children's Feelings of Personal Control as Related to Social Class and Ethnic Group," *Journal of Personality*, 31 (1963), 482–490.
37 Gordon, *Assimilation in American Life*.
38 H. P. McAdoo and J. L. McAdoo, eds., *Black Children: Social, Educational, and Parental Environments* (Beverly Hills: Sage Publications, 1985).
39 J. E. Blackwell, *The Black Community: Unity and Diversity*, 2nd ed. (New York: Harper and Row, 1985).

40 J. A. Banks, "An Exploratory Study of Assimilation, Pluralism, and Marginality: Black Families in Predominantly White Suburbs," document resume in *Resources in Education*. ERIC document 257–175.

41 E. P. Martin and J. M. Martin, *The Black Extended Family* (Chicago: The University of Chicago Press, 1978).

42 J. W. Moore and H. Pachon, *Mexican Americans*, 2nd ed. (Englewood Cliffs, N.J.: Prentice-Hall, 1976).

43 B. G. Cox and M. Ramírez, "Cognitive Styles: Implications for Multiethnic Education," in *Education in the 80s: Multiethnic Education*, ed. J. A. Banks (Washington, D.C.: National Education Association, 1981), pp. 61–71.

44 R. E. Slavin, *Cooperative Learning* (New York: Longman, 1983); E. G. Cohen, *Designing Groupwork: Strategies for the Heterogeneous Classroom* (New York: Teachers College Press, 1986).

45 J. A. Banks, *Teaching Strategies for Ethnic Studies*, 4th ed. (Boston: Allyn and Bacon, 1987).

CHAPTER 23

LESSONS FROM RESEARCH WITH LANGUAGE-MINORITY CHILDREN (1994)

Luis C. Moll and Norma González

Lupita, a third-grade student, pulled up a chair to a table and sat next to some classmates. She was doing research on the Sioux as part of a broader classroom project studying Native Americans, and had spent part of the morning selecting books from the school library with information about that cultural group. The students themselves had selected Native Americans as the general topic of study and were doing independent and collaborative research on their particular groups of choice. Lupita had already written several questions about the Sioux that would serve to guide her study. These questions were all in Spanish, her first language; the books she selected were all in English, her rapidly evolving second language (Moll & Whitmore, 1993).

Eventually, with some assistance from the teacher, for the texts were difficult, Lupita was able to read portions of the books that contained relevant information to answer her questions, and she translated the information into Spanish so that she could incorporate it later into an essay summarizing her findings. Her classmate, Yolanda, doing research on the Yaquis, had developed a questionnaire in Spanish to interview a teacher aide who is Yaqui and trilingual in Yaqui, Spanish, and English. She would also write her report in Spanish but other children chose English, for they had the option of using either language as needed to complete their tasks.

In yet another activity within this same classroom, a group of children decided to read a set of story books the teacher had assembled about the topic of war and how they affect people's lives (Moll, Tapia, & Whitmore, 1993). As the children read the books and discussed them among themselves and with the teacher, they struggled in understanding realistic but fictional accounts of events about other people, at other places, and in other times. They borrowed from each other's experiences in making sense of the stories, relating them to their own lives, and evaluating the worthiness of the books. All of the books were in English, however, they could have easily been in Spanish.

Lupita, Yolanda, and several of their classmates in this bilingual third-grade classroom are well on their way to becoming literate in two languages. Furthermore, they are becoming competent in specific literate practices that will help them to consciously and intentionally use their bilingualism as a means to accomplish personal, academic, or intellectual tasks. These third-grade children can formulate their own research questions, search for and document their sources of information, abstract relevant information from multiple texts, conduct interviews to supplement their readings, and produce texts that summarize and communicate what they have learned.

They can also read novels and stories and discuss the events, characters, styles, even the writer's craft, and relate the stories to their own experiences to make sense of them, or to reevaluate their experiences (Moll, Tapia, & Whitmore, 1993). And they can do this at will, and if bilingual, they can do it in two languages. In brief, these children are developing the wherewithal to access not one, but two social, cultural, and literate worlds as resources for their thinking and development (Moll & Dworin, in press; Moll & Whitmore, 1993).

To be sure, the literacy practices sketched above, and the classroom dynamics which support them, are not very common with working-class students. They clash with the constraints of the instructional "status quo" for working-class children in the United States, bilingual or otherwise, and the limiting perceptions of their intellectual or academic capabilities. We have reviewed these issues elsewhere (e.g., Moll, 1992; Moll & Dworin, in press), especially the limitations imposed by an educational system stratified by social class (Oakes, 1986), the lack of access to rigorous academic work (e.g., Olsen & Minicucci, 1992), and the narrow uses of literacy typical of these settings (for related issues, see Allington, 1994). Rather than concentrate on these constraints, however, in this paper we present projects that are challenging the status quo, that are shaping these constraints by creating alternative conditions for these children to use literacy and learn in either their first or second language.

These studies (among several that we could include), conducted independently in different regions of the United States and with different ethnolinguistic and age groups, highlight both teachers and children as active learners using language and literacy as tools for inquiry, communication, and thinking. The role of the teachers is to enable and guide activities that involve students as thoughtful (and literate) learners in socially and academically meaningful tasks. Central to each of the studies and the point we want to emphasize in this article is the strategic use of cultural resources for learning. These resources may include parents participating as knowledgeable "informants" in a lesson or project, a community location as a key research site, or addressing through reading and writing social issues of importance to the students and teachers. This emphasis on active research and learning leads to the realization that these children (and their communities) contain ample resources, which we term "funds of knowledge," that can form the bases for an education that addresses broader social, academic, and intellectual issues than simply learning basic, rudimentary skills.

Given this broad scope and emphasis, the research is by necessity interdisciplinary, and in the specific studies reported here, it involves close collaboration between teachers and researchers in questioning how children are being taught and in proposing alternative methods of instruction. Although these studies relied primarily on qualitative (Jacob, 1987) or interpretive (Mehan, 1992) approaches to educational research, including ethnographic methods of study, the researchers departed considerably from the detached, passive spectator stance that usually characterizes these approaches (cf. Ely, 1991) by participating actively in developing new arrangements for learning.

We begin with work that we have conducted with Latino (predominantly Mexican) and African-American households and classrooms in Tucson, Arizona (e.g., González et al., 1993; Moll & Greenberg, 1990; Moll, Amanti, Neff, & González, 1992). Here we define what we mean by funds of knowledge and how we are using this concept in our work. In particular, we will emphasize the teacher's research on household dynamics. We then summarize the research of Warren, Rosebery, and Conant (Warren, Rosebery, & Conant, 1989; Warren, Rosebery, & Conant, 1994) with Haitian children in the Boston area, and their use of collaborative inquiry in the teaching and learning of science. We follow with the work of Mercado (1992) on the forming of research "teams" with Puerto Rican and African-American students in New York City, and conclude with the research of McCarty and colleagues (McCarty, Wallace, Lynch, & Benally, 1991; see also, Lipka & McCarty, in press; McCarty, 1989) with Navajo children in Arizona that challenges the common and stereotypical notion of Native American children as somehow passive, noninquisitive learners.

As we review these studies, our focus will not be on reading and writing processes per se but on how broader classroom conditions can be created that shape what it means to be literate in these settings. And in each case, becoming literate means taking full advantage of social and cultural resources in the service of academic goals.

A "funds of knowledge" perspective

The centerpiece of our work is the collaboration with teachers in conducting household research (González et al., 1993; Moll et al., 1992). We start with the assumption that there are important (cultural) resources for teaching in the school's immediate community, but that one needs both theory and method to locate, identify, and document these resources. Furthermore, we also assume that it is one thing to identify resources but quite another to use them fruitfully in classrooms, so that collaboration with teachers (and pedagogical theory) is indispensable.

In contrast to other efforts at teacher-research (e.g., Lytle & Chochran-Smith, 1990), we do not start with the classroom as the unit of study, although that is our eventual goal. We take a "mediated" approach, starting elsewhere, usually by studying households. There are some compelling reasons for taking this approach. For one, having strangers scrutinize one's teaching is not a very good way of creating a working relationship between teachers and researchers. Goodson (1991) has made a similar point by arguing that making classroom practice the starting point of a research collaboration can deflect the participatory process:

> I wish to argue that to place the teachers' classroom practice at the centre of the action for action researchers is to put the most exposed and problematic aspect of the teachers' world at the centre of scrutiny and negotiation. In terms of strategy, . . . I think it is a mistake to do this. I say it is a mistake to do this—and this may seem like a paradox—particularly if we wish to ultimately seek reflection about and change in the teachers' practice. (p. 141)

The initiation of teacher-researchers into household, rather than classroom, analysis provides the context for collaboration in a number of overlapping arenas. In the first place, teachers are presented with a body of social theory that allows them to reconceptualize the households of "minority" children (more on this issue below). In addition, by approaching these households as qualitative researchers, teachers are offered a nonevaluative framework that helps them to go beyond surface images of families. Secondly, the household analysis also serves as a sort of "rite of passage" as the teachers study unfamiliar settings which they cannot assume they know or understand. The contrast between the familiar (the classroom) and the unfamiliar (the household), especially when teachers do not live in the community in which they teach, is analogous to an anthropologist entering an unknown community. This contrast becomes an issue even when the teachers are themselves members of the community. In such cases, the task becomes that of "making the familiar strange" in order to observe and document processes that are less salient or "visible" to the "insider." All teachers, minority or otherwise, have found that entering the households as researchers, rather than as "teacher," produces a discernible reorientation to household dynamics and processes (González & Amanti, 1992; González et al., 1993).

The theoretical orientation of our "fieldwork" is toward documenting the productive activities of households and what they reveal about families' funds of knowledge. Particularly important in our work has been the analysis of households as "strategizing units": how they function as part of a wider economy, and how family members obtain and distribute their material and intellectual resources through strategic social ties or networks, or through other adaptive arrangements (see, e.g., Vélez-Ibáñez, 1988; Vélez-Ibáñez & Greenberg, 1992). We have learned that in contrast to classrooms, households never function alone or in isolation; they are always connected to other households and institutions through diverse social networks. These social networks not only facilitate different forms of economic assistance and labor cooperation that help families avoid the expenses involved in using secondary institutions, such as plumbing companies or automobile repair shops, but serve important emotional and service functions, providing assistance of different types, for example, in finding jobs, with child-care and rearing, or other problem-solving functions.

It is primarily through these social networks that family members obtain or share what we have termed "funds of knowledge." We have defined funds of knowledge as those historically accumulated and culturally developed bodies of knowledge and skills essential for household or individual functioning and well-being (Greenberg, 1989; Moll & Greenberg, 1990). As households interact within circles of kinship and friendship, children are "participant-observers" of the exchange of goods, services, and symbolic capital which are part of each household's functioning (see, e.g., Andrade & Moll, 1993).

The knowledge and skills that such households (and their networks) possess are extensive. For example, many of the families know about repairs, carpentry, masonry, electrical wiring, fencing, and building codes, in general, knowledge related to jobs in the working-class segment of the labor market. Some families have knowledge about the cultivation of plants, folk remedies, herbal cures, midwifery, and first aid procedures, usually learned from older relatives. Family members with several years of formal schooling have knowledge about (and have worked in) archeology, biology, education, engineering, and mathematics. From the documentation and (theoretical) analysis of funds of knowledge, one learns not only about the extent of the knowledge found among these working-class households, but about the special importance of the social and cultural world, and of social relations, in the development of this knowledge (Moll, Tapia, & Whitmore, 1993).

What is the source of these funds of knowledge? We have concentrated primarily on documenting the social and labor history of the families. Much of a household's knowledge is related to its origins and, of course, to family members' employment, occupations, or work, including labor specific to household activities. To make this discussion more concrete, consider the following case examples drawn from one of our studies (adapted from Moll & Greenberg, 1990; names are pseudonyms):

> The Aguilars and the Morales are typical cross border families with rural roots, part of an extended family—Mrs. Aguilar is Mr. Morales' sister—that came to Tucson from the northern Sonoran (Mexico) towns of Esqueda and Fronteras. The Morales had a parcel of land on an *ejido*. Mr. Aguilar's father had been a cowboy, and had worked on a large ranch owned by the descendants of a governor of Sonora in the 19th century. Like his father, Mr. Aguilar is a cowboy. Although he worked for a time in construction after coming to the United States, he is currently employed on a cattle ranch near Pinal, Arizona where he spends five to six days a week, coming home only on Tuesdays. Like Mr. Aguilar, Mr. Morales initially found work in construction, but unlike his brother-in-law, he eventually formed his own company: Morales Patio Construction. This family concern also employs his son as well as his daughter-in-law as their secretary/bookkeeper. Nevertheless, the Morales' rural roots remain strong, even idealized. In their backyard, the Morales have recreated a "rancho" complete with pony and other animals. Moreover, the family owns a small ranch north of Tucson which serves as a "recreation center" and locus for learning. They take their children and grandchildren not just to help with the chores, running the tractor, feeding animals, building fences, but more importantly to teach them the funds of knowledge entailed in these old family traditions which cannot be learned in an urban context.

A second example is from a family with an urban background:

> The Zavalas are an urban working class family, with no ties to the rural hinterland. They have seven children. Their eldest daughter, however, no longer lives at home, but with her boyfriend and son. Mr. Zavala is best characterized as an entrepreneur. He works as a builder, part-time, and owns some apartments in Tucson and properties in Nogales. Mrs. Zavala was born in Albuquerque, New Mexico, in 1950 but came to Tucson as a young child. She left school in the 11th grade. Mr. Zavala was born in Nogales, Sonora in 1947, where he lived until he finished the 6th grade. His father too was from Nogales. His father had little education, and began to work at the age of 9 to help support the family. His family, then, moved to Nogales, Arizona where he went to school for another two years, When he was 17, Mr. Zavala left home and joined the army, and spent two years stationed on military bases in California and Texas. After his discharge, he returned to Nogales, Arizona and worked for a year installing television cable and heating and cooling ducts. In 1967, Mr. Zavala came to Tucson, first working as a house painter for six months, then in an airplane repair shop where he worked for three years. In 1971, he opened a washing machine and refrigerator repair shop, a business he had for three years. Since 1974, Mr. Zavala works in construction part time, builds and sells houses, and he owns four apartments (two of which he built in the backyard of his house).

Everyone in the Zavala's household, including the children, is involved in informal sector economic activities to help the family. Juan, for example, who is in the sixth grade, has a bicycle shop in the back of the house. He buys used bicycle parts at the swap meet and assembles them to build bicycles, which he sells at the yard sales his family holds regularly. He is also building a go-cart, and says he is going to charge kids 15 cents per ride. His sisters, Carmen and Conchita, sell candies that their mother buys in Nogales to their schoolmates. The children have used the money they have earned to buy the family a video recorder.

Teachers have reported to us the transformative potential of viewing households from a funds of knowledge perspective (González et al., 1993). One implication, and a most important one, is debunking ideas of working-class, language minority households as lacking worthwhile knowledge and experiences. These households, and by implication, these communities, are often viewed solely as places from which children must be saved or rescued, rather than places that, along with problems (as in all communities), contain valuable knowledge and experiences that can foster the children's development.

A second implication is in understanding the concept of culture from a more dynamic, "processual" view, not as a group of personality traits, folk celebrations, foods, or artifacts, but as the lived practices and knowledge of the students and their families. As Rosaldo (1989) notes, "from a processual perspective, change rather than structure becomes society's enduring state, and time rather than space becomes its most encompassing medium" (p. 103). The fact that many minority students live in ambiguous and contradictory circumstances favors a perspective in which attention is directed toward the interaction between individual agency and received structures. In this way, the actual and everyday experiences of students' lives are privileged over uniform, integrated and standardized cultural norms. Cathy Amanti, one of the teacher-researchers in the project, explains it as follows:

> Participating in the project helped me to reformulate my concept of culture from being very static to more practice-oriented. This broadened conceptualization turned out to be the key which helped me develop strategies to include the knowledge my students were bringing to school in my classroom practice. It was the kind of information elicited through the questionnaires that was the catalyst for this transformation. I sought information on literacy, parenting attitudes, family and residential history, and daily activities. But I was not looking for static categories, or judging the household's activities in these areas according to any standards—my own or otherwise. . . . If our idea of culture is bound up with notions of authenticity and tradition, how much practice will we ignore as valueless and what will we say to our students? But if our idea of culture is expanded to include the ways we organize and make sense of all our experiences, we have many more resources to draw upon in the classroom. (González & Amanti, 1992, p. 8)

In addition to providing evidence of the repositories of knowledge found in these homes, teachers have drawn on the insights gained from household visits and analysis in a number of ways. For example, one teacher learned that many of her students' households had extensive knowledge of the medicinal value of plants and herbs. She was able to draw on this ethnobotanical knowledge in formulating a theme unit that reflected local knowledge of the curative properties of plants. Another teacher, after visiting a household that regularly participated in trans-border activities in northern Mexico, discovered that her student commonly returned from these trips with candy to sell. Elaborating on this student's marketing skills, an integrated unit emerged which spun around various aspects of candy and the selling of candy. Students adopted an inquiry-based approach to investigate the nutritional content of candy, a comparison of U.S. and Mexican candy, sugar processing, and developed a survey and graphing unit on favorite candies. In both instances, individuals met during the household visits became participants, visiting the classrooms to contribute (in either English or Spanish) their knowledge or experiences (González, Amanti, & Floyd, 1994; Moll et al., 1992).

In other cases, the involvement of the parents has followed an unexpected trajectory. In one special case involving an African-American household, the research visits revealed that the father, in addition to his regular job as a gardener, had a wealth of musical and theatrical knowledge that was tapped for the production of a full-scale musical in the school. This father wrote lyrics and composed music and script that featured eight original songs, described by the teacher as "songs that these children will carry with them for the rest of their lives" (Hensley, 1994). Other than the skills learned in staging the musical, a unit on sound and music was developed that focused on the acoustical properties of sound, the construction of various musical instruments and ethnomusicology. Interestingly, a written survey sent by the school inquiring about household skills had not been returned by this family, but the personal and interested contact of the teacher was key in revealing and using this storehouse of talents.

One further development marks this case study as illustrative of the "catalytic" potential of this method. During an initial interview, the Johnsons (a pseudonym for this family) had indicated disinterest in the school's PTA. However, as Mr. Johnson became a frequent school visitor (on his weekly day off, we should add), carrying his musical instruments, other teachers noticed him and asked about his presence. Soon they were requesting that he visit their classrooms, and his visibility extended into other areas of school life. By the end of the school year, Mr. Johnson had been elected PTA president, proposing an ambitious agenda of community involvement in school matters. This case example effectively points out yet another area of potential that can be harnessed by transcending the boundaries of the school and making inroads into the funds of knowledge of the community.

Another teacher sought to build on the inquiry process itself, involving students themselves as "ethnographers" and developing a survey of the languages spoken in the school (Craig, 1994). The students prepared the questionnaire, piloted and revised it, and organized themselves into teams that would collect the information from teachers in the school. They also tabulated the data, and noticing inconsistencies in the results, revised the questionnaire to obtain additional data that would confirm (or not) earlier results. They also prepared a report to communicate to others in the school their findings.

Doing science in Haitian Creole

Inquiry-based instruction is also the central theme of the research reported by Warren, Rosebery, and Conant (1989, 1994). The goal of the work was to develop a collaborative approach to science for students in a Haitian Creole bilingual program in Boston. As the authors pointed out, science instruction for working-class language minority students, when offered at all, takes the most limited and traditional forms, and it is often subordinated to the goal of developing the students' English language. In contrast, their approach, called Cheche Konnen ("search for knowledge" in Haitian Creole), involved the students in the conduct of science, especially in developing investigations and scientific ways of thinking, talking and acting: "students are encouraged to pose their *own* questions, collaboratively plan and implement research to explore those questions, collect analyze and interpret data, build and revise theories, draw conclusions, and make decisions based on their research" (Warren et al., 1989, p. 2, emphasis in original). In developing and implementing these activities, oral and written language (in Creole and English) and mathematics played indispensable mediating roles in communicating ideas and in thinking scientifically. Central to their approach was the work of the teachers in guiding, facilitating, and supporting the students' research activities and discussions.

In one of their case studies, for example, the students and the teachers (with the help of the researchers) in a seventh-grade classroom designed and conducted an investigation into aquatic ecosystems, the goal of which was to "develop an understanding of the concept of an ecosystem through observation and analysis of the physical, chemical and biological forces and relationships affecting aquatic life in a local pond, stream or river" (Warren et al., 1989, p. 34). As part of their research, the class decided to carry out a field study of a local pond near the city's reservoir. Several class sessions were spent planning a "Field Guide" for the conduct of the study, and the students (with the teacher's assistance) generated a set of questions about the pond that they wanted to investigate, such as the depth of the pond at different places, the animals that live there, whether the water is safe to drink, the cleanliness of the pond, and whether the pond had always been the same size (p. 35).

These questions motivated their inquiry, and lead to theory development, collection and analysis of data, revisions of theory, and further research questions and follow-up activities. The students met in language groups (Creole and English) to discuss their research, divide the labor and responsibilities, plan experiments, decide on the kinds of data needed to answer their questions, and develop instruments to record their findings. For instance, some of the students collected temperature readings at various depths and at different locations in and around the pond, recording the various temperatures on the board for discussion and the generation of hypotheses. In doing so, they noticed a discrepancy between the air and the water temperature at different depths. The following trilingual discussion ensued among children and adults:

> Teacher Assistant (in English): O.K. These were the results Martine (one of the students) found. Can anybody explain why they think? What the changes were about? Why weren't they the same?
>
> Martine (in Creole): Why above the water was, where when I first came the air was 20 was because it was a bit warm out and also the air. . . .
>
> Teacher Assistant (in English): O.K., what Martine is saying, she's saying that when we came to the pond it was pretty warm outside and that's why he thinks it was 20. What do people think? Why would the water be, I don't understand why the water would be different from the air.
>
> Martine (in Creole): Because the water, the sun doesn't hit the bottom of the water.
>
> Mario (in English): The sun wasn't going to the bottom of the water.
>
> Lorenzo (in Spanish): The water on top is hot, because the sun hits it, but the water in the bottom is . . .
>
> ESL Teacher (in English): Alright! Lorenzo got, just got that. See if you try to get it! The temperature, can I translate for Lorenzo. He told me in Spanish.

The water on top of the pond is warmer than deeper down because the sun heats up the water on the top.

Teacher Assistant (in English): O.K., that's just what Mario was saying. O.K., great. Is that true? Did anybody measure the water down below?

Student: We did.

(from Warren, Rosebery, & Conant, 1989, p. 38)

The discussion continued as children and teachers shared ideas, made sense of the data, and developed new questions, especially when their data revealed that the water 5 feet under was warmer, not colder than the water on the surface. How could this be? The teachers and children proposed new ideas for the discrepancy in temperatures and designed a new experiment to obtain more precise data to answer their questions. During the activity, the students also wrote (in addition to the Field Guide) their findings and interpretations, displaying more sophistication in their interpretations as the research progressed (for details, see Rosebery, Warren, and Conant, 1992; Warren, Rosebery, & Conant, 1989).

Researching the research process

This third example borrows from a project conducted with sixth-grade Puerto Rican and African-American students in New York City (Mercado, 1992). As with the two studies summarized above, it represents a collaborative effort, in this instance between a single researcher and a teacher, involving students in "authentic," real investigations about issues that matter to them and to the community. A key, and unusual, component of this work is that the students and teacher not only conceptualized and conducted research projects, but presented their work at research conferences, an often overlooked aspect of student inquiry. As part of the work, the class designated Friday "Research Day," and devoted two 90-minute sessions, one in the morning and one in the afternoon, to the activities and discussions related to their projects. The initial question posed to the students was straight-forward: What would you like to learn about in this research project? (p. 170). The students responded with a long list of questions, including issues such as where and how to obtain resources to help the poor and the homeless, questions about drugs and alcohol abuse, the etiology of diseases, crime and child abuse, early pregnancies, women and employment, and food shortages (and one student who wanted to know about lava). They then organized themselves into research teams and gave their teams names that related to the issues under investigation (e.g., Teen Pregnancy Association).

The Friday meetings were also used to discuss the work of other researchers in the field (not summaries or condensations, but their actual articles) or specific topics of concern (e.g., writing bibliographic references), and to demonstrate or model how research is done. Mercado (1992) described it as follows:

> By showing students how I am documenting the research activities of this class, we have the opportunity to reflect on and discuss what occurred during our previous meeting, as well as to explore how ethnographic procedures may be used by the students in their own work. In addition, bringing in copies of my typed field notes/logs and data summaries for their examination, allows me to validate my recorded data and obtain additional perceptions of and reactions to occurrences I had noted. The significance of this procedure had been discussed and students are well aware that ethnographic researchers

must verify the accuracy of their information. In fact, they enjoyed "correcting" my data, as they refer to it. (p. 171)

The students also functioned as collaborators by serving as "scribes" and taking notes on the proceedings. These meetings, then, served as a research study group, where the student-researchers discussed issues raised by their work, examined the literature, and used each other and the adults (including community members) as consultants in developing their investigations. They also submitted written summaries of their activities and plans for future action.

Particularly striking are the insights the students developed through their participation in research. Among the most important is an ongoing redefinition of themselves as learners. Although some are reluctant to label themselves researchers, they have come to understand that through their inquiries they have access to special information that others might lack, and that they are indeed capable of doing the intellectual work necessary to conduct an investigation, and deal with the problems and frustrations of the work. The students (with the help of the researcher and teacher) have also presented their work and ideas at professional research conferences (including a conference in another state) and to students in teacher education programs, experiencing the anxieties and satisfaction of sharing one's work with interested others, and benefiting from comments about their work. In turn, the students have helped the researcher and the teacher realize more clearly the importance of social relationships in developing, conducting, and sustaining a research effort, that is, in creating a social context for thinking and for inquiry.

The students' work on the project contrasts sharply with the type of schooling that they most frequently encounter, the rote-like instruction characteristic of their experiences in classrooms. The students are quite aware that this type of instruction helps define school for them; that teachers simply, as two students expressed it, "put work on the board, and we do it" (p. 187). As Mercado (1992) describes it, "This [perception of schooling] was brought out in early January when, in preparing for our first presentation, I asked students to tell me what was so different about our work together, as they had been insisting. Rebecca [one of the students] explained that Marcy [the classroom teacher] and I give students 'the idea and let (them) find out the information and say how (they) feel.' In other words, we allowed them to 'discover' for themselves, a word she also used, and we respected their views" (pp. 187–188). As the author concluded, these students have learned to work, talk, and make presentations like researchers, and in doing so, learn that they are fully capable of more advanced work than they are usually allowed to perform in schools.

Challenging the notion of Native American styles of learning

This challenge of the typical view of students in also central to the final example, which we borrow from the analysis of McCarty and her colleagues of the Navajo bilingual program in Rough Rock, Arizona (McCarty, Wallace, Lynch, & Benally, 1991; see also, Lipka & McCarty, in press). This program has a long history and has played an intricate and critical role in the development of the community it serves, including becoming its chief local employer (McCarty, 1989). McCarty and others (1991) describe the introduction into the program of a bilingual social studies curriculum emphasizing open-ended questioning, analytical reasoning, and active student participation and verbalization. A major aim of the curriculum was to develop the children's concepts and problem-solving abilities in the context of culturally salient experiences and topics, while promoting competency in Navajo and English. For example, an organizing concept in the curriculum was that of *K'é*, meaning kinship and clanship in Navajo. In the first two grades the students examined this concept in relation to their interactions with family and relatives, progressing in the third and fourth grades to the analysis of the interactions of people in the community and with the natural environment, and in the older grades encompassing a critical understanding of the concept in relation to other groups of people, nations and governments.

As the authors report it, within this framework the students could examine the development of Navajo society from local, tribal, and national perspectives, exploring in increasing complexity the concepts of interaction, change, and causality. Throughout, the students were encouraged to do research, use reading and writing as tools of inquiry, and contribute their ideas as part of classroom discussions. Interestingly, several Navajo teachers resisted the introduction of the curriculum on the basis that Navajo students would not respond to an inquiry-based curriculum and that they needed scripted drills to develop basic skills. It was only after a successful demonstration of the curriculum in action, with the students actively participating, that the teachers agreed that the curriculum was feasible and useful, and decided to implement it.

The teachers reported that the emphasis on inquiry generated active participation and verbalization in both languages from the children. That it allowed the children, through their own interactions and explorations, to use their knowledge to solve new problems, in ways that are very similar to the other studies summarized above. The authors point out that the activities in the curriculum were also analogous to other Navajo community-based experiences that support and expect experimentation on the part of the children, as well as the sharing of knowledge.

What about the often-documented passive responses of Navajo and other Native American children in schools? McCarty and her colleagues suggest that these are responses to constraining (and ubiquitous) forms of instruction that are also, as we have pointed out, common with working-class children in other locations, not indications of a general (context-free), culturally based, nonanalytical "style" of learning. In these researchers' words, in contrast to passive students, "in classrooms where talk is shared between teachers and students, where the expression of students' ideas is sought and clearly valued, where students' social environment is meaningfully incorporated into curricular content, and where students are encouraged to use their cultural and linguistic resources to solve new problems, Native American students respond eagerly and quite verbally to questioning, even in their second language" (p. 53).

The mediating roles of literacy

All of the projects summarized above seek to build, each in a very different way, on the cultural resources of the students and their communities, on their funds of knowledge, if you will. In this final section we want to return to the literacy practices with which we started this paper to propose a model of how these practices are essential in gaining access to funds of knowledge for academic learning and, conversely, how transcending the classroom is essential in maintaining these literate classroom practices within working-class settings. In brief, our point is as follows: None of these innovations will last unless teachers are able to overcome the intellectual limits of traditional schooling for these children. A major limitation of most classroom innovations is that they do not require (or motivate) teachers or students to go beyond the classroom walls to make instruction work. Consequently, sooner or later, the classroom comes under the control of the status quo—in the case of working-class students, the status quo means rote-like, low level instruction. Capitalizing on cultural resources for teaching allows both teachers and students to continually challenge the status quo, especially in terms of how the students are using literacy as a tool for inquiry and thinking, and to refurbish their learning with new topics, activities, and questions.

In Figure 23.1 we depict the key elements of a transformed (mediated) model of classroom instruction. Clearly, as shown in the studies summarized above, the social relationships between teacher and students (and among students) are central to the success of such classrooms, thus they form the base of the triangle. They are also central in defining what it means to be literate within these classrooms, what Reder (1994) calls the "modes of engagement" with literacy. Of central concern with language minority children is whether they are limited to learning only the rudimentary uses of reading and writing, as is typically the case, or whether they are supported in developing various modes of engagement, especially what Wells (1990) refers to as "epistemic" engagements with text: where text is treated to create, develop, or interpret knowledge or new meanings (see also Wells & Chang-Wells, 1992).

Thus, as shown in Figure 23.1, the relationships between teacher and students always mediate the students' engagements with texts, as well as what literacy comes to mean for them within the classroom. In most classrooms, especially with working-class students, those relationships are bounded, restricted, and often determined by the characteristics of commercial products, such as basal readers, worksheets, and exercises. So, in this sense, teacher–student relationships not only mediate, but are mediated by the types of texts found in these classrooms, as well as by what students are asked to do with texts, whether in one or two languages.

We have suggested that a key element in fostering epistemic engagements with texts is developing the children's literate competencies in two languages, as done by Lupita in our example. But these positive outcomes of bilingualism (and literacy) are far from automatic. Consider that bilingual education in the United States is primarily a working-class phenomenon, so that these classrooms form part of a broader, stratified system of instruction, with implications we have already reviewed. How can we overcome these constraints? One way is for teachers and students to use literacy to connect with resources outside the class-room. In all of the examples presented earlier, the uses of literacy were inseparable

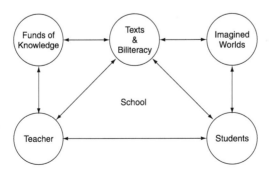

Figure 23.1 Transformed model of classroom instruction

from collaborative interactions developed for appropriating and transforming cultural resources for learning.

Thus, our model portrays at least two ways (there are certainly many more) that we can establish these mediated relationships between texts and social world: by helping students to enter (access, manipulate, use) both "real" and "imagined" worlds. The connection to the "real" world is through the analysis of funds of knowledge. We highlighted the role of teachers, equipped with both theory and method, in visiting households and establishing the necessary social relationships to learn from the families. This "ethnographic" approach helps teachers confirm that there are indeed important cultural resources in the households that in great part constitute the school's community and, as important, it helps teachers develop a theory of how to identify and access them for teaching.

Certainly, the starting point for the use of funds of knowledge for teaching need not be the household visits, this connection can also be mediated. For example, it might be a specific classroom activity (e.g., a science lesson about plants) that motivates the search for resources (e.g., an expert) from the community. And certainly, not all classroom activities need make an immediate connection to household knowledge. But the point is that both teachers and students know and appreciate that the funds of knowledge are there and that their relevance for classroom learning, and for developing various modes of engagement with literacy, can be readily established.

Now, these connections to funds of knowledge may only take place in English, if need be, but that would certainly limit the view of what is available within the community, and limit the possibilities of involvement by parents and others. Monolingualism (and monoliteracy) can be an annoying constraint in these bilingual contexts. Biliteracy, in contrast, creates the expanded possibility of accessing funds of knowledge from the lived experiences of not only one but two (or more) social worlds, most pertinently the funds of knowledge of the immediate and bilingual ethnolinguistic communities of the school.

A second, mediated connection between text and the social world is through literature, by helping students enter an imagined (but still social and cultural) world (cf. Smith, 1985). Here, biliteracy also serves an important "amplifying" function, allowing teachers and students access to literate resources in not one but in two languages, be it English and Spanish, or Navajo and English, as the case may be. These literate sources allow students to access knowledge and experiences not found in the immediate community. But this connection can also be mediated in important ways. For example, as illustrated in Figure 23.1, students can learn how to make use of funds of knowledge from their communities to address new issues or problems found in the literature, or use the knowledge from the literature to rethink issues in the community, thus providing alternatives (and new mediated connections) for thinking that would otherwise not exist. Developing these imagined worlds facilitated by literature are an extremely important function of literacy, whether we are dealing with students experiencing vicariously the horrors of war (Moll, Tapia, & Whitmore, 1993; see also, Crowell, 1993), or with science and the creation of theories (stories) about real life and possible worlds (Warren, Rosebery, & Conant, 1994).

Notice how the primary characteristic of our model has to do with the expanded possibilities facilitated by developing mediated and literate relationships. The educational emphasis is on the students' novel use of cultural resources, including people, ideas, and technologies, to facilitate and direct their intellectual work. A goal of the teacher within this social system is to teach the children how to exploit these resources in their environment, how to become, through literacy, conscious users of the funds of knowledge available for their thinking and development.

Conclusion

We have summarized four projects that attempt to make use of cultural resources for instruction, each in an unique way. And we have suggested that these projects also serve as "catalysts" to challenge the status quo by creating conditions and activities for novel uses of literacy by teachers and students. We have also highlighted the important mediating functions of literacy, especially in two languages, in helping learners establish novel connections between texts and social worlds to obtain or create knowledge and transform it for meaningful purposes.

To be sure, there is much that we left out of our discussion, such as the critical role of discourse in creating teacher-student relationships and what it means to be literate, or discussions about peer relations, outcomes or assessment. But our purpose was to provoke thought about alternative arrangements for literacy, and expanded considerations of how to become literate in classrooms by considering mediated connections with other sociocultural worlds, whether real or imagined. In so doing, as Wallace (1989) puts it, one moves "beyond minimal interpretations of literacy as the ability to read and write to a view of literacy as a resource which offers possibilities of access to what has been said and thought about the world, of the kind which day-to-day spoken interactions can less readily offer" (p. 7).

We believe that the documentation of funds of knowledge, especially by teachers and students, provides the necessary theoretical and empirical base to continue this work. But, to be frank, we also lament that we have to spend so much of our careers documenting competence, when it should simply be assumed, suggesting that "language minority" students have the intellectual capabilities of any other children, when it should simply be acknowledged, and proposing instructional arrangements that capitalize fully on the many strengths they bring into classrooms, when it should simply be their right.

References

Allington, R. (1994). What's special about special programs for children who find learning to read difficult? *Journal of Reading Behavior, 26*, 95–115.

Andrade, R. A. C., & Moll, L. C. (1993). The social worlds of children: An emic view. *Journal of the Society for Accelerative Learning and Teaching, 18*(1&2), 81–125.

Craig, M. (1994, April). *Students as ethnographers.* Paper presented at the meeting of the Society for Applied Anthropology, Cancun, Mexico.

Crowell, C. (1993). Living through war vicariously with literature. In L. Patterson, K. Smith, C. Santa, & K. Short (Eds.), *Teachers as researchers: Reflection and action* (pp. 51–59). Newark, DE: International Reading Association.

Ely, M. (1991). *Doing qualitative research: Circles within circles.* London: Falmer.

González, N., & Amanti, C. (1992, November). Teaching ethnographic method to teachers; Successes and pitfalls. Paper presented at the meeting of the American Anthropological Association, San Francisco.

González, N., Amanti, C., & Floyd, M. (1994). Redefining "teachers as researchers": The research/practice connection. Manuscript submitted for publication.

González, N., Moll, L. C., Floyd-Tenery, M., Rivera, A., Rendón, P., Gonzáles, R., & Amanti, C. (1993). Learning from households: Teacher research on funds of knowledge. *Educational Practice Report.* Santa Cruz: Center for the Study of Cultural Diversity and Second Language Learning, University of California.

Goodson, I. (1991). Teachers' lives and educational research. In I. Goodson & R. Walker (Eds.), *Biography, Identity and Schooling: Episodes in Educational Research* (pp. 137–149). London: Falmer.

Greenberg, J. B. (1989, April). *Funds of knowledge: Historical constitution, social distribution, and transmission*. Paper presented at the meeting of the Society for Applied Anthropology, Santa Fe, NM.

Hensley, M. (1994, April). *From untapped potential to creative realization: Empowering parents of multicultural backgrounds*. Paper presented at the meeting of the Society for Applied Anthropology, Cancun, Mexico.

Jacob, E. (1987). Qualitative research traditions: A review. *Review of Educational Research, 57*(1), 1–50.

Lipka, J., & McCarty, T. L. (1994). Changing the culture of schooling: Navajo and Yup'ik cases. *Anthropology and Education Quarterly, 25,* 266–284.

Lytle, S., & Cochran-Smith, M. (1990). Learning from teacher research: A working typology. *Teachers College Record, 92*(1), 83–103.

McCarty, T. L. (1989). School as community: the Rough Rock demonstration. *Harvard Educational Review, 59,* 484–502.

McCarty, T. L., Wallace, S., Lynch, R. H., & Benally, A. (1991). Classroom inquiry and Navajo learning styles: A call for reassessment. *Anthropology and Education Quarterly, 22*(1), 42–59.

Mehan, H. (1992). *Understanding inequality in schools: The contribution of interpretive approaches. Sociology of Education, 65,* 1–20.

Mercado, C. (1992). Researching research: A classroom-based student-teacher-researcher collaborative project. In A. Ambert and M. Alvarez (Eds.), *Puerto Rican children on the mainland: Interdisciplinary perspectives* (pp. 167–192). New York: Garland.

Moll, L. C. (1992). Bilingual classrooms and community analysis: Some recent trends. *Educational Researcher, 21*(2), 20–24.

Moll, L. C., Amanti, C., Neff, D., & González, N. (1992). Funds of knowledge for teaching: Using a qualitative approach to connect homes and classrooms. *Theory into Practice, 31*(2), 132–141.

Moll, L. C., & Dworin, J. (in press). Biliteracy in classrooms: social dynamics and cultural possibilities. In D. Hicks (Ed.), *Child discourse and social learning*. Cambridge, England: Cambridge University Press.

Moll, L. C., & Greenberg, J. (1990). Creating zones of possibilities: combining social contexts for instruction. In L. C. Moll (Ed.), *Vygotsky and education* (pp. 319–348). Cambridge, England: Cambridge University Press.

Moll, L. C., Tapia, J., & Whitmore, K. (1993). Living knowledge: The social distribution of cultural resources for thinking. In G. Salomon (Ed.), *Distributed cognitions: Psychological and educational considerations* (pp. 139–163). Cambridge, England: Cambridge University Press.

Moll, L. C., & Whitmore, K. (1993). Vygotsky in educational practice. In E. Forman, N. Minick, & C. A. Stone (Eds.), *Contexts for learning: Sociocultural dynamics in children's development* (pp. 19–42). New York: Oxford.

Oakes, J. (1986). Tracking, inequality, and the rhetoric of school reform: Why schools don't change. *Journal of Education, 168,* 61–80.

Olsen, L., & Minicucci, C. (1992, April). *Educating limited English proficient students in secondary schools: Critical issues emerging from research in California schools*. Paper presented at the meeting of the American Educational Research Association, San Francisco.

Reder, S. (1994). Practice-engagement theory: A sociocultural approach to literacy across languages and cultures. In B. Ferdman, R. Weber, & A. Ramírez (Eds.), *Literacy across languages and cultures* (pp. 33–74). Albany, New York: SUNY.

Rosebery, A., Warren, B., & Conant, F. (1992). Appropriating scientific discourse: Findings from language minority classrooms. *Journal of the Learning Sciences, 2*(1), 1–94.

Rosaldo, R. (1989). *Culture and truth: The remaking of social analysis*. Boston: Beacon.

Smith, F. (1985). A metaphor for literacy: creating worlds or shunting information? In D. R. Olson, N. Torrance, & A. Hildyard (Eds.), *Literacy, language, and learning* (pp. 195–213). Cambridge, England: Cambridge University Press.

Vélez-Ibáñez, C. G. (1988). Networks of exchange among Mexicans in the U.S. and

Mexico: Local level mediating responses to national and international transformations. *Urban Anthropology, 17*(1), 27–51.

Vélez-Ibáñez, C. G. & Greenberg, J. (1992). Formation and transformation of funds of knowledge among U.S. Mexican households. *Anthropology and Education Quarterly, 17*(1), 27–51.

Wallace, C. (1989). Participatory approaches to literacy with bilingual adult learners. *Language Issues, 3*(1), 6–11.

Warren, B., Rosebery, A., & Conant, F. (1989). *Cheche Konnen: Science and literacy in language minority classrooms* (Report No. 7305). Cambridge, MA: Bolt, Beranek & Newman.

Warren, B., Rosebery, A., & Conant, F. (1994). Discourse and social practice: Learning science in a language minority classroom. In D. Spener (Ed.), *Adult biliteracy in the United States* (pp. 191–210). Washington, DC: Center for Applied Linguistics.

Wells, G. (1990). Talk about text: Where literacy is learned and taught. *Curriculum Inquiry, 20*, 369–405.

Wells, G., & Chang-Well, G. L. (1992). *Constructing knowledge together: Classrooms as centers of inquiry and literacy.* Portsmouth, NH: Heinemann.

APPENDIX 1: OTHER SUGGESTED READINGS

Cervantes, R. A. (1984). Ethnocentric pedagogy and minority student growth: Implications for the common school. *Education and Urban Society, 16*(3), 274–293.

Daniel, W. G. (1964). Problems of disadvantaged youth, urban and rural. *Journal of Negro Education, 33*(3), 218–224.

Fordham, S., & Ogbu, J. (1986). Black students' school success: coping with the "burden of acting white". *The Urban Review, 18*(3), 176–206.

Fuller, M. L., & Ahler, J. (1987). Multicultural education and the monocultural student: A case study. *Action in Teacher Education, 9*(3), 33–40.

Gay, G. (1985). Implications of selected models of ethnic identity development for educators. *Journal of Negro Education, 54*(1), 43–55.

Hilliard, A. (1992). Behavioral style, culture, and teaching and learning. *Journal of Negro Education, 61*(3), 370–375.

Holmes, B. J. (1982). Black students' performance in the national assessments of science and mathematics. *Journal of Negro Education, 51*(4), 392–405.

Larke, P. J. (1991). Multicultural education: A vital investment strategy for culturally diverse youth groups. *SAEOPP,* 11–22.

Ogbu, J. (1995). Cultural problems in minority education: Their interpretations and consequences—Part One: Theoretical Background. *Urban-Review, 27*(4), 271–297.

Trueba, H. T. (1988). Culturally based explanations of minority students' academic achievement. *Anthropology & Education, 19*(2), 271–287.

Wagner, H. (1981). Working with the culturally different student. *Education, 101*(4), 353–358.

APPENDIX 2: JOURNAL PUBLISHERS AND CONTACT INFORMATION

Action in Teacher Education
Association of Teacher Educators
1900 Association Drive, Suite ATE
Reston, VA 20191–1502
(703)620–2110; (703)620–9530
http://www.ate1.org

American Association of Colleges for Teacher Education
1307 New York Avenue, NW Suite 300
Washington, DC 20005–4701
(202)293–2450; (202)457–8096 (Fax)
www.aacte.org

American Educational Research Association
1230—17th Street NW
Washington, DC 20036
(202)223–9485, × 100; (202)775–1824
http://aera.net

American Journal of Education
University of Chicago Press
Permissions Department
1427 East 60th Street
Chicago, IL
(773)702–6096; (773)702–9756

American Sociological Association
1307 New York Avenue, NW Suite 700
Washington, DC 20005–4701
Jill Campbell
Publications Manager
(202)383–9005, × 303; (202)638–0882
www.asanet.org

Anthropology and Education
Anthropology and Education Quarterly
University of California Press
Journals and Digital Publishing Division
2000 Center Street, Suite 303
Berkeley, CA 94704

Association for Supervision and Curriculum Development
1703 N. Beauregard Street
Alexandria, VA 22311–1714
(703)578–9600; (703)575–5400 (Fax)
www.ascd.org

Banks, Cherry A. McGee
Professor, Education
University of Washington, Bothell
18115 Campus Way NE Room UW1 244
Bothell, WA 98011–8246

Banks, James A.
University of Washington
Box 353600, 110 Miller Hall
Seattle, WA 98195–3600
(206)543–3386; (206)542–4218 Fax
http://faculty.washington.edu/jbanks

Comparitive Education Review
University of Chicago Press
Permissions Department
1427 East 60th Street
Chicago, IL
(773)702–6096; (773)702–9756

Curriculum and Teaching
James Nicholas Publishers
PO Box 244
Albert Park, Australia, 3206

Education
Dr. George E. Uhlig
PO Box 8826
Spring Hill Station
Mobile, AL 36689

Education and Urban Society
Corwin Press, Inc.
2455 Teller Road
Thousand Oaks, CA 91320–2218
(805)499–9734; (805)499–0871 (Fax)
http://www.sagepub.com

Educational Horizons
National Association for Ethnic Studies, Inc. &
American Cultural Studies Department
Western Washington University
516 High Street—MS 9113
Bellingham, WA 98225–9113
(360)650–2349; (360)650–2690 (Fax)

Educational Leadership
Association for Supervision and Curriculum Development
PO Box 79760
Baltimore, MD 21279–0760
(703)578–9600; 1–800–933–2723; (703)575–5400 Fax
www.ascd.org

Educational Research Quarterly
113 Greenbriar Drive
West Monroe, LA 71291
(318)274–2355
hashway@alphagram.edu

Educators for Urban Minorities
Long Island University Press (No longer in operation)
Eugene E. Garcia, Ph.D.
Vice President Education Partnerships
Professor of Education
Arizona State University
Eugene.Garcia@asum.edu

English Journal
1111 W. Kenyon Road
Urbana, IL 61801–1096
(217)328–3870; (217)328–9645 (Fax)
http://www.ncte.org

Exceptional Children
Council for Exceptional Children
Permissions Department
1110 North Glebe Road Suite 300
Arlington, VA 22201–5704
(703)264–1637

FOCUS
Joint Center for Political Studies
1301 Pennsylvania Avenue, NW
Washington, DC 20004
(202)626–3500

Ford Foundation
320 East 43rd Street
New York, NY 10017

Gibson, Margaret A.
Professor of Education and Anthropology
Department of Education
University of California, Santa Cruz
1156 High Street
Santa Cruz, CA 95064
(831)459–4740; (831)459–4618 (Fax)

Harvard Educational Review
Harvard Graduate School of Education
8 Story Street, 1st Floor
Cambridge, MA 02138
(617)495–3432; (617)496–3584 (fax)
www.hepg.org
+
HarperCollins Publishers
10 East 53rd Street
New York, NY 10022
(212)207–7000

Interchange
Nel van der Werf
Assistant Rights and Permissions/Springer
Van Godewijckstraat 30
PO Box 17
3300 AA Dordrecht
The Netherlands
31 (0) 78 6576 298; 31 (0) 78 6576 323 (Fax)
Nel.vanderwerf@springer.com
www.springeronline.com

Journal of Curriculum Studies
Routledge (Taylor & Francis, Inc.)
4 Park Square, Milton Park
Abingdon, Oxon OX14 4RN United Kingdom
44–1235–828600; 44–1235–829000 (Fax)
http://www.routledge.co.uk

Journal of Curriculum and Supervision
Association for Supervision and Curriculum Development
1703 North Beauregard Street
Alexandria, VA 22311–1714
(703)578–9600/(800)933–2723; (703)575–3926 (Fax)
http://www.ascd.org

Journal of Teacher Education
American Association of Colleges for Teacher Education
1307 New York Avenue NW Suite 300
Washington, DC 20017–4701
(202)293–2450; (202)457–8095 (Fax)
www.aacte.org

Journal of Research and Development in Education
Julie P. Sartor, Editor
Office of the Associate Dean for Research,
Technology, & External Affairs
UGA College of Education
(706)542–4693; (706)542–8125 (Fax)
jsartor@uga.edu

Journal of Negro Education
Howard University Press
Marketing Department
2600 Sixth Street, NW
Washington, DC 20059
(202)806–8120; (202)806–8434 (Fax)

Journal of Literacy Research (formerly *Journal of Reading Behavior*)
Lawrence Erlbaum Associates, Inc.
10 Industrial Avenue
Mahwah, NJ 07430–2262
(201)258–2200; (201)236–0072 (Fax)

Journal of Educational Thought
University of Calgary
Faculty of Education – Publications Office
2500 University Drive N.W.
Education Tower, Room 1310
Calgary, Alberta, Canada T2N 1N4
(403)220–7499/5629; (403)284–4162 (Fax)
www.ucalgary.ca

Journal of Teacher Education
American Association of Colleges for Teacher Education
1307 New York Avenue NW 300
Washington, DC 20005–4701
(202)293–2450; (202)457–8095 (Fax)
www.aacte.org

Language Arts
The National Council of Teachers of English
1111 W. Kenyon Road
Urbana, IL 61801–1096
(217)278–3621
permissions@ncte.org

Momentum
National Catholic Educational Association
1077—30 Street, NW Suite 100
Washington, DC 2007
(202)337–6232; (202)333–6706 (Fax)
nceaadmin@ncea.org

Multicultural Education
Gaddo Gap Press
3145 Geary Boulevard PMB 275
San Francisco, CA 94118
(414)666–3012; (414)666–3552
http://www.caddogap.com

National Catholic Educational Association
1077—30 Street, NW Suite 100
Washington, DC 20007
(202)337–6232; (202)333–6706 (Fax)
nceaadmin@ncea.org

National Council for the Social Studies
8555 Sixteenth Street, Suite 500
Center for Multicultural Education
Silver Spring, MD 20910
(301)588–1800 × 122;
(301)588–2049 Fax

National Educational Service
1252 Loesch Road
PO Box 8 Department V2
Bloomington, IN 47402

Negro Educational Review
NER Editorial Offices
School of Education
1601 East Market Street
Greensboro, NC 27411
Alice M. Scales (scales@pitt.edu)
Shirley A. Biggs (biggs@pitt.edu)

Peabody Journal of Education
Lawrence Erlbaum Associates
10 Industrial Avenue
Mahwah, NJ 07430–2262

Phi Delta Kappan
Phi Delta Kappa International
408 N. Union Street
PO Box 789
(812)339–1156; 800–766–1156; (812)339–0018 fax

Race, Class, and Gender
Southern University at New Orleans (No Response)
Carl contact Jean Belkhir (jbelkhir@uno.edu)

Radical Teacher
Center for Critical Education
PO Box 382616
Cambridge, MA 02238
Saul Slapikoff, Permissions Editor
slap2@comcast.net

Researching Today's Youth: The Community Circle of Caring Journal
Dr. Carlos E. Cortes
Professor Emeritus
Department of History
University of California,
Riverside, CA 92521–0204
(951)827–1487
(951)827–5299 fax
carlos.cortes@ucr.edu

Review of Educational Research
American Educational Research Association
1230—17th Street NW
Washington, DC 20036–3078

Sage Publications, Inc.
Corwin Press, Inc
2455 Teller Road
Thousand Oaks, CA 91320
(805)410–7713; (805)376–9562 (Fax)
permissions@sagepub.com

Southeastern Association of Educational Opportunity Program Personnel (SAEOPP)
75 Piedmont Avenue NE
Suite 408
Atlanta, GA 30303–2518
(404)522–4642

Teachers College Record
Blackwell Publishing
PO Box 805
9600 Garsington Road
Oxford OX4 2ZG United Kingdom
44 (0) 1865 776868; 44 (0) 1865 714591 Fax
www.blackwellpublishing.com

Teacher Education and Special Education
Dr. Fred Spooner, Editor
Teacher Education and Special Education
SPCD/College of Education
University of North Carolina at Charlotte
Charlotte, NC 28223

(704)687–8851; (704)687–2916 Fax
fhspoone@email.uncc.edu

The American Scholar
1606 New Hampshire Avenue NW
Washington, DC 20009
(202)265–3808; (202)265–0083

The Educational Forum
Kappa Delta Pi
3707 Woodview Trace
Indianapolis, IN 46268–1158

The High School Journal
The University of North Carolina Press
PO Box 2288
Chapel Hill, NC 27515–2288
(919)966–3561; (919)966–3829
www.uncpress.unc.edu

The Journal of Educational Research
Heldref Publications
1319 Eighteenth Street, NW
Washington, DC 20036–1802
(202)296–6267; (202)296–5146 (Fax)
www.heldref.org

The New Advocate
Christopher-Gordon Publishers, Inc.
1502 Providence Hwy, Suite 12
Norwood, MA 02062–4643
(781)762–5577; (781)762–7261
http://www.christopher-gordon.com

The Social Studies
Heldref Publications
1319 Eighteenth Street, NW
Washington, DC 20038–1802
(202)296–6267; (202)296–5149 (Fax)
permissions@heldref.org

The Teacher Educator
Ball State University
Teachers College
TC 1008
Muncie, IN 47306
(765)285–5453; (765)285–5455

The Urban Review
Nel van der Werf
Assistant Rights and Permissions/Springer
Van Godewijckstraat 30
PO Box 17
3300 AA Dordrecht
The Netherlands
31 (0) 78 6576 298; 31 (0) 78 6576 323 (Fax)
Nel.vanderwerf@springer.com
www.springeronline.com

Theory into Practice
Lawrence Erlbaum Associates, Inc.
10 Industrial Avenue
Mahwah, NJ 07430–2262

Viewpoints in Teaching and Learning
Indiana University
School of Education
Education Building 109
Bloomington, IN 47405

Young Children
National Association for the Education of Young Children
1313 L Street, NW, Suite 500
Washington, DC 20036–1426
(202)232–8777; (202)328–1846 (Fax)
http://www.naeyc.org

PERMISSION CREDITS

Part 1: Attribution Theory and its Legacy in Research on Students

Ronald W. Henderson, "Social and Emotional Needs of Culturally Diverse Children." *Exceptional Children*, 46:8 (May 1980), 598–605. Copyright © 1980 by the Council for Exceptional Children. Reprinted with permission.

Audrey J. Schwartz, "A Comparative Study of Values and Achievement: Mexican-American and Anglo Youth." *Sociology of Education*, 44:4 (Fall 1971), 438–462. Copyright © 1971 by the American Sociological Association. Reprinted with permission.

John U. Ogbu, "Minority Status and Schooling in Plural Societies." *Comparitive Education Review*, 27:2 (June 1983), 168–190. Copyright © 1983 by the University of Chicago Press. Reprinted with permission.

Gwendolyn C. Baker, "Motivating the Culturally Different Student." *Momentum*, 14 (February 1983). 45–46. Copyright © 1983 by the National Catholic Educational Association. Reprinted with permission.

Patricia J. Larke, "Multicultural Education: A Vital Investment Strategy for Culturally Diverse Youth Groups." *SAEOPP* (Spring 1991), 11–22. Copyright © 1991 by the Southeastern Association of Educational Opportunity Program Personnel (SAEOPP). Reprinted with permission.

Part 2: Single Group Studies

Russell L. Young and Valerie Ooka Pang, "Asian Pacific American Students: A Rainbow of Dreams." *Multicultural Education*, 3:2 (Winter 1995), 4–7. Copyright © 1995 by Caddo Gap Press. Reprinted with permission.

Grace Kao, "Asian Americans As Model Minorities? A Look at Their Academic Performance." by the *American Journal of Education*, 103 (February 1995), 121–159. Copyright © 1995 by the *American Journal of Education*. Reprinted with permission.

Robert K. Chiago, "Making Education Work for the American Indian." *Theory into Practice*, 20:1 (1981), 20–25. Copyright © 1981 by Lawrence Erlbaum. Reprinted with permission.

Donna Deyhle, "Navajo Youth and Anglo Racism." *Harvard Educational Review,* 65:3 (1995), 403–444. Copyright © 1995 by the President and Fellows of Harvard College. Reprinted with permission.

Robert W. Sizemore, "Do Black and White Students Look for the Same Characteristics In Teachers?" *Journal of Negro Education,* 50:1 (1981), 48–53. Copyright © 1981 by Howard University Press. Reprinted with permission.

Diane Scott-Jones, and Maxine L. Clark, "The School Experiences of Black Girls: The Interaction of Gender, Race, and Socioeconomic Status." *Phi Delta Kappan* (March 1986), 520–526. Copyright © 1986 by Phi Delta Kappa International. Reprinted with permission.

Cathy A. Pohan and Norma J. Bailey, "Opening the Closet: Multiculturalism That Is Fully Inclusive." *Multicultural Education,* 5:1 (Fall 1997), 12–15. Copyright © 1997 by Caddo Gap Press. Reprinted with permission.

Roberta W. Ginsberg, "In the Triangle/Out of the Circle: Gay and Lesbian Students Facing the Heterosexual Paradigm." *The Educational Forum,* 64 (Fall 1999), 46–56. Copyright © 1999 by Kappa Delta Pi. Reprinted with permission.

Part 3: Intersections of Race, Class, and Gender

Carlos Cortes, "Mixed-Race Children: Building Bridges to New Identities." *Researching Today's Youth: The Community Circle of Caring Journal,* 3:2 (1999), 28–31. Copyright © 1999 National Educational Service. Reprinted by permission of Carlos E. Cortes.

Thomas H. Hawkes and Norma F. Furst, "Race, Socio-Economic Situation, IQ, and Teacher Ratings of Students Behavior as Factors Relating to Anxiety in Upper Elementary School Children." *Sociology of Education,* 44 (Summer 1971), 333–350. Copyright © 1971 by the American Sociological Association. Reprinted with permission.

Carl A. Grant and Christine E. Sleeter, "Race, Class, and Gender in Education Research: An Argument for Integrative Analysis." *Review of Educational Research,* 56:2 (Summer 1986), 195–211. Copyright © 1986 by the American Educational Research Association. Reprinted with permission.

Carl A. Grant and Christine E. Sleeter, "Race, Class, and Gender and Abandoned Dreams." *Teachers College Record,* 90:1 (Fall 1988), 19–40. Copyright © 1988 by Blackwell Publishing. Reprinted with permission.

Sonia Nieto, "Lessons from Students On Creating a Chance to Dream." *Harvard Educational Review,* 64:4 (Winter 1994), 392–426. Copyright © 1994 by the President and Fellows of Harvard College. Reprinted with permission.

Part 4: Matching the Needs of Diverse Students to Elements of Schooling

Margaret A. Gibson, "Reputation and Respectability: How Competing Cultural Systems Affect Students' Performance in School." *Anthropology and Education,* 13:1 (1982), 3–27. Copyright © 1982 by the Council on Anthropology and Education. Reprinted with permission.

Jim Cummins, "Empowering Minority Students: A Framework for Intervention." *Harvard Educational Review,* 56:1 (February 1986), 18–36. Copyright © 1986 by the President and Fellows of Harvard College. Reprinted with permission.

Sarah Deschenes, Larry Cuban, and David Tyack, "Mismatch: Historical Perspectives on Schools and Students Who Don't Fit Them." *Teachers College Record,* 103:4 (2001), 525–547. Copyright © 2001 by Teachers College, Columbia University. Reprinted with permission.

James A. Banks, "Ethnicity, Class, Cognitive, and Motivational Styles: Research and Teaching Implications." *Journal of Negro Education,* 57:4 (1988), 452–466. Copyright © 1988 by Howard University Press. Reprinted with permission.

Luis C. Moll and Norma González, "Lessons from Research with Language-Minority Children." *Journal of Reading Behavior,* 26:4 (1994), 439–456. Copyright © 1994 by Lawrence Erlbaum. Reprinted with permission.

AUTHOR INDEX

SUBJECT INDEX